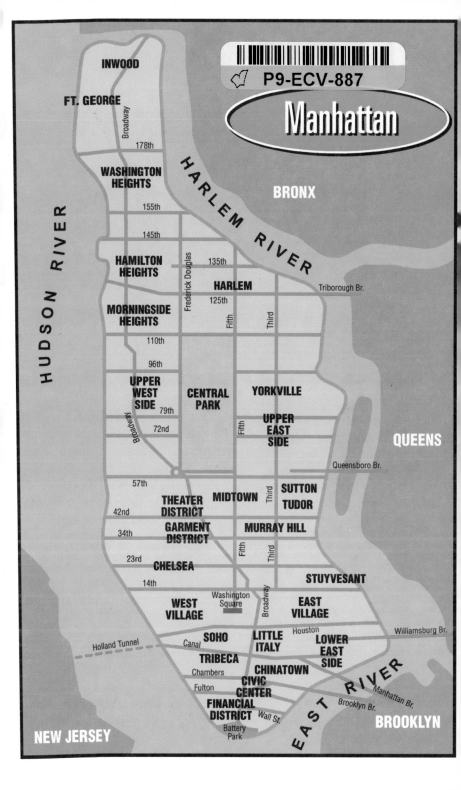

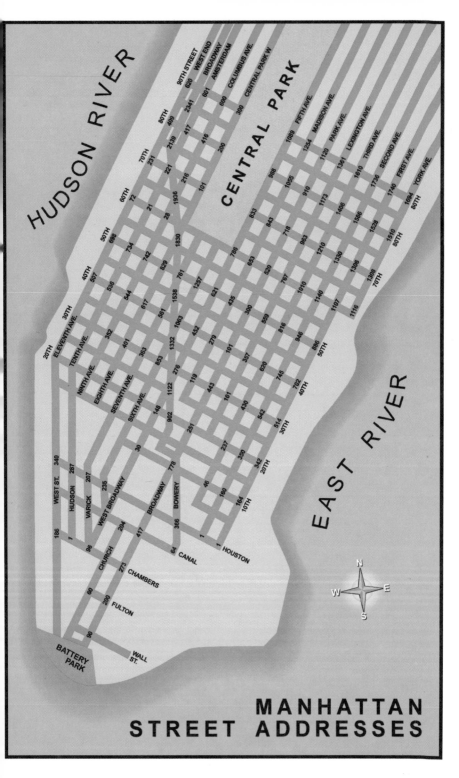

MANHATTAN
STREET ADDRESSES

GERRY FRANK'S

Where to Find It, Buy It, Eat It in New York

GERRY FRANK'S

Where to Find It, Buy It, Eat It in New York

Gerry's Frankly Speaking

P.O. Box 2225
Salem, OR 97308
503/585-8411
800/NYC-BOOK (800/692-2665)
Fax: 503/585-1076
E-mail: gerry@teleport.com
www.gerrysfranklyspeaking.com

Contact us for additonal copies and
special quantity prices.

Printed in the United States of America
Library of Congress Catalog Card Number 80-7802

ISBN (10): 1-879333-18-X
ISBN (13): 978-1-879333-18-5

First Edition 1980
Second Edition 1981
Third Edition 1983
Fourth Edition 1985
Fifth Edition 1987
Sixth Edition 1989
Seventh Edition 1991
Eighth Edition 1993
Ninth Edition 1995
Tenth Edition 1997
Eleventh Edition 1999
Twelfth Edition 2001
Thirteenth Edition 2003
Fourteenth Edition 2005

No fees were paid or services rendered in exchange for inclusion in
this book.

Although every effort was made to ensure that all information was
accurate and up-to-date at the time of publication, neither the publisher
nor the author can be held responsible for any errors, omissions, or
adverse consequences resulting from the use of such information. It is
recommended that you call ahead to verify the information contained in
individual business listings.

Contents

III. WHERE TO FIND IT: MUSEUMS, TOURS, AND OTHER EXPERIENCES

IV. WHERE TO FIND IT: NEW YORK'S BEST FOOD SHOPS

V. WHERE TO FIND IT: NEW YORK'S BEST SERVICES

VI. WHERE TO BUY IT: NEW YORK'S BEST STORES

VII. WHERE TO "EXTRAS"

From the Author . . .

Dear Readers,

This is the 25th-anniversary edition of a book that I first wrote on a bit of a whim after years of sharing my New York secrets with my friends. I'd been coming to New York every few weeks for 30 years, and I always kept notes on where to stay, shop, eat, and explore. Turning those notes into a book seemed like a natural thing to do way back in 1980, so I self-published *Where to Find It, Buy It, Eat It in New York* and took it into the bookstores that used to line Fifth Avenue, begging store owners to give me a little shelf space. Little did I know that it would become the best-selling complete guidebook to New York, with more than one million copies sold!

When I first started visiting New York, men wore hats, women wore gloves, and everyone dressed up for dinner and the theater. In the more than 50 years since then, whole areas have been torn down and rebuilt, stores that seemed like they would last forever have become footnotes in history, and several generations have come and gone through the city's offices, restaurants, and neighborhoods. This city has seen great sadness and great joy, shared tragedy and savored triumph, and in many ways has changed dramatically.

Despite all the changes, however, New York remains the single most interesting, exciting, challenging, and diverse city in the world. It has an energy and vitality unmatched anywhere. And it has something for just about everyone: world-class museums, high fashion, foreign films, incredible restaurants, innovative chefs, cutting-edge design, and every kind of music, theater, and art. You name it, New York has it!

This book is different things to different people. To native New Yorkers, it is a friend to reminisce with and to find something they didn't know about before. To those who live here, it is a great resource for everything from rug cleaners to consignment stores. And to the millions of people who visit New York every year, it is a one-stop source for everything the title suggests: where to find it, buy it, and eat it in this remarkably rich and diverse city.

The heart of this book is my collection of personal notes and opinions. Nobody pays to be included, and I am the final judge of what goes in and what does not. That said, however, I am indebted to several people: my researchers, Carrie Klein and Grace McMillan; my superb editor, Parke Puterbaugh; my extremely able and extraordinarily decent book assistant, Cheryl Johnson, and her husband, Jim; my incredibly organized executive assistant and friend, Linda Wooters; and my always positive and efficient helper, Linda Chase. Tim Prock, a talented graphic artist, created the cover, and the unfailingly patient Tom and Carole Stinski tackled the typesetting. I am grateful as well to my mentors and friends, Esther Benovitz and Bryan Miller.

Whether you're planning your first visit to New York or have lived here all of your life, I hope you will find some magic in these pages. I love New York. I hope you do, too!

Gerry Frank.

Gerry Frank

I. In and Around the World's Greatest City

GETTING TO NEW YORK

So you're headed for New York! Whether you're traveling 90 miles from Philadelphia or 9,000 miles from Singapore, you're in for a wonderful treat. But first you'll need to get here.

AIRPORTS—New York City is served by three major airports, and more than 90 million people pass through them every year. **LaGuardia Airport** is the most frequently used for domestic flights, while **John F. Kennedy International Airport** (also referred to as "JFK" or "Kennedy") has flights to and from just about every nation. Both airports are in the borough of Queens. **Newark Liberty International Airport** (commonly called "Newark"), across the Hudson River in New Jersey, handles an increasingly large volume of domestic and international flights. The most common ways of traveling between Manhattan and these airports are by taxicab, shuttle bus, and private car or limousine.

Taxi lines form in front of most terminals at all three airports, and the exits to them are usually well marked with signs that say "Ground Transportation." These lines are legitimate and generally move quickly. Assuming you don't run into bad traffic, a cab trip between LaGuardia and midtown will take about half an hour and cost roughly $25, plus bridge toll and tip. The trip between Kennedy and anywhere in Manhattan can take as long as an hour and costs a flat fee of $45, plus bridge or tunnel toll and tip. A taxi between Newark and Manhattan can also take as long as an hour and costs as much as $60 (the metered fare plus a $5 surcharge for any destination on the East Side of Manhattan and another $5 surcharge anywhere in New York during rush hour or on weekends between noon and 6), plus tolls and a $1 surcharge for each piece of luggage over 24 inches. If you have a preference for which route to take into or out of Manhattan, tell the driver in advance. And be forewarned: although they are required by law to do so, cab drivers in Manhattan often don't like taking people to the airports because it's sometimes hard to get quick fares back. In fact, New York cabbies aren't even allowed to pick up passengers at Newark.

If taxi fares seem a little steep, there are less expensive alternatives. Several companies run **shuttle buses** and **vans** between Manhattan and the airports. If you're alone and going to a major hotel in midtown, you can really save money by taking a shuttle. But it may not be worth it if there are others in your party to share a cab, if you're in a hurry, or if you're headed to a friend's apartment or an out-of-the-way hotel. Shuttle-bus tickets and schedules are available at the ground transportation desks at all three airports.

Shuttle-bus options to and from LaGuardia and Kennedy airports include **Express Shuttle** (212/315-3006, 800/451-0455), **New York Airport Service** (718/875-8200, 800/872-4577, www.nyairportservice.com), and **SuperShuttle** (212/258-3826, 800/622-7000, . www.supershuttle.com). SuperShuttle also takes passengers to and from Newark, as does **Olympia Airport Express** (212/964-6233, 800/451-0455). Most of the shuttle buses serving Kennedy and Newark are slightly more expen-sive than the ones serving LaGuardia, but all of them are under $20. For a complete list of options and prices, call the Port Authority's **Air-Ride** recording (800/247-7433) or go to www.panynj.gov.

The long-awaited **AirTrain** is now an option from both Kennedy and Newark. For $7 you can take AirTrain from Kennedy to the Howard Beach or Jamaica subway stops and then take a subway into Manhattan. If you're in a hurry and willing to pay a little more, you can also take the Long Island Railroad into Penn Station. From Newark, you can take AirTrain to the Newark Rail Link Station and then ride either Amtrak or New Jersey Transit into Penn Station. Call 800/626/7433 or go to www.panynj.gov/airtrain for detailed information.

If you really want to save money and are in no hurry, **public transporta-tion** is also an option. For $3, you can take the M60 bus from LaGuardia to the corner of Lexington Avenue and 125th Street or Broadway and 116th Street and then any one of a half dozen subway lines into midtown and other parts of Manhattan. The same $3 will get you to Kennedy via subway (the E and F lines) and bus (the Green Line Q-10), but it takes almost two hours.

Don't Say I Didn't Warn You

Under no circumstance should you follow someone who asks if you want a taxi or limousine ride inside or outside the terminal. The crowd offering taxis and limousines can be quite daunting, and their offers may seem tempting if the airport is jammed, but you'll end up paying far more than you should and will have absolutely no recourse.

A fourth option is calling a private **car service** or **limousine** ahead of time. A driver will meet you at the gate or in the baggage claim area, holding up a sign with your last name on it. Depending on your personality, this will make you feel important, embarrassed, or a little bit of both. Be forewarned that a car or limo service can get pretty pricey, particularly if the driver has to wait because your flight is delayed. (They charge for waiting time.) Costs to and from LaGuardia run anywhere from $25 plus tip, if you want a sedan and everything goes smoothly, to well over $100, if there are delays or you request a limousine. Prices are higher to and from Kennedy and Newark. You can also secure a sedan or limousine after you've arrived by going to the ground trans-portation desks at any of the three airports.

TRAINS—Dozens of Amtrak trains come in and out of New York City every-day. Service is concentrated in the Northeast Corridor, between Washington and Boston, but you can catch trains between New York and Florida, Chicago, or even Seattle and many cities in Canada. Trains arrive and depart Pennsyl-vania Station (commonly referred to as **Penn Station**), underneath Madison Square Garden between 31st and 33rd streets and Seventh and Eighth avenues. Penn Station is a major subway hub. You also can find a legitimate and well-organized taxicab line immediately outside the station on Seventh Avenue. Under no circumstances should you follow someone who comes up to you inside or outside Penn Station asking if you need a taxi or help with your bags.

You can choose between the Acela Express, sleeping cars, and other kinds of Amtrak service. Multi-day excursion passes are also available. Although the station is much improved from its dilapidated state a decade ago and actually includes an enclosed waiting area for ticketed Amtrak passengers in the middle of the main concourse, it's still not a place you will want to spend much time. (Call Amtrak at 800/872-7245 or go to www.amtrak.com for fare and schedule information.) Train service to and from Connecticut and suburban New York is run by **MetroNorth** (800/638-7646, www.mta. nyc.ny.us/mnr) through the wonderfully reborn Grand Central Station.

DRIVING—If you can avoid driving to or in New York, by all means do so. Otherwise, you will end up paying exorbitant prices for tolls and parking (and your mental health will inevitably suffer, too). The fact that most New Yorkers don't own cars ought to tell you something! Traffic in and around the metropolitan area is horrendous, and drivers are extraordinarily aggressive. Once you're in New York, the only time you may possibly need a car is if you want to leave for a day or two—and then you can rent one, as many New Yorkers do. The public transportation system in New York is extremely efficient, inexpensive, and used frequently by just about everyone.

If you still aren't convinced or have no alternative, get a map before setting out and study it carefully. The three major approaches to the city involve the New England Thruway (I-95), the New York State Thruway (I-87), and the New Jersey Turnpike (I-95). Expect long waits during rush hour at the bridges and tunnels leading in and out of Manhattan. Turn to AM radio stations 770, 880, or 1010 for area traffic reports to help you decide which approach to take. Expect to pay a hefty toll for whichever bridge or tunnel you choose. And no matter what else you do, avoid rush hour (actually rush hours, as they occur in the morning and afternoon) and Sunday afternoon.

Don't Say I Didn't Warn You, Part Two
   Single-occupancy vehicles are now banned from entering Manhattan between 6 and 10 a.m. on weekdays via all access routes. If you're traveling alone in Manhattan during those times, you can take the subway, the bus, or a taxi. Given the absence of below-ground traffic, the subway is definitely the fastest alternative.

GETTING TO KNOW NEW YORK

   In case you haven't already figured it out, this book isn't really about New York. It isn't even about New York City. It's about Manhattan. Most people (including me) use New York, New York City, "the city," and Manhattan synonymously. But New York is one of the Northeast's largest states, and New York City actually comprises five separate boroughs: Manhattan, Brooklyn, the Bronx, Queens, and Staten Island. Of those five boroughs, only the Bronx is attached to the mainland. Manhattan and the other three are all islands.

A LITTLE HISTORY—Now that you know we're talking only about the island of Manhattan, a little history may help make sense of how the city is laid out. Native Americans were the first known residents of this area. Italian explorer Giovanni da Verrazano (for whom the Verrazano Narrows Bridge, linking Brooklyn and Staten Island, is named) sailed into New York Harbor in 1524 and "discovered" Manhattan for his French patron, King Francis I. In 1609, a trader for the Dutch East India Company named Henry Hudson sailed into the harbor and up the river that now bears his name. The first permanent European settlement in Manhattan, a Dutch trading post called Nieuw Amsterdam, was established in 1625 at the very southern tip of the island, where Battery Park is today. The story you've probably heard since childhood is true, at least to the extent that the various parties understood each other's intentions and expectations: rights to the island were "bought" by the Dutch West India Company a year later from local Indians with inexpensive beads, cloth, and other goods. It was renamed New York in 1664 after the British— in the person of Charles II's brother, the Duke of York—gained control of the still-tiny settlement.

It's hard to imagine today, but such areas as midtown and even Greenwich Village were way out in the country for another 150 years. Indeed, Wall Street is so named because a wall of logs was erected there in the mid-17th century to protect the farms in lower Manhattan from the wilderness beyond. New York's population—which numbered only 60,000 as late as 1800—remained concentrated on the southern tip of the island, while most of Manhattan was used for country estates and farmland or just left as forests and wilderness. Indeed, pigs were roaming around Wall Street well into the 19th century. When a commission headed by engineer John Randall, Jr., laid out a grid system for the largely undeveloped area from Houston Street north to 155th Street in 1807, most residents thought it entirely unnecessary.

THE RANDALL PLAN—For those trying to find their way around Manhattan, the so-called Randall Plan is a godsend. The streets below Houston (pronounced *House*-ton), particularly those below Canal Street, meander like the Dutch farm trails they once were. Even the relatively straight ones were not built for 21st-century traffic. World-famous Wall Street, for example, is narrower than the typical suburban driveway. Truth be told, not much about the city's layout makes sense south of 14th Street. If you're ever at the corner of West 4th Street and West 10th Street in Greenwich Village, you'll know what I mean!

Thanks to the Randall Plan, however, everything north of 14th Street is just about as simple as a major city can be. With the exception of Broadway— originally a well-worn footpath and now one of the country's longest streets, extending from the southern tip of Manhattan to the capital city of Albany — and some of the streets in northern Manhattan, the streets and avenues are laid out in a north-south, east-west grid. All of the east-west streets are numbered, as are many of the north-south avenues. In general, most avenues are one-way and alternately northbound and southbound. Most streets are one-way as well: the even-numbered ones tend to be eastbound, and the odd-numbered ones westbound. Two-way exceptions include such major east-west thoroughfares as Canal, Houston, 14th, 23rd, 34th, 42nd, 57th, 72nd, 79th, 86th, 96th, 110th, and 125th streets. (See the "Key to Addresses" section for help with finding a specific address.)

EAST SIDE, WEST SIDE—Starting just north of Washington Square Park at about 8th Street in Greenwich Village, Fifth Avenue divides the city into east and west sides. Broadway, built on an old Algonquin Indian trade route, acts as the east-west dividing line south of Washington Square, although it runs a little east of where Fifth Avenue would be. That east-west distinction is important, as most addresses in New York reflect it. For example, 125 East 52nd Street and 125 West 52nd Street are two distinct locations several blocks apart.

Let's start with the East Side of the city. Moving east from Fifth Avenue toward the East River, you'll cross Madison Avenue, Park Avenue (called Park Avenue South below 34th Street and Fourth Avenue below that), Lexington Avenue (called Irving Place between 14th and 20th streets), Third Avenue, Second Avenue, and First Avenue. Madison Avenue doesn't start until 23rd Street, while Lexington Avenue begins as Irving Place at 14th Street. Sutton Place starts at 51st Street between First Avenue and the river, turns into York Avenue at 60th Street, and stops at 92nd streets. East End Avenue runs between York Avenue and the river from 79th to 90th streets. All of these avenues run north-south, parallel to Fifth Avenue. FDR Drive ("The FDR" to locals) hugs the river along the east side of the island.

The West Side of Manhattan is a bit more confusing. Moving west from Fifth Avenue toward the Hudson River, you'll find Avenue of the Americas (or Sixth Avenue, as everyone still calls it, despite the official name change in the 1950s), Seventh Avenue, Eighth Avenue (known as Central Park West north of 59th Street), Ninth Avenue (Columbus Avenue north of 59th Street), Tenth Avenue (Amsterdam Avenue north of 59th Street), and Eleventh Avenue (West End Avenue between 59th Street and its end at 107th Street). You'll also find Broadway meandering about the West Side above 23rd Street. Avenue of the Americas and Seventh Avenue both stop at the south end of Central Park. Riverside Drive runs parallel to West End Avenue near the Hudson River north of 72nd Street. All of these avenues run north-south and parallel to Fifth Avenue (except Broadway, which meanders diagonally before more or less straightening out around 79th Street). The Henry Hudson Parkway (also known as the West Side Highway and sometimes called Twelfth Avenue around midtown) runs along the entire west side of the city.

Central Park occupies land between 59th and 110th streets, further dividing Manhattan's East and West sides. Fifth Avenue runs along the east side of the park, and everything east of it is known as the Upper East Side. Central Park West runs along the west side of the park, and everything west of it is known as the Upper West Side. Both the Upper East Side and Upper West Side are largely residential, although most of the north-south avenues have plenty of shops and stores.

NORTHERN MANHATTAN—The avenues on the East Side remain fairly consistent as they move north of Central Park into the area known as East (or Spanish) Harlem. Lenox Avenue (which soon becomes Malcolm X Boulevard) picks up where Avenue of the Americas left off below the park. Adam Clayton Powell, Jr. Boulevard picks up where Seventh Avenue left off. Central Park West becomes Frederick Douglass Boulevard. Amsterdam Avenue, Broadway, and Riverside Drive all extend into Northern Manhattan, while such major roads as Convent Avenue, St. Nicholas Avenue, Edgecombe Avenue, and Fort Washington Avenue are exclusive to Harlem and the northern tip of Manhattan.

Key to Addresses

So how do you find an address in Manhattan? Manhattan phone directories and other publications generally include cross-street information as part of their address listings. If you have an address without a cross street, however, here's a reliable system for figuring it out:

AVENUES—If you have a numerical address on one of the north-south avenues, you can determine the approximate cross street by dropping the last number, dividing the remainder by two, and adding or subtracting the number indicated.

Avenue A, B, C, or D	Add 3
First Avenue	Add 3
Second Avenue	Add 3
Third Avenue	Add 10
Lexington Avenue	Add 22
Fourth Avenue/Park Avenue South	Add 8
Park Avenue	Add 35
Madison Avenue	Add 26

Fifth Avenue
• addresses up to 200	Add 13
• between 201 and 400	Add 16
• between 401 and 600	Add 18
• between 601 and 774	Add 20
• between 775 and 1286	Subtract 18
• between 1289 and 1500	Add 45
• addresses up to 2000	Add 24
Avenue of the Americas/Sixth Avenue ..	Subtract 12
Lenox Avenue/Malcolm X Boulevard ..	Add 110
Seventh Avenue	Add 12
Adam Clayton Powell, Jr. Boulevard ...	Add 20

Broadway
• addresses up to 754 are below 8th Street	
• between 754 and 858	Subtract 29
• between 859 and 958	Subtract 25
• addresses above 1000	Subtract 30
Eighth Avenue	Add 10
Ninth Avenue	Add 13
Columbus Avenue	Add 60
Tenth Avenue	Add 14
Amsterdam Avenue	Add 60
Eleventh Avenue	Add 15
West End Avenue	Add 60
Convent Avenue	Add 127
St. Nicholas Avenue	Add 110
Manhattan Avenue	Add 100
Edgecombe Avenue	Add 134
Fort Washington Avenue	Add 158

Central Park West and Riverside Drive have formulas of their own. To find the cross street for a building on Central Park West, divide the address by 10 and add 60. To find the cross street for a building on Riverside Drive up to 165th Street, divide the address by 10 and add 72.

A word of caution: because certain addresses—particularly those on Fifth, Madison, and Park avenues—are thought to be particularly prestigious, many buildings use them even if their entrances are actually on a side street. This is most common in midtown and along Fifth Avenue on the Upper East Side. If you can't find an address, look around the corner.

CROSS STREETS—Numbered cross streets run east-west. Addresses on them are easy to find. Allow for a little variation below 23rd Street (because Madison, Eleventh, and Twelfth avenues have yet to begin) and throughout the city whenever Broadway is involved.

EAST SIDE

1 to 49	between Fifth Avenue and Madison Avenue
50 to 99	between Madison Avenue and Park Avenue
100 to 149	between Park Avenue and Lexington Avenue
150 to 199	between Lexington Avenue and Third Avenue
200 to 299	between Third Avenue and Second Avenue
300 to 399	between Second Avenue and First Avenue
400 to 499	between First Avenue and York Avenue

WEST SIDE BELOW 59th STREET

1 to 99	between Fifth Avenue and Avenue of the Americas
100 to 199	between Avenue of the Americas and Seventh Avenue
200 to 299	between Seventh Avenue and Eighth Avenue
300 to 399	between Eighth Avenue and Ninth Avenue
400 to 499	between Ninth Avenue and Tenth Avenue
500 to 599	between Tenth Avenue and Eleventh Avenue
600 and up	between Eleventh Avenue and Twelfth Avenue

WEST SIDE ABOVE 59th STREET

1 to 99	between Central Park West and Columbus Avenue
100 to 199	between Columbus Avenue and Amsterdam Avenue
200 to 299	between Amsterdam Avenue and West End Avenue
Above 300	between West End Avenue and Riverside Drive

Odd-numbered addresses on east-west streets are on the north (uptown) side, while even-numbered ones are on the south (downtown) side.

Five area codes and 11 digits!

The proliferation of cell phones, pagers, fax machines, and dial-up modems has meant that three new area codes—917, 347, and 646—have been added to 212 (Manhattan) and 718 (New York's other four boroughs). Whether you're calling across the street or out to Staten Island, all calls now require dialing 11 digits: the numeral 1, plus the area code and phone number.

Neighborhoods

It may be hard for visitors to think of a city of millions in this fashion, but New York is really a collection of small neighborhoods. Some are more famous than others, and their borders may ebb and flow over the years, but each has a history and flavor all its own. To get a full sense of this wonderful city, I encourage you to visit as many neighborhoods as possible. From north to south, they include:

INWOOD AND WASHINGTON HEIGHTS—Home to General George Washington's forces during the Revolutionary War, these neighborhoods cover all of Manhattan north of about 151st Street. Racially and ethnically mixed, they have been home to generations of immigrants and now include everything from trendy to middle-class and poor areas. Several large and remarkably unspoiled parks, Yeshiva University, the Dyckman Farmhouse, The Cloisters, Columbia-Presbyterian Hospital, and Audubon Terrace are all in this area, as is the entrance to the George Washington Bridge. As the name implies, Washington Heights contains some surprisingly steep sections.

New York and Presidential History

Few places in our country have the rich history of New York. Whether you're interested in Colonial America, the Revolutionary War, the Civil War, the history of immigration, the labor movement, or the civil rights movement, New York is just brimming with stories and sights.

Presidential history buffs will want to know that:

- General George Washington used the Morris-Jumel Mansion (Edgecombe Ave at 160th St) as his headquarters during the Battle of Harlem Heights and gave his farewell address to his troops at Fraunces Tavern (54 Pearl St).
- President George Washington was inaugurated at Federal Hall National Memorial (26 Wall St).
- Republican presidential candidate Abraham Lincoln gave an historic anti-slavery speech that many consider the turning point in his campaign at Cooper-Union (30 Cooper Square) in 1860. Five years later, his body lay in state in the City Hall rotunda (Chambers St at Broadway).
- President Ulysses S. Grant and his wife are buried at Grant's Tomb in Riverside Park (Riverside Dr at 122nd St).
- President Theodore Roosevelt was born on East 20th Street (now the Theodore Roosevelt Birthplace National Historic Site, at 28 E 20th St).
- President Herbert Hoover lived in the tower at the Waldorf-Astoria (301 Park Ave) for many years after he left the White House.
- President Dwight Eisenhower was President of Columbia University (Broadway at 116th St) before he sat in the Oval Office.
- Former President Bill Clinton's offices are located at 55 West 125th Street in Harlem.

HARLEM—There are actually two Harlems: East Harlem (also called Spanish Harlem) and Harlem proper. East Harlem begins at about 96th Street and runs along the east side of the island to its northern tip. The population of this area is predominantly Latino, and Spanish is spoken more frequently than English here. El Museo del Barrio is on the southwestern edge of East Harlem.

Harlem itself occupies a small corridor in the middle of the island at the top of Central Park (at 110th Street) and then extends north and west of the famous and always busy 125th Street. That thoroughfare has again become a major shopping and entertainment hub, thanks in large part to the leadership of former NBA star Magic Johnson. The population of Harlem is almost entirely African-American, and the historic neighborhood is known around the world as a center of African-American music, politics, and culture. Harlem includes both middle-class and poor areas. Here you'll find the Schomburg Center for Research in Black Culture, the Apollo Theater, Abyssinian Baptist Church, and the Studio Museum of Harlem, as well as the office of former President Bill Clinton.

West *What* Street?

Even native New Yorkers have trouble keeping up with all the honorary street names scattered throughout the city. Leonard Bernstein Way? West 65th Street between Broadway and Amsterdam, just north of Avery Fisher Hall. But what about such less familiar eminences as Josh Rosenthal Way? West 72nd Street between Columbus Avenue and Central Park West. Joe Horvath Street? West 52nd Street between Tenth and Eleventh avenues. Abraham Kazan Street? Down on Grand Street, on the Lower East Side. R. Lonnie Williams Place? Go uptown to East 104th Street.

MORNINGSIDE HEIGHTS—This relatively small but vibrant area runs between Morningside Drive and the Hudson River from 110th Street to 124th Street. The stretch of Broadway between those streets is the neighborhood's economic heart. The area is dominated by three large and well-known institutions: Columbia University, Riverside Church, and the Cathedral Church of St. John the Divine. Grant's Tomb is across from Riverside Church, at 122nd Street in Riverside Park. The neighborhood is full of students and professors from all over the world.

UPPER WEST SIDE—This primarily residential area extends west of Central Park to the Hudson River from Columbus Circle at 59th Street all the way north to 110th Street. The Upper West Side is home to such famous apartment buildings as the Dakota and the Ansonia. The neighborhood is racially and ethnically mixed, and its residents pride themselves for being politically progressive and tending toward the bohemian (although by downtown standards, Upper West Siders are decidedly conventional).

Like a lot of Manhattan neighborhoods, the Upper West Side is brimming with children and families. Thanks in large part to entrepreneur Donald Trump, even the once grim Columbus Circle, at the southwest corner of Central Park, has been reborn with the new Time Warner Center and the so-called Shops at Columbus Circle. A little further north, the ABC Studio (where its talk shows and soap operas are taped) and Lincoln Center dominate the low and high ends of cultural life, respectively. The fabulous food stores Fairway and Zabar's are landmarks a bit further north. So are the American Museum of Natural History and the New-York Historical Society. Barnes & Noble at Broadway and 82nd Street is a major fixture in the neighborhood as well. Columbus Avenue, Amsterdam Avenue, and Broadway are lined with stores, while Central Park West, West End Avenue, and Riverside Drive are almost exclusively residential. The most elegant living areas of the Upper West Side are on Central Park West and the cross streets in the high 60s, the 70s, and the low 80s. Although even many longtime New Yorkers may suppose there's little worth doing between 96th Street and Harlem, that area—particularly on Broadway—is alive with good restaurants, neighborhood shopping, and great jazz clubs.

UPPER EAST SIDE—Best known for art museums, galleries, and upscale boutiques, the Upper East Side is also the city's most prestigious old-money residential neighborhood. It covers the area east of Central Park from Fifth Avenue to the East River between 59th and 96th streets. Fifth Avenue (also known as Museum Mile) is dominated by such famous institutions as the Metropolitan, Guggenheim, and Cooper-Hewitt museums. It is also home to a large number of expensive apartment buildings, former mansions, and foreign consulates, as well as many of Manhattan's elite private schools. On Madison Avenue you'll find the Whitney Museum and lots of galleries, all sorts of chic international designers and retailers in the 60s and lower 70s, and upscale boutiques and shops in the upper 70s and lower 80s. Park Avenue and most of the cross streets are home to residential buildings and such institutions as the Asia Society and the Americas Society. From Lexington Avenue east to the river above 75th Street—an area known as Yorkville—rents go down a bit. You'll find Gracie Mansion, the mayor's residence in Carl Schurz Park, overlooking the river at about 88th Street. Bloomingdale's has long been a major retail force at the southern end of the Upper East Side.

Times Change

Believe it or not, part of the old **Hell's Kitchen** (the gentrified name is now **Clinton**) has morphed into a wonderful neighborhood for restaurants, international food stores, and great bakeries. Look on Ninth Avenue between the high 30s and low 50s.

MIDTOWN—Squarely in the middle of the island south of 59th Street, midtown Manhattan is one of the busiest places on earth on weekdays and is almost deserted, except for tourists, on Sundays. (During Christmas season, tourists and natives alike flock to midtown.) The area extends from 42nd to 59th streets between Third and Seventh avenues. Fifth Avenue, home to the most expensive rental real estate in the world, is the heart of midtown and one of the world's most famous shopping areas. The flagship stores of Tiffany's, F.A.O. Schwarz, Saks Fifth Avenue, and Bergdorf Goodman are all here, as are such pop-culture icons as Niketown and The Gap. Many stately mansions once lined this part of Fifth Avenue, but only a few remain and none still serves as a residence.

St. Patrick's Cathedral and several other famous churches are also on Fifth Avenue in midtown. St. Bartholomew's is on Park Avenue, and the stately Central Synagogue is on Lexington Avenue. Landmark buildings like the Citicorp Center, Trump Tower, Rockefeller Center, and the Chrysler Building dominate the skyline. Carnegie Hall, the Ed Sullivan Theater, and Radio City Music Hall occupy the western edge of midtown. The once-elegant 57th Street, on the north edge of midtown, is definitely a little less exclusive these days, as stores like Swatch, Sunglass Hut, and Victoria's Secret sit side-by-side with Chanel, Prada, and Louis Vuitton. Grand Central Station, the New York Public Library, and Bryant Park mark midtown's southern edge.

CLINTON—Home to the Hell's Kitchen Gang a century ago, this neighborhood was once among the most violent and dangerous in the nation. It stretches south from 59th Street to 34th Street between Eighth Avenue and the Hudson River. Led by the startling transformation of the Times Square area into a family-friendly tourist mecca, much of Clinton has been gentrified. The always crowded and still scruffy Port Authority Bus Terminal is on Eighth Avenue in the southern part of this neighborhood. Ninth Avenue, particularly in the high 30s and low 40s, is home to a lot of ethnic grocers, bakers, and butchers. The west end of 42nd Street boasts some very good off-Broadway theaters. The Jacob K. Javits Convention Center and most of the city's passenger-ship terminals are located here along the Hudson River. Long considered one of the few "affordable" neighborhoods in New York, this area has seen lots of high-rise construction in recent years and plans are in the works for much more.

MURRAY HILL—Covering the East Side from 42nd Street south to 34th Street, Murray Hill begins at Park Avenue and runs to the East River. This area is almost entirely residential, and the nicest part can be found around Park Avenue in the upper 30s. The only real visitor attractions are the Morgan Library and the incredible Science, Industry, and Business Library in the old B. Altman Building at Madison Avenue and 34th Street.

Only in New York!
   The newsstand at the corner of Broadway and 32nd Street—an area close to the Diamond District and known for its sizable Korean business population—may be the only one in the world that sells newspapers in Hebrew, Korean, and English.

CHELSEA—As it has been, this area remains one of Manhattan's hottest. Still a largely residential neighborhood despite its increasing number of galleries, it extends from 34th Street down to 14th Street between Avenue of the Americas and the Hudson River. Madison Square Garden and Penn Station are in the northeast corner of Chelsea, but it's the southern part of the neighborhood that has really taken off. Surprisingly quiet and relatively clean, the southwestern part of Chelsea has lots of turn-of-the-century townhouses and small apartment buildings. It's also home to the lovely grounds of the General Theological Seminary and the Chelsea Piers development. What's really gotten the city's attention, however, are the almost 200 galleries that have migrated to the western edge of Chelsea, between 20th and 26th streets. Meanwhile, the southeastern edge of Chelsea, particularly where Chelsea and the Flatiron District overlap along Avenue of the Americas in the high teens and low 20s, has become what it was a century ago: a retailing hub. Such superstores as Bed Bath & Beyond, Barnes & Noble, and Burlington Coat Factory occupy buildings that once housed famous department stores.

FLATIRON DISTRICT—Named for the historic Flatiron Building, an architectural curiosity at the intersection of Broadway and Fifth Avenue at 23rd Street, this area was known as Ladies' Mile in the late 19th century for its elegant department stores. (A famous jingle at the time: "From 8th Street down, the men are earning it. From 8th Street up, the women are spending it.") Those department stores went out of business a century ago, but the buildings and the neighborhood are again alive and well, thanks in large part to an influx of superstores. The Flatiron District runs between Park Avenue South and Avenue of the Americas from 23rd Street down to 14th Street. Avenue of the Americas is really thriving, and parts of Fifth Avenue in this area also have undergone a resurgence. The Church of the Transfiguration (affectionately known as "the Little Church Around the Corner"), the Marble Collegiate Church, and the Empire State Building are all just north of here.

GRAMERCY PARK—This aging but still pleasant neighborhood was once the city's most elegant residential area. It covers the area from Park Avenue South to Second Avenue between 34th Street and 14th Street. The nicest part is Gramercy Park itself. The city's only remaining private park, it is bounded by Park Avenue South, Third Avenue, and 20th and 21st streets. A stroll down Irving Place, which runs from the park south to 14th Street, can be very pleasant indeed. The Flatiron District and the Gramercy Park area meet at Union Square, a lively area that is home to the city's largest and most popular Greenmarket. The New York Police Academy and Theodore Roosevelt's birthplace are on the western edge of Gramercy Park, and Stuyvesant Square Park occupies both sides of Second Avenue between 15th and 17th streets. Two huge planned residential areas, Stuyvesant Town and Peter Cooper Village, abut the East River, as does Bellevue Hospital.

Harlem is Hot!

In the 25 years that I've been writing this book, the fortunes of certain neighborhoods have definitely risen and fallen dramatically. Property values have gone through the roof in the northern part of the Upper West Side in recent years, and Harlem is experiencing another renaissance. The renovated **Apollo Theater** (253 W 125th St) is full of energy almost every night, the **Studio Museum** (144 W 125th St) showcases luminaries in the art world, and the **Schomburg Center for Research in Black Culture** (515 Malcolm X Blvd) has become a world-class research institution.

Spend a day in Harlem and discover some lesser-known treasures like **The Brownstone** (2032 Fifth Ave), *the* cafe and boutique for independent clothing designers; **Hue-Man Bookstore and Cafe** (2319 Eighth Ave), the city's best and biggest selection of African-American children's books; and **Wimps Southern Style Bakery, Sky Cafe and Martini Bar** (29 W 125th St), which offers a mouth-watering selection of fabulous baked goods and an upstairs bar. Former President Bill Clinton's office is at 55 West 125th Street.

Manhattan hot spots include **Clinton Street**, the new **Restaurant Row** on the Lower East Side, **West 14th Street** in the Meatpacking District, and **Smith Street** in Brooklyn.

MEATPACKING DISTRICT—This is one of the city's most bizarre and fascinating neighborhoods. I'm not suggesting that the average tourist would want to wander around here. However, the neighborhood west of Ninth Avenue (from 15th Street south to Gansevoort Street, between Chelsea and the West Village) is being shaped by a collision of interesting forces. Traditionally this dirty, architecturally uninteresting area has been the home of New York's meatpacking industry, as well as a great deal of prostitution. But the number of meatpacking businesses has dropped precipitously and community action has forced much of the prostitution elsewhere. Meanwhile, artists, bar owners, ultra-trendy boutiques and fashion designers, and even young families are attracted by the neighborhood's relatively cheap rents. The result is a weird mix of trendy bars, fashionable boutiques, wholesale meatpacking plants, transvestites, and Midwestern tourists seeking to be chic. There's even an ultramodern (and ultra-costly) new hotel—the Gansevoort—for all the beautiful people.

EAST VILLAGE—About 150 years ago the Astors, the Vanderbilts, and others of the city's elite lived here, but today the East Village is among the city's funkiest and, surprisingly, most livable neighborhoods. It lies between Avenue B and Broadway from 14th Street down to Houston Street. Alphabet City (the avenues in the eastern part of the East Village that have letters for names) and Tompkins Square are much tamer than they were a decade ago, and many parts have become gentrified to the point of being family-friendly, but they're still home to some offbeat and colorful nightclubs, shops, and people. The area along 6th Street between First and Second avenues is a thriving ethnic enclave known as Little India. The area around 7th Street and Third Avenue is home to a great many Ukrainian immigrants, and Stuyvesant Street is a gathering spot for young people from Japan. The Ukrainian Museum, St. Mark's in the Bowery, and Grace Church are all in the northern part of the East Village. Old Merchant's House, the last remnant of the East Village of yesteryear, is on the neighborhood's western edge.

GREENWICH VILLAGE—Although Greenwich Village is best known today for the beatniks and jazz clubs of the 1950s, it's also true that Edgar Allan Poe, Walt Whitman, Edna St. Vincent Millay, Frederic Church, and Edward Hopper all lived here at one time or another. In fact, this area has been among the city's most vibrant centers of culture (and *counter*culture) since relatively affluent New Yorkers began moving here in the early part of the 19th century to avoid the health epidemics of the increasingly crowded city to the south. Greenwich Village covers most of the area from Broadway west to the Hudson River between 14th Street and Houston Street. The section from Seventh Avenue to the river is known to locals as the West Village, and the part west of Ninth Avenue is the Meatpacking District. The beautiful Jefferson Market Library, the Forbes Magazine Galleries, New York University, and lots of interesting shops and nightclubs are located here, as is the always lively Washington Square Park and its famed arch. If you're going to spend time walking around here, relax and enjoy the Village without worrying about exactly what street you're on. The streets down here are confusing at best, but the area is small and you can't really get lost.

SOHO—Short for *So*uth of *Ho*uston, Soho went from being the center of New York in the middle of the 19th century to an almost entirely abandoned wasteland in the middle of the 20th century. Discovered by artists looking for inexpensive space in the 1960s and by upscale boutiques and retailers in the 1990s, it's now so trendy—that is to say, crowded and overrun with designer boutiques and tourists—that many artists, galleries, and now even some of the same high-end retailers who flocked to the area just a few years ago have moved to other parts of town. That said, it's still an energetic and dynamic neighborhood, and the recent addition of a Bloomingdale's on Broadway has been a shot in the arm for area retailers. Soho begins several blocks south of Washington Square Park on Houston Street and runs south to Canal Street between Broadway and Avenue of the Americas. The neighborhood comes alive on weekends and in the evening. Almost everything down here stays open later than similar establishments in the rest of the city. Many of the neighborhood's commercial galleries are concentrated on and around West Broadway (a separate street four blocks west of Broadway) between Houston and Broome streets.

TRIBECA—Shorthand for *Tri*angle *Be*low *Ca*nal, Tribeca used to be a rather dull and dirty commercial district but is becoming both residential and every bit as chic as Soho. It covers the area from Canal Street south to Chambers Street between Broadway and the Hudson River. Although it doesn't look as upscale as you might expect and can be very confusing for outsiders wandering around, Tribeca is home to emerging and established artists, commercial galleries, converted loft apartments, movie stars (Robert DeNiro's Tribeca Film Center has become a fixture down here), some good restaurants, and a growing number of boutiques.

Where are the Shopping Districts?

While most of the dozens of distinct shopping districts that once defined New York are gone or in precipitous decline, a few "only in New York" areas—shopping and otherwise—are worth noting:

- **Diamond District**—Jewelers and gem-cutters are concentrated on 47th Street between Fifth Avenue and Avenue of the Americas.
- **Financial District** (a.k.a. "Wall Street")—Banks, investment firms, and stock markets are headquartered between Broadway and Water Street from Maiden Lane to Exchange Place.
- **Flower District**—Located on West 28th Street between Avenue of the Americas and Seventh Avenue, this is the place to pick up fresh flowers and plants.
- **Museum Mile**—Some of New York's finest museums are strung along Fifth Avenue from 70th to 106th streets.
- **Theater District**—Renowned on- and off-Broadway theaters occupy Broadway and Eighth Avenue from 44th to 48th streets and on 42nd Street between Ninth and Tenth avenues.
- **Crystal District**—The five-block stretch of Madison Avenue between 58th and 63rd streets is home to Steuben, Swarovski, Baccarat, Daum, and Lalique.

You'll also find a cluster of **kitchen-supply stores** on the Bowery north of Delancey and Grand streets; **women's shoes** on 8th Street between Fifth Avenue and Avenue of the Americas; and several good **stationery stores** on 18th Street between Fifth Avenue and Avenue of the Americas.

CHINATOWN—This neighborhood's 150,000 residents, who occupy roughly 40 square blocks, make up the largest concentration of Chinese outside of Asia. Because it is always growing and increasingly overlaps such neighborhoods as Little Italy and the Lower East Side, Chinatown has boundaries nobody can quite agree how to define. Roughly speaking, it runs from Grand Street south to Worth Street, between Broadway and Allen Street. Its busiest streets are Canal, Mott, and Pell. If you've ever been to Hong Kong or southern China, you'll be overwhelmed by the similarities between those places and this neighborhood. Look for all sorts of wonderful food stores, as well as the Museum of Chinese in the Americas and the marvelous Chinese New Year parade and celebration.

NOLITA—Short for *No*rth of *L*ittle *Ita*ly, Nolita is a tiny neighborhood packed with vibrant restaurants, galleries, and boutiques. The entire neighborhood lies between Houston and Kenmare streets on Mulberry, Lafayette, Mott, and Elizabeth streets.

LITTLE ITALY—No longer home to many Italian immigrants and seemingly shrinking a little more every year as Chinatown and the newer Nolita expand, this area nonetheless remains the emotional heart of the entire region's Italian-American population, many of whom return for weddings, funerals, holidays, and other special occasions. Mulberry Street (better known as Via San Gennaro) around Grand Street forms the heart of Little Italy and is known for its restaurants and festivals.

Riding in Style

Next time you're feeling a little claustrophobic on a subway car, think of August Belmont, Jr., who financed construction of the IRT—the city's first subway line—between City Hall and 145th Street. He loved using the subway system but not with everyone else. Belmont had his very own subway car, complete with a rolltop desk, Tiffany glass, and a galley. It even had a name: the *Mineola*.

LOWER EAST SIDE—Many people use the Lower East Side as a geographic umbrella for Chinatown, Little Italy, and the Bowery, but I know it as a distinct neighborhood where generations of Eastern European and other immigrants first settled in overcrowded tenements and worked in sweatshops so their children could have better lives. (Many newer immigrants still live and work here in conditions that are not as much improved as you might think, although the immigrants and longtime retailers are being pushed out by yuppies looking for "affordable" housing and the increasing rents that follow them.) I also know it as what has historically been the best place in Manhattan to shop for high-quality clothing, household goods, and accessories at a discount. Because some of the area's businesses still are run by religiously observant Jews, they are closed on Friday afternoon and Saturday. Sunday is *the* shopping day here. Canal and Orchard streets are the area's heart, but the Lower East Side extends broadly from Houston to Canal streets and from the Sara D. Roosevelt Parkway east to Ludlow Street. The area still looks pretty run-down and many of the old stores are really struggling, but some of the old-timers are becoming more retail-savvy as their shops are increasingly interspersed with hip clubs, chic boutiques, art galleries, and new restaurants. Make sure to stop by the Lower East Side Tenement Museum and the Eldridge Street Synagogue to get a sense of the area's rich history.

DOWNTOWN—This area is a little hard to define except to say that it's centered around City Hall. Very roughly speaking, it runs from Chambers Street south to Fulton Street and from West Broadway east to Pearl Street. Many mom-and-pop stores and major chains are sited here, and its streets are always busy. St. Paul's Chapel, the Woolworth Building, the entrance to the Brooklyn Bridge pedestrian walkway, and the beautifully restored City Hall Park are all reasons to spend a little time here. Despite lots of improvements recently, this area always seems dirtier than the rest of the city. The South Street Seaport is located just east of downtown, and it's an easy walk south to Wall Street and Battery Park.

LOWER MANHATTAN—Extending from Wall Street and other parts of the Financial District south to Battery Park, this is the oldest part of New York City and was home to the World Trade Center. The hardest hit by the lingering aftermath of the terrorist attacks of September 11, 2001, it remains a very sober place. Things are very compact and vertical down here: the streets are as narrow as the buildings are tall. The boat to the Statue of Liberty and Ellis Island leaves from near Castle Clinton National Monument in Battery Park, and the Staten Island Ferry's terminal is just east of the park. While in Lower Manhattan, look for the exceptional Museum of the American Indian, Trinity Church, the Federal Hall National Memorial, Fraunces Tavern Museum, the Museum of American Financial History, New York Unearthed, the new home of the New York City Police Museum, and the New York Stock Exchange.

Need Directions?

   Go to *www.hopstop.com* for directions to any street address in New York via the subway, bus system, or on foot. Like the New York Transit system's version of MapQuest, this website renders obsolete all those maps you tried not to let anyone see you reading, but some of the full-size maps are still best if you're plotting out an itinerary.

BATTERY PARK CITY—A planned residential area built entirely on the landfill created when the original World Trade Center site was excavated in the 1970s, this collection of high-rise apartment buildings sits on the western side of Manhattan's southern tip, starting a bit north of Battery Park itself. The World Financial Center, where a lot of its residents work, is planted squarely in the middle of this neighborhood, and the Museum of Jewish Heritage is at its southern tip. Of course it's important to note that the World Trade Center sat on this neighborhood's eastern edge, and its absence has created a devastating hole, both physically and emotionally. While work to build a memorial on the site and to rebuild some of the surrounding area is ongoing, that hole will be there for many years to come.

GETTING AROUND NEW YORK

   Because it is an island and cannot sprawl outward, New York is compact and easier to navigate than most of the world's other large cities. You have a range of choices for how to get around, listed here in order of personal preference.

WALKING—Without question, this is my favorite way to get around New York. It may seem a little overwhelming at first (particularly in midtown at rush hour), and you'll stick out like a sore thumb if you wait on the curb for the "walk" signs, but walking is definitely the best way to see the city and get a sense of its neighborhoods. Often, especially in midtown on a weekday, walking is also the fastest way to travel ten or more blocks. Walking north-south (uptown or downtown), 20 blocks are equivalent to one mile. Most east-west (crosstown) blocks, particularly those between Fifth and Seventh avenues, are much longer. Unless you have small children in tow or are trying to get from Columbia University (at 116th Street) to New York University (at 4th Street), walking is the least expensive and most interesting way to travel. Just be aware of traffic and wear comfortable walking shoes!

SUBWAY—Some visitors and natives love to ride the subway, while others will do anything to avoid it. The roughly 3.5 million people who ride subways every weekday know that it's usually the fastest and most efficient way to travel in the city. As those numbers suggest, the subway can get very crowded. If you get claustrophobic, stay away from the subway around rush hour. And always hold on tightly to the hands of children who are with you. Thanks to an ongoing anti-grafitti campaign, a beefed-up police presence, an increasingly well-enforced ban on panhandling, and lots of renovations, the experience also has become significantly more pleasant.

Attention Older Visitors!
    If you have trouble climbing long flights of stairs, avoid the subway! Most stations have steep stairways and few have elevators. Buses, on the other hand, can kneel to ease access from the curb, and newer ones have ramps instead of stairs. By law, taxi drivers are required to help disabled passengers and cannot start the meter until passengers are safely settled.

The subway system is the result of a merger of private lines like the BMT and the IRT that sprang up over a century ago. Some of the stations and cars are quite old, so don't expect the relative luxury of BART in San Francisco or the Metro in Washington, D.C. Its 714 miles of track connect every borough except Staten Island. In Manhattan, the system is concentrated south of 110th Street (particularly below 59th Street). Maps of the system are available at station booths and are posted in most subway cars and stations. If you need to study a map, I suggest doing so in your hotel room or some other private place so as not to advertise the fact that you don't know where you're going. You'll also find a detailed map of the subway system in the front section of the Manhattan Yellow Pages.

The stairs leading down to most subway stations are almost always on a corner, marked by signs with a big "M" or "MTA." It's important to know that some are closed on weekends and others are marked for "uptown" or "downtown" access only. Unlike those in some of the other boroughs, Manhattan's subway stations are underground. (This should be noted by anyone who has trouble climbing stairs, as there are lots of steep ones in the subway system and few elevators.) You'll typically find station booths at the bottom of the stairs. Inside the station, signs point to the appropriate platform for uptown (sometimes "Bronx-bound") or downtown (sometimes "Brooklyn-bound") trains. Keep an eye out for express trains—they're great time-savers if you want to go where they're going, since they make limited stops. Some trains, such as the F line, run "express" in Queens but become "local" in Manhattan. The line number or letter, "local" or "express," and the name of the last stop are written on the side of each subway car, but maps are the best source of such information.

If you pay per ride, the subway costs $2 ($1 for senior citizens 65 and over with identification and free for up to three children under 44 inches tall with a fare-paying adult). Thanks to the **MetroCard** system, you can buy an unlimited seven-day pass for $24 or a 30-day pass for $76. You can also buy a one-day Fun Pass for $7, but it's available only from MetroCard vending machines, certain MetroCard merchants, and major visitor centers. A $10 card will get you 6 rides for the price of 5, while a $20 card will get you 12 for the price of 10.

While MetroCards can be purchased for cash only at station booths, major credit cards and debit cards can be used in the automated, multilingual vending machines inside the stations. (Be sure to press the Start button or you'll stand there wondering why the machine won't work!) MetroCards are also available at Rite Aid stores, Associated and D'Agostino supermarkets, Hudson News branches, and other locations throughout the city.

For all its great features, the MetroCard has one drawback worth mentioning: to discourage misuse of unlimited-ride cards, you cannot use the Fun Pass or any multiday, unlimited-ride pass again within 18 minutes of entering or leaving a given subway station. That can be frustrating if you get off at the wrong stop or are running a quick errand.

Some general subway rules:
- Once you've passed through the turnstiles and are inside a station, you can transfer between lines or ride for as long as you like. And if you're using a MetroCard, you can even transfer for free onto a bus within two hours with the same card—or anytime you want if you're using an unlimited-ride card!
- Station names are written on the walls of the stations and are announced inside subway cars, but the former are sometimes obscured and the latter are often garbled, so stay on your toes. If you miss your stop, you can get off and go back.
- Some lines stop running for a couple hours in the early morning and many have less frequent or different service at night and on weekends, but all stations in the system are served by some train on a regular basis 24 hours a day, seven days a week.

If you have questions or a problem, call the Metropolitan Transit Authority at 718/330-1234. (Non-English speakers can call 718/330-4847.)

Two subway strategies worth mentioning:
- Take an express to the stop closest to your destination and then wait for a local to take you the rest of the way. You can always get on one line and then switch trains to get to your destination. This works particularly well on the 4, 5, and 6 lines on the East Side, for example, as only the 6 makes local stops in midtown while the 4 and 5 go all the way down to Bowling Green. So, for instance, you can board the 6 in midtown and switch to a 4 or 5 at 42nd Street, 34th Street, or wherever else the lines meet.
- Wait for the next train if an arriving one is packed. Chances are there's a less crowded train right behind it. Your ride could be significantly more pleasant if you wait a minute or two. This also holds true for buses.

Finally, a word about safety. The Metropolitan Transit Authority has worked hard to clean up stations and the graffiti in them, as well as signifi-cantly reduce the number of system breakdowns. Still, subway stations and the cars themselves are sometimes dirty, and all sorts of strange people wan-der through them. Statistically, however, the system is no more dangerous than any other mode of transportation. Indeed, like crime in New York gen-erally, crime in the subway has fallen sharply. But do use common sense.

- *Don't* ride late at night or very early in the morning, particularly if you're alone.
- *Don't* enter deserted stations.
- *Don't* ride in an otherwise empty car.
- *Don't* wear flashy jewelry.
- *Don't* wander around aimlessly.
- *Don't* stand too close to the tracks.
- *Don't* use the bathroom inside any station.
- *Do* stick close to the designated off-hours waiting area if you're riding at an off-peak hour so that an attendant can keep an eye on you.
- *Do* watch your wallet or purse, particularly when riding in crowded cars.

Be Forewarned: Don't Try to Get a Cab at 5 p.m.!

As ridiculous as it sounds, the hardest time of day to catch a cab is late afternoon—right around quitting time and just before dinner. Why? Because cab drivers typically work a 12-hour shift, and 4:30 or 5 p.m. is the end of the day shift. If you're making dinner reservations or need to be somewhere in late afternoon, plan accordingly!

TAXIS—All officially licensed medallion taxicabs in New York are yellow, have the words "NYC Taxi" and fare information written on their side doors, and post their medallion number in a box on the roof. Inside you'll see a meter and the driver's license (with his or her picture) and medallion number dis-played on the dashboard, usually on the passenger's side. The city, particu-larly outside midtown, is full of unregulated "cars for hire" (a.k.a. gypsy cabs) that are not legally allowed to pick up people south of 96th Street. Still, they sometimes try to do just that.

I strongly encourage you to stick with medallion cabs. The cost of a ride in a medallion cab is calculated per trip rather than per person, which means that a short trip for four adults in a cab can actually be cheaper than a bus or subway ride. That said, however, fares can add up quickly, particularly if you're stuck in heavy traffic. The charge begins at $2.50 the moment you get in and costs 40 cents for every one-fifth of a mile driven and every 90 seconds the cab sits in traffic. In general, the meter should "click" every four blocks when you're going north-south and every block when you're going east-west. You pay for any tolls, and there's a 50-cent surcharge for rides made between 8 p.m. and 6 a.m. and a $1 surcharge on rides between 4 p.m. and 8 p.m. on weekdays. The meter in the front keeps a running total of the fare, and the driver is required to give you a receipt, if requested. A tip of between 15% and 20% of the fare is standard, and payment is generally expected in cash. Drivers often cannot make change for bills larger than $20 (and are not required to).

Drivers *are* required to take you anywhere within the five boroughs of

New York City, to Westchester and Nassau counties, and to Newark Airport. That's the law, but the reality is that many cab drivers will make a fuss if you want to go to one of the airports, out to one of those suburban counties, or even to lower-income neighborhoods in Manhattan. Moreover, be forewarned that drivers can charge double the metered fare once they leave the city limits, plus tolls. If you have a problem, jot down the driver's name and medallion number and contact the New York City Taxi and Limousine Commission (221 W 41st Street, New York, NY 10036; 212/221-8294, www.nyc. gov/html/tlc) to complain. These folks take their oversight responsibilities seriously.

So how do you go about hailing a cab? Stand on or just off a curb and stick your arm up and out. If the number (but not the "off-duty" sign) is lit in the rectangular box on a cab's roof, it's empty and looking for business. Finding a cab in a snowstorm, in midtown, on a rainy Friday afternoon or any day around 5 p.m. is difficult, but you usually won't have trouble finding one in most parts of the city at most times of day. If you do have trouble, go to a major hotel or join the cab line at Penn Station, Grand Central Station, or Port Authority Bus Terminal. If you want the driver to take a particular route (it's a good idea to know exactly where you're going), say so when you get in. Assuming it isn't raining, I also suggest giving the driver the closest intersection rather than a street address as your destination. This will save both time and money. Passengers ride in the back seat, although the driver will usually let one person ride up front if there are four in your party. A final note: a recent law requires drivers to help disabled passengers and prohibits them from starting the meter until such passengers are safely settled.

Get Off the Sidewalk!

   The only New Yorkers allowed to ride bikes on the sidewalk are children under 12. Everyone else must be on the street. All bike riders and skaters under 14 are required by law to wear a helmet.

BUSES—In the earliest editions of this book, I wrote that the only reasons to take a city bus are if you have a lot of time and are afraid of the alternatives. A friend who rode the bus every day objected strongly. First of all, she pointed out, the city's blue-and-white buses are wheelchair-accessible (which the subway decidedly is not) and "elderly friendly" in that the driver can lower the stairs at the entrance for anyone who has trouble climbing high steps. Some of the city's newest buses are even "low-floor" models, with loading ramps instead of stairs. Buses are also "stroller friendly," insofar as the doors don't close automatically and there are only a few steps to climb and descend.

Precisely because people who take the bus aren't in a hurry, they tend to be friendlier than subway riders and often will give an older person or a harried parent their seat. Buses are very safe and usually don't attract the strange people who still sometimes habituate subway cars and stations. Because there is a driver, you can ask questions or get directions. And because the bus stops frequently and you can always see where you're going, it's a good and relatively cheap way to get a flavor of the city. I still find the system frustratingly slow (the average speed of the M96, a bus traversing the length of 96th Street, has been clocked at 4.3 miles per hour at midday), but buses do have some redeeming features, and their popularity has increased so dramatically that there are now some double-length ("articulated") buses traveling busier routes.

Buses run up and down most avenues and on most major cross streets beween 6 a.m. and midnight. Uptown buses stop every two or three blocks, and crosstown buses stop on every block—assuming someone is waiting at a bus stop or a bus rider has pushed the yellow tape to alert the driver that a stop is requested. Many bus lines have a "limited stop" version that stops every ten blocks or so at major intersections; an orange "limited" sign is clearly visible in their front windshields. At a minimum, you can spot a bus stop by its blue sign and route numbers. The city has renovated and added more "Guide-a-Ride" signs and route maps, making the entire system much more user-friendly.

Many stops are used by more than one route, so check the screen on the front or side of each bus for its route number or simply ask the driver. Your fare entitles you to one bus transfer, and you should request the transfer ticket from the driver when you board (unless you're paying with a Metrocard, in which case you can transfer automatically within two hours). The transfer is good only for a continuous trip, which means that you cannot get off and then board another bus on the same route. If you're using a MetroCard, you can transfer onto a subway within two hours.

If you pay per ride, the bus costs $2 ($1 for senior citizens 65 and over with identification and free for up to three children under 44 inches tall with a fare-paying adult). You need exact change and the machine cannot accept bills. Thanks to the **MetroCard** system, you can buy unlimited-ride passes or multiple-ride ones. For more information, see the previous section on the subway, or go to any subway station.

My Best Advice
- Everybody is in a hurry. You don't need to be. Slow down and savor the sights and sounds of Manhattan.
- Give yourself permission to wander without an agenda in a neighborhood like the West Village or the Upper East Side.
- The subway is by far the fastest and most efficient way to get around the city, but do not use it if you have trouble using stairs.

You can get a map of Manhattan bus routes on most buses (ask the driver or look for boxes by the front and back doors) and at most subway token booths. You will also find a detailed map of the bus system in the Manhattan Yellow Pages. The map details where buses run, frequency of service, and which bus to take to major museums and other attractions. If you have questions about how to get from one place to another via bus, call the Metropolitan Transit Authority between 6 a.m. and 9 p.m. at 718/330-1234 or go to www.mta.nyc.ny.us.

CAR SERVICES—If you're wondering about the large number of Lincoln Town Cars and other black sedans in midtown and the Financial District, they are car services. Unlike taxicabs, which cruise the streets looking for business, car services are available only by reservation and often are exclusively for corporate clients. If you're in New York on business, your company may arrange to have you picked up from the airport and shuttled around town by one of these services. Chances are you will be given an account number and pay with a voucher provided by either your company or the driver. A client's name and car number will typically be posted in the window of the car, and you'll be told in advance what to look for.

Some car services and limousine companies take reservations from individuals. **Carey Limousine NY** (212/599-1122, 800/336-4646) is among the larger and more reputable companies. You can have a car meet you at the airport, be shuttled around town for a day, or simply arrive and depart from the opera in style. The cost is calculated by the hour or the trip rather than by mileage, so make sure you agree on a price before making a commitment. Reservations are required. Make them at least a day in advance and call to confirm several hours before you expect to leave. If you want a specific type of car or limousine, say so when you're making reservations. These car services are on the high end of the business. You'll find lots of gypsy cabs and low-end car services in the outer boroughs and outside midtown, but I suggest avoiding them. Just so you know, licensed limousines are required to post a diamond-shaped decal on the right side of their windshield. On it will be an eight-digit number bookended by the letters T and C.

Don't Miss

Everyone has their list of favorites in New York, but here are a few places that you just *shouldn't* miss if you're visiting this great city:
* Ellis Island and the Statue of Liberty
* Lower East Side Tenement Museum and Orchard Street
* Frick Collection
* Metropolitan Museum of Art
* Grand Central Station
* Museum of the City of New York—especially the Rockefeller Rooms
* Museum of Modern Art
* Central Park
* The Cloisters
* St. Patrick's Cathedral
* Ground Zero
* Radio City Music Hall
* Cathedral Church of St. John the Divine

DRIVING—If you read my comments earlier in this chapter, you already know that I *strongly* recommend against driving in New York. Leave the hassles and headaches to cab and bus drivers. The parking regulations alone ought to discourage you. There are alternate-side-of-the-street rules, special rules for several dozen official holidays, and weekend rules. For information, go to www.nyc.gov/html/dot. And that's assuming you can find a space. (The average rental cost of a parking space in an underground lot in midtown is more than $500 a month!) Illegal parking can cost upwards of $200—and that's *after* you've paid for the towing and impoundment of your vehicle. If you can't find a space on the street or want the security of a garage, you're going to pay big bucks. Forty dollars a day is not uncommon.

Hundreds of thousands of cars, taxis, trucks, and other vehicles come into Manhattan every day. While the speed limit on city streets is 30 miles per hour unless otherwise posted, it's little wonder that the average speed of traffic going uptown or downtown is less than 10 mph . . . and the average crosstown speed is half that! If you must drive, I recommend becoming a member of AAA or some other major automobile club and getting all the information they have about traffic laws and driving in the city. Whatever else you do, make sure you know where you're going and be prepared for a lot of honking. Drivers in New York are not very patient.

II. Where to Eat It: Manhattan a la Carte

During the day, visitors like to do different things in New York: wandering through museum galleries, shopping at chic boutiques along Madison Avenue, taking trips to the Empire State Building or to the Statue of Liberty —the list goes on and on. But there's one thing everyone does when they come to New York: go out for meals. This is a restaurant town, certainly the best restaurant town in this country and possibly in the world.

Over the years, I've been asked more questions about restaurants than any other topic. What's the best French restaurant? Who makes the best pizza in town? Where can I get a good Sunday brunch? Where can I get a good meal for a decent price? What's the best restaurant with a view in New York? These are just a few of the questions I've tried to answer in the following pages.

Here are a few things to keep in mind as you begin to think about dining in New York:

- People in New York eat later than they do in the rest of the country. Prime dinner hour is 8 p.m. Many are still eating by 10 p.m.
- Reservations matter. Make them in advance, be nice to the person taking them, and confirm them before you go.
- If you can't get a reservation, drop by anyway. If there is no space, consider eating at the bar.
- Dress appropriately. While most restaurants in New York are far more casual than they once were, a few still have dress codes. At no time in any restaurant should men wear hats!
- Ask the wine steward and waiter for their suggestions. Just be wary of high-priced specials.
- Tip appropriately. An easy rule of thumb is to double the tax (which is 8.25%) for adequate service. Good, attentive service deserves a 20% tip. For really excellent service, a tip of 25% of the pre-tax bill is absolutely appropriate.

Everyone has a list of things that bother them about a restaurant. Here's mine:

- Haughty greeting or no greeting at all.
- Being forced to wait at the bar when tables are available.
- Overly chatty waiters who provide their life histories.
- Sloppy, unkempt wait staff.
- Being offered pepper with every course.
- Greasy, dirty menus.

- Being asked repeatedly, "Is everything all right?"
- Waiters who scrape food off plates in front of diners.
- Having to ask more than once for the check.
- Unclean restrooms.

Before I explain how I approach reviews and recommendations, let me first offer a few caveats. I am not a professional restaurant critic. I do own a restaurant and gourmet cake shop in Oregon, and I definitely have some strong opinions about what makes a good operation. I care deeply about service and presentation. Like anyone who is paying for their meal—and in New York you'll generally pay a lot more than you would back home—I care most about whether my food looks and tastes good. Those are the criteria I've used to evaluate the hundreds of New York restaurants I've included in the following pages.

You should know that the New York restaurant scene changes daily. Even some restaurants that seem to be fixtures one day can be gone the next. Trendy chefs bounce around sometimes, and new restaurants open and close with remarkable speed. With all that in mind, however, I've included a list of restaurants by neighborhood, as well as extensive lists of places I think offer the best in a given food category. In addition, I've authored nearly 300 full-length restaurant reviews, which begin on page 82. Those restaurants each fall into one of four price categories for dinner, excluding drinks and tax:

Inexpensive: $15 and under per person
Moderate: $16 to $34 per person
Moderately expensive: $35 to $45 per person
Expensive: $46 and up per person

If you have a particularly good experience or strongly disagree with any of my comments, please let me know. Also contact me if a favorite spot is not covered in this book.

Bon appetit!

Quick Reference Guide

(Note: Reference to Sunday simply means that a given restaurant is open on Sunday.)

CENTRAL PARK AREA

Alain Ducasse (Essex House, a Westin Hotel, 155 W 58th St): French
Atelier (Ritz-Carlton New York, Central Park, 50 Central Park S): Continental, Sunday
Café Botanica (Essex House, a Westin Hotel, 160 Central Park S): American, Sunday
Manhattan Ocean Club (57 W 58th St): Seafood, Sunday
Sarabeth's Kitchen (40 Central Park S): American/Continental, Sunday
Tavern on the Green (Central Park W at 67th St): Continental, Sunday

CHELSEA

The Biltmore Room (290 Eighth Ave): Continental, Sunday
Chelsea Bistro & Bar (358 W 23rd St): French, Sunday
Da Umberto (107 W 17th St): Italian
F&B Güdtfood (269 W 23rd St): European street food, Sunday
Frank's (410 W 16th St): Steak, Sunday
Gascogne (158 Eighth Ave): French, Sunday

La Bottega (Maritime Hotel, 88 Ninth Ave): Italian, Sunday
La Lunchonette (130 Tenth Ave): French, Sunday
Moran's Chelsea (146 Tenth Ave): American, Sunday
Porters (216 Seventh Ave): American, Sunday
Raymond's Cafe (88 Seventh Ave): Continental, Sunday

CHINATOWN

Golden Unicorn (18 East Broadway): Chinese, Sunday

EAST HARLEM

Rao's (455 E 114th St): Italian

EAST SIDE/UPPER EAST SIDE

Annie's (1381 Third Ave): American, Sunday
Arabelle (Hotel Plaza Athenee New York, 37 E 46th St): Continental, Sunday
Aureole (34 E 61st St): New American
Bravo Gianni (230 E 63rd St): Italian, Sunday
Cafe Boulud (Surrey Hotel, 20 E 76th St): French, Sunday
Cafe Sabarsky (Neue Galerie, 1048 Fifth Ave): Vietnamese, Sunday
Daniel (60 E 65th St): French
davidburke & donatella (133 E 61st St): Continental, Sunday
Demarchelier (50 E 86th St): French, Sunday
Elio's (1621 Second Ave): Italian, Sunday
Etats-Unis (242 E 81st St): American, Sunday
Fred's at Barneys New York (660 Madison Ave, 9th floor): American, Sunday
Geisha (33 E 61st St): Japanese
Gino (780 Lexington Ave): Italian, Sunday
Il Riccio (152 E 79th St): Italian, Sunday
Il Vagabondo (351 E 62nd St): Italian, Sunday
Jackson Hole Burgers (various locations): Burgers, Sunday
Jacques (204 E 85th St): French, Sunday
John's Pizzeria (408 E 64th St): Italian, Sunday
King's Carriage House (251 E 82nd St): Continental, Sunday
Le Boeuf à la Mode (539 E 81st St): French, Sunday
Lentini (1562 Second Ave): Italian, Sunday
Le Refuge (166 E 82nd St): French, Sunday
Manhattan Grille (1161 First Ave): Continental, Sunday
Mark's Restaurant (The Mark Hotel, 25 E 77th St): French, Sunday
Nicola's (146 E 84th St): Italian, Sunday
92 (Wales Hotel, 45 E 92nd St): American, Sunday
Our Place (1444 Third Ave): Chinese, Sunday
Paola's (245 E 84th St): Italian, Sunday
Park Avenue Cafe (100 E 63rd St): American, Sunday
Payard Patisserie & Bistro (1032 Lexington Ave): French
Pinocchio (1748 First Ave): Italian, Sunday
Post House (Lowell Hotel, 28 E 63rd St): Steak, Sunday
Primavera (1578 First Ave): Italian, Sunday
Restaurant 343 (343 E 85th St): American, Sunday
Sarabeth's at the Whitney (Whitney Museum of American Art, 945 Madison Ave): American/Continental, Sunday
Sarabeth's Kitchen (1295 Madison Ave): American/Continental, Sunday

Serendipity 3 (225 E 60th St): American, Sunday
Sette Mezzo (969 Lexington Ave): Italian, Sunday
Sistina (1555 Second Ave): Italian, Sunday
Taste (1413 Third Ave): American, Sunday
Tony's Di Napoli (1606 Second Ave): Italian, Sunday
Vinegar Factory (431 E 91st St): American, Sunday
Vivolo (140 E 74th St): Italian, Sunday

EAST VILLAGE

Danal (90 E 10th St): French, Sunday
Hearth (403 E 12th St): American, Sunday
I Coppi (432 E 9th St): Italian, Sunday
Jack's Luxury Oyster Bar (246 E 5th St): Seafood
Second Avenue Kosher Delicatessen and Restaurant (156 Second Ave):
    Deli, Sunday

FLATIRON DISTRICT/GRAMERCY PARK/LOWER BROADWAY/ UNION SQUARE

Blue Smoke (116 E 27th St): Barbecue, Sunday
Blue Water Grill (31 Union Square W): Seafood, Sunday
Bolo (23 E 22nd St): Spanish, Sunday
Candela (116 E 16th St): American, Sunday
Caviar & Banana (12 E 22nd St): South American, Sunday
City Bakery (3 W 18th St): Bakery/Cafe, Sunday
Craft (43 E 19th St): American, Sunday
Eleven Madison Park (11 Madison Ave): French/American, Sunday
Fleur de Sel (5 E 20th St): French, Sunday
Gramercy Tavern (42 E 20th St): American, Sunday
Houston's (378 Park Ave S): American, Sunday
La Petite Auberge (116 Lexington Ave): French, Sunday
Les Halles (411 Park Ave S): French, Sunday
MetroCafe & Wine Bar (32 E 21st St): American, Sunday
Morrell's Wine Bar (900 Broadway): American
Olives New York (W New York Union Square, 201 Park Ave S): Continental,
    Sunday
Rolf's (281 Third Ave): German, Sunday
T Salon & T Emporium (11 E 20th St): Teahouse, Sunday
Tabla (11 Madison Ave): Indian, Sunday
Tocqueville (15 E 15th St): American, Sunday
Union Square Cafe (21 E 16th St): American, Sunday
Veritas (43 E 20th St): Continental, Sunday

GREENWICH VILLAGE/WEST VILLAGE

Babbo (110 Waverly Pl): Italian, Sunday
Blue Hill (75 Washington Pl): American, Sunday
Blue Ribbon Bakery (35 Downing St): American, Sunday
Cafe Topsy (575 Hudson St): Continental, Sunday
Camaje (85 MacDougal St): French, Sunday
Chez Jacqueline (72 MacDougal St): French, Sunday
Chez Michallet (90 Bedford St): French, Sunday
Citron (228 Bleecker St): American, Sunday
Cucina Stagionale (289 Bleecker St): Italian, Sunday

Gonzo (140 W 13th St): Italian, Sunday
Good (89 Greenwich Ave): American, Sunday
Gotham Bar & Grill (12 E 12th St): American, Sunday
Il Mulino (86 W 3rd St): Italian
Jarnac (328 W 12th St): French, Sunday
John's Pizzeria (278 Bleecker St): Italian, Sunday
La Ripaille (605 Hudson St): French, Sunday
Le Gigot (18 Cornelia St): French, Sunday
Minetta Tavern (113 MacDougal St): Italian, Sunday
One if by Land, Two if by Sea (17 Barrow St): Continental, Sunday
Paris Commune (99 Bank St): French, Sunday
Pó (31 Cornelia St): Italian, Sunday
(The Famous) Ray's Pizza of Greenwich Village (465 Ave of the Americas):
    Pizza, Sunday
Strip House (13 E 12th St): Steak, Sunday
Tartine (253 W 11th St): Continental, Sunday
Wallsé (344 W 11th St): Austrian, Sunday

LINCOLN CENTER

Gabriel's Bar & Restaurant (11 W 60th St): Italian
Picholine (35 W 64th St): Mediterranean, Sunday
Rosa Mexicano (61 Columbus Ave): Mexican, Sunday

LOWER EAST SIDE

A.O.C. Bedford (14 Bedford St): Continental, Sunday
Clinton St. Baking Co. & Restaurant (4 Clinton St): American, Sunday
Freeman's (2 Freeman Alley): Continental, Sunday
Katz's Delicatessen (205 E Houston St): Deli, Sunday
Le Quinze (132 W Houston St): French, Sunday
Schiller's (131 Rivington St): American, Sunday
71 Clinton Fresh Food (71 Clinton St): American, Sunday
Tasting Room (72 E 1st St): Continental

MEATPACKING DISTRICT

Markt (401 W 14th St): Belgian, Sunday
Pastis (9 Ninth Ave): French, Sunday
Spice Market (403 W 13th St): Asian, Sunday

MIDTOWN EAST

Angels Ristorante (1135 First Ave): Italian, Sunday
Aquavit (65 E 55th St): Scandinavian, Sunday
Artisanal (2 Park Ave): Bistro/Brasserie, Sunday
Bellini (208 E 52nd St): Italian
BLT Steak (106 E 57th St): Steak
Bouterin (420 E 59th St): French, Sunday
Brasserie (100 E 53rd St): French, Sunday
Cafe Centro (MetLife Building, 200 Park Ave): Continental
Cafe Indulge (561 Second Ave): American/Bakery, Sunday
Capital Grille (Chrysler Center, 155 E 42nd St): Steak, Sunday
Chin Chin (216 E 49th St): Chinese, Sunday
Cucina & Co. (MetLife Building, 200 Park Ave, lobby): Italian
Dawat (210 E 58th St): Indian, Sunday

Dining Commons (City University of New York Graduate Center, 365 Fifth Ave, 8th floor): American
Docks Oyster Bar and Seafood Grill (633 Third Ave): Seafood, Sunday
El Parador Cafe (325 E 34th St): Mexican, Sunday
F&B Güdtfood (150 E 52nd St): European street food, Sunday
Fifty Seven Fifty Seven (Four Seasons Hotel New York, 57 E 57th St, lobby level): American, Sunday
Four Seasons (99 E 52nd St): Continental
Frank's Trattoria (371 First Ave): Italian, Sunday
Fresco by Scotto (34 E 52nd St): Italian
Grand Central Oyster Bar and Restaurant (Grand Central Station, 42nd St at Vanderbilt Ave, lower level): Seafood
Hatsuhana (17 E 48th St and 237 Park Ave): Japanese
Houston's (Citicorp Center, 153 E 53rd St): American, Sunday
Il Postino (337 E 49th St): Italian, Sunday
Jimmy Sung's (219 E 44th St): Chinese, Sunday
La Grenouille (3 E 52nd St): French
Le Périgord (405 E 52nd St): French, Sunday
Lever House (390 Park Ave): American, Sunday
L'Impero (45 Tudor City Pl): Italian
Maloney & Porcelli (37 E 50th St): American, Sunday
March (405 E 58th St): American, Sunday
Marchi's (251 E 31st St): Italian
Michael Jordan's the Steak House NYC (Grand Central Station, 42nd St at Vanderbilt Ave): Steak, Sunday
Morton's of Chicago (551 Fifth Ave): Steak, Sunday
Mr. K's (570 Lexington Ave): Chinese, Sunday
Oceana (55 E 54th St): Seafood
Palm One (837 Second Ave): Steak, Sunday
Palm Too (840 Second Ave): Steak, Sunday
Park Bistro (414 Park Ave S): French, Sunday
Pershing Square (90 E 42nd St): American, Sunday
Pietro's (232 E 43rd St): Italian
P.J. Clarke's (915 Third Ave): American/Bistro, Sunday
Rare Bar & Grill (Shelburne Murray Hill, 303 Lexington Ave): American, Sunday
Ristorante Grifone (244 E 46th St): Italian
Rosa Mexicano (1063 First Ave): Mexican, Sunday
San Pietro (18 E 54th St): Italian
Shun Lee Palace (155 E 55th St): Chinese, Sunday
Smith & Wollensky (797 Third Ave): Steak, Sunday
Sparks Steakhouse (210 E 46th St): Steak
Tao (42 E 58th St): Asian, Sunday
Tropica (MetLife Building, 200 Park Ave, lobby): Seafood
Turkish Kitchen (386 Third Ave): Turkish, Sunday
Typhoon Brewery (22 E 54th St): Thai
United Nations Delegates Dining Room (United Nations, First Ave at 46th St): Continental
Vong (200 E 54th St): Thai, Sunday
Water Club (500 E 30th St): American, Sunday
Zarela (953 Second Ave): Mexican, Sunday

MIDTOWN WEST

Abboccato (136 W 55th St): Italian, Sunday
Baldoria (249 W 49th St): Italian, Sunday
Beacon (25 W 56th St): American, Sunday
Ben Benson's Steak House (123 W 52nd St): Steak, Sunday
Bond 45 (154 W 45th St): Italian, Sunday
Brasserie 8½ (9 W 57th St): French, Sunday
Brasserie LCB (60 W 55th St): French, Sunday
Brooklyn Diner USA (212 W 57th St): Eclectic, Sunday
Bryant Park Grill (25 W 40th St): American/Continental, Sunday
Carmine's (200 W 44th St): Italian, Sunday
Carnegie Delicatessen and Restaurant (854 Seventh Ave): Deli, Sunday
Del Frisco's Double Eagle Steak House (McGraw-Hill Building, 1221 Ave
   of the Americas): Steak, Sunday
44 & X Hell's Kitchen (622 Tenth Ave): American, Sunday
Gaby (44 W 45th St): French, Sunday
Il Gattopardo (33 W 54th St): Italian, Sunday
Keens Steakhouse (72 W 36th St): American, Sunday
Le Bernardin (155 W 51st St): French
Le Biarritz (325 W 57th St): French
Le Rivage (340 W 46th St): French, Sunday
Mangia è Bevi (800 Ninth Ave): Italian, Sunday
McCormick & Schmick's (1285 Ave of the Americas): Seafood, Sunday
The Modern (Museum of Modern Art, 9 W 53rd St): Continental, Sunday
Nobu 57 (40 W 57th St): Japanese, Sunday
Osteria del Circo (120 W 55th St): Italian, Sunday
Our Place Shanghai Tea Garden (141 E 55th St): Chinese, Sunday
Palm West Side (250 W 50th St): Steak, Sunday
Patsy's (236 W 56th St): Italian, Sunday
Redeye Grill (890 Seventh Ave): American, Sunday
Remi (145 W 53rd St): Italian, Sunday
René Pujol (321 W 51st St): French
Roundtable (Algonquin Hotel, 59 W 44th St, lobby): American, Sunday
Rue 57 (60 W 57th St): French, Sunday
Sea Grill (19 W 49th St): Seafood
Shelly's New York (104 W 57th St): American, Sunday
Tony's Di Napoli (147 W 43rd St): Italian, Sunday
Trattoria Dell'Arte (900 Seventh Ave): Italian, Sunday
21 Club (21 W 52nd St): American
Uncle Jack's Steakhouse (440 Ninth Ave): Steak, Sunday
Woo Chon (10 W 36th St): Korean, Sunday

SOHO/LITTLE ITALY

Balthazar (80 Spring St): French, Sunday
Bistro les Amis (180 Spring St): French, Sunday
Blue Ribbon (97 Sullivan St): Eclectic, Sunday
Butter (415 Lafayette St): New American
Country Cafe (69 Thompson St): French/Moroccan, Sunday
Cupping Room Cafe (359 West Broadway): American, Sunday
Fiamma Osteria (206 Spring St): Italian, Sunday
Giorgione (307 Spring St): Italian, Sunday
Il Cortile (125 Mulberry St): Italian, Sunday

Kittichai (60 Thompson St): Thai, Sunday
Le Jardin Bistro (25 Cleveland Pl): French, Sunday
Mezzogiorno (195 Spring St): Italian, Sunday
O'Nieal's Grand Street (174 Grand St): Continental, Sunday
Provence (38 MacDougal St): French, Sunday
Raoul's (180 Prince St): French/Bistro, Sunday
Savore (200 Spring St): Italian, Sunday
Spring Street Natural Restaurant (62 Spring St): Health, Sunday
Woo Lae Oak Soho (148 Mercer St): Korean, Sunday
Zoë (90 Prince St): American, Sunday

THEATER DISTRICT/TIMES SQUARE

Barbetta (321 W 46th St): Italian, Sunday
DB Bistro Moderne (55 W 44th St): French, Sunday
Ellen's Stardust Diner (1650 Broadway): Diner, Sunday
Orso (322 W 46th St): Italian, Sunday
Ruby Foo's (1626 Broadway): Chinese, Sunday

TRIBECA/DOWNTOWN/FINANCIAL DISTRICT

Acappella (1 Hudson St): Italian
Bayard's (1 Hanover Square): French
Bouley (120 West Broadway): French, Sunday
Bridge Cafe (279 Water St): American, Sunday
Capsouto Frères (451 Washington St): French, Sunday
Chanterelle (2 Harrison St): French
Danube (30 Hudson St): Austrian
Fresh (105 Reade St): American
Il Bagatto (192 E 2nd St): Italian, Sunday
Il Giglio (81 Warren St): Italian
MarkJoseph Steakhouse (261 Water St): Steak
Montrachet (239 West Broadway): French
Nobu (105 Hudson St): Japanese, Sunday
Nobu Next Door (105 Hudson St): Japanese, Sunday
Roy's New York (New York Marriott Financial Center Hotel, 130 Washington St): Pan-Pacific, Sunday
Scalini Fedeli (165 Duane St): Italian
66 (241 Church St): Chinese, Sunday
Tribeca Grill (375 Greenwich St): American, Sunday
2 West (Ritz-Carlton New York, Battery Park, 2 West St): American, Sunday
Walker's (16 N Moore St): Pub, Sunday

WEST SIDE/UPPER WEST SIDE

Alouette (2588 Broadway): French, Sunday
Asiate (Mandarin Oriental New York, 80 Columbus Circle): French/Japanese, Sunday
Big Nick's (2175 Broadway): Burgers/Pizza, Sunday
Café Gray (Time Warner Center, 10 Columbus Circle, 3rd floor): Continental
Carmine's (2450 Broadway): Italian, Sunday
'Cesca (164 W 75th St): Continental, Sunday
Compass (208 W 70th St): American, Sunday
Docks Oyster Bar and Seafood Grill (2427 Broadway): Seafood, Sunday

Fairway Cafe & Steakhouse (2127 Broadway): American, Sunday
Good Enough to Eat (483 Amsterdam Ave): American, Sunday
Jean Georges (Trump International Hotel, 1 Central Park W): Continental, Sunday
Jean-Luc (507 Columbus Ave): French, Sunday
John's Pizzeria (260 W 44th St): Italian, Sunday
La Boite en Bois (75 W 68th St): French, Sunday
Les Routiers (568 Amsterdam Ave): French, Sunday
Métisse (239 W 105th St): French, Sunday
Ocean Grill (384 Columbus Ave): Seafood, Sunday
Ouest (2315 Broadway): American, Sunday
Ruby Foo's (2182 Broadway): Chinese, Sunday
Sarabeth's Kitchen (423 Amsterdam Ave): American/Continental, Sunday
Shun Lee Cafe/Shun Lee West (43 W 65th St): Chinese, Sunday

OUTSIDE MANHATTAN

Brooklyn
  Peter Luger Steak House (178 Broadway, at Driggs Ave): Steak, Sunday
  River Cafe (1 Water St, Brooklyn Bridge): American, Sunday

Queens
  Park Side (107-01 Corona Ave, at 51st Ave): Italian, Sunday

An Exclusive List: Hundreds of the Best Taste Treats in New York City (Eat In and Takeout)

Antipasto bar: **Da Umberto** (107 W 17th St) and **Trattoria Dell'Arte** (900 Seventh Ave)
Appetizers, gourmet: **Russ & Daughters** (179 E Houston St)
Apple crisp: **Yura & Co.** (1645 Third Ave and 1292 Madison Ave)
Apple ring (holidays): **Lafayette** (26 Greenwich Ave)
Artichoke: **La Lunchonette** (130 Tenth Ave)
Baba au rhum: **Alain Ducasse** (55 W 58th St)
Babka: **Gertel's Bake Shop** (53 Hester St)
Bacon: **The Kitchenette** (80 West Broadway and 1272 Amsterdam Ave)
Baguettes: **Amy's Bread** (75 Ninth Ave and 672 Ninth Ave), **La Baguette Shop** (106 University Pl), and **Tribakery** (186 Franklin St)
Bakery goods, kosher: **Crumbs Bake Shop** (321½ Amsterdam Ave)
Banana split: **Blue Ribbon Bakery** (33 Downing St)
Baskets, gift and corporate: **Basketfull** (276 Fifth Ave, Suite 201), **Corporate Amenities** (134 W 29th St), and **Manhattan Fruitier** (105 E 29th St)
Bean curd: **Fong Inn Too** (46 Mott St)
Beef, braised (menu special): **Danube** (30 Hudson St)
Beef, cut to order (affordable): **Florence Meat Market** (5 Jones St)
Beef, fillet of (menu special): **King's Carriage House** (251 E 82nd St)
Beef and veal (premium): **Lobel's Prime Meats** (1096 Madison Ave)
Beef cheeks (menu special): **Fleur de Sel** (5 E 20th St)
Beef Wellington: **One if by Land, Two if by Sea** (17 Barrow St)
Belgian nut squares: **Duane Park Patisserie** (179 Duane St)
Bialys: **Kossar's Bialys** (367 Grand St)

Biscuits, blueberry-peach: **Taylor's Prepared Foods** (523 Hudson St and 156 Chambers St)
Biscuits, pepper: **Vesuvio Bakery** (160 Prince St)
Blintzes: **Cafe Edison** (228 W 47th St)
Boeuf Bourguignon (menu special): **Country Cafe** (69 Thompson St)
Bomboloncini (fried doughnuts with fillings): **Osteria del Circo** (120 W 55th St)
Bouillabaisse: **Payard Patisserie & Bistro** (1032 Lexington Ave) and **Pearl Oyster Bar** (18 Cornelia St)
Boules, sourdough: **Silver Moon Bakery** (2740 Broadway)
Bratwurst: **Schaller & Weber** (1654 Second Ave)
Bread, banana: **O Mai** (158 Ninth Ave)
Bread, chocolate: **Amy's Bread** (75 Ninth Ave and 672 Ninth Ave)
Bread, Indian: **Dawat** (210 E 58th St)
Bread, Irish soda: **Zabar's** (2245 Broadway)
Bread, just-baked: **Pasha** (70 W 71st St)
Bread, rye and country white: **Blue Ribbon Bakery Market** (14 Bedford St)
Bread, Semolina raisin fennel: **Amy's Bread** (75 Ninth Ave and 672 Ninth Ave)
Bread, whole-wheat: **Dean & Deluca** (560 Broadway)
Brioche: **Chez Laurence Patisserie** (245 Madison Ave) and **Lipstick Cafe** (885 Third Ave)
Brownies, best: **Fat Witch Bakery** (75 Ninth Ave) and **Sarabeth's Kitchen** (1295 Madison Ave, 423 Amsterdam Ave, and 945 Madison Ave at Whitney Museum of American Art)
Buns, sticky: **William Greenberg Jr. Desserts** (1100 Madison Ave) and **Sarabeth's Kitchen** (423 Amsterdam Ave)
Burrito, breakfast: **Kitchen Market** (218 Eighth Ave)
Burritos: **Burritoville** (1487 Second Ave and other locations), **Harry's Burrito Junction** (241 Columbus Ave and other locations), **Nacho Mama's Burritos** (2893 Broadway), **Samalita's Tortilla Factory** (1429 Third Ave), and **Taqueria de Mexico** (93 Greenwich Ave)
Burritos (to go): **Benny's Burritos** (113 Greenwich Ave and 93 Ave A)
Butcher: **Balducci's** (155-A W 66th St)
Butcher, Eastern European: **Kurowycky Meat Products** (124 First Ave)
Cabbage, pickled with pork and noodles: **Ollie's Noodle Shop and Grill** (200 W 44th St)
Cacik: **Turkish Kitchen** (386 Third Ave)
Cake: **E.A.T.** (1064 Madison Ave), **Edgar's Cafe** (255 W 84th St), and **Ferrara** (195 Grand St)
Cake, Belgian chocolate: **King's Carriage House** (251 E 82nd St)
Cake, blackout: **Gertel's Bake Shop** (53 Hester St, weekends only) and **Serendipity 3** (225 E 60th St)
Cake, Bohemian: **Cupcake Cafe** (522 Ninth Ave)
Cake, buttercream and chocolate: **Moishe's Bakery** (115 Second Ave)
Cake, carrot: **Carrot Top Pastries** (3931 Broadway and 5025 Broadway)
Cake, chocolate: **Cafe Lalo** (201 W 83rd St), **Hard Rock Cafe** (1501 Broadway), **Second Avenue Kosher Delicatessen and Restaurant** (156 Second Ave), and **Soutine Bakery** (104 W 70th St)
Cake, chocolate meringue with chocolate mousse: **Soutine Bakery** (104 W 70th St)
Cake, chocolate mousse: **City Bakery** (3 W 18th St)

Cake, chocolate mud: **Umanoff & Parsons** (467 Greenwich St)

Cake, chocolate raspberry: **Caffe Roma** (385 Broome St)

Cake, chocolate soufflé: **Taylor's Prepared Foods** (523 Hudson St and 156 Chambers St)

Cake, white coconut and marshmallow meringue: **Magnolia Bakery** (401 Bleecker St)

Calamari: **Turkish Kitchen** (386 Third Ave)

Calzone: **Little Italy Gourmet Pizza** (1 E 43rd St)

Candy, Asian: **Aji Ichiban** (167 Hester St)

Candy (bonbons): **Teuscher Chocolates** (620 Fifth Ave and 25 E 61st St)

Candy (butter crunch): **Mondel Chocolates** (2913 Broadway)

Candy (caramels): **Fifth Avenue Chocolatiere** (510 Madison Ave)

Candy (fruit jellies): **La Maison du Chocolat** (1018 Madison Ave)

Candy (jelly beans): **Myzel Chocolates** (140 W 55th St)

Cannelle: **Payard Patisserie & Bistro** (1032 Lexington Ave)

Cannelloni: **Giambelli** (46 E 50th St) and **Piemonte Homemade Ravioli Company** (190 Grand St)

Cannoli: **De Robertis Pastry Shop & Caffe** (176 First Ave)

Carpaccio: **Cipriani Downtown** (376 West Broadway)

Cassoulet: **L'Absinthe** (227 E 67th St)

Caviar: **Caviar Russe** (538 Madison Ave), **Caviarteria** (Trump Building, 502 Park Ave), **Firebird** (365 W 46th St), **Petrossian** (182 W 58th St), and **Sable's Smoked Fish** (1489 Second Ave)

Caviar (best prices): **Russ & Daughters** (179 E Houston St) and **Zabar's** (2245 Broadway)

Caviar, Urbani: **Cucina & Co.** (Macy's, 151 W 34th St, cellar)

Ceviche (marinated seafood): **Rosa Mexicano** (1063 First Ave and 61 Columbus Ave)

Champagne: **Flute** (40 E 20th St and 205 W 54th St), **Garnet Liquor** (929 Lexington Ave), and **Gotham Wines** (2517 Broadway)

Cheese, mozzarella: **DiPalo Fine Food** (200 Grand St)

Cheese, ricotta: **Alleva Dairy** (188 Grand St)

Cheese selection: **Grace's Marketplace** (1237 Third Ave), **Zabar's** (2245 Broadway), and **Murray's Cheese Shop** (257 Bleecker St)

Cheesecake: **Mitchel London Foods** (22-A E 65th St and 458 Ninth Ave), **S&S Cheesecake** (222 W 238th St, Bronx), **Two Little Red Hens** (1652 Second Ave), and **Yura & Co.** (1645 Third Ave and 1292 Madison Ave)

Cheesecake, almond: **Il Mulino** (86 W 3rd St)

Cheesecake, combination fruit: **Eileen's Special Cheesecake** (17 Cleveland Pl)

Cheesecake, ricotta: **Primavera** (1578 First Ave)

Chicken, beggar's (order in advance): **Shun Lee Palace** (155 E 55th St) and **Shun Lee West** (43 W 65th St)

Chicken, Dijon: **Zabar's** (2245 Broadway)

Chicken, fried: **Beppe** (45 E 22nd St), **Jezebel** (630 Ninth Ave), and **M&G Diner** (383 W 125th St)

Chicken, grilled: **Da Nico** (164 Mulberry St)

Chicken, Murray's free-roaming: sold in top-quality meat markets all over the city

Chicken, parmesan: **Il Mulino** (86 W 3rd St)

Chicken, roasted: **davidburke & donatella** (133 E 61st St), **Mitchel London Foods** (22A E 65th St and 458 Ninth Ave), and **Montrachet** (239 West Broadway)

Chicken, tandoori: **Curry in a Hurry** (119 Lexington Ave)
Chicken dishes: **International Poultry** (983 First Ave)
Chicken hash: **21 Club** (21 W 52nd St)
Chicken-in-a-pot: **Fine & Schapiro** (138 W 72nd St)
Chicken salad: **China Grill** (60 W 53rd St)
Chicken salad, curry or walnut: **Petak's** (1246 Madison Ave)
Chili: **Manhattan Chili Company** (1500 Broadway)
Chinese vegetables: **Kam Man** (200 Canal St)
Chocolate, gratin of (seasonal): **Daniel** (60 E 65th St)
Chocolate Bruno: **Blue Ribbon** (97 Sullivan St)
Chocolate desserts: **ChikaLicious** (203 E 10th St) and **Four Seasons Hotel** (57 E 57th St)
Chocolate eclairs: **Patisserie Claude** (187 W 4th St)
Chocolate tasting: **Gramercy Tavern** (42 E 20th St) and **Payard Patisserie & Bistro** (1032 Lexington Ave)
Chocolate truffles: **La Maison du Chocolat** (1018 Madison Ave)
Cholent: **Second Avenue Kosher Delicatessen and Restaurant** (156 Second Ave)
Chops, mutton: **Keens Steakhouse** (72 W 36th St)
Choucroute garnie: **Maureen's Passion** (1200 Lexington Ave)
Clam chowder: **Aquagrill** (210 Spring St)
Clam chowder, New England: **Pearl Oyster Bar** (18 Cornelia St)
Clambake: **Clambakes by Jim Sanford** (205 W 95th St; call 212/865-8976)
Clams: **Umberto's Clam House** (178 Mulberry St)
Clams, baked: **Frank's Trattoria** (371 First Ave)
Cobbler, strawberry rhubarb (seasonal): **Gramercy Tavern** (42 E 20th St)
Cocas (flatbread pizzas from Catalonia): **Pipa** (38 E 19th St)
Cod, roast: **Gramercy Tavern** (42 E 20th St)
Coffee, iced: **Oren's Daily Roast** (several locations)
Coffee beans: **Porto Rico Importing Company** (201 Bleecker St, 107 Thompson St, and 40½ St. Marks Pl) and **Zabar's** (2245 Broadway)
Condiments: **Adriana's Caravan** (78 Grand Central Terminal Market, Grand Central Station, 42nd St at Vanderbilt Ave)
Congee (traditional Chinese rice porridge): **Wong's Rice and Noodle Shop** (86 Mulberry St)
Cookies, butter: **CBK of New York** (226 E 83rd St, 212/794-3383; by appointment only)
Cookies, chocolate chip: **City Bakery** (3 W 18th St), **Hampton Chutney Co.** (68 Prince St), **Jacques Torres Chocolate Haven** (350 Hudson St), **Levain Bakery** (167 W 74th St), **Ruby et Violette** (457 W 50th St), and **Taylor's Prepared Foods** (523 Hudson St and 156 Chambers St)
Cookies, chocolate chubbie: **Sarabeth's Kitchen** (423 Amsterdam Ave, 1295 Madison Ave, and 945 Madison Ave, at Whitney Museum of American Art) and **Sarabeth's Bakery** (75 Ninth Ave)
Cookies, chocolate hazelnut meringue: **De Robertis Pastry Shop & Caffe** (176 First Ave)
Cookies, chocolate turtles: **Yura & Co.** (1645 Third Ave and 1292 Madison Ave)
Cookies, fortune (themed): **Gifted Ones** (150 W 10th St)
Corn on the cob, cheese-smeared: **Cafe Habana** (17 Prince St)
Cornbread: **Moishe's Bakery** (115 Second Ave) and **107 West** (2787 Broadway)
Corned beef: **Katz's Delicatessen** (205 E Houston St)

Corned beef hash: **Broadway Diner** (590 Lexington Ave) and **Carnegie Delicatessen and Restaurant** (854 Seventh Ave)

Cotton candy: **Four Seasons** (99 E 52nd St)

Couscous (in summer or by request): **Provence** (38 MacDougal St)

Crab: **Pisacane Midtown** (940 First Ave)

Crab, soft shell (seasonal): **New York Noodle Town** (28 Bowery)

Crab cakes: **Acme Bar & Grill** (9 Great Jones St) and **Tropica** (MetLife Building, 200 Park Ave)

Crab claws, stone: **Shelly's New York** (104 W 57th St)

Cream puffs: **Choux Factory** (865 First Ave)

Crème brûlée (best): **Barbetta** (321 W 46th St), **Lumi** (963 Lexington Ave), and **Tribeca Grill** (375 Greenwich St)

Crepes: **Palacinka** (28 Grand St)

Croissants: **City Bakery** (3 W 18th St), **Fauchon** (442 Park Ave, 1000 Madison Ave, and 138 Third Ave), and **Le Pain Quotidien** (100 Grand St and 1131 Madison Ave)

Croissants, almond: **Butterfield Market** (1114 Lexington Ave) and **Marquet Patisserie** (15 E 12th St)

Crudo (raw fish Italian-style): **Bar Tonno** (17 Cleveland Pl), **Cru** (24 Fifth Ave), **Esca** (402 W 43rd St), **Lure Fishbar** (142 Mercer St), and **Pace** (121 Hudson St, by request)

Cupcakes: **Buttercup Bake Shop** (973 Second Ave), **Crumbs Bake Shop** (321½ Amsterdam Ave), **Cupcake Cafe** (522 Ninth Ave), **Kitchenette** (1272 Amsterdam Ave), **Magnolia Bakery** (401 Bleecker St), **Mitchel London Foods** (22A E 65th St and 458 Ninth Ave), **Out of the Kitchen** (456 Hudson St), **Polka Dot Cake Studio** (312 Bleecker St), and **William Greenberg Jr. Desserts** (1100 Madison Ave)

Curry: **Baluchis** (193 Spring St), **Brick Lane Curry House** (342 E 6th St), and **Tabla** (11 Madison Ave)

Custard, frozen (self-serve): **Custard Beach** (2 World Financial Center)

Danishes: **Chez le Chef** (127 Lexington Ave)

Dates, piggyback: **Pipa** (ABC Carpet & Home, 38 E 19th St)

Delicatessen assortment: **Dean & Deluca** (560 Broadway), **Grace's Marketplace** (1237 Third Ave), and **Zabar's** (2245 Broadway)

Dessert, all-natural frozen: **PAX Gourmet Deli** (109 E 59th St)

Dessert, frozen low-calorie: **Tasti D-Lite** (1115 Lexington Ave and other locations)

Doughnuts: **Fisher & Levy** (875 Third Ave), **Krispy Kreme** (six locations), and **Per Se** (10 Columbus Circle)

Doughnuts, whole-wheat: **Cupcake Cafe** (522 Ninth Ave)

Duck: **Apple Restaurant** (17 Waverly Pl)

Duck, Beijing: **Shun Lee Palace** (155 E 55th St)

Duck, braised: **Quatorze Bis** (323 E 79th St) and **Tang Pavilion** (65 W 55th St; order in advance)

Duck, corned with rye-crisp appetizer: **WD-50** (50 Clinton St)

Duck, Peking: **Home's Kitchen** (22 E 21st St), **Our Place** (1444 Third Ave), **Peking Duck House Restaurant** (28 Mott St), **Shun Lee Palace** (155 E 55th St), and **Shun Lee West** (43 W 65th St)

Duck, roasted: **Four Seasons** (99 E 52nd St)

Duck, tea-smoked: **Grand Sichuan** (six different locations)

Dumplings: **Chef Ho Dumpling House** (148 W 49th St), **Chin Chin** (216 E 49th St), **Excellent Dumpling House** (111 Lafayette St), **Joe's Shang-**

hai (9 Pell St), and **Peking Duck House Restaurant** (28 Mott St)

Dumplings, chicken: **Chiam** (160 E 48th St)

Dumplings, Shanghai: **Goody's** (1 East Broadway)

Egg cream: **Carnegie Delicatessen and Restaurant** (854 Seventh Ave), **EJ's Luncheonette** (447 Amsterdam Ave and 1271 Third Ave), and **Tom's Restaurant** (782 Washington Ave, Brooklyn)

Eggs, fresh Jersey: stands at 72 E 7th St (Thurs only: 7 to 5:30) and 1750 Second Ave

Eggs, Scotch: **Myers of Keswick** (634 Hudson St)

Eggs, soft-boiled: **Le Pain Quotidien** (100 Grand St and 1131 Madison Ave)

Empanadas: **Ruben's** (64 Fulton St, 15 Bridge St, and 505 Broome St)

Escargots: **Artisanal** (2 Park Ave) and **Town** (15 W 56th St)

Espresso: **Caffe Dante** (79-81 MacDougal St), **Caffe Reggio** (119 Mac-Dougal St), and **Chez Laurence Patisserie** (245 Madison Ave)

Fajitas: **Zarela** (953 Second Ave)

Falafel: **Alfanoose** (8 Maiden Lane), **Moishe's Street Cart** (46th St at Ave of the Americas), and **Sahara East** (184 First Ave)

Fish, Chilean sea bass: **Cellini** (65 E 54th St, when available)

Fish, cod (battered): **A Salt & Battery** (112 Greenwich Ave)

Fish, fresh: **Central Fish Company** (527 Ninth Ave) and **Citarella** (1313 Third Ave and 2135 Broadway)

Fish, grilled: **Estiatorio Milos** (125 W 55th St)

Fish, pickled herring: **Sable's Smoked Fish** (1489 Second Ave)

Fish, smoked: **Russ & Daughters** (179 E Houston St) and **Barney Green-grass** (541 Amsterdam Ave)

Fish, sturgeon: **Barney Greengrass** (541 Amsterdam Ave) and **Sable's Smoked Fish** (1489 Second Ave)

Fish, tuna steak: **Gotham Bar & Grill** (12 E 12th St), **Omen** (113 Thompson St), and **Union Square Cafe** (21 E 16th St)

Fish, tuna tartare: **Tropica** (MetLife Building, 200 Park Ave)

Fish, turbot (seasonal): **Jean Georges** (1 Central Park W) and **Montrachet** (239 West Broadway)

Fish & chips: **A Salt & Battery** (112 Greenwich Ave and 80 Second Ave), **BLT Fish** (21 W 17th St), and **Telephone Bar & Grill** (149 Second Ave)

Flatbreads: **Kalustyan's** (123 Lexington Ave)

Foie gras: **Balthazar** (80 Spring St), **Daniel** (60 E 65th St), **Gascogne** (158 Eighth Ave), **Gramercy Tavern** (42 E 20th St), **Le Bernardin** (155 W 51st St), **Le Périgord** (405 E 52nd St), **Park Avenue Cafe** (100 E 63rd St), and **Veritas** (43 E 20th St)

Fondue: **La Bonne Soupe** (48 W 55th St)

Food and kitchen equipment (best all-around store): **Zabar's** (2245 Broadway)

French fries: **Atomic Wings** (528 Ninth Ave), **Cafe de Bruxelles** (118 Greenwich Ave), **Cafe de Paris** (924 Second Ave), **Cafe Loup** (105 W 13th St), **Grand Saloon** (158 E 23rd St), **The Harrison** (355 Greenwich St), **Les Halles** (411 Park Ave S and 15 John St), **Market Cafe** (496 Ninth Ave), **Michael's** (24 W 55th St), **Pampa** (768 Amsterdam Ave), **Pastis** (9 Ninth Ave), **Petite Abeille** (466 Hudson St), **Pfiff** (35 Grand St), and **Steak Frites** (9 E 16th St)

Fries, steak: **Balthazar** (80 Spring St) and **Montparnasse** (230 E 51st St)

Frites (French fries with mayonnaise): **Pommes Frites** (123 Second Ave)

Fruits and grains: **Nature's Gifts** (1297 Lexington Ave and 320 E 86th St)
Fruits and vegetables: **Balducci's** (155-A W 66th St) and **Fairway Cafe & Steakhouse** (2127 Broadway)
Fruit dessert plate: **Primavera** (1578 First Ave)
Game: **Ottomanelli's Meat Market** (285 Bleecker St) and **Da Umberto** (107 W 17th St)
Gelati: **Caffe Dante** (81 MacDougal St)
Gelato, homemade: **Fiamma Osteria** (206 Spring St)
Gingerbread house (one week notice): **Chez le Chef** (127 Lexington Ave)
Gnocchi, potato: **Hearth** (403 E 12th St)
Goat, roast baby: **Primavera** (1578 First Ave)
Goulash: **Mocca Hungarian** (1588 Second Ave)
Gourmet food: **Grace's Marketplace** (1237 Third Ave)
Groceries, discount: **Gourmet Garage** (453 Broome St, 301 E 64th St, 2567 Broadway, and 117 Seventh Ave S)
Guacamole: **Manhattan Chili Company** (1500 Broadway) and **Rosa Mexicano** (1063 First Ave)
Haggis (Scottish dish made of sheep innards): **St. Andrew's** (120 W 44th St)
Halibut, steamed: **Le Bernardin** (155 W 51st St)
Hamburgers: **burger joint at Le Parker Meridien** (119 W 57th St), **Corner Bistro** (331 W 4th St), **DB Bistro Moderne** (55 W 44th St), and **Jackson Hole Burgers** (232 E 64th St and other locations)
Hamburgers, Roquefort: **Burger Heaven** (9 E 53rd St)
Hen, Cornish: **Lorenzo and Maria's Kitchen** (1418 Third Ave)
Herbs and spices: **Adriana's Caravan** (Grand Central Station)
Heros: **Hero Boy** (492 Ninth Ave) and **Italian Food Center** (186 Grand St)
Heros, sausage: **Manganaro Grosseria Italiana** (488 Ninth Ave)
Horseradish, kosher: **The Pickle Guys** (49 Essex St)
Hot chocolate: **City Bakery** (3 W 18th St), **Jacques Torres Chocolate Haven** (66 Water St), **Lunettes et Chocolat** (25 Prince St), **Payard Patisserie & Bistro** (1032 Lexington Ave), and **Vosges Haut-Chocolat** (132 Spring St)
Hot dogs: **Brooklyn Diner USA** (212 W 57th St), **Crif Dogs** (113 St. Mark's Pl), **Dawgs on Park** (178 E 7th St), **F&B Güdtfood** (269 W 23rd St and 150 E 52nd St), **Gray's Papaya** (402 Ave of the Americas, 539 Eighth Ave, and 2090 Broadway), **Old Town Bar** (45 E 18th St), and **Papaya King** (179 E 86th St)
Hot dogs (most expensive): **Old Homestead** (56 Ninth Ave)
Huitlacoche (Mexican specialty): **Rosa Mexicano** (1063 First Ave and 61 Columbus Ave)
Hummus (best): **Hoomoos Asli** (100 Kenmare St)
Ice cream: **Ciao Bella** (27 E 92nd St and 285 Mott St), **Emack & Bolio's** (389 Amsterdam Ave and 56 Seventh Ave), **Petrossian** (182 W 58th St), and **Serendipity 3** (225 E 60th St)
Ice cream, caramel (menu special): **Gramercy Tavern** (42 E 20th St)
Ice cream, nougatine (by request): **Payard Patisserie & Bistro** (1032 Lexington Ave)
Ice cream sundae: **Brooklyn Diner USA** (212 W 57th St)
Ice cream sundae ("Forbidden Broadway"—awesome!): **Serendipity 3** (225 E 60th St)
Ice cream sundae, sesame: **Bôi** (246 E 44th St)

Indian snacks: **Lassi** (28 Greenwich Ave)

Jambalaya: **107 West** (2787 Broadway)

Juice, fresh-squeezed: **Candle Cafe** (1307 Third Ave)

Kebabs: **Turkish Cuisine** (631 Ninth Ave) and **Turkish Kitchen** (386 Third Ave)

Kielbasa spring roll: **Pat Pong** (93 E 7th St)

Knishes: **Murray's Sturgeon Shop** (2429 Broadway)

Kobe beef: **Megu** (62 Thomas St) and **Riingo** (205 E 45th St)

Lamb, rack of: **Gotham Bar & Grill** (12 E 12th St), **March** (405 E 58th St), and **Shun Lee Palace** (155 E 55th St)

Lamb shank: **Bolo** (23 E 22nd St) and **Molyvos** (871 Seventh Ave)

Lamb stew: **Bouterin** (420 E 59th St)

Lasagna: **Noi Italian Bistro** (271 Bleecker St) and **Via Emilia** (240 Park Ave S)

Latino hot drinks: **Mosaico** (175 Madison Ave)

Latkes: **Just Like Mother's** (110-60 Queens Blvd, Forest Hills, Queens)

Lemonade: **Lexington Candy Shop** (1226 Lexington Ave) and **Pyramida** (401 E 78th St)

Liver, chopped: **Fischer Brothers** (230 W 72nd St) and **Second Avenue Kosher Delicatessen and Restaurant** (156 Second Ave)

Liverwurst: **The Modern** (Museum of Modern Art, 9 W 53rd St)

Lobster: **Docks Oyster Bar and Seafood Grill** (2427 Broadway and 633 Third Ave)

Lobster, live: **Blue Ribbon Sushi** (119 Sullivan St)

Lobster bisque (catering): **Neuman & Bogdonoff** (212/228-2444; by request)

Lobster roll: **BLT Fish** (21 W 17th St) and **Pearl Oyster Bar** (18 Cornelia St)

Lollipops, cheesecake: **davidburke & donatella** (133 E 61st St)

Macaroni and cheese: **Shelly's New York** (104 W 57th St)

Marinara sauce: **Patsy's** (236 W 56th St)

Meat (best service): **H. Oppenheimer Meats** (2606 Broadway) and **Jefferson Market** (450 Ave of the Americas)

Meat (German deli cold-cut selection): **Schaller & Weber** (1654 Second Ave)

Meat and poultry (best prices): **Empire Purveyors** (883 First Ave)

Meatballs: **Il Gattopardo** (33 W 54th St)

Meatloaf: **Ouest** (2315 Broadway)

Mexican foodstuffs: **Kitchen Market** (218 Eighth Ave)

Meze (Turkish tapas-like appetizer): **Beyoglu** (1431 Third Ave)

Milkshakes: **Comfort Diner** (214 E 45th St)

Moussaka: **Periyali** (35 W 20th St)

Mousse, chocolate (best): **Bistrot Margot** (26 Prince St)

Mozzarella, smoked: **Joe's Dairy** (156 Sullivan St)

Mozzarella and ricotta: **Russo and Son** (344 E 11th St)

Mücver (zucchini pancakes): **Turkuaz Restaurant** (2637 Broadway)

Muffins: **Between the Bread** (145 W 55th St) and **The Muffins Shop** (222 Columbus Ave)

Muffins, corn: **107 West** (2787 Broadway)

Muffins, pear-walnut: **Soutine Bakery** (104 W 70th St)

Mushrooms, grilled portobello: **Giovanni Venticinque** (25 E 83rd St)

Mushrooms, wild: **Grace's Marketplace** (1237 Third Ave)

Mussels: **Jubilee** (347 E 54th St and 329 W 51st St) and **Markt** (401 W 14th St)

Nachos: **Benny's Burritos** (93 Ave A and 113 Greenwich Ave)

Napoleon: **Ecco** (124 Chambers St)

Natural foods: **Whole Foods Market** (2421 Broadway and other locations)

Noodles: **Honmura An** (170 Mercer St) and **Sammy's Noodle Shop & Grill** (453 Ave of the Americas)

Noodles, Asian: **Republic** (37 Union Sq W)

Noodles, cold with hot sesame sauce: **Sung Chu Mei** (615 Hudson St)

Noodles, green tea: **Ten Ren Tea & Ginseng** (79 Mott St)

Noodles, Shanghai-style: **Shun Lee Palace** (155 E 55th St)

Noodles, soba: **Soba Nippon** (19 W 52nd St)

Nuts: **A.L. Bazzini Co.** (339 Greenwich St)

Oatmeal: **Sarabeth's Kitchen** (1295 Madison Ave, 423 Amsterdam Ave, and 945 Madison Ave, at Whitney Museum of American Art)

Olive oils: **Oliviers & Co.** (249 Bleecker St)

Olives: **International Grocery** (543 Ninth Ave)

Onion rings: **Cornerstone Grill** (327 Greenwich St), **Home Restaurant** (20 Cornelia St), **Palm One** (837 Second Ave), **Palm Too** (840 Second Ave), and **Palm West Side** (250 W 50th St)

Osso Buco: **Il Mulino** (86 W 3rd St)

Oyster stew: **Grand Central Oyster Bar Restaurant** (Grand Central Station)

Oysters Rockefeller (occasional): **City Hall** (131 Duane St)

Paella: **Bolo** (23 E 22nd St) and **Sevilla** (62 Charles St)

Pancakes: **Friend of a Farmer** (77 Irving Pl) and **Vinegar Factory** (431 E 91st St; Sunday brunch)

Pancakes, blue corn: **Mesa Grill** (102 Fifth Ave)

Pancakes, kimchi: **Dok Suni's** (119 First Ave)

Pancakes, potato: **Rolf's** (281 Third Ave)

Pancakes, raspberry: **Veselka** (144 Second Ave)

Panini: **'ino** (21 Bedford St)

Panna cotta (dessert, occasional): **Gramercy Tavern** (42 E 20th St)

Pasta: **Arqua** (281 Church St), **Bottino** (246 Tenth Ave), **Cafe Pertutti** (2888 Broadway), **Caffe Buon Gusto** (236 E 77th St), **Cinque Terre** (22 E 38th St), **Col Legno** (231 E 9th St), **50 Carmine** (50 Carmine St), **Fresco by Scotto** (34 E 52nd St), **Gabriel's Bar & Restaurant** (11 W 60th St), **Il Monello** (1460 Second Ave), **Il Valentino** (330 E 56th St), **Paola's** (245 E 84th St), **Pinocchio** (1748 First Ave), **Teodora** (141 E 57th St), and **Todaro Brothers** (555 Second Ave)

Pasta, angel hair: **Piemonte Homemade Ravioli Company** (190 Grand St) and **Nanni's** (146 E 46th St)

Pasta, handmade egg: **Balducci's** (155-A W 66th St)

Pasta (inexpensive): **La Marca** (161 E 22nd St)

Pasta, Venetian: **Remi** (145 W 53rd St)

Pastrami: **Artie's Delicatessen** (2290 Broadway), **Carnegie Delicatessen and Restaurant** (854 Seventh Ave), and **Katz's Delicatessen** (205 E Houston St)

Pastrami, salmon: **Park Avenue Cafe** (100 E 63rd St)

Pastries: **Bleecker Street Pastry** (245 Bleecker St) and **Financier** (3-4 World Financial Center and 62 Stone St)

Pastries, French: **La Bergamote** (169 Ninth Ave)

Pastries, Hungarian: **Hungarian Pastry Shop** (1030 Amsterdam Ave)

Pastries, Italian: **LaBella Ferrara Pastry** (108-110 Mulberry St) and **Rocco Pastry Shop** (243 Bleecker St)

Pastries, Japanese traditional: **Minamoto Kitchoan** (608 Fifth Ave)

Paté: **Zabar's** (2245 Broadway)

Peanut butter: **Peanut Butter & Co.** (240 Sullivan St)

Pickles, kosher: **The Pickle Guys** (49 Essex St)

Pickles, sour or half-sour: **Guss' Pickles** (85-86 Orchard St) and **Russ & Daughters** (179 E Houston St)

Pie, apple: **William Greenberg Jr. Desserts** (1100 Madison Ave) and **Yura & Co.** (1645 Third Ave and 1292 Madison Ave)

Pie, apple crumb: **Cupcake Cafe** (522 Ninth Ave) and **Wimp's Sky Cafe** (29 W 125th St)

Pie, banana cream: **Sarabeth's Kitchen** (423 Amsterdam Ave, 1295 Madison Ave, and 945 Madison Ave, at Whitney Museum of American Art)

Pie, cheddar-crust apple (autumn only): **Little Pie Company** (424 W 43rd St)

Pie, cherry crumb (summer only): **Magnolia Bakery** (401 Bleecker St)

Pie, clam: **Lombardi's** (32 Spring St)

Pie, duck shepherd's: **Balthazar** (80 Spring St)

Pie, key lime: **Little Pie Company** (424 W 43rd St) and **Union Square Cafe** (21 E 16th St; menu special)

Pie, pecan: **Magnolia Bakery** (401 Bleecker St)

Pie, sweet potato: **Wimp's Sky Cafe** (29 W 125th St)

Pie, walnut sour-cream apple: **Little Pie Company** (424 W 43rd St)

Pies: **E.A.T.** (1064 Madison Ave)

Pig's feet (menu special): **Daniel** (60 E 65th St)

Pistachios: **Bazzini** (339 Greenwich St)

Pizza (by the slice): **Pizza 33** (201 E 33rd St)

Pizza, designer: **Paper Moon Milano** (39 E 58th St)

Pizza, gourmet: **apizz** (217 Eldridge St)

Pizza, grilled: **Gonzo** (140 W 13th St)

Pizza, Neapolitan: **Sal's & Carmine's Pizza** (2671 Broadway) and **Stromboli Pizzeria** (112 University Pl)

Pizza, Sicilian: **Sal's and Carmine's Pizza** (2671 Broadway)

Popcorn: **Dale & Thomas Popcorn** (1592 Broadway and 2170 Broadway)

Popovers: **Popover Cafe** (551 Amsterdam Ave)

Pork: **H. Oppenheimer Meats** (2606 Broadway)

Pork, braised: **Daniel** (60 E 65th St)

Pork buns: **Mei Lai Wah Coffee House** (64 Bayard St)

Pork, European-style cured: **Salumeria Biellese** (378 Eighth Ave)

Pork and chicken buns: **Lung Moon Bakery** (83 Mulberry St)

Pork chops, smoked: **Yorkville Packing House** (1560 Second Ave)

Pork shank: **Maloney & Porcelli** (37 E 50th St)

Potato chips: **Vinegar Factory** (431 E 91st St)

Potatoes, mashed: **Mama's Food Shop** (200 E 3rd St) and **Union Square Cafe** (21 E 16th St)

Pretzels, Martin's: **Greenmarket** (various locations, 315/628-4927)

Pretzels and cookies, hand-dipped chocolate: **Evelyn's Chocolates** (4 John St)

Prime rib: **Fresco by Scotto** (34 E 52nd St) and **Smith & Wollensky** (201 E 49th St)

Produce, fresh: **Fairway Market** (2127 Broadway)

Pudding, rice: **Marti Kebab** (238 E 24th St) and **Rice to Riches** (37 Spring St)

Quiche: **Chez Laurence Patisserie** (245 Madison Ave)

Ravioli: **DiPalo Fine Food** (200 Grand St), **Osteria del Circo** (120 W 55th St), **Piemonte Homemade Ravioli Company** (190 Grand St), and **Ravioli Store** (75 Sullivan St)

Ravioli, steamed Vietnamese: **Indochine** (430 Lafayette St)

Ribs: **Brother Jimmy's BBQ** (1485 Second Ave), **Hog Pit BBQ** (22 Ninth Ave), and **Sylvia's** (328 Lenox Ave)

Ribs, baby back: **Baby Buddha** (753 Washington St), **Mesa Grill** (102 Fifth Ave), and **Ruby Foo's** (1626 Broadway and 2182 Broadway)

Ribs, braised short beef: **Daniel** (60 E 65th St) and **Deborah** (43 Carmine St)

Rice: **Rice** (227 Mott St)

Rice, fried: **Ollie's** (1991 Broadway)

Rice, sticky, with mango: **Vong** (200 E 54th St)

Risotto: **Four Seasons** (99 E 52nd St) and **Risotteria** (270 Bleecker St)

Rugelach: **Margaret Palca Bakes** (191 Columbia St, Brooklyn) and **Ruthy's Cheesecake and Rugelach Bakery** (75 Ninth Ave)

Salad, Caesar: **Pearl Oyster Bar** (18 Cornelia St) and **Post House** (28 E 63rd St)

Salad, egg: **Murray's Sturgeon Shop** (2429 Broadway)

Salad, lobster: **Sable's Smoked Fish** (1489 Second Ave)

Salad, seafood: **Gotham Bar & Grill** (12 E 12th St)

Salad, tuna: **Cosi Sandwich Bar** (numerous locations), **Murray's Sturgeon Shop** (2429 Broadway), and **Todaro Brothers** (555 Second Ave)

Salad, warm white bean: **Caffe Grazie** (26 E 84th St)

Salad, whitefish: **Barney Greengrass** (541 Amsterdam Ave)

Salad bar: **Azure** (830 Third Ave) and **City Bakery** (3 W 18th St)

Salmon filets, Norwegian: **Sea Breeze** (541 Ninth Ave)

Salmon, smoked: **Aquavit** (65 E 55th St), **Murray's Sturgeon Shop** (2429 Broadway), and **Sable's** (1489 Second Ave)

Sandwich, avocado: **Olive's** (120 Prince St)

Sandwich, bacon, lettuce, and tomato (BLT): **Eisenberg's Sandwich Shop** (174 Fifth Ave) and **Good** (89 Greenwich Ave; summer only)

Sandwich, beef brisket: **Second Avenue Kosher Delicatessen and Restaurant** (156 Second Ave) and **Smith's Bar & Restaurant** (701 Eighth Ave)

Sandwich, cheese-steak: **BB Sandwich Bar** (120 W 3rd St) and **Wogie's Bar & Grill** (39 Greenwich Ave)

Sandwich, chicken: **Ranch 1** (315 Seventh Ave and other locations)

Sandwich, *croque monsieur*: **Payard Patisserie & Bistro** (1032 Lexington Ave)

Sandwich, Cuban: **Margon Restaurant** (136 W 46th St)

Sandwich, flatbread: **Cosi Sandwich Bar** (numerous locations)

Sandwich, French dip: **Sandwich Planet** (534 Ninth Ave)

Sandwich, green (spinach or broccoli rabe): **Tony Luke's Old Philly Style Sandwiches** (576 Ninth Ave)

Sandwich, grilled cheese: **Grilled Cheese** (168 Ludlow St) and **Say Cheese** (649 Ninth Ave)

Sandwich, grilled chicken breast: **Ranch 1** (315 Seventh Ave and other locations)

Sandwich, grilled portobello: **Zoë** (90 Prince St)

Sandwich, loin of pork: **Bottino** (246 Tenth Ave)

Sandwich, pastrami on rye: **Katz's Delicatessen** (205 E Houston St)

Sandwich, pig (pulled pork): **Hard Rock Cafe** (1501 Broadway)

Sandwich, po'boy: **Two Boots** (37 Ave A and other locations)

Sandwich, *poulet roti* (roast chicken): **Chez Brigitte** (77 Greenwich Ave)
Sandwich, turkey: **Viand Coffee Shop** (1011 Madison Ave)
Sandwiches (many varieties): **Call Cuisine** (1032 First Ave)
Sardines, marinated (occasional): **Oceana** (55 E 54th St)
Satays: **Typhoon Brewery** (22 E 54th St)
Sauerkraut: **Katz's Delicatessen** (205 E Houston St)
Sausage, European-style: **Kurowycky Meat Products** (124 First Ave) and **Mandler's** (26 E 17th St)
Sausage, Italian: **Corona Heights Pork Store** (107-04 Corona Ave, Queens)
Sausages, freshly made (over 40 kinds!): **Salumeria Biellese** (376 Eighth Ave; selection varies daily)
Scallops: **Le Bernardin** (155 W 51st St)
Schnecken: **William Greenberg Jr. Desserts** (1100 Madison Ave)
Scones: **Mangia** (50 W 57th St), **The Muffins Shop** (222 Columbus Ave), and **Tea & Sympathy** (108-110 Greenwich Ave)
Seafood dinners: **Le Bernardin** (155 W 51st St) and **Le Pescadou** (18 King St)
Shrimp, grilled: **Periyali** (35 W 20th St)
Shrimp Creole: **Jezebel** (630 Ninth Ave)
Sliders (mini burgers): **Sassy's Sliders** (1530 Third Ave)
Snacks, soups, and sandwiches: **Serendipity 3** (225 E 60th St)
Sorbet: **Atelier** (50 Central Park S), **La Boite en Bois** (75 W 68th St), and **La Maison du Chocolat** (1018 Madison Ave; summer only)
Soufflé: **Capsouto Frères** (451 Washington St)
Soufflé, Grand Marnier: **La Grenouille** (3 E 52nd St)
Soufflé, lime: **Gramercy Tavern** (42 E 20th St)
Soup, black bean: **Union Square Cafe** (21 E 16th St)
Soup, chicken: **Brooklyn Diner USA** (212 W 57th St), **Bubby's** (120 Hudson St), **Craft** (47 E 19th St), **Fred's at Barneys New York** (660 Madison Ave), **Pastrami Queen** (1269 Lexington Ave), **Second Avenue Kosher Delicatessen and Restaurant** (156 Second Ave), **Teresa's** (103 First Ave), and **Via Emilia** (240 Park Ave S)
Soup, Chinese: **Chao Chow** (111 Mott St)
Soup, duck: **Kelley & Ping** (127 Greene St)
Soup, French onion: **La Bonne Soupe** (48 W 55th St) and **Le Singe Vert** (160 Seventh Ave)
Soup, hot and sour: **Shun Lee Cafe** (43 W 65th St)
Soup, hot yogurt: **Beyoglu** (1431 Third Ave)
Soup, *kimchi chigae* (spicy stew with beef, tofu, and pork): **Do Hwa** (55 Carmine St)
Soup, matzoh ball: **Second Avenue Delicatessen and Restaurant** (156 Second Ave)
Soup, minestrone: **Il Vagabondo** (351 E 62nd St) and **Trattoria Spaghetto** (232 Bleecker St)
Soup, noodle: **Chao Chow** (111 Mott St)
Soup, pumpkin (seasonal): **Mesa Grill** (102 Fifth Ave)
Soup, split pea: **Cafe Edison** (228 W 47th St) and **Joe Jr.** (482 E 6th St and 167 Third Ave)
Soup, tapioca noodle: **Bao Noodles** (391 Second Ave)
Soup, tomato: **Sarabeth's Kitchen** (423 Amsterdam Ave, 1295 Madison Ave, and 945 Madison Ave, at Whitney Museum of American Art)
Soup, white borscht (weekends): **Teresa's** (80 Montague St, Brooklyn)

Soybeans: **Soy** (102 Suffolk St)

Spaghetti, housemade: **L'Impero** (45 Tudor City Place)

Spareribs, Chinese: **Fu's** (972 Second Ave) and **66** (241 Church St)

Spices: **Adriana's Caravan** (78 Grand Central Terminal Market, Grand Central Station, 42nd St at Vanderbilt Ave), **Aphrodisia** (264 Bleecker St), **International Grocery** (543 Ninth Ave), and **Kalustyan's** (123 Lexington Ave)

Spinach pies, Greek: **Poseidon Bakery** (629 Ninth Ave)

Spring rolls, crab: **Vong** (200 E 54th St)

Squab, roasted stuffed: **Daniel** (60 E 65th St)

Squid, grilled stuffed: **I Trulli** (122 E 27th St)

Steak, Black Angus and French fries: **Steak Frites** (9 E 16th St)

Steak, Cajun rib: **Morton's of Chicago** (551 Fifth Ave) and **Post House** (28 E 63rd St)

Steak, grilled ribeye: **Restaurant Charlotte** (145 W 44th St)

Steak, hanger: **Pastis** (9 Ninth Ave)

Steak, pepper: **Chez Josephine** (414 W 42nd St)

Steak, Porterhouse: **Manhattan Grille** (1161 First Ave), **Morton's of Chicago** (551 Fifth Ave), and **Porters** (216 Seventh Ave)

Steak fries: **Balthazar** (80 Spring St) and **Montparnasse** (230 E 51st St)

Steak tartare: **21 Club** (21 W 52nd St)

String beans, Chinese-style: **Tang Tang** (1328 Third Ave)

Strudel: **Mocca Hungarian** (1588 Second Ave)

Sushi, *omakase* ("astonish me"): **Taka** (61 Grove St)

Sweetbreads: **Casa Mono** (52 Irving Place) and **Métisse** (239 W 105th St)

Swordfish, charbroiled: **Morton's of Chicago** (551 Fifth Ave)

Tacos: **Gabriela's** (685 Amsterdam Ave), **Maya** (1191 First Ave), **Mexicana Mama** (525 Hudson St), and **Rosa Mexicano** (1063 First Ave and 61 Columbus Ave)

Tamales: **Rosa Mexicano** (1063 First Ave and 61 Columbus Ave) and **Zarela** (953 Second Ave)

Tapas: **Azafran** (77 Warren St), **Bolo** (23 E 22nd St), **Casa Mono & Bar Jamone** (52 Irving Pl), **El Cid** (322 W 15th St), **Il Buco** (47 Bond St), **ñ** (33 Crosby St), **Oliva** (161 E Houston St), **Pipa** (ABC Carpet & Home, 38 E 19th St), **Solera** (216 E 53rd St), **Suba** (109 Ludlow St), **Tia Pol** (205 Tenth Ave), and **Xunta** (174 First Ave)

Tart, apple: **Gotham Bar & Grill** (12 E 12th St), **Marquet Patisserie** (15 E 12th St), and **Quatorze Bis** (323 E 79th St)

Tart, chocolate: **Le Bernardin** (155 W 51st St)

Tart, fruit: **Ceci-Cela** (55 Spring St) and **Payard Patisserie & Bistro** (1032 Lexington Ave)

Tart, fruit and vegetable: **Once Upon a Tart** (135 Sullivan St)

Tart, lemon: **Margot Patisserie** (2109 Broadway)

Tartufo: **Il Corallo** (172-176 Prince St), **Il Vagabondo** (351 E 62nd St), **Manhattan Grille** (1161 First Ave), and **Sette Mezzo** (969 Lexington Ave)

Tea, loose (130 kinds): **Alice's Tea Cup** (102 W 73rd St)

Tempura: **Inagiku** (Waldorf-Astoria Hotel, 301 Park Ave)

Tequila: **Dos Caminos** (373 Park Ave S)

Tiramisu: **Biricchino** (260 W 29th St), **Caffe Dante** (79 MacDougal St), and **Mezzogiorno** (195 Spring St)

Tong shui (Chinese soup): **Sweet-n-Tart Cafe** (76 Mott St)

Tonkatsu: **Katsuhama** (11 E 47th St)

Torte, Sacher: **Duane Park Patisserie** (179 Duane St, special order)
Tortillas, corn: **Pure Food and Wine** (54 Irving Pl)
Tripe alla parmigiana: **Babbo** (110 Waverly Pl)
Truffles: **Black Hound** (170 Second Ave), **La Maison du Chocolat** (25 E
    73rd St), and **Teuscher Chocolates** (620 Fifth Ave and 25 E 61st St)
Veal chops: **Daniel** (60 E 65th St)
Veal rib chop: **Baldoria** (249 W 49th St)
Veal stew (menu special): **Pierre au Tunnel** (250 W 47th St)
Vegan foods: **Whole Earth Bakery & Kitchen** (130 St. Mark's Pl)
Vegetables, raw: **Estiatorio Milos** (125 W 55th St)
Vegetarian combo: **Hudson Falafel** (516 Hudson St)
Vegetarian meals: **Natural Gourmet Cookery School** (48 W 21st St)
Venison (seasonal): **Chanterelle** (2 Harrison St)
Waffles, Belgian: **Cafe de Bruxelles** (118 Greenwich Ave), **Le Pain Quoti-
    dien** (1131 Madison Ave), and **Petite Abeille** (107 W 18th St)
Waffles, pumpkin: **Sarabeth's Kitchen** (1295 Madison Ave, 423 Amsterdam
    Ave, and 945 Madison Ave, at Whitney Museum of American Art)
Wagashi (gelatinous sweet confection): **Minimoto Kitchoan** (608 Fifth Ave)
Whiskeys, malt: **Soho Wines & Spirits** (461 West Broadway)
Wines, French: **Park Avenue Liquors** (292 Madison Ave) and **Quality
    House** (2 Park Ave)
Wines, German: **First Avenue Wines & Spirits** (383 First Ave)
Zabaglione: **Il Monello** (1460 Second Ave)

Bagels

Absolute Bagels (2788 Broadway)
Bagel City (720 W 181st St)
Bagel Works (1229 First Ave)
Bagel Zone (50 Ave A)
Bagels on the Square (7 Carmine St)
Columbia Hot Bagels (200 W 44th St)
Ess-a-Bagel (359 First Ave and 831 Third Ave)
H&H Bagels (2239 Broadway and 639 W 46th St)
H&H Midtown Bagels East (1551 Second Ave)
Lenny's (2601 Broadway)
Murray's Bagels (500 Ave of the Americas)
Pick-a-Bagel (1101 Lexington Ave)

Barbecued Meats

Big Wong (67 Mott St): Chinese style
Biscuit BBQ Joint (367 Flatbush Ave, Brooklyn)
Blue Smoke (116 E 27th St): Danny Meyer does it again!
Bone Lick Park (75 Greenwich Ave): ribs and pork smoked over fruit
    woods and hickory
Brother Jimmy's West (428 Amsterdam Ave): ribs, sandwiches, good sauce
Brothers Bar-BQ (225 Varick St): smoked ribs
Copeland's (547 W 145th St): Harlem setting
Daily Chow (2 E Second Ave): Mongolian
Dallas BBQ (1265 Third Ave, 27 W 72nd St, 21 University Pl, and 132 Sec-
    ond Ave): big and busy, but still only fair in quality
Hog Pit BBQ (22 Ninth Ave)

Kang Suh (1250 Broadway)
Pearson's Texas BBQ (71-04 35th Ave, Queens)
Shun Lee Cafe (43 W 5th St): classy Chinese
Sylvia's (328 Lenox Ave): reputation better than the food
Virgil's Real Barbecue (152 W 44th St): big, brassy, mass-production
Woo Chon (8-10 W 36th St): Korean

Breakfast

For the real morning-meal power scenes, hotels are the preferred locations. The biggest names:

Four Seasons Hotel, Fifty Seven Fifty Seven (57 E 57th St): excellent pancakes
Le Parker Meridien Hotel, Norma's (118 W 57th St)
Paramount Hotel (235 W 46th St)
Peninsula New York Hotel (700 Fifth Ave)
Regency (540 Park Ave)
Royalton (44 W 44th St)

Other places with excellent day-starters:

Amy Ruth's (113 W 116th St)
Balthazar (80 Spring St)
Brasserie (100 E 53rd St)
Bright Food Shop (216 Eighth Ave)
Bubby's (120 Hudson St)
Café Botanica (Essex House, a Westin Hotel, 160 Central Park S)
Carnegie Delicatessen and Restaurant (854 Seventh Ave): The cheese blintzes only have a half-million calories!
City Bakery (3 W 18th St)
Columbus Bakery (474 Columbus Ave): sinful cheese Danishes and yummy croissants
Comfort Diner (214 E 45th St)
Cucina & Co. (MetLife Building, 200 Park Ave): commuter-convenient
Delmonico's (56 Beaver St)
District (Muse Hotel, 130 W 46th St)
E.A.T. (1064 Madison Ave): breads are great (and expensive)
EJ's Luncheonette (447 Amsterdam Ave)
Ellen's Stardust Diner (1650 Broadway)
Fairway Cafe & Steakhouse (2127 Broadway): fresh-tasting food in sizable portions
Fitzer's (Fitzpatrick Manhattan Hotel, 687 Lexington Ave): Irish breakfast
14 Wall Street Restaurant (14 Wall St)
Friend of a Farmer (77 Irving Pl): late pancake feast
Grey Dog's Coffee (33 Carmine St)
Heartbeat (W New York, 149 E 49th St): breakfast for "well-being"
Jerry's (101 Prince St)
Kitchen Market (218 Eighth Ave): south of the border
Kitchenette (80 West Broadway)
Michael's (24 W 55th St)
Nice Matin (201 W 79th St)
NoHo Star (330 Lafayette St)
Once Upon a Tart (135 Sullivan St)
Pastis (9 Ninth Ave): haven for weekday breakfasts in the Meatpacking District

Payard Patisserie & Bistro (1032 Lexington Ave)
Pigalle (790 Eighth Ave)
Pink Tea Cup (42 Grove St): country breakfasts
Popover Cafe (551 Amsterdam Ave)
Rue 57 (60 W 57th St)
Sarabeth's Kitchen (423 Amsterdam Ave, 1295 Madison Ave, and 945 Madison Ave, at Whitney Museum of American Art)
Schiller's (131 Rivington St)
Tramway Coffee Shop (1143 Second Ave)
Veselka (144 Second Ave)
Viand Coffee Shop (300 E 86th St, 673 Madison Ave, and 1011 Madison Ave): crowded, but great value
Viet-Nam Banh Mi So 1 (369 Broome St)

Brunch

Annie's (1381 Third Ave)
Aquagrill (210 Spring St)
Balthazar (80 Spring St)
Barney Greengrass (541 Amsterdam Ave)
Beacon (25 W 56th St)
Blue Ribbon Bakery (33 Downing St)
Café Botanica (Essex House, a Westin Hotel, 160 Central Park S)
Café Gray (Time Warner Center, 10 Columbus Circle)
Cafe Habana (17 Prince St)
Cafe Lalo (201 W 83rd St)
Cafe Luluc (214 Smith St, Brooklyn)
Capsouto Frères (451 Washington St)
Cendrillon (45 Mercer St): Filipino flavors
Church Lounge (2 Ave of the Americas)
Crystal Fountain (Grand Hyatt Hotel, 109 E 42nd St)
Cupping Room Cafe (359 West Broadway)
Danal (90 E 10th St): luscious French toast
davidburke & donatella (133 E 61st St)
Eleven Madison Park (11 Madison Ave)
Fifty Seven Fifty Seven (57 E 57th St)
5 Ninth (5 Ninth Ave)
Five Points (31 Great Jones St)
Florent (69 Gansevoort St)
Friend of a Farmer (77 Irving Pl)
Good (89 Greenwich Ave)
Good Enough to Eat (483 Amsterdam Ave)
Iridium (44 W 63rd St): Dixieland jazz band
Isabella's (359 Columbus Ave)
Jones (41 Greenwich Ave)
Mark's Restaurant (25 E 77th St): classy
Mercadito (179 Ave B)
Nice Matin (201 W 79th St)
Odeon (145 West Broadway)
Olives New York (W New York Union Square, 201 Park Ave S)
Paris Commune (411 Bleecker St): Bohemian West Village bistro
Park Avenue Cafe (100 E 63rd St)
Pig'n Whistle (922 Third Ave): traditional Irish breakfast, too

Provence (38 MacDougal St)
Prune (54 E 1st St): inspired weekend brunch
River Cafe (1 Water Street, Brooklyn)
Sarabeth's Kitchen (1295 Madison Ave, 423 Amsterdam Ave, and 945 Madison Ave, at Whitney Museum of American Art)
Spring Street Natural Restaurant (62 Spring St)
Tartine (253 W 11th St)
Tavern on the Green (Central Park at 67th St): for entertaining out-of-town guests
Town (15 W 56th St)
Tribeca Grill (375 Greenwich St)
Vinegar Factory (431 E 91st St)
Water Club (500 E 30th St)

Burgers

aka Cafe (49 Clinton St)
Bar 89 (89 Mercer St)
Better Burger (565 Third Ave)
Big Nick's (2175 Broadway): You'll love it!
Blue Ribbon Bakery (33 Downing St)
Brasserie 360 (200 E 60th St): convenient for Bloomingdale's shoppers
Burger Heaven (20 E 49th St, 536 Madison Ave, and 9 E 53rd St)
burger joint at Le Parker Meridien (118 W 57th St)
Cafe de Bruxelles (118 Greenwich Ave)
Chelsea Grill (135 Eighth Ave)
Chumley's (86 Bedford St)
Corner Bistro (331 W 4th St)
DB Bistro Moderne (City Club Hotel, 55 W 44th St)
Fanelli's Cafe (94 Prince St)
44 (Royalton Hotel, 44 W 44th St)
Great Jones Cafe (54 Great Jones St)
Hard Rock Cafe (1501 Broadway)
Home Restaurant (20 Cornelia St)
J.G. Melon (1291 Third Ave)
Jackson Hole Burgers (232 E 64th St, 521 Third Ave, 1611 Second Ave, 1270 Madison Ave, and 517 Columbus Ave)
Keens Steakhouse (72 W 36th St)
Knickerbocker Bar and Grill (33 University Pl)
McDonald's (160 Broadway): atypically classy
MetroCafe & Wine Bar (31 E 21st St)
Michael Jordan's the Steak House NYC (Grand Central Station, 42nd St at Vanderbilt Ave)
Odeon (145 West Broadway)
Old Town Bar (45 E 18th St)
P.J. Clarke's (915 Third Ave)
Pastis (9 Ninth Ave)
Patroon (160 E 46th St)
Paul's Palace (131 Second Ave)
Popover Cafe (551 Amsterdam Ave)
Prime Burger (5 E 51st St)
Rare Bar & Grill (Shelburne Murray Hill, 303 Lexington Ave)
Rue 57 (60 W 57th St)

Smith & Wollensky (797 Third Ave)
Soup Burg (922 Madison Ave)
21 Club (21 W 52nd St)
Union Square Cafe (21 E 16th St)
White Horse Tavern (567 Hudson St)
Wollensky's Grill (201 E 49th St)
Zoë (90 Prince St)

Cheap Eats

A (947 Columbus Ave)
aka Cafe (49 Clinton St)
Alias (76 Clinton St)
Alouette (2588 Broadway)
Back Stage Eatery (3 E 47th St)
Bereket (187 E Houston St)
Beyoglu (1431 Third Ave)
Big Nick's (2175 Broadway)
Bistrot Margot (26 Prince St)
burger joint at Le Parker Meridien (118 W 57th St)
Cabana Carioca (123 W 45th St)
Cafe Cafe (470 Broome St)
Cafe de Bruxelles (118 Greenwich Ave)
Cafe Edison (Hotel Edison, 228 W 47th St)
Cafe Orlin (41 St. Mark's Pl)
Cafe Riazor (245 W 16th St)
Caffe Vivaldi (32 Jones St)
Carmine's (2450 Broadway)
Casa Adela (66 Ave C)
Chez Brigitte (77 Greenwich Ave)
City Bakery (3 W 18th St)
Coffee Shop (29 Union Sq W)
Comfort Diner (214 E 45th St)
Corner Bistro (331 W 4th St)
Cosette (163 E 33rd St)
Cucina Stagionale (289 Bleecker St)
Cupcake Cafe (522 Ninth Ave)
Curry & Curry (153 E 33rd St)
Dakshin Indian Bistro (741 Ninth Ave)
Danal (90 E 10th St)
Dining Commons (City University of New York Graduate Center, 365 Fifth
    Ave, 8th floor)
Dom's (202 Lafayette St)
East Village Cheese (40 Third Ave)
Edgar's Cafe (255 W 84th St)
El Cid (322 W 15th St)
Euzkadi (108 E 4th St)
F&B Güdtfood (269 W 23rd St and 150 E 52nd St)
First Avenue Coffee Shop (1433 First Ave)
Frank (88 Second Ave)
Go Sushi (3 Greenwich Ave)
Golden Unicorn (18 East Broadway)
Grano Trattoria (21 Greenwich Ave)

Gray's Papaya (402 Ave of the Americas, 539 Eighth Ave, and 2090 Broadway)
Hallo Berlin (402 W 51st St)
Havana Chelsea (190 Eighth Ave)
Havana New York (27 W 38th St)
Hoi An (135 West Broadway)
Home Restaurant (20 Cornelia St)
House of Pita (32 W 48th St)
Hummus Place (109 St. Mark's Pl)
Il Bagatto (192 E Second Ave)
Inside (9 Jones St)
Ivy's Cafe (154 W 72nd St)
Jasmine (1619 Second Ave)
Jean Claude (137 Sullivan St)
John's Pizzeria (278 Bleecker St and other locations)
Katz's Delicatessen (205 E Houston St)
Kitchenette (80 West Broadway)
La Flor de Broadway (3401 Broadway)
Le Gamin (183 Ninth Ave and 536 E 5th St)
Le Tableau (511 E 5th St)
Lil' Frankie's Pizza (19 First Ave)
Little Havana (30 Cornelia St)
Luke's Bar & Grill (1394 Third Ave)
Market Diner (572 Eleventh Ave)
McDonald's (160 Broadway)
Nam (110 Reade St)
Nam Phuong (19 Ave of the Americas)
Nha Trang (87 Baxter St)
107 West (2787 Broadway)
Pakistan Tea House (176 Church St)
Paul's Palace (131 Second Ave)
Peep (177 Prince St)
Pho Bang (6 Chatham St)
Pigalle (790 Eighth Ave)
Pinch, Pizza by the Inch (416 Park Ave S)
Pommes Frites (123 Second Ave)
Popover Cafe (551 Amsterdam Ave)
Pret à Manger (287 Madison Ave)
Prime Burger (5 E 51st St)
Sapporo (152 W 49th St)
Second Avenue Kosher Delicatessen and Restaurant (156 Second Ave)
Shopsin's General Store (54 Carmine St): an original!
Sirtaj (36 W 26th St)
Sosa Borella (460 Greenwich St and 832 Eighth Ave)
Sotto Cinque (1644 Second Ave)
Spring Street Natural Restaurant (62 Spring St)
Supper (156 E 2nd St)
Suzie's (163 Bleecker St)
Sweet-n-Tart Cafe (20 Mott St)
Sylvia's (328 Lenox Ave)
Tanti Baci Caffe (135½ Seventh Ave S)
Tartine (253 W 11th St)
Tavern on Jane (31 Eighth Ave)

Tea & Sympathy (108 Greenwich Ave)
Thai Thai Eatery (78 E 1st St)
Tiny's Giant Sandwich Shop (127 Rivington St)
Tossed (295 Park Ave S)
Turkish Cuisine (631 Ninth Ave)
Uncle Moe's (14 W 19th St)
Urban Roots (51 Ave A)
Veselka (144 Second Ave)
Viand Coffee Shop (300 E 86th St, 673 Madison Ave, and 1011 Madison
    Ave)
'wichcraft (49 E 19th St)
Zula Restaurant (1260 Amsterdam Ave)
Zum Schneider (107-109 Ave C)

Cheese Plates

Alain Ducasse (Essex House, a Westin Hotel, 155 W 58th St)
Artisanal (2 Park Ave)
Babbo (110 Waverly Pl)
Chanterelle (2 Harrison St)
Craft (43 E 19th St)
Daniel (60 E 65th St)
Eleven Madison Park (11 Madison Ave)
Gramercy Tavern (42 E 20th St)
Jean Georges (Trump International Hotel, 1 Central Park W)
La Grenouille (3 E 52nd St)
Osteria del Circo (120 W 55th St)
Picholine (35 W 64th St)
Solera (216 E 53rd St)
Tasting Room (72 E 1st St)

Coffeehouses

Big Cup (228 Eighth Ave)
Cafe la Fortuna (69 W 71st St)
Cafe Lalo (201 W 83rd St)
Cafe Mozart (154 W 70th St)
Caffe Dante (79 MacDougal St)
Caffe Roma (385 Broome St)
Caffe Vivaldi (32 Jones St)
Chez Laurence Patisserie (245 Madison Ave)
City Bakery (3 W 18th St)
Cupcake Cafe (522 Ninth Ave)
Cupping Room Cafe (359 West Broadway)
Dean & Deluca (9 Rockefeller Plaza)
Ferrara (195 Grand St)
Fluff (751 Ninth Ave)
French Roast (78 W 11th St)
Hungarian Pastry Shop (1030 Amsterdam Ave)
Jack's Stir Brewed Coffee (138 W 10th St)
Le Figaro Cafe (184 Bleecker St)
Le Pain Quotidien (1131 Madison Ave, 38 E 19th St, at ABC Carpet Home,
    and other locations)
Lipstick Cafe (885 Third Ave)
Once Upon a Tart (135 Sullivan St)

Oren's Daily Roast (many locations)
Sarabeth's Kitchen (1295 Madison Ave, 423 Amsterdam Ave, and 945 Madison Ave, at Whitney Museum)
Sensuous Bean (66 W 70th St)
71 Irving Place (71 Irving Pl)
Veselka (144 Second Ave)

Crepes

Le Gamin (183 Ninth Ave and 536 E 5th St)
Mon Petite Cafe (801 Lexington Ave)
Serendipity 3 (225 E 60th St)

Delis

Amy's Bread (75 Ninth Ave)
Artie's Delicatessen (2290 Broadway)
Back Stage III (807 Lexington Ave)
Barney Greengrass (541 Amsterdam Ave)
Ben Ash Delicatessen (857 Seventh Ave)
Ben's Kosher Deli (209 W 38th St)
Carnegie Delicatessen and Restaurant (854 Seventh Ave)
Cosi (many locations)
Dile Punjab Deli (170 Ninth Ave)
E.A.T. (1064 Madison Ave)
Ess-a-Bagel (831 Third Ave and 359 First Ave)
Fine & Schapiro (138 W 72nd St)
Food Exchange (120 E 59th St)
Garden of Eden (7 E 14th St, 310 Third Ave, and 162 W 23rd St)
Grace's Marketplace (1237 Third Ave)
Hadleigh's (1900 Broadway)
Katz's Delicatessen (205 East Houston St)
Junior's (Grand Central Station, 42nd St at Vanderbilt Ave)
Likitsakos Market (1174 Lexington Ave)
M&O Market (124 Thompson St)
Out of the Kitchen (456 Hudson St)
Samad's (2867 Broadway)
Sarge's Deli (548 Third Ave)
Second Avenue Kosher Delicatessen and Restaurant (156 Second Ave)
Stage Deli (834 Seventh Ave)
Village Farm & Grocery (146 Second Ave)
Yura & Company (1645-1659 Third Ave and 1292 Madison Ave)
Zabar's (2245 Broadway)

Delivery

Il Bagatto (192 E 2nd St)
Schiller's (131 Rivington St)
Vivolo (140 E 74th St)

Desserts

Asiate (80 Columbus Circle)
Bouley (120 West Broadway)
Cafe Ferrara (195 Grand St): Italian gelati

Cafe Lalo (201 W 83rd St): best European-style cafe!
Cafe Pertutti (2888 Broadway): a waist-expanding experience
Cafe Sabarsky (Neue Galerie, 1048 Fifth Ave)
ChikaLicious (203 E 10th St)
Cupcake Cafe (522 Ninth Ave)
davidburke & donatella (133 E 61st St): New World comfort
Gramercy Tavern (42 E 20th St)
Hearth (403 E 12th St): simple pleasure
Jean Georges (1 Central Park West): hyper-creative desserts
Magnolia Bakery (401 Bleecker St): wonderful cupcakes and more
Once Upon a Tart (135 Sullivan St)
Payard Patisserie & Bistro (1032 Lexington Ave): You'll pay a bit more
    and enjoy it more, too!
Petrossian (182 W 58th St)
Rocco (181 Thompson St)
Schiller's (131 Rivington St): Old World comfort
Serendipity 3 (225 E 60th St): an institution for the young and young-at-heart
Veniero's (342 E 11th St)
WD-50 (50 Clinton St)
Zabar's Cafe (2245 Broadway): big treats, low prices

Dim Sum

The serving of small tea pastries called *dim sum* originated in Hong Kong and has become a delicious Chinatown institution. Although dim sum is usually eaten for brunch, some restaurants also serve it as an appetizer before dinner. Dim sum items are brought over to your table on rolling carts, and you simply point at whatever looks good. This eliminates the language barrier and encourages experimentation. When you're finished, the small plates you've accumulated are counted and the bill is drawn up. Some of the most popular dim sum dishes include:

Cha Siu Bow (steamed barbecued pork buns)
Cha Siu So (flaky buns)
Chun Guen (spring rolls)
Dai Tze Gau (steamed scallop and shrimp dumplings)
Don Ta (baked custard tarts)
Dow Sah Bow (sweet bean paste-filled buns)
Fancy Fans (meat-filled pot sticker triangles)
Floweret Siu Mai (meat-filled dumplings)
Four-Color Siu Mai (meat-and-vegetable-filled dumplings)
Gau Choi Gau (pan-browned chive and shrimp dumplings)
Gee Cheung Fun (steamed rice-noodle rolls)
Gee Yoke Go (savory pork triangles)
Ha Gau (shrimp dumplings)
Jow Ha Gok (shrimp turnovers)
Pot Sticker Kou The (meat-filled dumplings)
Satay Gai Tran (chicken satay)
Siu Mai (steamed pork dumplings)
Tzay Ha (fried shrimp ball on sugarcane)

For the most authentic and delicious dim sum in New York, try the following:

Dim Sum Go Go (5 East Broadway)
Golden Unicorn (18 East Broadway): an especially fine selection
HSF (46 Bowery and 578 Second Ave)
Jing Fong (20 Elizabeth St)
Mandarin Court (61 Mott St)
Nice Restaurant (35 East Broadway)
Oriental Pearl (103 Mott St)
Our Place (141 E 55th St and 1444 Third Ave)
Ping's Seafood (22 Mott St)
Ruby Foo's (2182 Broadway and 1626 Broadway)
Shun Lee Cafe (43 W 65th St)
66 (241 Church St)
Sun Hop Shing Tea House (21 Mott St)
Sweet-n-Tart Cafe (20 Mott St)
Tai-Hong-Lau (70 Mott St)
Triple 8 Palace (59 Division St)

Diners

Broadway Diner (590 Lexington Ave)
Brooklyn Diner USA (212 W 57th St): outstanding
Ellen's Stardust Diner (1650 Broadway)
Empire Diner (210 Tenth Ave)
Market Diner (572 Eleventh Ave)
Moondance Diner (80 Ave of the Americas)

Dining and Dancing

Supper Club (240 W 47th St): vintage 1940s with big bands
Tavern on the Green (Central Park W at 67th St): great setting
World Yacht Cruises (Pier 81, 41st St at Hudson River): nonstop party

Dining Solo

Aquavit (65 E 55th St)
Babbo (110 Waverly Pl)
Broadway Diner (590 Lexington Ave)
Cafe de Bruxelles (118 Greenwich Ave)
Cafe S.F.A. (Saks Fifth Avenue, 611 Fifth Ave)
Carnegie Delicatessen and Restaurant (854 Seventh Ave)
Caviar Russe (538 Madison Ave)
Chez Napoleon (365 W 50th St)
Coffee Shop (29 Union Sq)
Col Legno (231 E 9th St)
Cupcake Cafe (522 Ninth Ave)
Elephant & Castle (68 Greenwich St)
Gotham Bar & Grill (12 E 12th St)
Grand Central Oyster Bar Restaurant (Grand Central Station, 42nd St at Vanderbilt Ave, lower level)
J.G. Melon (1291 Third Ave)
Jackson Hole Burgers (232 E 64th St, 521 Third Ave, and 1611 Second Ave)
Joe's Shanghai (9 Pell St)
Kitchenette (80 West Broadway)
La Bonne Soupe (48 W 55th St)

La Caridad (2199 Broadway)
Lipstick Cafe (885 Third Ave)
Mayrose (920 Broadway)
Pepolino (281 West Broadway)
Raoul's (180 Prince St)
Republic (37 Union Square W)
Sarabeth's Kitchen (1295 Madison Ave, 423 Amsterdam Ave, and 945 Madison Ave, at Whitney Museum of American Art)
Savoy (70 Prince St)
Second Avenue Kosher Delicatessen and Restaurant (156 Second Ave)
Stage Deli (834 Seventh Ave)
Trattoria Dell'Arte (900 Seventh Ave)
Tropica (MetLife Bldg, 200 Park Ave)
Union Square Cafe (21 E 16th St)
Viand Coffee Shop (300 E 86th St, 673 Madison Ave, and 1011 Madison Ave)
Zoë (90 Prince St)

Dog Friendly

Brew Bar (327 W 11th St)
Cafe Pick Me Up (145 Ave A)
Christina's (606 Second Ave)
11th Street Bar (510 E 11th St)
Zum Schneider (107-109 Ave C)

Don't Bother

Too many restaurants spoil the real reason for dining out: to get a good meal in a comfortable setting at a fair price. With so many great choices in Manhattan, why waste time and money on mediocre ones? Many restaurants on the following list are well known and popular, but I feel you can get better value elsewhere.

Angelo's of Mulberry Street: The portrait of former president Reagan is their only claim to fame.
B Bar & Grill: The servers are as disinterested as you will be in the food.
Bice: very noisy, very unimpressive
Bill Hong's: Time to retire graciously before exorbitant prices make it necessary.
Bistro du Vent: Following the mob can sometimes lead you astray.
Cafe des Artistes: The paintings remain appealing, but the beauty of the food is starting to fade.
Chiam: charming in every way except the most important: the food
Cipriani Downtown: expensive journey to Italy
City Crab: Amateurish service and mediocre food are enough to make anyone crabby.
City Grill: big menu, big crowd, not so big taste
Crispo: The anticipation is far better than the reality.
Cru: This room has had its ups and downs, and so does the present operation.
Cub Room: needs a lot of mothering
Django: The name, the setting, and the platters are different, but different doesn't always mean good.

Felidia: a small, dismal shadow of its former self

Foley's Fish House: An exciting view overlooking Times Square is spoiled by unexciting chow.

Frére Jacques: unrealized potential as a French dining destination

Giovanni Venticinque: haughty treatment and high prices

Giorgio's of Gramercy: utterly unmemorable

Island Burgers and Shakes: overpraised, unattractive hole-in-the wall

Jefferson: *Minimalist* accurately describes this place—the decor, table settings, food, and service. Everything except the tab.

La Mirabelle: nice people, but tired menu and surroundings

Le Clown: I'd be clowning if I claimed there was anything appealing about this bare-boned bistro.

Les Halles Brasserie: nothing to excite the taste buds

Le Veau d'Or: Heaven help the stranger.

Lotus: dark, deafening, and disappointing

LUPA: very uneven in both food and service

Maroons: Jamaican and Southern cooking that strays far from its origins.

Meet: This Meatpacking District eatery is not much of a place to meet or eat meat.

Metrazur: The train left a long time ago!

Mickey Mantle's: a strikeout

No. 1 Chinese: It's dark, mysterious, and cavernous—and that's about all.

Old Homestead: *Old* is the best description.

Rothmann's Steakhouse & Grill: Why spend bucks at this rather amateurish place when there are so many good alternatives?

Savoy: uncomfortably cute, unappealing plates

Shula's Steak House: A famous name on the door doesn't guarantee a great meal. Besides, the prices are ridiculous and the place is dull.

Swifty's: unpleasant greeting, snobby atmosphere

Triomphe: small in size, value, and service

Village: uninspired cooking in an uninspired space

Waikiki Wally's: Hawaii is nothing like this place . . . thank goodness! Macadamia nut growers would be aghast at the namesake chicken.

Wolfgang's Steakhouse: Wolfgang Zwiener (formerly of Peter Luger's) now has his own place, but I'm sorry to report it doesn't quite make the grade.

Eating at the Bar or Pub

Beacon (25 W 56th St)
Cafe de Bruxelles (118 Greenwich Ave)
China Grill (52 W 53rd St)
Cipriani Dolci (Grand Central Station, 42nd St at Vanderbilt Ave)
Delmonico's (56 Beaver St)
Emerald Inn (205 Columbus Ave): pre-Lincoln Center
Fanelli's Cafe (94 Prince St)
Five Points (31 Great Jones St)
Gotham Bar & Grill (12 E 12th St)
Grace (114 Franklin St)
Gramercy Tavern (42 E 20th St)
Hallo Berlin (402 W 51st St)
Keens Steakhouse (72 W 36th St)
Markt (401 W 14th St)
Mesa Grill (102 Fifth Ave)

Old Town Bar (45 E 18th St)
Patroon (160 E 46th St)
Penang (109 Spring St)
Petrossian (182 W 58th St)
Rain (100 W 82nd St)
Redeye Grill (890 Seventh Ave)
Spotted Pig (314 W 11th St)
Steakhouse at Monkey Bar (Hotel Elysee, 60 E 54th St)
Typhoon Brewery (22 E 54th St)
Union Square Cafe (21 E 16th St)
Wollensky's Grill (201 E 49th St)
Zoë (90 Prince St)

Family-Style Dining

Carmine's (2450 Broadway and 200 W 44th St)
Marchi's (251 E 31st St)
Sambuca (20 W 72nd St)
Szechuan Hunan (1588 York Ave)
Tony's Di Napoli (1606 Second Ave)

Fireside

All-State Cafe (250 W 72nd St)
Barbetta (321 W 46th St)
Bayard's (1 Hanover Square)
Chelsea Bistro & Bar (358 W 23rd St)
Chumley's (86 Bedford St)
Commune (12 E 22nd St)
Cornelia Street Cafe (29 Cornelia St)
Gramercy Tavern (42 E 20th St)
Hunter's (1397 Third Ave)
I Trulli (122 E 27th St)
Keens Steakhouse (72 W 36th St)
Molly's Pub and Shebeen (287 Third Ave)
Moran's Chelsea (146 Tenth Ave)
One if by Land, Two if by Sea (17 Barrow St)
Per Se (10 Columbus Circle)
René Pujol (321 W 51st St)
Savoy (70 Prince St)
Shaffer City Oyster Bar & Grill (5 W 21st St)
Vivolo (140 E 74th St)
Ye Waverly Inn (16 Bank St)

Foreign Flavors

Some commendable ethnic establishments do not have full writeups in this chapter. Here are the best of the more exotic eateries, arranged by cuisine:

Afghan: **Afghan Kebab House** (764 Ninth Ave)
Argentine: **Chimichurri Grill** (606 Ninth Ave) and **Sosa Borella** (460 Greenwich St and 832 Eighth Ave)
Asian: **Lucky Cheng's** (24 First Ave) and **Rain** (100 W 82nd St)
Australian: **Eight Mile Creek** (240 Mulberry St), **Public** (210 Elizabeth St), and **Sunburnt Cow** (137 Avenue C)

Austrian: **Cafe Sabarsky** (Neue Galerie, 1048 Fifth Ave) and **Wallsé** (344 W 11th St)

Belgian: **Cafe de Bruxelles** (118 Greenwich Ave) and **Petite Abeille** (466 Hudson St)

Brazilian: **Cabana Carioca** (123 W 45th St), **Cafe Colonial** (1376 Elizabeth St), **Churrascaria Plataforma** (221 West Broadway and 316 W 49th St), **Circus** (808 Lexington Ave), **Emporium Brazil** (15 W 46th St), and **Ipanema** (13 W 46th St)

Caribbean: **Bambou** (243 E 14th St), **Cabana** (1022 Third Ave), **Ideya** (349 West Broadway), **Negril Village** (70 W 3rd St), and **Tropica** (MetLife Building, 200 Park Ave)

Chilean: **Pomaire** (371 W 46th St)

Chinese: **Au Mandarin** (200-250 Vesey St), **Baby Buddha** (753 Washington Ave), **Big Wong** (67 Mott St), **Chin Chin** (216 E 49th St), **China Fun** (246 Columbus Ave), **Fu's** (972 Second Ave), **Golden Unicorn** (18 East Broadway), **Grand Sichuan International** (229 Ninth Ave, 745 Ninth Ave, and 227 Lexington Ave), **HSF** (46 Bowery), **Hunan Park** (235 Columbus Ave), **Jing Fong** (20 Elizabeth St), **Joe's Ginger** (113 Mott St), **Joe's Shanghai** (9 Pell St), **Kam Chueh** (40 Bowery), **Mr. K's** (570 Lexington Ave), **New Green Bo** (66 Bayard St), **Oriental Garden** (14 Elizabeth St), **Oriental Pearl** (103 Mott St), **Ping's Seafood** (22 Mott St), **Shanghai Cuisine** (89-91 Bayard St), **Shun Lee Palace** (155 E 55th St), **Shun Lee West** (43 W 65th St), **66** (241 Church St), **Tang Pavilion** (65 W 55th St), **Ten Pell Restaurant** (10 Pell St), **Wu Liang Ye** (36 W 48th St), **Xing** (785 Ninth Ave), and **Yumcha** (29 Bedford St)

Cuban: **Cafe Con Leche** (424 Amsterdam Ave), **La Caridad** (2199 Broadway), **Little Havana** (30 Cornelia St), and **Victor's Cafe** (236 W 52nd St)

East European: **Caviarteria** (Delmonico Hotel, 502 Park Ave), **Danube** (30 Hudson St), **Petrossian** (182 W 58th St), **Sammy's Roumanian** (157 Chrystie St), and **Veselka** (144 Second Ave)

Ethiopian: **Ghenet** (284 Mulberry St), **Meskerem** (468 W 47th St), and **Queen of Sheba** (650 Tenth Ave)

Filipino: **Elvie's Turo-Turo** (214 First Ave)

French: see restaurant write-ups

German: **Hallo Berlin** (402 W 51st St), **Heidelberg Restaurant** (1648 Second Ave), **Rolf's** (281 Third Ave), **Silver Swan** (41 E 20th St), and **Zum Schneider** (107 Avenue C)

Greek: **En Plo Estiatorio** (103 W 77th St), **Estiatorio Avra** (141 E 48th St), **Estiatorio Milos** (125 W 55th St), **Gus' Place** (149 Waverly Pl), **Ithaka** (308 E 86th St), **Likitsakos Market** (1174 Lexington Ave), **Meltemi** (905 First Ave), **Molyvos** (871 Seventh Ave), **Onera** (222 W 79th St), **Periyali** (35 W 20th St), **Pylos** (128 E 7th St), **Snack** (105 Thompson St), **Thalassa** (179 Franklin St), **Uncle Nick's** (747 Ninth Ave), and **Viand Coffee Shop** (300 E 86th St, 673 Madison Ave, and 1011 Madison Ave)

Hungarian: **Mocca Hungarian** (1588 Second Ave)

Indian: **Banjara** (97 First Ave), **Bay Leaf** (49 W 56th St), **Bengal Express** (789 Ninth Ave), **Bukhara Grill** (217 E 49th St), **Chola** (232 E 58th St), **Darbar** (152 E 46th St), **Dawat** (210 E 58th St), **Devi** (8 E 18th St), **Diwan** (148 E 48th St), **Haveli** (100 Second Ave), **Indian Bread Co.** (194 Bleecker St), **Indus Valley** (2636 Broadway), **Jewel of India** (15 W 44th

St), **Kalustyan's Cafe** (115 Lexington Ave), **Minar** (5 W 31st St), **Mirchi** (29 Seventh Ave S), **Rose of India** (308 E 6th St), **Salaam Bombay** (317 Greenwich St), **Shaan** (57 W 48th St), **Surya** (302 Bleecker St), **Tabla** (11 Madison Ave), **Taj Mahal** (318 E 6th St), **Tamarind** (41-43 E 22nd St), and Utsav (1185 Ave of the Americas)

Indonesian: **Bali Nusa Indah** (651 Ninth Ave)

Irish: **Neary's** (358 E 57th St) and **Thady Con's** (915 Second Ave)

Italian: see restaurant write-ups

Jamaican: **Jamaican Hot Pot** (2260 Adam Clayton Powell, Jr. Blvd) and **Maroons** (244 W 16th St)

Japanese: **Benihana** (120 E 56th St), **Bond Street** (6 Bond St), **Chikubu** (12 E 44th St), **Donguri** (309 E 83rd St), **Hatsuhana** (17 E 48th St), **Honmura An** (170 Mercer St), **Inagiku** (Waldorf-Astoria Hotel, 301 Park Ave), **Japonica** (100 University Pl), **Jewel Bako** (239 E 5th St), **Kai** (822 Madison Ave), **Kiiroi Hana** (20 W 56th St), **Kuruma Zushi** (7 E 47th St), **Mana** (646 Amsterdam Ave), **Megu** (62 Thomas St), **Menchanko-Tei** (43 W 55th St), **Minimoto Kitchoan** (608 Fifth Ave), **Nadaman Hakubai** (Kitano Hotel, 66 Park Ave), **Nobu** and **Nobu Next Door** (105 Hudson St), **Omen** (113 Thompson St), **Ono** (18 Ninth Ave), **Ozu** (566 Amsterdam Ave), **Sakagura** (211 E 43rd St), **Seo** (249 E 49th St), **Sugiyama** (251 W 55th St), **Sumile** (154 W 13th St), **Sushi Samba** (275 Park Ave S and 87 Seventh Ave S), and **Sushi Yasuda** (204 E 43rd St)

Korean: **Cho Dang Gol** (55 W 35th St), **Do Hwa** (55 Carmine St), **Dok Suni's** (119 First Ave), **Gam Mee Ok** (43 W 32nd St), **Hangawi** (12 E 32nd St), **Kang Suh** (1250 Broadway), **Kori** (253 Church St), **Kum Gang San** (49 W 32nd St), **New York Kom Tang** (32 W 32nd St), **Won Jo** (23 W 32nd St), **Woo Chon** (8-10 W 36th St), and **Woo Lae Oak Soho** (148 Mercer St)

Lebanese: **Al Bustan** (827 Third Ave)

Malaysian: **New Malaysia Restaurant** (48 Bowery) and **Penang** (109 Spring St)

Mediterranean: **Antique Garage** (41 Mercer St), **Chez Es Saada** (42 E 1st St), **L'Orange Bleue** (430 Broome St), **Marseille** (630 Ninth Ave), **Provence** (38 MacDougal St), and **Zanzibar** (645 Ninth Ave)

Mexican: **Alamo** (304 E 48th St), **Dos Caminos Soho** (475 West Broadway), **El Parador Cafe** (325 E 34th St), **El Rey del Sol** (232 W 14th St), **Ernesto Restaurant** (2277 First Ave), **Fresco Tortillas** (766 Ninth Ave), **La Hacienda** (219 E 116th St), **Maya** (1191 First Ave), **Mexicana Mama** (525 Hudson St), **Mexican Radio** (19 Cleveland Pl), **Mi Cocina** (57 Jane St), **Miracle Grill** (415 Bleecker St), **Rinconcito Mexicano** (307 W 39th St), **Rosa Mexicano** (1063 First Ave and 61 Columbus Ave), **Taqueria de Mexico** (93 Greenwich Ave), **Tortilla Flats** (767 Washington St), **Tulcingo del Valle Restaurant** (665 Tenth Ave), **Zarela** (953 Second Ave), and **Zocalo** (174 E 82nd St)

Middle Eastern: **Bread and Olive** (24 W 45th St), **Cleopatra's Needle** (2485 Broadway), **Layla** (211 West Broadway), and **Moustache** (265 E 10th St)

Moroccan: **Zerza Bar** (304 E 6th St)

Pan-Latino: **Calle Ocho** (446 Columbus Ave), **Flor's Kitchen** (149 First Ave), **Paladar** (161 Ludlow St), **Pampa** (768 Amsterdam Ave), **Sucelt Coffee Shop** (200 W 14th St), **Sugar Bar** (254 W 72nd St), and **Victor's Cafe** (236 W 52nd St)

Persian: **Persepolis** (1423 Second Ave)
Polish: **Christine's** (208 First Ave) and **Teresa's** (103 First Ave)
Portuguese: **Alfama** (551 Hudson St) and **Pao** (322 Spring St)
Puerto Rican: **La Taza de Oro** (96 Eighth Ave)
Russian: **Firebird** (365 W 46th St), **Russian Samovar** (256 W 52nd St), and **Uncle Vanya** (315 W 54th St)
Scottish: **St. Andrew's** (120 W 44th St)
South American: **Cafe Habana** (17 Prince St) and **Patria** (250 Park Ave S)
Southwestern: **Agave** (140 Seventh Ave S)
Spanish: **Azafran** (77 Warren St), **Bolo** (23 E 22nd St), **Cafe Español** (172 Bleecker St), **Cafe Riazor** (245 W 16th St), **El Cid** (322 W 15th St), **El Faro** (823 Greenwich St), **Flor de Mayo** (484 Amsterdam Ave), **Marichu** (342 E 46th St), **Olé Restaurant** (434 Second Ave), **Pintxos** (510 Greenwich St), **Pipa** (ABC Carpet & Home, 38 E 19th St), **Solera** (216 E 53rd St), **Tio Pepe** (168 W 4th St), and **Toledo** (6 E 36th St)
Swedish: **Aquavit** (65 E 55th St)
Thai: **Holy Basil** (149 Second Ave), **Jeeb** (154 Orchard St), **Land Thai Kitchen** (450 Amsterdam Ave), **Peep** (177 Prince St), **Pongsri Thai** (106 Bayard St), **Prem-on Thai** (138 W Houston St), **Regional Thai Sa-Woy** (1479 First Ave), **Royal Siam Thai** (240 Eighth Ave), **Siam Grill** (592 Ninth Ave), **Thai House Cafe** (151 Hudson St), **Thailand Restaurant** (106 Bayard St), **Topaz** (127 W 56th St), and **Vong** (200 E 54th St)
Tibetan: **Tibetan Kitchen** (444 Third Ave), **Tibet Shambala** (488 Amsterdam Ave), and **Tsampa** (212 E 9th St)
Turkish: **Ali Baba** (212 E 34th St), **Beyoglu** (1431 Third Ave), **Dervish** (146 W 47th St), **Layla** (211 West Broadway), **Maia** (98 Avenue B), **Pasha** (70 W 71st St), **Sip Sak** (928 Second Ave), **Turkish Cuisine** (631 Ninth Ave), **Turkish Kitchen** (386 Third Ave), **Üsküdar** (1405 Second Ave), and **Zeytin** (519 Columbus Ave)
Vietnamese: **Cyclo** (203 First Ave), **Le Colonial** (149 E 57th St), **MeKong** (44 Prince St), **Miss Saigon** (1425 Third Ave), **Monsoon** (435 Amsterdam Ave), **Nam Phuong** (19 Ave of the Americas), **Nha Trang** (87 Baxter St), **Pho Viet Huong** (73 Mulberry St), **Rain** (100 W 82nd St), and **River** (345 Amsterdam Ave)

French Bistros

Balthazar (80 Spring St)
Banania Cafe (241 Smith St, Brooklyn)
Bar Tabac (128 Smith St, Brooklyn)
Cafe Boulud (20 E 76th St)
Chelsea Bistro & Bar (358 W 23rd St)
Epiceri (170 Orchard St)
Flea Market Cafe (131 Ave A)
Fleur de Sel (5 E 20th St)
Jean Claude (137 Sullivan St)
Jo Jo (160 E 64th St)
Le Gigot (18 Cornelia St)
Le Jardin Bistro (25 Cleveland Pl)
Montrachet (239 West Broadway)
Pastis (9 Ninth Ave)
Payard Patisserie & Bistro (1032 Lexington Ave)
Raoul's (180 Prince St)

Rue 57 (60 W 57th St)

Game

Game is generally offered in winter months or by special request.

Aquavit (65 E 55th St)
Aureole (34 E 61st St)
Babbo (110 Waverly Pl)
Blue Hill (75 Washington Pl)
Cafe Boulud (Surrey Hotel, 20 E 76th St)
Chanterelle (2 Harrison St)
Daniel (60 E 65th St)
Danube (30 Hudson St)
Eleven Madison Park (11 Madison Ave)
Four Seasons (99 E 52nd St)
Gascogne (158 Eighth Ave)
Il Cantinori (32 E 10th St)
Il Mulino (86 W 3rd St)
Jean Georges (Trump International Hotel, 1 Central Park W)
Le Périgord (405 E 52nd St)
March (405 E 58th St)
Mesa Grill (102 Fifth Ave)
Montrachet (239 West Broadway)
Ouest (2315 Broadway)
Park Bistro (414 Park Ave)
Picholine (35 W 64th St)
Primavera (1578 First Ave)
River Cafe (1 Water St, Brooklyn)
Union Square Cafe (21 E 16th St)

Healthy Fare

Angelica Kitchen (300 E 12th St)
Dine by Design (325 E Houston St)
Four Seasons (99 E 52nd St): expensive
Heartbeat (149 E 49th St)
Honmura An (170 Mercer St)
Josie's Restaurant and Juice Bar (300 Amsterdam Ave)
Popover Cafe (551 Amsterdam Ave)
Quantum Leap (226 Thompson St)
Spring Street Natural Restaurant (62 Spring St): your best bet
Time Cafe (380 Lafayette St)
Zen Palate (663 Ninth Ave and other locations)

Hotel Dining

One of the most notable changes on the Manhattan restaurant scene over the last decade has been the resurgence of hotel dining. No longer are on-premises eateries just for the convenience of registered guests. Now they are destinations for those who desire a less trendy scene with a bit more atmosphere. Here are some of the best.

Algonquin Hotel (59 W 44th St): **Roundtable** and **Oak Room** (evening cabaret)
Carlyle Hotel (35 E 76th St): **Dumonet** (overpriced)

City Club Hotel (55 W 44th St): **DB Bistro Moderne** (Daniel Boulud's urbane bar-restaurant)

Essex House, a Westin Hotel (160 Central Park S): **Cafe Botanica** (casual, view of Central Park) and **Alain Ducasse** (very expensive, exceptional food)

Four Seasons Hotel (57 E 57th St): **Fifty Seven Fifty Seven** (superb dining)

Giraffe (365 Park Ave S): **Barna**

Hilton New York (135 Ave of the Americas): **New York Marketplace** (casual, deli-like) and **Etrusca** (Italian, dinner only)

Hilton Times Square (234 W 42nd St): **Restaurant Above and Pinnacle Bar** (breathtaking views, creative American menu with Italian accents

Hotel Elysee (60 E 54th St): **Steakhouse at Monkey Bar** (great history and excellent American cuisine)

Hotel Gansevoort (18 Ninth Ave): **Ono**

Inn at Irving Place (54 Irving Pl): **Lady Mendl's Tea Salon** (very proper)

Kimberly Hotel (145 E 50th St): **George O'Neill's of New York** (classic steakhouse)

Kitano (66 Park Ave): **Nadaman Hakubai** (Japanese) and **Garden Cafe**

Le Parker Meridien Hotel (118 W 57th St): **burger joint** (lobby), **Norma's** (breakfast and brunch), and **Seppi's** (classic French bistro)

Library (299 Madison Ave): **Branzini**

Lowell Hotel (28 E 63rd St): **Pembroke Room** and **Post House** (very good meat and potatoes, next door)

Mandarin Oriental New York (80 Columbus Circle): **Asiate** (view is great, food is so-so)

Mark Hotel, The (25 E 77th St): **Mark's Restaurant** (one of the very best French)

Millennium Broadway and Premier Tower (145 W 44th St): **Restaurant Charlotte** (American menu)

New York Marriott Financial Center Hotel (85 West St): **85 West**

New York Helmsley Hotel (212 E 42nd St): **Mindy's**

New York Marriott Marquis (1535 Broadway): **The View** (top floor, revolving; New York-centric menu) and **Katen Sushi Bar** (Japanese cuisine with modern decor)

New York Palace Hotel (455 Madison Ave): **Istana** (lobby)

Pierre Hotel (2 E 61st St): **Cafe Pierre** (stately and beautiful)

Plaza Athenee New York (37 E 64th St): **Arabelle** (dignified)

Regency (540 Park Ave): **540 Park Restaurant** (power scene) and **The Library** (informal)

Ritz-Carlton New York, Battery Park (2 West St): **2 West** (new American)

Ritz-Carlton New York, Central Park (50 Central Park S): **Atelier** (French)

Royalton (44 W 44th St): **44** (chic, favorite of publishing moguls)

Shelburne Murray Hill (303 Lexington Ave): **Rare Bar & Grill** (elegant burger spot)

Sheraton Manhattan Hotel (790 Seventh Ave): **Russo's Steak & Pasta**

Sheraton New York Hotel (811 Seventh Ave): **Streeter's** (cafe) and **Hudson's Sports Bar & Grill**

Shoreham (33 W 55th St): **The S Bar**

Soho Grand Hotel (310 West Broadway): **Grand Bar & Lounge** (upscale bar menu)

St. Regis New York (2 E 55th St): **Astor Court** (You can't do better!)

Surrey Hotel (20 E 76th St): **Cafe Boulud** (French-American)

Swissôtel New York—The Drake (440 Park Ave): **Q56** (attractive room, great onion soup and tarts)
Trump International Hotel (1 Central Park W): **Jean Georges** (Donald Trump's personal gem)
Waldorf-Astoria Hotel (301 Park Ave): **Bull & Bear** (British atmosphere), **Inagiku** (Japanese), **Oscar's** (cafeteria), and **Peacock Alley** (reopening late 2005)
Wales Hotel (1295 Madison Ave): **Sarabeth's Kitchen** (delightful)
Warwick New York Hotel (63 W 54th St): **Mural on 54**
W New York (541 Lexington Ave): **Heartbeat** (healthy American)
W New York Times Square (1567 Broadway): **Blue Fin** (seafood)

Kosher

Abigael's on Broadway (1407 Broadway): Located in the basement of the old Gourmet Center headquarters for Ladies' Sportswear), it is arguably the best kosher restaurant in Manhattan.
Abigael's at the Museum of Jewish Heritage (36 Battery Place): Celebrity chef Jeffrey Nathan overseas the Abigael's group, providing creative Kosher cooking.
American Cafe (160 Broadway): a hole-in-the-wall sandwich shop whose biggest draw is location, as there are very slim pickings downtown
Cafe at Makor (35 W 67th St): Makor is a meeting place designed for interaction.
Cafe Roma Pizza (175 W 90th St)
Cafe Weissman (Jewish Museum, 1109 Fifth Ave): In the basement of the museum, which was the old Felix Warburg mansion, this intimate spot is a kosher oasis on Museum Row. It's also close to Mt. Sinai Hospital.
Caravan of Dreams (405 E 6th St): natural, raw, and vegetarian East Village kosher restaurant
Circa NY (22 W 33rd St and 5 Dey St): This upscale cafeteria lunch spot has everything from sushi to create-your-own salads and hot lasagna—all delicious!
Circa 26 (601 W 26th St, 8th floor): very elegant dairy spot
Circa at the JCC in Manhattan (Jewish Community Center, 334 Amsterdam Ave): The Circa experience meets JCC ambience; clearly the most upscale snack bar at any JCC in the country.
Colbeh (43 W 39th St): For an unusual experience, try Persian kosher.
Darna (600 Columbus Ave): Darna's accents are Spanish, Moroccan, and Mideastern couscous, with a splash of medieval decor.
Date Palm Cafe (Center for Jewish History, 15 W 16th St): light but expensive vegetarian and dairy fare within the museum complex
Diamante Cafe (8 E 48th St): one of the busiest lunch spots in New York City
Diamond Dairy (4 W 47th St, mezzanine): Watching the diamond trade is worth the price of a meal, and the Jewish mother style of cooking will warm your insides and make you nostalgic. Even if it's July, get the soup.
Dimple (11 W 30th St): Dimple has been proclaimed the cheapest kosher spot in the Tri-State area, and it's filling.
Domani Ristorante (1590 First Ave): Located on the ground floor of an elegant townhouse, Domani boasts impeccable service and perfect food. Divas singing arias complete the atmosphere.
Dougie's Bar-B-Que & Grill (247 W 72nd St): The ribs are as good as kosher gets, and the original store has spawned a franchise.

Eden Wok (127 W 72nd St): great kosher Chinese restaurant with sushi bar

Essex on Coney Downtown (17 Trinity Pl): Just the aroma is enough to entice you.

Estihana (221 W 79th St): the closest kosher eatery to the Museum of Natural History

Galil (1252 Lexington Ave): This small Israeli meat restaurant serves surprisingly large portions of Middle Eastern specialties.

Haikara Grill (1016 Second Ave): the first and still the best Japanese kosher steakhouse

Hartley Kosher Deli (Columbia University, 101 Hartley Hall, 116th St at Amsterdam Ave): This kosher university dining hall is open to the public.

Jerusalem II (1375 Broadway): Crowds keep coming back to one of the first and best pizza, falafel, and salad bars in town.

Judaica Treasures (226 W 72nd St): a hidden treasure in the basement of a Judaica store

Le Marais (150 W 46th St): This French steakhouse, with a butcher store at the front, sets the standard.

Levana Restaurant (141 W 69th St): Levana is one of a relative few restaurants that's appeared in every edition of this book.

Mendy's Galleria (115 E 57th St): huge portions, fantastic food, and friendly service

Mendy's Rockefeller Plaza (30 Rockefeller Plaza, 48th St at Fifth Ave)

My Most Favorite Dessert Company Cafe (120 W 45th St): Expensive pasta, fish, salads, and desserts are all delectable.

Pizza Cave (218 W 72nd St and 1376 Lexington Ave): Kids in the know say Pizza Cave is the very best.

Tevere (155 E 84th St): old family Italian Jewish recipes and great traditions

Va Bene (1589 Second Ave): superb pastas

Vegetarian Paradise 3 (33-35 Mott St): Set in the heart of Chinatown, this vegetarian spot with rabbinical supervision is quintessential New York.

Village Green Moroccan (96 Third Ave): The menu offers authentic Moroccan grill specialties, great soups, and chumus without peer.

Yonah Schimmel's Knishes (137 E Houston): Yes, knishes are still served up at the same place the business started 150 years ago. A Yonah Schimmel knish is a mound of vegetable or kasha surrounded by flaky dough.

Late Hours

The city that never sleeps . . .

Balthazar (80 Spring St)

Baraonda (1439 Second Ave)

Bereket (187 East Houston St)

Big Nick's (2175 Broadway)

Blue Ribbon (97 Sullivan St)

Blue Ribbon Sushi (119 Sullivan St and 278 Fifth Ave)

Cafeteria (119 Seventh Ave)

Cafe Lalo (201 W 83rd St)

Carnegie Delicatessen and Restaurant (854 Seventh Ave)

Coffee Shop (29 Union Square W): open 22 hours a day, to be exact

Empire Diner (210 Tenth Ave)

Florent (69 Gansevoort St)

Frank (88 Second Ave)

French Roast (78 W 11th St)
Gam Mee Ok (43 W 32nd St)
Gray's Papaya (2090 Broadway)
Green Kitchen (1477 First Ave)
Han Bat (53 W 35th St)
Kum Gang San (49 W 32nd St)
Lahore (132 Crosby St)
L'Express (249 Park Ave S)
Market Diner (572 Eleventh Ave)
Mas (39 Downing St)
Odessa (119 Ave A)
P.J. Clarke's (915 Third Ave)
Sarge's Deli (548 Third Ave)
Veselka (144 Second Ave)
Viand Coffee Shop (300 E 86th St)
Won Jo (23 W 32nd St)

Munching at the Museums

American Folk Art Museum (45 W 53rd St): cafe
American Museum of Natural History (Central Park W at 79th St): food court
Asia Society (Park Ave at 70th St): Garden Court Cafe
Guggenheim Museum (1071 Fifth Ave): Museum Cafe
International Center of Photography (1133 Ave of the Americas): cafe
Jewish Museum (1109 Fifth Ave): Cafe Weissman
Metropolitan Museum of Art (1000 Fifth Ave): Cafeteria (basement) and Petrie Court Cafe (looks onto Central Park)
Museum of Modern Art (9 W 53rd St): The Modern and three other great Danny Meyer operations
Neue Galerie (1048 Fifth Ave): Cafe Sabarsky
Scandinavia House Galleries (58 Park Ave): Cafe AQ
Whitney Museum of American Art (945 Madison Ave): Sarabeth's Kitchen

Offbeat

Afghan Kebab House (764 Ninth Ave and 1345 Second Ave): kebab
Barney Greengrass (541 Amsterdam Ave): You're in the 1940s!
Becco (355 W 46th St)
Brother Jimmy's BBQ (1485 Second Ave): great ribs
Coco Pazzo (23 E 74th St): crazy chef!
Great Jones Cafe (54 Great Jones St): eclectic
Khyber Pass (34 St. Mark's Pl): Afghan
Nobu and Nobu Next Door (105 Hudson St): Oriental delight
NoHo Star (330 Lafayette St): diner
Rao's (455 E 114th St): way uptown
Sammy's Roumanian (157 Chrystie St): Lower East Side
Sylvia's (328 Lenox Ave): soul food
Veselka (144 Second Ave): Polish-Ukrainian

Old-timers

1783: **Fraunces Tavern** (54 Pearl St)
1794: **Bridge Cafe** (279 Water St)
1851: **Bayard's** (1 Hanover Square)

1864: **Pete's Tavern** (129 E 18th St)
1868: **Old Homestead** (56 Ninth Ave)
1885: **Keens Steakhouse** (72 W 36th St)
1887: **Peter Luger Steak House** (178 Broadway, Brooklyn)
1888: **Katz's Delicatessen** (205 E Houston St)
1890: **P.J. Clarke's** (915 Third Ave)
1906: **Barbetta** (321 W 46th St)
1913: **Grand Central Oyster Bar Restaurant** (Grand Central Station, 42nd
    St at Vanderbilt Ave, lower level)
1920: **Ye Waverly Inn** (16 Bank St)
1926: **Palm One** (837 Second Ave)
1927: **Minetta Tavern** (113 MacDougal St)
1929: **21 Club** (21 W 52nd St)

Outdoor Bars

Baraza (133 Ave C)
Bubby's (120 Hudson St)
Bull McCabe's (29 St. Marks Pl)
Caliente Cab Co. (61 Seventh Ave S)
Casimir (103-105 Ave B)
Chelsea Brewing Company (Pier 59, West St at 18th St)
Finnegan's Wake (1361 First Ave)
Hallo Berlin (626 Tenth Ave)
International Bar (120½ First Ave)
Iris and B. Gerald Cantor Roof Garden (Metropolitan Museum of Art,
    1000 Fifth Ave)
Luna Park (1 Union Square E)
Metro Grill Roof Garden (Hotel Metro, 45 W 35th St)
Miracle Grill (112 First Ave)
O'Flaherty's Ale House (334 W 46th St)
Revival (129 E 15th St)
Ryan's Irish Pub (151 Second Ave)
St. Bart's (109 E 50th St)
Sweet & Vicious (5 Spring St)
White Horse Tavern (567 Hudson St)

Outdoor Dining

Aquagrill (210 Spring St)
August (359 Bleecker St)
Barbetta (321 W 46th St)
Barolo (398 West Broadway)
Bateaux New York (Pier 62 at Chelsea Piers, 23rd St at Hudson River)
Bello Giardino (71 W 71st St)
Blue Water Grill (31 Union Sq W)
Bottino (246 Tenth Ave)
Bouterin (420 E 59th St)
Bryant Park Grill (25 W 40th St)
Cafe Centro (200 Park Ave)
Cafe la Fortuna (69 W 71st St)
Caffe Dante (79 MacDougal St)
Cascina (647 Ninth Ave)
Central Park Boathouse (Central Park, off Fifth Ave at 72nd St)
City Lobster & Crab Company (121 W 49th St)

Da Silvano (260 Ave of the Americas)
Druids (736 Tenth Ave)
Empire Diner (210 Tenth Ave)
Falai (68 Clinton St)
Gascogne (158 Eighth Ave)
Gavroche (212 W 14th St)
Gigino (Wagner Park, 20 Battery Pl)
Grocery (288 Smith St, Brooklyn)
Grotto (100 Forsyth St)
Home Restaurant (20 Cornelia St)
Hudson Beach Cafe (Riverside Park)
Il Gattopardo (33 W 54th St)
I Trulli (122 E 27th St)
Il Monello (1460 Second Ave)
Jackson Hole Burgers (232 E 64th St)
Jean Georges (Trump International Hotel, 1 Central Park W)
Le Jardin Bistro (25 Cleveland Pl)
Lombardi's (32 Spring St)
Luna Park (1 Union Square E)
March (405 E 58th St)
Mezzogiorno (195 Spring St)
Miracle Grill (112 First Ave)
Moda (135 W 52nd St)
New Leaf Cafe (Fort Tryon Park, Margaret Corbin Dr at 190th St)
Ono (Hotel Gansevoort, 18 Ninth Ave)
Pampa (768 Amsterdam Ave)
Pampano (209 E 49th St)
Paradou (8 Little West 12th St)
Pastis (9 Ninth Ave)
Patois (255 Smith St, Brooklyn)
Patroon (160 E 46th St)
Pete's Tavern (129 E 18th St)
Porters (216 Seventh Ave)
Provence (38 MacDougal St)
Pure Food and Wine (54 Irving Pl)
Radio Perfecto (190 Ave B)
Rialto (265 Elizabeth St)
River Cafe (1 Water St, Brooklyn)
Roc Restaurant (190-A Duane St)
Rock Center Cafe/The Rink Bar (Rockefeller Center, 20 W 50th St)
San Pietro (18 E 54th St)
Sel et Poivre (853 Lexington Ave)
79th Street Boat Basin Cafe (Riverside Park, West End Ave at 79th St)
Shake Shack (Madison Square Park, Madison Ave at 23rd St)
Sheep Meadow Cafe (Central Park, Fifth Ave at 69th St)
SouthWest NY (225 Liberty St)
Spring Street Natural Restaurant (62 Spring St)
Sushi Samba 7 (87 Seventh Ave S)
Tabla (11 Madison Ave)
Tartine (253 W 11th St)
Tavern on the Green (Central Park W at 67th St)
Terrace 5 (Museum of Modern Art, 9 W 53rd St)
Terrace in the Sky (400 W 119th St)

Time Cafe (380 Lafayette St)
Trattoria Dell'Arte (900 Seventh Ave)
United Nations Delegates Dining Room (United Nations, First Ave at 46th St, 4th floor)
Va Tutto (23 Cleveland Pl)
Water Club (30th St at East River)
White Horse Tavern (567 Hudson St)
World Yacht Cruises (Pier 81, 41st St at Hudson River)
Yaffa (97 St. Mark's Pl)

Oyster Bars

Blue Ribbon (97 Sullivan St)
Docks Oyster Bar and Seafood Grill (2427 Broadway and 633 Third Ave)
Grand Central Oyster Bar Restaurant (Grand Central Station, 42nd St at Vanderbilt Ave, lower level)
Pearl Oyster Bar (18 Cornelia St)
Shaffer City Oyster Bar & Grill (5 W 21st St)

Personal Favorites

Babbo (110 Waverly Pl): fabulous food
Barbetta (321 W 46th St): charming surroundings
Blue Ribbon (97 Sullivan St): great value
Café Gray (10 Columbus Circle): a great New York chef
Gotham Bar & Grill (12 E 12th St): Everything is good.
Gramercy Tavern (42 E 20th St): the "in" place
Il Mulino (86 W 3rd St): Italian heaven!
Jackson Hole Burgers (232 E 64th St, 521 Third Ave, 1611 Second Ave, 1270 Madison Ave, and 517 Columbus Ave): the best burgers
La Grenouille (3 E 52nd St): beautiful
Le Périgord (405 E 52nd St): impeccable
March (405 E 58th St): imaginative
Mark's Restaurant (The Mark Hotel, 25 E 77th St): the way hotel dining should be
Nobu (105 Hudson St): Japanese food at its best
One if by Land, Two if by Sea (17 Barrow St): romantic
Park Side (107-01 Corona Ave, Queens): Come here to eat!
Piccolo Angolo (621 Hudson St): like family
Primavera (1578 First Ave): superb service
River Cafe (1 Water St, East River, Brooklyn): Oh, that view!
Smith & Wollensky (797 Third Ave): old-time flavor
Union Square Cafe (21 E 16th St): justly famous

Picnic Lunches

China Fun (1239 Second Ave and 246 Columbus Ave)
Dean & Deluca (560 Broadway, 9 Rockefeller Plaza, and 75 University Pl)
Mark's Restaurant (The Mark Hotel, 25 E 77th St)
Murray's Cheese Shop (257 Bleecker St)
2 West (Ritz-Carlton New York, Battery Park, 2 West St)
Virgil's Real Barbecue (152 W 44th St)

Pizza

Angelo's (117 W 57th St)
apizz (217 Eldridge St)

Arturo's Pizzeria (106 W Houston St)
Beacon (25 W 56th St)
Da Ciro (229 Lexington Ave)
Da Nico (164 Mulberry St)
De Marco's (146 W Houston St)
Denino's (524 Port Richmond Ave, Staten Island)
Fred's at Barneys New York (10 E 61st St)
Giorgione (307 Spring St)
Grimaldi's (19 Old Fulton St)
Il Corallo (176 Prince St)
Isola (485 Columbus Ave)
Joe's (233 Bleecker St and 7 Carmine St)
John's Pizzeria (278 Bleecker St, 260 W 44th St, and 408 E 64th St)
Lento's (7003 Third Ave)
Lil' Frankie's Pizza (19 First Ave)
Lombardi's (32 Spring St)
Luca Lounge (220 Ave B)
Luigi's (1701 First Ave)
Mezzogiorno (195 Spring St)
Naples 45 (200 Park Ave)
Nick & Toni's Cafe (100 W 67th St)
Orso (322 W 46th St)
Osteria del Circo (120 W 55th St)
Patsy's Pizza Pizzeria (2291 First Ave)
Sal's & Carmine's Pizza (2671 Broadway)
Serafina (29 E 61st St and 38 E 58th St)
Stromboli Pizzeria (112 University Pl)
Sullivan Street Bakery (73 Sullivan St)
Totonno Pizzeria Napolitano (1544 Second Ave)
Trattoria Dell'Arte (900 Seventh Ave)
Two Boots (37 Ave A and 74 Bleecker St)
Una Pizza Napoletana (349 E 12th St)

Power Meals

Alain Ducasse (Essex House, a Westin Hotel, 155 W 58th St)
Ben Benson's Steak House (123 W 52nd St)
Cafe Pierre (Pierre Hotel, 2 E 61st St)
Daniel (60 E 65th St)
Delmonico's (56 Beaver St)
Dumonet (Carlyle Hotel, 35 E 76th St)
Fives (Peninsula New York Hotel, 700 Fifth Ave)
Four Seasons (99 E 52nd St)
Gabriel's Bar & Restaurant (11 W 60th St)
Gotham Bar & Grill (12 E 12th St)
Il Mulino (86 W 3rd St)
Jean Georges (Trump International Hotel, 1 Central Park West)
La Grenouille (3 E 52nd St)
Le Bernardin (155 W 51st St)
Maloney & Porcelli (37 E 50th St)
Michael's (24 W 55th St)
Morton's of Chicago (551 Fifth Ave)
Nobu and Nobu Next Door (105 Hudson St)
Palm One (837 Second Ave)

Park Avenue Cafe (100 E 63rd St, at Park Ave)
Primavera (1578 First Ave)
Regency (540 Park Ave)
Sette Mezzo (969 Lexington Ave)
Smith & Wollensky (797 Third Ave)
21 Club (21 W 52nd St)

Pre-Theater

It is best to let your waiter know when you sit down that you are attending the theater so that service can be adjusted accordingly. Also, if it is raining, allow extra time for getting a taxi. Some restaurants have specially priced pre-theater dinners.

Aquavit (65 E 55th St)
Arqua (281 Church St)
Barbetta (321 W 46th St)
Beacon (25 W 56th St)
Becco (355 W 46th St)
The Biltmore Room (290 Eighth Ave)
Café Botanica (Essex House, a Westin Hotel, 160 Central Park S)
Café Gray (10 Columbus Circle)
Cafe Un Deux Trois (123 W 44th St)
Carmine's (2450 Broadway and 200 W 44th St)
Chez Josephine (414 W 42nd St)
ChikaLicious (203 E 10th St)
Dawat (210 E 58th St)
Esca (402 W 43rd St)
Fifty Seven Fifty Seven (57 E 57th St)
Firebird (365 W 46th St)
44 (Royalton Hotel, 44 W 44th St)
Four Seasons (99 E 52nd St)
Gino (780 Lexington Ave)
Hearth (403 E 12th St)
Hell's Kitchen (679 Ninth Ave)
Indochine (430 Lafayette St)
La Boite en Bois (75 W 68th St)
Limoncello (777 Seventh Ave)
Marchi's (251 E 31st St)
Momofuku (163 First Ave)
Ollie's Noodle Shop and Grill (200-B W 44th St, 2315 Broadway, and 1991 Broadway)
Orso (322 W 46th St)
Picholine (35 W 64th St)
Red Cat (227 Tenth Ave)
Sandwich Planet (534 Ninth Ave)
Spice Market (403 W 13th St)
Tavern on the Green (Central Park W at 67th St)
Thalia (828 Eighth Ave)
Tropica (MetLife Building, 200 Park Ave)

Prix-Fixe Lunches

Cafe Boulud (20 E 76th St)

Eleven Madison Park (11 Madison Ave)
Gotham Bar & Grill (12 E 12th St)
Nobu (105 Hudson St)
21 Club (21 W 52nd St)
Vong (200 E 54th St)

Pubs and Bars

Anotheroom (249 West Broadway)
APT (419 W 13th St): hidden
Arlene's Grocery (95 Stanton St)
Back Page Sports Bar (1472 Third Ave): football
Balcony Bar (Metropolitan Museum of Art, 1000 Fifth Ave): culture
Baraonda (1439 Second Ave): international
Bar East (1733 First Ave): down-to-earth
Bar 89 (89 Mercer St): renowned for unisex glass bathrooms
Barrow's Pub (463 Hudson St)
Bar Seine (Hotel Plaza Athenee, 37 E 64th St)
Bemelmans Bar (Carlyle Hotel, 353 E 76th St): old-school hotel bar
Blarney Rock Pub (137 W 33rd St)
Blue Fin (W New York Times Square, 1567 Broadway): best pre-theater
Boat Basin Cafe (79th St at Hudson River): view with a bar
Bourbon Street (407 Amsterdam Ave): football
Brandy Library (25 N Moore St): fine liquor
Bull & Bear (Waldorf-Astoria Hotel, 301 Park Ave)
Bungalow 8 (515 W 27th St): celebrity watering hole
Buster's Garage (180 West Broadway): sports
Campbell Apartment (Grand Central Station, 42nd St at Vanderbilt Ave, off West Balcony): unique
Cellar Bar (Bryant Park Hotel, 40 W 40th St): new hotel bar
Chelsea Brewing Company (Pier 59, West St at 18th St): big place, big steaks
Chibi's Bar (238 Mott St): Japanese hideaway
Chumley's (86 Bedford St): an old speakeasy in the Village
Coda (Hanover Trust, 34 E 34th St): bar in a bank
Corner Bistro (331 W 4th St): great burgers
Danube (30 Hudson St): Austrian
d.b.a. (41 First Ave): relaxed, "best bar" list (130 single-malt Scotches, 50 tequilas, etc.)
Dive Bar (732 Amsterdam Ave): tall half-pounder
Duvet (45 W 21st St): perfect for an office party
Eleven Madison Park (11 Madison Ave)
ESPN Zone (1472 Broadway): sports
Feinstein's at the Regency Hotel (540 Park Ave): sophisticated cocktail-sipping and people watching
Fondue (303 E 80th St)
40/40 Club (6 W 25th St): sports
Four Seasons Hotel Bar (57 E 57th St)
Frank's (85 Tenth Ave)
Ginger Man (11 E 36th St): huge beer selection
Good World Bar & Grill (3 Orchard St)
Gramercy Tavern (42 E 20th St)

Grand Bar & Lounge (Soho Grand Hotel, 310 West Broadway): recently renovated hotel bar
The Grotto (Michelangelo Hotel, 152 W 51st St)
Heartland Brewery (1285 Ave of the Americas and 35 Union Square W): Try the charcoal stout.
Heights Cafe (84 Montague St, Brooklyn)
Hotel Roger Williams (131 Madison Ave)
Hudson Bar and Books (636 Hudson St): reading
Jack Dempsey (61 Second Ave)
Jean-Luc (507 Columbus Ave): great after-work bar
Jeremy's Ale House (228 Front St)
Jimmy's Bait Shack (1644 Third Ave): football
Jimmy's Corner (140 W 44th St)
Keens Steakhouse (72 W 36th St)
King Cole Bar (St. Regis New York, 2 E 55th St)
Lenox Lounge (288 Malcolm X Blvd): Harlem lounge and jazz club
Level V (675 Hudson St): high-energy dance floor
The Library (Regency, 540 Park Ave): class
Living Room (W New York Times Square, 1567 Broadway): tourists
Lobby Lounge (Mandarin Oriental New York, 80 Columbus Circle): phenomenal Central Park views
Mark's Bar (The Mark Hotel, 25 E 77th St)
McCormack's (365 Third Ave): soccer and football
McQuaid's Public House (589 Eleventh Ave)
Morgan's Bar (237 Madison Ave): great ambience
Mundial (505 E 12th St): soccer
Mustang Sally's (324 Seventh Ave): basketball
Night Cafe (938 Amsterdam Ave)
No Idea (30 E 20th St)
North Square Lounge (Washington Square Hotel, 103 Waverly Pl)
Oak Room (Algonquin Hotel, 59 W 44th St)
Oasis (W New York, 541 Lexington Ave)
Old Town Bar (45 E 18th St): burgers
The Park (118 Tenth Ave): people watching
Park Avenue Country Club (381 Park Ave S)
Parlour (250 W 86th St)
Peculiar Pub (145 Bleecker St): 500 beers!
Pen Top Bar & Terrace (Peninsula New York Hotel, 700 Fifth Ave): rooftop
Peter McManus Cafe (152 Seventh Ave)
Pete's Tavern (129 E 18th St): New York's oldest continuously operating pub
Pianos (158 Ludlow St): busy
P.J. Clarke's (915 Third Ave)
Play-by-Play (4 Penn Plaza): sports
Prime 54 (RIHGA Royal Hotel, 151 W 54th St)
Proof (239 Third Ave): football and basketball
Pussycat Lounge (96 Greenwich St): dancing
Rao's (455 E 114th St)
Rinnade Lounge (Hilton Times Square, 234 W 42nd St)
Rise (Ritz-Carlton New York, Battery Park, 2 West St, 14th floor): view
Route 85A (85-A Ave A): a true bar
Rudy's Bar & Grill (627 Ninth Ave)

Sakagura (211 E 43rd St): Japanese restaurant bar
Scruffy Duffy's (743 Eighth Ave): sports
Ship of Fools (1590 Second Ave): football
66 Water (66 Water St, Brooklyn): bar, restaurant, club, gallery
Smith's Bar & Restaurant (701 Eighth Ave): stand-up bar
Smoke Jazz Club & Lounge (2751 Broadway): best jazz bar
Spotted Pig (314 W 11th St): London-style gastro-pub
Steakhouse at Monkey Bar (Hotel Elysee, 60 E 54th St)
Subway Inn (143 E 60th St): cheapo
Swift Hibernian Lounge (34 E 4th St): 26 beers on tap
Tabla Bar (11 Madison Ave): fancy bar menu
Table 50 (643 Broadway): decent dance floor
Times Square Brewery (160 W 42nd St): in the middle of it all
Tonic and the Met Lounge (727 Seventh Ave): boxing
Town Bar (Chambers Hotel, 15 W 56th St): good service
Trailer Park Lounge (271 W 23rd St): turkey burgers
12:31 (12 E 31st St): cozy
Uncle Ming's (225 Ave B, 2nd floor): mysterious
Vazac's Horseshoe Bar, a.k.a. **7B** (108 Ave B): hockey
The View Lounge (New York Marriott Marquis, 1535 Broadway): rotating
    rooftop views
Waterfront Ale House (540 Second Ave): great Belgian beer, good food
Westside Brewing Company (340 Amsterdam Ave)
The Whiskey (1567 Broadway): see and be seen
Wollensky's Grill (201 E 49th St)
Xunta (174 First Ave): tapas bar

Romantic

Aureole (34 E 61st St)
Barbetta (321 W 46th St)
Bouterin (420 E 59th St)
Bridge Cafe (279 Water St)
Cafe Pierre (Pierre Hotel, 2 E 61st St)
Cafe Trévi (1570 First Ave)
Caffe Reggio (119 MacDougal St)
Caffe Vivaldi (32 Jones St)
Capsouto Frères (451 Washington St)
Chanterelle (2 Harrison St)
Chez Josephine (414 W 42nd St)
Danal (90 E 10th St)
Erminia (250 E 83rd St)
Firebird (365 W 46th St)
Four Seasons (99 E 52nd St)
I Trulli (122 E 27th St)
Il Buco (47 Bond St)
Il Cortile (125 Mulberry St)
Jean Georges (Trump International Hotel, 1 Central Park W)
King Cole Bar (St. Regis New York, 2 E 55th St)
Lady Mendl's Tea Salon (Inn at Irving Place, 56 Irving Pl)
La Grenouille (3 E 52nd St)
Le Périgord (405 E 52nd St)
March (405 E 58th St)

Mark's Restaurant (The Mark Hotel, 25 E 77th St)
The Modern (Museum of Modern Art, 9 W 53rd St)
One if by Land, Two if by Sea (17 Barrow St)
Paola's (245 E 84th St)
Provence (38 MacDougal St)
River Cafe (1 Water St, Brooklyn)
Scalinatella (201 E 61st St)
Tavern on the Green, Crystal Room (Central Park W and 67th St)
Water Club (500 E 30th St)
Zoë (90 Prince St)

Sandwiches

Amy's Bread (672 Ninth Ave)
Bread Market & Cafe (485 Fifth Ave)
Cafe Gitane (242 Mott St)
Call Cuisine (1032 First Ave)
Carnegie Delicatessen and Restaurant (854 Seventh Ave)
City Bakery (3 W 18th St)
Cosi Sandwich Bar (11 W 42nd St, 685 Third Ave, 38 E 45th St, 1633
    Broadway, and 60 E 56th St)
Cucina & Co. (MetLife Building, 200 Park Ave)
Deb's (200 Varick St)
E.A.T. (1064 Madison Ave)
Eisenberg's Sandwich Shop (174 Fifth Ave)
Faicco's (260 Bleecker St)
Good and Plenty to Go (410 W 43rd St)
Italian Food Center (186 Grand St)
La Table O & Co. (92 Prince St)
Manganaro's Hero Boy (105 Sullivan St)
Mangia (50 W 57th St)
Nicky's Vietnamese Sandwiches (150 E 2nd St)
Once Upon a Tart (135 Sullivan St)
Popover Cafe (551 Amsterdam Ave)
Salumeria Biellese (378 Eighth Ave)
Sandwich Planet (534 Ninth Ave)
Sosa Borella (460 Greenwich St and 832 Eighth Ave)
Sullivan Street Bakery (73 Sullivan St)
Telephone Bar & Grill (149 Second Ave)
Terramare (22 E 65th St)
Todaro Brothers (555 Second Ave)
Tony Luke's Old Philly Style Sandwiches (576 Ninth Ave)
Union Square Cafe (21 E 16th St)
'wichcraft (49 E 19th St)

Seafood

Aquagrill (210 Spring St)
Aquavit (65 E 55th St)
BLT Fish (21 W 17th St)
Blue Fin (W Times Square, 1567 Broadway)
Blue Ribbon (97 Sullivan St)
Blue Water Grill (31 Union Square W)
Bridge Cafe (279 Water St)

Captain's Table (860 Second Ave)
Coast (110 Liberty St)
Docks Oyster Bar and Seafood Grill (2427 Broadway and 633 Third Ave)
Esca (402 W 43rd St)
Estiatorio Milos (125 W 55th St)
Grand Central Oyster Bar Restaurant (Grand Central Station, 42nd St at
    Vanderbilt Ave, lower level)
Kuruma Zushi (7 E 47th St)
Le Bernardin (155 W 51st St)
Lure Fishbar (142 Mercer St)
Manhattan Ocean Club (57 W 58th St)
Mary's Fish Camp (64 Charles St)
McCormick & Schmick's (1285 Ave of the Americas)
Mermaid Inn (96 Second Ave)
Oceana (55 E 54th St)
Ocean Grill (384 Columbus Ave)
Oriental Garden (14 Elizabeth St)
Pearl Oyster Bar (18 Cornelia St)
Primola (1226 Second Ave)
Remi (145 W 53rd St)
Sea Grill (19 W 49th St)
Shore (41 Murray St)
Trata Estiatorio (1331 Second Ave)
Tropica (MetLife Building, 200 Park Ave)
Westville (210 W 10th St)

Shopping Breaks

To replenish your energy, here are some good places to eat in the major
Manhattan stores:

ABC Carpet & Home (888 Broadway, 212/473-3000): **Le Pain Quotidien**
    (bakery & cafe), **Lucy Mexican Barbecue** (Nuevo Latino), and **Pipa**
    (South American)

Barneys New York (660 Madison Ave, 212/833-2200): **Fred's** (upscale)

Bergdorf Goodman Men (745 Fifth Ave, 212/753-7300): **Cafe 745** (salads
    and sandwiches)

Bergdorf Goodman (women's store, 754 Fifth Ave, plaza level, 212/753-
    7300): **Goodman** (salads and sandwiches)

Bloomingdale's (1000 Third Ave, 212/705-2000): **40 Carrots** (metro level,
    casual dining and good yogurt), **59 & Lex** (midlevel, casual dining), **Le
    Train Bleu** (6th floor, French cuisine), and **Showtime Cafe** (7th floor,
    casual American)

Lord & Taylor (424 Fifth Ave, 212/391-3344): **An American Place** (5th
    floor, American) and **Signature Cafe** (6th floor, American)

Macy's (151 W 34th St, 212/695-4400): **Au Bon Pain** (street level and 8th
    floor, French bakery cafe), **Cucina Express Marketplace** (cellar, comfort
    food), **Grill Restaurant & Bar** (cellar, American menu), and **Starbucks**
    (3rd floor, coffee)

Saks Fifth Avenue (611 Fifth Ave, 212/753-4000): **Cafe S.F.A.** (8th floor,
    tasty American cuisine, classy)

Takashimaya (693 Fifth Ave, 212/350-0100): **Tea Box Cafe** (lower level,
    Oriental flavor)

Soups

Chez Laurence Patisserie (245 Madison Ave)
Hale & Hearty Soups (849 Lexington Ave)
Second Avenue Kosher Delicatessen and Restaurant (156 Second Ave)
Soup Kitchen International (259-A W 55th St)
Sweet-n-Tart Cafe (20 Mott St)
Tea Den (940 Eighth Ave)
Veselka (144 Second Ave)

Southern Flavors and Soul Food

Acme Bar & Grill (9 Great Jones St)
Amy Ruth's (113 W 116th St)
Bayou (308 Lenox Ave)
Biscuit BBQ Joint (367 Flatbush Ave, Brooklyn)
Brother Jimmy's BBQ (1485 Second Ave)
Bubby's (120 Hudson St)
Cafe Con Leche (424 Amsterdam Ave)
Cajun (129 Eighth Ave)
Chantale's Cajun Kitchen (510 Ninth Ave)
Comfort Diner (214 E 45th St and 25 E 23rd St)
Copeland's (547 W 145th St)
Great Jones Cafe (54 Great Jones St)
Jezebel (630 Ninth Ave)

Are you feeling under the weather? How about a bowl of chicken soup? Some of the best bowls in the city are served here:

Artie's Delicatessen (2290 Broadway)
Brooklyn Diner USA (212 W 57th St)
Carnegie Delicatessen and Restaurant (854 Seventh Ave)
Fine & Schapiro (138 W 72nd St)
Kitchenette (80 West Broadway)
Second Avenue Kosher Delicatessen and Restaurant (156 Second Ave)
Zabar's (2245 Broadway): Saul Zabar himself is there to make sure it's just like his grandmother's.

Londel's Supper Club (2620 Frederick Douglass Blvd)
M&G Diner (383 W 125th St)
Manna's (2331 Frederick Douglass Blvd)
Miss Maude's Spoonbread Too (547 Lenox Ave)
107 West (2787 Broadway)
Pink Tea Cup (42 Grove St)
Shark Bar (307 Amsterdam Ave)
Sister's Cuisine (47 E 124th St)
Sylvia's (328 Lenox Ave)

Steaks

Angelo and Maxie's (233 Park Ave S): reasonable prices
Ben Benson's Steak House (123 W 52nd St)
Bistro le Steak (1309 Third Ave): inexpensive and good

BLT Steak (106 E 57th St)
Bull & Bear (Waldorf-Astoria Hotel, 301 Park Ave)
Churrascaria Plataforma (Belvedere Hotel, 316 W 49th St)
Cité (120 W 51st St)
Del Frisco's Double Eagle Steak House (1221 Ave of the Americas)
Frank's (85 Tenth Ave)
Frankie and Johnnie's (269 W 45th St)
Gallagher's (228 W 52nd St)
Hacienda de Argentina (339 E 75th St)
Keens Steakhouse (72 W 36th St)
Le Marais (150 W 46th St): kosher
Maloney & Porcelli (37 E 50th St)
Manhattan Grille (1161 First Ave)
MarkJoseph Steakhouse (261 Water St)
Michael Jordan's the Steak House NYC (Grand Central Station, 42nd St
   at Vanderbilt Ave)
Morton's of Chicago (551 Fifth Ave)
Nick & Stef's Steakhouse (9 Penn Plaza)
Old Homestead (56 Ninth Ave)
Palm One, Palm Too, and Palm West Side (837 Second Ave, 840 Second
   Ave, and 250 W 50th St)
Patroon (160 E 46th St): outrageously expensive
Peter Luger Steak House (178 Broadway, Brooklyn): a tradition since 1887
Pietro's (232 E 43rd St)
Post House (Lowell Hotel, 28 E 63rd St)
Ruth's Chris Steak House (148 W 51st St)
Smith & Wollensky (797 Third Ave)
Soho Steak (90 Thompson St)
Sparks Steakhouse (210 E 46th St)
Steak Frites (9 E 16th St)
Strip House (13 E 12th St)

Sushi

Since the early 1980s, sushi bars have been a favorite of the fashionable
set. To this day, New Yorkers love to wrap their chopsticks around succulent
slivers of raw or cooked fish on rice. Although many are content to order
assortments concocted by the chef, true sushi aficionados prefer to select by
the piece.   To tailor your next sushi platter to your own tastes, here's what
you need to know:

Amaebi (sweet shrimp)
Anago (sea eel)
California roll (avocado and crab)
Hamachi (yellowtail)
Hirame (halibut)
Ika (squid)
Ikura (salmon roe)
Kappa maki (cucumber roll)
Maguro (tuna)
Nizakana (cooked fish)
Saba (mackerel)
Sake (salmon)

Tekka maki (tuna roll)
Toro (fatty tuna)
Umeshiso maki (plum roll)
Unagi (freshwater eel)
Uni (sea urchin)

Give any of these a try for sushi:

Aki (181 W 4th St)
Avenue A Sushi (103 Ave A)
Blue Ribbon Sushi (119 Sullivan St)
Bond Street (6 Bond St)
Ebisu (414 E 9th St)
Gari (370 Columbus Ave)
Geisha (33 E 61st St)
Hatsuhana (17 E 48th St)
Honmura An (170 Mercer St)
Inagiku (Waldorf-Astoria Hotel, 301 Park Ave)
Japonica (100 University Pl)
Jewel Bako (239 E 5th St)
Kai (Ito En, 822 Madison Ave)
Kuruma Zushi (7 E 47th St, 2nd floor)
March (405 E 58th St)
Masa (10 Columbus Circle, 4th floor)
Megu (62 Thomas St)
Nadaman Hakubai (Kitano Hotel, 66 Park Ave)
Nippon (155 E 52nd St)
Nobu and Nobu Next Door (105 Hudson St)
Ruby Foo's (2128 Broadway)
Sapporo East (245 E 10th St)
Shabu-Tatsu (216 E 10th St)
Sugiyama (251 W 55th St)
Sushi a Go-Go (1900 Broadway)
Sushiden (19 E 49th St and 123 W 49th St)
Sushi Hana (1501 Second Ave)
Sushi of Gari (402 E 78th St)
Sushi Rose (248 E 52nd St)
Sushi Samba (87 Seventh Ave)
Sushi Seki (1143 First Ave)
Sushi Yasuda (204 E 43rd St)
Sushi Zen (108 W 44th St)
Taka (61 Grove St)
Takahachi (85 Ave A)
Tomoe Sushi (172 Thompson St)
Tsuki (1410 First Ave)
Yama (92 W Houston St, 40 Carmine St, and 122 E 17th St)

Takeout

Beacon (25 W 56th St)
Cafe Español (172 Bleecker St)
Cucina Vivolo (138 E 74th St)
Demarchelier (50 E 86th St)
Diwan (148 E 48th St)
It's a Wrap (2012 Broadway)

Jacques Brasserie (204-206 E 85th St)
Jubilee (347 E 54th St)
L'Absinthe (227 E 67th St)
Lorenzo and Maria's Kitchen (1418 Third Ave)
Maria Pia (319 W 51st St)
Molyvos (871 Seventh Ave)
Musette (228 Third Ave)
Pepe Verde (559 Hudson St)
Schiller's (131 Rivington St)
Sushi a Go-Go (1900 Broadway)
Sushi Zen (108 W 44th St)
Tio Pepe (168 W 4th St)
Tossed (295 Park Ave S)
Turkuaz Restaurant (2637 Broadway)

Teatime

Astor Court (St. Regis New York, 2 E 55th St)
Cafe S.F.A. (Saks Fifth Avenue, 611 Fifth Ave, 8th floor)
Carlyle Hotel Gallery (35 E 76th St)
Cha-an (230 E 9th St, 2nd floor)
Cocktail Terrace (Waldorf-Astoria Hotel, 301 Park Ave)
Danal (90 E 10th St)
Fifty Seven Fifty Seven (Four Seasons Hotel, 57 E 57th St)
Gotham Lounge (Peninsula New York Hotel, 700 Fifth Ave)
Harlem Tea Room (1793-A Madison Ave)
Ito En (822 Madison Ave)
King's Carriage House (251 E 82nd St)
Lady Mendl's Tea Salon (Inn at Irving Place, 56 Irving Pl)
Mark's Restaurant (The Mark Hotel, 25 E 77th St)
McNally Robinson (50 Prince St)
Payard Patisserie & Bistro (1032 Lexington Ave)
Pembroke Room (Lowell Hotel, 28 E 63rd St)
Plaza Athenee New York (37 E 64th St)
Podunk (231 E 5th St)
Rotunda (Pierre Hotel, 2 E 61st St)
Salon de Thé (Fauchon, 442 Park Ave)
Sarabeth's Kitchen (423 Amsterdam Ave and 1295 Madison Ave)
Sweet Melissa (276 Court St)
Tea & Sympathy (108 Greenwich Ave)
Tea Box Cafe (Takashimaya, 693 Fifth Ave)
Teany (90 Rivington St)
T Salon & T Emporium (11 E 20th St)
Waldorf-Astoria Hotel (301 Park Ave)
Yaffa's Tea Room (19 Harrison St)

Top-Rated Restaurants

Alain Ducasse (Essex House, a Westin Hotel, 155 W 58th St)
Aureole (34 E 61st St)
Babbo (110 Waverly Pl)
Barbetta (321 W 46th St)
Blue Ribbon Sushi (119 Sullivan St and 278 Fifth Ave)
Bouley (120 West Broadway)
Cafe Boulud (20 E 76th St)

Chanterelle (2 Harrison St)
Craft (43 E 19th St)
Daniel (60 E 65th St)
Danube (30 Hudson St)
Four Seasons (99 E 52nd St)
Gotham Bar & Grill (12 E 12th St)
Gramercy Tavern (42 E 20th St)
Il Mulino (86 W 3rd St)
Jean Georges (Trump International Hotel, 1 Central Park W)
La Grenouille (3 E 52nd St)
Le Bernardin (155 W 51st St)
Le Périgord (405 E 52nd St)
March (405 E 58th St)
The Modern (Museum of Modern Art, 9 W 53rd St)
Montrachet (239 West Broadway)
Nobu and Nobu Next Door (105 Hudson St)
Oceana (55 E 54th St)
Park Avenue Cafe (100 E 63rd St)
Peter Luger Steak House (178 Broadway, Brooklyn)
Post House (Lowell Hotel, 28 E 63rd St)
Primavera (1578 First Ave)
River Cafe (1 Water St, Brooklyn)
71 Clinton Fresh Food (71 Clinton St)
Sugiyama (251 W 55th St)
Sushi of Gari (402 E 78th St)
Sushi Yasuda (204 E 43rd St)
Union Square Cafe (21 E 16th St)

Vegetarian Choices

Angelica Kitchen (300 E 12th St)
Barbetta (321 W 46th St)
Benny's Burritos (113 Greenwich Ave and 93 Avenue A)
Better Burger (178 Eighth Ave and 561 Third Ave)
Cafe Boulud (20 E 76th St)
Candle Cafe (1307 Third Ave)
Caravan of Dreams (405 E 6th St)
Chennai Garden (129 E 27th St)
Chola (232 E 58th St)
Counter (105 First Ave)
Gobo (401 Ave of the Americas)
Green Table (Chelsea Market, 75 Ninth Ave)
Hangawi (12 E 32nd St)
Koi (175 Second Ave)
Moda (135 W 52nd St)
Monte's Trattoria (97 MacDougal St)
Park Bistro (414 Park Ave S)
Planet One (76 E 7th St)
Pure Food and Wine (54 Irving Pl)
Quantum Leap (226 Thompson St)
Quintessence (353 E 78th St, 566 Amsterdam Ave, and 263 E 10th St)
Rice (227 Mott St)
Salute! Restaurant and Bar (270 Madison Ave)

Snack (105 Thompson St)
Souen (28 E 13th St and 210 Ave of the Americas)
Spring Street Natural Restaurant (62 Spring St)
Surya (302 Bleecker St)
Two Boots (37 Ave A and other locations)
Vatan (409 Third Ave)
Village Natural (46 Greenwich Ave)
Whole Earth Bakery & Kitchen (130 St. Mark's Pl)
Zen Palate (633 Ninth Ave and 34 Union Sq E)

View

Alma (187 Columbia St, Brooklyn): magical rooftop garden
Asiate (Mandarin Oriental New York, 80 Columbus Circle): 35th floor of
    Time Warner Center
Metropolitan Museum of Art (1000 Fifth Ave): rooftop bar
Peninsula New York Hotel (700 Fifth Ave): sky bar and open-air terrace
    among lofty midtown skyscrapers
Rise (Ritz-Carlton New York, Battery Park, 2 West St): indoor-outdoor lounge
    on the 14th floor
River Cafe (1 Water St, Brooklyn): A window seat affords that breathtaking
    view of the downtown skyline you've always seen on postcards and in
    movies.
Tavern on the Green (Central Park W at 67th St): Magical!
Top of the Tower (3 Mitchell Pl): an art deco penthouse delight
United Nations Delegates Dining Room (First Ave at 42nd St, visitors'
    entrance)
The View (New York Marriott Marquis, 1535 Broadway): revolves high
    above Times Square
Water Club (500 E 30th St, at East River): Savor the view with Sunday
    brunch.
World Yacht Cruises (Pier 81, 41st St at Hudson River): Manhattan from
    the water

Wine Bars

Ara (24 Ninth Ave)
Artisanal (2 Park Ave)
Barbaluc (135 E 65th St)
Eleven Madison Park (11 Madison Ave)
Enoteca I Trulli (124 E 27th St)
Il Posto Accanto (190 E 2nd St)
'ino (21 Bedford St)
'inoteca (98 Rivington St)
I Tre Merli (463 West Broadway)
MetroCafe & Wine Bar (32 E 21st St)
Paradou (8 Little West 12th St)
Proseccheria (447 Third Ave)
Punch & Judy (26 Clinton St)
Rhone (63 Gansevoort St)
Veritas (43 E 20th St)
Xicala Wine & Tapas Bar (151-B Elizabeth St)

New York Restaurants: The Best in Every Price Category

ABBOCCATO
136 W 55th St (bet Ave of the Americas and Seventh Ave)
Breakfast, Lunch, Dinner: Daily   212/265-4000
Expensive   www.abboccato.com

The Livanos family is well-known and well-respected in the restaurant business in New York; they own this newish Italian dining spot, so one comes expecting big things. Well, there are big things here if you like your Italian dishes rather fussy. Personally, I am more of a purist, so I found some items a bit overwhelming. Most of the appetizers, especially the pastas, are excellent and their breadsticks fabulous. But vanilla-scented veal cheeks with chocolate? Choose carefully and you could end up with a delicious rack of lamb or roasted veal shank. The dessert menu is a dream: ten choices, including homemade gelati. The sizable tab, however, will quickly bring you back down to earth.

ACAPPELLA
1 Hudson St (at West Broadway)   212/240-0163
Lunch: Mon-Fri; Dinner: Mon-Sat   www.acappella-restaurant.com
Moderately expensive

Acappella is a classy, upscale—in atmosphere, food, and pricing—Tribeca diningroom with a highly professional staff that provides a very special dining experience. It's a good place for a romantic interlude, for an important business lunch, or to experiment with some unique Northern Italian dishes. You'll find homemade pastas, risotto, calamari, fish, veal scaloppine, veal chops, Kobe beef, breaded breast of chicken, and prime steak on the menu. Forget the more ordinary desserts and splurge on the homemade Italian cheesecake or chocolate truffle torte.

ALAIN DUCASSE
Essex House, a Westin Hotel
155 W 58th St   212/265-7300
Dinner: Mon-Sat   www.alain-ducasse.com
Extremely expensive

A meal here is definitely an experience. In a magnificent setting, it is thoughtful to the last detail (even a stool at chairside for a lady's bag), with superb table settings and a rarefied atmosphere. The staff almost outnumbers the diners (just 65 are seated per meal). I counted over 20 at work in the bustling kitchen alone. The restaurant also has a cozy alcove where special diners can see how all the famous dishes are put together. There is no question that dining here will be something you'll long remember, but methinks more for the size of the tab than for the taste of the fine caviars. To be fair, there are some great dishes. The Maine lobster, 48-hour chicken, and seared tuna are special, as are the dessert soufflés and cheese plate. Different seasonal menus are available. And the candy cart is magnificent! But with prices in the range of several hundred dollars—even for lunch—and wine tabs that would make a Wall Street baron think twice, most folks will opine that Alain Ducasse was fun to see and experience but would hesitate for a return visit unless they win the lottery. For a party of up to 12, you can reserve a private diningroom with your own waiter, sommelier, pre-menu consultation, and private entrance.

ALOUETTE
2588 Broadway (bet 97th and 98th St)   212/222-6808
Dinner: Daily   www.alouettenyc.com
Moderate

Looking for a bustling eatery on the Upper West Side where prices are within reason and the food is good? Well, Alouette is made even more desirable by a friendly and helpful staff. Seating is provided in smallish quarters on the street floor, and more tables are available on the mezzanine. You'll find many French specialities to start: *paté de foie gras de canard*, onion soup *gratinee,* escargots, and a delicious warm goat cheese *tartelette*. Seafood dishes are available, but it is in the steak category that Alouette really shines. Hanger steak and sirloin are both excellent choices, with superb *pommes frites* (as you would expect) and a coconut-infused spinach side dish. Pretend you are in Paris and enjoy the cheese plate for dessert.

ANGELS RISTORANTE
1135 First Ave (bet 62nd and 63rd St)   212/980-3131
Daily: 11:30 a.m.-11:30 p.m.   www.angelsnyc.com
Moderate

For years Angels has been one of the most popular East Side Italian restaurants. They bring consistency to the preparation of their homemade pastas, breads, cheeses, salads, and exotic appetizers. Entree offerings include a variety of fish and meat dishes. Known for huge portions and good service, Angels is an experience not to be missed. Stroll around the corner and find a variety of homebaked goodies, ready-to-eat pastas, and sandwiches for takeout or delivery from **Wings on Angels** (212/371-8484).

I don't know if folks come to **AMA** (48 MacDougal St, 212/358-1707) for the excellent Italian food—from the Puglia region—or to gaze upon the restaurant's most attractive partner, Donatella Arpaia. You might also see her at **Bellini** (208 E 52nd St), another classic Italian beauty. In any case, uptowners are flocking to this smallish Soho establishment, and all seem to enjoy the looking and the tasting. By the way, *ama* is Italian for love!

ANNIE'S
1381 Third Ave (bet 78th and 79th St)   212/327-4853
Breakfast: Mon-Fri; Lunch, Dinner: Daily
Inexpensive to moderate

Doesn't anyone in Manhattan go out for breakfast or lunch on Saturday? It would seem that way, with most restaurants pulling the shades until dinnertime. Not at Annie's. The daily brunch menu finds this place hopping with neighborhood regulars who know they can get a good meal at a sensible price. On the brunch menu are tasty eggs, omelets, frittatas, cereals, and homemade baked items. Lunch and dinner menus regularly feature tasty soups and salads, sandwiches, pastas, steaks, chicken, burgers, and seafood. Don't pass up the delicious beef short ribs for dinner! If you can imagine desserts under $7 in inflated New York, then look at what Annie offers: homemade apple pie, tarts, gelati, and sorbets. No wonder this is such a popular place. Even standing in line is a pleasure when you get value like this! Delivery is free from 57th to 96th streets between East End and Fifth avenues.

A.O.C. BEDFORD
14 Bedford St (at Ave of the Americas and Houston St)
Dinner: Daily   212/414-4764
Moderate to moderately expensive   www.aocbedford.com

First, what does that strange name mean? Well, the letters "A.O.C." in France, "D.O.C." in Italy, and "C.O." in Spain designate products that exhibit the finest qualities and characteristics of a given geographical area. This is a warm, quaint room in an area where you would not expect to find a classy operation. A.O.C. Bedford is certainly A-OK in the kitchen but loses points quickly with the poorly trained and generally inept personnel at the front of the house, including the manager on duty (at least when I was there). The menu changes seasonally. By all means order lamb, if offered. A nice touch is the cheese course, offering some unusual soft cheeses from all over the world. The Spanish blue cheese was especially good. The dessert selection is small but adequate, with crepes suzette the best choice. If you would like to spend some quality time in a cozy setting with a special date, consider A.O.C. Bedford.

AQUAVIT
65 E 55th St (bet Park and Madison Ave)   212/307-7311
Lunch: Mon-Fri (also Sat in cafe); Dinner: Daily; Brunch: Sun
Expensive   www.aquavit.org

Owner Hakan Swahn and chef Marcus Samuelson have relocated their spectacular Scandinavian restaurant a few blocks east, and their fabulous menu survived the move. In a very sophisticated setting, such delicious dishes as scallops, foie gras, smoked salmon, seared gravlax, and their famous smoked Arctic char are served on huge white plates. There is more: a great seafood stew, duck breast, and short ribs. The lunch salads and sandwiches are very special. For dessert try the Arctic Circle (a goat cheese parfait), apple sorbet, or warm chocolate ganache. Aquavit is as authentic a North Sea setting as you will find in this country. Make an evening out of your visit here!

ARABELLE
Hotel Plaza Athenee New York
37 E 64th St (bet Madison and Park Ave)   212/606-4647
Breakfast: Daily; Lunch, Dinner: Tues-Sat; Brunch: Sun
Moderately expensive to expensive   www.arabellerestaurant.com

Dining in this attractive room is a civilized experience. It is elegant and charming, and the adjacent lounge is one of the classiest places in Manhattan. For starters, try real French onion soup (in the lounge), sauteed Hudson Valley foie gras, or sashimi ahi tuna. If you still have room, entree winners include pan-roasted Atlantic halibut, pork and shrimp dumplings, beef tenderloin, and a tasty Maine lobster salad. By all means, try the warm valrhona chocolate soufflé (order at the start of your meal) for dessert. The wait staff is unusually attentive and professional.

ARTISANAL

2 Park Ave (at 32nd St)   212/725-8585
Lunch: Mon-Fri; Dinner: Daily; Brunch: Sat, Sun
Moderate to moderately expensive

Imagine a combination bistro, brasserie, and *fromagerie*, and you'll have a clear picture of this exciting operation. Being a cheese lover, I found the menu and the attractive in-house takeout cheese counter first-rate. There is much more! The crab and avocado salad is a wonderful way to start. Pricey seafood platters include lobster, clams, scallops, oysters, shrimp, sea urchin, and more. Several fondues are offered, including a classic Swiss and a wonderful stilton and sauterne. Seafood specialties include soft-shell crabs (in summer), cod, and Dover sole. Heartier appetites will be sated by grilled lamb chops, several steak items, and daily offerings. Cruise the cheese counter and load up your plate from a selection of 250 of the world's best for dessert. Seating is comfortable in a spacious room, service is highly informed and refined, and the energy level is high. Great wine selection, too!

How long since you've been on West Houston Street and nearby blocks? What a change from the Lower East Side of former days. They are even getting a Whole Foods Market! And the restaurant scene there is no less than amazing. One of the newest, cleanest, and best (worth a trip from uptown) is **Falai** (68 Clinton St, 212/253-1960). The cuisine is Italian, the outdoor patio is most inviting, the chicken-in-a-pot is fabulous, the homemade breads are among the best I have ever tasted, and the profiteroles are "to die for." The sorbet is also first-class.

ASIATE

Mandarin Oriental New York
80 Columbus Circle (at 60th St)   212/805-8881
Breakfast, Lunch, Dinner: Daily   www.mandarinoriental.com
Expensive

I greatly admire the Mandarin Oriental hotel group, whose original hotel in Hong Kong has been my favorite resting place for decades. So when the news came that they were coming to New York, I lit up. As far as the restaurant is concerned, that light faded quickly. In the first place, they may claim "there are no reservations for six weeks," but that is baloney. I have walked in several times to see a multitude of empty tables. And the much-trumpeted French-Japanese cuisine of chef Noriyuki Sugie is nothing you will remember for long. On the plus side, the 35th-floor view is absolutely fabulous! That is the only reason I would visit Asiate.

ATELIER

Ritz-Carlton New York, Central Park, 50 Central Park S
(at Ave of the Americas)
Breakfast, Dinner: Daily   212/521-6125
Expensive

With a great location right on Central Park, a name that denotes top quality and service, and a room that is executed in sparkling good taste, Atelier is among the city's best hotel restaurants. Executive chef Alain

Allegretti brings top French experience. The salads are delicious and meats formidable, but it is in the seafood department that the place really shines. This is definitely a room for those on an expense account or looking to cement a relationship. A tasting menu, with little change from a $100 bill, is available, as well as a nice selection of caviar (don't ask the price!) and innovative desserts by pastry chef Eric Hubert. The staff is very accommodating and not the least bit snobbish.

> Not too hungry? Try the following for small plates:
> **Amuse** (108 W 18th St, 212/929-9755)
> **Matsuri** (369 W 16th St, 212/243-6400)
> **Nice Matin** (201 W 79th St, 212/873-6423)

AUREOLE
34 E 61st St (bet Madison and Park Ave)   212/319-1660
Lunch: Mon-Fri; Dinner: Mon-Sat   www.aureolerestaurant.com
Expensive

Owner-chef Charlie Palmer usually does a fine job with the preparation of his dishes, which are beautifully served by personnel who are more than a little impressed that they work here. If you manage to get seated without a questionable wait at the bar and are lucky enough to sit on the first floor, with its seasonal garden views, you are fortunate. Best bets are the game dishes. Desserts look better than they taste. Personally, I would take my hard-earned money someplace where the staff appreciates the business. On the plus side, the four-course tasting luncheon is a good value.

BABBO
110 Waverly Pl (near Washington Square)   212/777-0303
Dinner: Daily   www.babbonyc.com
Moderate to moderately expensive

Surely you have heard about Babbo! For many years 110 Waverly Place has been one of my favorite dining addresses. First it was the legendary Coach House, and now it is the magnificent Italian watering spot Babbo, which means "daddy" in the native tongue. It has become one of the most respected houses of fine Italian dining in New York, and a reservation here is one of the toughest in Manhattan. The townhouse setting is warm and comfortable, the service is highly professional, and an evening at Babbo is one you will savor for a long time! Most everything is good, but I especially recommend sweetbreads, grilled ribeye steak for two, and beef cheek ravioli. Wonderful desserts include chocolate hazelnut cake, saffron panna cotta, pistachio and chocolate *semifreddo*, and the ever-popular cheese plate. Best of all is the assortment of homemade gelati and sorbetti.

BALDORIA
249 W 49th St (bet Eighth Ave and Broadway)   212/582-0460
Lunch: Mon-Fri; Dinner: Daily   www.baldoriamo.com
Moderately expensive

New Yorkers in the know head way uptown to Rao's, on 114th Street. Although getting a reservation at Rao's can be a problem, a midtown offshoot of this famous Italian eatery is a definite winner. The seasonings and sauces at Baldoria make almost every dish memorable. There are mussels and clams to start, wonderfully fresh seasonal salads, a good selection of pastas, and especially delectable spaghetti dishes. The meatballs are sensational! Their lemon chicken is one of the best I have ever tasted. If fresh peach *semifreddo* is on the menu, try it for dessert; otherwise I recommend Italian cream puffs with espresso cream and chocolate caramel sauce. The place is busy, but an abundance of personnel will make sure you are well taken care of.

The Stars Shine Bright!

The most prestigious restaurant award—four stars from the *New York Times*—has been awarded to just five Manhattan restaurants:

Le Bernardin (155 W 51st St): March 1986
Jean Georges (1 Central Park W): June 1997
Daniel (60 E 65th St): March 2001
Per Se (10 Columbus Circle, 4th floor): September 2004
Sushi Masa (141 E 47th St): December 2004

BALTHAZAR
80 Spring St (at Crosby St)   212/965-1414
Breakfast, Lunch, Dinner: Daily; Brunch: Sat, Sun
Moderate   www.balthazarny.com

Balthazar is a popular destination at any time of the day (or night, as they serve late). The setting—with old mirrors, ceiling fans, and a yellow tin roof—is unique, and the food is quite good, considering the size of the operation. The personnel are harried but well-trained, and you will not wait for your water glass to be filled. Excellent bakery items shine at breakfast; be sure to pick up some tasty bread next door at their bakery on your way out. At lunch and dinner you can enjoy delicious seasonal salads, sandwiches, cheeses, *panini*, fabulous French onion soup, *brandade*, escargots, steak *frites*, and an abundant seafood selection (including a seafood bar). For dessert the *tarte tatin* is a must. This brasserie is fun and different, and its takeout menu is a plus.

BARBETTA
321 W 46th St (bet Eighth and Ninth Ave)   212/246-9171
Lunch, Dinner, Supper: Tues-Sun   www.barbettarestaurant.com
Moderate to expensive

Barbetta is one of those special places you'll find only in New York, and owner Laura Maioglio is a very special person, as well. It is an elegant restaurant serving Piemontese cuisine. Piemonte is located in the northern part of Italy, and the cuisine reflects that charming part of the country. You can dine here in European elegance. One of New York's oldest restaurants, Barbetta will celebrate its 100th anniversary in 2006. Amazingly, it's still owned by the family that founded it. One of the special attractions is dining alfresco in the garden during the summer. The main diningroom and private party rooms are magnificent! They offer an a la carte luncheon menu, as well as a four-course pre-theater dinner menu, which includes fish specialties, *scottiglia*, and a number of other selections that are served expeditiously so you can make opening curtain. If you have more time and can enjoy a leisurely dinner, think about the *crespelle* (almost a meal in itself), handmade ravioli, or the fabulous quail's nest of *fonduta* with white truffles. Barbetta specializes in fish and game dishes that vary daily. Try the squab prepared with foie gras and chestnuts. Other selections include rabbit, beef braised in red wine with polenta, and a delicious rack of venison. Sixteen desserts are prepared daily, including several chocolate offerings, an assortment of cakes, tarts, and fruits, and one of the best panna cottas in the city. Barbetta's extraordinary wine list, featuring 1,750 wines, was awarded first prize in 2005 by *Wine Enthusiast* and is an eight-time winner of the *Wine Spectator* Award of Excellence.

BAYARD'S
1 Hanover Square (bet Pearl and Stone St)   212/514-9454
Dinner: Mon-Sat   www.bayards.com
Expensive

Get out your map! This is a most unusual and hard-to-find setting for a restaurant. The building is India House, a private club in the Financial District for members only during lunch. The facilities open to the general public at night and for private parties. For an extra treat, ask for a tour of Bayard's private party rooms. The decor is New England nautical, and the rooms are exceptionally nice. This would be a good place to celebrate a special occasion. Prices are high, but so is value. The dishes are high-quality, and an enormous selection is available. Chef Eberhard Müller grows his own produce. Appetizers range from sauteed foie gras to a selection of chilled oysters from both coasts. On to the marvelous Maine lobster salad or seared Atlantic salmon. Your choice from among a dozen desserts includes a cheese dish, soufflés, homemade sorbets, and ice cream. Service is very professional. A *prix fixe* menu is available.

BEACON
25 W 56th St (bet Fifth Ave and Ave of the Americas)
Lunch: Mon-Fri; Dinner: Daily; Brunch: Sat, Sun   212/332-0500
Moderately expensive   www.beaconnyc.com

In a huge space divided into intimate sections, Beacon serves some of the tastiest open-fire-cooked dishes in the city. If you can get a seat in the room by the open kitchen ("the pit"), it is a fascinating show. With over 200 seats and an expansive menu for lunch and dinner, the staff have been well trained to provide superior service. Over a dozen appetizers (from grilled quail to oysters on the half shell), sandwiches, salads, steaks, chops, seafood, and pasta are available at noon. The seafood selection increases at night, as do the meat offerings. The wood-roasted chops and veal dishes are special. Several game dishes are listed on the dinner menu. Dessert soufflés add a festive ending to a great meal. All breads and rolls are made in-house and are available for purchase.

BELLINI
208 E 52nd St (bet Second and Third Ave)   212/308-0830
Lunch: Mon-Fri: Dinner: Mon-Sat   www.bellinirestaurantnyc.com
Moderately expensive

You might call the cuisine at this classic Italian beauty "all in the family." The head lady at Bellini is Donatella Arpaia. Her father, Lello Arpaia, is a well-known chef, and her brother Dino is also in the business. Donatella has successfully stepped out on her own with Bellini. Her menus take into account the current interest in healthy platters. Specialties include thinly sliced raw tuna with dill, grilled sirloin steak, and a number of Neapolitan specialties. Even the appetizers (such as grilled portobello mushrooms) and fresh salads are a treat. For traditionalists, Bellini gnocchi served with Bolognese sauce is sure to please. For dessert, warm chocolate hazelnut cake is a can't-miss treat. In addition to the glamorous owner, other attractions include businesslike waiters, tables that are far enough apart to permit conversation, and a noise-dampening ceiling.

BEN BENSON'S STEAK HOUSE
123 W 52nd St (bet Ave of the Americas and Seventh Ave)
Lunch: Mon-Fri; Dinner: Daily   212/581-8888
Moderately expensive   www.benbensons.com

For years Ben Benson's has been a favorite of the meat-and-potato set, and with justification. The atmosphere is macho-clubby, and the food is uniformly good. Unlike some other steakhouses, service is courteous and efficient. The menu is what you would expect: sirloin steak, filet mignon, T-bone, prime rib, chops, and the like. But Ben Benson's also offers seafood, chicken, calves liver, and chopped steak. A special veal chop steak-style offers 22 ounces of indulgence. The soups are great! Wonderful potatoes, onion rings, or healthy spinach will complete the stomach-filling experience. Daily lunch specials include lobster cakes, grilled chicken breast, roast beef hash, and chicken pot pie. Don't come looking for bargains. Ben treats you well, and you pay well in return!

Bianca (5 Bleecker St, 212/260-4666), a small Italian neighborhood restaurant, has been getting a lot of attention. The lasagna is great, the mashed potatoes sinful, and the tartufo almost the real thing. Take cash, as no credit cards are accepted. The tab is modest, so this shouldn't be a problem.

BIG NICK'S
2175 Broadway (at 77th St)   212/362-9238
Daily: 24 hours   www.bignicks.citysearch.com
Inexpensive

For those readers who believe this book deals only in pricey places, I would argue that is simply not true! Take Big Nick's, for example. This unfancy, inexpensive place offers good food at low prices. Breakfasts are super, and they serve lots of salads and sandwiches for lunch. The burgers are sensational. There is a special selection for diet-watchers. Filo pastries and meat, cheese, and spinach pies are all specialties. There are pizzas, baked potatoes served any way you want, delicious cakes and pies, homemade baklava, and yogurt. The service is friendly, and they offer free delivery. They've been at it since 1962 with no publicity.

THE BILTMORE ROOM
290 Eighth Ave (bet 24th and 25th St)   212/807-0111
Dinner: Daily (bar open until 4 a.m.)   www.thebiltmoreroom.com
Expensive

Old-timers certainly remember the great Biltmore Hotel, where generations of New Yorkers arranged to meet under the famous clock. (Incidentally, the favorite spot to gather in downtown Portland, Oregon, was "under the clock" at Meier and Frank, my family's department store.) Some of the favorite features from that wonderful old building have been incorporated into this restaurant, jazzing up a retreat that seems completely out-of-place in an unattractive neighborhood. You enter through the Biltmore's famous iron gate and revolving doors, and inside you can warm yourself by a fireplace where a replica of the famous clock sits above the mantel. Vintage marble gives a classy look to a place where the atmosphere is a bit better than the Asian-themed food. Still, there are some delicious dishes, including the giant prawns in sarong appetizer and Thai marinated free-range chicken (with delicious sesame whipped potatoes) entree. For dessert, try warm chocolate torte with praline ice cream or soufflé (order early).

BISTRO LES AMIS
180 Spring St (at Thompson St)   212/226-8645
Lunch, Dinner: Daily   www.bistrolesamis.com
Moderate

Bistro les Amis is a delightful bistro worth stopping by in the middle of a Soho shopping or gallery excursion. In the warmer months, doors open to the sidewalk, and the passing parade is almost as inviting as the varied menu. French onion soup with gruyere is a must, and salmon marinated with fresh dill and herbs is just as good. Lunch entrees include sandwiches and fresh salads. In the evening, seafood and steak dishes are available. The steak *frites* with herb butter are first-class. There's nothing very fancy about this bistro —just good food with an extra touch of friendly service.

BLT STEAK
106 E 57th St (bet Park and Lexington Ave)   212/752-7470
Dinner: Mon-Sat   www.bltsteak.com
Moderately expensive to expensive

No, BLT does not stand for the popular bacon, lettuce, and tomato sandwich. It stands for Bistro Laurent Tourondel, and Tourondel's considerable talents in the kitchen have made this French/American steakhouse one of the best in Manhattan. The delicious popovers served at the start absolutely melt in your mouth! Most of the pricey salads are big and healthy, and the soups are filling and hearty. Save room for the main show: hanger steak, Kobe flat-iron steak, filets, New York strip steak, and more. You have your choice of seven great sauces to accompany your meat entree. Also on the menu: fish, shellfish, and potatoes done eight different ways. (I could make an entire meal of those potato choices!) The rack of lamb is superb. Chocolate tart smothered with almond milk ice cream is one of the best desserts in Manhattan. A smallish chocolate chip cookie arrives compliments of the chef.

BLUE HILL
75 Washington Pl (at Ave of the Americas)   212/539-1776
Dinner: Daily   www.bluehillnyc.com
Moderate to moderately expensive

Dramatic it is not. Comfortable it is—barely. Solid it is—in spades. Blue Hill is named for a farm in the Berkshires inhabited by a member of the owner's family. The restaurant reflects the chef's solid upbringing with David Bouley. The smallish menu, with only a half dozen appetizers and entrees, does include some spectacular standouts and changes periodically. Poached duck is a specialty. If your evening plans involve intimate conversation, forget Blue Hill, as eavesdropping is inevitable and rampant. The chocolate bread pudding ("chocolate silk") is the best and really the only dessert worth the calories. This is one of those spots that older relations may especially enjoy, as it is very civilized.

BLUE RIBBON
97 Sullivan St (bet Spring and Prince St)   212/274-0404
Daily: 4 p.m.-4 a.m.
Moderate

Blue Ribbon is one of the most popular spots in Soho, with a bustling bar scene and people lining up for its limited number of tables. Regulars appreciate the exceptional food in this unpretentious restaurant. There is a raw bar to attract seafood lovers, along with clams, lobster, crab, boiled crawfish, and the house special "Blue Ribbon Royale." One can choose from two dozen appetizers, including barbequed ribs, smoked trout, caviar, and chicken wings. Entrees are just as wide-ranging: sweetbreads, catfish, tofu ravioli, fried chicken and mashed potatoes, burgers, and more. How the smallish kitchen can turn out so many dishes is amazing, but they certainly do it well. Don't come for a relaxed evening; this is strictly an all-American culinary experience. Those who experience hunger pangs after midnight will appreciate the late hours. Try the sushi at their nearby **Blue Ribbon Sushi** (119 Sullivan St, 212/343-0404)

Did you ever imagine that you might be able to have dinner at the Rockefeller family mansion in Pocantico Hills, New York? Well, now you can. For a really superb experience, make reservations far in advance for **Blue Hill at Stone Barns** (914/366-9600,www.bluehillstonebarns. com). Only 80 guests are accommodated in what was once a cow barn. Executive chef Michael Anthony presides over a kitchen that serves a *prix fixe* dinner from about $48 to $75. Brunch is served on Sundays. Many of the ingredients are grown on the estate.

BLUE RIBBON BAKERY
35 Downing St (at Bedford St)   212/337-0404
Lunch, Dinner: Daily; Brunch: Sat. Sun
Moderate

Another Blue Ribbon operation! The rustic breads at this cafe and bakery are excellent, and there is so much more. Downstairs, customers may dine in a fantastic grotto-like atmosphere, complete with two small diningrooms, a wine cellar, and wonderful fresh-bread aroma. The upstairs and downstairs menus feature sandwiches, steaks, seafood, cheeses, grill items, veggies and yummy desserts, including profiteroles.

BLUE SMOKE
116 E 27th St (bet Lexington Ave and Park Ave S)   212/447-7733
Lunch, Dinner: Daily   www.bluesmoke.com
Moderate

Leave it to Danny Meyer to fill a real void in the Manhattan dining scene. There are legions of barbecue lovers who find it difficult to get real down-home ribs with all the trimmings in the Big Apple. Blue Smoke is not just a barbecue place; it is a scene, with an ultra-busy bar attracting trendsetters. In addition to ribs, you'll find chili, smoked beef brisket, tasty sandwiches, pit baked beans, and more. This place is fun and different, and Meyer has added another star to his culinary crown.

BLUE WATER GRILL
31 Union Square W (at 16th St)   212/675-9500
Lunch, Dinner: Daily; Brunch: Sun   www.brguestrestaurants.com
Moderate

This seafood restaurant really knows the ocean and all the edible creatures that inhabit it! The Blue Water Grill is a highly professional operation (except for their phone system). Superbly trained personnel operate a building that once served as a bank and is now a *very* bustling restaurant. Wonderful appetizers include lobster bisque, grilled baby octopus, and real Maryland crab cakes. Tuna, salmon, and swordfish are prepared several ways. Lobsters and oysters (several dozen varieties) are fresh and tasty. For those who want to stick to shore foods, there are pastas, chicken dishes, and grilled filet mignon. A half dozen sensibly priced desserts include a seasonal fruit plate and warm valrhona chocolate cake with vanilla ice cream.

BOLO
23 E 22nd St (bet Broadway and Park Ave S)   212/228-2200
Lunch: Mon-Fri; Dinner: Daily   www.bolorestaurant.com
Moderate to moderately expensive

The menu at Bolo is not a copy of the namesake restaurant at the Ritz Hotel in Madrid, but it does encompass contemporary Spanish as well as Southwestern flavors in an attractive and comfortable setting. The atmosphere and personnel are upbeat, as the folks here want your meal to be both tasty and fun. The dozen or so tapas are delicious. Try the chicken and shellfish paella. The logistics are a miracle, with the tiny kitchen turning out a bevy of wonderful and sometimes seasonal dishes.

BOND 45
154 W 45th St (bet Ave of the Americas and Seventh Ave)
Lunch, Dinner: Daily   212/869-4545
Moderate to moderately expensive   www.bond45.com

In the middle of the Theater District, busy restaurateur Shelly Fireman has created another huge dining hall. Billed as an Italian kitchen steak and seafood room, Bond 45 is named for the old Bond men's store that used to occupy this site. The antipasto bar at the entrance makes a mouth-watering beginning. Beyond that there are salads, mozzarella, carpaccio dishes, oysters, clams, cured meats, pastas, steaks, and so on. If it's Italian, Bond 45 has it, with osso buco a house specialty. An overabundance of wait personnel ensures prompt service. For an unusual treat, try the crispy cheese-filled focaccia. But be advised that the dessert selection doesn't live up to the rest of the fare.

BOULEY

120 West Broadway (at Duane St)   212/964-2525
Lunch, Dinner: Daily   www.bouleyrestaurants.com
Expensive

When Manhattan is being battered by a blizzard and this restaurant is still packed, you know Bouley must be something special! One can describe Bouley in many ways: subdued, plush, and elegant, with superb service and magical French/American food. For a dining experience like no other, this must be right at the top of the list. David Bouley is at his very best in the kitchen, but he obviously has trained the crew to meet his high standards. I suggest letting the captain order for you. Tasting menus are offered, and there are many seasonal treats. Day-boat fish from Cape Cod is a specialty, as are fabulous desserts like valrhona chocolate soufflé. Bring your appetite, your best friend or significant other, and your platinum credit card.

The best chefs in Manhattan
Aix: **Didier Virot**
Alain Ducasse: **Tony Esnault**
Alto and L'Impero: **Scott Conant**
Babbo: **Mario Batali** and **Gina DePalma** (pastry chef)
Bouley: **David Bouley**
Cafe Boulud and Daniel: **Daniel Boulud**
Café Gray: **Gray Kunz**
'Cesca: **Tom Valenti**
Craft: **Karen DeMasco** (pastry chef)
Cru: **Shea Gallante**
Dumonet: **Jean-Louis Dumonet**
Fiamma Osteria: **Michael White**
Gotham Bar & Grill: **Alfred Portale**
Gramercy Tavern: **Tom Colicchio**
Jean Georges and Jo Jo: **Jean Georges Vongerichten**
The Modern: **Gabriel Kreuther**
Nobu: **Nobu Matsuhisa**
Per Se: **Jonathan Benno**
Picholine: **Terrance Brennan**
RM: **Rick Moonen**

BOUTERIN

420 E 59th St (near First Ave)   212/758-0323
Dinner: Daily   www.bouterin.com
Moderately expensive

Very quietly, in one of the most pleasant dining settings in Manhattan, Antoine Bouterin has created a French country restaurant with style and class. The flowers and accessories in the room add to the enjoyment of the *provençal* theme. And what goodies he produces: crispy duck, lemon sole, crab cakes with red pepper sauce, candy lamb stew, red snapper with shallot crust, and bouillabaisse Marseille-style are just a few of the treats. Save room for the signature desserts: Grandmother's Floating Island, with fresh berries, or the soufflés. For the health conscious, vegetarian dishes are available.

BRASSERIE
100 E 53rd St (bet Park and Lexington Ave)   212/751-4840
Breakfast: Mon-Fri; Lunch, Dinner: Daily
Moderate   www.restaurantassociates.com

For years the Brasserie was a round-the-clock operation, but alas the night owls must now get their orders in a bit earlier. In attractive quarters, with a grand central staircase, sexy lighting, and a bar that offers all manner of goodies, the Brasserie now closes at 1 a.m. During its 18-hour day, you can find good, if not exceptional, food with a variety of choices, most with a French flair. Among them are grilled dishes, short ribs, *pot-au-feu*, steamed mussels with *frites*, and daily specials. But the real winners are good old onion soup, burgers, and salad nicoise. Desserts (except the beignets) are tasteless.

Score big in the stock market? You might celebrate at these spots where deep pockets are a necessity. Dinner is well over $100 per person, without drinks.
Alain Ducasse (Essex House, a Westin Hotel, 155 W 58th St)
Daniel (60 E 65th St)
Jean Georges (1 Central Park W)
Masa (10 Columbus Circle)
Per Se (10 Columbus Circle)

BRASSERIE 8½
9 W 57th St (bet Fifth Ave and Ave of the Americas)   212/829-0812
Lunch: Mon-Sat; Dinner: Daily; Brunch: Sun (summer hours vary)
Moderately expensive   www.restaurantassociates.com

The interior almost beats the dining at this dramatic restaurant. Descending a long spiral staircase, you enter a spectacular room filled with comfy chairs, an attractive bar, a wall of Léger stained glass, and a collection of signed Matisse prints. Even the tableware is pleasing. Main-course winners include crab cakes, roast chicken, grilled sea scallops, grilled veggie salad, and Maine lobster salad. Specials are offered daily. Friday's seafood bouillabaisse is worth a special visit. Great desserts include chocolate soufflé with malt ice cream. On top of everything, these folks seem genuinely happy to greet their diners.

BRASSERIE LCB
60 W 55th St (bet Fifth Ave and Ave of the Americas)
Lunch, Dinner: Daily   212/688-6525
Moderately expensive

Leave it to Jean-Jacques Rachou! His former endeavor, La Côte Basque, was a New York institution for many years. Now he has opened a charming brasserie in the same room but with an updated French look. The result is a busy, informal house with superb professional service and excellent food. You'll find all the favorite French dishes: platters of fruit *de mer*, *choucroute*, *cassoulet*, *boeuf Bourguignon*, Dover sole, quenelles, and more. Tasty French fries accompany some of the dishes. Fish is also featured: salmon, halibut, red snapper, and lobster. A huge selection of rich and delicious desserts completes a satisfying meal. This is a place for fun and celebration, and you won't be disappointed.

BRAVO GIANNI
230 E 63rd St (bet Second and Third Ave)   212/752-7272
Lunch: Mon-Fri; Dinner: Mon-Sun
Moderately expensive

Fans of Bravo Gianni—and there are many—may be upset that I've included it in this book. They want to keep it a secret. It's so comfortable and the food so good that they don't want it to become overcrowded and spoiled. But it doesn't look like there's any real danger of that happening as long as Gianni himself is on the job. The not-too-large room is pleasantly appointed, with beautiful plants on every table. The atmosphere is intimate. And what tastes await you! You can't go wrong with any of the antipasto selections or soups. They have the best ravoli in town. But save room for the *tortellini alla panna*, *fettuccine con ricotta*, or roast baby lamb; no one does them better. I can recommend every dish on the menu, with top billing going to the fish dishes and rack of lamb. Marvelous desserts, many of them made in-house, will surely tempt you. Legions of loyal customers come back again and again, and it's easy to see why.

BRIDGE CAFE
279 Water St (under Brooklyn Bridge)   212/227-3344
Lunch: Mon-Fri: Dinner: Daily; Brunch: Sun   www.bridgecafe.com
Moderate

Dyed-in-the-wool New Yorkers know this as one of Manhattan's treasures. As a matter of fact, the Bridge Cafe—located north of South Street Seaport, beneath the Brooklyn Bridge—has been in operation since 1794, making it the oldest business establishment in the city. Over the decades (nay, centuries!) it has housed its share of brothels and saloons. Great dishes include buffalo steak, lobster pot pie, and vegetable strata. There is nothing fancy about this place—just good food and especially pleasant personnel. Don't leave without trying the banana chocolate bread pudding. On Sundays the French toast will get you off to a great start!

BROOKLYN DINER USA
212 W 57th St (bet Broadway and Seventh Ave)   212/977-1957
Breakfast, Lunch, Dinner, Late Supper: Daily
Moderate   www.brooklyndiner.com

Brooklyn Diner USA (which is located in Manhattan) is worth a visit. With all-day dining, an expansive menu, pleasant personnel, better-than-average diner food, and reasonable prices, this place is a winner. You can find just about anything your heart desires: breakfast fare, sandwiches (the cheeseburger is a must), salads, hearty lunch and dinner plates, homemade desserts, and good drinks. Their muffins are moist, flavorful, and outrageously good. A tile floor and comfortable booths add to the authentic diner ambience.

BRYANT PARK GRILL
25 W 40th St (bet Fifth Ave and Ave of the Americas)
Lunch: Mon-Fri; Dinner: Daily; Brunch: Sat, Sun   212/840-6500
Moderate   www.arkrestaurants.com

A handy location in midtown, a refreshing view of Bryant Park, and a sensible, family-friendly menu make this a popular destination. Although the menu changes with the seasons, one can count on a good selection of soups, salads, steak, and seafood items at lunch and dinner. A *prix fixe* pre-theater menu is available daily from 5 to 7 with three courses—handy for those going to shows nearby. The $25 *prix fixe* weekend brunch is popular, too. Personnel are unusually friendly and especially child-oriented. The four kiosks in the park offer different dishes.

BUTTER
415 Lafayette St (bet 4th St and Astor Pl)   212/253-2828
Dinner: Mon-Sat   www.butterrestaurant.com
Moderately expensive

Noisy and fun, Butter prides itself on turning out exceptional dishes. The appetizer menu includes oysters, rare tuna, and sweetbreads. For entrees, I recommend any of the seafood dishes and the outstanding grilled organic rib-eye. Creamed spinach is done the way it should be! A dozen desserts will appeal to the sweet tooth. The warm banana bread is a must if it's on the menu. Informal downstairs dining is available.

With all the expensive restaurants in the city, it is reassuring to find some that have reasonable price tags. A few suggestions:
Crispo (240 W 14th St, 212/229-1818)
Supper (156 E 2nd St, 212/477-7600)
Via Emilia (240 Park Ave S, 212/505-3072)

CAFÉ BOTANICA
Essex House, a Westin Hotel
160 Central Park S   212/484-5120
Breakfast, Lunch, Dinner: Daily; Brunch: Sat, Sun
Moderate

Chalk up another winner for the increasing number of good dining spots in Manhattan hotels. Café Botanica overlooks Central Park, offering magnificent table settings to go along with the tasty fare. Villeroy and Boch's "Botanica" pattern is the theme, and along with the colorful chairs and the light and airy feel, it makes for one of Manhattan's most attractive diningrooms. Start with spicy crab cakes or a selection of cold appetizers. On to a veal, steak, or rack of lamb platter. It's a wonderful place for a special buffet breakfast or lunch—the closest thing to a private diningroom in Central Park! At lunch a three-course *prix fixe* menu goes for $26, and for dinner a pre-theater *prix fixe* dinner menu is offered from 5 to 7.

CAFE BOULUD
Surrey Hotel
20 E 76th St   212/772-2600
Lunch: Tues-Sat; Dinner: Daily   www.danielnyc.com
Moderately expensive

Boulud is a famous name in Manhattan food circles. If you are one of the "ladies who lunch" or like to look at those who do, then this is the place for you. The food is quite good, though the room is rather drab and I sometimes find the attitude unappealing. Once seated, however, you'll enjoy the innovative menu. There are always vegetarian selections, world cuisines (every season highlights a different area), traditional French classics and country cooking, and menu items inspired by the "rhythm of the seasons." A two- or three-course *prix fixe* menu is available at lunch. Dinner prices are higher, but remember this place belongs to *the* Daniel Boulud, one of the nation's best chefs. Unfortunately he isn't in the kitchen here, because he is busy doing great things at Daniel.

CAFE CENTRO
MetLife Building
200 Park Ave (45th St at Vanderbilt Ave)   212/818-1222
Lunch: Mon-Fri; Dinner: Mon-Sat   www.restaurantassociates.com
Moderate

Power brokers lunch here! Restaurant Associates (a major player in the city) has created a brasserie with excellent food at reasonable prices. One is greeted by a gas-fired working rotisserie and a beautiful open kitchen that's spotlessly clean and efficient. There are *prix fixe* dinners, if you so desire. The menu changes daily, but I can always find such favorites as chicken pie *bisteeya* (with almonds, raisins, and orange-flower essence), a light and tasty dish. There is a hefty seafood platter, excellent steaks and French fries, and daily roasts. Crusty French bread is laid out in front of you. Other specialties include sea bass, penne pasta, and a moist, flavorful roast chicken. The pastry chef obviously has a chocolate bias (good for him!). *La marquise au chocolat*, bittersweet chocolate mousse, *soufflé chaud au chocolat*, valrhona bittersweet chocolate ice cream, and crème brûlée with caramel sauce are just a sampling. Adjoining the diningroom is a busy beer bar that serves light sandwiches and appetizers.

> A very satisfying Saturday or Sunday brunch can be enjoyed at **Cafe de Bruxelles** (118 Greenwich Ave, 212/206-1830). What to order? Belgian waffles, of course, which come with delicious Belgian fries and a green salad.

CAFÉ GRAY
Time Warner Center
10 Columbus Circle, 3rd floor   212/823-6338
Breakfast, Lunch, Dinner: Mon-Sat   www.cafegray.com
Moderately expensive

Celebrity chef Gray Kunz, who once was the headman at Lespinasse, again has a winner on his hands. In a dramatic setting at the new Time Warner Center, he has created a room that is warm and interesting (the open kitchen is between diners and the park view), with memorable food and friendly solicitous service. All of this comes without the outrageous prices charged at other New York City rooms. The menu changes periodically, so I suggest conferring with your server about the specials.

CAFE INDULGE
561 Second Ave (at 31st St)   212/252-9750
Breakfast, Lunch, Dinner: Daily: Brunch: Sat, Sun
Inexpensive to moderate

The fresh-baked goods are tasty, reasonably priced and attractive. I particularly recommend the flourless chocolate cake and the devil's food cake with chocolate frosting. But there is much more at this cozy, unpretentious hideaway! The three-egg omelets are excellent, and nearly three dozen varieties are offered. Breakfast pastries, especially scones, are also excellent. Sugar-free muffins will please dieters. For light meals you'll find wraps, salads, sandwiches, and pastas. Burgers are a specialty, as are smoothies and a variety of cafe drinks. For a special treat, try the grilled portobello mushroom sandwich. Dinners at comfortable prices include steaks, lamb chops, grilled chicken, baked meatloaf, lasagna, and filet of sole.

CAFE SABARSKY
Neue Galerie
1048 Fifth Ave (at 86th St)   212/288-0665
Breakfast, Lunch, Dinner: Wed-Mon   www.cafesabarsky.com
Moderate

The setting is quaint, the personnel gracious, the prices right, and the German-Austrian food delicious. How do these sound? For breakfast, Sabarsky Frühstück (Viennese Mélange, orange juice, soft-boiled eggs, and Bavarian ham) or other tasty selections. For lunch or dinner, pea soup with mint, paprika sausage salad, crepes with smoked trout, Bavarian sausage, späetzle with mushrooms and peas, or Hungarian beef goulash. Cafe Sabarsky also serves sandwiches, sensational sweets (like Viennese dark chocolate cake and apple strudel), Viennese coffees, and much more. P.S. As you can imagine, the place is crowded. Come early and expect a wait! There is music on Wednesday and Thursday afternoon and Thursday and Friday evening.

It's no wonder that **Cafe Lalo** (201 W 83rd St, 212/496-6031) is a madhouse at all hours. For delicious, reasonably priced sandwiches and other light meals, this room is first-rate. The selection of desserts can only be described as awesome!

CAFE TOPSY
575 Hudson St (bet 11th St and Bank St)   646/638-2900
Breakfast, Lunch: Tues-Sun; Dinner: Daily; Brunch: Sun
Moderate   www.cafetopsy.com

There's nothing fancy either in atmosphere or presentation at Cafe Topsy, just wholesome food at reasonable prices. Soups, salads, and entrees are all excellent. I recommend the shrimp, stews, and brisket of beef cooked in Guinness beer with onion and chive mashed potatoes. The real charm is the home-style English cooking, along with the friendly, casual servers. The popular Topsy burger comes with caramelized onions, cheddar cheese, and fries. All desserts are homemade.

CAMAJE
85 MacDougal St (bet Bleecker and Houston St)   212/673-8184
Daily: 12 noon-12 midnight; Brunch: Sat, Sun   www.camaje.com
Inexpensive

Abigail Hitchcock knows how to cook a great meal. In tiny quarters (capacity 20 or so), this cozy French bistro can evoke memories of some wonderful little place you may have discovered in Paris. Camaje is one of those New York restaurants few know about; however, diners who do know it return often. From the moment delicious crusty bread arrives to the excellent homemade desserts, everything is wholesome and tasty. I don't think I've ever had a better sandwich than their shrimp salad and avocado. There's three-onion soup *gratinee*, smoked trout salad, a half-dozen sandwiches, crostini, small plates, meat and fish entrees, and veggie side dishes. You can create your own three-ingredient crepe, if you desire. By all means, try one of their crepes *sucrées* for dessert; my favorite was a chocolate ice cream crepe with caramel sauce. Another plus is the large selection of quality teas. For a change, their iced tea is the real thing. Cooking classes are offered three times a week.

Beware of Restaurant Pricing Ripoffs!
- Check your bill to verify the price of wine you selected. Also make sure it's the correct vintage when delivered to the table.
- Bottled water is grossly overpriced.
- Look to see if gratuities have been added to the bill, and double-check the math.
- Daily specials are usually more expensive than regular menu items, so proceed with caution.
- Ask to make sure an offered birthday cake or slice is complimentary.
- Add up the items on your bill to ensure that the total charge is correct.
- Be sure to read the fine print about surcharges.

CANDELA
116 E 16th St (near Irving Pl)   212/254-1600
Dinner: Daily; Brunch: Sun   www.candelarestaurant.com
Moderate

Romance abounds at Candela! The only thing missing is King Arthur arriving on horseback with his Knights of the Round Table. As you might guess from the name of this unique establishment in the Union Square area, Candela is awash with candles . . . everywhere. The effect is quite dramatic, with a high ceiling and brick walls with Mediterranean touches. Waiters are attired in ill-fitting and ugly outfits. But the American menu is special, the service is prompt and efficient, and the dishes are fairly priced. The winners: excellent salads, a superb seafood platter (three tiers for two or more hungry patrons), and tasty homemade pasta dishes. Try the standout valrhona chocolate cake with malted-milk-ball ice cream and dark chocolate and milk chocolate malt sauces. Despite the high energy and noise level, you'll not regret your visit. Private parties may be held here during the day.

CAPITAL GRILLE
Chrysler Center, Trylon Towers
155 E 42nd St (bet Lexington and Third Ave)   212/953-2000
Lunch: Mon-Fri; Dinner: Mon-Sun   www.thecapitalgrille.com
Moderately expensive

With all the top-drawer steakhouses in Manhattan, it's amazing they are all so busy. This one is stunningly decorated with Philip Johnson's glass-and-steel pyramids. The room exudes comfort and congeniality, and this is underscored by a wait staff that is welcoming, pleasant, efficient, and informed. Some say this is a Republican establishment, but no one asks for political affiliation and I found them to be super-nice to everyone. The midtown location is handy, the menu is full of the usual appetizers, soups, and salads (a good bet for lunch), and the steaks and chops are fabulous. There are five potato dishes, all first-class. Desserts are good—I liked the flourless chocolate espresso cake—but not overly memorable.

If you know someone who works for **Condé Nast**, ask to meet him or her for lunch at the fabulous cafeteria on the fourth floor of their building at 4 Times Square. (Breakfast is also offered.) In a titanium-sheathed room designed by Frank Gehry, one can find nearly everything to make a memorable meal: a tempting salad bar, hot and cold entrees, sandwiches, good-looking desserts, and much more. The cost is inexpensive (about $6 for an average lunch), but only Condé Nast employees can pick up the very reasonable tab. The parade of models is quite something, as is the whole scene.

CAPSOUTO FRÈRES
451 Washington St (south of Canal St; entrance at 135 Watts St)
Lunch: Tues-Fri; Dinner: Daily; Brunch: Sat, Sun   212/966-4900
Moderate   www.capsoutofreres.com

Capsouto Frères just gets better and better. In 1891, when the building it's in was constructed, this was an "in" area. Now it is hot all over again, and the Landmark Building is still a beauty. Serving contemporary French cuisine, three brothers operate a classic establishment, complete with ceiling fans, wooden tables, good cheer, and tasty plates. An assortment of savory soufflés is very popular. At noon a special *prix fixe* lunch is offered, or you can order from an a la carte menu laden with salads, fish, meat, and pasta dishes. In the evening, they offer more of the same, along with quail, duckling, and first-rate sirloin steak. They are known for their signature dessert soufflés. This bistro is a great setting for a casual evening with good friends who like to live it up!

CARMINE'S
2450 Broadway (bet 90th and 91st St)   212/362-2200
Lunch, Dinner: Daily
200 W 44th St (bet Seventh and Eighth Ave)   212/221-3800
Lunch, Dinner: Daily
Moderate   www.carminesnyc.com

Time to treat the gang or the whole family? Call Carmine's for reservations and show up famished. You won't be disappointed! Carmine's presents Southern Italian-style family dining with huge portions and zesty seasonings. Not only are the platters full, they are delicious. If you are coming with fewer than a half-dozen friends or family, show up early. The wait can be as long as an hour, as they will not reserve tables for smaller parties after 7 p.m. Menu choices run the gamut of pastas, chicken, veal, seafood, and tasty Italian appetizers such as calamari. Wall signs explain the offerings. There is also a delivery menu.

CARNEGIE DELICATESSEN AND RESTAURANT
854 Seventh Ave (at 55th St)   212/757-2245, 800/334-5606
Breakfast, Lunch, Dinner: Daily (6:30 a.m.-4 a.m.)
No credit cards
Moderate   www.carnegiedeli.com

There's no city on earth with delis like New York's, and Carnegie is one of the best. Its location in the middle of the hotel district makes it perfect for midnight snacks. Everything is made on the premises, and free delivery is offered between 7 a.m. and 3 a.m. within a five-block radius. Where to start? Your favorite Jewish mother didn't make chicken soup better than the Carnegie's homemade variety. It comes with matzo balls, golden noodles, rice, kreplach, or kasha. There's more: Great blintzes. Open-faced sandwiches, hot and delicious. Ten different deli and egg sandwiches. A very juicy burger with all the trimmings. Lots of fish dishes. Corned beef, pastrami, and rare roast beef. An unequaled choice of egg dishes. Salads. Side orders of everything from hot baked potatoes to potato pancakes. Outrageous cheesecake topped with strawberries, blueberries, or cherries (or just served plain). Desserts from A to Z—even Jell-O.

CAVIAR & BANANA
12 E 22nd St (at Broadway)   212/353-0500
Dinner: Daily
Expensive

This Brazilian-inspired "brasserio" certainly offers something different for Manhattan diners. Give it a try if you hunger for South America. The tab can be outrageous, though they say many of the dishes are meant to be shared. You'll find a large assortment of tapas, *carioca* bread (Brazilian crispy pizza), and delicious appetizers like a giant ravioli dish and grilled Hudson River foie gras. There are also Brazilian coconut stews, grilled *churrascos* (like strip steak or beef tenderloin served with five sauces), and a large selection of side dishes. Entrees such as sauteed shrimp and roasted quail (a specialty) will have the whole table talking. Now, what does the crazy name mean? Well, their "caviar" is actually tapioca spiked with soy sauce while the "banana" is thin strips of deep-fried plantain.

'CESCA
164 W 75th St (at Amsterdam Ave)   212/787-6300
Dinner: Daily   www.cescanyc.com
Moderate to moderately expensive

Chef Tom Valenti has created another Upper West Side winner (along with Ouest)! You'll love 'Cesca's atmosphere (a former hotel lobby that is both intimate and attractive), highly skilled and accommodating wait staff, and food, which is deliciously Italian from start to finish. Some suggestions: marinated baby artichokes and fresh ricotta, roasted mushrooms, and garlic soup to start. The homemade potato gnocchi is great. Save room for main course standouts like swordfish and the very tender (and huge) grilled lamb loin chops. Daily specials are offered, with the popular meatloaf featured on Tuesday. From the superb Italian bread at the start to rich desserts like buttermilk panna cotta and honey goat's milk gelato, dining here is a real treat.

CHANTERELLE
2 Harrison St (at Hudson St)   212/966-6960
Lunch: Tues-Sat; Dinner: Mon-Sat   www.chanterellenyc.com
Expensive

For civilized dining, this is a must! For over 25 years I have been a great admirer of Chanterelle. Karen and David Waltuck have created something unique and special for Manhattan diners. All the ingredients are here: magnificent decor, extremely professional service, wonderful food, and owners who look after every detail. Of course, nothing this good comes cheaply, and Chanterelle's dinners can be tough on the pocketbook. However, the *prix fixe* lunch is a real treat. As the menu changes often, there are many specials. Ask Karen (who is out front) or David (in the kitchen) to suggest a menu. The seafood dishes are extra special. Their grilled seafood sausage is rightly famous. If you have room after all this, the cheese selection is superb. A mousse, soufflé, or an unusual flavor of ice cream are great for dessert, and the petit fours (served with coffee) make all others seem mundane.

CHELSEA BISTRO & BAR
358 W 23rd St (bet Eighth and Ninth Ave)   212/727-2026
Dinner: Daily
Moderate

Cozy up to a working brick fireplace! Chelsea offers a number of trendy eating establishments, and this is one of the best. It used to be a cave, but now it is a bustling bistro. In a comfortable space that includes an attractive glass-enclosed French garden room, this well-run house has a menu that will please both adventurous and conservative diners. For appetizers, there is a cassoulet of snails, grilled baby calamari, and a tart of goat cheese and onions. Seafood entrees include lightly smoked Atlantic salmon and Chilean sea bass. The niçoise salad is hard to beat. Other specialties include hanger steak in red wine sauce, dry-aged ribeye steak for two, roasted duck, and marinated chicken. All items are seasonal. At dessert time, the tarts really shine. Ask about daily specials.

CHEZ JACQUELINE
72 MacDougal St (bet Bleecker and Houston St)   212/505-0727
Dinner: Daily; Brunch: Sat, Sun   www.chezjacqueline.com
Moderate

Chez Jacqueline is a very popular neighborhood French bistro, and no wonder. The atmosphere and service are appealingly relaxed. All ages seem to be happy here: young lovers hold hands, and seniors have just as good a time on a special evening out. Popular appetizers are fish soup, snails, and goat cheese salad. As you might expect from a French house, the rack of lamb and veal dishes are excellent. My favorite is the hearty beef stew in red wine, tomato and carrot sauce. For dessert, try the caramelized apple tart.

CHEZ MICHALLET
90 Bedford St (at Grove St)   212/242-8309
Dinner: Daily; Brunch: Sun   www.chezmichallet.com
Moderate

Imagine you are sitting at the window of a quaint little restaurant in a picturesque French country village. The place has 14 tables, the decor is eclectic, the kitchen is tiny . . . but the food and service are wonderful. All this is true at Chez Michallet, except you are looking out on the corner of Bedford and Grove streets in Greenwich Village. The friendly waiters couldn't be more helpful in explaining the varied menu: steak, salmon, duck, lamb, veal, chicken, fish . . . anything your heart desires. There is even a special pre-theater menu. Desserts are good as well. Choose from tarts, a great chocolate truffle cake, crème brûlée, profiteroles, and fresh berries. For a perfectly satisfying and relaxing evening, this charmer is hard to beat.

CHIN CHIN
216 E 49th St (bet Second and Third Ave)   212/888-4555
Lunch: Mon-Fri; Dinner: Daily
Moderate to moderately expensive

Chin Chin is a very classy Chinese restaurant whose ambience and price reflect a superior cooking style. There are two rooms and a garden in back. The soups and barbecued spareribs are terrific starters. Chin Chin house specialties include Grand Marnier prawns and orange beef. I'd concentrate on the seafood dishes, though you might also try the wonderful Peking duck dinner, with choice of soup, crispy duck skin with pancakes, fried rice, poached spinach, and homemade sorbet and ice cream. The menu is much the same for lunch or dinner. A reasonable *prix fixe* lunch is available.

CITRON
228 Bleecker St (bet Ave of the Americas and Carmine St)
Lunch: Mon-Fri; Dinner: Daily; Brunch: Sat, Sun   212/924-9717
Moderate   www.citron-restaurant.com

Gavin Citron has trained his people well! Dive into a selection of small plates at this American contemporary restaurant, situated in proper Village surroundings. I'd come just for the crème brûlée French toast with Kentucky bourbon maple syrup! Other winners: Maine lobster crab rolls, tuna tartare, and burgers. For heavier dishes, try the braised short ribs or smoked double lamb chops. Cheese dishes are a specialty. Finish with rice pudding or bittersweet chocolate mousse.

CITY BAKERY
3 W 18th St (at Fifth Ave)   212/366-1414
Breakfast, Lunch: Daily
Moderate

The taste buds tingle the moment you walk into the bustling City Bakery (which is really not a bakery but a buffet operation). Your eyes and stomach will savor the fresh-looking salad bar, the tempting hot entrees, chocolate room, hearty sandwiches, yummy pastries, and much more. I am impressed with the well-trained personnel, who keep displays well stocked, tables clean, and checkout counters running efficiently. For a casual, moderately priced meal in unfancy surroundings, this is a good deal.

CLINTON ST. BAKING CO. & RESTAURANT
4 Clinton St (at Houston St)   646/602-6263
Breakfast, Lunch, Dinner: Mon-Sat; Brunch: Sat, Sun
Moderate   www.greatbiscuits.com

Clinton Street may be a bit out of the way—it's on the Lower East Side
—but the trip is worth it if you want wholesome food at very reasonable
prices. At breakfast you will find homemade granola, pancakes, French toast,
biscuit sandwiches, omelets, and more. For lunch, homemade soups, salads,
eggs, and sandwiches are featured. The evening menu includes delicious
homemade potato chips, oysters, a butcher's salad, halibut, macaroni and
cheese, rib steak, and garlic chicken. Homemade cakes and pastries are
available all day. Extra thick shakes, sundaes, and sodas are a feature of
their fountain. The atmosphere may be a bit dull, but the food certainly isn't.

COMPASS
208 W 70th St (at Amsterdam Ave)   212/875-8600
Lunch: Mon-Fri; Dinner: Daily; Brunch: Sun
Moderately expensive   www.compassrestaurant.com

Compass has been moving in the right direction the past few years, giving
the Upper West Side another winner. Now the excellent food is comple-
mented by a superb service staff put together by Al Lopez. The personnel
are polite and efficient. Most everything on the menu is good, but the veal
chops, sirloin, and braised short ribs are special. A tasty selection of over a
dozen cheeses for dessert is the perfect ending to an outstanding meal.

It is not too often that your author gets really excited about a Japanese restaurant, but this one—**Megu** (62 Thomas St, 212/964-7777,
www.megunyc.com)—absolutely deserves top billing. The theme here
is pricey modern Japanese. The selection of dishes, the adept service,
the romantic and compelling atmosphere—all add to a truly superb dining experience. Of course there is sushi in abundance, but the star of the
menu is thin slices of Kobe beef that one can cook over a hot rock. The
Japanese version of a Caesar salad is delicious. Even the desserts (yes,
in a Japanese restaurant) are plentiful and fanciful. Go! Lunch is available Monday through Friday. Just don't let the inexperienced door
personnel tell you that all tables are reserved—baloney!

COUNTRY CAFE
69 Thompson St (bet Spring and Broome St)   212/966-5417
Lunch, Dinner: Daily; Brunch: Sat, Sun   www.countrycafesoho.com
Moderate

You have to know what you're looking for to find this tiny Soho establishment. Once inside, you'll appreciate the no-nonsense approach to French
country dining. The service and atmosphere could easily be transplanted to
any small village in France. The menu would fit right in as well, with items
like homemade country paté with onion and fruit chutney; a fabulous country salad with croutons, lardons, blue cheese, and walnuts; vegetable cous-

cous; snails in garlic butter; and one of the city's best steaks *au poivre* with real homemade French fries. I love the informality of the place, the sizable portions, and the obvious delight the young staff takes in showing guests what it is like to be treated by some real homebodies. *Bon appetit!*

> When a craving strikes for great pastries and quiches, head down to **Ceci Cela** (55 Spring St, 212/274-9179). Laurent Dupal and Herve Grall dish up some of the area's best breakfasts and light lunches in casual surroundings.

CRAFT
43 E 19th St (bet Park Ave S and Broadway)   212/780-0880
Dinner: Daily
Expensive

You can pretend you are a chef here! Unlike any restaurant you've ever seen, Craft is worth visiting for a number of reasons. The atmosphere is conducive to good eating, and the help is particularly friendly. Most of all, the way you order is unique. It is all a la carte. The menu is divided into sections: fish and shellfish, meats, vegetables, mushrooms, potatoes, grains, and beans. You can put together any combination you find appealing, and the plates won't overwhelm your appetite. Chef-owner Tom Colicchio came from the Gramercy Tavern, and the expertise shows. Even the dessert selection is great: wonderful cheeses, pastries, custards, fruits, ice creams, and sorbets (with many sauces available). If you're not terribly hungry or there are picky eaters in the group, head to Craft. **Craftbar** (900 Broadway) is more casual than Craft, with a contemporary New American menu and composed dishes.

CUCINA & CO.
MetLife Building, lobby
200 Park Ave (45th St at Vanderbilt Ave), lobby   212/682-2700
Breakfast, Lunch, Dinner: Mon-Fri
(takeout open 7 a.m.-9 p.m.; Sat: 8-4) www.restaurantassociates.com
Moderate

Hidden between three hyped restaurants (Tropica, Naples 45, and Cafe Centro) in the bowels of the huge MetLife Building, Cucina & Co. is a treasure. The takeout counter is one of the best in mid-Manhattan: all sorts of prepared foods, sandwiches, salads, great cookies and cakes, breads, and whatever else you might want to take back to the home or office. Adjoining is a bustling, crowded cafe that serves first-class food at reasonable prices for such a prime location. You will find delicious burgers (served on sesame brioche rolls), baked pastas, quiches, seafood, health food dishes, and a good selection of dessert items. The service is fast and the personnel highly professional. They have to be in order to serve so many people during rush hours! I heartily recommend this place, especially for lunch. You'll also find Cucina & Co. in prime real estate at 30 Rockefeller Center (212/332-7630), and in Macy's Cellar (212/868-2388).

CUCINA STAGIONALE
289 Bleecker St (at Seventh Ave)   212/924-2707
Lunch, Dinner: Daily
Inexpensive

When you serve good food at a low price, word gets around. So it's no wonder there's a line in front of this small Greenwich Village cafe almost any time of day. Its name translates as "seasonal kitchen," and the seasonal specialties are real values. It's a bare-bones setup, with seating for only a few dozen hungry folks. Service is impersonal and nonprofessional, but who cares at these prices? Innovative Italian cuisine—tasty, attractive, and filling—is served, and you can do very well on a slim budget. Recommended appetizers include smoked salmon with endive and radicchio, and sauteed wild mushrooms. For a few pennies more, you can get a large dish of linguine or ravioli. I'm constantly asked about inexpensive places that serve quality food, and I have no hesitation recommending this spot. One word of warning: don't go if it's raining, because you'll probably have to wait outside to get seated.

A dessert bar? That is what **ChikaLicious** (203 E 10th St, 212/995-9511) calls itself. It is a tiny room, with bar stools and several tables, with *prix fixe* dessert choices for $12, and a wine pairing for $7 more. Choices include a cheesecake, two chocolate dishes, cheeses, and more. Portions are miserly, the tastes leave a lot to be desired, and the plates look too fussy to be truly inviting.

CUPPING ROOM CAFE
359 West Broadway (bet Broome and Grand St)   212/925-2898
Breakfast, Lunch: Mon-Fri; Dinner: Daily; Brunch: Sat, Sun
Moderate   www.cuppingroomcafe.com

It is easy to see why the Cupping Room Cafe is one of the most popular places in Soho to meet and dine. In a noisy, convivial atmosphere, with close-together tables and a bar where you can drink and/or eat, all the news of the area is exchanged. The diverse food offerings at lunch and dinner include pastas, seafood, chicken, steaks, and vegetarian dishes. But breakfast and brunch are where they really shine: freshly baked pastries, fruit and cheese, waffles, pancakes, wonderful French toast, and eggs and omelets. Eggs Benedict can be customized. For lighter dining, there are soups, sandwiches, burgers, and salads. Be sure to ask about daily dessert items; most are delicious, fresh, reasonably priced, and caloric. Entertainment is offered some evenings, as is a *prix fixe* dinner.

DANAL
90 E 10th St (bet Third and Fourth Ave)   212/982-6930
Lunch: Mon-Fri; Dinner: Daily; Brunch: Sat, Sun;
Tea: Fri-Sat (by reservation)
Moderate

Here are my guidelines for a good eating spot: The bread is fresh, crisp, and warm. Vegetables are not overcooked. Salads are cool, and the house salad is not just a pile of lettuce. If homemade ice cream is served, it is rich and creamy and has no ice particles in it. Sorbets are equally delicious.

Finally, the owner is on the job. Danal meets all of the above criteria with fly-ing colors. The location is the East Village, on a safe, quiet street. The atmo-sphere is what the owner calls "country French." I would call it homey mix-and-match. The service is understated and friendly, with no pretense. The uniformly delicious dishes are served in right-sized portions. Entrees at Danal are typical French country Mediterranean bistro fare. The menu varies daily but features something tasty for any appetite.

DANIEL
60 E 65th St (bet Madison and Park Ave)   212/288-0033
Dinner: Mon-Sat   www.danielnyc.com
Expensive

Daniel Boulud deserves to feel immensely proud of his four-star, $10 mil-lion classical French country restaurant. Despite all the hype and intense scrutiny of every aspect of his dream, this accomplished chef has achieved perfection. If you are ready to have an absolutely superb dining experience and money doesn't matter, then join the often long waiting list for a table in the space of the former Mayfair Hotel lobby and the old Le Cirque restau-rant. The setting resurrects the original 1920s look, with neoclassical details. The result is an unusually pleasant feeling, with the light and hum of the room adding to the joy of each delicious platter. The wait staff is highly pro-fessional and knowledgeable. Signature dishes change by the season. It might be a duo of roasted beef tenderloin and braised short ribs (the best I have ever tasted), roasted squab, or roasted filet of venison. Desserts are works of art. Don't miss the cheese selection! Every time I visit this restaurant I don't want the meal to end, and I can't think of a higher compliment.

Although Manhattan has not been known for great barbecue estab-lishments, a relatively new one has shown great promise. **Daisy May's BBQ USA** (623 Eleventh Ave, 212/977-1500) offers takeout and cater-ing but no inside seating. Best bet: Kansas City sweet and sticky ribs, which are tender and delicious. And there is much more: beef short ribs, bourbon half chicken, beef and pork sandwiches, baked beans, creamy cole slaw, peaches in bourbon, and superb mashed sweet potatoes with brown sugar. Prices are easy on the pocketbook.

DANUBE
30 Hudson St (bet Duane and Reade St)   212/791-3771
Dinner: Mon-Sat   www.bouleyrestaurants.com
Expensive

If you are looking for a purely Austrian restaurant, then this may not sat-isfy. But if you want a dining experience with a *touch* of Austria, done with class in magnificent surroundings, then by all means book a reservation at Danube. The decor is spectacular, with all the ingredients of a plush Euro-pean drawing room: Venetian stucco, ebony paneling, velvet and ultrasuede fabrics, beautiful lighting fixtures. You will appreciate the magic created in the kitchen, too. Tyrolean wine soup, great Austrian cheese ravioli, and roasted sweet organic beets make great starters. Beef cheeks are braised in a wine sauce with chive späetzle. The veal wiener schnitzel with Austrian crescent potatoes will have you dreaming about Vienna's Imperial Hotel. I could make an entire meal from the great dessert offerings here. Between courses, special items periodically arrive at the table.

DA UMBERTO
107 W 17th St (at Ave of the Americas)   212/989-0303
Lunch: Mon-Fri; Dinner: Mon-Sat
Moderate to moderately expensive

Da Umberto is for serious Italian diners. This Tuscan trattoria is a feast for the eyes as well as the palate. A groaning table of inviting antipasto dishes greets guests; one could easily make an entire meal just from this selection. All of the platters look so fresh and healthy! Vittorio Assante himself is around much of the time, ensuring that the service is as good as the food. One can look into the glass-framed kitchen at the rear to see how real professionals work. The three-color salad is a house specialty. On to well-prepared pastas, fish, veal, game (in season), or chicken. Your waiter will have many specials, like calamari *ripieni,* to detail. If you have room, the chocolate truffle cake and tiramisu are the best of the dessert selections.

DAVIDBURKE & DONATELLA
133 E 61st St (bet Park and Lexington Ave)   212/813-2121
Lunch: Mon-Fri; Dinner: Daily; Brunch: Sun   www.dbrestaurant.com
Moderately expensive

Let's start at the end! To me, the real joy of this establishment from famed chef David Burke and Donatella Arpaia are the desserts. Butterscotch panna cotta, coconut layer cake, dark chocolate and praline torte, and a dollhouse stove full of yummy candy are all created by an excellent pastry chef. Of course there are other attractions at this popular spot, which seems to me more of a ladies' dining choice. If I had to choose one word to describe the place, it would be *fussy.* Their chef's salad is absolutely the best I have ever tasted. I also like the way bread is served, warm in a small pan like a muffin. The menu changes periodically. A white limousine is parked outside for smokers!

DAWAT
210 E 58th St (bet Second and Third Ave)   212/355-7555
Lunch: Mon-Sat; Dinner: Daily   www.restaurant.com/dawat
Moderate

Ms. Madhur Jaffrey, a highly respected cookbook author, creates innovative Indian dishes that set Dawat apart as one of the best Indian restaurants in the city. There are numerous good seafood choices, including a sensational entree called Shrimp Konju Pappaas. Chicken, goat, and lamb dishes are other favorites, as is an attractive choice of vegetarian dishes. Different varieties of excellent breads are available. Don't pass up Jaffrey's desserts, which are unusually good for an Indian restaurant.

DB BISTRO MODERNE
55 W 44th St (bet Fifth Ave and Ave of the Americas)   212/391-2400
Lunch: Mon-Sat; Dinner: Mon-Sun   www.danielnyc.com
Moderate to moderately expensive

Renowned restaurant impressario Daniel Boulud's latest venture is, for him, a more casual dining experience. Even burgers are served, and they are very good. (At $29, they should be!) Of course, this is no ordinary hamburger. It is ground sirloin filled with short ribs, foie gras and black truffles, served on a parmesan bun and accompanied by delicious, light *pommes soufflés* presented in a silver cup. Diners have their choice of two rooms with a bar-type setup between them that is comfortable for singles. The stylish menu is divided into sections like *thon* (tuna), *saumon* (salmon), *canard* (poultry), and *boeuf* (beef), offering several items in each category. For dessert, the cheese selection is a real winner, as are any of Daniel's specialties that use berries and other fresh fruit.

DEL FRISCO'S DOUBLE EAGLE STEAK HOUSE
McGraw-Hill Building
1221 Ave of the Americas (at 49th St)   212/575-5129
Lunch: Mon-Fri; Dinner: Daily
Expensive

Del Frisco's provides a good meal with accommodating service in a setting where both the ceiling and prices are high. Fresh, warm bread is brought to the table as you enjoy a seafood appetizer or great beefsteak tomato and sliced onion salad. Steaks, chops, veal dishes, and lobster are all first-rate, while accompanying side dishes are large and uneven. In-house desserts include bread pudding with Jack Daniel's sauce, crisp chocolate soufflé cake with raspberries, and strawberries Romanoff with vanilla ice cream. All are winners. This establishment is inviting, except when it comes to price. Isn't $16.95 for a shrimp cocktail a bit steep? To be frank, I also found myself wondering whether every dish is freshly cooked for each diner.

DEMARCHELIER
50 E 86th St (at Madison Ave)   212/249-6300
Lunch, Dinner: Daily   www.demarchelierrestaurant.com
Moderate

For years diners have come to this French bistro for two reasons: good food and no pretense. If you like solid French fare like fresh artichokes and fresh asparagus in season, crusty bread, *paté de campagne*, salad niçoise, and grilled shrimp with honey, you'll love Demarchelier. Steak dishes are also a specialty. Service is extremely efficient and prompt—ideal if you are in a rush for lunch. Takeout dishes are available, too.

DINING COMMONS
City University of New York Graduate Center
365 Fifth Ave (at 34th St), 8th floor   212/817-7953
Breakfast, Lunch: Mon-Fri (express coffee shop on 1st floor)
Inexpensive

The Dining Commons offers excellent food in comfortable surroundings at affordable prices. Continental breakfasts—featuring muffins, Danishes, croissants, bagels, and more—are available. Lunches feature deli sandwiches, salads, and some hot entrees. It is possible to eat heartily for under $10, and both eat-in and takeout are available. The facility is open to faculty, students, and the general public. Students get a discount with CUNY identification cards. This is no run-of-the-mill fast-food operation. Restaurant Associates does a particularly good job of offering tasty, adequate portions without fancy touches.

DOCKS OYSTER BAR AND SEAFOOD GRILL
2427 Broadway (bet 89th and 90th St)   212/724-5588
Lunch: Mon-Sat; Dinner: Daily; Brunch: Sun

633 Third Ave (at 40th St)   212/986-8080
Lunch: Mon-Fri; Dinner: Daily; Brunch: Sat, Sun
Moderate

For those who appreciate a great raw bar, sail right up Broadway to the original Docks or to a larger, newer operation on Third Avenue. At both lunch and dinner you'll find fresh swordfish, lobster, tuna, Norwegian salmon, red snapper, and other seafood specials. The crab cakes are outstanding. At dinner, the raw bar offers four oyster and two clam selections. For a lighter meal, try steamers in beer broth or mussels in tomato and garlic. Delicious smoked sturgeon and whitefish are available. Docks has a special New England clambake on Sunday and Monday nights. Mississippi mud pie is a fitting way to finish your culinary cruise. The atmosphere is congenial, and so are the professional waiters.

Folks wait even in cold, wet weather to get into **EJ's Luncheonette** (1271 Third Ave, 212/472-0600), where breakfast, lunch, and dinner are served daily. You'll find great flapjacks, waffles, omelets, sandwiches, burgers, baked items, salads, and everything in between. In addition to a huge menu, especially at breakfast, you'll enjoy the very reasonable prices. Free delivery, too!

ELEVEN MADISON PARK
11 Madison Ave (at 24th St)   212/889-0905
Lunch: Mon-Fri; Dinner: Daily; Brunch: Sat, Sun
Expensive

When Danny Meyer runs a restaurant, you can be sure it will be a classy operation. Eleven Madison Park is no exception. In a soaring space previously used for business meetings, an attractive dining facility has been created with an intimate wine bar and several private meeting rooms. The cuisine is American/continental. Appetizers lean toward seafood: a seasonal shellfish assortment, flash-seared squid, tuna *cru*, and for lunch, a salad of Maine lobster. Foie gras is a specialty. Braised shoulder of duck, seared Arctic char, and prime aged rib of beef are excellent main-course choices. Save room for the platter of tiny cookies and cakes. A meal would not be complete without a journey into the past glory of this building and area by studying the archival photographs featured throughout.

ELIO'S
1621 Second Ave (at 84th St)   212/772-2242
Dinner: Daily
Moderate to moderately expensive

For years Elio's has been *the* classic clubby Upper East Side diningroom for those who are recognizable, as well as those who aspire to be! In not so fancy surroundings, with waiters who greet regulars as if they are part of the family, tasty platters of beef carpaccio, clams, mussels, stuffed mushrooms, and minestrone are offered as starters. Lots of spaghetti and risotto dishes follow, along with seafood (their specialty), liver, scaloppine, and the usual Italian assortment. For dessert, try the delicious sorbets. Half the fun is watching the not-so-subtle eye contact among diners. But the food is excellent, and it is easy to see why Elio's is a neighborhood favorite.

ELLEN'S STARDUST DINER
1650 Broadway (at 51st St)   212/956-5151
Breakfast, Lunch, Dinner: Daily   www.ellensstardustdiner.com
Inexpensive to moderate

Come here for good food and a singing wait staff! Ellen's fits right into the neighborhood. A casual, fun, and noisy spot, it serves satisfying food the traditional American way. Trains are the theme of the decor; a track circles the balcony, with a locomotive and cars that would thrill any railroad buff. The breakfast menu includes bagels and muffins, along with tasty buttermilk pancakes, Belgian waffles, French toast, and omelets. For the rest of the day, comfort foods are the order: salads and sandwiches, burgers, chicken pot pie, meatloaf, barbecue baby back ribs, turkey, and steak. There is more: egg creams, shakes, malts, and a nice selection of caloric desserts. Be sure to ask that your shake be made "thick"! Delivery is available.

EL PARADOR CAFE
325 E 34th St (bet First and Second Ave)   212/679-6812
Lunch, Dinner: Daily
Moderate

A restaurant that has been in business for over four decades in New York is obviously pleasing customers. At El Parador, delicious Mexican food is served in a fun atmosphere at down-to-earth prices. Moreover, they are some of the nicest folks in the city. Warm nachos are put on the table the minute you arrive; from there, you have a choice of specialties. There are quesadillas, Spanish sausages, and black bean soup to start. Delicious shrimp and chicken dishes follow. Create your own tacos and tostaditas, if you like. How about stuffed jalapenos? El Parador has over 50 brands of premium tequila, and they make what many consider the best margaritas in New York. It really is the granddaddy of New York's Mexican restaurants.

ETATS-UNIS
242 E 81st St (bet Second and Third Ave)   212/517-8826
Dinner: Daily
Moderate to moderately expensive

Etats-Unis is like a large family diningroom. There are only 14 tables and a busy kitchen where the Rapp family produces some of the best food this side of your grandmother's! Appetizers, entrees, and desserts (usually about five of each) change every evening and are uniformly delicious. It's very wholesome food, not cute or fancy but served professionally in portions that are substantial but not overwhelming. Fresh homemade bread is an attraction. Try date pudding or chocolate soufflé for dessert. The tab is not cheap, but in order to support an operation with limited hours and few tables, the Rapps have to make every meal count. A bar/cafe across the street is open for lunch (except Sunday). The entire room is available for private parties.

F&B GÜDTFOOD
150 E 52nd St (bet Lexington and Third Ave)   212/421-8600
269 W 23rd St (bet Seventh and Eighth Ave)   646/486-4441
Lunch, Dinner: Daily   www.gudtfood.com
Inexpensive

Güdtfood means "good food," of course. This place is unlike any other.
There are no tables, which means you eat counter style. And what do you
eat? European street food like British fish and chips, steak French *frites*,
Belgian *pommes*, Swedish meatballs . . . you get the idea. Kids' menus and
healthy vegetarian items are also available. For dessert there are apple
beignets and churros, French ice creams, and sorbets. The people-watching
is pretty good, and the prices are even better! A great place for kids' parties.

FAIRWAY CAFE & STEAKHOUSE
2127 Broadway (at 74th St), upstairs   212/595-1888
Breakfast and Lunch: Daily (as Fairway Cafe);
Dinner: Daily (after 5:30 p.m., as Fairway Steakhouse)
Moderate   www.fairwaymarket.com

Most folks know of Fairway as a busy market, but there is more. Take
the stairway by the entrance, and you'll find a rather bare-bones room
that serves unbelievably good food—much of it of the comfort variety—at
comfortable prices. Breakfasts include eggs, pancakes, omelets, smoked
salmon, and the like. For lunch: soups, salads, and sandwiches are extremely
good values for the quality offered. In the evening the place turns into a modestly priced steakhouse, with complete steak dinners—your choice of cut,
plus salad, soup, vegetables, and more for $40. There are chops, rack of lamb,
short ribs, fish, chicken, even spaghetti. All desserts are modestly priced at
$5. An extensive catering menu is available.

FIAMMA OSTERIA
206 Spring St (bet Ave of the Americas and Sullivan St) 212/653-0100
Lunch: Mon-Fri; Dinner: Daily
Moderate to moderately expensive   www.brguestrestaurants.com

Some restaurants just make you feel good when you enter. Located on a
busy Soho street, Fiamma is one of them. They have a flair for tasty Italian
dishes that include fresh seafood, excellent chicken, tender meat, and wonderful pastas like ricotta cheese tortelli and handmade pasta quills (when
available). The duck breast is tender and appealing. As for desserts, imagine
choosing dark chocolate praline cake, caramel zabaglione with a milk-
chocolate rum center, or homemade gelati and sorbets. A delicious selection
of Italian cheeses is also available.

FIFTY SEVEN FIFTY SEVEN
Four Seasons Hotel New York
57 E 57th St (bet Park and Madison Ave), lobby level   212/758-5757
Breakfast, Lunch, Dinner: Daily; Brunch: Sun
Moderate to moderately expensive   www.fourseasons.com

When the name Four Seasons is on the door, you can be assured that the
service on the inside is something special. So it is at Fifty Seven Fifty Seven,
one of Manhattan's star hotel diningrooms. The room is highlighted by hand-
some cherry floors with mahogany inlays, ceilings of Danish beechwood, and

bronze chandeliers. The tabletops match the floor in material and design. Served in an informal yet elegant atmosphere, the food has the authority of classic American cooking. The menu changes by season, featuring some exceptionally well-thought-out pasta entrees. Salads and fish are good lunch choices. Taste and personal attention, not the ego of a famous chef, are what makes this room tick. A thoughtful touch is the offer of rapid service for "power breakfast" guests.

FLEUR DE SEL
5 E 20th St (bet Fifth Ave and Broadway)   212/460-9100
Lunch: Mon-Sat; Dinner: Daily   www.fleurdeselnyc.com
Moderately expensive (lunch), expensive (dinner)

Some restaurants immediately create a buzz, and Fleur de Sel is one of them. Chef-owner Cyril Renaud does interesting and exciting things with a constantly changing menu. The plates are all well presented. The charming exposed-brick room features some of Renaud's own oil paintings. Lobster salad with avocado is different and delicious. Entrees tend to be on the rich, exotic side, so your meat-and-potato husband may prefer to go elsewhere. However, those with more adventurous palates will find marinated beef cheeks to be tender and delicious. To be honest, I found Fleur de Sel worthy of a visit but not the unabashed raves it has received. By the way, the chocolate tart soufflé with vanilla ice cream and white chocolate caramel ganache are both magnificent. Dinner is *prix fixe*. A luncheon tasting menu is available, too.

44 & X HELL'S KITCHEN
622 Tenth Ave (at 44th St)   212/977-1170
Dinner: Daily; Brunch: Sat, Sun
Moderate to moderately expensive

The Hell's Kitchen area is an unlikely place for a first-rate restaurant, but this one qualifies in spades! Boasting a menu of "reinvented American classics" served in a rather sterile white-on-white atmosphere, this spot literally sparkles with tasty dishes presented in a most professional manner. There is an abundance of polite, well-trained servers and helpers. Your every desire seems to be their uppermost concern as they parade their clever *Heaven* (on the front) and *Hell* (on the back) T-shirts. The bisque of butternut squash was so good I just about licked the bowl. Other classy starters: Mediterranean chopped salad, pan-seared scallops, and crab fritters. Don't miss the buttermilk fried chicken, the super burger with outstanding fries, a hefty casserole of Maine lobster, comfortable tomato meatloaf, or melt-in-your-mouth barbecued salmon. Delicious apple crisp and white chocolate bread pudding are stars on the dessert menu.

FOUR SEASONS
99 E 52nd St (bet Park and Lexington Ave)   212/754-9494
Lunch: Mon-Fri; Dinner: Mon-Sat   www.fourseasonsrestaurant.com
Expensive

If you ever find yourself entertaining a visitor of style and substance from abroad who has never tasted an American meal, the magnificent Four Seasons restaurant should be your top choice. It is elegant and awe-inspiring in its simplicity and charm. Two separate dining areas—the Grill Room and the Pool Room—are different in menu and appeal. The dark suits (translation: business and media heavy hitters) congregate at noon in the Grill Room, where the waiters know them by name and menu preference (baked potatoes, great salads, steak tartare, or burgers). The Pool Room, set beside an actual marble pool, is more romantic and feminine. Ladies who lunch and couples who want to dine with the stars are right at home with superb service, a wonderful duck entree, and a dessert menu that can only be described as obscene. Individual soufflés in coffee cups are a splendid treat.

FRANK'S
410 W 16th St (bet Ninth and Tenth Ave)   212/243-1349
Lunch: Mon-Fri; Dinner: Daily   www.franksnyc.com
Moderate

The Molinari family—the third generation in a business that started in 1912—has kept up the quality and appeal of this popular spot. Customers are usually folks with large appetites! Reservations are suggested, as the place is very popular. There are great pastas, huge steaks, superb prime rib, fresh fish, veal, lamb, and really good French fries. New York cheesecake is the preferable dessert choice.

Biergartens (beer gardens):
Hallo Berlin (626 Tenth Ave, 212/977-1944)
Zum Schneider (107 Avenue C, 212/598-1098)

FRANK'S TRATTORIA
371 First Ave (bet 21st and 22nd St)   212/677-2991
Lunch, Dinner: Daily   www.frankstrattoria.com
Inexpensive

It's true in New York, just as it is anywhere else in the country, that no one knows great, cheap places to eat better than the boys in blue. Manhattan's finest are some of the best customers of this modest trattoria, and it is easy to see why. The menu runs the gamut of Florentine dishes, each prepared to order and served piping hot (as is the bread, which is always a good sign). There is a large seafood selection, plus steaks, lobster, chops, and chicken. You can choose from over 20 pizzas, served whole or by the piece. Everyone here is informal and friendly, and Frank is delighted that the good word about his place has spread beyond the neighborhood regulars.

FRED'S AT BARNEYS NEW YORK
660 Madison Ave (at 60th St), 9th floor   212/833-2200
Lunch, Dinner: Daily; Brunch: Sat, Sun
Moderate to moderately expensive

It would be a tossup as to which is better at Fred's—the food or the people watching. This is definitely a place where the "beautiful people" like to see and be seen. You'll find the dishes ample and delicious, and they should be at the prices charged. Selections include seafood dishes, pastas, salads, comfort food (like an excellent Tuscan pot roast), pizzas, and sandwiches. French fries are served Belgian-style and are quite tasty. There's no shortage of selections or calories on the dessert menu. I just wonder if all those skinny model types really finish their meals! I find it hard to say good things about Barneys these days, but their restaurant is definitely first-class.

FREEMAN'S
2 Freeman Alley (at Rivington St bet Bowery and Chrystie St)
Dinner: Daily; Brunch: Sat, Sun   212/420-0012
Moderate   www.freemansrestaurant.com

Freeman's is a place you don't want to miss—even though it is almost impossible to locate. It used to be a halfway house. Freeman's is crowded, noisy, and unpretentious. It has extra-friendly service personnel, clean restrooms, a great bar and bartender, and a nice kitchen. But most of all, it has really delicious food. You must start with "Devils on Horseback": Stilton-stuffed prunes wrapped in bacon and served piping hot. Then there is a delicious hot artichoke dip with crisp bread. (All the breads are great.) Organic poached chicken with carrots and celery in parsley broth is outstanding, as are the roasted pork loin and seared filet mignon. A dish of marinated beets with dill will add a special touch. Desserts are just okay, but a visit here is so unique you can overlook your sweet tooth!

FRESCO BY SCOTTO
34 E 52nd St (bet Madison and Park Ave)   212/935-3434
Lunch: Mon-Fri; Dinner: Mon-Sat   www.frescobyscotto.com
Moderate to moderately expensive

Things are hopping at Fresco, especially during the noon hour. Even with the pressure of folks in a hurry, the staff is courteous and efficient. They take rightful pride in serving outstanding dishes prepared by executive chef Steven Santoro. His background shows with the kinds of plates offered: delicious homemade pastas, a number of grilled dishes (including great grilled veal chops), eggplant and zucchini pie, a 32-ounce steak, and braised short ribs that will melt in your mouth. Wonderful potato side dishes include garlic mashed, basil whipped, mashed sweet, and smashed Yukon Gold potatoes. For dessert, try the key lime panna cotta or bombolini filled with vanilla cream. After a meal here, you will understand why modern Tuscan cuisine is so popular. Next door, **Fresco on the Go** (40 E 52nd St) offers homemade muffins, croissants, scones, sticky buns, Danishes, Belgian waffles, homemade pancakes, granola and yogurt, eggs to order, and espresso or cappuccino for breakfast. Lunch consists of sandwiches (meatball, eggplant parmesan, prosciutto, and mozzarella), pizzas, soups, salads, fresh pastas, homemade desserts, and ice cream. Private parties from 20 to 150 are welcome all day long.

FRESH
105 Reade St (bet Church St and West Broadway)   212/406-1900
Lunch: Mon-Fri; Dinner: Mon-Sat   www.freshshorecoast.com
Moderate

The minute you walk into Fresh, your taste buds will begin working; the place is attractive, friendly, and inviting. All of this is a reflection of the personality of the charming executive chef/owner Daniel Angerer. Daniel has put together a top-notch seafood house that runs the gamut from appetizers like lobster tartare, crispy Florida shrimp, salads, soup, fried clams, raw bar (oysters, sashimi, ceviche, and crab claws), and a dozen fresh entrees. You'll find wild salmon, grilled sea bass, paella, haddock, pine nut-crusted St. Peters fish, and more. A flourless chocolate cake completes a great meal. If you're really hungry, try the seven-course tasting menu. Wow!

GABRIEL'S BAR & RESTAURANT
11 W 60th St (bet Broadway and Columbus Ave)   212/956-4600
Lunch: Mon-Fri; Dinner: Mon-Sat   www.gabrielsbarandrest.com
Moderate

Gabriel's is a winner for dining in the Lincoln Center area. You are greeted by an extremely friendly host, Gabriel Aiello, while "Gabriel . . . Gabriel" plays in the background. And what good food and drink! Delicious bread. Fresh melon and blood-orange mimosa. A fine assortment of Italian appetizers. Then on to really first-class pastas (like tagliatelle with peppers), chicken, steaks, and grilled seafood dishes. The in-house gelati creations are among New York's best, as is the flourless chocolate torte. To cap it all off, Gabriel's offers more than a dozen unusual teas (like peach melba, raspberry, and French vanilla). Gabriel doesn't have to blow his own horn; his satisfied customers are happy to do it for him! Private party facilities are available.

You'll always see a crowd at **French Roast** (78 W 11th St, 212/533-2233) in Greenwich Village. Why? The food is good, the price is right, the service is prompt, and the place is open 24 hours a day.

GABY
44 W 45th St (bet Fifth Ave and Ave of the Americas)   212/782-3040
Breakfast, Lunch, Dinner: Daily
Moderate

Gaby is a convenient stop in busy midtown Manhattan, open from early morning until late in the evening. The theme is French, and they do well with a full menu of French favorites. Foie gras and snails are popular starters. The French onion soup has a double cheese crust. For a delicious and filling lunch item, I recommend the Maine lobster club sandwich. Open-faced crisp French sandwiches topped with salmon, tuna, or buffalo mozzarella are available. However, the real star is their traditional crème brûlée —just about the best in the city.

GASCOGNE
158 Eighth Ave (at 18th St)   212/675-6564
Lunch: Tues-Fri; Dinner: Daily; Brunch: Sat, Sun
Moderate   www.gascognenyc.com

Hearty appetites and southwest French cooking spell happiness with a capital *H* at this intimate Chelsea bistro. There's no fuss or fancy affectations by the capable and friendly waiters, who will happily explain the fine points of the rather limited menu. Salads are popular. Foie gras lovers will be in heaven. The main-course menu features duck, cassoulet, quail, and roasted rabbit. Seafood dishes are especially tasty. All desserts are made in-house and show imagination. There are sorbets, fruit tarts, soufflés, and some unusual ice cream flavors (prune, Armagnac, and chocolate mint). A small dining area is available downstairs, but it is rather claustrophobic. The garden is charming. If you are longing for an extensive French dining experience, take a look at the pre-theater *prix fixe* menu. By the way, Gascony is the only region in the world where Armagnac, a brandy distilled from wine, is produced.

GEISHA
33 E 61st St (bet Park and Madison Ave)   212/813-1112
Lunch: Mon-Fri; Dinner: Mon-Sat   www.geisharestaurant.com
Moderately expensive to expensive

Although sushi is the name of the game here, Geisha also does well with other offerings. You can choose from an assortment of menus, including regular fusion and sushi. The excellent sushi rolls include a salmon crunch roll (salmon skin, tuna shiso, and shaved bonito), caterpillar roll (saltwater eel, toasted sesame seeds, and avocado), and the signature Geisha roll (served with lobster honey miso dressing and shiso vinagrette). The house is divided into a downstairs bar area and main upstairs diningroom, plus the adjacent tatami (family) room, decorated with rich kimono fabrics. Main courses run the gamut from skate, salmon, halibut, and cod to filet mignon and rack of lamb. A number of tasty salads are just right for lunch. Unlike the desserts, the collection of green teas is special.

GINO
780 Lexington Ave (at 61st St)   212/758-4466
Lunch, Dinner: Daily
Cash only (checks accepted if known on premises)
Moderate

As you survey the crowd at this New York institution, you can tell immediately that the food is great. Why? Because this Italian restaurant is filled with native New Yorkers. You'll see no tourist buses out front. The menu has been the same for years: a large selection of popular dishes (over 30 entrees!) from antipasto to soup, pasta to fish. There are daily specials, of course, but you only have to taste such regulars as chicken a la Capri, Italian sausages with peppers, or scampis a la Gino to get hooked. Gino's staff has been here forever, taking care of patrons in an informed, fatherly manner. The best part comes when the tab is presented. East Side rents are always climbing, but Gino has resisted price hikes by taking cash only and serving delicious food that keeps the tables full. No reservations are accepted, so come early.

GIORGIONE
307 Spring St (bet Greenwich and Hudson St)   212/352-2269
Lunch: Mon-Fri; Dinner: Daily; Brunch: Sun
Moderate

You know when the name Deluca (as in Dean & Deluca) is involved, it will be a quality operation. Giorgio Deluca is one of the partners in this attractive high-tech establishment, which features shiny metal-top tables and an inviting pizza oven that turns out some of the best pies in the area. This is a very personal restaurant, with Italian dishes like you'd find in mother's kitchen in the Old Country: carpaccio, prosciutto, ravioli, risotto, and linguine. The minestrone is as good as I have tasted anywhere. Pizzas come in eight presentations. Finish with a platter of tasty Italian cheeses or pick from the appealing dessert trolley. A raw bar is also available.

GOLDEN UNICORN
18 East Broadway (at Catherine St)   212/941-0911
Breakfast, Lunch, Dinner, Dim Sum: Daily
Inexpensive

Golden Unicorn prepares the best dim sum outside of Peking! This bustling, two-floor, Hong Kong-style Chinese restaurant serves delicious dim sum every day of the week. Besides delicacies from the rolling carts, diners may choose from a wide variety of Cantonese dishes off the regular menu. Pan-fried noodle dishes, rice noodles, and noodles in soup are house specialties. Despite the size of the establishment (they can take care of over 500 diners at one time), you will be amazed at the fast service, cleanliness, and prices. This is one of the best values in Chinatown.

GONZO
140 W 13th St (bet Ave of the Americas and Seventh Ave)
Dinner: Daily   212/645-4606
Moderate

It is a wonder that more restaurants don't understand that what diners really want is tasty food served in a fun atmosphere with competent service. All of this is available at Gonzo, a popular place in Manhattan. Seating is available in front, at the bar, and in the smallish, attractive back room. Grilled pizzas are big, and a number of them are available at a modest tab. There are also chopped salads, sliced meat and cheese plates, real Italian pastas, and a nice selection of meat and fish entrees. My choices: braised shortribs of beef (it literally falls off the bone) and fresh grilled whole fish, which varies each day. Veggie lovers will savor a dozen or more side-dish offerings, a number of them grilled. Chef-owner Vincent Scotto knows what the younger crowd likes, and he caters to them.

GOOD
89 Greenwich Ave (bet Bank and 12th St)   212/691-8080
Lunch: Tues-Fri; Dinner: Daily; Brunch: Sat, Sun
Moderate   www.goodrestaurantnyc.com

Good is a casual, friendly, take-your-time establishment. It is a popular weekend destination for locals, especially for brunch. The solid, contemporary American fare is served by very friendly personnel. The brunch menu highlight is the "Good Breakfast": a heaping plate of eggs and choice of pancakes, home fries, and bacon or sausage. Burgers are tasty, and pork tenderloin and house-smoked pulled pork are good bets for dinner.

GOOD ENOUGH TO EAT
483 Amsterdam Ave (at 83rd St)   212/496-0163
Breakfast, Lunch: Mon-Fri; Dinner: Daily, Brunch: Sat, Sun
Inexpensive

New York is a weekend breakfast and brunch town, and you cannot do better than Good Enough to Eat in both categories. Savor the apple pancakes, four-grain pancakes with walnuts and fresh bananas, and chocolate chip and coconut pancakes. There is more: French toast, waffles, six kinds of omelets, four scrambled egg dishes, corned beef hash, homemade Irish oatmeal, fresh-squeezed orange juice, and homemade sausage. The lunches in this homey and noisy room—which has been open for over two decades, with tile floor and wooden tables and bar—feature inexpensive and delicious salads, burgers (juicy and delicious), pizzas, and sandwiches. More of the same is served for dinner, plus meatloaf, turkey, pork chops, fish, and roast chicken plates. A children's menu is available, and an outdoor cafe is popular in the nice weather. This is comfort food at its best, all the way through wonderful home-made pies, cakes, and ice creams.

GOTHAM BAR & GRILL
12 E 12th St (bet Fifth Ave and University Pl)　　212/620-4020
Lunch: Mon-Fri; Dinner: Daily　　www.gothambarandgrill.com
Moderately expensive

For over two decades Gotham Bar & Grill has been recognized as one of New York's best. Dining here can be summed up in one word: *exciting*! It is not inexpensive, but every meal I have had has been worth the tab. However, there is a really good *prix fixe* lunch deal. You may also eat at the bar. Alfred Portale is one of the most talented chefs in the city. The modern, spacious, high-ceilinged space is broken by direct spot lighting on the tables. Fresh plants lend a bit of color. There are great salads (try the seafood), excellent free-range chicken, and superior grilled salmon and roast cod. Each entree is well seasoned, attractively presented, and delicious. The rack of lamb is one of the tastiest served in town. Desserts are all made in-house; try the carrot cake or unique ice cream flavors.

GRAMERCY TAVERN
42 E 20th St (bet Park Ave S and Broadway)　　212/477-0777
Lunch, Dinner: Daily
Expensive

Everyone loves this place, and it is no mystery why. When you combine an outstanding and innovative operator like Danny Meyer, a highly trained staff, an unusually attractive space, and prices in line with excellent food, the public will respond. Every detail reflects superb taste. The ceiling is a work of art, the private party room is magnificent, and there isn't a bad seat in the house. Singles are in heaven here, and the light menu (including a fabulous cheese selection) adds strength to possible conquests. The menu changes often, but you can't go wrong with the large selection of seafood appetizers and entrees. The corn chowder is worth a visit in itself. If roasted loin and braised shank of lamb is on the menu, grab it! Desserts are fabulous, espe-cially the chocolate ones! If you are entertaining out-of-town guests, I highly recommend this place for a showcase dinner. The Tavern menu also has some delicious offerings, like the wood-grilled veggie Dagwood.

GRAND CENTRAL OYSTER BAR AND RESTAURANT
Grand Central Station (42nd St at Vanderbilt Ave), lower level
Mon-Fri: 11:30-9:30; Sat: 12-9:30　　212/490-6650
Moderate　　www.oysterbarny.com

Native New Yorkers know about the nearly century-old institution that is the Oyster Bar at Grand Central. A midtown destination once popular with commuters and residents, it has been restored and is doing quite nicely again. (They serve over 2,000 folks a day!) The young help are most accommo-dating, and the drain on the pocketbook is minimal. The menu boasts more than 72 seafood items (with new entrees daily), 20 to 30 varieties of oysters, a super oyster stew, clam chowder (Manhattan and New England), oyster pan roast, bouillabaisse, *coquille St. Jacques*, Maryland crab cakes (Wednesday special), Maine lobsters, 75 wines by the glass, and marvelous homemade desserts.

HATSUHANA
17 E 48th St (bet Fifth and Madison Ave)   212/355-3345
237 Park Ave (at 46th St)   212/661-3400
Lunch, Dinner: Mon-Fri   www.hatsuhana.com
Moderate

Hatsuhana has a longstanding reputation as one of the best sushi houses in Manhattan. One can sit at a table or at the sushi bar and get equal attention from the informed help. There are several dozen appetizers, including broiled eel in cucumber wrap and chopped fatty tuna with aged soybeans. Next try the salmon teriyaki or any number of tuna or sushi dishes. Forget about desserts and concentrate on the exotic appetizer and main dish offerings.

HEARTH
403 E 12th St (at First Ave)   646/602-1300
Dinner: Daily   www.restauranthearth.com
Moderately expensive

In a cozy atmosphere in the East Village, with an open kitchen and pleasant personnel, Hearth is one of those places where the clientele seem more focused on their dining companion than the food. Nevertheless, the New American/Tuscan dishes are done well, even if the prices seem a bit inflated. The black sea bass, guinea hen, and sirloin steak are very popular. The menu changes every season. All in all, it's a good place for that must-talk-to-date evening (but avoid the back room).

Those little Spanish appetizers known as tapas are big. People like to order three or four plates to share, and some can make complete meals. Sangria is the favorite liquid accompaniment. The best tapas in Manhattan can be found at the following:

Casa Mona (52 Irving Pl, 212/253-2773): very good
Kaña Tapas Bar (324 Spring St, 212/343-8180)
Ñ 33 Crosby (33 Crosby St, 212/219-8856)
Pipa (ABC Carpet & Home, 38 E 19th St, 212/677-2233)
Xunta (174 First Ave, 212/614-0620): outstanding

HOUSTON'S
Citicorp Center   212/888-3828
153 E 53rd St (bet 54th and Third Ave)
378 Park Ave S (bet 26th and 27th St)   212/689-1090
Lunch, Dinner: Daily   www.houstons.com
Moderate to moderately expensive

If you are meeting someone for a business lunch, the two Houston's locations are very handy. Houston's serves really good burgers, sandwiches, and salads. For heartier appetites, the barbecued ribs, seared tuna steak, and prime rib roast can't be beat. I could make a meal out of their giant baked potato with all the trimmings. Apple walnut cobbler will finish off a meal that will be certain to expedite any deal you're trying to make. Best of all, you will be served in attractive surroundings by pleasantly enthusiastic personnel.

I COPPI
432 E 9th St (bet First Ave and Ave A)   212/254-2263
Lunch: Sat, Sun; Dinner: Daily   www.icoppinyc.com
Moderate

The husband and wife team of Lorella Innocenti and John Brennan have created a charming Tuscan restaurant in the East Village with tasty food to match the appealing atmosphere. They have brought talent from the Old Country to ensure that the breads are authentic. A brick pizza oven adds a special touch. Outstanding luncheon dishes on a menu that changes seasonally may include Tuscan-style omelets or thin egg noodles with *bolognese* sauce. Pastas, grilled striped bass, roasted rabbit, and grilled sirloin steak are excellent dinner choices, if offered. Save room for gelati, sorbet, or Tuscan cheese for dessert. The heated and canopied outdoor garden is especially inviting. No need to rush uptown to fancier and pricier Tuscan restaurants; this one is as professional as I have found anywhere in the city.

Grilled Cheese (168 Ludlow St, 212/982-6600) serves just what the name suggests! You can order from a menu of over a half-dozen grilled-cheese sandwiches or design your own. Soups and salads are also available, but you've got to have a designer grilled cheese sandwich! Grilled Cheese is open daily from 11 a.m. to almost midnight.

IL BAGATTO
192 E 2nd St (bet Ave A and B)   212/228-0977
Dinner: Tues-Sun (closed Aug)
Inexpensive

One of Manhattan's best bargains, Il Bagatto is the place to come if you're feeling adventurous. Housed in tiny digs in an area you would hardly call compelling, the doors open to an extremely popular Italian trattoria. The owners have discovered the rules of success: being on the job and ensuring that every dish tastes just like it came out of mama's kitchen. About a dozen tables upstairs (and in the lounge) are always filled, so it's best to call ahead for reservations. There's delicious spaghetti, homemade gnocchi with spinach, tortellini with meat sauce (made from their own secret recipe), and wonderful tagliolini with seafood in a light tomato sauce. Other menu offerings include chicken, carpaccio, salads, and always a few specials. They deliver, too (212/228-3710).

IL CORTILE
125 Mulberry St (bet Canal St and Hester St)   212/226-6060
Lunch, Dinner: Daily   www.ilcortile.com
Moderate

Little Italy is more for tourists than serious diners, but there are some exceptions. Il Cortile is an oasis of tasty Italian fare in an attractive and romantic setting. A bright and airy garden area in the rear is the most pleasant part of the restaurant. The menu is typical Italian, with just about anything you could possibly want. Entree listings include fish, chicken, and veal dishes, plus excellent spaghetti, fettuccine, and ravioli. Sauteed vegetables like bitter broccoli, hot peppers, mushrooms, spinach, and green beans are specialties of the house. One thing is for certain: the waiters zip around like they are on roller skates. Service is excellent and expeditious. If you can fight through the gawking visitors, you will find Il Cortile worth the effort!

IL GATTOPARDO
33 W 54th St (bet Fifth Ave and Ave of the Americas)   212/246-0412
Lunch, Dinner: Daily
Expensive

Yes, Il Gattopardo is expensive, but it's certainly worth the tariff. This is the kind of place that appeals to serious gourmets, as food and service leave little to be desired. The room is not fancy; it is, in fact, rather claustrophobic. In the nice weather, the outdoor patio is charming. Very interesting appetizers that vary from time to time include beef and veal meatballs wrapped in cabbage, scallops, and shrimp salad. Among the many pastas, homemade *scialatielli* is delicious. Main-course highlights include Neapolitan meatloaf, herb-crusted rack of lamb, fish and shellfish stew, and much more. For dessert, warm chocolate cake with ice cream is sinful.

With more folks visiting Cuba, there is renewed interest in the cuisine of this country. One of the best Manhattan locations for creating your own paella or tasting delicious Havana-style barbecued ribs with mango ginger sauce is **Havana Central** (22 E 17th St, 212/414-4999). Jeremy Merrin, a hands-on partner, welcomes diners with counter service at breakfast and lunch, and tables at dinner. The price is right, and vegetarians will feel right at home.

IL GIGLIO
81 Warren St (bet West Broadway and Greenwich St)   212/571-5555
Lunch: Mon-Fri; Dinner: Mon-Sat   www.ilgigliorestaurant.com
Moderate

If you can find this place, you will be delighted to discover a bright, clean, classy operation that serves absolutely great Northern Italian food. Smallness is a virtue here, as the two dozen tables are looked after by a crew of highly trained, tuxedo-clad waiters, most of whom have been on the premises since its opening. Specials are almost as numerous as menu items (be sure to ask for prices), and by all means look over the display of fresh fruits, desserts, and other goodies by the entrance. The scampi and veal dishes are superb, and few places in Tribeca (or elsewhere in Manhattan) do pasta any better. Moreover, all desserts are made in-house.

IL MULINO
86 W 3rd St (bet Sullivan and Thompson St)   212/673-3783
Lunch: Mon-Fri; Dinner: Mon-Sat
Moderately expensive

Those who live to eat will not want to miss Il Mulino. Never mind that reservations usually must be made a week or so in advance. Never mind that it's always crowded, the noise level is intolerable, and the waiters nearly knock you down as you wait to be seated. It's all part of the ambience at Il Mulino, one of New York's best Italian restaurants. Your greeting is usually

"Hi, boss," which gives you the distinct impression that the staff is accustomed to catering to members of the, uh, "family." When your waiter finally comes around, he'll reel off a lengthy list of evening specials with glazed eyes. On the other hand, a beautiful, mouth-watering display of these specials is arrayed on a huge entrance table. After you're seated, the waiter delivers one antipasto after another while he talks you into ordering one of the fabulous veal dishes with portions bountiful enough to feed King Kong. Osso buco is a favorite dish. By the time you finish one of the luscious desserts, you'll know why every seat in the small, simple diningroom is kept warm all evening.

> Don't miss the great panini at **'inoteca** (98 Rivington St, 212/614-0473).

IL POSTINO
337 E 49th St (bet First and Second Ave)   212/688-0033
Lunch: Mon-Sat; Dinner: Daily
Expensive

It is nice to splurge on occasion, if what you get is really worth the extra bucks. Il Postino does have a rather hefty price structure, but the offerings rival the best in Manhattan! The setting is comfortable and not showy. You'll be impressed by the captains, who can recite a lengthy list of specials without hesitation. You have your choice of ground-level tables or a slightly raised balcony; I have found the latter to be more comfortable. An extraordinarily tasty bread dish and assorted small appetizer plates get things off to a good start. Next, sensational pastas—like linguine with three kinds of clams or freshly made tagliolini with mushrooms—should not be missed. The chicken in a baked crust is very satisfying, and the roasted loin of veal for two is also top-grade. The sorbets, whose taste is straight from the homeland, finish a memorable gourmet experience. Incidentally, lunch is equally tasty and easier on the wallet.

IL RICCIO
152 E 79th St (bet Third and Lexington Ave)   212/639-9111
Lunch, Dinner: Daily
Moderate

There's nothing fancy here—just darn good Italian fare. Il Riccio is consistent, so you can count on leaving satisfied and well fed. Spaghetti with crabmeat and fresh tomato is one of my favorites. So is thinly sliced beef with truffled pecorino cheese and breaded rack of veal. Also offered are Dover sole and grilled sardines with broccoli. The patio is a small and comfortable place to dine in the nice weather. Service is unfailingly pleasant. Fruit tarts are homemade and delicious, and marinated peaches (when available) are the signature dessert.

IL VAGABONDO
351 E 62nd St (bet First and Second Ave)   212/832-9221
Lunch: Mon-Fri; Dinner: Daily
Inexpensive

Il Vagabondo is a good spot to recommend to your visiting friends, and many folks consider it their favorite restaurant! This bustling restaurant has been popular with knowledgeable New Yorkers since 1965. The atmosphere is strictly old-time, complete with white tablecloths, four busy rooms, and an even busier bar. You may have spaghetti, ravioli, and absolutely marvelous veal or chicken *parmigiana*. There is no pretense at this place, which is a great spot for office parties. You will see happy faces, compliments of a delicious meal and the reasonable bill. Save room for the great Bocce Ball Dessert (*tartufo*). Il Vagabondo, you see, is the only restaurant in New York with an indoor bocce court!

Doughnuts for dessert at a restaurant? You'll find yummy ones at **Riingo** (205 E 45th St), **Wallsé** (344 W 11th St), and **Schiller's** (131 Rivington St).

JACK'S LUXURY OYSTER BAR
246 E 5th St (bet Bowery and Second Ave)   212/673-0338
Dinner: Mon-Sat
Moderate to moderately expensive

Owners Jack and Grace Lamb are surely inventive! I'm not quite sure where the "luxury" part figures in to their tiny outlet, which once was a residence. The cramped quarters include a downstairs room and bar that seats just over a dozen, a narrow stairway that constantly tests the dexterity of the affable staff, a minuscule kitchen, and another small diningroom (with fireplace) on the second floor. What Jack's lacks in space is made up for in the quality of the dishes: fresh oysters (done six ways), fabulous barbecued lobster, littleneck clams, glazed quail, and more. Sit at the raw bar or squeeze in at a table—you'll be well taken care of. All but one dessert (bananas Foster) are great.

JACKSON HOLE BURGERS
232 E 64th St (bet Second and Third Ave)	212/371-7187
521 Third Ave (at 35th St)	212/679-3264
1611 Second Ave (at 84th St)	212/737-8788
1270 Madison Ave (at 91st St)	212/427-2820
517 Columbus Ave (at 85th St)	212/362-5177
69-35 Astoria Blvd, Jackson Heights	718/204-7070
35-01 Bell Blvd, Bayside	718/281-0330
Lunch, Dinner: Daily	www.jacksonholeburgers.com
Inexpensive	

You might think that a burger is a burger. But having done hamburger taste tests all over the city, I've chosen Jackson's as one of the best. Each one weighs at least seven juicy, delicious ounces. You can get all kinds: pizza burger, Swiss burger, English burger, or a Baldouni burger (mushrooms, fried onions, and American cheese). Or try an omelet, Mexican items, salads, or grilled chicken breast. The atmosphere isn't fancy, but once you sink your teeth into a Jackson Hole burger, accompanied by great onion rings or French fries and a homemade dessert, you'll see why I'm so enthusiastic (as is former President Bill Clinton). Free delivery and catering are available.

JACQUES
204 E 85th St (bet Second and Third Ave)   212/327-2272
Lunch, Dinner: Daily; Brunch: Sat, Sun
Moderate

It is easy to understand why this bistro is so popular with folks in the neighborhood. It is cozy, friendly, moderately priced, and serves great food. In addition, Jacques himself is one of the friendliest proprietors in town. All of the classic French dishes are available: onion soup, steak *au poivre,* crème brûlée, cheeses, and a wonderful chocolate soufflé with Tahitian vanilla ice cream. There are also several outstanding seafood dishes. Mussels are prepared six ways. Moreover, this bistro is intimate, making it a great place for private parties.

JARNAC
328 W 12th St (at Greenwich St)   212/924-3413
Dinner: Tues-Sun   www.jarnacny.com
Moderate

Owner Tony Powe grew up in Jarnac, France, and that locale is the seed for his tiny and charming West Village bistro with a clear corner view of the street. With talented chef Maryann Terillo at his side, Tony's plain, no-hype establishment makes the diner concentrate on the ever-changing menu. For such a small place, the selection is sizable: hearty soups, fresh salads, great beef short ribs, top-notch cassoulet, and other choices. A well-chosen cheese course is an extra attraction. The dozen or so tables are filled with Village regulars. Because there is such a variety of dishes, every one seems fresh and innovative, and clean-cut, informed servers add to the pleasure of the meal. The desserts, however, don't live up to the rest of the menu.

JEAN GEORGES
Trump International Hotel
1 Central Park W (bet 60th and 61st St)   212/299-3900
Breakfast: Daily (in cafe); Lunch: Mon-Fri;   www.jean-georges.com
Dinner: Mon-Sat; Brunch: Sun
Very expensive

Jean Georges Vongerichten has created a French dining experience in a setting that can only be described as cool, calm, and calculating. I mean *calculating* in the sense that one is put into a frame of mind to sample *haute cuisine* at its best in a very formal diningroom that's awash with personnel. In keeping with any operation bearing the Trump name, the hype at Jean Georges continues. But to be honest, if price is unimportant, you can't do better. The cafe, **Nougatine**, is a bit less intimidating. The New French menu changes regularly. Come ready to be educated!

JEAN-LUC
507 Columbus Ave (bet 84th and 85th St)   212/712-1700
Dinner: Daily
Moderate to moderately expensive

If energy, noise, and making the scene are important to you, then this is a place to try. Jean-Luc, despite some strange decorative touches, does have one particularly strong suit: the wait staff and service personnel are superbly energized. A dirty plate or half-filled glass is taken care of immediately. Ed "Jean-Luc" Kleefield is on the spot, making sure that the right people get the right treatment. (If you're not known here, you may have to wait awhile.) This Upper West Side attraction has some exceptionally tasty dishes: steamed artichokes with a flavorful vinaigrette dressing, Black Angus filet mignon (though the mounds of French fries taste like they came from McDonald's), New Zealand rack of lamb and diced vegetable stew, and many excellent seafood items. Alas, for a French operation, the bread basket is noticeably poor, and their desserts are just so-so.

JIMMY SUNG'S
219 E 44th St (bet Second and Third Ave)   212/682-5678
Lunch, Dinner: Daily   www.jimmysungs.com
Moderate

For over two decades Jimmy Sung has been a talented player in the highly competitive world of Chinese restaurants in Manhattan. Sung's can seat over 250 customers in the main area, and seven exceptionally attractive private diningrooms can accommodate groups of various sizes. The cuisine includes Hunan, Canton, Shanghai, and Manchurian dishes that range from mild to very spicy. Some of Jimmy's favorites: vegetarian pie with house pancakes, Japanese sushi, sauteed frog legs with garlic sauce, and a seafood combination. An experienced staff of chefs and waiters provide a personal touch at this busy spot. The next time the office plans a get-together, consider Jimmy Sung's. On top of everything, prices are very affordable.

JOHN'S PIZZERIA
278 Bleecker St (bet Ave of the Americas and Seventh Ave)
                                        212/243-1680
260 W 44th St (bet Eighth Ave and Broadway)   212/391-7560
408 E 64th St (bet First and York Ave)   212/935-2895
Daily: 11:30 a.m. to midnight
Moderate   www.johnspizzeria.com

Pete Castelotti (there is no John) is known as the "Baron of Bleecker Street." However, he brought his John's Pizzeria to the Upper West Side and the Upper East Side so that more New Yorkers can taste some of the best brick-oven pizza in the city. John's offers 54 (count 'em) varieties, from cheese and tomatoes to a gut-busting extravaganza of cheese, tomatoes, anchovies, sausage, peppers, meatballs, onions, and mushrooms. John's does homemade spaghetti, cheese ravioli, and manicotti well, too. The surroundings on Bleecker Street are a bit shabby. Things are higher-class uptown; in fact, the enormous 44th Street location is a renovated former church.

KATZ'S DELICATESSEN
205 E Houston St (at Ludlow St)   212/254-2246
Sun-Tues: 8 a.m.-9:30 p.m.; Wed, Thurs: 8 a.m.-10:30 p.m.;
Fri, Sat: 8 a.m.-2:30 a.m.
Inexpensive

If you're experiencing hunger pangs on the Lower East Side, try Katz's Delicatessen. It is a super place whose hand-carved and overstuffed sandwiches are among the best in town. Mainstays include pastrami, hot dogs, corned beef, and potato pancakes. Prices are reasonable. Go right up to the counter and order—it is fun watching the no-nonsense operators slicing and fixing—or sit at a table where a seasoned waiter will take care of you. Try dill pickles and sauerkraut with your sandwich. Incidentally, Katz's is a perfect place to sample the unique "charm" of the Lower East Side. While you wait for a table or discover that the salt and pepper containers are empty and the catsup is missing, you'll know what I mean. Catering (at attractive rates) and private party facilities are available.

KEENS STEAKHOUSE
72 W 36th St (bet Fifth Ave and Ave of the Americas)
Lunch: Mon-Fri; Dinner: Daily   212/947-3636
Moderate   www.keenssteakhouse.com

One of the most reliable long-time Manhattan restaurants is Keens Steakhouse, a unique New York institution. I can remember going there decades ago, when those in the garment trade made Keens their lunch headquarters. This has not changed. Keens still has the same attractions: the bar reeks of atmosphere, and there are great party facilities and fine food to match. Keens has been a fixture in the Herald Square area since 1885. For some time it was for "gentlemen only," and although it still has a masculine atmosphere, ladies feel comfortable and welcome. The famous mutton chop with mint is the house specialty, but other delicious dishes include steak, lamb, and fish. For the light eater, especially at lunch, there are some great salads. Lobster has been added to the menu. They do seasonal single-malt Scotch tastings from fall to spring and stock one of the largest single-malt collections in New York. If you have a meat-and-potato lover in your party, this is the place to come. Make sure to save a little room for the deep-dish apple pie.

Egg Cream

A New York invention, the egg cream is generally credited to Louis Auster, a Jewish immigrant who owned a candy store at Stanton and Cannon streets during the early part of the 20th century. Mostly to amuse himself, he started mixing carbonated water, sugar, and cocoa until he concocted a drink he liked. It was such a hit that Schraft's reportedly offered him $20,000 for the recipe. Auster wouldn't sell and secretly continued making his own syrup in the back room of his store. When he died, his recipe went with him. Some years later, Herman Fox created another chocolate syrup, which he called Fox's U-Bet. Fox's brand is regarded as the definitive egg cream syrup to this day.

KING'S CARRIAGE HOUSE
251 E 82nd St (bet Second and Third Ave)   212/734-5490
Lunch: Mon-Sat; Dinner: Daily
Moderately expensive

Even some folks in the immediate neighborhood are unaware of this sleeper. King's is indeed an old carriage house, remade into a charming two-story dining salon that your mother-in-law will love. The mood is Irish manor house, with the menu changing every evening. In a quaint setting with real wooden floors, you dine by candlelight in a very civilized atmosphere. The luncheon menu stays the same: salads, sandwiches, and lighter fare. Afternoon tea is a treat. The continental menu in the evening may feature grilled items (like loin of lamb). On Sundays, it is a roast dinner (leg of lamb, loin of pork, chicken, or tenderloin of beef). The *prix fixe* menu is a really good value. Personally, I found the Stilton cheese with a nightcap of ruby port absolutely perfect for dessert, but you may prefer chocolate truffle cake or rhubarb tart.

KITTICHAI
60 Thompson St (at Broome St)   212/219-2000
Lunch: Mon-Fri: Dinner: Daily   www.kittichairestaurant.com
Moderately expensive

If you like sophisticated Thai food, come to Kittichai. No egg rolls here! One's eyes rest as much on the tableware, the black-draped service personnel, and the fish tank as on the food. As is true in most Thai restaurants, seafood is high on the list. Marinated monkfish is a splendid starter, and the seafood soup is a must on a cold evening. The salad of banana blossom, artichokes, and roasted chili was a pleaser at my table. Don't overlook the chocolate (cocoa powder) baby back ribs marinated in Thai spices. For entrees, Chilean sea bass and wok-fried chicken with roasted cashew nuts are winners. Kittichai's curries are exceptional. Champagne mango with sticky rice is an unusual dessert. Honestly, I found this place a bit overdone, both in attitude and dishes. But you do get a peek at the mystique of Thailand.

LA BOITE EN BOIS
75 W 68th St (near Columbus Ave)   212/874-2705
Lunch: Tues-Sat; Dinner: Daily; Brunch: Sun
No credit cards
Moderate

You don't have to pronounce the name of this restaurant properly to have a good time! It packs them in every evening for obvious reasons: delicious food, personal service, and moderate prices. Salads are unusual, and the country paté is a great beginner. For an entree, I recommend fillet of snapper, roast chicken with herbs, or *pot-au-feu.* The atmosphere is intimate, and all the niceties of service are operative from start to finish. Desserts are made in-house; try one of their sorbets. Call for reservations, since La Boite en Bois is small and popular.

LA BOTTEGA
Maritime Hotel   212/243-8400
88 Ninth Ave (at 17th St)   www.themaritimehotel.com
Breakfast, Lunch, Dinner: Daily; Brunch: Sat, Sun
Moderate

In the nice weather, outside dining at La Bottega is very pleasant. At other times, the inside seating at this downtown hotel offers a relaxing spot for business meetings. The food is basic Italian, moderately priced, with no surprises. Pizzas, pastas, and salads are the main offerings. Sliced prosciutto with seasonal fruit is one of the best light dishes. Several flavors of gelato are on the dessert menu.

LA GRENOUILLE
3 E 52nd St (bet Fifth and Madison Ave)   212/752-1495
Lunch, Dinner: Tues-Sat   www.la-grenouille.com
Expensive

La Grenouille remains a special place that must be seen to be believed. Beautiful fresh flowers herald a unique, not-to-be-forgotten dining experience. The food is as great as the atmosphere, and although prices are high, it's worth every penny. Celebrity-watching adds to the fun. You'll see most of the famous faces at the front of the room. The professional staff serves a complete French menu. Be sure to try the cold hors d'oeuvres, which are a specialty of the house. So are the lobster dishes, sea bass, and poached chicken. Nowhere in New York are sauces any better. Don't miss the superb dessert soufflés. The tables are very close together, but what difference does it make when the people at your elbows are so interesting?

LA LUNCHONETTE
130 Tenth Ave (at 18th St)   212/675-0342
Lunch, Dinner: Daily
Inexpensive to moderate

La Lunchonette proves that you don't have to be fancy to succeed, as long as you serve good food. In an unlikely location, this popular spot offers some of the tastiest French dishes around: snails, sauteed portobello mushrooms, and lobster bisque to start, and omelets, grilled lamb sausage, sauteed calves liver, and more for entrees. On Sunday evenings, live music is a feature. You'll be pleasantly surprised when the bill comes!

LA PETITE AUBERGE
116 Lexington Ave (at 28th St)   212/689-5003
Lunch: Mon-Fri: Dinner: Daily
Moderate

Genuine French cooking in this area is not easily found, but this smallish, unpretentious restaurant is worth a casual lunch or dinner visit. Extra friendly personnel will lead you through the usual French favorites, like onion soup and escargots. But there is much more: frog legs, roast duck, filet mignon, rack of lamb, and filet of sole. Delicious soufflés are the best way to finish a satisfying meal.

LA RIPAILLE
605 Hudson St (at 12th St)   212/255-4406
Lunch, Dinner: Daily; Brunch: Sun
Moderate

This small, bright, Parisian-style bistro in the West Village (complete with fireplace) makes a cozy spot for an informal meal. You might want to enjoy a cocktail on the lovely outdoor terrace. The chef puts his heart into every dish. Entrees are done to perfection; the seafood is always fresh (try bass in champagne and fine herbs), and they do an excellent job with rack of lamb and duck *magret*. White chocolate is a house favorite; at least half of the dessert offerings use it as an ingredient. Proudly displayed at the front of the room are rave notices from a number of New York gourmets.

LE BERNARDIN
155 W 51st St (near Seventh Ave)   212/489-1515
Lunch: Mon-Fri; Dinner: Mon-Sat   www.le-bernardin.com
Expensive

There has to be one place that tops every list, and among seafood palaces Le Bernardin holds that spot. Owner Maguy LeCoze and chef Eric Ripert make this house extremely attractive to the eye and very satisfying to the stomach. Wonderfully fresh oysters and clams are a great way to start. Whatever your heart desires from the ocean is represented on the entree menu. What distinguishes La Bernardin is presentation. Signature dishes change nightly and might include yellowfish tuna (appetizer), monkfish, halibut, and skate. *Prix fixe* lunch is $49; dinner is $92. The dessert menu usually includes a cheese assortment and superb chocolate dishes.

The **Hungarian Pastry Shop** (1030 Amsterdam Ave, 212/866-4230) is a cafe *and* bakery! The wonderful cakes (linzer tarts are my favorite) are only part of the appeal. The cafe serves all sorts of waist-expanding items, along with delicious Viennese coffee.

LE BIARRITZ
325 W 57th St (bet Eighth and Ninth Ave)   212/245-9467
Lunch: Mon-Fri; Dinner: Mon-Sat   www.lebiarritz.com
Moderate

New York is full of neighborhood restaurants, and Le Biarritz is one of the best. Happily, nothing changes here. It seems like home every evening as regulars claim most of the seats in this warm, smallish eatery. The place has been at the same location and in the same hands for nearly four decades. Gleaming copper makes any eating establishment look inviting, and you'll see a first-rate collection of beautiful French copper cooking and serving pieces. If you're in the mood for escargots to start, the chef prepares them well. You might also try French onion soup or crepes a la Biarritz (stuffed with crabmeat). Entrees include frog legs *provençale,* duck in cherry sauce with wild rice, and all kinds of chicken, lamb, beef, veal, and fish dishes, each served with fresh vegetables. Desserts are homemade and very good. The reasonably priced dinners include soup, salad, and choice of dessert. I recommend Le Biarritz if you are going to a Broadway show or an event at Lincoln Center.

LE BOEUF À LA MODE
539 E 81st St (bet York and East End Ave)   212/249-1473
Dinner: Daily
Moderately expensive

My idea of a perfect restaurant is Le Boeuf à La Mode. This Upper East Side French bistro has been pleasing New Yorkers for decades, and rightfully so. The owners know the recipe for success: warm, comfortable surroundings, pleasant and informed service, and outstanding and reliable food, all at prices that will not decimate one's pocketbook. The classic French fare includes snails in garlic butter, sauteed shrimp, classic French onion soup, outstanding grilled baby lamb chops, and filet mignon. To top it off, the dessert cart is so appetizing you'll want to order one of each! A restaurant does not have to be new and trendy to be worth a visit. Visit Le Boeuf à La Mode and you'll think you've taken a trip to Paris.

LE GIGOT
18 Cornelia St (bet Bleecker and 4th St)   212/627-3737
Lunch, Dinner: Tues-Sun; Brunch: Sat, Sun
American Express and cash only
Moderate

This is a charming, romantic 30-seat bistro in the bowels of the Village. Most taxi drivers have never heard of Cornelia Street, so allow extra time if you come by cab. Once you're here, the cozy atmosphere and warm hospitality of the ladies who greet and serve combine with hearty dishes that will please the most discerning diner. My suggestion for a memorable meal: bouillabaisse or, in winter, *le boeuf Bourguignon* (beef stew in red wine with shallots, bacon, carrots, mushrooms, and potatoes). Snails or patés make delicious starters. Tasty desserts like upside-down apple tarts and flambéed bananas with cognac are offered. Le Gigot is a lot less expensive than its counterpart in Paris but just as appealing.

Italian Specialties

Bruschetta: slices of crispy garlic bread, usually topped with tomatoes and basil

Carpaccio: thin shavings of raw beef topped with olive oil and lemon juice or mayonnaise

Risotto: creamy rice-like pasta, often mixed with shellfish and/or vegetables

Saltimbocca: Thinly sliced veal is topped with prosciutto and sage, then sauteed in butter and slow-simmered in white wine. The name means "jumps in your mouth."

Zabaglione: a dessert sauce or custard made with egg yolks, marsala, and sugar; also known as *sabayon* in France

---

LE JARDIN BISTRO
25 Cleveland Place (bet Kenmare and Spring St)   212/343-9599
Lunch, Dinner: Daily; Brunch: Sat, Sun   www.lejardinbistro.com
Moderate

It is no wonder this charming downtown restaurant has thrived over the years, because it is an excellent operation in every way. The setting, particularly by the garden, is homey and pleasant. The service is unobtrusive and friendly. The menu prices offer good value. You'll find many French favorites: onion soup, tuna tartare, niçoise salad, and more to start. For the main course, I'd suggest bouillabaisse (fish stew), breast of duck, or rack of lamb. For dessert, the profiteroles (vanilla ice cream in puff pastry) are New York's best, mainly because of the fabulous chocolate sauce. Don't miss this one!

LENTINI
1562 Second Ave (at 81st St)   212/628-3131
Dinner: Daily   www.lentinirestaurant.com
Moderately expensive

How refreshing to enjoy an evening at a civilized establishment where the atmosphere is conducive to pleasant conversation and where staff members are incredibly well-trained and well-mannered. (I was really impressed when a waiter wordlessly handed me a clean napkin after I accidentally dropped mine on the floor.) Lentini's prices are not out-of-line with the quality of food served, and every dish can be counted on for quality and attractive presentation. Brothers Giuseppe (the executive chef) and Vincenzo Lentini are to be congratulated for a menu that reflects the best of Italy, whether it is a superb pasta, a choice broiled veal chop, or breaded fried calamari. Try the Sicilian-style *cassata* for dessert.

Sirio Maccioni promises a new venue for his famed **Le Cirque** restaurant in the Bloomberg building (58th St at Lexington Ave) in early 2006. The facility will have a main diningroom and lounge, mezzanine, and private diningroom on the second floor.

LE PÉRIGORD
405 E 52nd St (bet First Ave and East River)   212/755-6244
Lunch: Mon-Fri; Dinner: Daily   www.leperigord.com
Expensive

Is it time for a really special evening? *Civilized* is the word to describe Le Périgord. It is like dining in one of the great rooms of Manhattan in the "good old days," but with a distinctively modern presence. From gracious host Georges Briguet to the talented chef, everything is class personified. Gentlemen must wear jackets. Every captain and waiter has been trained to perfection. Fresh roses and Limoges dinner plates adorn every table. But this is just half the pleasure of the experience. Every dish—from the magnificent cold appetizer buffet that greets guests to the spectacular dessert cart—is tasty and memorable. You may order a la carte, of course. Soups are outstanding. Dover sole melts in your mouth. A fine selection of game is available in winter. Roasted free-range chicken, served with the best potato dish I have ever tasted (*bleu de gex* potato gratin), should not be missed; neither should the roasted spiced duck breast. The chocolate mousse is without equal in Manhattan. The luxurious setting of Le Périgord makes one appreciate what gracious dining is really all about.

LE QUINZE
132 W Houston St (bet MacDougal and Sullivan St)   212/475-1515
Lunch, Dinner: Daily   www.lequinze.com
Moderate

In a rather shabby area, this delightful French bistro is a great retreat for a Sunday brunch, especially in nice weather. In addition to the usual brunch items—eggs, salads, soups—they serve delicious sandwiches and more. During the week, braised beef cheeks and grilled salmon are top sellers. By the way, the French onion soup is exceptional and could well make a full meal.

LE REFUGE
166 E 82nd St (bet Third and Lexington Ave)   212/861-4505
Dinner: Daily   www.lerefuge.com
Moderate

In any other city, Le Refuge would be one of the hottest restaurants in town. But aside from folks in the neighborhood, few seem to have heard of it. This charming, three-room French country restaurant offers excellent food, professional service, and delightful surroundings. The front room is cozy and comfortable, and the rear sections provide nice views and pleasant accommodations. A back garden is open in the summer. This is another house where the owner is the chef, and as usual, it shows in the professionalism of the presentations. Specialties of the house: duck with fresh fruit, bouillabaisse *de crustaces*, and couscous Mediterranean with shrimp. Finish off your meal with crème brûlée, profiteroles, or chocolate truffle cake. You'll find happy hour prices at the bar all night long.

LE RIVAGE
340 W 46th St (bet Eighth and Ninth Ave)   212/765-7374
Lunch, Dinner: Daily   www.lerivagenyc.com
Moderate

Le Rivage is one of the survivors along the highly competitive "restaurant row" of 46th Street. They endure by serving French food that's well prepared and reasonably priced. Escargots, onion soup, *coq au vin rouge*, and peach melba are all delectable and well-presented. Besides, the atmosphere and the pleasant attitude of the servers puts one in the proper frame of mind to enjoy a Broadway show.

LES HALLES
411 Park Ave S (bet 28th and 29th St)   212/679-4111
Daily: noon to midnight   www.leshalles.net
Moderate

Les Halles has struck a responsive chord on the New York restaurant stage. Probably this is because the establishment provides the necessary ingredients for success in today's restaurant sweepstakes: tasty food in an appealing atmosphere at reasonable prices. Specialties like blood sausage with apples, lamb stew, and fillet of beef are served in hefty portions with fresh salad and delicious French fries. Harried waiters try their best to be polite and helpful, but they are not always successful, as tables turn over more rapidly than at most fast food outlets. If a week in Paris is more of a dream than a reality, then you might settle for mussels (ten ways), snails, onion soup, and classic cassoulet at this busy establishment. Unless you love tarts, the dessert selection is a disappointment. (Note: Their butcher shop by the front door is open daily.) The quieter **Les Halles Downtown** (15 John St, 212/285-8585) has much the same menu.

LES ROUTIERS
568 Amsterdam Ave (bet 87th and 88th St)   212/874-2742
Dinner: Daily   www.les-routiers.com
Moderate

A small French bistro set amid scruffy-looking storefronts is a happy find on the Upper West Side. This is the real thing, with a changing contemporary French menu and genuine ambience. There are snails and mussels with wine, patés, duck, seafood, steaks, breast of chicken—all the things you might find in the French heartland. Salads are almost a meal in themselves. An enticing selection of sweet things is available; look at the dessert table as you enter.

LEVER HOUSE
390 Park Ave (at 54th St)   212/888-2700
Lunch, Dinner: Daily   www.leverhouse.com
Expensive to very expensive

The space is grand and the menu sophisticated, but the prices are stratospheric. This former Lever Co. products display area has been heavily visited by all manner of critics, whose views run the gamut. The claim of "no tables until 11 p.m."—often told to prospective diners—is ridiculous; you can walk in any evening and find ample seating. The clientele is hardly dressed for a special occasion; it looks more like the crowd at your favorite neighborhood watering hole. The personnel are nice enough, seemingly well-schooled, and eager to please. But Lever House fails to deliver on the main reason for coming—extraordinary food. The scallops, short ribs, lamb, and many other dishes are merely good—*period*. I found the milk and dark chocolate tart with malted vanilla ice cream to be the best part of the evening. (Incidentally, the private dining area overlooking the main diningroom looks like a marvelous venue for a private party—that is, if a rich uncle is picking up the tab.)

> Just in case you are in the mood for an omelet that has six eggs, a lobster, and ten ounces of sevruga caviar, rush over to **Norma's** (Le Parker Meridien Hotel, 118 W 57th St, 212/708-7460). Oh, I forgot to mention the price: $1,000. The budget version (one ounce of caviar) goes for a mere $100.

L'IMPERO
45 Tudor City Pl (bet 42nd and 43rd St)   212/599-5045
Lunch: Mon-Fri; Dinner: Mon-Sat   www.limpero.com
Expensive

Tucked away in Tudor City Place, L'Impero is like a Tiffany jewel wrapped up in that famous blue box. This 1928 landmark room in the United Nations area is for serious diners. The theme is rustic Italian, but the menu will appeal to diverse tastes. Chef Scott Conant changes the menu seasonally. The pastas are uniformly delicious; homemade spaghetti is recommended. Tuna poached in olive oil is superb, as is baby goat. I particularly enjoyed choosing a cheese plate from a mouth-watering selection of nearly a dozen varieties. The gelati is authentic. For a different dessert try sesame cannoli with orange mascarpone mousse and blood orange sorbet. Get a rich relative to pick up the check, especially if you succumb to the magnificent tasting menu.

MALONEY & PORCELLI
37 E 50th St (bet Park and Madison Ave)   212/750-2233
Lunch, Dinner: Daily   www.maloneyandporcelli.com
Expensive

If your accountant wrangles you a tax refund, take him or her to Maloney & Porcelli! Most everything is expensive: the ambience, the platters, and (yes) the check. But the meat dishes—fabulous sirloin steaks and crackling pork shank—are wonderful. It is a temptation to fill up on the great bread basket; instead, try first-rate appetizers like the pizzas, crab cakes, and pastrami salmon. Lobster dishes are a specialty, particularly the "Angry Lobster." For dessert, my vote goes to the chocolate brownout cake. Their private diningroom is a great facility for an office party or wedding reception.

MANGIA È BEVI
800 Ninth Ave (at 53rd St)   212/956-3976
Lunch, Dinner: Daily   www.mangiaebevirestaurant.com
Inexpensive to moderate

This is definitely not the spot for a relaxing, intimate, refined meal. But it is a top choice for delicious food at unbelievably low prices (for Manhattan). The noise level is almost unbearable, the tables allow you to instantly become friendly with strangers and the waiters are very casual and surprisingly helpful. The abundant antipasto platter, overflowing with nearly a dozen choices, is a house specialty. This rustic trattoria also features a large selection of pastas, fish, meat dishes, salads and a bevy of in-season veggies. Brick-oven pizza lovers will be in seventh heaven with pleasing combinations and equally pleasing prices. There's nothing special about desserts, except the homemade tiramisu. It is easy to see why colorful Mangia è Bevi is one of the most popular destinations along Ninth Avenue.

MANHATTAN GRILLE
1161 First Ave (at 64th St)   212/888-6556
Lunch: Mon-Fri; Dinner: Daily; Brunch: Sat, Sun
Moderate to moderately expensive   www.themanhattangrille.com

This classy continental steakhouse has been a hit for quite some time. It is indeed an attractive, pleasant place to dine. The steaks are large and delicious, as are the lamb chops and prime rib. Even the seafood, especially the filet of sole, is worth trying. Among the veal dishes, veal piccata is particularly good. Accompany your choice with excellent cottage fries. For dessert, the *tartufo* equals any I've tasted in Italy (except Tre Scalini's in Rome), and the cheesecake melts in your mouth. A pre-theater menu is available daily before 6:15 p.m. A *prix fixe* menu is available daily from 9 p.m. until closing.

MANHATTAN OCEAN CLUB
57 W 58th St (bet Fifth Ave and Ave of the Americas)   212/371-7777
Lunch: Mon-Fri; Dinner: Daily   www.manhattanoceanclub.com
Moderately expensive to expensive

Alan Stillman (of Smith & Wollensky fame) has come up with another winner! In a two-story setting, seafood lovers are treated to the very best and freshest seafood. Their "Shellfish Bouquet" (lobster, crab, shrimp, and oysters) is unforgettable. The Ocean Club clam chowder is a great warmer-upper. An oyster tasting complete with caviar is sensational. Ask about daily seafood specials like steamed black sea bass and Dover sole. For the non-seafood diners in your party, the filet mignon is superb. To cap it all off, try chocolate soufflé with fudge sauce and toasted almond ice cream for dessert.

MARCH
405 E 58th St (bet First Ave and Sutton Pl)   212/754-6272
Dinner: Daily
Moderately expensive

If you want to be spoiled, start here. This attractive, romantic, and renovated townhouse with high ceilings and teak floors offers regal dining in three rooms on lower levels, plus a summer rooftop terrace. Executive chef Wayne Nish and partner Joseph Scalice have raised the art of dining to perfection. Create your own *prix fixe* meal of up to seven courses from over 30 choices. It is well worth the tab, for the sky is the limit when it comes to service and quality. Their rack of lamb is A+ and then some. The fact that March remains so busy is a tribute to the format. An attractive, glass-enclosed back porch overlooks a small garden in this Sutton Place neighborhood.

French Specialties

Bouillabaise: French seafood stew

Confit: goose, duck, or pork that has been salted, cooked, and preserved in its own fat

Coulis: a thick, smooth sauce, usually made from vegetables but sometimes from fruit

En croute: anything baked in a buttery pastry crust or hollowed-out slice of toast

Foie gras: duck or goose liver, usually made into a paté

Tartare: finely chopped and seasoned raw beef, often served as an appetizer

---

MARCHI'S
251 E 31st St (near Second Ave)   212/679-2494
Dinner: Mon-Sat (special hours for private parties)
Moderate   www.marchirestaurant.com

Marchi's has been a New York fixture since 1930, when it was established by the Marchi family in an attractive brownstone townhouse. Three sons are on hand, lending a homey flavor to the restaurant's three diningrooms and garden patio (a great spot for a private dinner). It's almost like eating at your favorite Italian family's house, especially since there are no menus. Bring a hearty appetite to take full advantage of a superb feast. The first course is a platter of antipasto—including radishes, *finocchio,* and Genoa salami—plus a salad of tuna, olives, and red cabbage. The second is an absolutely delicious homemade lasagna. The third is crispy deep-fried fish. Side orders of cold beets and string beans with fish are light and tempting. The entree is delicious roast chicken and veal served with fresh mushrooms and a tossed salad. Dessert consists of fresh fruit, cheese, lemon fritter, and sensational *crostoli* (crisp fried twists sprinkled with powdered sugar). The price tag is reasonable. Come to Marchi's for a unique, leisurely meal and an evening you will long remember. In the summer, dining alfresco is a wonderful option.

MARKJOSEPH STEAKHOUSE
261 Water St (off Peck Slip)   212/277-0020
Lunch: Mon-Fri; Dinner: Mon-Sat   www.markjosephsteakhouse.com
Moderately expensive

If the trendy uptown steakhouses turn you off, then head downtown—with good directions, as Water Street turns into Pearl Street near this location—to a comfortable, homey neighborhood room that is high on quality meat and low on attitude. The room is filled with folks in casual garb, more interested in delving into a huge, juicy steak than wondering who's sitting at the next table. Some of the personnel (including a few who came over from Peter Luger) are all business. If you're dining with a group or family, the seafood combination platter (lobster, shrimp, clams, calamari, and mussels) is a great place to start. Porterhouse steak and filet mignon are highly recommended. Baked or hash brown potatoes are great side dishes. At lunch, the half-pound burgers are wonderful, as is the signature steak sandwich. If there's still room for dessert, opt for the tartufo or the MarkJoseph special. You'll be surprised at its contents!

New Yorkers are lining up to fill their lunch plates with items from a growing number of attractive and well-stocked delis and buffets that offer eat-in or takeout sandwiches, soups, drinks (including smoothies), huge salad bars, hot entrees, and a good selection of desserts. The advantages are obvious: quick service, reasonable prices, and tasty food. Here are several I recommend:

Amy's Bread (75 Ninth Ave, 212/462-4338)
Azure (830 Third Ave, 212/486-8080)
Ben's Kosher Deli (209 W 38th St, 212/398-2367)
Bonsignour Cafe (35 Jane St, 212/229-9700)
Churrascaria Plataforma (Belvedere Hotel, 316 W 49th St, 212/245-0505)
City Bakery (5 W 18th St, 212/366-1414)
City Market Cafe (918 Third Ave, 212/546-9315)
Dimple (11 W 30th St, 212/643-9464)
Food Exchange (120 E 59th St, 212/759-0656)
Garden of Eden (310 Third Ave, 212/228-4681; 162 W 23rd St, 212/675-6300; and 7 E 14th St, 212/255-4200)
Hadleigh's (1900 Broadway, 212/580-0669)
Mangia (50 W 57th St, 212/582-5882; 16 E 48th St, 212/754-7600; 22 W 23rd St, 212/647-0200; and 40 Wall St, 212/425-4040)
Minado (6 E 32nd St, 212/725-1333)
North Village Deli Emporium (74 Eighth Ave, 212/229-0887)

MARK'S RESTAURANT
The Mark Hotel
25 E 77th St (bet Fifth and Madison Ave)   212/879-1864
Breakfast, Lunch, Dinner: Daily; Brunch, Sun
Moderately expensive   www.themarkhotel.com

You'd be hard pressed to find better hotel dining than this fine French-American restaurant. Refined, professional service, beautiful appointments, fresh flowers, and gorgeous china add up to a delightful experience. The menu is seasonal, with fresh seafood always available. Imported caviars and oysters are a specialty. You don't have to be a hotel guest to partake of this room's charm. Afternoon tea is an occasion!

MARKT
401 W 14th St (at Ninth Ave)   212/727-3314
Lunch: Mon-Fri; Dinner: Daily; Brunch: Sat, Sun
Moderate   www.marktrestaurant.com

In a building that once housed a fish market, Markt presents an attractive, large, and noisy room with a distinctive Belgian flavor. The huge bar is a good place to get a feel for the restaurant. A menu feature is *waterzooi,* a classic Belgian stew that can be prepared with chicken and veggies, fresh fish, or lobster. The several lobster dishes offered are among the best in the house. You'll also find seafood, Belgian beef stew, rabbit, steak, and more. A raw bar offers a good selection of shrimp, crab, lobster, and periwinkles, as well as a variety of oysters. Mussels are popular, too. Don't pass up the great Belgian fries. Dessert specials vary every day, but the trio of Belgian dark, white, and milk chocolate mousse is tops.

MCCORMICK & SCHMICK'S
1285 Ave of the Americas (at 52nd St)   212/459-1222
Lunch: Mon-Fri; Dinner: Daily   www.mccormickandschmick.com
Moderate to moderately expensive

I can recognize a great seafood house, as my home is on the Pacific coast. Oregon-based McCormick & Schmick's seafood restaurant chain has landed an operation in Manhattan, and it is a dandy. The fresh seafood sheet lists over 30 treats from the world's waterways, all prepared with imagination and care. And the prices, unlike those at some of the so-called class seafood houses in Manhattan, are very much within reach of the average pocketbook. What's good and special: pan-fried Willapa Bay yearling oysters, nine varieties of oysters on the half-shell, Massachusetts steamer clams, Atlantic salmon, and Dungeness crab legs sauteed with mushrooms, artichoke hearts, and sherry. Two dozen seafood specialty entrees run the gamut from cashew-crusted red tilapia from Ecuador to Nantucket Bay scallops and mahi-mahi from Costa Rica. There are also ample choices for non-seafood diners. Don't miss the dessert tray to complete a memorable meal!

MÉTISSE
239 W 105th St (bet Amsterdam Ave and Broadway)   212/666-8825
Dinner: Daily
Moderate

Columbia University personnel call this home! This Upper West Side French bistro does all the good things you would expect, but it is the atmosphere that adds so much to a dinner at Métisse. The place is quiet and restful, the waiters unobtrusive, the cuisine satisfying, and the check reasonable. Salads are fresh, entrees varied (many seafood dishes, steaks, and chops). For dessert, napoleons top off a fine meal.

METROCAFE & WINE BAR
32 E 21st St (bet Park Ave S and Broadway)   212/353-0800
Lunch, Dinner: Daily   www.metrocafenyc.com
Moderate

Quality and reasonable prices are the draws at MetroCafe. In addition to a complete menu, wine lovers will delight in 125 wines by the glass and 21 wine flights. Other attractions: a good selection of Kobe steaks and dim sum.

You can dine on fresh salads, ten-inch thin-crust personal pizza pies, filling sandwiches, pastas, excellent chargrilled burgers, and a selection of comfort foods like meatloaf, fish and chips, grilled chicken *paillard*, and grilled filet of salmon. Desserts are tasty, and the atmosphere is family-friendly.

MEZZOGIORNO
195 Spring St (near Ave of the Americas)   212/334-2112
Lunch, Dinner: Daily   www.mezzogiorno.com
Moderate

Florence, Italy, is one of the world's most charming cities, not only because of its abundance of great art, but also for the wonderful small restaurants on every street corner. At Mezzogiorno, a Florence-style trattoria in New York, the food is comparably good (though some of the art is questionable). The place is busy and noisy, and tables are so close together that conversation is impossible. The decor is best described as "modern Florence." Check out the unusual writing on the ceiling, done by master fresco artist Pontormo. Better yet, keep your eyes on the food. The salad selection is outstanding, and their lasagna is one of the best. Mezzogiorno is also famous for pizza. You'll find all the ingredients for a wonderful make-believe evening in Florence.

MICHAEL JORDAN'S THE STEAK HOUSE NYC
23 Vanderbilt Ave (at Grand Central Station)   212/655-2300
Lunch, Dinner: Daily   www.theglaziergroup.com
Moderately expensive

The refurbished Grand Central Station has come back to life, and Michael Jordan's establishment is one more reason to visit this historic building, even if you are not catching a train. Michael and his partners have provided another good New York steakhouse. The menu is very much what you would expect: steaks, chops, lobster, and salmon. You'll fill up on the sizable portions, but if you feel especially hungry, try the sliced tomatoes and sweet onion appetizer. Forget about calories and order the special French fries as a side dish. For a change, desserts are reasonably priced. They include brownie ice cream sundae and a fabulous 12-layer chocolate cake.

MINETTA TAVERN
113 MacDougal St (near Bleecker St)   212/475-3850
Lunch, Dinner: Daily
Moderate

How about taking your guests to a Northern Italian restaurant where both the coat-and-tie and meat-and-potato set feel comfortable? Established in 1937, Minetta Tavern has been serving excellent food for generations in Greenwich Village. Located on the spot where Minetta Brook wandered through Manhattan in the early days, this tavern was made famous by Eddie "Minetta" Sieveri, a friend of many sports and stage stars of yesteryear. Dozens of old pictures adorn the walls of this intimate, scrupulously clean tavern, where professional personnel serve no-nonsense Italian food at attractive prices. Grilled mushrooms, steamed clams, or homemade *tortellacci* are good ways to get the juices flowing. If you'd like something a bit heftier, veal and various chicken dishes are available. Chocolate mousse cake, profiteroles, and other pastries cap off a satisfying meal.

THE MODERN
Museum of Modern Art
9 W 53rd St (bet Fifth Ave and Ave of the Americas)   212/333-1220
Cafe 2—Breakfast, Lunch, Dinner: Daily
Terrace 5—Breakfast, Lunch, Dinner: Daily
                              www.unionsquarehospitalitygroup.com
Moderate (Cafe 2 and Terrace 5)
Bar Room—Lunch, Dinner: Daily
Dining Room—Dinner: Mon-Sat
Moderate to moderately expensive (Bar Room and Dining Room)

Leave it to Danny Meyer to produce something classy and special, something that is "only in New York." Others would shudder at the logistics of creating four different venues, all opening at the same time, with the myriad problems that accompany any new venture. Danny has pulled it off superbly. The Museum of Modern Art is, of course, a great venue for these operations, and all four are unique in their own right. The Bar Room is busy, clubby, fun, and swinging. You can eat at the bar (great soups, salads, brasserie food). The adjoining Dining Room, which is a bit more formal, has a great view of the sculpture garden, with Meyer's typical haute cuisine. It is a special-occasion room. Up on the second floor, Cafe 2 offers a spectacular array of cured meats and cheeses, vegetable plates, pastas, soups, and salads; it is casual and very busy. Terrace 5, on the fifth floor, is a great place for resting tired feet while enjoying delicious chocolates, cakes, and sandwiches. In the nice weather the terrace outside offers spectacular midtown views.

BLT Fish (21 W 17th St, 212/691-8888) is relatively new and it is great. Outstanding features include a blackboard for daily oyster selections, a raw bar, wonderful garlic bread, a large selection of fish, fresh Maine lobsters, homemade pies, and other yummy desserts.

MONTRACHET
239 West Broadway (bet White and Walker St)   212/219-2777
Lunch: Fri; Dinner: Mon-Sat;   www.myriadrestaurantgroup.com
Moderately expensive

Montrachet has been a fixture for years in Tribeca, and its popularity is well deserved. Anything Drew Nieporent touches has a special magic. You'll find superb dishes of seafood, game, and meat prepared by chef Chris Gesualdi. The menu changes periodically, but you can hope that such specialties as endive salad with pears and walnuts, Chilean sea bass, and foie gras are available when you visit. The signature dessert, crème brûlée, is one of the best in the city. Service is highly professional, and the $20 *prix fixe* lunch on Friday is a winner. Montrachet has a world-class wine list. On Monday nights the restaurant will let you BYOB (bring your own bottle) without any corkage fee. The evening has created a very convivial atmosphere among wine lovers.

MORAN'S CHELSEA
146 Tenth Ave (at 19th St)   212/627-3030
Lunch, Dinner: Daily   www.moransny.com
Moderate

In a building that's nearly 200 years old, Moran's has seen a lot of history, including time as a speakeasy and as a Jewish lodging house during Prohibition days. Time has been good to this exceptionally charming tavern, complete with fireplaces in every room, hardwood paneling, large and attractive party facilities, and a cozy bar, all done with touches of copper everywhere you look. The old tin ceiling adds a special dimension. On to the food: fresh seafood, aged chops, lobster, crab cakes, prime rib, and shepherd's pie are just a few of the specialties. You'll also find excellent burgers, fresh salads, and a few pastas. If you are looking for a unique venue for a party or celebration in groups of 20 to 250, I strongly suggest you take a look here. The personnel are friendly and accommodating.

While exploring downtown, visiting Ground Zero, Wall Street, or other places of interest, take time to enjoy a pleasant meal. One of the more attractive places to have a casual lunch is **Cassis on Stone** (52 Stone St, 212/425-3663). Outdoor seating is provided in the nice weather, and a takeout menu is available. Nearby is **Financier** (62 Stone St, 212/344-5600), an attractive spot serving a light lunch menu and French pastry items all day and into the early evening.

MORTON'S OF CHICAGO
551 Fifth Ave (at 45th St)   212/972-3315
Lunch: Mon-Fri; Dinner: Daily
Moderately expensive to expensive

Now, this is a real steakhouse! These folks are experts, with units all over the country. Every member of the highly efficient staff has been trained in the Morton's manner. At the start of your meal, you are shown a cart with samples of entree items: fresh vegetables, lobster, and whatever else happens to be featured. Every dish is fully explained. Appetizers are heavy in the seafood department: shrimp, oysters, smoked salmon, sea scallops, and salads are attractive and appetizing. The steaks and chops are so tender you can cut them with a fork. They arrive promptly, too, which is not the case in many steakhouses. There are several potato choices, including wonderful hash browns. Sauteed spinach with mushrooms and steamed broccoli and asparagus are fresh and tasty. Top it all off with a delicious soufflé—chocolate, Grand Marnier, lemon, or raspberry—that's large enough for two hungry diners.

MR. K'S
570 Lexington Ave (at 51st St)   212/583-1668
Lunch, Dinner: Daily   www.mrksnyc.com
Moderately expensive to expensive

Mr. K's is a very classy Chinese diningroom where high-powered politicos (especially Republicans) come to dine. All manner of goodies will whet the appetite: Shanghai spring rolls, dumplings, and a delicious seafood dish of sauteed crab, shrimp, and scallops. Of course, there is chicken and corn chowder; in my opinion, no Chinese dinner is complete without it. What else? Share an assortment of plates with your table partners: lemon chicken, Peking duck, honey-braised pork ribs, sesame beef, crispy sea bass, and sesame prawns with shiitake mushrooms. If you like hot dishes, go for the firecracker prawns with Szechuan sauce!

NICOLA'S
146 E 84th St (bet Lexington and Third Ave)   212/249-9850
Dinner: Daily
Moderately expensive

Upper-crust New Yorkers who like a clubby atmosphere and good food —which are not often found together—love this place! At times the noise level rivals that of a Broadway opening. In a setting of rich wood with framed familiar faces on the walls, no-nonsense waiters serve delicious platters of pasta, veal, chicken, fish, and steak. There are daily Italian specials in every category, and each is inviting. Concentrate on the main part of your meal, as desserts show little imagination.

> Looking for a quick bite in midtown? Try **Lyn's Cafe** (12 W 55th St, 212/397-2020). You'll find breakfast items, fresh baked goods, sandwiches, health foods, good soups and burgers, pizzas, and more. I especially like the selection of jumbo muffins.

92
Wales Hotel   212/828-5300
45 E 92nd St (at Madison Ave)
Lunch: Mon-Fri: Dinner: Daily; Brunch: Sat, Sun
Moderate

If you're in the mood to escape fancy diningrooms, complicated dishes, and overbearing service, 92 is the place to go. The hamburger and turkey burger fit right into the brasserie setting. Salads are fresh and satisfying. Special dishes like chicken pot pie, crab cakes, and pork tenderloin are featured nightly and change seasonally. Try the lasagna special on Sundays! Bring the family and save room for dessert, which is the best part of the experience.

NOBU
105 Hudson St (near Franklin St)   212/219-0500
Lunch: Mon-Fri; Dinner: Daily   www.myriadrestaurantgroup.com

NOBU NEXT DOOR
105 Hudson St (near Franklin St)   212/334-4445
Dinner: Daily

NOBU 57
40 W 57th St (bet Fifth Ave and Ave of the Americas)
Opening in late 2005
Moderately expensive

Now there are three Nobus in Manhattan! These restaurants are must-visits for anyone who likes Japanese cuisine. There is a bevy of talent: the management expertise of Drew Nieporent, the setting by the David Rockwell Group, and most of all, the great cuisine of Chef Nobu Matsuhisa. These restaurants are considered the gold standard for Japanese cuisine. You receive a traditional Japanese welcome as you progress to the comfortable sushi bar. The menu includes hot and cold dishes, special dinner entrees (salmon, scallops, chicken, and tenderloin of beef), plus tempura, sashimi, and sushi dinners. There's also kushiyaki (two skewers), salads, soups, sushi rolls, and desserts like the Bento Box (warm valrhona chocolate soufflé cake). The ambience is unique, the people-watching is as fabulous as the food, and the pricey tab is worth every penny. To take care of the overflow crowds, Nobu Next Door serves equally good dishes with a no-reservations policy. It also has a raw bar and a fine selection of noodle dishes. The new 57th Street location will occupy nearly 13,000 square feet on two levels.

OCEAN GRILL
384 Columbus Ave (bet 78th and 79th Ave)   212/579-2300
Lunch, Dinner: Daily; Brunch: Sat, Sun   www.brguestrestaurants.com
Moderate

Ship ahoy! Ocean Grill is one of the few good seafood restaurants on the Upper West Side, and in the nice weather, the passing parade visible from outside tables is fun to watch. Quite popular with young professionals, the place is noisy, too. The food is good, not great, with littleneck clams topping the list. For a party, chilled shellfish platters—offering a selection of lobster, clams, oysters, shrimp, and more—are appropriate. A wood-burning grill offers Scottish salmon, big-eye tuna, mahi-mahi, and wild striped bass. A moderately priced "sunset" menu is available, with such attractions as crab cakes, lobster bisque, and seafood Cobb salad. For brunch, goat cheese quiche and blueberry, banana, and buttermilk pancakes are good bets.

Mama's Food Shop (200 E 3rd St, 212/777-4425) is an inexpensive and tasty destination for homemade dishes like meatloaf, grilled salmon, and fried, roasted and grilled chicken. Sides include mashed potatoes, macaroni and cheese, honey-glazed sweet potatoes, green beans, Swiss chard, and turnips. Don't miss the banana cream pie! Takeout, delivery, and catering are available.

OCEANA
55 E 54th St (bet Park and Madison Ave)   212/759-5941
Lunch: Mon-Fri; Dinner: Mon-Sat   www.oceanarestaurant.com
Expensive

When you save enough dough to take a cruise, you want to do it the right way and book passage on a really fabulous ship. Well, the same is true if you want a really first-rate seafood meal with price being no object. Oceana is just that kind of place. This midtown townhouse offers several floors of classy dining, with relatively new chef Cornelius Gallagher putting out a terrific three-course *prix fixe* dinner at a terrific price ($72). The menu changes frequently, and the seafood catches are so fresh they practically swim to the table. For entrees I'd suggest striped bass, Icelandic cod, or crispy Maine skate. The gnocchi is a blue-ribbon winner! The sticky toffee pudding and pumpkin strudel with ice cream are don't-miss desserts.

OLIVES NEW YORK
W New York Union Square
201 Park Ave S (at 17th St)   212/353-8345
Breakfast: Daily; Lunch: Mon-Fri; Dinner: Daily; Brunch: Sat, Sun
Moderate   www.toddenglish.com

For yuppies, this is *the* place! The trendy crowd seems to like the New England influence of Todd English's open-kitchen charmer. A spirited and jazzy atmosphere combines with superbly trained personnel and great food to make a pleasant dining experience. Portions are big, with delicious pastas high on the list. If your tastes are not too fancy, the burgers are very good and the peanut butter pancakes at brunch are "to die for." For dessert I recommend a vanilla or strawberry soufflé.

> Fish lovers, take note: **Esca** (402 W 43rd St, 212/564-7272) is one of Manhattan's very best seafood restaurants. With an emphasis on Southern Italian seafood and pastas, this attractive establishment in the Theater District is deservedly always crowded.

ONE IF BY LAND, TWO IF BY SEA
17 Barrow St (bet Seventh Ave and 4th St)   212/228-0822
Dinner: Daily   www.oneifbyland.com
Expensive

If romance is the intent of your evening out, then I heartily recommend this restaurant. The candlelight, fireplace, flowers, and background piano music all add to the ambience. One If By Land, Two If By Sea is housed in an 18th-century carriage house once owned by Aaron Burr. Allow extra time to find this place, as Barrow Street (one of the West Village's most charming) is generally unknown to taxi drivers. Besides, there's no sign out front! Tables at the front of the balcony are particularly appealing. You can't go wrong with rack of lamb or breast of duck. Individual beef Wellington is usually excellent, as is the spice-roasted lobster. A *prix fixe* seven-course tasting menu is available. Their classic crème brûlée is a favorite dessert.

O'NIEAL'S GRAND STREET
174 Grand St (bet Centre and Mulberry St)   212/941-9119
Lunch, Dinner: Daily; Late Night Menu: Thurs-Sat www.onieals.com
Moderate

This legendary and historic speakeasy, with its secret tunnel to the old police headquarters, evokes memories of days long past. Housed beneath a 150-year-old hand-carved mahogany ceiling, this bar, lounge, and restaurant is reminiscent of another time. O'Nieal's achieved additional celebrity as a backdrop on HBO's *Sex and the City*. They also serve one of the best burgers. You'll find marinated grilled yellowfin tuna, Cobb salad, hangar steak *au poivre*, scallion risotto, and more. For dessert, try the Four Devils chocolate soufflé cake (named after the four devils intricately carved on the ceiling). Service at O'Nieal's is friendly and efficient.

ORSO
322 W 46th St (bet Eighth and Ninth Ave)   212/489-7212
Lunch, Dinner: Daily; Brunch: Sun   www.orsorestaurant.com
Moderate

This restaurant features the same menu all day long, which is great for those with unusual dining hours and handy for theatergoers. Orso is one of the most popular places on midtown's "restaurant row," so if you're planning a six o'clock dinner, be sure to make reservations. The smallish room is cozy and comfortable. It's watched over by a portrait of Orso, a Venetian dog who is the mascot for this Italian bistro. The kitchen is open in the back, allowing diners to see the experienced staff at work. The changing menu offers many good appetizers, including cold roast veal and grilled eggplant salad. A variety of pizzas and some excellent pasta dishes are also offered. For an entree, you can't go wrong with the popular sauteed calves liver. The strawberry tiramisu, one of many homemade desserts, will finish off a great meal. A special Sunday brunch menu is available.

Asian Specialties

Dim sum: a whole meal of succulent nibblers, such as steamed dumplings, shrimp balls, and savory pastries

Egg foo yung: thick, savory pancakes made of eggs, vegetables, and meat, often slathered with a rich, broth-based sauce

General Tso's chicken: breaded and deep-fried chicken chunks tossed in a spicy-sweet sauce

Moo shu: stir-fried shredded meat, vegetables, and seasonings, scrambled with eggs and rolled (usually by the diner) inside thin pancakes

Peking duck: After air is pumped between a duck's skin and flesh, the bird is coated with honey and hung up until the skin dries and hardens. The duck is then roasted, cut into pieces, and served with scallions and pancakes or steamed buns.

Sashimi: sliced raw fish served with daikon (Japanese radish), wasabi (Japanese horseradish), pickled ginger, and soy sauce

Sukiyaki: stir-fried pieces of meat (and sometimes vegetables, noodles, or tofu) flavored with soy sauce, dashi (Japanese fish stock), and mirin (sweet rice wine)

Sushi: raw fish or vegetables placed atop vinegared rice or served inside rolls wrapped in nori (sheets of dried seaweed)

Tempura: fried, battered seafood and vegetables

Teriyaki: beef or chicken marinated in a sauce of rice wine, soy sauce, sugar, and seasonings, then grilled or stir-fried

---

OSTERIA DEL CIRCO
120 W 55th St (bet Ave of the Americas and Seventh Ave)
Lunch: Mon-Sat; Dinner: Daily   212/265-3636
Moderately expensive   www.osteriadelcirco.com

Were it not for the fact that the owners are the sons of legendary Sirio Maccioni (of Le Cirque fame), this establishment might just be written off as another Italian restaurant. But here we have three brothers—Mario, Marco, and Mauro (and mother Egidiana)—operating a classy establishment with a friendly, circus-themed ambience, atypical Italian menu, and a bit of Le Cirque's magic. The tastiest items include great pizzas and salads, satisfying soups, and unusual pastas. A unique dessert is an Italian favorite called *bomboloncini:* small vanilla-, chocolate- and marmalade-filled doughnuts.

OUEST
2315 Broadway (at 84th St)   212/580-8700
Dinner: Daily   www.ouestny.com
Moderate

Ouest is overflowing with happy locals enjoying one of the best rooms in the city. The comfortable booths, the open kitchen, the cozy (if dark and noisy) balcony, and the pleasant serving staff combine to make Thomas Valenti's jewel first-class. This is not surprising, as Valenti gained experience at Alison on Dominick St and Butterfield 81 on the Upper East Side. The bistro menu is just as inviting as the semicircular tables, with appetizer choices like smoked duck breast with crispy eggs and bitter greens, goat cheese ravioli, and several fresh salads. The braised short ribs melt in your mouth. Nightly specials include braised lamb shanks on Monday and Tuesday, and meatloaf like your mother served on Sunday. From delicious warm bread to rich chocolate cake for dessert, the whole experience is pure pleasure.

Certainly one of the most popular breakfast foods is French toast. To get the best in New York City, try **Clinton St. Baking Co. & Restaurant** (4 Clinton St, 646/602-6263) or **Silverleaf Tavern** (43 E 38th St, 212/973-2550), where the dish is particularly delicious and unusual.

OUR PLACE
1444 Third Ave (at 82nd St)   212/288-4888
Lunch, Dinner: Daily; Brunch: Sat, Sun   www.ourplaceuptown.com
Moderate

Our Place is not a typical Chinese restaurant. Classy service, moderate prices, and delicious food have been its trademarks for over a decade. Appreciative Upper East Siders have kept its two spotlessly clean diningrooms filled for nearly every meal. Single diners obviously enjoy the atmosphere and feel comfortable here. You'll find many of your favorite Chinese dishes on the menu. I've enjoyed wonton soup, moo shu pork, tangerine beef, Szechuan chicken, duck-wrapped lettuce with pine nuts, and home-style chicken casserole. Free delivery is offered in a wide area. Prices are as comfortable as the chairs.

OUR PLACE SHANGHAI TEA GARDEN
141 E 55th St (bet Lexington and Third Ave)   212/753-3900
Lunch, Dinner: Daily   www.ourplace-teagarden.com
Moderate

Shanghai flavors are usually a bit more complex than other Chinese dishes, and this is surely true at this clean and first-rate Oriental room. Shanghai specialties include "Lion's Head" (giant meatballs and vegetable hearts in brown sauce), sauteed squid, and Shanghai-style braised pork shoulder. Besides the Shanghai specialties, there are the usual Chinese dishes, with an excellent assortment of dumplings, soups, chicken, and duck. Their barbecued honey spare ribs are the best in the city. Service is highly efficient and professional. If you want to take the family out for a tasty meal at a reasonable price, I suggest coming here.

PALM ONE
837 Second Ave (at 44th St)
212/687-2953

PALM TOO
840 Second Ave (at 44th St)
212/697-5198

PALM WEST SIDE
250 W 50th St (bet Eighth Ave and Broadway)
212/333-7256
Lunch: Mon-Fri; Dinner: Daily   www.thepalm.com
Expensive

Even with all the excellent new steakhouses in Manhattan, steak and lobster lovers still have a special place in their hearts for the Palm, which started as a speakeasy in 1926. All three locations have much the same atmosphere. They're noted for huge, delicious steaks, chops, and lobsters. Don't miss the terrific Palm fries—homemade potato chips—or onion rings. These are earthy spots, so don't get too dressed up. Indolent waiters are part of the scene.

PAOLA'S
245 E 84th St (bet Second and Third Ave)   212/794-1890
Lunch: Dinner: Daily   www.paolasrestaurant.com
Moderate

There is a new look at Paola's, a wonderful place for a romantic evening! The Italian home cooking is first-class, with Paola herself in the kitchen. Great homemade filled pastas, superb veal dishes, and tasty hot vegetables (like baby artichoke hearts) are house specialties. Be advised that they don't spare on the garlic! Mirrors reflect the warmth and flicker of candles, and the lady of the house will charm any guest. Top off your reasonably priced meal with a rich chocolate mousse.

Eat in the East Village!
    Here are some suggestions:
Chickpea (23 Third Ave, 212/254-9500): pita parlor
Dumpling Man (100 St. Mark's Pl, 212/505-2121): dumplings
Grand Sichuan (19-23 St. Mark's Pl, 212/529-4800): Chinese
Klong (7 St. Mark's Pl, 212/505-9955): Thai
Korean Temple (81 St. Mark's Pl, 212/979-9300): Seoul food
Miss Williamsburg Portavia (228 E 10th St, 212/228-5355): lasagna
St. Mark's Market (21 St. Mark's Pl, 212/253-7777): Korean deli-
    style

PARIS COMMUNE
99 Bank St (at Greenwich St)   212/929-0509
Dinner: Daily; Brunch: Sat, Sun
Moderate

Paris Commune is a popular gathering spot in the West Village, where regulars outnumber visitors every night. The French/Continental menu includes pastas, salads, steaks, and seafood. The new location provides much needed additional seating. The staff is prompt and efficient. Dining by candlelight with an adjoining fireplace is a big attraction. The weekend brunch features spectacular French toast, along with the usual fare. Delicious dishes include a great vegetable frittata. Their homemade cheesecakes are good and rich.

PARK AVENUE CAFE
100 E 63rd St (at Park Ave)   212/644-1900
Lunch: Mon-Fri; Dinner: Daily; Brunch: Sun
Moderately expensive   www.parkavenuecafe.com

Park Avenue Cafe, whose windows face Park Avenue and walls favor a folk-art look, is a showpiece for expert restaurateur Alan Stillman. (He also has his hand in the Post House, Cité, Manhattan Ocean Club, and Smith & Wollensky.) Stillman obviously is a man of eclectic tastes. Chef Neil Murphy offers innovative American cuisine with offerings that run the gamut from greenleaf spinach soup to crispy Chatham cod and Maine lobster tagine. Highly professional waiters make dining here an experience in classy customer care. The people-watching is great, and conversations at adjacent tables can be fascinating. (It's not eavesdropping when you can't help it!) Desserts are sensational!

PARK BISTRO
414 Park Ave S (bet 28th and 29th St)   212/689-1360
Lunch: Mon-Fri; Dinner: Mon-Sun
Moderate

The Park Bistro is full of smiling faces and more. This small, homey jewel of a diningroom specializes in authentic French cuisine from the Provence region. From the start, when warm and tasty bread is placed before you, to the finishing touch of rich and luscious homemade desserts (like chocolate napoleon), you are surrounded by attentive service and magnificent food. Don't miss the hangar steak or lamb stew. A professional team runs this place, and it shows.

PARK SIDE
107-01 Corona Ave (51st Ave at 108th St, Corona, Queens)
Lunch, Dinner: Daily   718/271-9274
Moderate

Do you want to show someone who claims to know everything about New York a spot he or she doesn't know? Would you like to eat on your way to or from LaGuardia or Kennedy Airport? Do you want a special meal in an unusual setting? Well, all of the above are excellent reasons to visit Park Side, in Queens. I make an exception in including a restaurant not in Manhattan because it is exceptional. Joseph Oliva runs a first-class, spotlessly clean restaurant that serves wonderful Italian food at very affordable prices. Start with garlic bread and then choose from two dozen kinds of pasta and an opulent array of fish, steak, veal, and poultry dishes. The meat is all prime-cut and fresh—nothing frozen. You'll also find polite, knowledgeable waiters in an informal atmosphere. Get a table in the garden room or the Marilyn Monroe room upstairs. Eat to your heart's content, and then be pleasantly surprised at the tab.

PASTIS
9 Ninth Ave (at Little West 12th St)   212/929-4844
Breakfast, Dinner: Daily; Lunch: Mon-Fri; Brunch: Sun
Moderate   www.pastisny.com

What a scene! In what was once a garage, a large area has been gutted and converted into a bar and dining space with touches that make it look as though it has been around for a long time. Keith McNally, who knows how to hype a restaurant, has turned a spot in the Meatpacking District into one of the most high-energy rooms in Manhattan. The huge bar is a sea of hundreds of young Turks—and some not so young—who come to see and be seen. The diningroom, if you can get in, serves reasonably good food to hordes who love the unbelievable noise level and classic bistro fare. A nice touch is a large long table in the center of the dining space for singles and others who do not want to wait in the reservation line. The menu includes oysters on the half shell, omelets, shellfish stew, roast lobster, sauteed chicken, braised beef, patés, good French fries, and their "Floating Island" dessert. The first question you will ask is "How did they cram all these people into this place?" After a few minutes, you'll understand that the crowd is all part of the attraction. Pastis offers delivery, too.

PATSY'S
236 W 56th St (bet Broadway and Eighth Ave)   212/247-3491
Lunch, Dinner: Daily   www.patsys.com
Moderate

For over half a century, the Scognamillo family has operated this popular eatery, specializing in Neapolitan cuisine. At present, the son and a grandson are taking care of the front of the house, while another grandson is following the family tradition in the kitchen. "Patsy" was an immigrant gentleman chef whose nickname graces a two-level restaurant. Each floor has its own cozy atmosphere and convenient kitchen. The family makes sure that every guest is treated as if they are in a private home; courtesy and concern are the name of the game. A full Italian menu is available, with numerous specials that include a different soup and seafood entree each day. If you can't find what you like among the two dozen pasta choices, you are in deep trouble! There are *prix fixe* lunch and dinner (pre-theater) menus as well.

PAYARD PATISSERIE & BISTRO
1032 Lexington Ave (bet 73rd and 74th St)   212/717-5252
Lunch, Tea, Dinner: Mon-Sat (bakery 7 a.m.-11 p.m.)
Moderate   www.payard.com

Francois Payard has created a winner! Everything about this place is appealing: the look of the bakery cases as you enter, the attractively presented appetizers and entrees, and informed service by a well-trained staff. Payard is a combination French bistro and pastry shop that works to perfection. When you pair an expert pastry chef like Francois with executive chef Philippe Bertineau, you're going to get the very best. If you want to take something home, choose from croissants, muffins, tea cakes, seasonal tarts, individual pastries, *gateaux*, petit fours, biscuits, handmade candies, and superb chocolates. Classic and seasonal ice creams and sherbets are offered. Prepared soups, salads, sandwiches, and other goodies are also available for takeout. But don't miss the opportunity to dine here, as Payard offers terrific appetizers, superb salads, homemade foie gras, seafood dishes, traditional bouillabaisse, steaks, and more.

PERSHING SQUARE
90 E 42nd St (at Park Ave)   212/286-9600
Breakfast, Lunch, Dinner: Daily; Brunch: Sat, Sun
Moderate   www.pershingsquare.com

In a space just opposite Grand Central Station, Pershing Square serves throngs of hungry local and traveling New Yorkers. The odd-shaped room is full of energy and conversation, much of it relating to the broad variety of menu offerings. For those who missed breakfast before boarding their train, Pershing Square offers Irish oatmeal, eggs Benedict, vanilla-bean brioche French toast, and great buttermilk pancakes. Omelets are a specialty. Lunch and dinner items include seafood dishes, boneless beef short ribs, roast chicken, steaks, and pastas. The grilled hamburger with a selection of cheeses and crisp steak fries is a winner any time of day. More serious seafood dishes —like seared sea scallops with sweet onions and sun-dried tomatoes, and pan-seared Atlantic salmon—are popular for dinner. Try chocolate mousse cake for dessert. A friendly wait staff and an attractive bar are pluses.

Restaurant Associates can be relied upon to operate first-class eating establishments. Their places include:

Brasserie (100 E 53rd St, 212/751-4840)
Cafe Centro (MetLife Building, 200 Park Ave, 212/818-1222)
Cucina & Co. (MetLife Building, 200 Park Ave, 212/682-2700)
Naples 45 (MetLife Building, 200 Park Ave, 212/972-7001)
Nick & Stef's Steakhouse (Madison Square Garden, 33rd St and Eighth Ave, 212/563-4444)
Rock Center Cafe (Rockefeller Center, 20 W 50th St, 212/332-7620)
Tropica (MetLife Building, 200 Park Ave, 212/867-6767)

PETER LUGER STEAK HOUSE
178 Broadway (at Driggs Ave), Brooklyn   718/387-7400
Lunch, Dinner: Daily   www.peterluger.com
Expensive

Folks don't go here for the ambience or service, but if it's steak you want, you simply can't do better. The menu makes it simple: your choices are steak for one, two, three, or four. The creamed spinach and steak sauce are out of this world. Tell your waiter to go easy on the whipped cream if you order dessert. Peter Luger is only a stone's throw from Manhattan (take the very first right off the Williamsburg Bridge), and the staff is accustomed to ordering cabs. Reservations are suggested well in advance.

PICHOLINE
35 W 64th St (bet Broadway and Central Park W)   212/724-8585
Lunch: Tues-Sat; Dinner: Daily
Moderately expensive to expensive

Terrance Brennan is a workhorse, and it shows in his attractive restaurant. The warm atmosphere is a perfect backdrop for the seasonal, Mediterranean-inspired plates. The many positives include outstanding service, delicious homemade breads, perfectly done fish dishes, superbly prepared game, one of the best cassoulets in the city, and daily classic cuisine specials. For lunch, a "sea" menu and an "earth" menu are offered. The wine room and small private party room are fabulous settings for a memorable evening. I always look forward to the magnificent cheese cart for dessert. Jackets are required for gentlemen.

PIETRO'S
232 E 43rd St (bet Second and Third Ave)   212/682-9760
Lunch: Mon-Fri; Dinner: Mon-Sat (closed Sat in summer)
Expensive

Pietro's is a steakhouse featuring Northern Italian cuisine. Everything is cooked to order. The menu features great salads (they claim to make New York's best Caesar salad), steaks, chops, seafood, chicken, and an enormous selection of veal dishes. Tell your companion not to bother dressing up. Bring an appetite, however, because portions are huge. Although steaks are the best known of Pietro's dishes, you will also find ten chicken and ten veal selections (marsala, cacciatore, scaloppine, piccata, *francaise,* etc.) and nine potato dishes. Prices border on expensive and service is boisterous, but you'll certainly get your money's worth. By the way, Pietro's is very child-friendly.

PINOCCHIO
1748 First Ave (bet 90th and 91st St)   212/828-5810
Dinner: Tues-Sun; Brunch: Sun
Moderate

There's no pretense at this place, which is for serious Italian dining. Mark Petrillo presides over this tiny 12-table etablishment on the Upper East Side, where wonderful home-style Italian food is served. There are numerous specials every night, and I suggest letting the boss order for you. You'll always find great pastas, like cheese-filled ravioli, tortellini Pinocchio (meat-filled tortellini with cream, peas, and prosciutto), several spaghetti dishes, and fettuccine alfredo. The dessert menu has improved.

Don't miss a visit to **Pop Burger** (58-60 Ninth Ave, 212/414-8686), where thick, creamy milkshakes, tasty burgers (large and small), and non-greasy French fries are the attractions. In the evening, the back-room pool hall and lounge offer a heartier menu.

P.J. CLARKE'S
915 Third Ave (at 55th St)   212/317-1616
Lunch, Dinner: Daily   www.pjclarkes.com
Moderate

P.J. Clarke's can rightfully be called a Manhattan institution. Every day at lunch and dinner the regulars are joined by hordes of visitors, guzzling at the bar, eyeing the raw bar, or fighting for a table in the back room. No one is disappointed with the sizable platters, great burgers, and fresh seafood. Service is highly professional, and the price is right. Daily specials include wonderful meatloaf with mashed potatoes on Thursday and prime filet mignon on Saturday. Upstairs, you'll be taken with the decor at the **Sidecar,** which has its own kitchen and entrance.

PÓ
31 Cornelia St (bet Bleecker and 4th St)   212/645-2189
Lunch: Wed-Sun; Dinner: Daily
Moderate

Steve Crane has found the formula for a successful eating establishment.

The space is crowded, but tables are not on top of each other. The service is family-friendly, informed, and quick. The food is hearty, imaginative and unusually tasty. The portions are king-size. The prices are right. No wonder the place is always busy! As I have noted before, if the bread is good, chances are what follows will be also. Pó has hearty, crusty, fresh Italian bread. The pastas—tagliatelle, tortellini, linguine, and a special or two—are huge. The tasting menus offer great value, with a six-course meal going for only $40. Pastas and some heavier entrees (like grilled salmon) are available for lunch, along with inventive sandwiches like marinated portobello with roasted peppers. An unusual and satisfying dessert called *affogato* consists of coffee gelato in chilled cappuccino with chocolate and caramel sauces.

> If you are worn out after a stressful day, try **The Pump** (40 W 55th St, 212/246-6844), an "energy food" restaurant. Healthy sandwiches, salads, and energy-filled plates are available daily for eat-in, takeout, and delivery. Shakes are mixed with fruit, juice, and nonfat frozen yogurt. Their special protein shakes will surely pump you up!

PORTERS
216 Seventh Ave (bet 22nd and 23rd St)   212/229-2878
Lunch, Dinner: Daily; Brunch: Sun   www.portersnyc.com
Moderate

No big name or trendy buzz at Porters, just good food in a clean and modest Chelsea location. It is very satisfying if you are looking for sensible, well-prepared food at affordable prices. Three-course luncheons for around $20 are popular. They also offer a nice selection of salads and fish, steak, and chicken dishes. At dinnertime, popular appetizers such as filet mignon carpaccio, salads, shellfish stew, great burgers, and coconut-crusted salmon are available. Yukon mashed potatoes are a smash, and the chocolate caramel pyramid is the dessert to try!

POST HOUSE
Lowell Hotel
28 E 63rd St   212/935-2888
Lunch: Mon-Fri; Dinner: Daily
Moderately expensive

This great Manhattan steakhouse is an "in" social and political hangout that serves excellent food in comfortable surroundings. The guest list usually includes many well-known names and recognizable faces. They are attracted, of course, by the good food and warm ambience. Hors d'oeuvres like crab-meat cocktail, lobster cocktail, and stone crabs are available in season, but the major draws are steak and lobster. Prices for the latter are definitely not in the moderate category; ditto for lamb chops. However, the quality is excellent, and the cottage fries, fried zucchini, hash browns, and onion rings are superb. Save room for the chocolate box (white and dark chocolate mousse with raspberry sauce). If you can walk out under your own steam after all this, you're doing well!

PRIMAVERA

1578 First Ave (at 82nd St)   212/861-8608
Lunch: Mon-Fri; Dinner: Daily   www.primaveranyc.com
Expensive

Primavera is one of my favorite places, and it keeps getting better! Owner Nicola Civetta is the epitome of class, and his wife, Peggy, is equally charming. They know how to make you feel at home and present a superb Italian meal. Don't come if you're in a hurry, as Primavera is geared toward relaxed dining. I could wax eloquently with descriptions of the dishes, but you can't go wrong no matter what you order. Let Nicola choose for you, as there are specials every day. To top it all off, they have one of the most beautiful desserts anywhere: a gorgeous platter of seasonal fruit that looks too good to eat. Primavera is always busy, so reservations are a must. A beautiful private party room is available.

Be sure to try **Bar Americain** (152 W 52nd St, 212/265-9700). The food is pure American and the quality is pure pleasure. Try the homemade potato chips.

PROVENCE

38 MacDougal St (at Prince and Houston St)   212/475-7500
Lunch, Dinner: Daily   www.provence-soho.com
Moderate

Here's a sliver of France in Manhattan! You won't quickly forget a visit to Provence, a Greenwich Village charmer. Tasty and wholesome food is professionally served at sensible prices. Garlic is another reason you won't forget this bistro. If you like its taste, you'll love Provence! The French country menu is served in several spaces: one noisy room by the bar, a more romantic area in the back, and a comfortable outside patio. You'll find dishes typical of the Provence region (fish and steamed vegetables) on the menu. If you like some of the signature dishes (*pot-au-feu,* cassoulet, bouillabaisse), call ahead to find out what is featured that evening. Wonderful French fries accompany certain dishes. Top it all off with one of their great desserts!

RAO'S

455 E 114th St (near First Ave)   212/722-6709
Dinner: Mon-Fri   www.raos.com
No credit cards
Inexpensive

Don't be put off by rumors about Rao's, such as a two-month wait for reservations. If you want to go to Rao's—an intimate old-time (1896) Italian restaurant—you should plan a bit in advance, however. The place is crowded all the time for two reasons: the food is great, and prices are ridiculously low. Don't walk or take a car; hail a taxi and get out in front of the restaurant, which is in Spanish Harlem. When you're ready to leave, they'll call a taxi. Frankie Pellegrino is a gregarious and charming host who makes guests feel right at home and will even sit at your table while you order. Be prepared for leisurely dining. While you're waiting, enjoy the excellent bread and warm atmosphere. Believe it or not, the Southern fried chicken (Rao's style) is absolutely superb and would be my number-one choice. (Hint: Try appearing unannounced at the door or call the same day, as tables are often available on the spur of the moment.)

RAOUL'S
180 Prince St (bet Sullivan and Thompson St)   212/966-3518
Dinner: Daily   www.raoulsrestaurant.com
Moderate

There are dozens of good places to eat in Soho, and Raoul's is one of the best. This long, narrow restaurant used to be an old saloon. There are paper tablecloths and funky walls covered with a mishmash of posters, pictures, and calendars of every description. The bistro atmosphere is neighborly, friendly, and intimate; the prices moderate; and the service attentive. The trendy clientele runs the gamut from jeans to fur coats. The house favorites are steak *au poivre* and paté *maison*. Raoul's is a natural for those whose days begin when the rest of us are ready to hit the sack.

Mexican Specialties

Ceviche: citrus-marinated raw fish
Chilis rellenos: mild to spicy chili peppers stuffed with cheese and fried in egg batter
Chorizo: spicy pork sausage
Empanadas: meat-filled pastries surrounded by a fat-laden crust
Enchiladas: soft corn tortillas filled with meat, vegetables, or cheese and topped with salsa and cheese
Fajitas: marinated beef, shrimp, chicken, and/or vegetables served in warm tortillas (often wrapped by the diner)
Paella: an elaborate saffron-flavored rice casserole that includes a variety of seafood and meats
Tamales: chopped meat and vegetables encased in cornmeal dough

---

RARE BAR & GRILL
Shelburne Murray Hill   212/481-1999
303 Lexington Ave (at 37th St)   www.rarebarandgrill.com
Breakfast, Lunch, Dinner: Daily
Moderate

If noise is your thing, you will be right at home at Rare. Inhabited by tables of yuppies and button-down business types, this restaurant literally vibrates with energy. The food is almost secondary to the scene, but the burgers are fabulous. They are served on Orwasher buns with a large choice of toppings. You can get a classic burger or order one of their more exotic types: Mexican, foie gras, Kobe beef, barbecued pork, turkey scallion, crab, shrimp, and vegetable. They also serve coconut shrimp, a French-fry tasting basket (cottage, shoestring, and sweet potato fries with three dipping sauces), salads, soups, and a huge banana split.

RAYMOND'S CAFE
88 Seventh Ave (bet 15th and 16th St)   212/929-1778
Lunch, Dinner: Daily; Brunch: Sat, Sun
Moderate

Some of the old haunts in the Chelsea area have lost their appeal, but Raymond's still has a lot going for it. Chef Raymond is obviously a perfectionist. The place is spotlessly clean with an up-to-date look, and the food is well presented and very tasty. Choices range from pastas and sandwiches at noon to delicious hot and cold appetizers, fresh seafood items, and a great grilled salmon steak at dinner. The weekend brunch features omelets, linguini dishes, and warm chicken salad. A private diningroom is available, and delivery is free within eight blocks. The early-bird dinner is a three-course bargain! Ask about their private party facilities.

Tribeca residents and visitors shouldn't miss a visit to **Bubby's** (120 Hudson St, 212/219-0666). First of all, the regular menu items are tasty and reasonably priced. The Sunday brunch is delicious and a real scene for the locals! Then there are the great pies: mile-high apple, sour cherry, key lime, and chocolate peanut butter. Homemade cakes, too! Delivery in the Tribeca area is free.

(THE FAMOUS) RAY'S PIZZA OF GREENWICH VILLAGE
465 Ave of the Americas (at 11th St)   212/243-2253
Sun-Thurs: 11 a.m.-2 a.m.; Fri, Sat: 11 a.m.-3 a.m.
Inexpensive

"Ray" and "pizza" are synonymous in Manhattan! Ray's is so popular that guests have asked them to ship pizzas to Midwestern relatives (and they will). No pizzeria in the Big Apple is any better than this one, supposedly featuring the *real* Ray. The pizza is gourmet at its best, and you can create your own from the many toppings offered. You can have a fresh slice, whole pizza, or Sicilian square. Kids love the baby pizzas. You won't leave hungry, as pizzas are a generous 18 inches. Take-and-bake personal pizzas—ten-inch pies that are all natural and handmade—bake in your oven in 12 minutes. Free delivery is available.

REDEYE GRILL
890 Seventh Ave (at 56th St)   212/541-9000
Lunch, Dinner: Daily; Brunch: Sat, Sun   www.redeyegrill.com
Moderately expensive

From the day it opened, this "home of the dancing shrimp bar" has been a busy place! The name attracted my attention, because I am a frequent coast-to-coast redeye flyer. When I first entered the place, I could see I had a lot of company. Owner Sheldon Fireman knows how to appeal to the eye, taking a cue from his very successful nearby Trattoria dell'Arte. Specialties include shrimp done in all shapes and sizes, smoked salmon, a huge seafood appetizer platter (at a huge price), a smoked fish bar, grilled fish, and pastas. There's more, too: weiner schnitzel, burgers, smoked fish, and egg dishes. The personnel are hip and helpful, but the scene is the major attraction. Live jazz is featured Tuesday through Saturday and during Sunday brunch.

REMI
145 W 53rd St (bet Ave of the Americas and Seventh Ave)
Lunch: Mon-Fri; Dinner: Daily   212/581-4242
Moderate

Come here for the best seafood risotto in town! Remi operates in a spectacular space in midtown, handy to hotels and theaters. In an unusually long room dominated by a dramatic 120-foot Venetian wall painting by Paulin Paris, the food soars as high as the setting. In the warm weather, the doors open up and diners can enjoy sitting at tables in the adjoining atrium. Waiters, chairs, and wall fabrics all match in attractive stripes. Antipasto like roasted quail wrapped in bacon will get you off to a delicious start. Main dishes are not of the usual variety. The spaghetti, linguine, and ravioli (stuffed with such items as shrimp, ricotta, and vegetables) can match any house in Venice. Of course, there are fish and meat dishes for more mainstream appetites. The chocolate-raspberry mousse cake is superb. Paddle on down (Remi means "oars") for a first-class experience! Takeout and delivery are available.

At **Pure Food and Wine** (54 Irving Pl, 212/477-1010) the food is not quite raw—but nothing is cooked over 117 degrees, so as not to destroy the food's enzymes. You will find a tasty selection of soups, salads, lasagna, ravioli, pizzas, and other choices. A juice bar is on the premises and takeout is available. Reservations are suggested.

RENÉ PUJOL
321 W 51st St (bet Eighth and Ninth Ave)   212/246-3023
Lunch, Dinner: Mon-Sat   www.renepujol.com
Moderate

First things first: order a chocolate soufflé right away for dessert! René Pujol is a very attractive French restaurant that makes an ideal spot for a pre-theater dinner or private party. It's always busy, and a large number of customers are regulars, which speaks well of a restaurant. One reason for René Pujol's success is that it's a family enterprise. The owners—the daughter and son-in-law of the retired René Pujol—are on the job, and the waiters are superb. Housed in an old brownstone, the restaurant has two warmly decorated, cozy, and comfortable diningrooms, complete with a working fireplace. There are attractive private party rooms upstairs, too. The menu is vintage French, with filet mignon, grilled Atlantic salmon, and tasty tarts being the specialties of the house. An award-winning wine list, too!

RESTAURANT 343
343 E 85th St (bet First and Second Ave)   212/717-6200
Lunch: Wed-Fri; Dinner: Daily; Brunch: Sat, Sun
Moderate to moderately expensive

343 is a relaxing retreat on the Upper East Side with no flash and no attitude. All of this is rather refreshing in today's frenetic Manhattan restaurant scene. Salads are fresh and healthy, especially baby spinach with delicious buttermilk Roquefort dressing. Some people claim the burgers are the best in the city, and they are very good indeed, being made from ground Black Angus sirloin. You can also have roast chicken, seafood, or steak. While desserts are not made in-house, Mississippi mud praline cheesecake is a winner.

RISTORANTE GRIFONE
244 E 46th St (bet Second and Third Ave)   212/490-7275
Lunch: Mon-Fri; Dinner: Mon-Sat   www.grifonenyc.com
Moderate to moderately expensive

New Yorkers get so hyped up about trendy new places that they tend to forget about old-timers that quietly continue to do a good job. Grifone is one of those. If you are looking for an attractive, comfortable, and cozy place to dine—one with impeccable service and great food—then try Grifone. The menu is Northern Italian; there are so many daily specials that you probably won't even look at the printed sheet, including a good selection of pasta, chicken, veal, fish, and beef dishes. A takeout menu is available as well. Quality never goes out of style; just ask the neighborhood regulars who flock here year after year.

If you feel like dropping by a restaurant for an after-theater dessert, try **Resette** (7 W 45th St, 212/221-7530) and order the warm rustic apple tart with almond-cinnamon cream, gelato, and caramel and vanilla sauces. This dish will make the whole evening worthwhile—even if the show wasn't very good!

RIVER CAFE
1 Water St (Brooklyn Bridge), Brooklyn   718/522-5200
Lunch: Mon-Sat; Dinner: Daily; Brunch: Sun
Moderately expensive

A visit here is a must, and don't forget to bring your camera! The River Cafe isn't in Manhattan, but it *overlooks* Manhattan, and that's the main reason to come. The view from the window tables is fantastic, awesome, romantic—you name it. There's no other skyline like it in the world. And so the River Cafe—just across the East River in the shadow of the Brooklyn Bridge—remains an extremely popular and sophisticated place. Call at least a week in advance to make reservations, and be sure to ask for a window table. This is a flag-waving special-occasion restaurant that's proud of its American cuisine. The seafood, lamb, and steak entrees are particularly good, and desserts are rich and fresh. The "Brooklyn Bridge," done in dark chocolate, is a dessert you will never forget.

ROLF'S
281 Third Ave (at 22nd St)   212/477-4750
Lunch, Dinner: Daily
Moderate

In a city with few good German restaurants, Rolf's is worth remembering. It's a colorful spot where several dozen tables and wooden benches perfectly complement the eclectic decor. Faux Tiffany lampshades, old pictures, tiny lights, strings of beads, and what-have-you add up to a charming and comfortable setting for tasty German dishes. The schnitzels, goulash, sauerbraten, boiled beef, veal shanks, and bratwurst are served in ample portions with delicious potato pancakes and sauerkraut. German, apple, and potato pancakes come with applesauce on the side. For dessert, save room for homemade apple strudel or Black Forest cake.

ROSA MEXICANO
1063 First Ave (at 58th St)   212/753-7407
61 Columbus Ave (at 62nd St)   212/977-7700
Lunch: Daily (at Columbus Ave location); Dinner: Daily
Moderate to moderately expensive   www.rosamexicano.com

This is, quite simply, classic Mexican cuisine. Start with the guacamole *en molcajete*; prepared fresh at the table, it is the best in town. There are also great appetizers, like small tortillas filled with sauteed shredded pork, small shrimp marinated in mustard and chili vinaigrette, and raviolis filled with sauteed chicken, tomato, and onion. Main course entrees include tasty (and huge) crepes filled with shrimp and a multi-layered tortilla pie. Grilled specialties like beef short ribs and skewered marinated shrimp are tempting. Even the desserts are first-class. Choose from a traditional flan, Mexican spongecake, or mango with ice cream. The atmosphere at these two locations is friendly, the energy level high, and the dining top-drawer.

Are you confused about all the Kobe beef items you are suddenly seeing on Manhattan menus? Well, the truth of the matter is that the Kobe designation really refers to the highly marbled beef, which can (and does) come from any place *except* Japan. (It even comes from my home state of Oregon!) Importation of Japanese beef was stopped in 2001 due to the mad cow scare. Kobe beef, in most cases, is tender and has a delicious flavor, even if the price tag is sizable. By the way, **Riingo** (205 E 45th St, 212/867-4200) serves a sensational sushi-style variation of Kobe beef.

ROUNDTABLE
Algonquin Hotel   212/840-6800
59 W 44th St, lobby level   www.algonquinhotel.com
Breakfast, Lunch, Dinner: Daily
Moderate to moderately expensive

The famous Roundtable at the Algonquin, where all manner of famous personalities in the arts, business, and politics would meet to exchange stories and repartee, is still alive and kicking! You can even reserve the famous table if your party numbers seven or more. The Roundtable reeks of days past, but the food is very good and the servers will shower you with loving care. Don't expect anything fancy, and instead just relax in the manner of the good old days (if that is what they really were!).

ROY'S NEW YORK
New York Marriott Financial Center Hotel
130 Washington St (bet Carlisle and Albany St)   212/266-6262
Breakfast: Daily; Lunch: Mon-Fri; Dinner: Mon-Sat
Moderate to moderately expensive   www.roysrestaurant.com

I have never seen operations run as efficiently as Roy's. This large one in Manhattan's Financial District brings to 24 the number he oversees all around the globe. The menu blends ideas from Europe (where Roy was trained) with popular ingredients from Asia and the Pacific. The changing menu includes items like wonderful coconut shrimp on a stick, grilled Szechuan baby back pork ribs, and Macadamia nut-crusted mahi-mahi with lobster butter sauce. Top it all off with hot chocolate soufflé or cherry *crostada*. Seats at the counter overlooking the kitchen will provide an extra dimension to your meal.

RUBY FOO'S
2182 Broadway (at 77th St)   212/724-6700
1626 Broadway (at 49th St)   212/489-5600
Lunch, Dinner: Daily; Brunch: Sun (uptown location)
Moderate   www.brguestrestaurants.com

What a scene this is! Upper West Siders have discovered Ruby Foo's in a big way. The two-level facility, which seats about 400 people, is packed. You'd better call for reservations or be prepared to spend an eternity at the bar. The same is true at the Times Square location. The place is billed as a dim sum and sushi palace; the best dishes are in the latter category. However, if you and your tablemates share glazed baby back ribs with Asian pear napa slaw, you will go home happy. There is a large selection of maki rolls: spicy tuna, fresh crabmeat, tempura shrimp, California crab, and many more. The seven different sushi platters are well-selected and great for a party. Hand rolls, soups, salads, and rice dishes are also featured. The crowd is hip, the noise level high, the food very good, and the value outstanding.

Eat in bed? You've probably tried that at home. Now it is possible to feast atop a mattress at some Manhattan restaurants. Unfortunately, you cannot spend the night!

B.E.D. (530 W 27th St, 212/594-4109) features 23 beds in the main dining space. The food is French/American with a Brazilian twist.
Duvet (45 W 21st St, 212/989-2121) has 25 beds, and groups can book private bedrooms. The cuisine is progressive American.
Highline (835 Washington St, 212/243-3339), located in the Meatpacking District, has beds that are used mainly for cocktails and hors d'oeuvres.
Ono (18 W 13th St, 212/660-6766), at Hotel Gansevoort, offers cocktails and hors d'oeuvres, outdoors as weather allows.

Oh, yes—these restaurants promise that sheets are changed after each use!

RUE 57
60 W 57th St (at Ave of the Americas)   212/307-5656
Lunch, Dinner: Daily; Brunch: Sat, Sun
Moderate (lunch) to moderately expensive (dinner)

With an extremely convenient location, friendly and accommodating service, and pleasant atmosphere, this Parisian brasserie is one busy place. When you combine a menu that encompasses soups and salads, oysters and clams, sushi, steaks, varied entrees (like salmon, chicken, risotto, and ravioli), plus daily specials, you have a winning attraction. The young ones will enjoy the great burgers. Lovers of Japanese cuisine will find sushi, sashimi, maki, and temaki. Don't pass up the beefsteak tomato salad with onions and Roquefort!

SAN PIETRO
18 E 54th St (bet Fifth and Madison Ave)   212/753-9015
Lunch, Dinner: Mon-Sat   www.sanpietro.net
Moderately expensive

A visit to classy San Pietro is like a vacation in southern Italy. The Bruno brothers have brought the joys of that part of the world to their upscale restaurant, which is popular with society mavens and the well-heeled. Fresh fruit and veggies are legendary, as is linguine with anchovy juice. Spaghetti dishes and *scialatelli* are special, too. A selection of fish, veal, and chicken dishes are very well crafted. On the down side, waiters can be offhand and even snooty if they think you're not a big tipper, and desserts leave a lot to be desired. However, if you want to enjoy tasty Italian dishes while seeing how the other half lives, San Pietro might just be your ticket!

SARABETH'S KITCHEN
423 Amsterdam Ave (at 80th St)   212/496-6280

1295 Madison Ave (at 92nd St)   212/410-7335
Breakfast, Lunch, Dinner: Daily

40 Central Park S (bet Fifth Ave and Ave of the Americas)
Breakfast, Lunch, Dinner: Daily; Brunch: Sat, Sun   212/826-5959
Moderate

SARABETH'S AT THE WHITNEY
Whitney Museum of American Art
945 Madison Ave (bet 74th and 75th St)   212/570-3670
Lunch: Tues-Fri; Brunch: Sat, Sun   www.sarabeth.com
Moderate

I am reminded of the better English tearooms when visiting one of Sarabeth's locations. Swinging it is not. Reliable it is. The big draw is the homemade quality of the dishes, including the baked items and excellent desserts. They also make gourmet preserves and sell them nationally. Menu choices include excellent omelets, porridge, or fresh fruit for breakfast, a fine assortment of light items for lunch, and fish, game, or meat dishes for dinner. The chocolate mousse cake, chocolate soufflé, warm berry bread pudding, and homemade ice cream are splendid desserts. Service is rapid and courteous. Look in on their bakery at 75 Ninth Avenue, too.

SAVORE
200 Spring St (at Sullivan St)   212/431-1212
Lunch, Dinner: Daily; Brunch: Sat, Sun
Moderate

Soho has no shortage of restaurants, many of them with a snooty attitude that's in keeping with the area. Savore has none of this. You come here for good, fresh food served in a casual and friendly atmosphere. It is a particularly attractive destination in the nice weather, when tables are placed outside. The menu offers a large selection of pastas, like hand-cut spaghetti with basil and roasted tomato. In true Tuscan fashion, salads are served after the main course. I am partial to their crème brûlée, which features a wonderful coffee flavor.

SCALINI FEDELI
165 Duane St (bet Greenwich and Hudson St)   212/528-0400
Lunch: Tues-Fri; Dinner: Mon-Sat
Expensive

This very upscale Italian restaurant is for those who want a truly classy and classic meal. The offerings are exotic: seared foie gras and roasted apples, and soft egg-yolk ravioli with ricotta and spinach . . . all to start! Then on to delicious braised short ribs of beef, breast of Muscovy duck, and wonderful tuna. Desserts are equally fabulous, like a flourless chocolate cake (cooked to order) with a trio of gelati or a warm caramelized apple tart in a baked fillo crust. Luncheons are a bit lighter. *Prix fixe* menus are the order of the day. As you look around this sedate establishment, you'll be impressed by the relative youth of some of the gourmet diners. A nice, private wine cellar room is available for parties.

A quick snack or meal at any time of day is a routine for many of us. New York eating establishments have come to recognize this trend. You can now find excellent comfort food stops all over Manhattan:

- **Danny Meyer's Shake Shack** (Madison Square Park, 23rd St bet Madison Ave and Broadway is a popular place, with long lines in the nice weather. And no wonder! Wonderful burgers, hot dogs, frozen custards, shakes, floats, and more.
- **Westville** (210 W 10th St) is a tiny stop with big flavors, serving salads, soups, burgers, hot dogs, sandwiches, complete platters, and yummy desserts. Brunch is served on weekends and holidays, with the usual bagel, egg, and breakfast dishes.
- Fast counter service is offered at **New York Burger Co.** (303 Park Ave). Choices include excellent burgers and fries, fresh salads, smoothies, and other good choices. The crowds are a good indication that this is a tasty spot!
- **Mary's Dairy** (171 W 4th St) is perfect for delicious homemade ice cream, sorbets, fancy dessert dishes, and more.
- For European street food, try **F&B Güdtfood** (269 W 23rd St and 150 E 52nd St). You'll find soups and salads, vegetable and *haute* dogs (a specialty), sweets, and more.

SCHILLER'S
131 Rivington St (at Norfolk St)   212/260-4555
Lunch: Mon-Fri; Dinner: Daily (open late); Brunch: Sat, Sun
Moderate   www.schillersny.com

There is no place quite like Schiller's in Manhattan; leave your pin stripes at home and bring the gang downtown. Keith McNally has created an unusual, fun, and deservedly popular munching and drinking spot in an area not renowned for exciting places. Known officially as Schiller's Liquor Bar, this place joins a group of busy brasseries, including his very "in" Balthazar. The atmosphere is rather Parisian and the service informal, with much emphasis on the wine selection: cheap, decent, and good vintages are offered, with prices to match. They serve good Bibb lettuce salads, excellent burgers, Welsh rarebit, modestly priced steaks, and rotisserie chicken, and daily specials are offered. For those who lament the lack of good German food in Manhattan, visit Schiller's on Thursday, when German sausages and wiener schnitzel are on special. Sticky toffee pudding and chocolate cream pie are two of the better desserts. Takeout and delivery are also offered.

SEA GRILL
19 W 49th St (at Rockefeller Plaza)   212/332-7610
Lunch: Mon-Fri; Dinner: Mon-Sat   www.restaurantassociates.com
Moderately expensive

You'll pay for the setting as well as the food at this Rockefeller Center seafood house, which overlooks the ice skating rink in winter and features open-air dining in the nice weather. Take advantage of the seafood bar (clams, oysters, shrimp, mussels, crab, and lobster) to start. Well-prepared but somewhat pricey main courses include tasty crab cakes, salmon, and Nantucket bay scallops. I love the desserts. The menu changes daily, but offerings include such delights as warm chocolate steamed pudding, warm apple tart, key lime pie, and "Palette of Sorbets." Rockefeller Center has been spruced up, and Sea Grill is one of its gems. Now if they could just lighten up on the prices!

SECOND AVENUE KOSHER DELICATESSEN AND RESTAURANT
156 Second Ave (at 10th St)   212/677-0606
Sun-Thurs: 7 a.m.-midnight (Fri, Sat till 3 a.m.)
Inexpensive   www.2ndavedeli.com

You've heard all about the great New York delicatessens; now try one of the really authentic ones, located in the historic East Village. From the traditional *k*'s—knishes, kasha varnishkes (buckwheat groats with pasta), and kugel—to boiled beef and chicken in the pot (with noodles, carrots, and matzo balls), no one does it quite like the Lebewohl family. Portions are enormous. Homemade soups, three-decker sandwiches (tongue and hot corned beef are sensational), deli platters, complete dinners—you name it, they've got it. The smell is overwhelmingly appetizing, the atmosphere is "caring Jewish mother," and they don't mind if you take your meal out instead of dining in the colorful back room. Don't leave without trying the chopped liver and warm apple strudel!

SERENDIPITY 3
225 E 60th St (bet Second and Third Ave)   212/838-3531
Sun-Thurs: 11:30 a.m.-12 a.m.; Fri: 11:30 a.m.-1 a.m.; Sat: 11:30 a.m.-
2 a.m.   www.serendipity3.com
Moderate

How does a "Golden Opulence Sundae" sound? It costs $1,000 and must be ordered a week in advance, but it actually has edible gold leaf! The young and young-at-heart rate Serenpidity 3 *numero uno* on their list of "in" places, as it has been for a half century. In an atmosphere of nostalgia set in a quaint, two-floor brownstone, this full-service restaurant offers a complete selection of delicious entrees, sandwiches, soups, salads, and pastas. The real treats are the fabulous desserts, including favorites like hot fudge sundaes and frozen hot chocolate (which can also be purchased in mix form to take home).

An added pleasure is the opportunity to browse a shop loaded with trendy gifts, books, clothing, and accessories. If you are planning a special gathering for the teens in your clan, make Serendipity 3 the destination!

SETTE MEZZO
969 Lexington Ave (at 70th St)   212/472-0400
Lunch, Dinner: Daily
Cash only
Moderate

Sette Mezzo is small, professional, and busy, and it makes a great spot for people-watching! There are no affectations in decor, service, or food preparation. This is strictly a business operation, with the emphasis on serving good food at reasonable prices. Don't worry about dressing up; many diners come casually attired to enjoy a variety of Italian dishes done to perfection. At noon the menu is tilted toward lighter pastas and salads. In the evening, all of the grilled items are excellent. Fresh seafood is a specialty. Ask about the special pasta dishes; some of the combinations are marvelous. For more traditional Italian plates, try veal chops, veal cutlets, stuffed baked chicken, or fried calamari and shrimp. All desserts are made in-house. They include several caloric cakes, tasty lemon tarts, sherbet, and ice cream.

71 CLINTON FRESH FOOD
71 Clinton St (at Rivington St)   212/614-6960
Dinner: Daily   www.71clintonfreshfood.com
Moderately expensive

The area is anything but fancy, the place is tiny, and tables are close together. Never mind. The food, wait staff, and dining experience at 71 Clinton are all superb. Wylie Dufresne and his associates present dishes pleasing to the eye and the tummy. You might start with trout tartare. Don't overlook the venison and sliced hangar steak entrees. Seafood offerings include poached monkfish, seared sea scallops, and crisp sea bass. For dessert, go for the warm chocolate cake with a peanut butter center and vanilla ice cream.

SHELLY'S NEW YORK
104 W 57th St (at Seventh Ave)   212/245-2422
Lunch, Dinner: Daily; Brunch: Sun   www.shellysnewyork.com
Moderate

Shelly Fireman is the consummate restaurant innovator. His various New York eateries are dramatic and unique, but all have a common thread: good food. Shelly's is no exception. In a space that was once a booming Horn and Hardart Automat (where you got your food through little mailbox-like windows), this bustling operation combines a cafe, a wine and raw bar, an American bar, and several unique diningrooms. In the nice weather, the open sidewalk windows showcase New York characters by the dozens. Inside, you'll find a grand array of oysters from both coasts, littleneck clams, lobster, shrimp salads, sandwiches, steaks, lamb chops, and moderately priced entrees. Stone crab claws are featured all year round. Don't miss the unusual and somewhat risque art scattered about the premises. A penthouse and roof garden terrace can accommodate up to 500 guests.

SHUN LEE CAFE/SHUN LEE WEST
43 W 65th St (bet Columbus and Central Park W)
Lunch: Sat, Sun; Dinner: Daily   212/769-3888, 212/595-8895
Moderate

Dim sum and street-food combinations are served in an informal setting at Shun Lee Cafe. It's a fun place where you can try some unusual and delicious Chinese dishes. A waiter comes to your table with a rolling cart and describes the various goodies. The offerings vary, but don't miss stuffed crab claws if they are available. Go on to the street-food items: delicious roast pork, barbecued spare ribs, a large selection of soups and noodle and rice dishes, and a menu full of mild and spicy entrees. Sauteed prawns with ginger and boneless duckling with walnut sauce are great choices. A vegetarian dish of shredded Chinese vegetables is cooked with rice noodles and served with a pancake (like moo shu pork, but without the meat). For heartier appetites, Shun Lee West—the excellent old Chinese restaurant that adjoins Shun Lee Cafe—is equally good. Some of the best Chinese food in Manhattan is served here. If you come with a crowd, family-style dining is available. Prices are a bit higher at the restaurant than in the cafe.

Restaurant Tipping Guide

Coat check	$1 per item
Maitre d'	$10 to $100 (depending on the occasion, restaurant and level of service you wish to receive; given before sitting at the table)
Wait staff	15% to 20% of the bill before taxes; 25% is appropriate for truly outstanding service
Sommelier	15% of the wine bill
Restroom	50¢ to $1 for handing you a towel or if you use any products or cosmetics

---

SHUN LEE PALACE
155 E 55th St (bet Lexington and Third Ave)   212/371-8844
Lunch, Dinner: Daily   www.shunleepalace.com
Moderate to moderately expensive

There are all manner of Chinese restaurants in Manhattan: The colorful Chinatown variety. The mom-and-pop corner operations. The over-Americanized establishments. The grand Chinese diningrooms. Shun Lee Palace belongs in the latter category, possessing a very classy and refined look. You are offered a delicious journey into the best of this historic cuisine. You can dine rather reasonably at lunch; a four-course *prix fixe* experience is available. Ordering from the menu (or through your captain) can be a bit pricier, but the platters are worth it. Specialties include beggar's chicken (24 hours advance notice required), curry prawns, and Beijing duck. There's much more, including casserole specials and spa cuisine. Yes, this is just about the nearest thing Manhattan has to a real Chinese palace.

SISTINA
1555 Second Ave (at 80th St)   212/861-7660
Lunch, Dinner: Daily
Moderate

The philosophy of this family operation is that the joy is in the eating, not the surroundings, and for that they get top marks. Because the atmosphere is pretty plain, one comes to Sistina for the food, and it can't be beat for classy Italian cooking. The specialty of the house is seafood; the Mediterranean red snapper and salmon are excellent dishes. There are also the usual choices of pasta, veal, and chicken, as well as daily specials.

> If you're looking for fun, interesting people, good food, and a place that's unique in New York, try **Sidecar** (205 E 55th St, 212/317-2044). It's upstairs from P.J. Clarke's, with a separate entrance. The fish and steaks are first-rate, and the setting—a former antique store—adds to the experience.

66
241 Church St (bet Leonard and Worth St)   212/925-0202
Lunch, Dinner: Daily   www.jean-georges.com
Moderate to moderately expensive

Leave it to Jean Georges Vongerichten to do something different, colorful, delicious, and thoroughly professional. He's turned his attention to Chinese food, served in a downtown setting that is clean, bold, attractive, and comfortable. Bright red banners add a special note. A long communal dining table also serves as a bar with intriguing back lighting. The Asian personnel are competent and attractive, though their uniforms are drab. Sensibly-sized portions of appetizers, dim sum, noodles and rice, vegetables, seafood, poultry, and fish leave one looking forward to the main dishes, which are likewise exciting and tasty. Entrees are served family-style at large tables. Especially recommended are barbecued beef short ribs, stir-fried shrimp, black bass, and lemon-sesame chicken. Modestly priced (for Jean Georges) desserts include almond tofu, valrhona chocolate cake, and a nice selection of sorbets and ice cream. This is definitely not your usual Chinese restaurant; in my opinion, it is a must-try.

SMITH & WOLLENSKY
797 Third Ave (at 49th St)   212/753-1530
Lunch, Dinner: Daily   www.smithandwollensky.com
Moderate to moderately expensive

When visitors to the Big Apple want a taste of what this great city is all about, there is no better spot than Smith & Wollensky. There is an abundance of space (two floors) and talented, helpful personnel. I always grade a place on the quality of their bread, and Smith & Wollensky's is great. There is no better lobster cocktail offered anywhere in the city. Outposts around the country (like Miami's South Beach) add to the authenticity of this house, along with the wonderful steaks, prime rib, and lamb chops. Every man in the family will love the place, and the ladies will appreciate the special attention paid to them. Come here when you and your guests are really hungry.

SPARKS STEAKHOUSE
210 E 46th St (bet Second and Third Ave)   212/687-4855
Lunch: Mon-Fri; Dinner: Mon-Sat
Moderately expensive

You come here to eat, period. This is a well-seasoned and popular beef restaurant with little ambience. For years, businessmen have made an evening at Sparks a must, and the house has not let time erode its reputation. You can choose from veal and lamb chops, beef scaloppine, and medallions of beef. There are a half-dozen steak items, like steak *fromage* (with Roquefort), prime sirloin, sliced steak with sauteed onions and peppers, and top-of-the-line filet mignon. Seafood dishes are another specialty. Rainbow trout, filet of tuna, and halibut steak are as good as you'll find in most seafood houses. The lobsters are enormous, delicious, and expensive. Skip the appetizers and desserts, and concentrate on the main dish. Private party rooms are available.

SPICE MARKET
403 W 13th St (at Ninth Ave)   212/675-2322
Lunch, Dinner: Daily   www.jean-georges.com
Moderate

Jean Georges Vongerichten has created another restaurant full of surprises! For atmosphere and mostly tasty Asian street food, this is one of the city's hot dining spots. Located in the trendy Meatpacking District, Spice Market is a charming space with tables surrounding an open area that leads to an inviting bar downstairs. The place looks like it could have been designed with ABC Carpet and Home merchandise, as the taste level is superior. As for the food, it is different and exciting. The Vietnamese spring rolls are yummy, the salads unusual and tasty, and the chicken skewer with peanut sauce outstanding. Other wonderful dishes: striped bass or cod with Malaysian chili sauce, onion- and chili-crusted short ribs that melt in your mouth, and a large selection of vegetables, noodles, and rice. Desserts are even better. Thai jewels and fruits with fresh coconut snow—one of the most famous street desserts in Thailand—is a must. Other sweet selections: warm rice pudding, palm sugar caramel flan, Ovaltine kulfi, and a really fabulous chocolate and Vietnamese coffee tart served with ice cream.

SPRING STREET NATURAL RESTAURANT
62 Spring St (at Lafayette St)   212/966-0290
Daily: 9 a.m.-11:30 p.m.; Fri, Sat until 12:30 p.m.; Brunch: Sat, Sun
Moderate   www.springstreetnatural.com

Before eating "naturally" became a big thing, Spring Street Natural Restaurant was a leader in the field. That tradition continues today after 30 years. In attractive surroundings, their kitchen provides meals prepared with fresh, unprocessed foods, and most everything is cooked to order. Neighborhood residents are regular customers, so you know the food is top-quality. Specials are offered every day, with a wide variety of organic salads, pastas, vegetarian meals, free-range poultry, and fresh fish and seafood. Try wonderful roasted salmon with creamy risotto and baby asparagus stalks. The best is saved for last: Spring Street believes in great desserts, like chocolate walnut pie, honey raspberry blueberry pie, and honey pear pie. The last two are made without sugar and dairy products.

STRIP HOUSE
13 E 12th St (bet Fifth Ave and University Pl)   212/328-0000
Dinner: Daily   www.theglaziergroup.com
Moderately expensive

The Strip House is a classy steakhouse with a sexy red ambience. If anything separates this place from others in this macho business, it is the attitude of the personnel. Everyone is friendly, helpful, and informed. Besides, the food is quite good. On the broiled side, there are New York strips, filet mignon, rib chops, Colorado lamb rack, and lobster. And there is seafood, chicken, and linguine. Daily specials might include duck breast, bouillabaisse, veal chops, Dover sole, and rabbit. Steamed littleneck clams make a nice appetizer, and a side of crisp goose-fat potatoes is tasty. I even liked the truffled cream spinach! The toughest part of dining here is choosing between chocolate profiteroles, chocolate fondue, and crepe soufflé for dessert.

TABLA
11 Madison Ave (at 25th St)   212/889-0667
Lunch: Mon-Fri; Bread Bar: Sat; Dinner: Daily
Moderate (downstairs) to expensive (upstairs)

In the New York restaurant world, no one is more respected than Danny Meyer. He takes his establishments and the city he calls home very seriously. His restaurants have become legends, with Gramercy Tavern and Union Square Cafe always at the top of the city's most popular venues. Those who like New Indian cuisine will find the upstairs room dramatic in decor and quite different in taste, with the option of a *prix fixe* menu. Downstairs, you'll find home-style Indian cooking and an a la carte menu.

> For those who like really intimate dining, try **Table d'Hote** (44 E 92nd St, 212/348-8125). The place is so tiny and the mix-and-match tables and chairs are so tightly squeezed together that you'll find it easier to sit down than leave after a full meal! By the way, this French bistro's food isn't bad!

TAO
42 E 58th St (bet Madison and Park Ave)   212/888-2288
Lunch: Mon-Fri; Dinner: Daily   www.taorestaurant.com
Moderate

Tao is billed as an Asian bistro, but it is much more than that. In a huge space that once served as a theater, a dramatic dining setting has been created with a huge Buddha looking down as you enjoy wonderful food at reasonable prices. Hordes of diners can be accommodated on two levels; a sushi bar and several regular bars are also available. Reservations are strongly recommended, as thirty-somethings make this their headquarters. A number of small plates are available to start, including Thai stuffed shrimp and squab lettuce wraps. Save room for a delicious steak: Kobe beef or filet mignon cooked at your table in a hot pot, or a marvelous wok-seared New York sirloin with shitake mushrooms that melts in your mouth. A $20 *prix fixe* lunch is offered daily. For dessert, try the molten chocolate cake with coconut ice cream. You'll love this place!

TARTINE
253 W 11th St (at 4th St)   212/229-2611
Lunch: Mon-Fri; Dinner: Daily; Brunch: Sat, Sun
Cash only
Moderate

Read carefully! Tartine will be your kind of place if you don't mind: (1) waiting outside in the rain, cold, or heat, (2) bringing your own drinks, (3) paying cash, and (4) having your dirty fork laid back down in front of you for the next course. All of this, of course, is secondary to the fact that this tiny spot (about 30 chairs) serves some of the tastiest dishes in the Village. There are soups, salads, quiches, and omelets, plus chicken, meat, and fish entrees at pleasing prices. The French fries are a treat. Desserts and pastries are baked on the premises. For about half the price of what you would pay uptown, you can finish your meal with splendid custard-filled tarts, a fabulous hazelnut-covered chocolate ganache, strawberry shortcake, or thinly sliced warm apples with cinnamon on puff pastry with ice cream. There is always a wait at dinner—a good sign, since neighborhood folks know what's best! If you want wine, you are encouraged to bring your own.

Dining in Harlem has improved. Here are some favorites:

Amy Ruth's (113 W 116th St, 212/280-8779): good breakfasts

Bayou (308 Lenox Ave, 212/426-3800): Creole cuisine

Copeland's (547 W 145th St, 212/234-2357): Try the Sunday gospel brunch.

Londel's Supper Club (2620 Frederick Douglass Blvd, 212/234-6114): jazz entertainment on weekends

Miss Maude's Spoonbread Too (547 Lenox Ave, 212/690-3100): pork chops and spoonbread, of course

Native (161 Lenox Ave, 212/665-2525): French-Moroccan

Rao's (455 E 114th St, 212/722-6709): famous Italian landmark

Revival (2367 Frederick Douglass Blvd, 212/222-8338): soul food

Settepani (196 Lenox Ave, 917/492-4806): deli and bakery specialties

Sylvia's (328 Lenox Ave, 212/996-0660): now larger, with soul food and entertainment

Yvonne (301 W 135th St, 212/862-1223): Southern specialties

TASTE
1413 Third Ave (at 80th St)   212/717-9798
Dinner: Daily   www.elizabar.com
Moderate to moderately expensive (dinner)

When it comes to quality food (with prices to match), there is no equal in Manhattan to Eli Zabar. Taste is his latest restaurant, and it has all the pluses and minuses you've come to expect from this gentleman. Dinners change nightly and feature such winners as sauteed duck livers, roasted artichoke hearts, wild Pacific salmon, pork chops, and quail. A wine bar, serving good wines that aren't too expensive by the glass, is an added feature. With his market just below, it looks like Taste is getting really fresh food. And the breads, as you would expect, are superb. The more informal **Taste Cafe** serves breakfast, lunch, and a weekend brunch.

TASTING ROOM
72 E 1st St (bet First and Second Ave)   212/358-7831
Dinner: Tues-Sat
Inexpensive to moderate

Don't blink or you will miss this tiny treasure! Renée (in front) and chef-husband Cohn Alevras (in the kitchen) treat just 25 guests for dinner with an ever-changing menu of very tasty dishes, along with a huge cache of wines —300 labels and over 2,000 bottles. I even noticed a large offering of great wines from my home state of Oregon. The menu is unusual: you can order either a small tasting plate or a larger share plate. The latter is fun if you are dining with a group. You'll find such sophisticated dishes as duck foie gras terrine, roasted partridge, chili-braised pork, and citrus-cured cod, all of it fresh and individually done. Renée is a charming hostess. Finish your meal with a piece of her mother's cheesecake, featuring wine-poached apricots and cherries topped with bee pollen.

TAVERN ON THE GREEN
Central Park W at 67th St   212/873-3200
Lunch: Mon-Fri; Dinner: Daily; Brunch: Sat, Sun
Moderate to moderately expensive   www.tavernonthegreen.com

There's no place like this back home! Tavern on the Green is a destination attraction. The setting in Central Park, with lights twinkling on nearby trees and glamorous inside fixtures, makes for dining experiences that residents and visitors alike never forget. Even though the operation is big and busy, the food and service are usually first-rate. Chef John Milito has a big job keeping this place hopping. If you are planning an evening that must be extra special, make reservations in the Crystal Room. Your out-of-town relatives will love it! Seasonal menus can be viewed online.

TOCQUEVILLE
15 E 15th St (bet Union Square W and Fifth Ave)   212/647-1515
Lunch: Mon-Sat; Dinner: Daily   www.tocquevillerestaurant.com
Moderately expensive

Tocqueville is a smallish restaurant tended with TLC by the husband-and-wife team of Marco Moreira and Jo-Ann Makovitzky. The result is outstanding. Innovative dishes are featured in a constantly changing menu. At lunchtime, a *prix fixe* menu is offered. "Billy Bi" soup (mussels in broth) is a superb way to start. On to the 60-second seared dry-aged sirloin. The warm apple tart is a wonderful finish. You'll have an absolutely fabulous meal, made all the more pleasant by a well-trained and accommodating staff. I fault only the not-very-warm bread and rather spartan decor, but those are minor flaws. This talented pair also operates **Marco Polo Caterers** (same phone number as Tocqueville), which offers an outstanding selection for home or business affairs. The owners will personally deliver the delicious food, and they can also take care of rental items, flowers, photographers, and professional service staff.

TONY'S DI NAPOLI
1606 Second Ave (at 83rd St)   212/861-8686
Dinner: Daily (open at 2 p.m. on Sat, Sun)
147 W 43rd St (Times Square)   212/221-0100
Lunch, Dinner: Daily   www.tonysdinapoli.com
Moderate

Tony's is not to be missed for great family-style dining. The kids will love it, as will your hungry husband or wife. So will your grandparents! The place is colorful, noisy, and busy. The Times Square location is a bit more subdued. Huge platters of appetizers, really delicious salads, pastas, chicken and veal dishes, broiled items, and seafood come piping hot and ready for the whole crew to dig into. Most everyone finds that they can't eat it all; you'll see lots of take-home boxes exiting these locations. Even the dessert menu is gigantic: cheesecakes, strawberry shortcake, sundaes, sorbets, and *tartufo* (almost the real thing). An outrageous fresh Godiva cappuccino is made with vanilla custard ice cream, espresso, cappuccino liqueur, and topped with Godiva chocolate liqueur. Sheer fun, believe me!

TRATTORIA DELL'ARTE
900 Seventh Ave (at 57th St)   212/245-9800
Lunch: Mon-Sat; Dinner: Daily; Brunch: Sun
Moderate   www.trattoriadellarte.com

The natives already know about Trattoria Dell'Arte, as the place is bursting at the seams every evening. A casual cafe is at the front, seats are available at the antipasto bar in the center, and the diningroom is in the rear. One would be hard-pressed to name a place at any price with tastier Italian food than is served here. The antipasto selection is large, fresh, and inviting; you can choose a platter with various accompaniments. There are daily specials, superb pasta dishes, grilled fish and meats, and salads. Wonderful pizzas are available every day. Special spa cuisine from Italy is a feature. The atmosphere and personnel are warm and pleasant. I recommend this place without reservation—although you'd better have one if you want to sit in the diningroom.

There is nothing quite like a glass of cold, fresh orange juice first thing in the morning. At **Great American Health Bar** (35 W 57th St, 212/355-5177), they squeeze it right in front of you.

TRIBECA GRILL
375 Greenwich St (at Franklin St)   212/941-3900
Lunch: Mon-Fri; Dinner: Daily; Brunch: Sun
Moderate   www.myriadrestaurantgroup.com

It hardly seems possible this place is 15 years old! Please note the address is Greenwich *Street,* not Avenue. The setting is a huge old coffee-roasting house in Tribeca. The inspiration is Robert DeNiro. The bar comes from the old Maxwell's Plum restaurant. The kitchen is first-class. The genius is savvy Drew Nieporent. Put it all together, and you have a winner. No wonder the people-watching is so good here! Guests enjoy a spacious bar and dining area, fabulous private screening room upstairs, a collection of paintings by Robert DeNiro, Sr., and banquet facilities for private parties. The food is stylish and wholesome. Excellent salads, seafood, veal, steak, and first-rate pastas are house favorites. One of the top dishes is seared tuna with sesame noodles. The tarts, tortes, and mousses also rate with the best. Their wine list (1,500 selections!) is world-class.

TROPICA
MetLife Building
200 Park Ave (45th St at Vanderbilt Ave), lobby   212/867-6767
Lunch, Dinner: Mon-Fri   www.restaurantassociates.com
Moderate

Realizing that most New Yorkers have limited time to spend over lunch, Tropica provides speedy and efficient service in addition to very tasty food. Dinner hours are a bit more relaxed in this bright, charming, tropical seafood house, which is hidden away on the concourse of the MetLife Building in midtown. Featured entrees include excellent tuna (in the sushi and sashimi assortment), seafood salads, and a variety of chicken, beef, and other seafood preparations. Stick to the fish and shellfish, and you'll be more than satisfied. The molten chocolate cake easily wins best dessert honors.

The **Time Warner Center** (10 Columbus Circle) is spectacular in almost every way. **The Mandarin Oriental New York** (see separate writeup of its **Asiate** restaurant) is superb. The **Equinox Health Club** is first-rate. The selection of retail stores is world-class. But when it comes to restaurants for the average diner, it is something else entirely.

I highly recommend **Café Gray** for atmosphere, value, great food, quality service, and the incredibly professional hand of Gray Kunz. As for the others, be prepared!

Masa is a very tiny Japanese restaurant owned by celebrated sushi chef Masayoshi Takayama. There is no question that the sushi is out-of-this-world, but so is the price. If you like sushi enough to spend $1,000 for dinner for two (including drinks), that is your choice. However, for a more reasonable tab and sushi that's nearly as good, **Bar Masa** is right next door.

Per Se, owner-chef Tom Keller's prize, has top-notch food and magnificent service, but prices are stratospheric.

V Steakhouse, a creation of famed chef Jean Georges Vongerichten, has the ambience of a dining salon in a fancy Las Vegas cathouse. It's downhill from there, with pretentious service and grandiose prices. Besides, I counted only six layers on their featured 14-layer chocolate cake!

T SALON & T EMPORIUM

11 E 20th St (bet Fifth Ave and Broadway) 212/358-0506
Daily: 10-8 888/NYC-TEAS
Moderate www.tsalon.com

Come here at teatime! Given renewed interest in tea, the unusual and enchanting T Salon will captivate tea addicts, as well as those who just want to experiment on an occasional basis. You will find green teas (light-colored Oriental tea with a delicate taste), oolong teas (distinctively peachy flavor), black teas (heavy, deep flavor and rich amber color), as well as white and red teas. Tea blending is a specialty. The T Salon is home of the new "pyramid pouch" tea bag. Proper afternoon tea with scones, sandwiches, and pastries is served daily. One can choose from 500 different teas. One of Manhattan's largest tea selections is sold upstairs, as are all kinds of attractively displayed and reasonably priced tea accessories. They host bridal and baby showers, book signings, and special events. This is one of the more unusual operations in Manhattan, again proving that no other city in the world is quite like the Big Apple!

TURKISH KITCHEN
386 Third Ave (bet 27th and 28th St)   212/679-6633
Lunch: Mon-Fri; Dinner: Daily; Brunch; Sun
Moderate   www.turkishkitchen.com

Turkey is in! I mean the country, as well as the food. This Turkish delight has great ethnic food and is absolutely spotless. Moreover, the staff exudes charm! There are all kinds of Turkish specialties, like zucchini pancakes, *istim kebab* (baked lamb shanks wrapped with eggplant slices), hummus, and tasty baked and grilled fish dishes. You can wash it all down with sour cherry juice from Turkey or *cacik*, a homemade yogurt. Turkish music is the Tuesday entertainment feature. This family-run Gramercy area operation is one of the best.

21 CLUB
21 W 52nd St (bet Fifth Ave and Ave of the Americas)   212/582-7200
Lunch: Mon-Fri; Dinner: Mon-Sat (closed Sat in summer)
Expensive to very expensive   www.21club.com

You know about 21. It has been around for a long time and has certainly established a reputation as a place to see and be seen. I can remember fascinating lunches there with my uncle, who was a daily diner. Alas, things have changed. Yes, there is still a gentleman at the door to give you the once over. Jackets are required. There are still 21 classics on the menu, even a not-so-lowly burger at $29. And the atmosphere is still quite special. But there the tradition ends, as far as I am concerned. The service is haughty, and the food is just okay. If your out-of-town guests simply *must* see this place and you're feeling flush, then go. Otherwise, the memories are better!

2 WEST
Ritz-Carlton New York, Battery Park
2 West St (at Battery Pl)   917/790-2525
Breakfast, Lunch, Dinner: Daily
Moderately expensive

The view is the thing here! Not that the food isn't very good, but the edibles are outclassed by the visual sights. The park and water view combines with the gorgeous indoor glass pieces and artwork to make a memorable feast for the eyes. The serving pieces are just as attractive, too. When you combine all of this with extremely fast and informed service and good food, I have no complaints. This room is just one of the hotel's dining choices, all of them done to Ritz-Carlton's standards of perfection. You'll find a rich selection of plates carefully designed and presented with local ingredients. I like the dessert plate; the chocolate tart is exceptional. If you're looking for a special place for afternoon tea, the adjoining Lobby Lounge is perfect.

TYPHOON BREWERY
22 E 54th St (bet Fifth and Madison Ave)   212/754-9006
Lunch: Mon-Fri; Dinner: Mon-Sat (limited bar menu on Sat)
Moderate

A bit of Bangkok has come to midtown Manhattan with this booming Thai eatery and brewery. The ground floor houses a huge bar with a vast selection of handcrafted American beers on draft and others (domestic and imported) in bottles. Daily specials are offered. A raw bar offers oysters from both coasts, as well as littleneck clams. All five Thai flavors—salty, sweet, sour, bitter, and spicy—are featured on the menu. Take your choice of selections in each category. Family-style platters add to the fun: great squid with garlic, delicious lemon-grass chicken, and superb seared monkfish in sour tamarind broth. Desserts aren't bad for a Thai house. Typhoon brûlées (Thai coffee crème, coconut jelly, apple tofu) head the list. It's crowded and fun but no place for those wearing hearing aids.

JAMES BEARD HOUSE
167 W 12th St (bet Ave of the Americas and Seventh Ave)
212/675-4984, www.jamesbeard.org

This is a real chefs' place! The legendary James Beard had his roots in Oregon, so anything to do with his life is of special interest to this author. He was a familiar personality on the Oregon coast, where he delighted in serving the superb seafood for which the region is famous. When Beard died in 1985, his Greenwich Village brownstone was put on the market and purchased by a group headed by Julia Child. Now the home is run by the nonprofit James Beard Foundation as a food and wine archive, research facility, and gathering place. It is the nation's only such culinary center. There are nightly dinners anyone can attend at which some of our country's best regional chefs show off their talents. For foodies, this is a great opportunity to have a one-on-one with some really interesting folks. Call for scheduled dinners.

UNCLE JACK'S STEAKHOUSE
440 Ninth Ave (at 34th St)   212/244-0005
Lunch: Mon-Fri; Dinner: Mon-Sun   www.unclejacks.com
Moderate (lunch) to expensive (steak dinners)

Entering this atmospheric steakhouse is like going back decades in time. The hand-carved mahogany bar, the antique light fixtures, the blackboard menu, and the private room (Jack's Parlor) make the place comfortable and colorful. You will be well taken care of, as the wait staff and captains are right on the job. Uncle Jack's is one of the few steakhouses in Manhattan that specialize in Kobe beef, which is famous for its tenderness and flavor. (Tao also has the item, but it's not a specialty.) As the beef is aged for 21 days and cooked to perfection, you can expect an equally grand price tag. Other menu items are what you would expect from a first-class steakhouse, and all are tasty and comfortably priced. For a gentlemen's evening out, a bachelor party, or office celebration, I can't imagine a more pleasant place. The bottled steak sauce is a must to take home!

UNION SQUARE CAFE
21 E 16th St (bet Fifth Ave and Union Square W)   212/243-4020
Lunch, Dinner: Daily   www.unionsquarecafe.com
Moderate

This is one of New York's most popular restaurants—and with good reason. The Stars and Stripes fly high here, as Union Square Cafe is very much an American restaurant (albeit with an Italian soul). The clientele is as varied as the food. Conversations are often oriented toward the publishing world, as well-known authors and editors are in attendance at lunch. The menu is creative, the staff unusually down-to-earth, and the prices very much within reason. Owner Danny Meyer offers such specialties as oysters Union Square, hot garlic potato chips, and wonderful black bean soup. For lunch, try the yellowfin tuna burger served on a homemade poppyseed roll. Dinner entrees from the grill are always delicious (tuna, shell steak, and veal). I go here just for the warm banana tart with honey-vanilla ice cream and macadamia nut brittle! Try a light afternoon cheese plate at the bar.

UNITED NATIONS DELEGATES DINING ROOM
United Nations Headquarters
First Ave at 46th St   212/963-7626, 212/963-7099 (banquets)
Lunch: Mon-Fri (open nights and weekends for special functions)
Moderate   www.aramark-un.com

Don't let the name or the security keep you away! The public can enjoy the international food and special atmosphere here. Conversations at adjoining tables are conducted in almost every language. The setting is charming, overlooking the East River. The room is large and airy, the service polite and informed. There is a large selection of appetizers, soups, salads, entrees, and desserts on the daily "Delegates Buffet." All of the dishes are attractively presented and very tasty. A huge table of salads, baked specialties, seafoods, meats, vegetables, cheeses, desserts, and fruits await the hungry noontime diner. Some rules apply: jackets required, jeans prohibited, and photo ID needed. (The room is used for private gatherings in the evening.) There isn't a more appetizing complete daily buffet available in New York.

After a long run on West 57th Street, the **Hard Rock Cafe** (1501 Broadway, 212/489-6565), has moved to the building that once housed the Paramount Theater. The new digs are twice the size of their former home, with room for over 700 diners.

VERITAS
43 E 20th St (near Park Ave S)   212/353-3700
Dinner: Daily   www.veritas-nyc.com
Moderately expensive

There are only 55 seats at Veritas, all of them kept warm for every meal. Getting to enjoy chef Scott Bryan's refreshingly simple dishes is definitely worth the wait. The world-class wine cellar stocks 1,300 bottles, ranging from $18 to $25,000. Like the food, the room is done in superb taste; every color and surface spells quality. Top dishes include seared foie gras, crisp sweetbreads, pepper-crusted venison, and roasted organic chicken that will melt in your mouth. Chocolate soufflé is a must for dessert. Finally someone has gotten the word that complex food combinations often just don't work. Simpler is better!

VINEGAR FACTORY
431 E 91st St (bet York and First Ave)   212/987-0885
Brunch: Sat, Sun   www.elizabar.com
Moderate

Savvy Upper East Siders quickly learned that weekend brunch at Eli Zabar's Vinegar Factory is delicious. Taste buds spring to alertness as you wander the packed aisles of the Vinegar Factory (a great gourmet store) on your way upstairs for Saturday or Sunday brunch. Don't expect bargain prices; after all, this is an Eli Zabar operation. But the quality is substantial. Wonderful breads (Eli is famous for them), a fresh salad bar, omelets, pizzas, pancakes, blintzes, and huge sandwiches are the order of the day. Your teens will love the massive portions, and you'll appreciate the fast, friendly service.

Steakhouses come and go, especially lately. Many of the new arrivals are quite good, but a true pioneer, **Smith & Wollensky** (797 Third Ave, 212/753-1530), continues to stand out as one of the very best. Steak and chop lovers will enjoy the comfortable atmosphere, top-quality meat, and informed service. Look around at the tables; some of New York's biggest deals have been made here.

VIVOLO
140 E 74th St (bet Park and Lexington Ave)   212/737-3533
Lunch: Mon-Fri; Dinner: Daily   www.vivolonyc.com
Moderate

Angelo Vivolo has created a neighborhood classic in an old townhouse converted into a charming two-story restaurant with cozy fireplaces and professional service. His empire includes **Cucina Vivolo** (138 E 74th St, 212/717-4700 and 222 E 58th St, 212/308-0222), which are specialty food shops. There are great things to eat at all three places. You can sit down and be pampered, have goodies ready for takeout, or place an order for delivery free of charge (from 66th to 80th St between York and Fifth Ave). The Cucina menu offers wonderful Italian specialty sandwiches made with all kinds of breads, as well as soups, cheeses, sweets, espresso, and cappuccino. A box lunch is also available. In the restaurant proper there are daily specials, pastas, stuffed veal chops, and much more. Vivolo serves over 60 scaloppine preparations. Save room for the cannoli *alla Vivolo,* a tasty version of this Italian classic.

VONG
200 E 54th St (bet Second and Third Ave)   212/486-9592
Lunch: Mon-Fri; Dinner: Daily   www.jean-georges.com
Moderate to moderately expensive

The atmosphere is Thai-inspired, with romantic and appetizing overtones. The ladies will love the colors and lighting, and the gentlemen will remember the great things Vong does with peanut and coconut sauces. I could make a meal of appetizers like chicken and coconut milk soup, prawn satay with oyster sauce, and raw tuna wrapped in rice paper. Order crispy squab or venison medallions, if available. A vegetarian menu is offered. For dessert I suggest passionfruit sorbet or warm chocolate cake. Dining here is a lot cheaper than a week at Bangkok's Oriental Hotel and just as delicious!

WALKER'S
16 N Moore St (at Varick St)   212/941-0142
Lunch, Dinner: Daily
Inexpensive

If you are looking for a glimpse of what old Manhattan was like, you'll love Walker's. In three crowded rooms, at tables covered with plain white paper so that diners can doodle with crayons, you will be served hearty food at agreeable prices. The regular menu includes homemade soups, salads, omelets (create your own), sandwiches, and quiches. Their burgers are big and satisfying. A dozen or so daily specials include fish and pasta dishes. For those coming from uptown, it is a bit of a project to get here. For those in the neighborhood, it is easy to see why Walker's is a community favorite, especially on Sunday jazz nights.

WD-50 (50 Clinton St, 212/477-2900) has a lot going for it. Owner Wylie Dufresne is a talented chef. His room is attractive: good lighting, unique restrooms, a dramatic semi-open kitchen. Many of the dishes are delicious, but unless you are one of those contemporary gourmets who enjoys unusual dishes served with equally unusual accompaniments—like pork belly with black soybeans and turnips—I would suggest heading elsewhere.

WALLSÉ
344 W 11th St (at Washington St)   212/352-2300
Dinner: Daily; Brunch: Sat, Sun   www.wallse.com
Moderate to moderately expensive

Ready for crispy cod strudel? Vienna it is not, but Kurt Gutenbrunner has brought a somewhat Austrian flavor to the West Village. The two dining-rooms are sparse but comfortable. The staff is pleasant and helpful, adding to the dining experience. Appetizers like foie gras terrine and chestnut soup with Armagnac prunes are seasonal favorites. Yes, there is wiener schnitzel with potato-cucumber salad. Great pastries for dessert: apple strudel, cheesecake, and Salzburger *nockerl*. The cheese selection is first-rate. Of couse, I'd rather be at Hotel Sacher in Vienna, but then getting to Wallsé is a lot less expensive.

WATER CLUB
500 E 30th St (at East River)   212/683-3333
Lunch: Mon-Sat; Dinner: Daily; Buffet Brunch: Sun
Moderately expensive   www.thewaterclub.com

Warning! Do not fill up on the marvelous small scones that are made fresh and served warm. They are the best things you have ever tasted, but they will diminish your appetite for the excellent meal to follow. The Water Club presents a magnificent setting on the river. The place is large and noisy, with a fun atmosphere that is ideal for special occasions. (They also have excellent private party facilities.) There is nightly piano music, as well as accommodations for a drink or light meal on the roof, weather permitting. A large selection of seafood appetizers is available. Entrees include numerous fish dishes, plus meat and poultry items. Homemade fruit sorbet and fresh-baked apple crisp (served at Sunday brunch) will round off a special meal. Be advised that getting here from the north can be confusing. (Exit FDR Drive at 23rd Street and make two left turns.)

> Here's one the kids will love! Dark tunnels, Martian men and women, interactive games, plus good food and drink—all can be found at **Mars 2112** (1633 Broadway, 212/582-2112). Menu offerings include out-of-this-world Interstellar Shrimp, Meteor Talapia, Pavonis Mons Chinese Chicken Salad, among others.

WOO CHON
10 W 36th St (off Fifth Ave)   212/695-0676
Daily: 10:30 a.m.-5 a.m.
Moderate

Look at the hours they keep at Woo Chon! This Korean restaurant is sparkling clean, friendly, and inviting. For a group dinner, order a variety of beef, pork, or shrimp dishes and have fun broiling them at your table. The sizzling seafood pancake is a winner! Accompanying dishes add a special touch to your meal. In addition to marinated barbecue items, there are such tasty delights as Oriental noodles and vegetables, traditional Korean herbs and rice served in beef broth, a variety of noodle dishes, and dozens of other Far East treats. If you are unfamiliar with Korean food, the helpful personnel will explain the dishes and how to eat them.

WOO LAE OAK SOHO
148 Mercer St (bet Prince and Houston St)   212/925-8200
Lunch, Dinner: Daily   www.woolaeoaksoho.com
Moderate to moderately expensive

In attractive Soho surroundings, one can choose from a large selection of hot and cold appetizers, as well as traditional Korean specialties. The best include Dungeness crab wrapped in spinach crepes and tuna tartare served over sliced Asian pears. Rice and side dishes such as seasoned seaweed, radish *kimchi,* and raw garlic are also available. The big draws are the barbecued items, cooked right at the table. Available for barbecuing are slices of beef, short ribs, chicken, lamb, pork, scallops, shrimp, tuna, veggies, and much more. The personnel are very helpful to beginners and seem genuinely pleased when diners show interest in their unusual menu.

> Pick up a quick bite from **Zeytinz Fine Food Market Place** (24 W 40th St, 212/575-8080), where they have gourmet sandwiches, wraps, paninis, pizzas, soups, and salads. Or try something from the cold buffet, sushi bar, or grill. Zeytinz offers specialty drinks like lattes and smoothies, a large selection of breakfast items, and custom-made cakes, tarts, and cookies. Catering, gift baskets, and delivery are available.

ZARELA
953 Second Ave (bet 50th and 51st St)   212/644-6740
Lunch: Mon-Fri; Dinner: Daily   www.zarela.com
Moderate

Zarela Martinez's family-style regional Mexican restaurant sets the standard for this type of cuisine in Manhattan. For lunch you'll find such tempting dishes as *flautas* (rolled chicken tacos), *tamales del dia*, guacamole, and delicious salads. A number of seafood, chicken, and meat dishes are also available. At dinner more *antojitos* are featured, including different varieties of fresh and dried chiles with assorted fillings and sauces. You'll also find sauteed shrimp, tuna steak, roasted half duck, pan-fried liver, and vegetable dishes. *Prix fixe* menus are available for lunch, dinner, and large groups. Even the desserts are great: chocolate crepes or Mexican fruit bread pudding with applejack-brandy butter sauce.

Do the words "Rainbow Room" bring back nostalgic memories of old New York? Well, you can still enjoy dinner from 5 to 11:30 daily at the **Rainbow Room Grill** (30 Rockefeller Plaza, 212/632-5100) high atop the city. This should be an "occasion" event, as prices can put a dent in the pocketbook.

ZOË
90 Prince St (bet Broadway and Mercer St)   212/966-6722
Lunch: Mon-Fri; Dinner: Tues-Sun; Brunch: Sat, Sun
Moderate   www.zoerestaurant.com

Once inventive and now at times routine, Zoë is still worth a visit. Zoë occupies an old building, and the original tiles and columns still show. The setting is attractive and particularly enjoyable for younger diners, who like to sit at the chef's counter and watch the interactive kitchen. There is a wood-burning grill, a wood-fueled pizza oven (used for lunch), and a rotisserie. The grill features delicious organic pork loin and steaks. The menu is contemporary American, with seasonal changes. It's worth saving room for the chocolate desserts!

Vegetarian diners who like classy Indian dishes should visit **Devi** (8 E 18th St, 212/691-1300). A lunch main course vegetarian meal is reasonably priced. In the evening a seven-course vegetable tasting menu is $55.

III. Where to Find It: Museums, Tours, and Other Experiences

A Week in New York

"I'm going to be in New York for a week. What do you recommend?" I've been asked that question a thousand times in the last 50 years, and I'm always torn about how to answer. You could spend an entire lifetime in New York and still never see and do everything this fabulous city has to offer. If you're here for a week, the first two things you need to do are gather information and make some choices.

When you're planning an itinerary, you need to know that certain places and areas are better visited on specific days—Soho on Saturday and the Lower East Side on Sunday, for example. Others shut down on Saturday (the Lower East Side), Sunday (Soho and most of midtown), all weekend (the Financial District), or Monday (many major museums and theaters). If your time is limited, pick a couple of things you really want to do or places you really want to see and build your days around them. Check the hours they're open and plan accordingly.

Every trip to New York is different, and each person will have a different list of favorites. If you have friends who know New York, by all means ask for their recommendations. The following itinerary for a week in New York combines my own favorites with some of the absolute "don't miss" classics. Whether you follow this outline, take a friend's suggestions, or make up your own, remember that part of the pleasure of New York is simply taking it all in at your leisure. Whatever else you do, spend a little time just walking around!

MONDAY: Getting Oriented
- Buy the current edition of *Time Out New York*, find a place to have coffee, and read the various "This Week in New York" sections.
- Go for a walk around your hotel.
- Take a Circle Line tour of Manhattan (Pier 83, W 42nd St at 12th Ave)
- Lunch at Smith & Wollensky (797 Third Ave)
- Walk along Madison Avenue in the 60s and 70s, checking out all the big name boutiques.
- Take a walk through Central Park.
- Dinner at Trattoria Dell'Arte (900 Seventh Ave)

TUESDAY: Museum Mile
- Breakfast at Sarabeth's Kitchen (1295 Madison Ave)
- Cooper-Hewitt National Design Museum (2 E 91st St)
- Solomon R. Guggenheim Museum (1071 Fifth Ave)
- Lunch in the new cafeteria at the Metropolitan Museum of Art (Fifth Ave bet 80th and 84th St)
- Metropolitan Museum of Art (see above)
- Whitney Museum of American Art (945 Madison Ave)
- Frick Collection (1 E 70th St)
- Dinner at Tao (42 E 58th St)
- Take in "The New Class Clown" comedy show at Caroline's on Broadway (Broadway at 50th St).

WEDNESDAY: Midtown
- Stroll through Rockefeller Plaza (Fifth Ave bet 49th and 51st St).
- Stop by St. Patrick's Cathedral (Fifth Ave at 51st St).
- Shop at Saks Fifth Avenue (611 Fifth Ave).
- Lunch at the Brasserie (101 E 53rd St)
- Take the 12:30 tour of Grand Central Station offered by the Municipal Art Society.
- Visit the New York Public Library (Fifth Ave bet 40th and 42nd St).
- Museum of Modern Art (11 W 53rd St)
- Dinner at The Modern (in the Museum of Modern Art)

THURSDAY: Heading North
- Start the day with a nosh at Zabar's (2245 Broadway).
- Stop by the Cathedral Church of St. John the Divine (Amsterdam Ave at 112th St).
- Stock up on sweets at Mondel Chocolates (2913 Broadway).
- Lunch at Cafe Lalo (201 W 83rd St)
- Spend the afternoon at The Cloisters (Fort Tryon Park).
- Dinner at McCormick & Schmick's (1285 Ave of the Americas)
- Go see a Broadway show. Be sure to get tickets well in advance from Americana Tickets!

FRIDAY: Heading South
- Take the first ferry from Battery Park to the Statue of Liberty and Ellis Island.
- Walk up the Battery Park Esplanade.
- Late lunch at Spice Market (403 W 13th St)
- Stop by St. Paul's Chapel (211 Broadway).
- Take a peek at the lobby of the Woolworth Building (233 Broadway).
- Take a leisurely late-afternoon stroll on the Brooklyn Bridge.
- Dinner at River Cafe (1 Water St, Brooklyn)
- Go see a performance at Lincoln Center. Be sure to get tickets well in advance from Americana Tickets!

SATURDAY: Chelsea and Soho
- Visit ABC Carpet & Home (888 Broadway).
- Go gallery hoping on and around West 22nd Street in Chelsea.
- Have a late-morning brunch at Blue Ribbon (97 Sullivan St).
- Go gallery hopping and shopping on and around West Broadway in Soho.
- Dinner at Balthazar (80 Spring St)

- Take a late-evening elevator ride up to the observation deck of the Empire State Building (Fifth Ave bet 33rd and 34th St).

SUNDAY: Lower East Side
- Lunch at Katz's Delicatessen (205 E Houston St)
- Take the noon tour ("Getting By: Immigrants Weathering Hard Times") at the Lower East Side Tenement Museum (97 Orchard St).
- Take the 1 p.m. walking tour of the Lower East Side sponsored by the Lower East Side Tenement Museum (see above).
- Visit the remarkable Eldridge Street Synagogue (12 Eldridge St).
- Dinner in Chinatown at Golden Unicorn (18 East Broadway)

Information on all of the places I've included in these itineraries can be found in other sections of this book. Whatever else you do during your visit, I have two final pieces of advice:

- Get to know the subway system. It is generally safe, reliable, convenient, inexpensive (particularly if you get a seven-day pass), and by far the most efficient way to travel in New York. If you take cabs everywhere you go, you'll burn both money and time.
- Slow down and enjoy yourself. New Yorkers move very fast. It is fun to get into the flow of things, but it is also good to slow down and take a look around. Don't get so focused on your destination that you fail to enjoy the journey. It's a remarkable city! Enjoy!

Auction Houses

Whether you're in the market for rare antiques or just looking for a fun experience, New York's auction houses can be a real treat. Look in the Weekend section of the Friday *New York Times* or the Arts and Leisure section of the Sunday *Times* for advertisements about auctions and previews at the auction houses listed below and others. The classified section of the *New York Times* also has an auction section, and all of Manhattan's auction houses are listed in the Manhattan Yellow Pages under "Auctioneers."

Before you go, think carefully about what it is that you're doing. If you just want to learn a little about the art world, simply show up, hang back, and take it all in. If you're even remotely serious about making a purchase, make sure you know the rules of the game. I strongly advise you to take full advantage of auction previews by ordering an auction catalog or going online. Attend some of the lectures and courses offered at the auction houses listed below to learn about a particular period or medium.

Finally, a word of warning: the people attending most auctions in New York are professionals. They know what they are looking for and what they want to pay, and sometimes they know each other. Auctions in New York are a one-of-a-kind experience and can be lots of fun. Just don't go expecting to beat the professionals.

CHRISTIE'S
20 Rockefeller Plaza (49th St bet Fifth Ave and Ave of the Americas)
212/636-2000
www.christies.com

This British auction house specializes in fine arts and antiques. Upcoming auctions are often open to the public for preview. Call ahead for schedule details. **Hours:** Monday through Friday from 9:30 to 5:30.

SOTHEBY'S
1334 York Ave (at 72nd St)   212/606-7000, www.sothebys.com

Arguably the most elite auction house in the world, this British institution also specializes in fine art and antiques. Like Christie's, Sotheby's is open for auction previews.

Christie's and Sotheby's dominate the auction world, both in New York and around the globe. Other reputable houses in New York include **Doyle New York** (212/427-2730, www.doylenewyork.com), **Tepper Galleries** (212/677-5300, www.teppergalleries.com), **Swann Auction Galleries** (212/254-4710, www.swanngalleries.com), and **Guernsey's** (212/794-2280, www.guernseys.com).

Films

Like any city, New York has a multitude of theaters for first-run movies. Indeed, most movies debut in New York and Los Angeles before opening anywhere else. (Depending on the size of the crowds they draw, some never do open elsewhere.) *The New Yorker, Time Out New York, New York* magazine, and the *New York Times'* Friday Weekend section and its Sunday Arts and Leisure section are all good places to look for what is playing and where, at any given time. You can also call 212/777-FILM (3456) for information about what movies are showing at virtually every theater in Manhattan and to purchase tickets by credit card at many of those theaters. If you're online, go to www.moviephone.com or www.newyork.citysearch.com.

If you're looking for an old movie, a foreign film, an unusual documentary, a 3D movie, or something out of the ordinary, try calling one of the following theaters. Most numbers connect you with a recording that lists current movies and times, ticket cost, and directions.

American Museum of Natural History's IMAX Theater (175-208 Central Park West, 212/769-5034)
Angelika Film Center and Cafe (18 W Houston St, 212/995-2000)
Anthology Film Archives (32 Second Ave, 212/505-5181)
Asia Society (725 Park Ave, 212/327-9276)
Austrian Cultural Forum (11 E 52nd St, 212/319-5300)
Film Forum (209 W Houston St, 212/727-8110)
Florence Gould Hall at the French Institute (55 E 59th St, 212/355-6160)
Japan Society (333 E 47th St, 212/752-0824)
Lincoln Plaza Cinema (1886 Broadway, 212/757-2280)
Loews Lincoln Square Theater (890 Broadway, 212/336-5000)
Makor (25 W 67th St, 212/601-1000)
Millennium (66 E 4th St, 212/673-0090)
Museum of Television and Radio (25 W 52nd St, 212/621-6800)
Quad Cinema (34 W 13th St, 212/255-8800)
Symphony Space (2537 Broadway, 212/864-5400)
Walter Reade Theater at Lincoln Center (165 W 66th St, 212/875-5600)
Whitney Museum of American Art (945 Madison Ave, 212/570-3676)

Like everything else, the price of movie tickets in New York tends to be higher than elsewhere in the country. If you purchase tickets over the phone, thus incurring a per-ticket surcharge, you'll spend more than $20 for two adults! In fact, you can spend $20 for two tickets at some movie theaters even if you buy at the box office. The second-run theaters, film societies, and museums usually charge a little less than the first-run theaters, however. For free open-air movies in the summer, try Bryant Park, Seward Park, and other parks throughout the city.

Finally, New York is home to dozens of popular film festivals. Probably the best known is the Film Society of Lincoln Center's **New York Film Festival**, held in late September and early October. This annual event showcases 20 films and gets more popular every year. Call the Walter Reade Theater box office at 212/875-5600 for more information. Look in *New York* magazine, *Time Out New York*, *The New Yorker*, or any daily newspaper for information on upcoming films and festivals.

Photo Ops!
  Of course there are thousands of great backdrops in New York, but here are several enduring favorites:

- **LOVE block** (Ave of the Americas at 55th St)
- **Prometheus statue** (Fifth Ave bet 50th and 51st St)
- **Rockefeller Plaza ice rink** (off Fifth Ave, bet 49th and 50th St)
- **Statue of Liberty** (off Battery Park)
- **Wall Street bull** (Broadway at Bowling Green)
- **Washington Arch** (Washington Square Park, Greenwich Village)

Flea Markets

Craft and street fairs pop up all over New York on weekends in spring, summer, and fall. If you hear about or just stumble onto one, by all means do some browsing. Real New Yorkers go to these, so you'll get a very different sense of the city and the people who live here than you would walking around midtown on a weekday. You'll also find everything from woven baskets made by somebody's relatives in Nigeria to socks and underwear sold at steep discounts. You'll also find some great food. That said, however, many street fairs look alike, and some neighborhoods have grown weary of them. Moreover, I suggest watching your pockets in a crowd.

In addition to these craft and street fairs, New York also has several regularly scheduled flea markets, as well as Greenmarkets. (See the "Fruits, Vegetables" section of Chapter IV for more information on these wonderful markets.) Take cash, don't be embarrassed to haggle a bit, and look around before buying anything—sometimes you'll see the same item at more than one place. Collectors and treasure hunters often go at the beginning of the day, when selections are best, while bargain hunters usually wait until the end of the day, when dealers may lower prices. Remember there are no guarantees or refunds.

The flea markets in the following list all are relatively well-established, although I highly recommend checking out the websites to be sure of the hours before making a plan for the day.

Annex Antiques Fair and Flea Market—This is probably the most famous of New York's many flea markets. Stylists, celebrities, and just plain folk all mingle every weekend hoping to find treasure amidst lots of hand-me-downs, castoffs, and just plain junk. The flea market operates on Avenue of the

Americas between 25th and 26th streets every weekend from 9 to 5. Admission is $1. The Antiques Garage (right around the corner at 112 West 25th Street) is part of the same operation and is open weekends from 6:30 to 5. Go to www.annexantiques.com for more information.

GreenFlea—This nonprofit operation runs two flea markets that benefit public schools. The larger is on the Upper West Side at Public School 87 and Intermediate School 44, on Columbus Avenue between 76th and 77th streets. Held all year on Sundays, it is open 10 to 6 from April to October and till 5:30 the rest of the year. The other is located in the West Village at the intersection of Charles and Greenwich streets (between West 10th and 11th streets. It is open 11 to 7 in warmer months and closed in winter. Both have a farmers market, plenty of independent vendors, and a wonderful international flair. Go to www.greenfleamarkets.com for more information.

Hell's Kitchen Flea Market—Run by the same folks who oversee the nearby Annex Antiques Fair and Flea Market, this newcomer to the flea market scene is open Saturday and Sunday from 10 to 6. In addition to fresh fruit and vegetables and all sorts of vendors, you can find food and music. This operation is on West 39th Street between Ninth and Tenth avenues. Go to www. hellskitchenfleamarket.com for more information.

Public School 183 Flea Market—Open Saturdays from 9 to 5:30, this decidedly upscale flea market is known for antiques and jewelry, as well as a terrific Greenmarket. It's held at Public School 183, on 67th Street between First and York avenues.

Union Square Farmers Market—This is the grandfather of all Greenmarkets. Open for business on Wednesday, Friday, and Saturday at the north end of Union Square (17th Street between Broadway and Park Avenue South), this popular market offers all sorts of fresh goodies: seasonal produce, baked goods, jams, jellies, and flowers.

Galleries

When people think of art, they sometimes think only of museums. While the art museums in New York are exceptional, anybody interested in art ought to think about visiting some commercial galleries, too. Galleries are places where potential buyers and admirers alike can look at the work of contemporary and 20th-century artists (a few galleries specialize in older works) at their own pace and without charge. Let me stress "admirers alike." A lot of people are afraid to go into galleries because they think they'll be expected to buy something or be treated poorly if they don't know everything there is to know about art. That just isn't true, and an afternoon of gallery hopping can be fun.

First decide what kind of art you want to see. New York has long been considered the center of the contemporary art world, and it follows that the city is home to literally hundreds of galleries of all sizes and styles. In general, the more formal and conventional galleries are on or close to Madison Avenue on the Upper East Side and along 57th Street. (You'll need to look up to find a lot of them, particularly on 57th Street.) Some of the less formal, avant-garde galleries tend to be in Soho on West Broadway, between Broome and Houston streets; on Greene Street between Prince and Houston streets; and on Prince Street, between Greene Street and West Broadway. Some of the latter are also in Tribeca.

As a general rule, artists who have yet to be discovered go where the rents are lower, and then more established artists and galleries follow. In the last ten years, the west end of Chelsea, as well as the northwest corner of the West Village on 14th Street (also known as the Meatpacking District), and even the Lower East Side on and around Rivington Street have joined the list of gallery hot spots. Chelsea alone is home to almost 200 galleries!

If you want to experience the diversity of the New York gallery scene, sample a couple galleries in each neighborhood. The Art Dealers Association of America (212/940-8590, www.artdealers.org) is a terrific resource if you have particular artists or areas of interest in mind.

Galleries are typically known for the artists they showcase. If you are interested in the work of just one artist, both the *New Yorker* and *New York* magazine contain listings of gallery shows by artists' names. Be sure to look at the dates, as shows sometimes change quickly. *Time Out New York* has a list of galleries by neighborhood in its "Arts" section, complete with descriptions of current shows. The Friday and Sunday editions of the *New York Times* are also good resources.

Most galleries are open Tuesday through Saturday from 10 or 11 a.m. to 5 or 6 p.m. Some close for a few weeks in summer.

Museums

New York is home to some of the most famous, interesting, and unusual museums in the world. Even if you don't think of yourself as a "museum person," I urge you to take a look at the following pages. As with so many other things in New York, there's something here for almost everybody! With a few exceptions, I've limited the following list to museums in Manhattan, but that does not mean that museums in the other boroughs aren't worth exploring. The **New York Transit Museum** in Brooklyn (718/243-8601, www.meta.nyc.ny.us/museum) is a must-see for train and subway buffs, while the **Brooklyn Museum of Art** (718/638-5000, www.brooklynart.org) is among the nation's oldest and largest art museums, with one of the best Egyptian collections in the world. The **New York Hall of Science** in Queens (718/699-0005, www.nyhallsci.org), the **Museum of the Moving Image** in Queens (718/784-0077, www.ammi.org), and the **Bronx Zoo** (718/367-1010, www.bronxzoo.org), also have lots of fans. The **Liberty Science Center** (201/200-1000, www.lsc.org), just across the Hudson River in Jersey City, New Jersey, is quite popular as well.

I've also not given full write-ups of some of the smaller museum gallery spaces in Manhattan, either because of their size, the narrow focus of their exhibits, or their abbreviated hours. That does not mean, however, that you might not find them well worth a visit. They include:

Americas Society Gallery (680 Park Ave, 212/249-8950, www.americas-society.org)
Austrian Cultural Forum (11 E 52nd St, 212/319-5300, www.acfny.org)
Chelsea Art Museum (556 W 22nd St, 212/255-0719, www.chelseaart museum.org)
China Institute (125 E 65th St, 212/744-8181, www.chinainstitute.org)
Drawing Center (35 Wooster St, 212/219-2166, www.drawingcenter.org)

Equitable Gallery (787 Seventh Ave, 212/554-4818)
French Institute/Alliance Française (22 E 60th St, 212/355-6100, www.
fiaf.org)
Grolier Club (47 E 60th St, 212/838-6690, www.grolierclub.org)
Japan Society (333 E 47th St, 212/832-1155, www.japansociety.org)
Museum of American Illustration (128 E 63rd St, 212/838-2560, www.
societyillustrators.org)
Museum of Biblical Art (1865 Broadway, 212/408-1200, www.american
bible.org)
Museum at FIT (Seventh Ave at 27th St, 212/217-5800, www.fitnyc.suny.
edu)
New York Unearthed (17 State St, 212/748-8628, www.southstseaport.org/
archeology/nyunearthed)
Nicholas Roerich Museum (319 W 107th St, 212/864-7752, www.roerich.
org)
PaineWebber Gallery (1285 Ave of the Americas, 212/713-2885)
Rose Museum at Carnegie Hall (154 W 57th St, 212/247-7800, www.
carnegiehall.org)
Rubin Museum of Art (150 W 17th St, 212/620-5000, www.rmanyc.org)
Scandinavia House Galleries (58 Park Ave, 212/879-9779, www.scandi
naviahouse.org)
Tibet House (22 W 15th St, 212/870-0563, www.tibethouse.org)

As a general rule, I suggest calling ahead. Some of the smaller museums and galleries close for days or even weeks for exhibit installation, and hours sometimes change. If you want to find out about current ex-hibits, look in the front of the *New Yorker*, the back of *New York* magazine, the "Museums" section of *Time Out New York*, *Museums New York*, or *Where New York* magazine (distributed free in most Manhattan hotel rooms).

One more piece of advice: if you want to see a particularly popular ex-hibit, plan well in advance and consider buying tickets online, as you'll avoid long lines.

Turn Off That Phone!
  New York City law requires that cell phones be turned off in all museums, galleries, theaters, and concerts. The fine for an ill-timed ring from your purse or pocket is $50! Now if they would just extend the ban to include restaurants and public transportation. . . .

AMERICAN FOLK ART MUSEUM
43 W 53rd St (bet Fifth Ave and Ave of the Americas)   212/265-1040
www.folkartmuseum.org

Although the small gallery space across from Lincoln Center remains open, the stunning new eight-story home of the American Folk Art Museum puts most of the collection back in midtown (where it began) with the Museum of Arts and Design and the renovated and expanded Museum of Modern Art. The skinny building is itself a work of art, with various galleries on the top four floors, a skylight capping the building, and art integrated throughout its many interesting spaces. The permanent and changing exhibitions offer stunning examples of 18th- and 19th-century folk art, as well as the work of self-taught artists from the 20th and 21st centuries. The enormous painted copper St. Tammany Weathervane is a particular treat, as is the two-story box of carved duck decoys by the open staircase. **Hours:** Tuesday through Sunday from 10:30 to 5:30 (until 7:30 on Friday). **Admission:** $9 for adults, $7 for students and seniors, and free for children under 12 (free for everyone on Friday after 5:30 p.m.).

"Drachmas, Doubloons, and Dollars: The History of Money" is the **American Numismatic Society**'s permanent display, housed since 2001 in the **Federal Reserve Bank** (33 Liberty St, bet Nassau and William St). Those wanting to study coins of a particular period or region should call the society's main office in northern Manhattan (212/234-3130) to arrange a personal visit.

AMERICAN MUSEUM OF NATURAL HISTORY
Central Park West (bet 77th and 81st St)   212/769-5100
                                                           www.amnh.org

If ever there was a perfect answer for what to do with children on a rainy day, this sprawling collection of 30 million (yes, *million*!) artifacts and specimens is it. You could spend an entire day on any one of the museum's four floors. (The main entrance puts you on the second floor.) Obtain a floor plan at the information desk and decide what you want to see, especially if time is limited. I also advise taking advantage of the coat check and going during the week to avoid often overwhelming weekend crowds. Exhibits include dinosaur and fossil halls; the Oceans Hall, with a whale suspended from the ceiling; a hall devoted to African mammals, including elephants; a display allowing some hands-on exploration of the natural world in New York itself; gems and minerals (keep an eye out for the Star of India sapphire); the Hall of Biodiversity; and fascinating displays about cultures from all over the globe. Hayden Planetarium, Rose Center for Earth and Space, and the Millstein Hall of Ocean Life are among the new and updated parts of the museum.

Guided tours of the museum's highlights are scheduled frequently throughout the day. You'll find a decidedly downscale cafeteria and the more pleasant Garden Cafe on the lower level, and another cafe on the fourth floor. The refurbished park on the north side of the museum is a grand place for a picnic. Request information about the IMAX Theater (212/769-5034) at the information desk. It costs extra, but whatever is showing is bound to be excellent. **Hours:** Sunday through Thursday from 10 to 5:45 (Friday until 8:45). **Admission:** $13 for adults, $10 for students and senior citizens, and $7.50 for children between 2 and 12 is suggested. Package prices are available if you want to see an IMAX movie or the space show at the Rose Center.

ASIA SOCIETY
725 Park Ave (at 70th St)   212/288-6400, www.asiasociety.org

The Asia Society is a nonprofit organization founded in 1956 in order to foster mutual understanding between Asian nations and the United States. Housed in a renovated and expanded building on Park Avenue, the Asia Society is the leading institution in the United States dedicated to the cultures of Asia and the Pacific. The society mounts traditional and contemporary art exhibitions, performances, films, lectures, and conferences to highlight the diversity of this remarkable part of the world. Free daily tours of the exhibitions are given. The galleries are well designed, the atmosphere is peaceful, and there are lots of great spaces for sitting and contemplating. A wonderful gift shop sits to the left of the admissions desk. **Hours:** Tuesday through Sunday from 11 to 6 (Friday until 9). **Admission:** $10 for adults, $7 for students and senior citizens, $5 for students, and free for children under 16.

> For years the large gallery space on the first and ground floors of 580 Madison Avenue was home to the IBM Gallery and later the Freedom Forum's "Newseum." However, IBM closed its gallery and the Newseum moved to the Washington, DC area several years ago. Maybe the third time is the charm! **The Dahesh Museum of Art** (212/759-0606, www.daheshmuseum.org), which formerly occupied a tiny space on Fifth Avenue, is now housed at 580 Madison Avenue (at 57th St). Dedicated to showcasing work by academically trained European artists of the 19th and early 20th centuries, the museum is fast becoming a midtown favorite, as are its cafe and gift shop!

BARD GRADUATE CENTER FOR STUDIES IN THE DECORATIVE ARTS, DESIGN, AND CULTURE
18 W 86th St (bet Central Park W and Columbus Ave) 212/501-3000
www.bgc.bard.edu

Tucked in a largely residential neighborhood on the Upper West Side, the Bard Graduate Center devotes three floors of its elegant beaux-arts townhouse to changing exhibitions of decorative arts. As is the case in many smaller museums and galleries in New York, half the pleasure of visiting here is simply being inside the building itself. Call ahead to learn about tours and public lectures. **Hours:** Tuesday through Sunday from 11 to 5 (Thursday until 8). **Admission:** $3 for adults, $2 for students and senior citizens, free for children under 12 accompanied by an adult.

CHILDREN'S MUSEUM OF MANHATTAN
212 W 83rd St (bet Broadway and Amsterdam Ave)   212/721-1234
www.cmom.org

"CMOM," as the locals call it, has lots of buttons to push, ladders to climb, and things to sort, touch, and examine. There's an early childhood center and play space for children four and under, as well as imaginative exhibits and the "WordPlay" exploration space. Older kids will appreciate the computer lab where they can use the latest digital technology to create their own designs. You know you're headed for a child-friendly place when a ramp instead of stairs leads up to the front entrance, but strollers must be checked at the entrance and food is not allowed in the museum. **Hours:** Wednesday through Sunday from 10 to 5 (summer and holiday hours are often extended). The museum is open to members at other times as well. **Admission:** $8 for adults and children, $5 for senior citizens, free for children under one.

THE CLOISTERS
Fort Tryon Park (at Henry Hudson Parkway North)   212/923-3700
www.metmuseum.org

Perhaps the finest medieval art museum in the world, the Cloisters is also one of the quietest and most beautiful places in all of Manhattan. Built on land donated by John D. Rockefeller, Jr. in the late 1930s, the museum incorporates large sections of cloisters and other pieces of buildings brought to the United States from southern France by sculptor George Grey Barnard. His collection was purchased by the Metropolitan Museum of Art with money donated for that purpose by Rockefeller in 1925, making The Cloisters a branch of the Metropolitan. The truly spectacular collection also includes carved wood and ivory, tapestries, and sculptures. The museum is quiet, peaceful, and rarely crowded, and its outdoor terrace and medieval gardens offer a great view of the Hudson River and the Palisades. A cafe is open in warmer months. Though it takes about an hour each way, the M4 bus delivers you right to the front entrance from Madison Avenue in midtown and back again via Fifth Avenue (the A subway line to 190th Street takes half the time). **Hours:** Tuesday through Sunday from 9:30 to 5:15 (4:45 from November through February). **Admission:** $15 for adults, $10 for students, $7 for senior citizens, free for children under 12 when accompanied by an adult. The fee entitles you to same-day admission to the Metropolitan Museum of Art.

Where is **Dia: Chelsea**? Closed—for now. The popularity of this cutting-edge museum's galleries has continued to grow since their 1987 opening in what was then a largely forgotten part of the city—the far western edge of Chelsea. Dedicated to public programming and exhibits that focus on modern art and artists, Dia: Chelsea became an engine of change in what is now a thriving gallery scene. But the facilities simply couldn't keep up. As this book was being written, the Dia Art Foundation's permanent collection—some 700 works by artists who emerged in the second half of the 20th century—is housed in a former Nabisco box factory just up the Hudson River in Beacon, New York, while Dia: Chelsea is closed for renovations. A plan is underway to move the entire facility a couple blocks south to the western edge of the Gansevoort Meat Market. For more information about the Dia Art Foundation and the current status of the project, go to www. diacenter. org.

COOPER-HEWITT NATIONAL DESIGN MUSEUM/
SMITHSONIAN INSTITUTION
2 E 91st St (bet Fifth and Madison Ave)   212/849-8400
www.ndm.si.edu

Founded by three granddaughters of Peter Cooper (their last name was Hewitt) as the Cooper Union Museum for the Arts of Decoration just before the turn of the century, this exceptional museum became part of the Smithsonian Institution in 1967 and was moved into Andrew Carnegie's Fifth Avenue mansion in 1976. Drawing from a permanent collection of almost a quarter million pieces involving every imaginable aspect of design, the museum's exhibitions change frequently. Outstanding lectures, workshops, tours, and gallery talks are developed around the exhibitions. Of course, part of the pleasure of a visit to the Cooper-Hewitt is seeing the Carnegie Mansion itself, including the spectacular Great Hall and Carnegie's personal library (which now houses the gift shop). Take time to look around—and up! In the warmer months, visit the outside garden, behind the reception desk. An expansion may be in the works. **Hours:** Tuesday through Thursday from 10 to 5, Friday from 10 to 9, Saturday from 10 to 6, and Sunday from 12 to 6. **Admission:** $10 for adults, $7 for senior citizens and students over 12, free for children under 12 accompanied by an adult and for Smithsonian Associates.

DYCKMAN FARMHOUSE MUSEUM
4881 Broadway (at 204th St)   212/304-9422
                                                www.dyckmanfarmhouse.org

This is the last surviving example of the sort of farmhouse built all over New York well into the 19th century. It is a real treat for anybody interested in the city's history in the decades following the Revolutionary War. The Dyckman family emigrated from the Netherlands to what were then the American colonies in the 17th century and had a thriving orchard in this area before the Revolutionary War. They were forced to flee during the war, and both their home and orchard were occupied and ultimately destroyed by British troops. When they returned to the area in 1784, the Dyckmans built this remarkable example of a Dutch-American farmhouse and later used the surrounding area for grazing cattle on their way to market downtown. The adjoining outbuildings no longer exist, but the house itself has been preserved and indeed was recently renovated.

You can get to Dyckman House from midtown by taking the A subway line to 207th Street and walking south on Broadway to 204th Street. (It's actually only a block, as there are no 205th and 206th streets.) You can also get there by taking the M1 bus up Madison Avenue to 125th Street and transferring to the M100, which will drop you off at the front door. **Hours:** Wednesday through Sunday from 10 to 4. **Admission:** $1 for adults, free for children under 12.

EL MUSEO DEL BARRIO
1230 Fifth Ave (bet 104th and 105th St)   212/831-7272
                                                        www.elmuseo.org

El Museo del Barrio—Spanish for "Museum of the Neighborhood"—is the only museum in New York devoted to the art and culture of Puerto Rico and Latin America. Located at the southern end of Spanish Harlem and the northern tip of Museum Mile, El Museo occupies part of the old Heckscher Building. El Museo, a special place devoted to the people and cultures of the surrounding community, features exhibitions of contemporary and traditional art, and sponsors all sorts of festivals, lectures, workshops, and outreach programs. Plans for expansion are underway for this imaginative place. **Hours:** Wednesday through Sunday from 11 to 5. Call for extended summer hours from May through September. **Admission:** Suggested admission of $6 for adults, $4 for students with ID and senior citizens, and free for children under 12 (additional prices for certain events).

ELLIS ISLAND MUSEUM OF AMERICAN IMMIGRATION
Ellis Island   212/363-3206, www.ellisisland.com

When you think of immigration to the United States, Ellis Island instantly comes to mind. At least one in every four Americans today can trace one or more relatives who came through the immigration processing center on the island between 1892 and 1954. Whether or not you're one of them, this is a "must see" museum. Located in the shadow of the Statue of Liberty in New York Harbor, Ellis Island was all but abandoned until a major portion was restored and opened to the public in 1990 as a National Park. (The restoration of another 30 buildings, including a hospital complex, is underway.) Walk through the moving display of photographs and artifacts brought to this country by immigrants, and you'll inevitably come across someone telling his children or grandchildren about what his family brought when they came to this country. Other displays retrace the steps the immigrants took once they arrived on the island and discuss immigration in the U.S. through the present.

To get to Ellis Island, take the Circle Line ferry from Battery Park. The ticket booth is in Castle Clinton, and the ferry makes stops at both Ellis Island and the Statue of Liberty. The best time to go is early in the morning on a weekday, as lines can get pretty long in the afternoon and on weekends due to crowds and security screenings. (For information on ferry sailings, call 212/269-5755.) The least expensive and most efficient way to get to Battery Park is by taking the N/R subway line to Whitehall Station or the 4/5 to the Bowling Green stop. **Hours:** Daily from 9 to 5 (extended hours in summer), although the last ferry leaves earlier and those times are subject to change. The Museum and the Statue of Liberty are closed on July 4 and December 25. **Admission:** $10 for adults, $8 for senior citizens 62 and over, and $4 for children 4 to 12. Time permitting, admission to both Ellis Island and the Statue of Liberty is included in the price of a ferry ticket. Headset rental for the audio tour is an additional $6 per person.

FORBES MAGAZINE GALLERIES
62 Fifth Ave (bet 12th and 13th St)   212/206-5548
www.forbesgalleries.com

Given the appeal of *The Antiques Roadshow* on PBS, it's amazing there aren't lines out the door of this Greenwich Village gem every day! More than 10,000 toy soldiers and other figurines, 500 toy boats and submarines, a tremendous collection of Monopoly games from as early as 1920, and 400 items from the House of Fabergé (including nine eggs) are among the treasures on display in these small but beautiful galleries. Everything on display was collected by the late Malcolm Forbes and his sons. It's worth noting that strollers are prohibited, children under 16 are not allowed without an adult, and no more than four children can accompany each adult. **Hours:** Tuesday, Wednesday, Friday, and Saturday from 10 to 4. (Call ahead for a reservation to join one of the guided tours offered on Thursday or to make sure the museum hasn't closed for a private luncheon or tour.) **Admission:** free.

FRAUNCES TAVERN MUSEUM
54 Pearl St (at Broad St)   212/425-1778
www.frauncestavernmuseum.org

If you're interested in Colonial and early U.S. history and culture, you'll really enjoy this often overlooked museum. The site of General George Washington's farewell address to his officers in 1783 and an anti-British meeting place before and during the Revolutionary War (it was built in 1719 as a private home), this tavern has seen many generations and much history come and go through its doors. The latest renovation brought a new restaurant downstairs, but upstairs you'll still find period rooms (including the room in which General Washington gave his historic address) with changing exhibitions on all sorts of topics in early American history and culture. Make sure to ask about movies, lunchtime and evening lectures, walking tours, and family craft projects on certain Saturdays. **Hours:** Tuesday through Friday from 12 to 5, Saturday from 10 to 5. **Admission:** $4 for adults, $3 for children and senior citizens, and free for children under 6.

FRICK COLLECTION
1 E 70th St (bet Fifth and Madison Ave)   212/288-0700
                                                            www.frick.org

This exceptionally elegant and peaceful mansion displays the late Henry Clay Frick's collection of paintings, sculpture, rugs, furniture, porcelain, and other artwork. Take time to wander around and look at the building itself —the moldings, the floors, the ceilings, the light fixtures, and the stairs—as well as the art. Built in 1914, this is one of the last great mansions on Fifth Avenue. Unlike the guards at a lot of other museums, those who work here are very knowledgeable and obviously proud of the building and the collection. Because the museum's temperature is kept at a constant 70 degrees, you'll be glad they require that all coats be checked (at no charge). Although this is not a place to take children (those under ten are not allowed), this beautiful and uncrowded museum is a real treat for art buffs and oglers alike. A free audio tour of the permanent collection is available in six languages, and a 22-minute slide presentation about the collection runs throughout the day. **Hours:** Tuesday through Saturday from 10 to 6, Sunday from 1 to 6. **Admission:** $12 for adults, $8 for senior citizens 62 and over, and $5 for students with ID.

HISPANIC SOCIETY OF AMERICA
Audubon Terrace (Broadway bet 155th and 156th St)   212/926-2234
                                                     www.hispanicsociety.org

Founded as a public museum and research library in 1904, this little-known place is home to a diverse and impressive collection of art and artifacts from the Iberian Peninsula (Spain and Portugal), as well as Latin America and the Philippines. The building—located directly across from the dramatic El Cid statue in the middle of Audubon Terrace—is beautiful, and the collection itself is astonishing. You'll find seals from the Roman Empire, a 15th-century silver processional cross from Barcelona, and paintings by such masters as Goya, Velázquez, and El Greco. Make sure to look at the beautiful tiles and mosaics in the walls on your way up the stairs between floors. You can take the M4 bus up Madison Avenue or the M5 bus up Avenue of the Americas to the museum and then take either back to Fifth Avenue in midtown. You can also take the 1 subway line from the West Side to 157th Street. **Hours:** The museum and library are open Tuesday through Saturday from 10 to 4:30. The museum is also open on Sunday from 1 to 4. The library is closed in August. **Admission:** free.

INTERNATIONAL CENTER OF PHOTOGRAPHY
1133 Ave of the Americas (at 43rd St)   212/857-0000, www.icp.org

If you're interested in photography, put the International Center of Photography (ICP) gallery at the top of your list of places to visit. Devoted to displaying photography as both art and historical record, this gallery has changing exhibits of work by photographers from all over the world, as well as photographs drawn from the center's permanent collection. Is is also a school and a center for working photographers. Complete with a cafe downstairs, this is a pleasant, unhurried spot to spend an afternoon without leaving midtown. **Hours:** Daily from 10 to 6 (Friday till 8). **Admission:** $10 for adults, $7 for students and senior citizens, $1 for children under 12, and "pay what you wish" for everyone on Friday evening from 5 to 8.

INTREPID SEA-AIR-SPACE MUSEUM
Pier 86 (46th St at Hudson River)   212/245-0072
                                                           www.intrepidmuseum.org

Though the water in the Hudson River is not particularly inviting and getting over here can seem like a big production, the trip is well worth the effort if you're interested in aircraft carriers, submarines, space exploration, and the like. The centerpiece is the giant *U.S.S. Intrepid,* an aircraft carrier that served in both World War II and the Vietnam War. The *U.S.S. Edison* (a destroyer used in Vietnam) and the *U.S.S. Growler* (a guided-missile submarine) are also stationed here. You can either take a self-guided audio tour or wander around by yourself, although the *Growler* and parts of the *Edison* are open only for scheduled guided tours. Galleries, display halls, video screens, and theaters are scattered throughout the complex. Kids will particularly like the two flight simulators (available for a hefty extra charge) in the back of the *Intrepid* and in the planes up on the deck.

You won't have much trouble finding the museum, as the *Intrepid* dominates this part of the river. The ticket booth and gift store are inside the main entrance and past the tanks, as is a McDonald's. The best way to get to the museum from midtown is via the M42 bus on 42nd Street (make sure it says "Piers" on the front). Stay aboard when it turns south on Eleventh Avenue, as it will then loop back around. **Hours:** Monday through Friday from 10 to 5, weekends (and most holidays) from 10 to 6. The ticket booth closes an hour before the museum. **Admission:** $16.50 for adults; $12.50 for veterans, reservists, and college students, students between 6 and 17 with ID cards, and senior citizens; $4.50 for children between 2 and 5. Disabled patrons are admitted for half price, and active-duty military personnel are admitted free of charge.

JEWISH MUSEUM
1109 Fifth Ave (at 92nd St)   212/423-3200
                                                          www.thejewishmuseum.org

Operated by the Jewish Theological Seminary of America and housed in yet another elegant Fifth Avenue mansion (donated by Felix Warburg's widow in 1947), the Jewish Museum displays the largest collection of Jewish art and Judaica in the United States. Some of the museum's collection was rescued from European synagogues and Jewish communities before World War II, and all of it is extremely well displayed. Renovated and expanded a decade ago, the museum has a large permanent exhibit tracing the Jewish experience —called "Culture and Continuity: The Jewish Journey"—on the third and fourth floors, as well as a variety of changing exhibits. A plaster sculpture by George Segal commemorating the Holocaust is a particularly moving part of the exhibit. It is tucked in a corner at the end and ought not be missed. Families will want to visit the children's gallery and ask about special family programs and workshops. Cafe Weissman, in the museum's basement, is a pleasant place for a light lunch or snack. **Hours:** Sunday through Wednesday from 11 to 5:45, Thursday from 11 to 8, and Friday from 11 to 3. The museum is closed on major Jewish holidays. **Admission:** $10 for adults, $7.50 for students and senior citizens, free for children under 12, and "pay what you wish" for everyone between 5 and 8 on Thursday evening. You can get a $2 discount on your admission if you present a recent ticket stub from the Museum of Jewish Heritage.

LOWER EAST SIDE TENEMENT MUSEUM
90 Orchard St (at Broome St)   212/431-0233, www.tenement.org

Founded in 1988, this unique museum is making an enormous contribution to the preservation of American social history and the urban immigrant experience. In the visitors center are permanent and changing exhibits, including a fabulous effort to give voice to the contemporary immigrant experience, as well as a theater. The centerpiece of this museum, however, is the tenement building. Home to as many as 7,000 people from more than 20 nations between 1863 and 1935, the tenement has had five of its apartments restored to different periods in their history. Together, these apartments offer a glimpse of what life was like in one of these incredibly crowded places—and what it *is* like for hundreds of thousands who still live this way today.

The museum's educators—who lead the various tenement tours Tuesday through Saturday all year long and on Mondays during the summer—are enormously well informed and dedicated. The Confino Program, a living-history tour in which families can interact with an actress portraying a resident of the Confino apartment, is also offered on Saturday and Sunday on the hour from noon to 3. Reservations are strongly encouraged (and are, in fact, required in advance for groups of ten or more). **Hours:** Monday from 11 to 5:30, Tuesday through Friday from 11 to 6, and weekends from 10:45 to 6. **Admission:** $13 for adults, $11 for senior citizens and students, and free for children under five. That fee includes admission to an audiovisual history of the site and a tour of the tenement building. Admission to the Confino Program is $12 for adults and $10 for students and senior citizens. Educational walking tours are offered on weekends for an additional charge.

MERCHANT'S HOUSE MUSEUM
20 E 4th St (bet Bowery and Lafayette St)   212/777-1089
www.merchantshouse.com

Home to a hardware merchant and his family for 100 years, this 1832 rowhouse now offers visitors a glimpse of life in an age when Greenwich Village was considered the suburbs. The house is filled with the family's original possessions and all the latest "modern" equipment of the period, including pipes for gas lighting. It is the only family home in New York City to survive intact, both inside and out, from the 1830s. The great effort and dedication of staff and volunteers has made that preservation possible, and those of us interested in the history of this grand city ought to be deeply grateful. A self-guided tour begins inside the front door, while docent-led tours are available Saturday and Sunday afternoons. **Hours:** Thursday through Monday from 12 to 5. **Admission:** $8 for adults, $5 for students and senior citizens, and free for children under 12. Monies go to support the building's ongoing restoration.

METROPOLITAN MUSEUM OF ART
Fifth Ave (bet 80th and 84th St)   212/535-7710
www.metmuseum.org

"The Met," as it is known to New Yorkers (not to be confused with the Metropolitan Opera), is one of those places you can visit a hundred times and never see the same thing twice. It is also one of the finest museums in the world. Whether you're interested in Egyptian tombs, Greek and Roman sculpture, paintings by the great Renaissance masters, African masks, Chinese and Asian art, Tiffany windows, or arms and armor from the Crusades, the depth and breadth of the Met's collections will take your breath away. Start by picking up a floor plan at one of the information desks in the main hall and mapping out your visit. Be sure to ask about the museum's half-dozen restaurants, bars, and cafes, including the redesigned cafeteria. Although the Met often has extremely popular special exhibits, I sometimes head for places with fewer people in order to wander and gaze at my own pace. If you want to avoid the crowds (almost 5 million people come through every year), the best time to visit is on weekday mornings. (It gets so crowded on Sundays that strollers are banned, as they are during special exhibitions.) Self-guided audio tours in English and other languages are available for an extra charge.

The Met also sponsors films, lectures, gallery talks, concerts, and other special programs. Pick up a seasonal program at one of the museum's information desks or visit the museum's website. If you come to New York frequently and like to visit the Met and its gift shops, consider becoming a National Associate. For a small annual fee, people who live outside a 200-mile radius of New York City can get free admission to both the Met and The Cloisters, a 10% discount at the Met's many gift shops, seasonal schedules, and a subscription to the museum's magazine. **Hours:** Sunday, Tuesday, Wednesday, and Thursday from 9:30 to 5:30; Friday and Saturday from 9:30 to 9 (and some holiday Mondays). **Admission:** $15 for adults, $10 for senior citizens, $7 for students, and free for children under 12 when accompanied by an adult. The fee entitles you to same-day admission to The Cloisters.

What Happened to the Morgan Library?
   One of my favorite little-known New York treasures—the library built by J. Pierpont Morgan (29 E 36th St, 212/685-0610, www.morgan library.org) to house his personal collection of art, manuscripts, books, and furniture— closed in 2003 for a major renovation and expansion. It is scheduled to open again in early 2006.

MORRIS-JUMEL MANSION
65 Jumel Terrace (at 160th St, east of St. Nicholas Ave) 212/923-8008
www.morrisjumel.org

Built in 1765 as a summer house for British Colonel Roger Morris and his wife, this graceful Palladian-style country house sits atop a hill overlooking the East River. It briefly served as General George Washington's headquarters in 1776 and later was home to Madame Eliza Jumel and her second husband, Aaron Burr. (Rumor has it that Madame Jumel's ghost has been spotted yelling at neighborhood children to be quiet from the second-floor balcony!) Throughout the house you'll find exceptional period furniture, including a 19th-century French mahogany directoire sleigh bed said to have belonged to Napoleon Bonaparte when he was First Consul of France. The surrounding neighborhood has definitely seen better days, but the mansion itself has been renovated. The grounds are particularly attractive in the spring and early summer. Take the M2 bus up Madison Avenue to the front of the mansion on Edgecombe Avenue, or take the A or C subway line to 163rd Street. **Hours:** Wednesday through Sunday from 10 to 4 (Monday and Tuesday by apointment only). **Admission:** $3 for adults, $2 for senior citizens over 60 and students with ID, free for children under 12 when accompanied by an adult.

MOUNT VERNON HOTEL MUSEUM & GARDEN
421 E 61st St (bet First and York Ave)   212/838-6878
www.mvhm.org

Known for years as the Abigail Adams Smith Museum, this terrific little time capsule—run by the Colonial Dames of America—will transport you back to the days when midtown Manhattan was a country escape for New Yorkers living at the southern end of the island. Constructed in 1799 as a carriage house and converted into the Mount Vernon Hotel in 1826, this museum shows what life in the building and in the city was like circa 1830. The staff and volunteer docents are enthusiastic and knowledgeable, and someone is always available to answer questions and point out interesting features of the hotel. If you're interested in social history or antiques, put this well-run and interesting museum at the top of your itinerary. **Hours:** Tuesday through Sunday from 11 to 4 (Tuesday evenings in June and July until 9). The museum is closed in August. **Admission:** $5 for adults, $4 for senior citizens and students, free for children under 12.

While the Museum of Modern Art got all the publicity for its temporary relocation and renovation, another Manhattan-based museum also made a move to Queens. The **Museum for African Art** (718/784-7700, www.africanart.org)—the only independent museum dedicated exclusively to the rich and diverse art of the African continent—has pulled up stakes at its Soho location and is now at 36-01 43rd Avenue in Long Island City. This is a real gem! If you go, be sure to check out the museum's gift shop and weekend programs.

MUSEUM OF AMERICAN FINANCIAL HISTORY
28 Broadway (bet Morris St and Battery Pl)   212/908-4110
www.financialhistory.org

Now affiliated with the Smithsonian Institution, this often overlooked museum offers visitors insight into the financial history of our country. Appropriately housed in the basement of the former site of John D. Rockefeller's Standard Oil Company headquarters (and Alexander Hamilton's law offices before that), it is not exactly a kid-friendly place. But if you're interested in the way our economy works, the Museum of American Financial History is a great place to start your tour around Wall Street. A real highlight: a working ticker-tape machine will actually spit your name out at the end of your visit. Be sure to check out the unusually well-conceived gift shop. **Hours:** Tuesday through Saturday from 10 to 4 (closed on national and stock market holidays). **Admission:** $2.

MUSEUM OF ARTS AND DESIGN
40 W 53rd St (bet Fifth Ave and Ave of the Americas)   212/956-3535
www.americancraftmuseum.org

This is an exciting, vibrant place with a new name—it was formerly the American Craft Museum—and big plans for a new location as well (at a redesigned 2 Columbus Circle in 2007). Dedicated to what its director calls "celebrating materials and creative processes," the museum showcases the work of established and emerging designers and artists. In addition to various changing exhibitions, the museum offers numerous hands-on workshops, public programs, and family classes for members and non-members alike. The store adjacent to the entrance has a marvelous selection of unusual items from contemporary American artists. **Hours:** Daily from 10 to 6 (Thursday until 8). **Admission:** $9 for adults, $6 for students and senior citizens, free for children under 12, and pay-as-you-wish on Thursday evening from 6 to 8.

Oregon Connections
Many New Yorkers likely couldn't place my home state of Oregon on a map, but like every other state in the nation, Oregon has made numerous contributions to this great city. Legendary chef James Beard had Oregon roots and brought our Pacific seafood to many of his menus. The 10,000-year-old Willamette meteor—on display in the Hall of the Universe at the Rose Center for Earth and Space—came from Oregon and remains sacred to the Confederated Tribes of the Grande Ronde. An Oregon architect—Brad Cloepfil, of Allied Works Architecture in Portland—is working on the redesign of the Huntington Hartford Building on Columbus Circle as a new home for the Museum of Arts and Design.

MUSEUM OF CHINESE IN THE AMERICAS
70 Mulberry St (at Bayard St), 2nd floor   212/619-4785
www.moca-nyc.org

Designed in the shape of a 15-sided traditional Chinese lantern, this is the first museum in the Western Hemisphere dedicated to preserving and interpreting the history and culture of Chinese immigrants and their descendants. Its stated mission is to reclaim, preserve, and broaden the understanding of the incredibly diverse story of Chinese people in the Americas. The museum's fascinating permanent exhibit—"Where Is Home? Chinese in the Americas"—combines the extraordinary with the ordinary to give visitors a glimpse into that story. If you're visiting Chinatown, this museum will offer some perspective on the world bustling around you on the streets below. **Hours:** Tuesday through Thursday and Saturday from 12 to 6, and Friday from 12 to 7. **Admission:** $3 for adults, $1 for senior citizens and students, and free for children under 12. Admission is free on Friday.

MUSEUM OF THE CITY OF NEW YORK
1220 Fifth Ave (bet 103rd and 104th St)   212/534-1672
www.mcny.org

Often overlooked by tourists and New Yorkers alike, this treasure is dedicated to the history of the city from the earliest European settlement through the present. Permanent exhibits include period rooms, an exquisite silver collection, toys and dollhouses, a firefighting gallery, an enormous number of model ships, and an exhibit on Broadway. The actual bedroom and dressing rooms from the home of John D. Rockefeller, Sr., on the museum's fifth floor, are truly breathtaking sights for anyone who likes antiques. (The sitting room is at the Brooklyn Museum.) Changing exhibits cover everything from the history of theater in New York to the city's many ethnic groups. The museum also offers an exceptionally diverse array of walking tours, children's programs, lectures, classes, and other events. Call the number listed above for more information, or pick up a seasonal schedule at the information desk right inside the entrance. **Hours:** Tuesday through Sunday from 10 to 5 (and some holiday Mondays). **Admission:** Suggested contributions of $7 for adults, $5 for senior citizens, students, and children, and $15 for families are strongly encouraged.

MUSEUM OF JEWISH HERITAGE: A LIVING MEMORIAL TO THE HOLOCAUST
36 Battery Place (just north of Battery Park)   646/437-4200
www.mjhnyc.org

A relative newcomer to the New York museum scene, this exceptional place fills a real void in the city. In addition to being a museum—and, when a $60 million expansion is completed, a classroom and theater space—it is also a memorial to Holocaust victims and survivors. New York is, after all, the heart of Jewish history and culture in the United States, and it is fitting that such a thoughtfully conceived and carefully constructed museum has its home here. The museum is composed of three parts, one on each floor. The first floor is dedicated to Jewish life a century ago, the second to the persecution of Jews and the Holocaust, and the third to modern Jewish life and renewal. The use of first-person narrative and testimonials is exceptionally moving and thought-provoking. Because of the sobering subject matter, this may not be a place for young children, and visitors should be prepared to take their time.

Two additional notes: the view of New York Harbor, Ellis Island, and the Statue of Liberty from the museum's third floor is extraordinary, and a visit to the gift shop is worthwhile. Security is very tight, and the rule against food in the galleries is strictly enforced. The museum was designed in the shape of a hexagon to memorialize the six-pointed Star of David and commemorate the 6 million Jews killed in the Holocaust. You'll recognize it immediately from its shape and the black gate surrounding the site, adjacent to Robert Wagner, Jr. Park at the southern end of Battery Park City. **Hours:** Sunday through Wednesday from 10 to 5, Thursday from 10 to 8, and Friday from 9 to 3 (till 5 during Daylight Savings Time). The museum closes early on the eve of Jewish holidays and is closed on all major Jewish holidays. **Admission:** $10 for adults, $7 for senior citizens, $5 for students, and free for children under 12 when accompanied by an adult. Advance tickets can be purchased by calling 646/427-4202.

MUSEUM OF MODERN ART
11 W 53rd St (bet Fifth Ave and Ave of the Americas)
212/708-9400, www.moma.org

It's back! The world's greatest collection of modern art and design finally moved back into its expanded and redesigned midtown home in late 2004.

Take a deep breath—the exorbitant admission price ($20 for adults!) is hard to take, but the gallery space has doubled, the architecture soars, and the art is every bit as fabulous as it ever was. Such masters as Matisse, Cezanne, Mondrian, and Picasso are all here, along with hundreds of other artists who defined the 20th century. Allow the better part of a day and definitely have lunch or dinner in one of the terrific new MoMA restaurants and cafes. **Hours:** Saturday through Monday, Wednesday, and Thursday from 10:30 to 5:30, Friday from 10:30 to 8. **Admission:** $20 for adults, $16 for senior citizens 65 and over with identification, $12 for full-time students with identification, and free for children under 16 when accompanied by an adult. The museum is also free on Fridays from 4 to 8, although limited tickets for free admission are available only on a first-come, first-serve basis at that time.

There is no way else to say it: admission fees to museums and other attractions in New York have gone sky high! If you are looking for a deal, consider buying a **CityPass**. For significantly less than the combined price of admission to each of the six places, you can purchase a pass good for one adult admission to the American Museum of Natural History, the Guggenheim Museum, the Museum of Modern Art, the Intrepid Air-Sea-Space Museum, the Circle Line sightseeing tour, and the Empire State Building. Not only will you save money, but you'll also bypass ticket lines. A CityPass for children is a particularly good deal. If you're interested, go to www.citypass.com or visit the ticket desk at any of the participating institutions.

THE MUSEUM OF SEX
233 Fifth Ave (at 27th St)   866/667-3969

I agonized about whether to include this recent arrival in the otherwise dignified list of museums in this chapter, particularly because it is among the most expensive museums in Manhattan. The entire affair (excuse the pun) is a bit tawdry, and the museum seems to exist on a shoestring. But crowds are streaming to the place, and its first exhibit at least tried to take itself seriously. So if you aren't shy about what really can only be described as at least softcore pornography, you may want to visit this two-floor museum just south of midtown. The free audiophone is worth using. Be forewarned that nobody under 18 is allowed in the museum. **Hours:** Monday, Tuesday, Thursday, and Friday from 11 to 6:30, Saturday from 10 to 9, and Sunday from 10 to 6:30. **Admission:** $17 for adults, $14 for students and seniors, and $12 for everyone on weekdays before 2.

MUSEUM OF TELEVISION AND RADIO
25 W 52nd St (bet Fifth Ave and Ave of the Americas)   212/621-6800
www.mtr.org

Television fans of all ages will definitely not want to miss this terrific place. Several galleries display changing exhibits on every imaginable aspect of television and radio, but the real reason to come is to watch a favorite television show. The museum's extensive collection includes 110,000 radio and television programs and advertisements, many of which are periodically screened for the public and all of which are available for individual viewing.

Indeed, the museum's computerized catalog makes more than six decades of radio and television shows immediately accessible. Give the museum a call to find out what's going on or stop by the front desk to reserve your own screening. I suggest going on a weekday, as the museum gets crowded on weekends. **Hours:** Tuesday through Sunday from 12 to 6 (Thursday until 8). The theater stays open on Friday until 9. **Admission:** $10 for adults, $8 for students with ID and senior citizens, and $5 for children under 14.

NATIONAL ACADEMY OF DESIGN
1083 Fifth Ave (bet 89th and 90th St)   212/369-4880
www.nationalacademy.org

Founded in 1825, this museum, fine arts school, and artists association was modeled after the Royal Academy in London. In addition to workshops and classes for artists, the National Academy of Design has changing exhibits of American and European paintings and other art. During the academy's "annual exhibition," some pieces are actually put up for sale. The museum occupies a surprisingly large townhouse, and wandering its three floors of galleries is a real pleasure. Winslow Homer, Thomas Eakins, and John Singer Sargent are just a few artists who have been members of the academy and whose work is part of its permanent collection. Docent-led tours are offered on Friday at 2. For information about the school itself, call 212/996-1908. **Hours:** Wednesday and Thursday from 12 to 5, Friday through Sunday from 11 to 6. **Admission:** $10 for adults and $5 for students, children under 16, and senior citizens.

The *New* New Museum

The **New Museum of Contemporary Art** (212/219-1222, www.new museum.org)—a showcase for contemporary artists and cutting-edge art —is in the midst of building a 60,000-square-foot exhibition space at 235 Bowery. While construction is going on, the museum has moved to a temporary space in the **Chelsea Art Museum** (556 W 22nd St).

NATIONAL MUSEUM OF THE AMERICAN INDIAN
1 Bowling Green (at the foot of Broadway)   212/514-3700
www.nmai.si.edu

Opened in 1994, the George Gustav Heye Center at the southern tip of Manhattan is home to one of the three branches of the National Museum of the American Indian that replaced the old Museum of the American Indian on Audubon Terrace. (The crown jewel of this trio opened on the National Mall in Washington, D.C., in 2004.) The changing exhibits are consistently well conceived and interesting. The spectacular building—the former Customs House—is worth visiting in and of itself. Take time to look up at the intricate detail in the ceilings, especially in the rotunda and library, and make sure to go down the exquisite (if a bit worn) staircase. Also be sure to visit at least one of the museum's two gift shops. **Hours:** Daily (except Christmas) from 10 to 5 (Thursday until 8). **Admission:** free.

NEUE GALERIE
1048 Fifth Ave (at 86th St)   212/628-6200
www.neuegalerie.org

It isn't every day that a museum opens along Fifth Avenue's Museum Mile, but then Ronald Lauder—the man responsible for bringing this boutique museum to life—isn't your ordinary art collector. Lauder is the former U.S. Ambassador to Austria and current chairman of Estee Lauder International. He and the late Serge Sabarsky—a longtime New York art dealer and namesake of the museum's popular Viennese cafe—shared a love of early 20th-century German and Austrian art and design. The museum is a reflection of that love, showcasing fine and decorative works in its two floors of gallery space. As with many museums in this part of New York, one of the pleasures of a visit is the turn-of-the-century mansion in which it is housed. Note that the museum is closed Tuesday through Thursday, although the cafe and shops are open. **Hours:** Friday from 11 to 9, Saturday through Monday from 11 to 6. **Admission:** $10 for adults and $7 for students and seniors. Children under 16 must be accompanied by an adult, and children under 12 are not admitted.

NEW YORK CITY FIRE MUSEUM
278 Spring St (bet Hudson and Varick St)   212/691-1303
www.nycfiremuseum.org

This museum, located in a turn-of-the-century firehouse, is dedicated to the history of firefighting and fire prevention. In addition to a relatively modern fire engine, a quite old ladder truck, a hand-pulled hand pump from 1820, and many other fire apparatuses, the museum displays pictures from fire stations all over New York, a collection of 19th-century leather fire buckets, and an assortment of badges. The darkest hour in the New York City Fire Department's history—the terrorist attacks of September 11, 2001—is remembered with an exhibition and a memorial to those brave fallen heroes who saved so many lives on that dreadful day. Older kids will love looking at the equipment, and most things are quite well displayed. Although the museum hopes to create a climbing and "hands on" exploring space for younger children in the future, "hands off" is the rule now. The museum is a bit out of the way, although less so since Soho has become a major tourist destination. Call ahead to make sure your visit won't coincide with that of a large school group. **Hours:** Tuesday through Saturday from 10 to 5, Sunday from 10 to 4. **Admission:** Suggested contribution of $5 for adults, $2 for students and senior citizens, and $1 for children under 12.

NEW YORK CITY POLICE MUSEUM
100 Old Slip (bet Water and State St)   212/480-3100
www.nycpolicemuseum.org

Almost a century ago, this beautiful building just off the East River was built for the New York City Police Department's 1st Precinct. Now, three decades after the precinct moved out from under a cloud of scandal, the NYPD has come back home with this excellent museum. Permanent exhibits include century-old mug shots, notorious criminals and the tools of their trade, police vehicles and uniforms, and a tribute to every NYPD officer killed in the line of duty throughout the city's history, including those who perished on September 11, 2001. Regular Saturday programs allow children to meet and interact with police officers and various NYPD units. The Firearms Training Simulator on the top floor allows visitors to test their judgment and response time in life-and-death situations through an interactive exhibit also used to train NYPD officers. And don't miss everyone's favorite photo op: the jail cell, complete with bunks and a latrine. The museum's bi-level gift shop, located on the east end of the first floor, is the only source in New York for officially licensed NYPD merchandise. **Hours:** Tuesday through Saturday from 10 to 5, Sunday from 11 to 5. **Admission:** A donation is suggested.

> The **New York Transit Museum** (718/243-8601, www.meta.info/mta/museum) has a small gallery and shop tucked behind the Grand Staircase in the Shuttle Passage of Grand Central Station. If you're a subway or train buff, a trip here can be great fun. It's open on weekdays from 8 to 8 and on weekends from 10 to 4. If that piques your interest, hop on a 2, 3, 4, or 5 subway line to Borough Hall Station in Brooklyn and visit the main museum (corner of Boerum Place and Schermerhorn Street, Brooklyn, 718/694-1600).

NEW-YORK HISTORICAL SOCIETY
2 W 77th St (at Central Park West)   212/873-3400
www.nyhistory.org

For two centuries, the New-York Historical Society has been what the *New York Times* once described as "New York City's archive and attic." The grand old institution is a real treasure trove, with more than half a million books; 2 million maps, manuscripts, and other documents; thousands of pieces of art; and John James Audubon's watercolor "Birds of America" series. While I'm a big fan of the Museum of the City of New York and encourage anyone interested in the city's history to spend time there, the New-York Historical Society also has tremendously deep archives and mounts a wide array of interesting exhibits in its grand space. Luman Reed's Picture Gallery (complete with Thomas Cole's *The Course of the Empire* and many of Audubon's works) and the library (open to those 18 and older) are great treats, as are the jam-packed display cases in the remarkable Henry Luce III Center for the Study of American Culture on the museum's fourth floor. **Hours:** Tuesday through Sunday from 10 to 6 (the library is open on those days from 10 to 5 but closed on Sunday). **Admission:** Suggested donation of $10 for adults and $5 for senior citizens, teachers, and students. Children under 12 are free when accompanied by an adult.

SOLOMON R. GUGGENHEIM MUSEUM
1071 Fifth Ave (bet 88th and 89th St)   212/423-3500
www.guggenheim.org

Housed in an enormous white spiral designed by Frank Lloyd Wright, the Solomon R. Guggenheim Museum is as famous for its building as for its collection. That is saying a lot, given a collection of 20th-century art that is arguably the best in the world. Chagall, Miro, Calder, Kandinsky, Picasso, and Gauguin are just a few of the artists whose work you'll encounter. Special exhibits featuring world-renowned collections and artists are mounted regularly, and gallery talks and other special events are held here. **Hours:**

Saturday through Wednesday from 10 to 5:45, Friday from 10 to 8. **Admission:** $15 for adults and $10 for senior citizens over 65 and students with ID. Children under 12 are admitted free but must be accompanied by an adult.

SOUTH STREET SEAPORT MUSEUM
209 Water St (at east end of Fulton St)   212/748-8600
                                                    www.southstseaport.org

This is both a traditional museum and a destination with a collection of exhibits, ships, stores, and restaurants spread throughout 11 square blocks of what was once the city's bustling port and economic center. You can walk around the South Street Seaport complex and look at everything from a distance without paying a dime, but admission to the museum includes the four-masted *Peking,* a light ship called the *Ambrose,* a tall ship called the *Wavertree* (accessible by tour only), several galleries with changing exhibitions, and a printer's shop. These places are worth the price of admission, particularly since your money supports educational outreach, historical research and preservation, urban archaeological programs, and programs for people with special needs. Stop by the visitors center at 12 Fulton Street or the ticket booth on Pier 16 to get a map and more information. On any given day (particularly in the warmer months), you'll find all sorts of special tours and activities throughout this fascinating complex. **Hours:** Daily from 10 to 5 (Thursday until 8) between April and October; Friday through Sunday from 10 to 5 between November and March. Restaurants and some stores stay open longer in summer. **Admission:** $8 for adults, $6 for senior citizens and students with identification, $4 for children 5 to 12, and free for children 4 and under.

Think of New York, and one of the first images that comes to mind is the skyline with its many skyscrapers. New York doesn't have the tallest building anymore. It may not even have the most tall buildings of any city. But this is where skyscrapers were born, and it's only fitting that the city is home to a museum dedicated to the subject. The **Skyscraper Museum** (212/945-6324, www.skyscraper.org) has bounced around several times since its inception in 1996, but rather ironically it now has a permanent home on the *ground floor* of the building that houses the Ritz-Carlton New York, Battery Park Hotel (2 West Street), across the street from the Museum of Jewish Heritage.

STUDIO MUSEUM IN HARLEM
144 W 125th St (bet Malcolm X and Adam Clayton Powell, Jr. Blvd)
                        212/864-4500, www.studiomuseuminharlem.org

This light and modern space is a real jewel. The name reflects its original mission to be a studio for working artists. It has evolved into a premier museum of visual art, exhibiting the work of local, national, and international artists of African descent. Renovations and expansions have made the museum's presence in the heart of Harlem even stronger. The museum mounts exhibits from its permanent collection and hosts traveling ones. It also offers lectures, gallery talks, performances, and other interpretive programs throughout the year. To get here from midtown, take the M101 bus up Third Avenue to the corner of the 125th Street and Malcolm X Boulevard. To return, board the M101 bus downtown from the opposite corner. You can also take a number of subway lines to the 125th Street stop and walk to the museum. **Hours:** Sunday and Wednesday through Friday from 12 to 6, Saturday from 10 to 6. **Admission:** Suggested donation of $7 for adults, $3 for students and senior citizens with identification, and free to children under 12 (free to everyone on the first Saturday of every month).

> **The Ukrainian Museum** (222 E 6th St, 212/228-0110, www. ukrainianmuseum.org), home to a popular exhibit of richly decorated Ukrainian eggs ("pysanka") each spring, has moved! Its expanded galleries (and a new Ukrainian cultural center) are a couple blocks down from the original spot in the East Village.

THEODORE ROOSEVELT BIRTHPLACE
28 E 20th St (bet Broadway and Park Ave)   212/260-1616
www.nps.gov/thrb

Tucked on a side street in a neighborhood often overlooked by New Yorkers and visitors alike (although the street was once among the city's most elegant), this wonderful brownstone is a reconstruction of Theodore Roosevelt's childhood home. The original building was torn down in 1916 but rebuilt by the president's sisters and wife using original blueprints and the house next door as a model. The rooms were then furnished and decorated largely as they had been in Teddy's childhood. Operated as a National Historic Site, the home is entered through the servants' entrance on the ground floor. Visitors browse a collection of pictures, clothing, and other items that belonged to the Roosevelt family in a wonderful wood-paneled room, then are taken through the living quarters on the second and third floors by a National Park Service guide. If you're interested in presidential history and the late 19th and early 20th centuries, or if you want to see how the wealthy lived in the 1850s and 1860s, put this museum on your itinerary. **Hours:** Tuesday through Saturday from 9 to 5 (tours begin on the hour until 4); closed on federal holidays. **Admission:** Tours cost $3 for adults and senior citizens, and are free for children 16 and under.

WHITNEY MUSEUM OF AMERICAN ART
945 Madison Ave (at 75th St)   212/570-3676, www.whitney.org

This museum has a decidedly modern focus, and its biennial exhibition is an eagerly awaited showcase for contemporary artists. However, the Whitney's collection also includes works by American artists from throughout this country's history. Several exhibits run concurrently, some focusing on a single artist and others built around a theme. If you're interested in gallery talks, special events, or what's on display at any given time, pick up a *This Week at the Whitney* schedule outside the museum's main entrance or drop by the information desk inside the front door. Also look here for some innovative family programs. A branch of Sarabeth's Kitchen, long a popular East Side restaurant, is located on the museum's lower level. If you want a brief retreat from the crowd, cool your heels on one of the comfortable benches in the museum's stairwells. **Hours:** Wednesday, Thursday, Saturday, and Sunday from 11 to 6, Friday from 1 to 9. **Admission:** $12 for adults, $9.50 for students with ID and senior citizens over 62, free for children under 12, and free for everybody on Friday evening from 6 to 9.

The small **Whitney Gallery and Sculpture Court at Altria** is located in the lobby of 120 Park Avenue, directly across 42nd Street from Grand Central Station. The gallery is open weekdays from 11 to 6 (until 7:30 on Thursday), and admission is free. The sculpture court, which doubles as a pleasant sitting area, is open Monday through Saturday from 7:30 a.m. to 9:30 p.m., Sunday from 11 to 7. Call 917/663-2453 for more information.

New, newer, newest!

Grand Central Station, Hayden Planetarium and the Millstein Hall of Ocean Life at the American Museum of Natural History, the Statue of Liberty, the Museum of Jewish History, and the Museum of Modern Art are just a few places around town that have had dramatic facelifts in recent years. And it seems that the work has just begun! The Museum of Arts and Design and the New Museum of Contemporary Art will soon have new homes; the remodeled Morgan Library will open shortly; and expansion plans are in the works at the Cooper-Hewitt and Lincoln Center. What an exciting time!

YESHIVA UNIVERSITY MUSEUM
15 W 16th St (bet Fifth Ave and Ave of the Americas)   212/294-8330
www.yumuseum.org

The Yeshiva University Museum has moved from the far reaches of Manhattan to the Center for Jewish History, just north of Greenwich Village. It houses an exceptional collection of paintings, books, religious artifacts, and other items related to Jewish life and culture. The museum mounts changing exhibitions in this beautiful and peaceful space. Look for special holiday events and workshops for adults, children, and families, as well as guided tours and gallery talks. **Hours:** Sunday, Tuesday, Wednesday and Thursday from 11 to 5. The museum is closed on major Jewish holidays. **Admission:** $6 for adults, $4 for children and senior citizens, and free for children under 5.

Places of Worship

Manhattan is home to some of the oldest, largest, and most famous churches and synagogues in the United States. These places, many of which are Episcopal churches—a relic of the city's life under British colonial rule—are integral to the social and architectural history of the city. Many of them allow people to come in and look around. (Remember that you are in a place of worship and always behave respectfully.) Here are some of my favorites.

ABYSSINIAN BAPTIST CHURCH
132 W 138th St (bet Frederick Douglass and   212/862-7474
Adam Clayton Powell, Jr. Blvd)   www.abyssinian.org

This church is one of the oldest in Harlem, and is home to one of the city's largest congregations. It was made famous by the late Adam Clayton Powell, Jr., its longtime minister and a U.S. congressman.

CATHEDRAL CHURCH OF ST. JOHN THE DIVINE
1047 Amsterdam Ave (at 112th St)   212/316-7540
www.stjohndivine.org

This magnificent Episcopal cathedral has been under construction for more than a century and will be among the largest Christian houses of worship in the world when (and if) it is completed sometime in this new century. The stonework, art, and stained glass are exceptional, as is the combination of Gothic, Romanesque, and Byzantine architectural styles. Even if you are not particularly interested in cathedrals, architecture, or religion, this somewhat out-of-the-way marvel is a must-see. To give you some sense of its scale, the Statue of Liberty could fit comfortably inside the main sanctuary. The rose window over the entrance is 40 feet in diameter!

CATHEDRAL OF THE HOLY TRINITY
319 E 74th St (bet First and Second Ave)   212/288-3215
www.thecathedral.goarch.org

This brick Greek Orthodox cathedral may not look so magnificent from the outside, but you'll think you're in ancient Greece once inside the lovely wooden doors.

CENTRAL SYNAGOGUE
Lexington Ave at 55th St   212/838-5122
www.centralsynagogue.org

This Reform synagogue is the oldest continuously used synagogue in the city. Completed in 1872, it was designed by Henry Fernbach and is a rare example of early Victorian religious architecture. The beautiful Moorish Revival exterior, complete with magnificent carved wooden doors and jaw-dropping tile work, is well worth a look. A fire in 1998 did extensive damage, but the congregation wasted no time rebuilding this gem while adding one of the city's most impressive organs.

CHURCH OF THE HOLY TRINITY
316 E 88th St (bet First and Second Ave)   212/289-4100
www.holytrinity-nyc.org

Near Gracie Mansion, this Episcopal church is a French Gothic marvel that dates back a hundred years. It's a favorite of classical music lovers because of its frequent winter concerts.

CHURCH OF THE TRANSFIGURATION
1 E 29th St (bet Fifth and Madison Ave)   212/684-6770
www.littlechurch.org

Known as "the little church around the corner," this Episcopal church is renowned for its marvelous programs of the music of Vivaldi and other composers. You'll find a lovely garden in front of this low-lying brick church and beautiful stained-glass windows inside.

FIRST PRESBYTERIAN CHURCH
12 W 12th St (at Fifth Ave)   212/675-6150, www.fpcnyc.org

A direct descendant of the first Presbyterian congregation in the United States, this church was built in 1846. (The original was on Wall Street.) The sanctuary has wooden pews with doors, a beautifully carved wooden pulpit that towers over the congregation, and a glorious blue rose window.

GRACE CHURCH
802 Broadway (bet 10th and 11st St)   212/254-2000
www.gracechurch.org

Built in 1846, this exquisite Episcopal church is one of several in New York designed by James Renwick, Jr. It is an elegant presence in the neighborhood and one of the most important examples of early Gothic Revival architecture in the country. The church is known for its daily prayer services, carved pulpit, and outstanding music.

God Meets Technology

Almost all houses of worship now have web pages. If you want to find out when services are held, what activities are going on at various churches, synagogues, and temples, or a little something about the history of these congregations, then spend a bit of time checking out their websites. Of course, you can also do it the old-fashioned way: the Manhattan Yellow Pages have extensive listings under the headings "Churches," "Synagogues," and "Religious Organizations." The Saturday *New York Times* also has advertisements for Catholic, Protestant, Ethical Culture, Unitarian, Universalist, Hindu, and Jewish services.

ISLAMIC CULTURAL CENTER OF NEW YORK
1711 Third Ave (bet 96th and 97th St)   212/722-5234

Opened in 1991, this sleek mosque and its grounds are hard to miss. The mosque dominates the skyline here. A gift to New York's Muslim community from several Islamic countries, it was built at an angle to face Mecca.

MARBLE COLLEGIATE CHURCH
1 W 29th St (at Fifth Avenue)   212/686-2770
www.collegiatechurch.org

This stately church was designed by Samuel Warner in 1854 and made famous by Dr. Norman Vincent Peale. It is an example of Early Romanesque Revival, and it draws its name from the Tuckahoe marble used in its construction. Its congregation is large and socially active.

RIVERSIDE CHURCH
490 Riverside Dr (bet 120th and 122nd St)   212/870-6700
www.theriversidechurchny.org

A gift of John D. Rockefeller, Jr., this interdenominational church was inspired by the famous Chartres Cathedral in France and can seat up to 2,500 people. Its 22-story bell tower dominates the northern end of Morningside Heights, and the 74-bell carillon can be heard throughout the area. From long before the civil rights movement and the Vietnam War up to the present, this church has been a center of social activism.

ST. BARTHOLOMEW'S CHURCH
109 E 50th St (at Park Ave)   212/378-0200, www.stbarts.org

Complete with a carved triple-arched portico (designed by architect

Stanford White) and a mosaic dome, this brick and stone Episcopal church is a midtown landmark. St. Bart's has a reasonably priced cafe (212/888-2664, www.cafestbarts.com) making it a great place to take a break from the crowds right in the middle of midtown.

ST. MARK'S IN THE BOWERY
131 E 10th St (at Second Ave)   212/674-6377

Constructed on the site of Peter Stuyvesant's personal chapel in 1799, this understated but elegant Episcopal church has lovely yards on either side. It is now the East Village but was once Stuyvesant's farm (or *bouwerie*, the Dutch word for farm).

ST. PATRICK'S CATHEDRAL
460 Fifth Ave (bet 50th and 51st St)   212/753-2261
www.ny-archdiocese.org

Designed by James Renwick, Jr., more than a century ago, this astonishing building is the largest Roman Catholic church in the United States and seat of the archdiocese of New York. The main organ has 9,000 pipes! The cathedral's steps along Fifth Avenue are a great place to rest your feet and watch the world go by.

St. Paul's Chapel was a gathering place for thousands fleeing the destruction of the World Trade Center on September 11, 2001, and a safe haven for rescue and clean-up workers. Today, in many ways, it is a living memorial to victims and survivors. An exhibit inside the church, "Unwavering Spirit: Hope and Healing at Ground Zero," offers glimpses into the physical and psychological devastation of that terrible day and those that followed. The exhibit is open Monday through Saturday from 10 to 6 and on Sunday from 9 to 4. Admission is free.

ST. PAUL'S CHAPEL
209 Broadway (bet Fulton and Vesey St)   212/602-0874
www.saintpaulschapel.org

As the dates on the gravestones in the surrounding cemetery might suggest, this Episcopal parish is housed in the oldest church building in the city. Its construction began in 1764 when New York was New Amsterdam. Though the interior may initially strike visitors as surprisingly plain, it is exceptionally elegant, understated, and lit by Waterford crystal chandeliers. Look for George Washington's pew in the north aisle. (He worshiped here on Inauguration Day 1789.)

ST. PETER'S LUTHERAN CHURCH
619 Lexington Ave (at 54th St)   212/935-2200, www.saintpeters.org

The only really modern church on this list, St. Peter's is nestled under the towering Citicorp Center. The church has an extensive program of jazz, opera, and other music on Sunday and during the week.

ST. THOMAS EPISCOPAL CHURCH
1-3 W 53rd St (at Fifth Ave)   212/757-7013
                                                www.saintthomaschurch.org

This beautiful church is best known for its magnificent music programs. The heart of these is the St. Thomas Choristers, who attend the country's only residential all-boy chorister school. They perform at many of the church's services. The incredibly ornate stone carvings on the church's exterior and its lovely doors and stately bell tower make it a real presence on Fifth Avenue.

SPANISH AND PORTUGUESE SYNAGOGUE
8 W 70th St (at Central Park W)   212/873-0300
                                                   www.shearith-israel.org

Home of the Orthodox Congregation Shearith Israel, founded in 1654 by descendants of Jews who fled the Spanish Inquisition, this synagogue was built in 1897. It contains remnants from its congregation's original synagogue, built on the Lower East Side in 1730. The Tiffany stained-glass windows are particularly impressive.

TEMPLE EMANU-EL
1 E 65th Street (at Fifth Ave)   212/744-1400, www.emanuelnyc.org

Built in 1929 and capable of seating 2,500 people, this is the largest Reform synagogue in the world. Stained-glass windows and mosaics grace the interior, and the limestone facade is a beautifully carved combination of Eastern and Western architectural styles. While the entrance is on 65th Street, be sure to look at the doors on Fifth Avenue.

TRINITY CHURCH
78-79 Broadway (at Wall St)   212/602-0800
                                                  www.trinitywallstreet.org

In the heart of the Financial District, this is the third Episcopal church to occupy a site on land donated by King William III of England in 1698. This building was completed in 1846, although the oldest headstones in its 2.5-acre graveyard date back to 1681. Alexander Hamilton is among the many historic figures buried here. Believe it or not, Trinity Church was the tallest building in Manhattan for much of the 19th century. The church offers a small museum, guided tours, and concerts, in addition to daily services.

Legend has it that Peter Minuit paid $24 in trinkets to purchase the island of Manhattan from Leni Lenape Indians at Bowling Green.

Sights and Other Places Worth a Look

Some of the places that make New York unique don't fit neatly into "Museums," "Places of Worship," or any of the other categories included in this book. Many can be visited without a guide or a formal agenda—indeed, simply walking around and gazing is pleasurable. A diverse lot, the following list includes some of the most famous, interesting, and unusual sights and places in Manhattan. Unless otherwise noted, admission is free.

AFRICAN BURIAL GROUND
Foley Square Park (bet Duane and Elk St, just north of City Hall)
www.africanburialground.com

A four-story black granite sculpture marks this otherwise unremarkable spot where the remains of several hundred black New Yorkers from the 18th century were unearthed in 1991. This out-of-the-way cemetery was long forgotten until backhoes dug it up while doing renovations in Lower Manhattan. A bronze medallion inscribed with the words of Maya Angelou's "Still I Rise" is on the ground. An interpretive center adjacent to the site is planned by the National Park Service.

Columbus Circle Gets a Facelift!
    It wasn't so long ago that Columbus Circle, at the southwest corner of Central Park, was a dreary collection of underused and unattractive buildings like the old coliseum on the west side and the odd Huntington Hartford building on the east side. With the opening of the Time Warner Center in 2004, however, all that has changed. A seven-level luxury mall—"The Shops at Columbus Circle"—is anchored by a 58,000-square-foot **Whole Foods Market**. Columbus Circle also boasts a 20,000-square-foot **Williams-Sonoma Grande Cuisine** store and demonstration kitchen, a huge new **Borders** bookstore, the new home for **Jazz at Lincoln Center**, and the luxury **Mandarin Oriental New York**.

ALWYN COURT APARTMENTS
180 W 58th St (at Seventh Ave)

Of all the magnificent apartment buildings in New York, this is my favorite to look at from outside. Built between 1907 and 1909 and recently renovated, it's a block north of Carnegie Hall. You could spend hours studying the elaborate carved terra cotta exterior. Its features include a crowned salamander—the symbol of Renaissance art patron Frances I, in whose style Alwyn Court was built. For the best view, cross the street.

BROOKLYN BRIDGE
East River (east of City Hall)

Spanning the East River between Manhattan and Brooklyn, this was the world's longest suspension bridge when built, and it remains one of the most spectacular. The 5,989-foot bridge took 15 years (1868–1883) and two generations of Roeblings to construct. After John Roebling, the engineer who designed the bridge, died from injuries sustained in an accident, his son Washington and wife Emily finished the project. To reach the bridge's bustling and historic promenade, go to the east side of the park (surrounding City Hall) and follow the bike signs. It's a surprisingly long walk—more than a mile from end to end—and a pretty noisy one too, but the views are well worth the effort. A word of caution: Stay in the pedestrian lane and watch out for bicycle riders zooming by!

CASTLE CLINTON NATIONAL MONUMENT
Battery Park (southern tip of Manhattan)   www.nps.gov/cac

Probably the best known of Manhattan's seven National Parks—it's the gateway to two others and headquarters for them all—Castle Clinton is a red circular building in Battery Park. It was built on what was once an island as part of a series of forts designed to defend New York Harbor at the beginning of the 19th century. Castle Clinton has been different things through the years: an entertainment center, an immigrant receiving station (8 million came through between 1855 and 1890), and home to the New York Aquarium. Today, Castle Clinton is where you buy tickets for the short boat rides to Ellis Island and the Statue of Liberty. It's worth taking a few minutes to visit the small museum detailing the site's history inside the door to your right. **Hours:** daily from 8:30 to 5.

The More Things Change . . .
The last peep shows have moved out of Times Square and even the seafood merchants are moving out of the old Fulton Fish Market, but some things in New York haven't changed. If it's nostalgia you want, try the **Waldorf-Astoria Hotel** (301 Park Ave), the overpriced **21 Club** (21 W 52nd St), or the **Grand Central Oyster Bar Restaurant**, inside Grand Central Station. You might also check out some of the old-time shops on the Lower East Side, like **Katz's Delicatessen** (205 E Houston St).

CENTRAL PARK ZOO
Fifth Ave at 64th St (behind The Arsenal)
212/439-9500, www.centralparkzoo.com

When people in New York hear the word *zoo*, they tend to think of the big one in the Bronx. But this animal-friendly replacement for the dilapidated zoo that was here for many years is well worth a visit. Divided by climate into three sections, this well-designed zoo includes an indoor rain forest, an outdoor temperate zone, and an indoor "Edge of the Icepack" exhibit. You'll find everything from a bat cave and a colony of leaf-cutter ants to Japanese snow monkeys and chinstrap penguins. There are even a couple of polar bears! **Tisch Children's Zoo**, located just north of the main zoo, has lots of spaces for preschoolers to climb and explore. It sponsors classes, workshops, and other events for children and families on weekends and in warmer months. A visit on a winter weekday can be enjoyable, too. The gift shop is nothing special, but the hot-dog and-French-fries crowd will love the small cafe. **Hours:** Weekdays from 10 to 5, weekends from 10 to 5:30 (daily 10 to 4:30 from November through March). The last tickets are sold half an hour before closing. **Admission:** $6 for adults, $1.25 for senior citizens, $1 for children between 3 and 12, free for children under 3. Children under 16 must be accompanied by an adult.

CHELSEA MARKET
75 Ninth Ave (bet 15th and 16th St)   www.chelsea.market.com

The huge brick building in this long-maligned section of Manhattan once housed the original Oreo cookie factory. It's now home to one of the city's most fashionable and popular shopping destinations. It isn't shoes or silks or antiques folks get in line for down here but food: fresh vegetables, soups, breads—you name it and you'll find it here. Look for kitchen stores, wine, and other shops as well, along with the offices of companies like NY1 News, Major League Baseball Productions, and Oxygen Media. And thanks to the purchase of more real estate across the street, the already enormous Chelsea Market is expanding. **Hours:** Weekdays from 8 to 8, weekends from 10 to 8.

> When you're standing in City Hall Park, look north to the **Municipal Building**. The five towers represent the five boroughs, but one is much higher than the others and is plated in gold. Guess which borough it represents! (Hint: You're standing in it.)

CHELSEA PIERS
Along the Hudson River (bet 17th and 23rd St)   212/336-6000
www.chelseapiers.com

When built at the beginning of the 20th century, Piers 59, 60, 61, and 62 on the Hudson River in Chelsea quickly became the destination for such elegant passenger ships as the *Lusitania and* the *Ile de France*. Indeed, the *Titanic* was headed for the Chelsea Piers when she sank in 1912. But when the length of ships increased in the 1930s and 1940s, new piers were built near 44th Street and those in Chelsea were largely abandoned. Thanks to a visionary developer, the Chelsea Piers have sprung back to life. The Chelsea Piers Sports & Entertainment Complex encompasses 1.7 million square feet of golf (yes, there's a year-round outdoor driving range in Manhattan!); ice skating, rollerblading and roller-skating rinks; batting cages; rock climbing; gymnastics; and other activities. There's more: restaurants, a 1.2-mile esplanade, a maritime center, and Silver Screen Studios (home to NBC's *Law and Order*).

> Here's a history test: Where was the nation's first capital? No, it wasn't Washington, D.C. or even Philadelphia. It was New York City! The building that once housed the entire federal government, now known as the **Federal Hall National Memorial** (212/825-6990, www.nps. gov/feha) closed in late 2004 for extensive renovations. At the intersection of Wall and Nassau streets, this remarkable landmark is scheduled to reopen in early 2006.

CHRYSLER BUILDING
405 Lexington Ave (bet 42nd and 43rd St)

One of New York's most recognizable sights, this art deco building housed the Chrysler Corporation at the dawn of the automobile age. Its stainless-steel spire is easy to spot, but take a closer look at the radiator-cap gargoyles (based on the then-current 1929 Chrysler) and the racing cars built into the relief. The Chrysler Corporation no longer maintains offices here and the interior isn't particularly interesting, but the lobby is open to the public.

CITY HALL PARK
City Hall (bet Broadway and Park Row)

Not so many years ago, a trip down to this area was to be avoided. Not anymore! City Hall has been beautifully renovated and the park surrounding is absolutely magnificent. In this spot where General George Washington once encamped his troops, you can sit on comfortable benches, stroll through gardens, and admire the wonderful fountain, which was brought back to this site after an 80-year stint in Crotona Park in Brooklyn.

CONSERVATORY GARDEN
Central Park (off Fifth Ave at 105th St)

www.centralpark.org

In warmer months, this elegant and peaceful spot is alive with color—and, since it's a popular site for wedding pictures, with wedding parties as well. The fountains, benches, and entrance gates once were part of Cornelius Vanderbilt's Fifth Avenue mansion. On Saturdays at 11 a.m. in spring, summer, and early fall, the Central Park Conservancy offers tours of the garden.

If you're a garden lover and are willing to venture out of the more traveled parts of Manhattan or even into the other boroughs, try these gems:

- **Brooklyn Botanical Gardens**: 1000 Washington Avenue, Brooklyn (718/623-7200, www.bbg.org)
- **Heather Garden**: Fort Tryon Park at Fort Washington Avenue in northern Manhattan (www.nycgovparks.org)
- **New York Botanical Garden**: Bronx River Parkway at Fordham Road, The Bronx (718/817-8700, www.nybg.org)
- **Wave Hill**: 675 W 252nd Street, The Bronx (718/549-3200, www.wavehill.org)

CUNARD BUILDING
25 Broadway (at Bowling Green)

Now serving as the Bowling Green branch of the U.S. Post Office, this often overlooked building near the foot of Broadway was the longtime home of the Cunard Steamship Line. Although the Cunard building was not erected until 1921, the Cunard Line is perhaps best known for its steamship *Lusitania*, which was sunk by a German U-boat off the coast of Ireland in 1915. Stand across the street and look for the triads and nautilus in the relief and for Poseidon himself over the door.

ELDRIDGE STREET SYNAGOGUE
12 Eldridge St (bet Canal and Division St)   212/219-0888
www.eldridgestreet.org

New York is full of time capsules, but this one, in what was once the largely Jewish Lower East Side and is now the edge of Chinatown, must be seen to be believed. This magnificently elaborate synagogue was home to more than a thousand worshipers at the turn of the 19th century. Although the orthodox Congregation K'hal Adath Jeshurun hasn't missed a Sabbath since the synagogue opened in 1887, its numbers steadily shrank in the middle of last century, and the building fell into such disrepair that pigeons were living in the sanctuary. Thanks to a few visionary and committed people, the synagogue has been saved, and a capital campaign is well on its way. **Hours:** Drop-in tours are given on Sunday on the hour from 11 to 3 and on Tuesday and Thursday at 11:30 and 2:30. **Admission:** $5 for adults, $3 for students, senior citizens, and children. All money goes to the synagogue's restoration.

EMPIRE STATE BUILDING
350 Fifth Ave (bet 33rd and 34th St)   212/736-3100
www.esbnyc.org

When people think of New York, this 102-story building is often the first image that comes to mind. Conceived as a great office building but almost bankrupted when it opened in 1931 because of the Great Depression, the Empire State Building soars above its neighbors just south of midtown. The neighborhood and the building itself are a bit grimy these days, and most of the staff are alternately bored or rude. However, this New York landmark draws almost 3 million visitors a year, and the views from the top live up to every expectation (assuming it's a relatively clear day or night). **Hours:** Daily from 9:30 to midnight (the last elevators go up at 11:15 p.m.). **Admission:** Tickets to the terrace and observation deck cost $13 for adults; $12 for those between 12 and 17, senior citizens, and active-duty military personnel with identification; and $8 for children between 6 and 11. Children 5 and under and active-duty military personnel in uniform are free.

FLATIRON BUILDING
175 Fifth Ave (bet 22nd and 23rd St)

This 22-story architectural oddity has been anchoring this intersection for a century. The prow of the building is said to sit on the windiest street corner in Manhattan. Its triangular shape and terra-cotta exterior have made it a familiar landmark, and the thriving neighborhood around it is known as the Flatiron District.

GRAND CENTRAL STATION
42nd St (bet Vanderbilt and Lexington Ave)
www.grandcentralterminal.com

This stunningly beautiful *beaux-arts* station was built at the turn of the 19th century during the great age of railroads. It replaced a station built by Cornelius Vanderbilt after steam engines were banned south of 42nd Street in 1854. Scores of commuter trains to Westchester County and Connecticut arrive and depart here. But the real reason for visitors to see Grand Central Station is the incredible cleaning and renovation it received in the 1990s. To say that the project was long overdue is an understatement—the ceiling hadn't been cleaned since 1944! And the results are amazing. Retail space has doubled. More recent arrivals like **Michael Jordan's the Steak House NYC** (yes, *that* Michael Jordan) and **Cipriani Dolci** have joined famous eateries like the **Grand Central Oyster Bar Restaurant**. Wine, lingerie, music, toy, and other great shops line the Lexington Avenue Passageway and other spots throughout this grand place. **Grand Central Books** is one of my favorites. **Grand Central Market,** on the Lexington Avenue side of the station, just south of the main lobby, is a destination in itself for those interested in fresh fruit, bread, seafood, meat, and the like. You'll even find New York's best food court (including a Two Boots pizza outlet), as well as clean, safe public bathrooms downstairs and a small **Transit Museum** gallery and gift shop behind the west stairs.

Purists need not fear: Grand Central does not feel like a giant shopping mall. With its breathtaking ceiling, chandeliers, and carved marble details, this is first and foremost an elegant peephole into New York's past, present, and future. The Municipal Art Society offers a fascinating free tour of the station at 12:30 on Wednesdays. (See the "Tours" section of this chapter for more information.) The most dramatic entrance to Grand Central Station is through the driveway off Vanderbilt Avenue (a small street just east of Madison Avenue) at 43rd Street. Incidentally, the original waiting room off Park Avenue has been cleaned and renovated, too, and is well worth a visit. While you're at it, spend a couple minutes at the Whisper Gallery outside the Oyster Bar. Stand in opposite corners facing the wall and try to hear each other whisper! **Hours:** The terminal itself is open daily from 5:30 a.m. to 1:30 a.m. **Grand Central Market** is open from 7 a.m. to 9 p.m. on weekdays, 10 to 7 on Saturday, and 11 to 6 on Sunday. Store and restaurant hours vary.

How many Yankees caps can we lose?

The lost-and-found department at Grand Central Station receives an average of 4,000 items every day. Laptop computers, cell phones, glasses, keys, and suit jackets turn up by the hundreds. Among the more unusual items in recent years: a movie script with the director's notes, an urn with human ashes, and Pete Seeger's banjo.

GRANT'S TOMB
Riverside Park (Riverside Dr at 122nd St)   212/666-1640
www.nps.gov/gegr

If you're an American history buff, you'll want to venture to the far reaches of the Upper West Side to visit the General Grant National Memorial—the not-so-subtle final resting place of President (and General) Ulysses S. Grant and his wife, Julia. When you're up at this lonely place—inspired by Napoleon's tomb in Paris and run today by the National Park Service—it's hard to imagine that a quarter million people filed through City Hall during the 48 hours Grant lay in state and that a million more lined Broadway to watch his coffin being transported. **Hours:** Daily from 9 to 5.

GROUND ZERO
Between Church, West, Liberty, and Vesey St

Ground Zero. Just the words evoke graphic pictures in our collective memory—painful and unshakable memories of the terrorist attacks on the World Trade Center on September 11, 2001. This is the place where 26,000 people a day rode the elevators to the observation deck on the 104th floor of Tower 2, where tens of thousands of people came to work in a 16-square-acre office complex with the world's tallest "twin" towers. Today, even as work begins on the memorial and other buildings that will fill this area in the future, there is still little but the retaining wall that continues to hold back the Hudson River and empty space—lots and lots of very empty space where thousands of men and women from 115 nations lost their lives and fires burned for three months.

If you want to visit Ground Zero, the first thing you should know is that there isn't much to see. A thousand people working 24 hours a day for months on end removed 1.8 million tons of debris, and now "the bathtub" at the World Trade Center's foundation is a big, gaping hole. There is an official Viewing Wall on Church Street and an historic display on Liberty Street, but the best viewing is from the glass-enclosed back wall of the World Financial Center, directly across West Street from the site. Construction will eventually begin on a memorial and replacement for the World Trade Center.

The memorial in St. Paul's Chapel is home to a particularly moving exhibit, "Unwavering Spirit: Hope and Healing at Ground Zero." St. Paul's Chapel (212/602-0874, www.stpaulschapel.org) is located adjacent to Ground Zero on Broadway between Fulton and Vesey streets.

New York-ese

Many places in America have their own special words and phrases that people from elsewhere can't understand. Here are some commonly heard in New York:

Bridge and tunnel crowd: a disparaging term for visitors from New Jersey; also "B&T crowd"

Coffee regular: coffee with milk and sugar

The FDR: Franklin Roosevelt Drive, an expressway running the length of Manhattan's East Side along the East River

Fuhgeddaboudit: Forget about it, as in "Don't mention it." It can also mean "No way."

The Garden: Madison Square Garden

The Island: Long Island

Houston: a street in lower Manhattan, pronounced HOUSE-ton

The Met: the Metropolitan Opera or Metropolitan Museum of Art

Shlep: as a verb, to drag or haul something; as a noun, a jerk

Shmeer: a smear of cream cheese, usually on a bagel

Slice: a piece of pizza

Soda: any carbonated beverage

HAUGHWOUT BUILDING
488 Broadway (at Broome St)

Considered by many architectural historians to be the finest example of cast-iron construction in the country, the Haughwout (pronounced how-it) was built in 1857 and contained one of Elisha Otis' first elevators. Originally home to E.V. Haughwout & Company—a silver, china, and porcelain manufacturer and retailer—the building fell on hard times around the turn of the 20th century and was almost demolished in the 1960s. Thanks to the Landmarks Preservation Commission and its current owners, it remains standing and has even been restored to some of its original grandeur.

IRISH HUNGER MEMORIAL
Vesey St at North End Ave   www.batteryparkcity.org/ihm

A half-acre memorial to the 1.5 million people who died in the Irish potato famines of 1845–52, this quiet, peaceful spot is tucked away in the shadow of the World Financial Center, overlooking the Hudson River and New York Harbor. The path is made of stones from all 32 of Ireland's counties, and the little stone cottage in the middle comes from County Mayo. Be sure to look around the base of the memorial for moving words about the Irish famines and others throughout history.

JEFFERSON MARKET LIBRARY
425 Ave of the Americas (at 10th St)   212/243-4334
www.nypl.org/branch/local/man/jmr.cfm

I've included this courthouse-turned-public library because it looks like a castle in a fairy tale and people are always wondering exactly what it is. Built in 1877 and modeled after Mad King Ludwig's Neuschwanstein in Bavaria, it was saved from years of neglect and abuse by community activists and is now one of the city's nicest (and most used) public libraries. A wonderful community garden grows on its south side during warmer months. A bit of trivia: the library's bell, thought to be the second largest in New York, was rung in 1995 for the first time in 97 years after long-awaited repairs. Prior to that it was rung to commemorate Admiral George Dewey's triumph in Manila Bay during the Spanish-American War. Thus the graffiti on the bell, which reads: "To hell with Spain—Remember the *Maine*—1898"!

LINCOLN CENTER
Columbus Ave bet 62nd and 65th St   212/875-5000
www.lincolncenter.org

Constructed between 1959 and 1969, this amazing complex includes Avery Fisher Hall, the New York State Theater, Alice Tully Hall, the Juilliard School of Music, the Guggenheim Bandshell, the Vivian Beaumont Theater, the Metropolitan Opera House, and a wonderful public library and small gallery devoted to the performing arts. Call the Lincoln Center events hotline at 212/546-2656 for current information.

MADAME TOUSSAUD'S
234 W 46th St (at Broadway)   212/246-8872, www.nycwax.com

For all the hype surrounding the opening of this London icon in the midst of Times Square a couple years back, I really expected to hate it. The prices are outrageous and seem to climb by the month, the signs and layout are confusing, and they make you exit through an incredibly shlocky gift shop. But I must admit the wax museum itself is fun. You'll see several hundred familiar faces, including New Yorkers Donald Trump and Rudolph Giuliani, sports greats Billie Jean King, Pelé, and Michael Jordan, world leaders Nelson Mandela and the Dalai Lama and movie stars Susan Sarandon and Woody Allen. If wax figures are your cup of tea, be sure to bring a camera: the photo ops are great! One word of warning: there is a lot of noise and gore in the section devoted to the period before the French Revolution, when Madame Toussaud was perfecting her craft. If you have children in tow, heed the signs and take the alternate route. Call 212/512-9600 for more information.

Hours: Daily from 10 to 8 (hours may be extended in summer and on holidays). **Admission:** $30 for adults, $24 for children 4 to 12, and $27 for senior citizens.

MADISON SQUARE GARDEN
31st to 33rd St bet Seventh and Eighth Ave   212/465-6741
                                                    www.thegarden.com

The only real sporting arena in Manhattan, Madison Square Garden plays host to everything from the Westminster Kennel Club's annual dog show and the Ringling Brothers and Barnum & Bailey Circus to professional basketball's New York Knicks and hockey's New York Rangers (assuming the NHL survives after the strike-cancelled 2004–05 season). There have been three other Madison Square Gardens; the one at this location opened in 1968. Penn Station—the terminal for Amtrak and New Jersey Transit, through which 750 trains pass every day—sits directly underneath "the Garden." You'll also find the Paramount Theater inside the complex. (For information about tours, see the "Tours" section of this chapter.)

Because of ongoing security concerns, the **New York Stock Exchange** is unfortunately no longer open to the public.

NEW YORK PUBLIC LIBRARY
Fifth Ave and 42nd St   212/930-0830, www.nypl.org

The main branch of the extraordinary New York Public Library is a treasure trove for researchers and architecture fans alike. This beautiful building is adjacent to Bryant Park. The marble stairs and open areas outside—a favorite brown-bag lunch spot for people who work in the area—are dominated by statues of two lions, Patience and Fortitude. You'll find a gallery with changing exhibits and a terrific gift shop on the first floor. But the greatest treat for tourists and even hard-to-impress New Yorkers is the stunning renovation of the Rose Main Reading Room (actually two connected rooms) on the library's third floor. This is where the Gilded Age meets the computer age, and the results are splendid. The nonprofit group Friends of the New York Public Library offers frequent tours of exhibits and the library itself. (For more information, stop by the desk in the lobby or see the "Tours" section of this chapter.) You're also free to wander alone and marvel at this glorious place. **Hours:** Monday, Thursday, Friday, and Saturday from 10 to 6; Tuesday and Wednesday from 11 to 7:30; Sunday from 1 to 6. (Hours in particular divisions may be shorter.)

NEW YORK PUBLIC LIBRARY FOR THE
PERFORMING ARTS
40 Lincoln Center Plaza   212/870-1630, www.nypl.org

Wedged between the Metropolitan Opera House and the Vivian Beaumont Theater in Lincoln Center, this branch of the New York Public Library houses a tremendous collection of music, plays, and other material related to the performing arts. It is also home to a small gallery with changing exhibits and a huge range of free public programs featuring authors, musicians, artists, and playwrights. **Hours:** Tuesday through Saturday from 12 to 6 (Thursday until 8).

PLAZA HOTEL
768 Fifth Ave (bet 58th and 59th St)

On the south side of Central Park South, just west of Fifth Avenue, this elegant old building is a sentimental and architectural favorite of many visitors and New Yorkers alike. A stroll through the lobby was always a stroll through wonderland. Although my favorite hotel in all of New York and maybe all the world was bought recently and is being converted into condos, some hotel rooms will remain.

On a Clear Day
When I first started writing this book, the observation deck atop the 68-story **RCA Building** at 30 Rockefeller Plaza was one of my favorite New York viewing spots. For a variety of reasons, it closed in 1986 and has been closed ever since. However, the building is now owned by GE and plans are in the works to reopen "Top of the Rock" to visitors in late 2005. Enter on 50th Street, west of Fifth Avenue.

RADIO CITY MUSIC HALL
1260 Ave of the Americas (at 50th St)   212/247-4777
                                                      www.radiocity.com

This 6,200-seat art deco wonder was the largest theater in the world when it was built in the early 1930s as part of the Rockefeller Center complex. Its murals and art alone are worth a visit, but Radio City is best known for its long-running Christmas show, featuring the Rockettes. This is yet another New York institution that has been renovated and refurbished in recent years. (If you're interested in taking a tour, see the "Tours" section of this chapter.)

ROCKEFELLER CENTER
47th to 52nd St bet Fifth and Seventh Ave   212/632-3974
                                                     www.rockefellercenter.com

The 19 buildings in Rockefeller Center stretch for blocks, but the heart of it all is off Fifth Avenue, between 49th and 50th streets. All sorts of interesting shops, the famed statue of Prometheus, the ice-skating rink, the *Today Show* studios, the legendary Rainbow Room, and the beautiful Channel Gardens are all here in the shadow of 30 Rockefeller Plaza. "30 Rock" is the home of NBC's network studios. (For information about the NBC Studio Tour, see the "Tours" section of this chapter.) In December, Rockefeller Center is home to the nation's most photographed Christmas tree. A lot of renovations have been done in the last decade to this famed complex, and people rave about the shopping. The downstairs food court is a welcome spot for budget-conscious tourists and local workers alike. Wonderful as the complex and its world-famous views may be, however, I find the whole layout a bit confusing and Rockefeller Center itself worth only a brief picture-taking stop.

ROOSEVELT ISLAND
In the East River, east of midtown   212/832-4555, www.rioc.com

If you want an experience even most New Yorkers haven't had, along with amazing views of the city's skyline, take the tram to Roosevelt Island in the middle of the East River. It leaves regularly from its station on Second Avenue between 59th and 60th streets and costs $2 per person each way. Although the 7,500 people who live here are only minutes from midtown Manhattan, they might as well be on another planet. Their island—which was at various times home to a hog pasture, a debtors' prison, and an insane asylum—is quiet, unhurried, and almost crime-free. For 10¢ you can take one of the elderly red buses that traverse the island from the tram station through a small shopping area to Lighthouse Park, on the island's northern end. Buy a map at the tram station and see the sights or just wander around. Be sure to walk along the island's west side to get a priceless view of the Manhattan skyline.

ROSE CENTER FOR EARTH AND SPACE
81st St at Central Park West (adjacent to the   212/769-5200
American Museum of Natural History)   www.amnh.org/rose

This companion to the Hayden Planetarium at the American Museum of Natural History has bells and whistles galore. In the Hall of the Universe, galaxies collide, supernovas explode, and telescopes beam back amazing images. In the Hall of Planet Earth, you can learn all about the Mothra Hydrothermal Field while tectonic plates collide and sulfide chimneys percolate with life. There's a fascinating multimedia display of the Big Bang, an exceptional display of relative scale in the universe, and even a "cosmic pathway" detailing the 13 billion-year evolution of our universe. Older children will be particularly taken with all the hands-on displays. Of course, the centerpiece of the Rose Center is the retooled Hayden Planetarium. The two space shows are fascinating, but be forewarned they may scare young children, and senior citizens might find all the standing and waiting a bit much. Also be forewarned of the stratospheric cost: a strongly suggested $22 for adults to take in the Rose Center, Hayden Planetarium, and American Museum of Natural History—and you can't choose to bypass the museum. **Hours:** The museum is open daily (except Thanksgiving and Christmas) from 10 to 5:45. The Rose Center stays open until 8:45 on Friday. Space shows are scheduled at various times from 10:30 to 4:30 (Fridays until 7:30). **Admission:** varies depending on package selected, but a minimum of $13 for adults without the Hayden Planetarium's space show and $22 with it.

SCHOMBURG CENTER FOR RESEARCH
IN BLACK CULTURE
515 Malcolm X Blvd (at 135th St)   212/491-2200, www.nypl.org

This branch of the New York Public Library is a comprehensive resource for scholars and others interested in the Harlem Renaissance, enduring African traditions, the civil rights movement, and a wide variety of topics associated with the African-American experience. It's also home to 300,000 prints and photographs, 10,000 pieces of art and artifacts, 5,000 hours of oral history, and (as part of a 75-year loan) many of Malcolm X's personal papers. While its two galleries are small and not in the best shape, you'll often find unique exhibits. The center's Langston Hughes Theater is used for performances and special programs. Call 212/491-2200 for more information. **Hours:** Tuesday and Wednesday from 12 to 8, Thursday and Friday from 12 to 6, Saturday from 10 to 6.

SCIENCE, INDUSTRY, AND BUSINESS LIBRARY
188 Madison Ave (at 34th St)   212/592-7000, www.nypl.org

Known around town as SIBL (as in the woman's name), this amazing library in the old B. Altman department store is among the most technologically advanced and user-friendly libraries in the world. Intended for use by the general public and business people, the library unites the New York Public Library system's collections of scientific, technological, mathematical, and business-related materials. This enormous archive comprises 1.2 million books, plus microfilm, microfiche, magazines, and journals. Whether you're interested in patents and trademarks, labor history, advertising practices, or how the Small Business Administration works, this is where to look for information. But don't expect to browse the stacks. With the exception of a circulating collection of 40,000 books on the first floor, everything is housed in electronically operated moving stacks. Each of the library's 500 seats is wired for laptop computer use, and 100 computer stations allow you to search electronic databases or go online. If you're interested in learning how to surf the Internet, sign up for one of the library's free classes offered through its Electronic Training Center. **Hours:** Tuesday through Thursday from 10 to 8, Friday and Saturday from 10 to 6.

There are 6,375 miles of streets in New York City. Twenty uptown/downtown blocks or 10 crosstown blocks are approximately equal to one mile.

SEVENTH REGIMENT ARMORY
643 Park Ave (at 66th St)

Most New Yorkers know this as a giant exhibition space in a prime location, but the Seventh Regiment Armory is also what the *New York Times* once called "a bit of New York in a bottle." The Seventh Regiment was founded in 1806 as a volunteer militia. Its members, a Who's Who of New York throughout the 19th century, built this armory as their headquarters in 1879. It includes rooms designed by famed architect Stanford White and decorated by Louis Comfort Tiffany, as well as paintings by such artists as Thomas Nast.

SONY WONDER TECHNOLOGY LAB
550 Madison Ave (at 56th St)   212/833-8100
www.sonywondertechlab.com

A brilliant public relations and merchandising ploy, this four-story interactive wonderland is a huge favorite among preteens and teenagers. Whether you want to try your hand at surgery or making a music video, you'll definitely find something to do and explore here. Best of all, it's free! The museum gets very crowded, especially on weekends and in summer. If you know when you want to visit, call 212/833-5414 to make advance reservations. **Hours:** Tuesday through Saturday from 10 to 5 (Thursday until 8), Sunday from 12 to 5.

SOUTH STREET SEAPORT
209 Water Street (at Fulton St)   212/748-8600, www.southseaport.org

This is the only place I've included in both the "Museums" section and this one, because it's a little of both. The main entrance to this popular area is at the east end of Fulton Street, but the area stretches for several blocks between Water Street and the East River. If you've ever been to Boston's Quincy Market or Baltimore's Inner Harbor, you'll recognize the concept of upscale shops, food courts, restaurants, and history all wrapped into one. South Street was one of the city's most important ports for many years, and this district was created more than two decades ago to preserve that history. You can stroll cobblestone streets, look at the early 19th-century buildings along Schermerhorn Row, and gaze at the tall ships. You can also buy a ticket to tour the ships and visit the seaport's galleries and children's center. (For a few extra dollars you also can take a cruise of New York Harbor in the warmer months.) A TKTS discount ticket booth that's often less crowded than other TKTS outlets lies just south of the main plaza on the corner of John and Front streets. Call 212/732-7678 for information about South Street Seaport and its special events. **Hours:** South Street Seaport Museum is open daily until 5 from April through October, and on weekends from November through March. Many shops and restaurants in the area are open late all year.

STATEN ISLAND FERRY
At the foot of Whitehall St in Lower Manhattan   718/727-2508
www.siferry.com

There are no better views of New York than those from the decks of these legendary ferryboats. The 22-minute trip is free, and boats leave from Manhattan and Staten Island every half hour during the week (a bit less frequently on weekends and holidays). Although the ferry terminal on the Manhattan side was a pretty dreary place for many years, the new Whitehall Terminal is itself almost worth the visit! To get there, take the 1/9 subway to South Ferry or the 4/5 to Bowling Green (on the southern tip of Manhattan, just east of Battery Park).

The Brooklyn Bridge was the first New York City bridge to be lit using electricity.

STATUE OF LIBERTY
In New York Harbor (south of Battery Park)   212/363-3200
www.nps.gov/stli

This 151-foot gift to the United States from France was built on Liberty Island in New York Harbor in 1886 and has been among New York's most recognized sights ever since. (Before the statue was erected, the island was used as a fort and later for hanging pirates!) Generations of immigrants still remember seeing Lady Liberty and her raised torch when they arrived at nearby Ellis Island. The Emma Lazarus sonnet "The New Colossus" ("Give me your tired, your poor/Your huddled masses yearning to breathe free"), which is carved onto its base, still expresses the most noble instincts of our country. To reach the Statue of Liberty, you must ferry over from Castle Clinton in Battery Park. For more information about the ferry (which also goes to Ellis Island), call 212/269-5755. Be forewarned: go early, particularly in the warmer months, as lines can grow long and security is tight. A timed pass is required to enter the recently renovated monument itself. A limited number of them are given out free of charge on a first-come, first-serve basis every day. You can reserve one in advance for a fee of $1.75 per ticket (866/ 782-8834, www.statuereservations.com). **Hours:** 8:30 to 5 in winter, 8:30 to 6:45 in summer (although the last boat leaves Castle Clinton at about 3). The Statue of Liberty is closed on July 4 and December 25. **Admission:** $10 for adults, $8 for senior citizens 62 and over, and $4 for children from 4 to 12. Time permitting, admission to both Ellis Island and the Statue of Liberty is included in the price of a ferry ticket.

STEINWAY & SONS
109 W 57th St (bet Ave of the Americas and Seventh Ave)
212/246-1100

New York is full of hidden treasures, and this is one of them. Part show-room and part monument to beauty and grace, this is not a place to bring little kids or big groups. The 1925 building is magnificent and the pianos so elegant that you don't need to be a music lover to appreciate their beauty and craftsmanship. Just down the street from Carnegie Hall, this also is the home of the Steinway "bank"—a collection of several dozen prime grand pianos from which visiting pianists can choose for their performances. **Hours:** weekdays from 9 to 6, Saturday from 9 to 5, and Sunday from 12 to 5.

Where Did They Go?
   Much has been made about the remarkable redevelopment of Times Square and the closure of its dozens of peep shows. When Peep-O-Rama, the last of them, closed in the summer of 2002 to make room for a new office tower, it signaled the end of an era. But don't be fooled: many of these businesses are still around. They just moved a couple of blocks west to Eighth Avenue!

TIMES SQUARE
42nd St at Broadway   www.timessquarenyc.org

When I first began writing this book, Times Square was among the most unpleasant places in Manhattan. It was synonymous with petty crime, pornography, and filth. Not anymore. In fact, it is increasingly hard to believe it's the same place. The Disney Company has reinvented West 42nd Street with the stunning success of *The Lion King* in the lovingly restored New Amsterdam Theater. An ever-growing number of tourist-oriented restaurants, megastores, hotels, and entertainment venues have opened here, including a McDonald's with 7,500 light bulbs in its marquee! The Times Square subway station (the city's busiest) has been redesigned, refurbished, and fitted for a 53-foot porcelain mural by Roy Lichtenstein. The Times Square Alliance runs a great tourist information center in the Embassy Theater on Seventh Avenue between 46th and 47th streets. Despite all the positive changes, be warned that the "new" Times Square still leaves something to be desired. It's wildly crowded with out-of-towners, the food is almost uniformly bad, prices are sky-high, and service tends to run from surly to incompetent.

TRUMP TOWER
725 Fifth Ave (bet 56th and 57th St)   212/832-2000

This 66-floor building is named for flamboyant financier Donald Trump.

Its six-story pink marble atrium—complete with galleries, shops, restaurants, outdoor gardens (on levels 4 and 5), and a dramatic waterfall—is open to the public and almost always crowded. Apartments begin on the 30th floor; tenants enter and leave via a separate entrance to avoid the crowds. **Hours:** daily between 8 a.m. and 10 p.m.

UNITED NATIONS
First Ave bet 42nd and 47th St   212/963-8687, www.un.org

The flags of member nations fly along the entire length of this complex, and you'll hear all sorts of languages spoken inside the UN and on surrounding streets. The main visitors entrance, between 45th and 46th streets, is well-marked and manned by UN guards. The park and plaza inside the gate offer wonderful views of the East River and comfortable benches. Once you've passed through a security checkpoint inside the main building, you can wander the enormous lobby, eat in the Delegates Dining Room, take a formal tour, or head downstairs to visit the UN post office and a great assortment of shops. An information desk in the main lobby provides daily schedules of meetings and events. Remember that those who work here are busy overseeing world affairs, so look around and ask questions but otherwise be quiet and respectful. **Hours:** Daily from 9 to 5 (closed weekends in January and February).

VERIZON BUILDING
140 West St (at Vesey St)

Built in 1926 as the headquarters for New York Telephone, this beautiful art deco landmark building actually withstood the collapse of two buildings on September 11, 2001. The North Tower collapsed on its Vesey Street facade and Number Seven World Trade Center fell on its eastern side. Despite tremendous damage, the folks at Verizon and the New York Landmarks Conservancy teamed up to bring the building back to life. Go into the lobby to see the beautiful ceiling murals and pause to consider the endurance of such beauty amid terrible destruction.

WASHINGTON ARCH
At the foot of Fifth Ave in Washington Square Park

Thanks to movies like *When Harry Met Sally*, you've probably seen this marble triumphal arch at the foot of Fifth Avenue, just south of 8th Street. Erected at the end of the 19th century, the marble arch replaced a wooden structure commemorating the inauguration of George Washington, who was sworn in as our nation's first president in New York.

WOOLWORTH BUILDING
233 Broadway (bet Barclay St and Park Pl)

Constructed of 17 million bricks, 28,000 tons of tile, and 53,000 pounds of bronze and iron hardware, this national landmark is among the city's most impressive office buildings. It's also become one of Manhattan's hottest residential properties, as the upper floors have been converted into condominiums. The cathedral-like lobby has extraordinary mosaics on its vaulted ceilings; it is a definite "don't miss" if you're in the area, although only a small part is open to the public for security reasons. Dime-store king F.W.

Woolworth paid $13.5 million in cash to have his namesake building erected in 1913, and it reigned as the world's tallest structure for more than a decade. Study the details and try to spot (under the south balcony) the gargoyle of Woolworth himself counting his nickels and dimes. **Hours:** The lobby is open 24 hours a day.

You can tell a real New Yorker from a wanna-be if he or she:

* Refuses to refer to Sixth Avenue as Avenue of the Americas.
* Refers to the MetLife Building as the PanAm Building.
* Has never been to either the Empire State Building or the Statue of Liberty.
* Has never bought a bagel at a grocery store.
* Doesn't flinch when the dinner bill exceeds $300 for two people but knows where to get a perfectly good meal for under $20.
* Doesn't own a car but rents one on weekends to go to Ikea and Home Depot—or doesn't have a driver's license at all.
* Never eats dinner before 8 p.m.
* Thinks Ohio is "out west."
* Knows the differences between Lombardi's and John's and has a strong opinion about which one is better.
* Buys the Sunday *New York Times* on Saturday night.
* Keeps a bike in the living room.
* Gives directions to cab drivers.
* Never rides a bus—but if he did, would get off through the back door.

WORLD FINANCIAL CENTER
At the Hudson River bet Vesey and Albany St   212/945-0505
www.worldfinancialcenter.com

In the heart of Battery Park City, the World Financial Center amazingly still stands after the destruction of the nearby World Trade Center on September 11, 2001. A proud but haunted survivor in this scarred area is the World Financial Center's Winter Garden. Ironically, the east windows of the World Financial Center, just upstairs from the Winter Garden, now offer the best view of Ground Zero. You'll find upscale stores and restaurants, great views of the Hud-son River, and some pleasant sitting areas both indoors and out. You'll also find the water taxi to Liberty State Park, not to mention some of the city's best children's playgrounds, just outside the World Financial Center along the Hudson River. Call 212/945-0505 for information about events and programs.

The spectacular **Winter Garden** at World Financial Center, Battery Park, looks better than ever after the 9/11 disaster. Besides gazing and resting and enjoying the river views, there is good eating and shopping. During the reconstruction period, more than 500 laborers worked to replace 60,000 square feet of tricolor Italian marble, 2,000 glass panes, and 16 43-foot-tall Washingtonia palm trees in the 10-story structure, and it took them only nine months. You'll find good eating at Cosi Sandwich Bar, Donald Sacks, Financier Patisserie, and P.J. Clarke's.

Tickets

Nowhere else in the world will you find such a wealth of performing arts. And no trip to New York is complete without taking in at least one play, musical, ballet, concert, or opera.

The trick, of course, is getting tickets. People have written entire books about how and where to get tickets, and others have made lucrative careers out of procuring them for out-of-towners. I've provided a variety of approaches for getting theater tickets and to find out about other performances. Keep your eye out for student and other discounts, but be aware that good deals for the best shows and performances are few and far between.

I'm often asked, "Where can I find a really reliable ticket broker?" Well, I have the answer: **Americana Tickets** (800/833-3121, 212/581-6660, www.americanatickets.com). For over 75 years, this business has been the one pointed to over and over for outstanding service. The third generation of the Radler family are outstanding people to deal with! Just a few of the advantages: premium seating for all theater, entertainment, concert, and sporting events in New York and worldwide; expert, professional agents; unique cancellation and exchange privileges; special offers for individuals and groups; hotel theater-desk locations (Marriott Marquis, Sheraton New York, Crowne Plaza Manhattan); great hours (8 a.m. to 8 p.m., seven days a week); and complimentary hotel, restaurant, limousine, and sightseeing reservations.

You can rely on **Surftix.com** (212/877-SURFTIX or sales@surftix. com) for all of your worldwide entertainment needs. They have sold over 16 million tickets and offer more than 10,000 events worldwide. When backed by such a successful business as Americana Tickets, they've got to be good.

BROADWAY

People may have different things in mind when they say they want to see a show. Some have their hearts set on great seats at a Saturday night performance of the hottest show on Broadway, while others are willing to sit anywhere to see anything. A lot of people fall somewhere between those extremes. In addition, some are willing to pay whatever it takes to see the show they want, while others just won't go if they can't pay less than full price. If the main purpose of your visit to the city is to see a particular show (or shows), make sure you have the tickets you want before leaving home so you're not disappointed.

Look in the Sunday Arts and Leisure section or the Friday Weekend section of the *New York Times,* the front pages of a current *New Yorker,* the Theater section of *Time Out New York,* or the back pages of a current *New York* magazine to find out where the play or musical you want to see is being performed. The front section of the Manhattan Yellow Pages has a list of Broadway and off-Broadway theaters and a map of the Theater District. **The Broadway Line** (888/276-2392 or 212/302-4111) tells what is playing and where, and also gives a quick plot summary.

Box Offices and Phone Orders—If you want to save a little money and pick your seat, go directly to the theater's box office with cash or a major credit card. Ask to see a diagram of the theater if it isn't posted, although most theaters are small enough to ensure that every seat has a good view. The best time to try is midweek. You can also check with the box office to learn if it releases day-of-performance "rush" tickets (most do, usually around 10 a.m.).

If you're willing to spend a little extra and let a computer pick what is in theory the "best available" seat, call the number or go to the website listed and have your credit card ready. Most numbers will be for **Telecharge** (212/239-6200, www.tele-charge.com) or **TicketMaster's Broadway Performance Line** (212/307-4100, www.ticketmaster.com). Both services charge a per-ticket handling fee in addition to the ticket price. Another option is stopping by the **Broadway Ticket Center** at the tourist information center in the Embassy Theater (on Seventh Avenue between 46th and 47th streets).

Be forewarned: full-price tickets to Broadway shows typically cost at least $50 and sometimes well over $100. Moreover, if the play or musical you want to see is really hot, it may be sold out the entire time you're in New York. In fact, a few really hot ones may be sold out months in advance.

A great addition to the New York theater world is **Theater Row**, a wonderfully conceived and renovated "multiplex" of off-Broadway theaters on 42nd Street between Ninth and Tenth avenues (212/714-2442). Other off-Broadway—and off-off and *really* way out—venues include:

Center Stage, NY: 48 W 21st St (212/929-2228)
The Flea: 41 White St (212/226-0051)
Soho Rep: 46 Walker St (212/941-8632)

CareTix—If you have your heart set on a particular show and cost is no obstacle, Broadway Cares/Equity Fights AIDS sells house seats for sold-out Broadway and off-Broadway shows for twice the box-office price. The extra money goes to a good cause and is a tax-deductible contribution. Call 212/840-0770 for more information.

TKTS Outlets—If you want to see a Broadway show but are flexible and have some free time, go to one of the TKTS outlets in Manhattan. Operated by the Theater Development Fund, these outlets sell whatever tickets happen to be left for various shows on the day of performance for half price or less (plus a $3 per-ticket charge). The most popular TKTS outlet is in Duffy Square, at 47th Street and Broadway. It's open from 3 to 8 Monday through Saturday (from 2 on Tuesday, when performances start an hour earlier at many theaters), from 10 to 2 on Wednesday and Saturday for matinee tickets, and from 11 to 7 on Sunday. A less crowded TKTS outlet is at the intersection of Front and John streets, just below South Street Seaport's main plaza. It's open Monday through Saturday from 11 to 6 and Sunday from 11 to 3:30. A list of shows for which tickets are available is posted in the window. Matinee tickets at this location go on sale the day *before* a performance. You must pay with cash or travelers' checks at both places.

The Theater Development Fund also offers extremely good deals on tickets to theater and other performances to its members. If you're a student, member of the clergy or armed forces (serving or retired), teacher, union member, or performing artist, send a stamped, self-addressed envelope for an application to Theater Development Fund, Attention: Application, 1501 Broadway, New York, NY 10036 (or go to www.tdf.org). All Broadway theaters offer a small number of deeply discounted tickets to people in wheelchairs and their companion or attendant. Call the theater box office directly for more information. Finally, standing-room-only tickets are sometimes available for sold-out performances on the day of the performance for between $10 and $20. Again, call the theater box office for more information.

Can You Be in Bed by Midnight?
The answer is yes, particularly with "Tuesdays at 7" on Broadway and earlier weekday curtain times at the New York Philharmonic. My advice for those accustomed to late curtain times in New York: check your tickets. The times they are a-changin'!

Off-Broadway and off-off-Broadway—In part because staging a Broadway production has become almost prohibitively expensive, off-Broadway and off-off-Broadway theater have really taken *off*. Thanks to a glut of talented actors and actresses in New York, such theater is typically excellent and often innovative. The front section of the Manhattan Yellow Pages lists off-Broadway theaters. Descriptions of what's playing off- and off-off-Broadway are published every Sunday in the *New York Times* Arts and Leisure section, in the back of *New York* magazine, and in *Time Out New York*. Tickets for off-Broadway and off-off-Broadway productions tend to be significantly less expensive, and TKTS outlets and twofers sometimes offer discounts.

OPERA AND CLASSICAL MUSIC

No other city in the world has as much music to choose from as New York! *Time Out New York* has an excellent listing of classical and opera performances, including locations, times, and ticket prices. Many New York-related websites, including several listed in the "For More Resources" section of Chapter VII, have comprehensive listings as well. Contact the **92nd Street Y** (212/996-1100, www.92y.org) if you're interested in chamber music or recitals by top performers. Otherwise, here's how to find schedule and ticket information at New York's top venues:

Carnegie Hall—You'll find individual musicians, out-of-town orchestras, and chamber music ensembles performing at Carnegie Hall all year. Try 212/247-7800, www.carnegiehall.org) between 11 and 6. A money-saving tip: At noon on the day of a concert, the box office releases a limited number of tickets for that evening's main hall performance for only $10 each.

Metropolitan Opera—The internationally renowned Met's season runs from fall through spring, and ticket sales are broken into three periods. Try the box office (212/362-6000, www.metopera.org), but be aware that orchestra seats can cost as much as $150! For a real bargain, bring cash to the Metropolitan's box office at 10 a.m. on Saturday, when standing-room-only tickets for the upcoming week's performances are sold for $16 each, one per person only.

New York City Opera—The season for this exceptional but often overshadowed opera runs through summer and early fall. For schedule and ticket information, try the box office (212/870-5570, www.nycopera.com) or TicketMaster (212/307-4100, www.ticketmaster.com). Standing-room-only tickets are sometimes available for $8 on the morning of a performance from the New York State Theater's box office in Lincoln Center.

New York Philharmonic—The Philharmonic's season runs from September through June. For schedule and ticket information, try CenterCharge (212/721-6500), the box office (212/721-6500), or the New York Philharmonic information line (212/875-5656, www.newyorkphilharmonic.org). If you're a student, call around 10:30 on the morning of a performance to see if they have any $10 "rush" tickets available.

DANCE AND BALLET

Ballet and dance companies have experienced tough times financially, but New York still is home to several world-class companies and a great many smaller ones. They include:

Alvin Ailey American Dance Theater (212/767-0590, www.alvin-ailey.org)
American Ballet Theater (212/362-6000, www.abt.org)
Dance Theatre of Harlem (212/690-2800, www.dancetheatreof harlem.org)
Dance Theater Workshop (212/691-6500, www.dtw.org)
New York City Ballet (212/870-5570, www.nycballet.com)
Paul Taylor Dance Company (212/431-5562, www.ptdc.org)

Time Out New York has a particularly good section on dance, including reviews and a day-by-day calendar of large and small performances by local and visiting companies. A number of major companies perform at the City Center of Music and Dance (131 West 55th Street). The Alvin Ailey American Dance Theater is now in its new Joan Weill Center for Dance (405 N 55th St). Call CitiTix (212/581-1212), go to the City Center website (www.citycenter.org), or visit an individual dance company's website for information about tickets and upcoming performances.

The major television networks all have street-level studios for their morning shows. Look for NBC's **Today Show** crowd on the sidewalk at 49th Street between Fifth Avenue and Avenue of the Americas. CBS's **Early Show** crowd gathers at the General Motors Building (Fifth Avenue at 59th Street), as do those who want to see **NFL Today** on Sunday mornings during football season (much to the irritation of neighbors in nearby apartment buildings). ABC's **Good Morning America** crowd assembles in Times Square at 44th Street and Broadway. CNN's **American Morning** originates in a former bank branch at Avenue of the Americas and 51st Street. People often show up before dawn, although cameras don't starting rolling until 7 a.m.

TELEVISION SHOW TAPINGS

Fine arts aside, there is one other kind of ticket everybody wants to get in New York: those that allow you to become part of the television studio audience for one of the many talk shows filmed here. I've listed some of the most popular shows and rules for getting free tickets.

Late Nite with Conan O'Brien—Tickets are available only by calling 212/664-3056. You can request up to four tickets every six months. Everyone attending must be at least 16. While they don't guarantee admission, standby tickets are distributed one per person at 9 a.m. on taping days under the "NBC Studios" sign on the 49th Street side of 30 Rockefeller Plaza.

Late Show with David Letterman—These are still among the hottest tickets in town, and you must be at least 18 to qualify for them. You can apply for these tickets by filling out a form at www.lateshowaudience.com or going in person to the Ed Sullivan Theater box office (Broadway between 53rd and 54th streets) between 9:30 and 12:30 on weekdays or 10 to 6 on weekends. Expect to wait at least six to eight months and probably longer. Standby tickets are sometimes distributed at 11 on the morning of a show by calling 212/247-6497 (*not* in person, as used to be the case). If you hear a recording, you'll know tickets have run out. Shows are taped Monday through Thursday. Bring a picture ID and jacket, as Dave insists that the theater be kept at a chilly 52° all year! Call 212/975-5853 for more information.

Saturday Night Live—Year in and year out, these remain the hardest tickets of all to get. A lottery is held every August from e-mails collected during the preceding 12 months, and each winner gets two tickets. If you want to be included in the lottery, send an e-mail to snltickets@nbc.com. Send only one e-mail per household, and realize there is no guarantee that you will get tickets in the following year. Standby tickets for the 8 p.m. dress rehearsal and the 11:30 p.m. live show are available at 7 a.m. on the day of the show (but show up around 5 a.m. if you really want them) at the 49th Street entrance to 30 Rockefeller Plaza. They do not guarantee entrance, and only one ticket is distributed per person over 16.

Looking for Main Street?

You won't find it in Manhattan. There is, however, a Main Street in each of the other boroughs and on Roosevelt Island.

Tours

No matter what your interest, price range, or schedule, New York has a tour for you. If you're interested in having a tour organized for your group, **Doorway to Design** (212/221-1111, www.doorwaytodesign.com), **Manhattan Passport** (212/861-2746, www.manhattanpassport.com), and **Viewpoint International** (212/246-6000, www.viewpointinternational.com) are all reputable outfits. The tours listed on the following pages are divided into three categories: tours of New York, tours of specific sights or neighborhoods, and individuals and companies that put together walking tours of New York. Because there are literally hundreds of tour guides and thousands of tours, there is no way to offer an exhaustive list. Rather, the following will give you an idea of some of the most popular and most interesting tours for individuals and small groups. As always, my advice is to call in advance.

If you want a particular kind of tour or a guide with special skills or areas of expertise, contact the **Guides Associations of New York** (212/969-0666).

The organization's website (www.NewYorkCityTourGuides.com) gives information about the city's licensed guides and their specialties, as well as practical details about the tours they offer.

TOURS OF NEW YORK
BIG APPLE GREETER
212/669-8159, www.bigapplegreeter.org

A volunteer service, this outfit will hook you up with a personal guide to New York. If you're looking for a really personalized introduction to this sometimes overwhelming city or a particular neighborhood, Big Apple Greeter may be right for you. And, it's free! You must give as much notice as possible, and tell them what part of New York you would like to see.

Sailing Up, Sailing Down

The Hudson and East rivers, which have long been engines of commerce of this region, became very polluted in the second half of the 20th century and were little used when I first began writing this book 25 years ago. No longer! Whether it's basic transportation or a nostalgic sail on a 100-year-old schooner, there are many options for getting out on the water. They include:

The Adirondack—This modern copy of a 19th-century pilot boat is docked at Pier 62 in the Chelsea Piers complex, on the Hudson River at 23rd Street (800/701-7245, www.scaranoboat.com/excursions).

New York Water Taxi—This water taxi makes regular stops for commuters and tourists alike at various West Side and Lower Manhattan locations (212/742-1969, www.nywatertaxi.com).

New York Waterway—This water-taxi service runs between various East River locations and Pier 11, near Wall Street (800/533-3799, www.newyorkwaterway.com).

The Pioneer—This wonderful 1885 schooner is docked at South Street Seaport (212/748-8786, www.southstseaport.org).

The Ventura—This 1921 sloop is docked at North Cove, near the World Financial Center in Battery Park City, as is the 1950 speedboat Petrel (212/786-1204, www.sailnewyork.com).

CIRCLE LINE
212/563-3200, www.circleline42.com

Particularly on warm days, the three-hour boat trip around the island of Manhattan on one of Circle Line's boats is a real treat. In addition to nice breezes, you'll get a good idea of how Manhattan is laid out. A guide offers commentary as the boat makes its way down the Hudson River, into New York Harbor, up the East River, across the top of the island via the Harlem River, and back down the Hudson. Trips depart Pier 83 (43rd Street at the Hudson River) daily between mid-March and December, with more trips added at the height of the season. In warmer months, tours also depart from Pier 16 at South Street Seaport. Tickets cost $28 for adults, $23 for senior citizens, and $15 for children under 12. Shorter tours are also available.

GRAY LINE
800/669-0051, 212/445-0848, www.graylinenewyork.com

If you're overwhelmed by New York and want to be shown the highlights from the safety and anonymity of a tour bus, try a Gray Line tour. The company offers a wide range of part- and full-day bus tours to various parts of Manhattan, including a marathon eight-and-a-half-hour "Manhattan Comprehensive" that goes from Harlem to Wall Street and even out to the Statue of Liberty and Ellis Island. Most tours run at least once a day, and some are offered in French, German, Italian, Portuguese, and Spanish, as well as English. Gray Line also offers a series of one- and two-day hop-on, hop-off packages. Look for the company's signature double-decker buses at tourist sights throughout the city. Tickets are available at the Gray Line office in the Port Authority Bus Terminal (42nd Street at Eighth Avenue), the Times Square Alliance's tourist information center (Seventh Avenue between 46th and 47th streets), and many hotel concierge desks.

The world's largest gothic cathedral is the **Cathedral Church of St. John the Divine**, and it's still under construction! The first stone was laid in 1892.

NEW YORK WATERWAY
800/533-3779; www.newyorkwaterway.com

Ninety-minute New York Harbor cruises, twilight cruises, and more are available from NY Waterway (Pier 78, 38th Street at Hudson River), as are full-day cruises to various spots up the Hudson River. Prices for the 90-minute harbor cruise, which runs throughout the year, are $20 for adults, $17 for senior citizens, and $10 for children. Prices vary for the other tours, which run only in warmer months.

TOURS OF SPECIFIC PLACES AND AREAS

I've said this before, but it bears repeating: The following list is by no means comprehensive. Literally hundreds of buildings, neighborhoods, museums, churches and synagogues, old homes, and even libraries offer tours. If you don't find what you're looking for here, check with your hotel concierge, browse the "Around Town" section of *Time Out New York*, or go to www.NewYorkCityTourGuides.com.

CARNEGIE HALL
212/903-9765, www.carnegiehall.org

Lincoln Center may have the Metropolitan Opera and the New York Philharmonic, but Carnegie Hall remains synonymous with classical music. If you want to take a look around during the day, one-hour tours are offered on weekdays during the season. The tour costs $9 for adults, $6 for students and senior citizens, and $3 for children under 12. Drop by the house manager's window inside the Carnegie Hall lobby at 153 West 57th Street, just off Seventh Avenue for more information. The box office opens at 11 a.m.

CATHEDRAL CHURCH OF ST. JOHN THE DIVINE
212/932-7347, www.stjohndivine.org

If you're interested in Gothic architecture or just want to see one of the most amazing places in all of New York, I urge you to take one of the weekly tours of this beautiful cathedral-in-progress. Located on Amsterdam Avenue at 112th Street, this Episcopal church makes a real effort to welcome people of all faiths. Tours are offered Saturday at 12:45 p.m. Although the "vertical tour" of the cathedral's hidden areas was canceled after a serious fire in 2001, it may be available again by the time you read this.

> If you want to see Central Park, Riverside Park, or any other part of New York by bike, go to www.transalt.org/calendar/century/rental for a fabulous listing of bike rentals available throughout the city. Prices range from $25 to $40 a day.

CENTRAL PARK
212/794-6564, www.centralparknyc.org/thingstodo/thisweek

The Central Park Conservancy leads a wide array of free tours in Central Park, including an hour-long "Views from the Past" tour, a tour of the Conservatory Garden in the summer and fall, a "Cross Park" tour, and more. The visitors information center at The Dairy (mid-park at 65th St) is a great place to start. The Audubon Society (212/310-6660, www.nycaudubon.org) gives birdwatching tours in the park as well. Call the visitors information center at The Dairy (212/794-6564) daily (except Monday) between 10 and 4 for more information about what's happening during any given week.

CNN STUDIO TOUR
866/426-6692, www.cnn.com/insidecnn

Spend 45 minutes learning about how news is gathered and how broadcasts are put together at CNN's New York studios at 10 Columbus Circle (the southwest corner of Central Park). The highlight for many kids is the most expensive for their parents: you can sit at an anchor desk, read the news off a teleprompter, and get a video of the performance ($22 for a DVD, $17 for a videotape). The tour is $15 for adults, $13 for senior citizens, $11 for kids between 4 and 12, and free for children under 3. Tours are available Monday through Saturday from 10 to 8 and Sunday from 10 to 5. Advance reservations are accepted.

ELDRIDGE STREET SYNAGOGUE
212/219-0888, www.eldridgestreet.org

This stunning synagogue was built by Eastern European immigrants at 12 Eldridge Street (between Canal and Division streets) on the Lower East Side in 1887. The building fell into disrepair in the middle of last century and is now being renovated. Fascinating tours are offered every Sunday on the hour between 11 and 3 and on Tuesday and Thursday at 11:30 and 2:30. Admission, which helps pay for the renovation, is $5 for adults and $3 for students, senior citizens, and children. They also have all sorts of specially designed tours and talks for student groups and children.

FEDERAL RESERVE BANK

212/720-6130, www.ny.frb.org

More than 20 countries keep their gold buried in the bedrock of Manhattan at the Federal Reserve Bank. Daily tours of this incredible institution are free, but reservations must be made at least a week in advance and children under 16 are not allowed. Be sure to look for the American Numismatic Society's display on the history of money. Call the Federal Reserve or send an e-mail to frbnytours@ny.frb.org for more information. The Federal Reserve Bank is located on Liberty Street between Nassau and Williams streets in Lower Manhattan.

> The Lower East Side has become a fascinating mix of new and old, trendy, and decidedly old-fashioned. While you're in the area, be sure to visit some of my favorite places! **Yonah Schimmel's Knishes** (137 E Houston St), **Sammy's Roumanian** (157 Chrystie St), **Russ & Daughters** (179 E Houston St), and **Guss' Pickles** (85-86 Orchard St) offer some only-in-New York taste treats. Go to **Fine and Klein** (119 Orchard St) for tremendous prices on an amazing selection of handbags and **Harris Levy** (278 Grand St) for excellent linens and service. These places have rich histories that go back several generations. Enjoy!

GRACIE MANSION

212/570-4751

Thanks to Fiorello LaGuardia, New York is one of the few cities in the U.S. with an official mayoral residence. Built in 1799, this historic mansion is one of the oldest continuously occupied homes in New York (well, sort of—current mayor Michael Bloomberg actually lives in an East Side townhouse). It's located in Carl Schurz Park, overlooking the East River (at 88th Street and East End Avenue). Morning and afternoon tours are offered on Wednesday by appointment in warmer months. Reservations are required and must be made far enough in advance to allow tickets to be mailed.

GRAND CENTRAL STATION

212/935-3960, www.grandcentralterminal.com

In addition to excellent walking tours, the Municipal Art Society conducts a 90-minute free tour of this beautiful building every Wednesday at 12:30. I highly recommend this popular tour. Grand Central Station is one of the city's real landmarks, and the society's tour conveys a sense of its grandeur and history while allowing you to see features most commuters don't even know exist. The tour meets at the information booth on the main concourse, directly across from the grand staircase. The Grand Central Partnership also offers a free tour of the neighborhood on Friday at 12:30 p.m. It meets at the Whitney Museum's small gallery, directly across 42nd Street from Grand Central Station (212/697-1245, www.grandcentralpartnership.org).

HARLEM

www.hometoharlem.com

Whether you want to visit a jazz club, stop by historic buildings like the Morris-Jumel Mansion and the Apollo Theater, or go to church on Sunday morning to hear a gospel choir, **Harlem Your Way!** (212/690-1687, www.harlemyourwaytours.com) specializes in customized tours for individuals and groups, family reunions, and other events.

LINCOLN CENTER
212/875-5350, www.lincolncenter.org

Tours of the magnificent auditoriums and concert halls at Lincoln Center are given at least four times a day between 10 and 4:30. Because the schedule is set only a day in advance, you must call for times on the day you want to tour the complex. The tour costs $12.50 for adults, $9 for students and senior citizens, and $6 for children 6 to 12. (If that seems steep, check out the prices of opera and concert tickets!) Lincoln Center stretches from 62nd to 65th streets along Columbus Avenue. The tour office is on the mezzanine level of the Metropolitan Opera House, directly in back of the main square.

LOWER EAST SIDE
212/226-9010, www.lowereastsideny.com

Sponsored by the Lower East Side Business Improvement District, this free two-hour tour will teach you all about this wonderful area's shops and retailing history. The tour meets on Sunday at 11 at Katz's Delicatessen (East Houston at Ludlow Street) from April through December. It lasts about two hours and is free.

At various times of year, dozens of New York's cultural institutions—including such heavyweights as the Metropolitan Museum of Art and lesser-known spots like the Caribbean Cultural Center—host special **"Insider's Hour"** tours. The New York City Opera, the New York Philharmonic, Jazz at Lincoln Center, Carnegie Hall, and even WNET (the area's flagship PBS station) all offer such tours as well. Look for a complete list at **NYC & Company** (810 Seventh Ave, 800/692-8474), or go to www.nycvisit.com and search for "Insider's Hour".

LOWER EAST SIDE TENEMENT MUSEUM
212/431-0233, www.tenement.org

I can't say enough about this wonderful museum and its docents. In addition to tours of the restored apartments in the tenement at 97 Orchard Street, the museum offers fascinating tours exploring the surrounding area's rich and diverse ethnic heritage on weekends in warmer months. Though not cheap, they're well worth the price. Tours leave from the museum's offices at the corner of Orchard and Broome streets.

MADISON SQUARE GARDEN
212/465-5800, www.thegarden.com

If you've always wanted to see the New York Knicks' locker room, this tour's for you! It's offered daily on the hour from 10 to 3. Be aware that schedules are frequently abbreviated, and access to certain areas is often limited because of events at the Garden. Tickets cost $17 for adults and $12 for children 12 and under, and are available at the Garden's box office.

METROPOLITAN OPERA
212/769-7020, www.metoperafamily.org/education

The Metropolitan Opera Guild offers 90-minute tours of this extraordinary place between the start of the opera season (around the end of September) and the end of the ballet season (in or around June) on weekday afternoons and Saturday mornings. Reservations should be made well in advance, but you can always call at the last minute to see if space is available or go on a standby basis. Tickets cost $10 for adults and $5 for full-time students.

NBC EXPERIENCE/STUDIO TOUR
212/664-3700, www.nbc.com

Children under six are not admitted, but anybody else can take an hour-long tour of NBC's television studios—$17.50 for adults and $15.50 for children and seniors. They've added lots of high-tech bells and whistles to this tour, but the quality still varies dramatically, depending on chance (what famous person happens to be getting off the elevator as you're getting on) and whether some big news event is breaking. The tour leaves every 15 minutes daily from 8:30 to 5 from NBC's lobby on 50th Street between Fifth Avenue and Avenue of the Americas.

The **New York Landmarks Conservancy** has published several books detailing self-guided walking tours in such neighborhoods as Lower Manhattan, the Upper East Side, Harlem, and the Flatiron District. Call 212/995-5260 or go to www.nylandmarks.org for more information.

NEW AMSTERDAM THEATER
212/282-2900, www.disney.go.com/disneytheatrical/newamsterdam

Tours of this beautifully restored theater—once home to the Ziegfeld Follies and now to *The Lion King*—offer a glimpse into Broadway's past and present. They're offered hourly on Monday and Tuesday between 10 and 5. Tickets are available at the theater's box office and cost $12 for adults and $5 for children under 12. Tours meet at the box office on 42nd Street between Seventh and Eighth avenues.

NEW YORK PUBLIC LIBRARY
212/930-0501, www.nypl.org

An informative free tour of the grand New York Public Library is offered Monday through Saturday at 11 and 2. It leaves from the Friends of the Library desk, to the right of the library's main entrance on Fifth Avenue at 41st Street. Tours of the changing exhibits in the library's Gottesman Hall are also offered daily except Sunday.

ON LOCATION TOURS
212/209-3370 (reservations only), www.sceneontv.com

This company offers tours of sites from such television shows as *Sex in the City*, *The Sopranos*, *Law and Order*, *Seinfeld*, and even *I Love Lucy*. Tours of the settings from various movies are offered as well. Available at various times throughout the week, tours last several hours and hop all around the city.

> Seth Kamil, Eric Wakin, and Kenneth Jackson—founders of Big Onion Walking Tours—have written a wonderful book outlining self-guided walking tours of New York. It's loaded with interesting details about this wonderful city. **The Big Onion Guide to New York City: The Historic Tours** is sold in bookstores, or you can call 212/439-1090 to order copies.

RADIO CITY MUSIC HALL
212/247-4777, www.radiocity.com

If you want to look inside this art deco treasure but don't want to attend a concert or other event, try one of the daily "Stage Door" tours. Tours run about an hour and are offered at various times, depending on the season. The cost is $16 for adults and $10 for children under 12. Tickets are available inside the main lobby, on the corner of Avenue of the Americas and 50th Street.

UNITED NATIONS
212/963-8687, www.un.org/tours

If you want to peek inside the chambers of the United Nations General Assembly and learn more about this incredible organization, tours begin about every half hour between 9:30 and 4:45 seven days a week (weekdays only in January and February). The tour costs $11.50 for adults, $8 for senior citizens, $7.50 for students, and $6.50 for children in grades one through eight. Children under five are not allowed on the tours, which last from 45 minutes to an hour and are offered in various languages. The visitors entrance to the United Nations is on First Avenue, between 45th and 46th streets, and the tour desk is directly across from the entrance, past the main lobby and down the hall.

WALDORF-ASTORIA HOTEL
212/872-1275

Get a dose of New York history and a peek behind the scenes of this landmark Park Avenue hotel. Tours are offered on the first Saturday of every month at 10:30 a.m. They are limited to 20 people, and advance reservations are required.

YANKEE STADIUM
718/579-4531, www.newyork.yankees.mlb.com

Even in the off-season, baseball fans can tour the dugout, press box, and clubhouse of "The House that Ruth Built" (which is, by the way, in the Bronx). If you're alone or with a few other people, simply show up at the stadium's press gate at noon daily (except on game days). If you're with a group of 12 or more, advance reservations are required. Tours cost $14 for adults and $7 for children 14 and younger and senior citizens 60 and older. More elaborate (and therefore more expensive) tours are also available.

> Babe Ruth hit his first home run in Yankee Stadium in the first game
> ever played there, on April 18, 1923.

WALKING TOURS

Time Out New York lists scheduled walking tours in its "Around Town"
section each week. Among the potential sources:

BIG ONION WALKING TOURS
212/439-1090, www.bigonion.com

Seth Kamil and his band of guides—most of them graduate students in
American history from Columbia University and New York University
—share their vast knowledge of New York through a wide array of walking
tours. Governor's Island, George Washington's New York, Historic Catholic
New York, and the Civil War and Draft Riots are just a few of the many
topics. You can even take a wildly popular tour of the Lower East Side on
Christmas Day. Most tours cost $15 for adults and $12 for senior citizens and
students. Some are a bit more and all can be arranged for private parties. All
tours last between two and two-and-a-half hours. While some of the guides
are more charismatic than others, all are well informed.

JOYCE GOLD'S HISTORY TOURS OF NEW YORK
212/242-5762, www.nyctours.com

Nowhere in the United States are past and present so closely quartered as
in New York, and few people are better able to convey that than historian
Joyce Gold. Her scheduled tours—which include such topics as the American Revolution, the Gilded Age of J. P. Morgan, and the Jewish Lower East
Side—are usually given on weekends in warmer months and cost $12. She is
also available for private tours.

MUNICIPAL ART SOCIETY
212/439-1049, www.mas.org/events/tours.cfm

This terrific advocacy group offers a wide array of thematic and area-
specific walking tours for people interested in the city's architecture and
history. Most tours are led by historians. The diverse topics include architectural oddities, immigrant New York, downtown skyscrapers, and subway art
and design. Tours are offered on different days at various places. Most last 90
minutes and cost $12 to $15 for adults (less for students and senior citizens).

MUSEUM OF THE CITY OF NEW YORK
212/534-1672, ext. 206, www.mcny.org

This museum's walking tours are very much in tune with the tenor of life
in the city. Typically held every other Sunday from April to October, tours
are led by experts and cost $15. Registration is required.

MY KIND OF TOWN NEW YORK
212/754-4500, www.mykindoftownny.com

The owner and founder of this wonderful little company shares my love of New York and my desire to make it as accessible for as many people as possible. The tours offered by this outfit—all of which are personalized, private, and done in the comfort of a Mercedes Benz sedan—begin with a few simple questions: Have you been here before? What do you want to see? What would help you feel confident here? The goal, of course, is for you to end up feeling like New York is your town, too—at least for a little while.

92ND STREET Y
212/415-5500, www.92y.org

This amazing institution offers walking tours to complement its frequent lectures and other programs, as well as open houses in historic areas. Prices vary, guides are knowledgeable, and tours are well run. They fill up quickly, and reservations are required.

URBAN PARK RANGERS
212/360-2774, www.nycgovparks.org

The city's Department of Parks and Recreation employs Urban Park Rangers, who give wonderful weekend walking tours of Central Park and other parks throughout Manhattan and the outer boroughs. Tours are free, and many are designed for children or families.

IV. Where to Find It: New York's Best Food Shops

Asian

ASIA MARKET
71½ Mulberry St (bet Canal and Bayard St)   212/962-2020
Daily: 8-7

Fresh fruit and vegetables, plus exotic herbs and spices from all over Asia, are the main attractions at Asia Market. You'll find items from Thailand, Indonesia, Malaysia, the Philippines, Japan, and China, plus a staff ready to explain how to prepare dishes from these countries. Asia Market provides produce to some of New York's best restaurants.

Bakery Goods

AMY'S BREAD
672 Ninth Ave (Hell's Kitchen)   212/977-2670
Mon-Fri: 7:30 a.m.-11 p.m.; Sat: 8 a.m.-11 p.m.; Sun: 9-6

75 Ninth Ave (Chelsea Market)   212/462-4338
Mon-Fri: 7:30 a.m.-8 p.m.; Sat: 8-7; Sun: 10-6

250 Bleecker St   212/675-7802
Mon-Thur: 7:30 a.m.-11 p.m.; Fri: 7:30 a.m.-12 a.m.;
Sat: 8 a.m.-12 a.m.; Sun: 8 a.m.-10 p.m.   www.amysbread.com

As the aroma of freshly baked bread and sweets drifts onto Ninth Avenue, locals and tourists alike line up outside of Amy's Hell's Kitchen location to sample the many treats for sale. An oasis in the heart of midtown, Amy's Bread is a cross between a Parisian *boulangerie* and a cozy Midwestern kitchen. Of course, you should come for the bread—Amy's signature semolina with golden raisins and fennel, the green olive *picholine*, or just a simple French baguette. One could eat three meals a day and in-between snacks at Amy's Bread. Among the goodies are grilled sandwiches, sticky buns, old-fashioned double layer cakes, and decadent brownies. The staff provides consistent, friendly service.

A. ORWASHER BAKERY
308 E 78th St (at Second Ave)   212/288-6569
Mon-Sat: 7-7; Sun: 9-4   www.orwashersbakery.com

Orwasher has occupied the same location and been run by the same family for nearly a century. Many of its breads are made from recipes handed down from father to son. You'll find Old World breads that once were commonly made in the local immigrant bakeries but are now extremely rare. Over 30 varieties are always available. Hearth-baked in brick ovens and made with natural ingredients, the breads come in a marvelous array of shapes and sizes—triple twists, cornucopias, and hearts, just to name a few. Be sure to sample the onion boards, rye, cinnamon raisin bread, and challah. It's almost as good as the home-baked variety. Best of all is the raisin pumpernickel, which comes in small rolls or loaves and is sensational when warm. The Irish soda bread is also special!

BILLY'S BAKERY
184 Ninth Ave (bet 21st and 22nd St)   212/647-9956
Mon-Thurs: 9 a.m.-11 p.m.; Fri, Sat: 9 a.m.- 12:30 a.m.;
Sun: 9 a.m.-11 p.m.   www.billysbakerynyc.com

You'll savor the mouth-watering vibes from the minute you walk in, as the baking is done right on the premises. Billy's presents a good assortment of tasty muffins, cakes, brownies, lemon squares, pies, and cheesecakes. The young staff is particularly helpful.

BREAD MARKET & CAFE
485 Fifth Ave (bet 41st and 42nd St)   212/370-7356
Mon-Fri: 6-6; Sat: 8-6

Freshness is the key! The bread is baked fresh daily in their rotating oven. You'll find very good San Francisco sourdough, French baguettes, sourdough focaccia, ciabatta, German pumpernickel, and much more. They make a wide variety of excellent sandwiches. Free delivery is offered.

Glossary for Bread Lovers

Bakers use these terms loosely:

Boule: round, domed bread
Baguette: long, thin loaf with soft interior and a crackly crust
Batard: short, slightly flattened baguette
Ciabatta: flat, rectangular Northern Italian bread with an airy interior and chewy crust
Ficelle: extra-thin baguette
Focaccia: flat, dense, and tender bread flavored with olive oil; from Liguria
Fougasse: chewy-crusted, rather flat sourdough wheat bread from Provence
Integrale: Italian term for "whole wheat"
Miche: round sourdough French bread
Pain au levain: dense, whole-wheat French sourdough bread with a very chewy crust
Pugliese: big, round bread with a very dark crust and light, airy interior
Sourdough: bread made from fermented dough saved for use as leaven

CAFE LALO
201 W 83rd St (at Amsterdam Ave)   212/496-6031
Mon-Thurs: 8 a.m.-2 a.m.; Fri: 8 a.m.-4 a.m.; Sat: 9 a.m.-4 a.m.;
Sun: 9 a.m-2 a.m.   www.cafelalo.com

In my opinion, this is the best dessert shop in town. You will be reminded
of a fine European pastry shop as you enjoy cappuccino, espresso, cordials,
and a large selection of delicious desserts. Cafe Lalo offers more than 100
choices, including cakes, cheesecakes, tarts, pies, and connoisseur cheese
platters. Yogurt and ice cream are also available, and soothing music makes
every calorie go down sweetly. Breakfasts and brunches are a treat. Delivery
throughout Manhattan is available.

COLUMBUS BAKERY
474 Columbus Ave (at 83rd St)   212/724-6880
Daily: 7:30 a.m.-10 p.m.

The Upper West Side has a quality bakery it can call its own! Columbus
Bakery sells great rosemary rolls, delicious onion rolls (terrific for burgers),
multigrain breads, really crusty sourdoughs, wonderful cakes, and pastries.
You can eat in or take out, but what a pleasure just to sit and smell those fresh
loaves. Catering is available.

CREATIVE CAKES
400 E 74th St (at First Ave)   212/794-9811
Mon-Fri: 8-4:30; Sat: 9-11   www.creativecakesny.com

Being in the "creative cake" business myself, I know all about making
special concoctions. Creative Cakes knows how to have fun using fine ingredients and ingenious patterns. Cake lovers are fans of the fudgy chocolate
cake with buttercream icing and sensational designs. Among other things,
Bill Schutz has replicated the U.S. Customs House in cake form for a Fourth
of July celebration. Prices are reasonable, and the results are sure to be a conversation piece at any party.

DESSERT DELIVERY
360 E 55th St (bet First and Second Ave)   212/838-5411
Mon-Fri: 8:30-7; Sat: 10-6   www.dessertdeliveryny.com

An unusual concept: Dessert Delivery sells only what they consider to be
the best pastry items made in the city. Created by different chefs, there are
chocolate-chip cookies, strawberry shortcake, cakes and cupcakes, and much
more. Delivery service—they say within two hours—is offered without
advance notification. For office parties or home celebrations, this is a very
good bet. Bill Clinton and Donald Trump think so, too!

DOUGHNUT PLANT
379 Grand St (bet Essex and Norfolk St)   212/505-3700
Tues-Sun: 6:30 a.m.-7 p.m. (or until they're gone)
                                              www.doughnutplant.com

Mark Israel has come a long way since delivering doughnuts on his
bicycle. Now he presides over an establishment that is truly unique, con-
cocting fluffy, fresh organic doughnuts made with spring water. The last time
I counted there were 26 flavors, including orange, malted milk, banana with

pecans, "Yankee" (with blueberry pin stripes), and rosewater (yes, with fresh rose petals)! Each doughnut is hand-cut, yeast-raised, and very large. They also serve cinnamon buns, sticky buns, and much more.

DUFOUR PASTRY KITCHENS
25 Ninth Ave (at 13th St)   212/929-2800
Mon-Fri: 9-5

This area is now one of New York's hottest! The air at Dufour is full of pastry flour, so don't wear your best black outfit. Moreover, all items are frozen, so you'll have to bake them yourself (instructions included). But these are the only drawbacks. You'll find delicious and sensibly priced pastry items of high quality at Dufour, which counts many fancy uptown restaurants among its customers. Chocolate and regular puff-pastry dough are available in sheets and in bulk. Wonderful hors d'oeuvres include bite-size, hand-filled "party bites" in flavors like fresh mushroom paté, Swiss cheese, and spinach.

To go to cupcake heaven, visit one of these:

Amy's Bread (672 Ninth Ave, 212/977-2670 and Chelsea Market, 75 Ninth Ave, 212/462-4338)
Buttercup Bake Shop (973 Second Ave, 212/350-4144)
Crumbs Bake Shop (321½ Amsterdam Ave, 212/712-9800)
Cupcake Cafe (522 Ninth Ave, 212/465-1530)
Kitchenette (1272 Amsterdam Ave, 212/531-7600 and 80 West Broadway, 212/267-6740)
Magnolia Bakery (401 Bleecker St, 212/462-2572)
William Greenberg Jr. Desserts (1100 Madison Ave, 212/744-0304)

FERRARA CAFE
195 Grand St (bet Mulberry and Mott St)   212/226-6150
Daily: 8 a.m.-midnight (Sat to 1 a.m.)   www.ferraracafe.com

This store in Little Italy is one of the largest little *pasticcerias* in the world. The business deals in wholesale imports and several other ventures, but the sheer perfection of their confections could support the whole business. Certainly, the atmosphere would never suggest that this is anything but a very efficiently run Italian bakery. Its **Old World Caffe** is famous for numerous varieties of pastry, light sandwiches, gelati, and coffee.

FLUFF
751 Ninth Ave (at 51st St)   646/289-3025
Mon-Wed: 7:30 a.m.-11 p.m.; Thur-Sat: 7:30 a.m.-midnight;
Sun: 8 a.m.-11 p.m.

Fluff has a lot going for it: handy location, nice surroundings, clean appearance, helpful personnel, reasonable prices, and (most of all) good food. This is a combination bakery-cafe offering breakfast items, sandwiches, salads, soups, crepes, and yummy desserts. You'll find beautiful cakes, cookies, brownies, lemon tarts, chocolate creations that melt in your mouth, peanut butter treats, and more.

GERTEL'S BAKE SHOP
53 Hester St (bet Essex and Ludlow St)   212/982-3250
Sun-Thurs: 6:30-5:30; Fri: 6:30-3

You simply must try Gertel's blackout cake! Customers who come here
are almost evenly divided between those who call it Ger*tel's* (accent on the
last syllable) and *Ger*tel's (as in girdles). Regardless, all agree that their cakes
and breads are among the best in New York. Locals prefer the traditional
babkas, strudels, and kuchens, but I find the chocolate rolls and aforementioned blackout cake to be outstanding. Tables are available for enjoying
baked goods, coffee, or a light lunch. From the regulars at these tables, one
can glean the choicest shopping tidbits on the Lower East Side. A final tip:
every Thursday and Friday, Gertel's makes potato kugels. People claim to
have come all the way from California for a Thursday kugel! During a slow
week, you can occasionally find one left over on a Sunday.

GLASER'S BAKE SHOP
1670 First Ave (bet 87th and 88th St)   212/289-2562
Tues-Fri: 7-7; Sat: 8-7; Sun: 8-3
Closed July and part of Aug

If it's Sunday, it won't be hard to find Glaser's. The line frequently spills
outside as people queue up to buy the Glaser family's fresh cakes and baked
goods. One isn't enough of anything here. Customers always walk out with
arms bulging. The Glasers have run their shop as a family business since
1902 at this same location, and they're justifiably proud of their breads,
brownies, cakes, cookies (try the chocolate chip!), and wedding cakes.

The best cheesecakes in New York:
Eileen's Special Cheesecake (17 Cleveland Pl, 212/966-5585, www.
eileenscheesecake.com)
Junior's (386 Flatbush Ave, Brooklyn, 718/852-5257)
Two Little Red Hens (1652 Second Ave, 212/452-0476, www.two
littleredhens.com)
Yura & Co. (1659 Third Ave, 212/860-8060)

H&H BAGELS
2239 Broadway (at 80th St)   212/595-8000
639 W 46th St (bet Eleventh and Twelfth Ave)   212/765-7200
Daily: 24 hours   www.hhbagels.com

If you find yourself out and about in the wee hours, you can get a fresh
hot bagel without having to wait in H&H's long daytime line. Regardless
of the hour, you can satisfy your hot bagel craving day or night at H&H,
which bakes the best bagels in Manhattan. They ship worldwide; call
800/NY-BAGEL for mail order.

KOSSAR'S BIALYS
367 Grand St (at Essex St)   212/473-4810
Sun-Thurs: 6 a.m.-8 p.m.; Fri: 6-3:30   877-4-BIALYS
                                                www.kossarsbialys.com

Tradition has it that the bialy derives its name from Bialystoker, where they were first made. Kossar's brought the recipe over from Europe almost a century ago, and their bialys, bagels, horns, and onion boards are fresh from the oven. The taste is Old World and authentic.

LE PAIN QUOTIDIEN
1131 Madison Ave (bet 84th and 85th St)	212/327-4900
Mon-Fri: 7:30-7; Sat, Sun: 8-7	
833 Lexington Ave (bet 63rd and 64th St)	212/755-5810
Mon-Fri: 7:30-7:30; Sat, Sun: 8-7:30	
100 Grand St (at Mercer St)	212/625-9009
Mon-Fri: 7:30-7:30; Sat, Sun: 8-7	
38 E 19th St (bet Park Ave and Broadway)	212/673-7900
Mon-Fri: 7:30-7:30; Sat, Sun: 8-7:30	
1336 First Ave (bet 71st and 72nd St)	212/717-4800
Daily: 7:30-7:30	
50 W 72nd St (bet Columbus and Park Ave S)	212/712-9700
Mon-Fri: 7:30-7; Sat, Sun: 8-7	
922 Seventh Ave (at 58th St)	212/757-0775
Mon-Fri: 7:30-8:30; Sat, Sun: 8:00 a.m.-8:30 p.m.	
10 Fifth Ave (at 8th St)	212/253-2324
Mon-Fri: 7:30-7:30; Sat-Sun: 8-7:30	www.painquotidien. com

Le Pain Quotidien traces its roots to Brussels, Belgium. It is a country-style bakery with long, wooden communal tables that serve customers breakfast, lunch, and light afternoon meals. European breads and pastries are sold at the counter. The meals offered are simple and the service very refined. You'll find delicious croissants, *pain au chocolate,* brioche, heaping bread baskets, Belgian sugar waffles, wonderful sandwiches (like Scottish smoked salmon with dill and Parisian ham with three mustards), an unusual Tuscan platter, crisp salads, and a wonderful board of French cheeses. Don't pass up the Belgian chocolate brownies!

If you can't find your favorite bagel (and cream cheese) at **Bagels on the Square** (7 Carmine St, 212/691-3041), it must not exist. This is a bagel lover's paradise!

LITTLE PIE COMPANY
424 W 43rd St (at Ninth Ave)	212/736-4780
Mon-Fri: 8-8; Sat: 10-7; Sun: 12-7	www.littlepiecompany.com

Former actor Arnold Wilkerson started baking apple pastries for private orders in his own kitchen. Now he and educator Michael Deraney operate a unique shop that makes handmade pies and cakes using fresh seasonal fruits. Although they specialize in apple pie (available every season), they also make fresh peach, cherry, blueberry, and other all-American fruit pie favorites, along with cream, meringue, and crumb pies. Stop by for a hot slice of pie a la mode and a cup of cider. Also available are delicious brownies, bars, muffins, fruit Danish, applesauce carrot cake, white coconut cake, chocolate cream pies, and cheescakes with wild blueberry, cherry, and orange toppings. No preservatives are used! Other offerings include croissants (ham, cheese, and turkey), and homemade "little" quiches. Little Pie Company has two other locations: a large eat-in American bakery at 407 West 14th Street (212/414-2324) and a spot in Grand Central Station (212/983-3538).

MAGNOLIA BAKERY
401 Bleecker St (at 11th St)   212/462-2572
Mon: noon-11:30; Tues-Thurs: 9 a.m.-11 p.m.; Fri: 9 a.m.-
12:30 a.m.; Sat: 10 a.m.-12:30 a.m.; Sun: 10 a.m.-11:30 p.m.

What a charming place! Everything is made right on the premises: layer cakes, pies, cupcakes, brownies, cookies, icebox desserts, and banana pudding. Birthday cakes are a specialty that come in various types and sizes. You won't go away hungry!

MOISHE'S HOMEMADE KOSHER BAKERY
115 Second Ave (bet 6th and 7th St)   212/505-8555
Sun-Thurs: 7 a.m.-9 p.m.; Fri: 7-5

Jewish bakery specialties are legendary, and they are done to perfection at Moishe's. The cornbread is prepared exactly as it was in the Old Country (and as it should be now), the pumpernickel is dark and moist, and the ryes are simply scrumptious. Black Russian pumpernickel bread is the house specialty, which cannot be bested in any old-fashioned Russian bakery. The cakes and pies are special, too! The owners are charming and eager to please, and they run one of the best bakeries in the city, with the usual complement of bagels, bialys, cakes, and pastries. By all means try the challah; Moishe's produces the best in town. The chocolate layer cakes are also superb. (Note: There is no cornbread or white bread on Friday.)

> When you mention cheesecake, natives in the know immediately sing the praises of **Junior's** (386 Flatbush Ave, 718/852-5257), a Brooklyn restaurant that's famous for it. You can get Junior's delicious treats, in many shapes and flavors, at Grand Central Station (212/JUNIORS), either near the waiting room on the main concourse or in Junior's restaurant, on the lower level.

MURRAY'S BAGELS
500 Ave of the Americas (bet 12th and 13th St)   212/462-2830
Mon-Fri: 6:30 a.m.-9 p.m.; Sat, Sun: 6:30 a.m.-7 p.m.

242 Eighth Ave (bet 22nd and 23rd St)   646/638-1335
Daily: 7 a.m.-10 p.m.   www.murraysbagels.com

Delicious hand-rolled, kettle-boiled and baked bagels—14 kinds of them!
—are featured, but there is much more. You'll also find smoked fish, spreads and schmears, deli items for sandwiches, plus soups and pastries. It's all available for eat-in, catering platters, or free home delivery (within limits).

POSEIDON BAKERY
629 Ninth Ave (bet 44th and 45th St)   212/757-6173
Tues-Sat: 9-7   www.poseidonbakery.com

Poseidon is a family-run bakery that produces Greek specialties. Tremendous pride is evident here. When a customer peers over the counter and asks about something, the response is usually a long description and sometimes an invitation to taste. There is homemade baklava, strudel, *katalf, trigona, tiropita* (cheese pie), spanakopita, *saragli*, and phyllo. They have cocktail-size frozen spinach, cheese, vegetable, and meat pies for home or parties. Poseidon was founded in 1922 by Greek baker Demetrios Anagnostou. Today it is run by his great grandson, Paul, to the same exacting standards. Poseidon's handmade phyllo is world-renowned.

SILVER MOON BAKERY
2740 Broadway (at 105th St)   212/866-4717
Mon-Fri: 7:30 a.m.-8 p.m.; Sat, Sun: 8:30-7
                                www.silvermoonbakery.com

Silver Moon presents delicious French, German, and Italian breads, French pastries and cakes, tarts, French macaroons, challah, brioche (fresh fruit, raspberry, raisin, and chocolate chip), muffins, scones, and much more. There are a few tables where you can enjoy a sandwich or quiche (pizzas, too, on Sunday) and watch the passing parade.

> Attention all bakers! **New York Cake & Baking Supply** (56 W 22nd St, 212/675-CAKE) is a treasure house of cake and chocolate supplies. The selection is vast, prices reasonable, and you'll find everything in the baking world for sale here. You can browse conveniently online (www.nycake.com) and then phone or fax your order.

STREIT'S MATZOS
150 Rivington St (bet Clinton and Suffolk St)   212/475-7000
Mon-Thurs: 9-4:30   www.streitsmatzos.com

Matzo is a thin, wafer-like unleavened bread. According to tradition, it came out of Egypt with Moses and the children of Israel when they had to flee so swiftly there was no time to let the bread rise. Through the years, matzoh was restricted to the time around Passover, and even when matzo production became automated, business shut down for a good deal of the year. But not today and not in New York. Streit produces matzo throughout the year, pausing only on Saturday and Jewish holidays to clean the machines. Streit allows a peek at the production, which is both mechanized and extremely primitive. Matzo is baked in enormous thin sheets that are later broken up. If you ask for a batch that's baking, they might break it right off the production line. They also offer noodles, wafers, ready-to-serve canned soups, potato products, Hanukkah products, and specialty dishes.

SULLIVAN STREET BAKERY
73 Sullivan St (bet Spring and Broome St)   212/334-9435
Daily: 7-7

533 W 47th St (bet Tenth and Eleventh Ave)   212/265-5580
Daily: 7-7   www.sullivanstreetbakery.com

Getting fresh, crusty, warm French loaves here is a must. If you savor really fresh authentic Italian country bread, this is also the place to go. Their sourdough is used by a number of restaurants, so you know it is first-rate. Sullivan Street Bakery carries the only flatbread *pizza bianca romana* (Roman-style white pizza) in Manhattan. Raisin-walnut bread is one of their specialties.

To score a real party or event hit, try the personalized cookies from **Eleni's Cookies** (Chelsea Market, 75 Ninth Ave, 212/255-7990, www. elenis.com).

SYLVIA WEINSTOCK CAKES
273 Church St (bet Franklin and White St)   212/925-6698
Mon-Fri: 9-4 (by appointment only)   www.sylviaweinstock.com

Sylvia Weinstock has been in the cake business for over two decades, so she knows how to satisfy customers who want the very best. Her trademark is floral decorations, which are almost lifelike! Although weddings are a specialty (two months notice is required), she will produce a masterpiece for any occasion, including hand-molded sugar figures.

VESUVIO BAKERY
160 Prince St (bet West Broadway and Thompson St)   212/925-8248
Mon-Thurs: 8 a.m.-10 p.m.; Fri-Sun: 8 a.m.-11 p.m.

It isn't every commercial bakery that eschews sugar, shortening, and preservatives, yet still manages to produce the tastiest Italian bread around. The new owner has maintained the ambience of this well-known bakery. Breakfast is served all day, paninis are a specialty, and classic breads are made fresh all day long.

Yes, there is even Indian fast food! Come try some items at **Indian Bread Co.** (194 Bleecker St, 212/228-1909). Hours are Mon-Thurs: 12-11; Fri, Sat: 12 noon to 1 a.m.; and Sun: 12-10.

WHOLE EARTH BAKERY & KITCHEN
130 St. Mark's Pl (bet First Ave and Ave A)   212/677-7597
Daily: 9 a.m.-midnight

This is a completely vegan establishment. It's the only Manhattan bakery using organic flours and organic, unprocessed sweeteners. They feature great pizza, lasagna, and soup, with daily selections of savory foods. Catering is available.

YONAH SCHIMMEL'S KNISHES
137 E Houston St (bet First and Second Ave)   212/477-2858
Sun-Thurs: 9-7; Fri, Sat: 9 a.m.-10 p.m.   www.knishery.com

Yonah Schimmel has been selling knishes for so long that his name is legendary. National magazines have written articles about him. Schimmel started out dispensing knishes among the pushcarts of the Lower East Side, and a Yonah Schimmel knish is still a unique experience. It doesn't look or taste anything like the mass-produced things sold at supermarkets, lunch stands, and New York ballgames. The knishes made here have a thin, flaky crust—almost like strudel dough—surrounding a hot, moist filling, and it is kosher. The best-selling filling is potato, but kasha (buckwheat), spinach, and a half-dozen others are also terrific. No two knishes come out exactly alike, since each is handmade. You can order by fax (212/477-2858) for delivery anywhere in the continental U.S.

Is your sweet tooth aching? Since 1894, **Veniero's** (342 E 11th St, 212/674-7070, www.venierospastry.com) has been serving Italian pastries, cakes, and gelati to satisfied customers. The quarters still have many of the original details, including hand-stamped metal ceilings and etched glass doors.

Beverages

B&E QUALITY
511 W 23rd Ave (bet Tenth and Eleventh Ave)   212/243-6559
Mon-Thurs: 8:30-6:30; Fri, Sat: 8:30-7

If you are planning a party and want to make a quantity purchase of beer and soda, this is a good place to go. B&E is a wholesale distributor but will pass along savings to retail customers. Some 500 beers from around the world are available, as well as kegs from over 15 breweries.

NEW YORK BEVERAGE WHOLESALERS
207 E 123rd St (bet Second and Third Ave)   212/831-4000
Mon-Fri: 8:30-6; Sat: 8:30-5   www.nybeverage.com

The *buy*-words here: tremendous variety and great prices. This outfit has one of the largest retail beer selections in Manhattan, with over 500 brands available, plus soda, mineral and natural waters, iced teas, and seltzers. They will deliver to your door, supply specialty imports, and work with you on any quantities needed. Call to place a delivery order, and don't forget the ice.

RIVERSIDE BEER AND SODA DISTRIBUTORS
2331 Twelfth Ave (at 133rd St)   212/234-3884
Mon-Sat: 9-5

This place mainly supplies wholesalers and large retail orders, but they are not averse to serving retail customers. Once you've made the trek up here, you might as well take advantage of the discount and buy in quantity.

British

MYERS OF KESWICK
634 Hudson St (bet Horatio and Jane St)   212/691-4194
Mon-Fri: 10-7; Sat: 10-6; Sun: noon-5   www.myersofkeswick.com

Peter and Irene Myers are to English food what Burberry, Church, and Laura Ashley are to English clothing. They've made it possible for you to visit "the village grocer" for imported staples and fresh, home-baked items you'd swear came from a kitchen in Soho—the London neighborhood, that is. Among the tins, a shopper can find Heinz treacle sponge pudding, trifle mix, ribena, mushy peas, steak and kidney pie, Smarties, Quality Street toffee, lemon barley water, chutneys, jams and preserves, and all the major English teas. Fresh goods include sausage rolls, steak and kidney pie, Scotch eggs, British bangers, and Cumberland sausages made daily. There are also cheeses (the double Gloucester is outstanding) and chocolates. For Anglophiles and expatriates alike, Myers of Keswick is a *luverly* treat.

Candy

CHOCOLATE BAR
48 Eighth Ave (bet Jane and Horatio St)   212/366-1541
Mon-Fri: 8:30 a.m.-10 p.m.; Sat: 9 a.m-10 p.m.; Sun: 10-7
                                                www.chocolatebarnyc.com

If, like your author, you are a chocoholic, you'll love the yummy brownies, handmade truffles, chocolate-covered peanut butter and jelly bars, cookies, and much more at the Chocolate Bar. Some of the best-known pastry chefs in New York, like Jacques Torres, contribute their talents to help customers expand their waistlines. Treats are available for eat-in or takeout.

DYLAN'S CANDY BAR
1011 Third Ave (at 60th St)   646/735-0078
Mon-Thurs: 11-9; Fri, Sat: 11-11; Sun: 11-7
                                                www.dylanscandybar.com

Ralph Lauren's daughter, Dylan, is in the candy business in a big way. Dylan's is a huge candy emporium, delighting grown-ups as much as kids. You'll find an old-fashioned soda fountain with custom-made ice cream flavors, a candy spa (for goodies like chocolate bath salts), the world's largest lollipop, 21 colors of M&Ms, Pez dispensers, and much more. This is a two-level operation, with stairs that look like gummies! A private party room with all kinds of candy activities—like designing your own candy picture frame —is available. The candy selection includes 5,000 types of sweets from all over the world.

ECONOMY CANDY
108 Rivington St (bet Essex and Ludlow St)   212/254-1531
Sun-Fri: 9-6; Sat: 10-5   800/352-4544 (outside New York)
                                                www.economycandy.com

The same family of owners has been selling everything from penny candies to beautiful gourmet gift baskets at Economy Candy since 1937. What a selection of dried fruits, candies, teas, jams, cookies, crackers, and chocolates —even sugar-free goodies! The best part is the price. You'll find much for your baking needs: almond paste, cocoas, baking chocolate, and glazed fruits. Old-time favorites that everybody loves include Pixie Sticks, candy buttons, wax lips, and ice cubes. Mail orders are filled efficiently and promptly; an online catalog is available.

JACQUES TORRES CHOCOLATE HAVEN
350 Hudson St (at King St)   212/414-2462
Mon-Sat: 9-7; Sun: 10-6   www.mrchocolate.com

Now you can see those delicious Jacques Torres bars and other creations actually being made right in front of you! In a hefty space that houses a factory, retail counter, and cafe, Jacques Torres will send the chocoholic in you to chocolate heaven.

LA MAISON DU CHOCOLAT
1018 Madison Ave (bet 78th and 79th St)   212/744-7117
Mon-Sat: 10-7; Sun: 12-6

30 Rockefeller Plaza   212/265-9404
Mon-Fri: 9:30-7; Sat: 10-7; Sun: 11-6   www.lamaisonduchocolat.com

What a place! Over 40 delicious variations of light and dark chocolates
are available under one roof. They carry French truffles, plain and fancy
champagnes, orangettes, coffee beans, chocolate-covered almonds, caramels,
candied chestnuts, and fruit paste. There's even a tea salon that serves pastries and drinks. Everything is made in Paris, and La Maison du Chocolat is
the first branch of the store outside of France. Prices are a cut above the
candy-counter norm, but then so are exotic flavors like September raspberries, freshly grated ginger root, raisins flamed in rum, marzipan with pistachio and kirsh, and caramel butter. What a way to go!

LEONIDAS
485 Madison Ave (bet 51st and 52nd St)   212/980-2608
Mon-Fri: 9-7; Sat: 12-7; Sun: 12-6   www.leonidas-chocolate.com

This is a U.S. franchise of the famous Belgian confectionary company and
a haven for those who appreciate exquisite sweets. Over 80 varieties of
confections—milk, white, and bittersweet chocolate pieces, chocolate orange
peels, solid chocolate medallions, fabulous fresh cream fillings, truffle fillings, and marzipan—are flown in fresh every week. Leonidas' pralines are
particularly sumptuous. Jacques Bergier, the genial owner, can make the
mouth water just describing his treasure trove. Best of all, prices are reasonable. Three retail locations of **Manon Cafe** (120 Broadway, 212/766-
6100; 3 Hanover Square, 212/422-9600; and 74 Trinity Pl, 212/233-1111)
serve coffee, espresso, cappuccino, sandwiches and salads, as well as
Leonidas' Belgian chocolates.

LI-LAC CANDY SHOP
40 Eighth Ave (at Jane St)   212/242-7374
Mon-Fri: 10-8; Sat: 12-8; Sun: 12-5

Grand Central Station (42nd St at Vanderbilt Ave)   212/370-4866
Mon-Fri: 7 a.m.-9 p.m.; Sat: 10-7; Sun: 11-6

Since 1923, Li-Lac has been *the* source for fine chocolate in Greenwich
Village. The most delicious creation is Li-Lac's chocolate fudge, made fresh
every day. If you tire of chocolate, maple walnut fudge is every bit as good.
Then there are pralines, mousses, French rolls, nuts, glacé fruits, and hand-
dipped chocolates, all made on-premises.

MARIEBELLE FINE TREATS & CHOCOLATES
484 Broome St (bet West Broadway and Wooster St)   212/925-6999
Mon-Sat: 11-7; Sun: 12-7   www.mariebelle.com

The heck with the diets; rush down to this delicious location! What awaits
you is thick European hot chocolate, homemade cookies and biscuits, a cocoa
bar, and wines. The exotic chocolate flavors are packed with class. What a
great gift for chocoholics!

MONDEL CHOCOLATES
2913 Broadway (at 114th St)   212/864-2111
Mon-Sat: 11-7; Sun: 12-6

Mondel has been a tasty gem in the neighborhood for about a half-century. Owner Florence Mondel's father founded the store. The aroma is fantastic! The chocolate-covered ginger, orange peel, nut barks, and turtles are especially good. I have routinely ordered their nonpareils. A dietetic chocolate line is offered.

Yum, yum, chocolate lovers! Don't miss these:

Burdick Chocolates (800/229-2419): mail order or delivery
Chocolate Bar (48 Eighth Ave, 212/366-1541): good prices
Christopher Norman Chocolates (212/402-1234, factory): carried at Bloomingdale's, Dean & Deluca, Whole Foods Market, and online (www.christophernormanchocolates.com)
Eric Girerd: Brooklyn Chocolate and Cocoa Co. (718/383-0853, www.wicked-chocolate.com)
F.A.O Schwarz (767 Fifth Ave, 212/644-9400, www.faoschwarz.com): chocolate and ice cream concoctions
Fifth Avenue Chocolatiere (510 Madison Ave, 212/935-5454)
Francois Payard (1032 Lexington Ave, 212/717-5252): carried at Henri Bendel
Jacques Torres Chocolate Haven (350 Hudson St, 718/875-9772): the "in" place
Kee's Chocolate (80 Thompson St, 212/334-3284)
La Maison du Chocolat (1018 Madison Ave, 212/744-7117 and 30 Rockefeller Center, 212/265-9404)
La Vergamote (169 Ninth Ave, 212/627-9010)
Laderach Chocolatier Suisse (800/231-8154): carried at Balducci's (Lincoln Square), Bloomingdale's, Dean & Deluca, and Macy's
Leonidas (485 Madison Ave, 212/980-2608)
Manhattan Fruitier (105 E 29th St, 212/686-0404)
Mariebelle Fine Treats & Chocolates (484 Broome St, 212/925-6999 and 25 Prince St, 212/925-8800)
Martine's (400 E 82nd St, 212/744-6289): carried at Bloomingdale's
Neuchatel Chocolates (55 E 52nd St, 212/759-1388 and 60 Wall St, 212/480-3766)
Page & Smith (42 E 59th St, 212/759-8560): unusual bittersweet chocolates imported from Chile
Richart Design et Chocolat (7 E 55th St, 212/371-9369)
Teuscher Chocolates of Switzerland (25 E 61st St, 212/751-8482 and 620 Fifth Ave, 212/246-4416)
Vosges Haut-Chocolat (132 Spring St, 212/625-2929): unusual combinations

---

NEUCHATEL CHOCOLATES
55 E 52nd St (bet Madison and Park Ave)   212/759-1388
Mon-Fri: 10-6

60 Wall St (bet William and Pearl St)   212/480-3766
Mon-Fri: 10-5:30

Neuchatel Chocolates is a class act—and you pay for the high quality. A discount is offered for orders over $1,000, and it's not difficult to earn it! The finest Swiss chocolates are prepared by hand from family recipes. The taste has been likened to velvety silk. There are 70 varieties of chocolate, with the house specialty being handmade truffles. The marzipan and pralines with fruit or nuts are also worth trying. Neuchatel's origins are Swiss, but the chocolates are created fresh in New York.

NEUHAUS CHOCOLATES
Saks Fifth Avenue
611 Fifth Ave (at 50th St), 8th floor   212/940-2891
Mon-Sat: 10-7 (Thurs till 8); Sun: 12-6

Grand Central Terminal (42nd St at Vanderbilt Ave)   212/972-3740
Mon-Fri: 10-7; Sat: 11-6   www.neuhauschocolate.com

In 1857, the same year my great-grandfather started his one-man store on the riverfront in Portland, Oregon, Jean Neuhaus established a pharmacy and confectionery shop in Belgium. Succeeding generations have produced some of the finest handcrafted, enrobed, and molded-design bittersweet, dark, and milk chocolates in the world. At Neuhaus' New York outlets, chocolates are still imported from Belgium. The showpiece is the Astrid Praline, named after the beloved late queen of Belgium; it is a sugar-glazed delight! Candy is sold in bulk, bars, pre-packs, and holiday and seasonal collections. Be sure to check out their fine assortment of truffles.

TEUSCHER CHOCOLATES OF SWITZERLAND
25 E 61st St (at Madison Ave)   212/751-8482
Mon-Sat: 10-5:45

620 Fifth Ave (Rockefeller Center)   212/246-4416
Mon-Sat: 10-6; Thurs: 10-7:30; Sun: 11-5

www.teuscherchocolate.com

If there was an award for "most elegant chocolate shop," it would have to go to Teuscher. These are not just chocolates; they're imported works of art. Chocolates are shipped weekly from Switzerland. They are packed into stunning handmade boxes that add to the decor of many a customer's home. The truffles are almost obscenely good. The superb champagne truffle has a tiny dot of champagne cream in the center. The cocoa, nougat, butter-crunch, muscat, orange, and almond truffles each have their own little surprise. Truffles are the stars, but Teuscher's marzipan, praline chocolates, and mints (shaped like sea creatures) are of similar high quality.

VOSGES HAUT-CHOCOLAT
132 Spring St (bet Greene and Wooster St)   212/625-2929
Mon-Sun: 11-8   www.vosgeschocolate.com

Does a truffle of milk chocolate, sweet Indian curry, and coconut turn you on? This is the place to get the "Naga Truffle," along with other really rich, exotic goodies. All truffles are handmade and boxed in containers that are as unusual as the flavors.

Catering, Delis, Food to Go

AGATA & VALENTINA
1505 First Ave (at 79th St)   212/452-0690
Daily: 8 a.m.-8:30 p.m.

This is a very classy expanded gourmet shop with an ambience that will make you think you're in Sicily. There are all kinds of good things to eat, with one counter more tempting than the next. In summer they have a sidewalk cafe. You'll love the great selection of gourmet dishes, bakery items, seafood, magnificent fresh vegetables, meats, cheeses, appetizers, cappuccino bar, candies, and gelati. Extra virgin olive oil is a house specialty.

AZURE
830 Third Ave (at 51st St)   212/486-8080
Daily: 24 hours

Azure's 125 feet of hot and cold offerings is a sight. What a salad bar! Of course, there is more: homemade soups, hot Italian sandwiches, stuffed baked potatoes, pizzas, sushi, and great muffins. Azure also offers healthy Mongolian grill fare.

BALDUCCI'S
155-A W 66th St (bet Broadway and Amsterdam Ave) 212/653-8320
Daily: 7 a.m.-9 p.m.   www.balduccis.com

Balducci is synonymous with food in Manhattan, especially when it comes to fresh fruits and vegetables. The Balduccis started their empire in 1946, offering fabulous selections of cakes and pastries, coffees, breads, meats, seafood, prepared entrees, and domestic and imported cheeses. You'll find a huge selection of Italian foodstuffs: focaccia, fresh-cut pastas and ravioli, sauces, and *taralli*. In the fresh produce area you'll find spectacular displays of offerings. It all looks so inviting! This uptown store carries on the family's quality tradition, with attractive displays and decor. Delivery is locally available.

BARNEY GREENGRASS
541 Amsterdam Ave (bet 86th and 87th St)   212/724-4707
Tues-Sun: 8-6 (takeout)
Tues-Fri: 8:30-4; Sat, Sun: 8:30-5 (restaurant)
Closed first two weeks of Aug   www.barneygreengrass.com

Those who like sturgeon like Barney Greengrass! This family business has occupied the same locale since 1929. Barney has been succeeded by his son Moe and grandson Gary, but the same quality gourmet smoked fish is still sold over the counter, just as it was in Barney's day. Greengrass lays claim to the title of "Sturgeon King," and few would dispute it. While sturgeon is indeed king, Greengrass also has other smoked-fish delicacies: Nova Scotia salmon, belly lox, and whitefish. There is more: caviar, pickled herring, and kippered salmon salad. The dairy/deli line—including vegetable cream cheese, great homemade cheese blintzes, homemade salads and borscht, and a smashing Nova Scotia salmon with scrambled eggs and onions—is world-renowned. In fact, because so many customers couldn't wait to get home to unwrap their packages, Greengrass started a restaurant next door.

BARRAUD CATERERS
405 Broome St (at Centre St)   212/925-1334
Mon-Fri. 10-6 (office hours)

Owner Rosemary Howe has an interesting background. She was born in India and grew up British, and is therefore familiar with Indian and Anglo-Indian food. Her training in developing recipes is on the French side. Because she was raised in the tradition of afternoon tea, she knows finger sandwiches and all that goes with them. Her menus are unique. All breads are menu-specific, every meal is customized from a lengthy list, a wine consultant is available, and consultations on table etiquette are given. Dinners focused on cheese and wine are a specialty. This is a real hands-on operation, with Rosemary taking care of every detail of your special brunch, tea, lunch, or dinner. She now specializes in degustation (tasting) menus, paired with appropriate wines for each course.

Bazzini (339 Greenwich St, 212/334-1280) is Tribeca's answer to the gourmet food business. You'll find a great showing of fine foods: meat, fish, produce, deli items, prepared foods to go, charcuterie, and more. There is an on-premises cafe, kids are welcome, kitchenware (dishes, flatware, linens, candles) is stocked, and nuts and dried fruits are a specialty. Delivery is available.

BUTTERFIELD MARKET
1114 Lexington Ave (bet 77th and 78th St)   212/288-7800
Mon-Fri: 7 a.m.-8 p.m.; Sat: 7:30-5:30; Sun: 8-5
www.butterfieldmarket.com

Upper East Siders have enjoyed the goodies at Butterfield for nearly a century. Highlights of this popular market include an excellent prepared foods section, produce, a good selection of quality specialty items, tasty pastries, charcuterie, attractive gift baskets, a terrific cheese selection, and a diet-busting candy and sweets section. Catering is a specialty, and service is personal and informed.

CAVIARTERIA
1012 Lexington Ave (bet 72nd and 73rd St)
Mon-Sat: 10-5:30; Sun: 11-5:30   212/759-7410, 800/4-CAVIAR
www.caviarteria.com

Caviarteria is the largest distributor of caviar in the U.S. It is known for high-quality products at reasonable prices. Much of the business is done by phone; shipments are packed with ice and handled responsibly. You will find paté de foie gras, Scottish and Swedish smoked salmon platters, and home-made biscotti. There is an on-premises restaurant and a caviar- and champagne-tasting bar. The restaurant, open Friday and Saturday, offers platters, crepes, and sandwiches. Delivery and catering are added services. Specialties include a Caspian caviar sampler, *club du roi* sandwiches, caviar crepes, and carpaccio. They also have a selection of gourmet foods and gifts.

CHARLOTTE'S CATERING
146 Chambers St (bet Greenwich St and West Broadway) 212/732-7939
Mon-Fri: 10-6 (office)   www.charlottescateringny.com

Quality is Number One! Charlotte's has developed an outstanding reputation for catering, with no detail too small for their careful attention. Their client list reads like a who's who. Charlotte's is a full-service catering establishment, from menus and music to flowers and waiters' outfits. Come here when you want real experts to handle wedding receptions, dinner dances, teas, luncheons, business meetings or dinners, and so forth. Specialties include wonderful tapas, a spa buffet menu, and outrageous desserts. They'll work parties outside of Manhattan as well.

CHELSEA MARKET
75 Ninth Ave (bet 15th and 16th St)   212/243-6005
Mon-Sat: 8 a.m.–9 p.m.; Sun: 10-8

In a complex of 18 former industrial buildings, including the old Nabisco Cookie Factory of the late 1800s, an 800-foot-long concourse houses one of the most unusual marketplaces in the city. The space is innovative, including a waterfall supplied by an underground spring. Among the nearly two dozen shops, you'll find **Amy's Bread** (big choice, plus a cafe); **Bowery Kitchen Supplies** (kitchen buffs will go wild!); **Chelsea Wholesale Flower Market** (really fresh cut flowers); **Chelsea Wine Vault** (climate-controlled); **Cleaver Company** (catering and event planning); **Ronnybrook Farms Dairy** (fresh milk and eggs); **buonItalia** (great Italian basics); **Hale & Hearty Soups** (dozens of varieties); **The Lobster Place** (takeout seafood); **Sarabeth's Bakery**; **Frank's Butcher**; **Manhattan Fruit Exchange** (for buying in bulk); **Goupil & DeCarlo Patisserie**; **Chelsea Thai** (wholesale and takeout); **Fat Witch Bakery** (brownies, goodies, gifts); and **Eleni's Cookies** (artfully iced sugar cookies, bagels, ice cream, and more). **Ruthy's Cheesecake and Rugelach Bakery** is outstanding!

Leave it to the Bromberg brothers (of Blue Ribbon fame) to open a place that specializes in quality at reasonable prices. **Blue Ribbon Bakery Market** (14 Bedford St, 212/337-0404) sells great homemade breads, farm and dairy products from surrounding areas; flour and bread-making ingredients; and (for takeout only) breads with a variety of delicious delicacies, like raw Mexican honey. No wonder the place is always jammed!

DEAN & DELUCA
560 Broadway (at Prince St)   212/431-1691
Daily: 10-8
1150 Madison Ave (at 85th St)   212/717-0800
Daily: 7 a.m.-8 p.m.   www.deananddeluca.com

Dean & Deluca is one of the great gourmet stores in the country. The temptations are extraordinary: fresh produce, a huge selection of cheeses, fresh bakery items, takeout dishes, coffees, magnificent pastries and desserts, housewares, books, and all kinds of meat, poultry, and fish products. An espresso and cappuccino bar is very popular. This part of the operation has been expanded into convenient smaller cafe locations at 75 University Place, the Paramount Hotel (235 W 46th Street), and 9 Rockefeller Plaza. A take-out shop and newsstand, **The Shack**, is located across from the flagship store on Broadway. Professional kitchen equipment is available to wholesale and retail customers, and a catering kitchen is on-premises.

DELMONICO GOURMET FOOD MARKET
320 Park Ave (at 50th St)	212/317-8777
55 E 59th St (bet Madison and Park Ave)	212/751-5559
375 Lexington Ave (at 42nd St)	212/661-0150
24 hours	

Each of these markets has gourmet groceries, fresh produce, pastries, bakery, a huge selection of cheeses, and much more. This is a good place if you are planning a catered event for your office or home. I like the ultra-clean surroundings and accommodating help. Don't miss the charcuterie selection and salad bars.

FAIRWAY
2127 Broadway (at 74th St)	212/595-1888
Daily: 6 a.m.-1 a.m.	
2328 Twelfth Ave (at 133rd St)	212/234-3883
Daily: 8 a.m.-11 p.m.	www.fairwaymarket.com

The popular institution known as Fairway made its name with an incredible selection of fruits and vegetables. They offer produce in huge quantities at very reasonable prices. The uptown store is newer and larger, stocking a wonderful array of cheeses, meats, bakery items, and more. Additions to the Broadway store include an on-premises bakery, a cafe, organically grown produce, expanded fish and meat departments, and a catering service. Fairway operates its own farm on Long Island and has developed a good relationship with area produce dealers. Both stores offer a full line of organic and natural grocery, health, and beauty items. There is an all-kosher bakery at the Harlem location. As you make your rounds on the Upper West Side, you can't go wrong by carrying a Fairway bag on one arm and a Zabar's bag on the other.

FINE & SCHAPIRO
138 W 72nd St (bet Broadway and Columbus Ave)
Daily: 10-10 212/877-2874, 212/877-2721
www.fineandschapiro. com

Ostensibly a kosher delicatessen and restaurant, Fine & Schapiro also offers great dinners for home consumption. Because of the high quality, they term themselves "the Rolls-Royce of delicatessens." That description is apt. Fine & Schapiro dispenses a complete line of cold cuts, hot and cold hors d'oeuvres, catering platters, and magnificent sandwiches—try the pastrami! Everything that issues from Fine & Schapiro is perfectly cooked and artistically arranged. The sandwiches are masterpieces; the aroma and taste are irresistible. Chicken in the pot and stuffed cabbage are among their best items.

FISHER & LEVY
875 Third Ave (at 53rd St, concourse level)   212/832-3880
Mon-Fri: 7:30-3:30 (call before 3 p.m. for dinner delivery)
www.fisherlevy.com

Chip Fisher and partner Thom Hamill have served the corporate catering needs of Manhattan with high-quality style and service for nearly two decades. They take care of big parties and solitary diners alike. Fisher & Levy will start your day with delicious breakfast items like coffee crumb-cake slices and fresh-baked blueberry scones. For lunch, dive into a juicy filet mignon sandwich with grilled red peppers or roasted turkey breast with honey glaze. In addition to delicious pizza, their small retail store in the food court offers sandwiches, soups, interesting pastas and vegetable salads, and Cobb salad. Don't miss such desserts as homemade bread pudding, gooey brownies, raspberry rugelach, and fabulous all-butter cookies.

Some of the best places for takeout and delivery by neighborhood:
East Village: **Max** (51 Avenue B, 212/539-0111)
Harlem: **El Toro Partido** (3431 Broadway, 212/281-1587)
Midtown East: **Chin Chin** (216 E 49th St, 212/888-4555)
Times Square: **Akdeniz** (19 W 46th St, 212/575-2307) and **Virgil's Real Barbeque** (152 W 44th St, 212/921-9663)
Union Square: **Grand Sichuan** (19-23 St. Marks Pl, 212/529-4800), **Second Avenue Kosher Delicatessen and Restaurant** (156 Second Ave, 212/677-0606)
Upper West Side: **Artie's Delicatessen** (2290 Broadway, 212/579-5959), **Gennaro** (665 Amsterdam Ave, 212/665-5348), and **Shun Lee West** (43 W 65th St, 212/595-8895)

GARDEN OF EDEN
162 W 23rd St (bet Ave of the Americas and
   Seventh Ave)   212/675-6300
7 E 14th St (bet University Pl and Fifth Ave)   212/255-4200
Daily: 7 a.m.-10 p.m.   www.gardenofedengourmet.com

These stores are both farmers markets and gourmet shops! The food items are fresh, appetizing, and priced to please. Moreover the stores are immaculate and well organized, and the personnel are exceptionally helpful. You'll find breads and bakery items, cheeses, veggies, meats, seafood, pastas, desserts and more. All manner of catering services are available, including suggestions for locations, rentals, and service. Platters of cheese, meats, fruit, vegetables, fish, paté, and breakfast are offered.

GLORIOUS FOOD
504 E 74th St (bet East River and York Ave)   212/628-2320
Mon-Fri: 9-5   www.gloriousfood.com

Glorious Food is at the top of many New Yorkers' lists when it comes to catering. They are a full-service outfit, expertly taking care of every small detail of your event. In business for over a quarter of a century, they have met most every challenge. Give 'em a try!

GOURMET GARAGE

453 Broome St (at Mercer St)	212/941-5850
Daily: 7 a.m.-9 p.m.	
301 E 64th St (at Second Ave)	212/535-6271
Daily: 7 a.m.-8:30 p.m.	
2567 Broadway (at 96th St)	212/663-0656
Daily: 7 a.m.-10 p.m.	
117 Seventh Ave S (at 10th St)	212/699-5980
Daily: 7 a.m.-10 p.m.	www.gourmetgarage.com

A working-class gourmet food shop is the best way to describe Gourmet Garage. These stores carry a good selection of in-demand items—including fruits and veggies, cheeses, breads, pastries, coffees, meats, and olive oils—at low prices. Organic foods are a specialty. Catering and gift baskets are available, and delivery service is offered in the Manhattan area for a nominal fee.

One of Manhattan's best food courts is located on the lower level of **Grand Central Station** (42nd St at Vanderbilt Ave). You'll find some of the city's best food purveyors, plus comfortable tables and chairs.

GRACE'S MARKETPLACE

1237 Third Ave (at 71st St)   212/737-0600
Mon-Sat: 7 a.m.-8:30 p.m.; Sun: 8-7   www.gracesmarketplace.com

Founded by Grace Balducci Doria and the late Joe Doria, Sr., Grace's Marketplace is one of the city's most popular food emporiums. Products, service, and ambience are top of the line. You'll find smoked meats and fish, cheeses, fresh pastas, homemade sauces, produce, a full range of baked goods, candy, coffee, tea, dried fruits, pastries, gourmet groceries, prepared foods, prime meats, and fresh seafood. They are also known for quality gift baskets and catering. Get a taste of Puglia at their restaurant, **Grace's Trattoria** (201 E 71st St, 212/452-2323). No visit to New York is complete without an excursion to Grace's!

GREAT PERFORMANCES

287 Spring St (bet Hudson and Varick St)   212/727-2424
Mon-Fri: 8:30-5:30   www.greatperformances.com

Great Performances has been creating spectacular events in the New York area for 20 years with the help of folks from the city's artistic community. Each division of this full-service catering company has a team of expert staff. They take pride in recruiting and maintaining the best and brightest the industry has to offer. Their people bring creativity, personality, and technical expertise to each event. From intimate dinner parties to gala dinners for thousands, Great Performances is a complete event-planning resource.

H&H MIDTOWN BAGELS EAST

1551 Second Ave (bet 80th and 81st St)   212/734-7441
Daily: 24 hours

Delicious bagels are made fresh right on the premises, and if you're lucky, you'll get 'em warm! But there is more: homemade croissants, assorted Italian cookies, soups, cold cuts, sandwiches, salads, salmon, lox, sturgeon, and pickled herring. The emphasis is on carryout, but tables are available for those who can't wait to dive in.

KELLEY & PING
127 Greene St (bet Houston and Prince St)   212/228-1212
340 Third Ave   212/871-7000
Lunch: Mon-Fri (11:30-5); Dinner: Daily (5:30 p.m.-11 p.m.)
www.kelleyandping.com

One of the fastest growing categories in foreign flavors is the exotic cuisine of Asia. Thai, Chinese, Vietnamese, Japanese, Malaysian, and Korean foods are popular in restaurants and at home. Kelley & Ping specializes in groceries and housewares from this part of the world. A restaurant is now a major part of the operation, and they do catering, too. If you have questions about how to prepare Asian dishes, these are the folks to ask.

MANGIA
50 W 57th St (bet Fifth Ave and Ave of the Americas) 212/582-5882
Mon-Fri: 7 a.m.-8 p.m.; Sat: 8-6
16 E 48th St (bet Fifth and Madison Ave)   212/754-7600
Mon-Fri: 7-7
40 Wall St (bet Broad and William St)   212/425-4040
Mon-Fri: 7-4   www.mangiatogo.com

At Mangia, the old European reverence for ripe tomatoes and brick-oven bread endures. This outfit offers four distinct services: corporate catering, with anything needed for an office breakfast or luncheon; a juice bar; a carry-out shop with an antipasti bar, soups, salads, sandwiches, entrees, sweets, and cappuccino; and a restaurant with full menu and made-to-order pastas. Prices are competitive, and delivery service is offered.

NEWMAN & LEVENTHAL
45 W 81st St (bet Central Park W and Columbus Ave)
By appointment only   212/362-9400

Having been a kosher caterer for nearly a century, this firm is known for unique menus and top quality. Be prepared to pay well for outstanding food.

NINTH AVENUE INTERNATIONAL FOODS
543 Ninth Ave (at 40th St)   212/279-1000
Mon-Sat: 7:30-6:30

Ninth Avenue is one great wholesale market of international cookery. Accordingly, Ninth Avenue International Foods is both a spice emporium and an excellent source for rudiments on which to sprinkle the spices. You will sacrifice frills for some of the best prices and freshest foodstuffs in town. Lamb can be special-ordered.

PETAK'S
1246 Madison Ave (bet 89th and 90th St)   212/722-7711
Mon-Fri: 7:30 a.m.-8 p.m.; Sat: 7:30-7; Sun: 9-7

Richard Petak, third-generation member of a family that has owned appetizer businesses in the South Bronx and New Jersey, made the leap to Manhattan. His "appy shop" was the first in the Carnegie Hill neighborhood in a long time. No neighborhood has truly arrived until it has a gourmet shop, and Petak's fills that need. There are all the appy standbys, such as salads (60 of them!), corned beef, pastrami, smoked fish, and all sorts of takeout foods. The store offers full corporate catering, a sushi chef, picnic hampers, and a full-service cafe/restaurant.

RUSS & DAUGHTERS
179 E Houston St (bet Allen and Orchard St)
Mon-Sat: 9-7; Sun: 8-5:30   212/475-4880, 800/RUSS-229
www.russanddaughters.com

One of my favorite places! A family business in its fourth generation, Russ & Daughters has been a renowned New York shop since it first opened its doors. They carry nuts, dried fruits, lake sturgeon, salmon, sable, and herring. Russ & Daughters has a reputation for serving only the very best. Six varieties of caviar are sold at low prices. Their chocolates are premium quality. They sell wholesale and over the counter, and ship anywhere. Many a Lower East Side shopping trip ends with a stop at Russ & Daughters. It is clean, first-rate, friendly—what more could you ask?

For those New Yorkers who don't find grocery shopping a pleasant pastime, there is hope. **Fresh Direct** (www.freshdirect.com) sells over 3,000 food items (organic and prepared) from their website. They also provide useful information like calorie counts, recipes, and cooking information. Prices are competitive, as they do not have a storefront or deal with middlemen. Delivery charges are reasonable.

SABLE'S SMOKED FISH
1489 Second Ave (bet 77th and 78th St)   212/249-6177
Mon-Fri: 8:30-7:30; Sat: 7:30-7:30; Sun: 7:30-5

Kenny Sze was the appetizers manager at Zabar's for many years, and he learned the trade well. He brings that knowledge to the Upper East Side, where he offers wonderful smoked salmon, lobster salad, Alaskan crab salad, sturgeon, caviar (good prices), cold cuts, cheeses, coffees, salads, fresh breads, and prepared foods. Sable's catering service can provide platters (smoked fish, cold cuts, and cheese), jumbo sandwiches, whole hams, cured meat, and more. Free delivery is offered in the immediate area, and they'll ship anywhere in the U.S. Cold cuts and chicken dishes are specialties. Tables for eat-in are available.

SALUMERIA BIELLESE
378 Eighth Ave (at 29th St)   212/736-7376
Mon-Fri: 6:30-6; Sat: 9-5   www.salumeriabiellese.com

This Italian-owned grocery store (with a restaurant in back) is also the only French charcuterie in the city. If that isn't contradiction enough, consider that the loyal lunchtime crowd thinks it's dining at a hero shop when it's really enjoying the fruits of a kitchen that serves many fine restaurants in the city. To understand how all this came about, a lesson in New York City geography is necessary. In 1945, when Ugo Buzzio and Joseph Nello came to this country from the Piedmontese city of Biella, they opened a shop a block away from the current one in the immigrant neighborhood Hell's Kitchen. (Today, this gentrified area is known as Clinton.) The two partners almost immediately began producing French charcuterie. Word spread among the chefs of the city's restaurants that Salumeria Biellese was producing a quality product that could not be duplicated anywhere. Buzzio's son Marc is one of three partners who run the business today. Offerings include sausages (pork, game, veal, lamb, and poultry), cured meats, and specialty patés.

SARGE'S
548 Third Ave (bet 36th and 37th St)   212/679-0442
Daily: 24 hours   www.sargesdeli.com

Sarge's isn't fancy, but it could feed an army, and there's much to be said for the taste, quality, and price. Sarge's will cater everything from hot dogs to hot or cold buffets for almost any size crowd. Prices are figured according to the number of people and type of food, and there are remarkably reasonable package deals. Sarge's also caters deli items and has an excellent selection of cold hors d'oeuvre platters, offering everything from canapes of caviar, sturgeon, and Nova Scotia salmon to shrimp cocktail. To make the party complete, Sarge's can supply utensils, condiments, and staff. Delivery is available.

SONNIER & CASTLE FOOD
532 W 46th St (bet Tenth and Eleventh Ave)   212/957-6481
Hours by appointment   www.sonnier-castle.com

This full-service caterer can provide assistance in finding locations, designer flowers, entertainment, and anything else a customer might need for a special gathering. Russ Sonnier and David Castle are young enough to be inventive yet mature enough to do a first-class job. Their menus incorporate French, Italian, Asian, and Mediterranean influences.

TAYLOR'S PREPARED FOODS AND BAKE SHOPS
523 Hudson St (bet 10th and Charles St)   212/378-2890
Daily: 7 a.m.-10 p.m.
156 Chambers St (bet West Broadway and Greenwich St)
Daily: 7-7   212/378-3401

These stores sell delicious pies and cakes, baked items like muffins and bagels, assorted salads, and hot takeout entrees. Breakfasts are a treat. A catering service for both informal and elegant affairs is available. Production companies may pick up their items as early as needed.

TODARO BROS.
555 Second Ave (bet 30th and 31st St)   212/532-0633
Mon-Sat: 6:30 a.m.-10 p.m.; Sun: 6:30 a.m.-9:30 p.m.
                                                www.todarobros.com

This is food heaven! An icon in the Kips Bay/Murray Hill area since 1917, Todaro Bros. carries the very best in specialty foods. Great lunch sandwiches, fresh mozzarella, sausages, and prepared foods are offered daily. Count on the fresh fish and meat to be of the highest quality. The cheese department offers a huge variety of imported varieties. The shelves are stocked with artisanal oil, vinegar, pasta, condiments, coffee, fresh produce, and exquisite pastries.

VINEGAR FACTORY

431 E 91st St (near York Ave)   212/987-0885
Daily: 7 a.m.-9 p.m.   www.elizabar.com
Brunch: Sat, Sun: 7-4

Located on the site of what used to be a working vinegar factory, this operation of Eli Zabar's has bearable prices on fresh produce, pizzas, fish, flowers, meats, desserts, seafood, cheeses, baked goods (including Eli's great bread), coffee, deli items, paper goods, books, and housewares. Breakfast and brunch (on weekends) are available on the balcony. This is one of the most intriguing food factories around! Catering is also offered.

> One of the must-visits in Paris is **Fauchon**, a famous market that upscale French shoppers swear by. Well, Fauchon has come to Manhattan with a shop at 442 Park Avenue (212/308-5919). There are candies, gelati, paninis, sauces, teas, foie gras, smoked salmon, Iranian caviar, and quiches. For an afternoon respite, tea and sandwiches are offered. There is a haughty air about the place, but then . . . it *is* Fauchon.

WHOLE FOODS MARKET

Time Warner Center
10 Columbus Circle   212/823-9600
4 Union Square S   212/673-5388
250 Seventh Ave (at 24th St)   212/924-5969
Daily: 8 a.m.-10 p.m.   www.wholefoods.com

Whole Foods is big, beautiful, and busy! If you can't find a particular food item here, it probably doesn't exist. In addition to all the usual things, this grocery superstore has a huge deli, a seafood selection, bakery, flowers, sushi, fresh juices, and all kinds of carry-out items. Thirty cashiers are on hand at the Time Warner location to ring up purchases.

ZABAR'S

2245 Broadway (at 80th St)   212/787-2000
Mon-Fri: 8-7:30; Sat: 8-8; Sun: 9-6
Mezzanine (housewares): Mon-Sat: 9-7:30; Sun: 9-6
                                                                  www.zabars.com

Zabar's is the foremost food-retailing operation in Manhattan. The Zabar family has been in the food business for decades, and Saul Zabar is carrying on the family tradition in a superb manner. Zabar's is known for vast assortments, great prices, and quality products. You will not find a better housewares department than their huge mezzanine operation. At street level there is an inviting bakery section, a huge showing of cheeses, a mouth-watering deli section, a renowned coffee selection (their coffee trade is among the largest in the world), sushi, prepared foods, smoked fish, appetizers, gift baskets, candy, and a value-priced cafe. A visit to Manhattan is not complete without a trip to Zabar's, and it is a part of daily life for residents. Hats off to Saul Zabar and managers Scott Goldshine and David Tait.

Cheese

ALLEVA DAIRY
188 Grand St (at Mulberry St)   212/226-7990, 800/4-ALLEVA
Mon-Sat: 8:30-6; Sun: 8:30-3   www.allevadairy.com

Alleva, founded in 1892, is the oldest Italian cheese store in America. The Alleva family has operated the business from the start, always maintaining meticulous standards. Robert Alleva oversees the production of over 4,000 pounds of fresh cheese a week: *parmigiano, fraschi, manteche, scamoize,* and *provole affumicale.* The ricotta is superb, and the mozzarella tastes like it was made on a side street in Florence. Quality Italian meats, an olive bar, and gift baskets are offered. A mail-order catalog is available.

Hot dogs! I love them! In my restaurant (**Gerry Frank's Konditorei**, 310 Kearney St, Salem, OR, 503/585-7070) we call them "Gerry's Franks!" For the best in Manhattan try:

Artie's Delicatessen (2290 Broadway, 212/579-5959)
Brooklyn Diner USA (212 W 57th St, 212/977-2280)
Crif Dogs (113 St Mark's Pl, 212/614-2728)
Dawgs on Park (178 E 7th St, 212/598-0667)
Gray's Papaya (2090 Broadway, 212/799-0243; 539 Eighth Ave, 212/904-1588; and 402 Ave of the Americas, 212/260-3532): inexpensive
Hallo Berlin (626 Tenth Ave, 212/977-1944 and a stand at 54th St and Fifth Ave)
Katz's Delicatessen (205 E Houston St, 212/254-2246)
Nathan's Famous (stands all over Manhattan)
Second Avenue Kosher Delicatessen and Restaurant (156 Second Ave, 212/677-0606)
Shake Shack (Madison Square Park, Madison Ave at 23rd St, 212/889-6600)

DIPALO FINE FOODS
200 Grand St (at Mott St)   212/226-1033
Mon-Sat: 9-6:30; Sun: 9-4

One word describes the cheeses and pastas offered at DiPalo: *superb.* If it's Italian, they carry it: olive oils, meats, and more. It's worth a trip to the Lower East Side for the goodies and friendly greetings.

EAST VILLAGE CHEESE
40 Third Ave (bet 9th and 10th St)   212/477-2601
Mon-Fri: 8:30-6:30; Sat, Sun: 8:30-6

Value is the name of the game. For years this store has prided itself on selling cheese at some of the lowest prices in town (cash only). They claim similar savings for whole-bean coffee, fresh pasta, extra-virgin olive oil, quiche, paté, and a wide selection of fresh bread. Good service is another reason to shop here.

IDEAL CHEESE SHOP
942 First Ave (at 52nd St)   212/688-7579
Mon-Sat: 8:30-6 (close Sat at 5 in summer)   800/382-0109
                                                   www.idealcheese.com

A great place! Hundreds of cheeses from all over the world are sold here. As a matter of fact, the owners are constantly looking for new items, just as is done in the fashion business. This store has been in operation since 1954, and many Upper East Siders swear by its quality and service. Members of the founding family are on hand to answer questions or prepare special platters and baskets. They carry gourmet items: olive oils, vinegars, mustards, gourmet coffees, biscuits, preserves, specialty meats, and olives. A catalog is available, and they will ship anywhere in the U.S.

JOE'S DAIRY
156 Sullivan St (bet Houston and Prince St) 212/677-8780
Tues-Fri: 9-6; Sat: 8-6

This is the best spot in town for fresh mozzarella. Anthony Campanelli makes it smoked, with prosciutto, and more.

If you believe that nutritional products can keep you looking younger, then visit **Dr. Nicholas Perricone** (791 Madison Ave, 866/791-7911). His store is full of foods, books, and advice.

MURRAY'S CHEESE SHOP
254 Bleecker St (at Leroy St) 212/243-3289
Mon-Sat: 8-7; Sun: 9-6 www.murrayscheese.com

One of the best cheese shops in Manhattan has a new home! Founded in 1940, Murray's offers wholesale and retail international and domestic cheeses of every description. Frank Meilak is the man to talk to behind the counter. Boy, does this place smell good! There is also a fine selection of cold cuts, prepared foods, cheesecakes, pasta, antipasti, bread, sandwiches, and specialty items. Owner Rob Kaufelt has built on the traditions of the city's oldest cheese shop. Special attractions include great party platters, gift baskets, and wholesale charge accounts for locals.

Chinese

GOLDEN FUNG WONG BAKERY
41 Mott St (at Pell St) 212/267-4037
Daily: 7:30 a.m.-8:30 p.m.

Golden Fung Wong is the real thing. Everyone from local Chinatown residents to the city's gourmands extol its virtues. The pastries, cookies, and baked goods are traditional, authentic, and delicious. Flavor is not compromised in order to appeal to Western tastes. The bakery features a tremendous variety of baked goods, and it has the distinction of being New York's oldest and largest "real" Chinese bakery.

KAM MAN FOOD PRODUCTS
200 Canal St (bet Mott and Mulberry St) 212/571-0330
Daily: 9-9 www.kammanfood.com

Kam Man is the largest Oriental grocery store on the East Coast. In addition to Chinese foodstuffs, they carry Japanese, Thai, Vietnamese, Malaysian, and Filipino products. Native Asians should feel right at home in this store, where all types of traditional condiments are available. All of the necessities for the preparation and presentation of Asian foods can be found, from sauces and spices to utensils and cookware. Tableware, too! For the health-conscious, Kam Man stocks a wide selection of teas and traditional Chinese herbal medicines. Prices are very reasonable. You needn't speak Chinese to shop here.

TONGIN MART
91 Mulberry St (at Canal St)   212/962-6622
Daily: 9-8

If a home-cooked Chinese dinner is on your itinerary, there's no better source than this store in Chinatown. Tongin Mart boasts that 95% of its business is conducted with the Chinese community. They have an open and friendly attitude, and great care is taken to introduce customers to the wide variety of imported Oriental food items, including Japanese, Thai, and Filipino products.

Coffee, Tea

BELL BATES NATURAL FOOD MARKET
97 Reade St (bet Church St and West Broadway)   212/267-4300
Mon-Fri: 9-7; Sat: 10-6   www.bellbates.com

Bell Bates is a hot-beverage emporium specializing in organic and natural foods and all manner of teas and coffees. The selection is extensive and prices are competitive. Bell Bates considers itself a complete food source, stocking health foods, vitamins, nuts, dried fruit, spices, herbs, and gourmet items. Ask for the marvelous Mrs. Sayage.

Harney & Sons Fine Teas (www.harney.com) are now available in Manhattan. **Adriana's Caravan** in Grand Central Station carries Harney's loose teas. **Eli's Manhattan** (1411 Third Ave) carries their tea bags. **Takashimaya** (693 Fifth Ave) sells their products, too.

EMPIRE COFFEE AND TEA COMPANY
568 Ninth Ave (bet 41st and 42nd St)   212/268-1220
Mon-Fri: 8-7; Sat: 9-6:30; Sun: 11-5   www.empirecoffeetea.com

Midtown java lovers have all wandered in here at one time or another. Empire carries an enormous selection of coffee (75 different types of beans), tea, and herbs. Because of the aroma and array of the bins, choosing is almost impossible. Empire's personnel are very helpful, but a perusal of their free catalog before visiting the shop might save you some time. Fresh coffee beans and tea leaves are available in bulk; everything is sold loose and can be ground. Empire also carries a wide selection of teapots and coffee and cappuccino machines. Gourmet gift baskets, too!

JAVA GIRL
348 E 66th St (bet First and Second Ave)   212/737-3490
Mon-Fri: 6:45 a.m.-7 p.m.; Sat, Sun: 8:30-7

The aroma of fresh-ground coffee that greets you upon entering this tiny place is overwhelming! For fine coffees, teas, and pastries, look no further. Java Girl has creative gift boxes as well.

JOE—THE ART OF COFFEE
141 Waverly Pl (bet Ave of the Americas and Seventh Ave)
Mon-Fri: 7 a.m.– 8 p.m.; Sat, Sun: 8-8   212/924-6750

Jonathan Rubinstein, an ex-talent agent, always wanted to share his passion for espresso, and now he has done it at one of the city's most unique spots. Espresso drinks, coffees, whole bean sales, and brewing equipment make a visit to Joe a must for the espresso fanatic.

Latte Lingo – and Other Coffee Terminology

A *tall* is any 12-ounce espresso drink, while a *grande* is 16 ounces, and a *venti* is 20 ounces. A *double* is any espresso drink with a second shot added. Finally, a *skinny* is any drink that uses nonfat milk.

Americano: a one- or two-ounce shot of espresso added to as much as seven ounces of hot water; an alternative to drip brewing, yielding a rich cup of gourmet coffee

Cafe au Lait: equal portions of drip coffee and steamed milk

Cafe Breve: a latte made with half-and-half instead of milk

Cafe Coretto: espresso to which liquor, typically brandy or coffee liqueur, has been added

Caffe Latte: a two-ounce shot of espresso combined with steamed milk and topped with a spoonful of milk froth

Caffe Mocha: a latte with an ounce of chocolate flavoring (either powder or syrup)

Cappuccino: a unique coffee drink, with equal parts steamed milk, coffee, and foamed milk; may be topped with cinnamon, nutmeg, chocolate sprinkles, or cocoa powder

Cappuccino (dry): a cappuccino with foam only, very little or no steamed milk added

Cappuccino (wet): a cappuccino with less foam and more steamed milk

Con Panna: espresso topped with whipped cream

Espresso: a coffee beverage produced by using pressure to rapidly infuse ground coffee with boiling water

Flavored Caffe Latte: a latte with an ounce of Italian syrup (such as almond, hazelnut, and vanilla) or liqueur

Granita: frozen Italian drink prepared with a granita machine (or *granitore*); can be made with espresso and milk or fresh fruits and juices

Shot, Straight Shot, Single Shot, Double Shot: espresso served straight up without milk or flavorings

---

McNULTY'S TEA AND COFFEE COMPANY
109 Christopher St (bet Bleecker and Hudson St)
Mon-Sat: 10-9; Sun: 1-7   212/242-5351, 800/356-5200
www.mcnultys.com

McNulty's has been supplying choosy New Yorkers with coffee and tea since 1895. Over the years they have developed a complete line that includes spiced and herbal teas, coffee blends ground to order, and coffee and tea accessories. They have a reputation for personalized gourmet coffee blends and work hard to maintain it. That reputation will take its toll on the pocketbook, but the blends are unique and the personal service is highly valued. McNulty's maintains an extensive file on customers' special blends.

M. ROHRS' HOUSE OF FINE TEAS AND COFFEES
303 E 85th St (near Second Ave)   212/396-4456
Mon-Thurs: 6 a.m.-9:30 p.m.; Fri, Sat: 6 a.m.-10 p.m.;
Sun: 6 a.m.-9 p.m.   www.rohrs.com

In 1996, M. Rohrs' turned a century old, and Donald Wright became the owner. Along with expanding the lines of tea and coffee, Wright brought a wide variety of honey, jam, cookies, and chocolates to the store. Rohrs' has a bar for espresso and an assortment of daily brewed coffees and teas, as well as easy Internet access. It truly is a village store in the big city. Wright, who is himself a great lover of coffee, claims to drink seven cups a day! He vows to carry on the store's tradition of Old World charm into its second century.

PORTO RICO IMPORTING COMPANY
201 Bleecker St (main store)   212/477-5421, 800/453-5908
Mon-Sat: 9-9; Sun: 12-7

40½ St. Marks Pl (coffee bar)   212/533-1982
Mon-Fri: 8-8; Sat: 9-8; Sun: 12-7

107 Thompson St (coffee bar)   212/966-5758
Mon-Thurs: 8-6; Fri: 8-7; Sat: 10-7; Sun: 10-6   www.portorico.com

In 1907, Peter Longo's family started a small coffee business in the Village. Primarily importers and wholesalers, they were soon pressured to serve the local community, so they opened a small storefront as well. As that operation gained a reputation for the best and freshest coffee available, it developed a loyal corps of customers. Since much of the surrounding neighborhood consists of Italians, the Longo family reciprocated their loyalty by specializing in Italian espressos and cappuccinos, as well as health and medicinal teas. Dispensed along with such teas are folk remedies and advice to mend whatever ails you. Today, the store remains true to its tradition. Peter has added coffee bars, making it possible to sit and sip from a selection of 150 coffees and 225 loose teas while listening to folklore or trying to select the best from the bins. All coffees are roasted daily in Porto Rico's own facility. (Hint: The inexpensive house blends are every bit as good as some of the more expensive coffees.)

SENSUOUS BEAN OF COLUMBUS AVENUE
66 W 70th St (at Columbus Ave)   212/724-7725, 800/238-6845
Mon, Thurs, Fri: 8:30-7; Tues, Wed, Sat: 8:30-6; Sun: 9:30-6
www.sensuousbean.com

In business long before the coffee craze started, this legendary coffee and teahouse carries 72 varieties of coffee and 52 teas. A coffee-of-the-month club is offered; after customers purchase ten pounds, they receive one pound free. The bulk bean coffees and loose teas come from all around the world. Teas from England, France, Germany, Ireland, and Taiwan are featured. They carry a large variety of green, white, chai, herbal, rooibos teas, and blending of loose tea, along with many organic and fair-trade coffees. They make lattes, cappuccinos, and espressos; steep teas; and offer many sweets, biscottis, and chocolates to accompany your drink.

TEN REN TEA & GINSENG CO.
75-79 Mott St (at Canal St)   212/349-2286
Daily: 10-8   www.tenrenusa.com

This company was founded a half-century ago and is the largest tea grower and manufacturer in East Asia. They sell green, oolong, jasmine, and black teas, plus tea sets and all manner of accessories. Various kinds of ginseng are also available as well as a delicious and chewy "bubble tea" containing tapioca pearls. Ten Ren means "heavenly love," and you might well fall in love with one of their flavors. Some can set you back $100 a pound!

Best pies in Manhattan

Apple: **City Bakery** (3 W 18th St, 212/366-1414) and **William Greenberg Jr. Desserts** (1100 Madison Ave, 212/744-0304)

Apple crumb: **Cupcake Cafe** (522 Ninth Ave, 212/465-1530)

Banana cream (seasonal): **Sarabeth's Kitchen** (423 Amsterdam Ave, 212/496-6280; 1295 Madison Ave, 212/410-7335; and 75 Ninth Ave, 212/989-2424)

Cherry crumb: **Glaser's Bake Shop** (1670 First Ave, 212/289-2562)

Chocolate peanut butter: **Bubby's** (120 Hudson St, 212/219-0666)

Classic pies: **Tuscan Square** (16 W 51st St, 212/977-7777): call ahead

Pecan: **Magnolia Bakery** (401 Bleecker St, 212/462-2572) and **Sweet Chef Southern Styles Bakery** (122 Hamilton Pl, 212/862-5909)

Pinolata: **Sullivan Street Bakery** (73 Sullivan St, 212/334-9435)

Sour cream apple-walnut, key lime, and seven other kinds: **Little Pie Company** (424 W 43rd St, 212/736-4780)

Strawberry rhubarb: **Buttercup Bake Shop** (973 Second Ave, 212/350-4144)

Foreign Foodstuffs (The best)

Chinese, Thai, Malaysian, Philippine, Vietnamese
Asia Market* (71½ Mulberry St)
Bangkok Center Grocery (104 Mosco St, at Mott St)
Chinese American Trading Company (91 Mulberry St)
Fong Inn Too (46 Mott St)
Hong Keung Seafood & Meat Market (75 Mulberry St)
Hung Chong Imports (14 Bowery)
Kam Kuo Foods (7 Mott St)
Kam Man Food Products* (200 Canal St)
Tea & Tea (157 2nd St)
Ten Ren Tea Ginseng Co.* (75-79 Mott St)
Thuan-Nguyen Market (84 Mulberry St)
United Noodles (349 E 12th St)

English
Myers of Keswick* (634 Hudson St)

German
Schaller & Weber* (1654 Second Ave)

Indian
Foods of India (121 Lexington Ave)
Kati Roll (99 MacDougal St)
Kalustyan's* (123 Lexington Ave)

Italian
DiPalo Fine Foods* (200 Grand St)
Todaro Bros.* (555 Second Ave)

Japanese
Katagiri & Company* (224 E 59th St)

Korean
Han Mi Reum (25 W 32nd St)

Polish
East Village Meat Market (139 Second Ave)

West African
West African Grocery (535 Ninth Ave)

*Detailed write-ups of these shops can be found in this chapter.

Where to Shop for Caviar
   We aim to please all palates and pocketbooks in this volume, including sophisticated tastes.
Bubble Lounge (228 West Broadway, 212/431-3433): the real thing, plus hundreds of champagnes and wines
Caviar Russe (538 Madison Ave, 212/980-5908): a luxury spot
Caviarteria (1012 Lexington Ave, 212/759-7410): I like everything about this place.
Firebird (365 W 46th St, 212/586-0244): housed in a re-creation of a pre-revolutionary Russian mansion
Petrossian (182 W 58th St, 212/245-2214): Providing ambience befitting the caviar set, this is a spectacular place to dine.
Zabar's (2245 Broadway, 212/787-2000): If good prices are important, then make this your first stop.

Types of Caviar
Beluga: Roe are large, firm, and well-defined, with a smooth, creamy texture.
Osetra: strong, with a sweet, fruity flavor
Sevruga: subtle, clean taste with crunchy texture

Fruits, Vegetables

GREENMARKET
51 Chambers St, Suite 1231 (office)   212/788-7900
Bowling Green (Broadway at Battery Pl)   www.cenyc.org
Tompkins Square (7th St at Ave A)
St. Mark's Church (10th St at Second Ave)
Abingdon Square (12th St at Hudson St)
Union Square (17th St at Broadway)
Tucker Square (Columbus Ave bet 65th and 66th St)
77th St (at Columbus Ave)
97th Street (bet Amsterdam and Columbus Ave)

175th St (at Broadway)
Balsley Park (Ninth Ave at 57th St)
Tribeca (Greenwich St bet Chambers and Duane St)
Dag Hammarskjold Plaza (47th St at Second Ave)
South Street Seaport (Fulton St bet Water and Pearl St)
Rockefeller Center (Rockefeller Plaza at 50th St)
Columbia University (Broadway at 115th St)
Downtown PATH (Vesey at Church St)

Starting in 1976 with just one location, these unique open-air markets have sprung up in various neighborhoods. They are sponsored and overseen by a nonprofit organization. Bypassing the middle man means prices are significantly less than at supermarkets. Another great advantage is that all produce (over 600 varieties), baked goods, flowers, and fish come straight from the sources. When the supply is gone, the stand closes for the day. Come early for the best selection. Call the listed office number to find out the address and hours of the nearest Greenmarket. Most are seasonal, operating from 8 to 3, although some stay open all year. (Note: Greenmarkets are not open every day, and hours may vary.)

Smoothies can be very healthy and low-calorie, too. If you're in the mood for a really good one, try **Smoothies** (642-A Lexington Ave, 212/593-1020), where you can create your own combination. They provide a list of remedies for almost every ailment (i.e., carrot, beet, and cucumber for headaches and carrot, celery, and parsley for diabetes).

Gift and Picnic Baskets

MANHATTAN FRUITIER
105 E 29th St (bet Park and Lexington Ave)
Mon-Fri: 9-5; Sat: deliveries only   212/686-0404, 800/841-5718
www.mfruit.com

Most fruit baskets are pretty bad, but this outfit makes tasty, great-looking masterpieces using fresh seasonal and exotic fruits. You can add such comestibles as hand-rolled cheddar cheese sticks, biscotti, and individually wrapped chocolates. Locally handmade truffles, fine food hampers, and fresh flowers are also available. Delivery charges in Manhattan are reasonable.

SANDLER'S
530 Cherry Lane   212/279-9779, 800/75-FRUIT
Floral Park, NY   www.sandlers.com
Mon-Fri: 9-5

Sandler's is a key source for scrumptious candies, delicacies, and some of the best chocolate chip cookies, even if they are not located in Manhattan. Yet they are even better known for gift baskets filled with fancy fresh fruits, natural cheeses, and gourmet delicacies. No one does it better!

Greek

LIKITSAKOS
1174 Lexington Ave (bet 80th and 81st St)   212/535-4300
Mon-Fri: 7 a.m.-9 p.m.; Sat, Sun: 8-8

Likitsakos is one of the better places in New York for Greek and international specialties, including salads, fruits, vegetables, grains, dips, and appetizers.

Health Foods

GARY NULL'S UPTOWN WHOLE FOODS
2421 Broadway (at 89th St)   212/874-4000
Daily: 8 a.m.-11 p.m.   www.garynullsuptownwholefoods.com

This is Manhattan's premier health food supermarket. Organic produce, fresh juices, discounted vitamins, and a full line of healthy supermarket products are featured. They deliver in Manhattan and ship anywhere in the world. A takeout deli offers rotisserie chicken, vegetarian entrees, and even popcorn. The deli and salad bar are organic and kosher.

Highlights in natural foods:

Bell Bates Natural Food Market (97 Reade St, 212/267-4300): herbs, coffees

Commodities Natural Market (165 First Ave, 212/260-2600): cheeses, good prices

Health Nuts (2611 Broadway, 212/678-0054): salad bar

Healthy Pleasures (93 University Pl, 212/353-3663): organic meats, produce

Integral Yoga Natural Foods (229 W 13th St, 212/243-2642): organic produce, baked items, yoga classes in same building

Lifethyme Natural Market (408-410 Ave of the Americas, 212/420-9099): salad bar, produce

Uptown Whole Foods (2421 Broadway, 212/874-4000): one of Manhattan's best; juice bar and kosher items

Whole Foods Market (Time Warner Center, 10 Columbus Circle, 212/823-9600; 4 Union Square S, 212/673-5388; and 250 Seventh Ave, 212/924-5969): salad bar, flowers, large selection

---

HEALTH & HARMONY
470 Hudson St (bet Barrow and Grove St)   212/691-3036
Mon, Tues, Thurs: 9-8:30; Wed, Fri: 9-8; Sat: 10-7:30; Sun: 11-7

A great find for the health-conscious! Health & Harmony stocks lots of good things to eat, organic produce, vitamins and herbs, and herbal remedies. They will also deliver.

INTEGRAL YOGA NATURAL FOODS
229 W 13th St (bet Seventh and Eighth Ave)   212/243-2642
Mon-Fri: 9 a.m.-9:30 p.m.; Sat, Sun: 9-8:30
                              www.integralyoganaturalfoods.com

Selection and quality abound in this clean, attractive shop, featuring a complete assortment of healthy, natural foods. Vegetarian items, packaged groceries, organic produce, bulk foods, and baked items are available at reasonable prices. A juice bar, salad bar, and deli are on-premises. They occupy the same building as a center that offers classes in yoga, meditation, and philosophy. Across the street is **Integral Apothecary** (234 W 13th St, 212/645-3051), a vegetarian, vitamin, and herb shop with a nutritional consultant on staff.

LIFETHYME NATURAL MARKET
408-410 Ave of the Americas (bet 8th and 9th St)   212/420-9099
Daily: 9 a.m.-10 p.m.

You'll find one of the area's largest selections of organic produce at this natural supermarket. In addition, there is an organic salad table, over 5,000 health-related books, a deli serving natural foods, a "natural cosmetics" boutique, a complete vegan bakery, and an organic juice bar. Located in two renovated 1839 brownstones in the heart of the Village, this busy shop also sells discounted vitamins, does catering, and offers custom-baked goods for dietary needs.

No question about it: the best yogurt in Manhattan is the coffee flavor served at **40 Carrots** on the metro level at **Bloomingdale's** (1000 Third Ave).

WHOLESOME MARKET
93 University Pl (bet 11th and 12th St)   212/353-FOOD
Daily: 7 a.m.-11 p.m.

You instantly feel healthy just walking in this place—and what a selection! Wholesome Market is a full-scale deli and health-products emporium. Entree items (like roasted chicken, lasagna, and fish) for takeout, healthy platters (organic steamed vegetables, salads, and soups), and delicious sandwiches are among the offerings. Delivery is free, an all-natural catering service is available, and fresh juice, all-natural muffins, organic and decaf coffees, and herbal teas are offered.

The best ice cream in Manhattan:

Bussola (65 Fourth Ave, 212/254-1940)

Chinatown Ice Cream Factory (65 Bayard St, 212/608-4170)

Ciao Bella (27 E 92nd St and 285 Mott St, 212/431-3591): gelati and sorbets

City Bakery (3 W 18th St, 212/366-1414): elegant flavors

Cold Stone Creamery (253 W 42nd St, 212/398-1882 and 1651 Second Ave, 212/249-7085): Super creamy! They'll custom-mix special ingredients right in front of you.

Cones, Ice Cream Artisans (272 Bleecker St, 212/414-1795): 36 flavors of ice cream and sorbet

Custard Beach (2 World Financial Center, 212/786-4707): many flavors of frozen custard

Emack & Bolio's (389 Amsterdam Ave, 212/362-2747 and 56 Seventh Ave, 212/727-1198): vanilla bean ice cream; Amsterdam Ave location open summer only

Fauchon (442 Park Ave, 212/308-5919)

Il Laboratorio del Gelato (95 Orchard St, 212/343-9922): gelati, sorbets

Il Gelatone (397 Third Ave, 212/481-2092): gelati

NYC Icy (21 Ave B, 212/979-9877): Italian ices

Payard Patisserie & Bistro (1032 Lexington Ave, 212/717-5252): top-grade gelati

Ronnybrook Farms Dairy (75 9th St, 212/741-6455): great flavors

Ice Cream and Other Goodies

CONES, ICE CREAM ARTISANS
272 Bleecker St (at Seventh Ave)   212/414-1795
Mon-Thurs, Sun: 1 p.m.-11 p.m.; Fri, Sat: 1 p.m.-1 a.m.

The D'Aloisio family brought their original Italian ice-cream recipes to Manhattan . . . and boy, are they good! Cones specializes in creamy gelati made with all-natural ingredients. Thirty-six flavors (try the coffee mocha chocolate chip) are carried, and fat-free fruit flavors are available. All are made daily on the premises, ensuring freshness and creamy goodness, and can be packed for takeout. Made-to-order ice-cream cakes are now available.

NEW YORK MILKSHAKE COMPANY
37 St. Mark's Pl (bet Second and Third Ave)   212/505-5200
Sun-Thurs: 11 a.m.-11 p.m.; Fri, Sat: 11 a.m.-2 a.m.

This place makes shakes and malts the way they should be! You can choose from 30 flavors or get low-fat frozen yogurt shakes. They also serve old-school Brooklyn egg creams, sandwiches, soups, and waffles.

Indian

KALUSTYAN'S
123 Lexington Ave (bet 28th and 29th St)
                                    212/685-3451, 800/352-3451
Mon-Sat: 10-8; Sun: 11-7   www.kalustyans.com

In 1944, Kalustyan's opened as an Indian spice store at its present location. After all this time, it is still a great spot. Many items are sold in bins or bales rather than prepackaged containers. The difference in cost, flavor, and freshness compared to regular grocery stores is extraordinary. The best indication of freshness and flavor is the store's aroma! Kalustyan's is both an Indian store and an Orient export trading corporation with a specialty in Middle Eastern and Indian items. There is a large selection of dried fruit, nuts, mixes, coffees and teas, and accessories.

> Here is an eclectic establishment! **Dile Punjab Deli & Electronics** (170 Ninth Ave, 212/647-9428) features Indian food, spicy Indian tea, herbal soup, and veggie dishes that they say "will keep the mind, body, and soul in full fitness."

Italian

RAFFETTO'S CORPORATION
144 W Houston St (bet Sullivan and MacDougal St)   212/777-1261
Tues-Fri: 9-6:30; Sat: 9-6

You can go to a gourmet market for pasta, but why not go straight to the source? Raffetto's has been producing all kinds of fresh-cut noodles and stuffed pastas since 1906. Though most of the business is wholesale, Raffetto's will sell their noodles, ravioli, mini-ravioli, tortellini, manicotti, gnocchi, and fettuccine to anyone. Variations include Genoa-style ravioli with meat and spinach, and Naples-style ravioli with cheese. More than ten homemade sauces are personally prepared by Mrs. Raffetto. Daily bread, dry pasta, and bargain-priced olive oils and vinegars are also featured.

RAVIOLI STORE
75 Sullivan St (bet Spring and Broome St)
Mon-Fri: 7-7; Sat, Sun: 11-7   212/925-1737, 877/NY-PASTA
                                       www.raviolistore.com

Since 1989, this factory has been producing some of New York's most unique ravioli and gourmet pasta products. Goat cheese ravioli in black peppercorn pasta is one of about a dozen unusual raviolis at this factory outlet. Various fresh pastas are available daily, along with sauces and cheeses.

A *hundred* flavors of gelati? Indeed, at **Il Laboratorio del Gelato** (95 Orchard St, 212/343-9922)! Their gelati is in the true Italian tradition and is made in-house. They also serve the real thing at **Otto Enoteca Pizzeria** (1 Fifth Ave, 212/995-9559) and **Vento** (675 Hudson St, 212/699-2400).

Japanese

KATAGIRI & COMPANY
224 E 59th St (bet Second and Third Ave)   212/755-3566
Mon-Wed, Sat: 10-7; Thurs, Fri: 10-9; Sun: 11-6   www.katagiri.com

Are you planning a Japanese dinner? Do you have some important clients you would like to impress with a sushi party? Katagiri features all kinds of Japanese food, sushi ingredients, and utensils. You can get some great party ideas from the helpful personnel. Delivery is available in Manhattan.

What to bring home or order from overseas:
Austria: rich tortes (Linzer is best)
Belgium: chocolates (can't beat Neuhaus!)
France: gourmet cuisine from the Fauchon shop in Paris
Germany: Stollen or *lebkuchen* are tops for the holidays.
Great Britain: fruitcakes (like the Brontë cake from York)
Greece: baklava from downtown Athens pastry shops
Hungary: *real* paprika
Ireland: Cashel blue cheese
Italy: packaged risotto from the Milan airport
Mexico: dried chilis
Netherlands: aged Gouda cheese
Spain: *turron* (almond-studded nougat bar)

SUNRISE MART
4 Stuyvesant St (at Third Ave), 2nd floor   212/598-3040
Sun-Thurs: 10 a.m.-11 p.m.; Fri, Sat: 10 a.m.-12 a.m.
494 Broome St (bet West Broadway and Wooster St)   212/219-0033
Daily: 10-10

In a part of the East Village that is home to an increasing number of young Japanese and stores that cater to them, these all-purpose grocery stores do a bustling business. Japanese is spoken more often than English, and many packages bear nothing but Japanese calligraphy. In addition to a wide range of snack foods and candy, they sell fruits, vegetables, meats, fish, and other grocery items. They also carry bowls, chopsticks, and items for the home. Sunrise Mart rents Japanese-language videos, too. A Japanese bake shop, **Panya Bakery** (10 Stuyvesant St, 212/777-1930), is next door to the original location.

Kosher

Note: see Restaurant chapter for additonal Kosher listings.

SIEGEL'S KOSHER DELI AND RESTAURANT
1646 Second Ave (bet 85th and 86th St)   212/288-3632
Daily: 10 a.m.-11 p.m.

If you are looking for a top kosher deli and gourmet appetizer store on the Upper East Side, you can't do better than Siegel's. They keep long hours (Sundays, too), and they also deliver. Featured are fresh, decorated turkey dishes; overstuffed sandwich platters; barbecued, roasted, and fried chicken platters; hors d'oeuvre selections; smoked fish platters; fresh baked breads and salad trays; and a large array of cakes, cookies, and fruit platters. The number of menu items is awesome, with nearly two dozen sandwiches, ten soups, dozens of salads, and side dishes ranging from potato and meat knishes to kugel and kishka.

Holyland Market (122 St. Mark's Pl, 212/477-4440, www.israeli market.com) is an excellent place for kosher meats, cheeses, and other hard-to-find Israeli imports.

Latin American

KITCHEN MARKET
218 Eighth Ave (bet 21st and 22nd St)   212/243-4433
Mon-Fri: 9 a.m.-11 p.m.; Sat, Sun: 11-11   www.kitchenmarket.com

This store features an extensive selection of Latin American food items. They also operate an adjacent Mexican/Asian restaurant next door, **Bright Food Shop** (216 Eighth Ave, 212/243-4433), and offer bulk prices online. If you want to know anything about Mexican foods, ask chef/owner Dona Abramson. Catering is available.

Liquor, Wine

ACKER, MERRALL & CONDIT
160 W 72nd St (bet Broadway and Columbus Ave)   212/787-1700
Mon-Sat: 9 a.m.-10 p.m.   www.ackerstore.com

This is the oldest operating wine and liquor store in America, having opened its doors in 1820. And what a place Acker, Merrall & Condit (AMC, for short) continues to be! There are in-store wine tastings Friday and Saturday afternoons. Wine seminars are offered to companies. Wine parties can be arranged in private residences for special occasions. Free delivery is available in Manhattan. This service-oriented firm stocks a good inventory of American wines and specializes in purchases from Bordeaux and the Rhine. The Wine Workshop—Acker, Merrall & Condit's special-events affiliate—offers wine-tasting classes and dinners that range in price from $40 to $1,295. AMC is the largest independent fine-wine auction company in the United States. They also have monthly Internet auction sales.

BEST CELLARS
1291 Lexington Ave (at 87th St)   212/426-4200
Mon-Thurs: 9:30-9; Fri, Sat: 9:30 a.m.-10 p.m.; Sun: 12-7
www.bestcellars.com

Are those expensive wines really worth the price? Can your guests tell the difference between various bottles? Best Cellars offers over 150 values, most under $15, and the personnel are very friendly and knowledgeable.

BURGUNDY WINE COMPANY
143 W 26th St (bet Ave of the Americas and Seventh Ave)
Mon-Sat: 10-7   212/691-9092
www.burgundywinecompany.com

One of the great pleasures of shopping in New York is knowing that there is a store for just about every specialty. The customer is the winner because the selection is huge and the price range is broad. Such is the case with Burgundy Wine Company, a compact and attractive store in Chelsea. These folks are specialists in fine Burgundies, Rhones, and Oregon wines, with over 2,000 labels to choose from. There are some great treasures in their cellars; ask the expert personnel. Tastings are offered all day Saturday, and Monday through Friday evening from 5 to 7.

CROSSROADS WINES AND LIQUORS
55 W 14th St (at Ave of the Americas)   212/924-3060
Mon-Sat: 9-8:30   www.crossroadswines.com

Crossroads carries 4,000 wines from all the great wine-producing countries. They stock rare, unique, and exotic liquors as well. Crossroads will special-order items, deliver, and help with party and menu planning. Their experienced staff has a passion for matching wines and foods. Best of all, their prices are as low as their low-key attitude.

GARNET LIQUORS
929 Lexington Ave (bet 68th and 69th St)   212/772-3211
Mon-Sat: 9-9; Sun: 12-6   800/USA-VINO (out of state)
www.garnetwine.com

You'll love Garnet's prices, which are among the most competitive in the city for specialty wines. If you're in the market for Champagne, Bordeaux, Burgundy, Italian, or other imported wines, check here first, as selections are impressive. They stock virtually everything except New York wines. Prices are good on other wines and liquors, too.

ITALIAN WINE MERCHANTS
108 E 16th St (bet Union Square E and Irving Pl)   212/473-2323
Mon-Fri: 10-7; Sat: 11-7   www.italianwinemerchant.com

If Italian wines are your thing, then Italian Wine Merchants should be your destination. You will find Italian wines exclusively, with specialties in cult and tightly allocated wines, many from undiscovered producers. Just wait until you see the place; it is class personified!

K&D FINE WINES AND SPIRITS
1366 Madison Ave (bet 95th and 96th St)   212/289-1818
Mon-Sat: 9-9   www.kdwine.com

K&D is an excellent wine and spirits market on the Upper East Side. Hundreds of top wines and liquors are sold at competitive prices. Occasional ads in local newspapers highlight special bargains.

Wine lovers will be interested in the **Windows on the World Wine School** (moved after the World Trade Center disaster to the New York Marriott Marquis, 1535 Broadway, 845/255-1456; www.wowws.com). Founder Kevin Zraly gives informative and entertaining lectures.

MISTER WRIGHT
1593 Third Ave (bet 89th and 90th St)   212/722-4564
Mon-Sat: 9 a.m.-9:30 p.m.; Sun: 1-7

Meet Mr. Wright! If you are interested in Australian wines, this shop has a nice selection. A neighborhood store for over three decades, Mister Wright has a reputation for fine stock at comfortable prices and extra-friendly Aussie service.

MORRELL & COMPANY
1 Rockefeller Plaza (49th St bet Fifth Ave and Ave of the Americas)
Mon-Sat: 10-7   212/688-9370
                                        www.morrellwine.com

Charming and well informed, Peter Morrell is the wine expert at this small, jam-packed store, which carries all kinds of wine and liquor. The stock is overwhelming, and a good portion of it must be kept in the wine cellar. However, it is all easily accessible, and the Morrell staff is amenable to helping you find the right bottle. The stock consists of spirits, including brandy liqueurs, and wine vintages ranging from old and valuable to young and inexpensive. While you are here, check out the **Morrell Wine Bar Cafe**, whose menu is inviting!

NANCY'S WINES FOR FOOD
313 Columbus Ave (at 75th St)   212/877-4040
Mon-Sat: 10-9; Sun: 12-6   www.nancyswines.com

These folks are pros at matching wines with food. Prices are reasonable, the selection is excellent, and they offer a "wine of the month" program. German white wines, "grower" champagnes, and boutique wines are specialties.

QUALITY HOUSE
2 Park Ave (bet 32nd and 33rd St)   212/532-2944
Mon-Fri: 9-6:30; Sat: 10-3; closed Sat in July, Aug
                                 www.qualityhousewines.com

Quality House boasts one of the most extensive stocks of French wine in the city, an equally fine offering of domestic and Italian wines, and selections from Germany, Spain, and Portugal. True to their name, this is a quality house, not a bargain spot. Delivery is available and usually free.

SHERRY-LEHMANN
679 Madison Ave (bet 61st and 62nd St)   212/838-7500
Mon-Sat: 9-7   www.sherry-lehmann.com

Sherry-Lehmann is one of New York's best-known wine shops, with an inventory of over 7,000 wines from all over the world. Prices run the gamut from $5 to $10,000 a bottle. This firm has been in business for seven decades, and it offers special services for their customers.

SOHO WINES AND SPIRITS
461 West Broadway (bet Prince and Houston St)   212/777-4332
Mon-Sat: 10-8   www.sohowines.com

Stephen Masullo's father ran a liquor store on Spring Street for over 25 years. When the neighborhood evolved into the Soho of today, sons Stephen, Victor, and Paul expanded the business and opened a stylish Soho establishment for wine on West Broadway. Now they are celebrating their own 25th anniversary! The shop is lofty. In fact, it looks more like an art gallery than a wine shop. Bottles are tastefully displayed, and classical music plays in the background. Soho Wines also has one of the largest selections of single-malt Scotch whiskeys in New York. Services include party planning and wine cellar advice.

American Bottles & Wine Spirits (300 E 78th St, 212/737-1588) is a handy name to know when you're having a party and run out of drinks! They are open daily till midnight (Sunday till 9).

VINO
121 E 27th St (bet Lexington Ave and Park Ave S)   212/725-6516
Mon-Sat: 12-10   www.vinosite.com

If Italian wine is your passion, then Vino is your store. You will find over 500 labels, many of them reasonably priced. The staff is extra friendly, and if you come at the right time, you might get a sample tasting.

VINTAGE NEW YORK
482 Broome St (at Wooster St)   212/226-9463
Mon-Sat: 11-9; Sun: 12-9
2492 Broadway (at 93rd St)   212/721-9999
Daily: 12-10   www.vintagenewyork.com

Vintage New York offers wines from dozens of New York wineries, along with local artisanal cheeses, patés, and other foods. Sampling is available daily in the tasting room or winebar. You'll also find wine-lifestyle accessories and can even create your own custom gift baskets of food and wine.

Meat, Poultry

FAICCO'S ITALIAN SPECIALTIES
260 Bleecker St (at Ave of the Americas)   212/243-1974
Tues-Thurs: 8:30-6; Fri: 8:30-7; Sat: 8-6; Sun: 9-2

An Italian institution, Faicco's carries delectable dried sausage, cuts of pork, and sweet and hot sausage. They also sell an equally good meat cuts for barbecue and an oven-ready rolled leg of stuffed pork. Pork loin, a house specialty, is locally famous. They also carry veal cutlets, veal chops, ground veal, veal for stew, a large selection of olive oils, and every ingredient needed to make an antipasto. If you're into Italian-style deli, try Faicco's first. And if you're pressed for time, take home their heat-and-eat chicken rollettes: breasts of chicken rolled around cheese and dipped in a crunchy coating. Prepared hot foods to take home—including lasagna, baby back ribs, and eggplant parmesan—are also available.

GIOVANNI ESPOSITO & SONS MEAT MARKET
500 Ninth Ave (at 38th St)   212/279-3298
Mon-Sat: 8-7:30

Family members still preside over an operation that has been at the same location since 1932. Whatever you need in the way of meat, you'll find it here at good prices. Their homemade Italian sausages are a specialty, and every kind you can imagine—breakfast, sage, garlic, smoked, hot dogs—is available. The cold cuts selection is awesome: bologna, liverwurst, pepperoni, salami, ham, turkey breast, American and Muenster cheese, and much more. Hosting a dinner? You'll find pork roasts, crown roasts, pork chops, spare ribs, slab bacon, tenderloins, sirloin steaks, short ribs, filet mignon, London broil, corned beef brisket, leg of lamb, pheasant, quail, and venison. Free home delivery is available in midtown for "modestly minimum orders."

> A West Village must: **Florence Meat Market** (5 Jones St, 212/242-6531). Everything is cut to order.

JEFFERSON MARKET
450 Ave of the Americas (at 10th St)   212/533-3377
Mon-Sat: 7:30 a.m-9 p.m.; Sun: 8 a.m.-8:30 p.m.

Quality and personal service are the bywords at Jefferson Market. Originally a prime meat and poultry market, Jefferson has grown into an outstanding full-line store. Second-generation family management ensures hands-on attention to service. Prime meats, fresh seafood, select produce, gourmet coffee, fancy groceries, Bell and Evans chicken, and fresh salads are all tempting. There are bakery, deli, cheese, produce, and fish sections. Delivery service is available. If you don't feel like cooking dinner, let Louis or John Montuori send you home with some delicious hot or cold prepared foods.

KUROWYCKY MEAT PRODUCTS
124 First Ave (bet 7th and 8th St)   212/477-0344
Mon-Sat: 8-6; closed Mon in July, Aug   www.sausagenyc.com

Erast Kurowycky came to New York from Ukraine in 1954 and opened this tiny shop the same year. Almost immediately it became a mecca and bargain spot for the city's Poles, Germans, Hungarians, Russians, Lithuanians, and Ukrainians. Many of these East European nationalities still harbor centuries-old grudges, but they all come to Kurowycky, where they agree on at least two things: the meats are the finest and prices are the best. A third-generation family member, Jaroslaw Kurowycky, Jr., runs the shop. Hams, sausages, meat loaves, and breads are sold. There are also condiments, including homemade Polish mustard, honey from Poland, sauerkraut, and a half-dozen other Ukrainian specialties.

Pointers for Meat Cuts

Chops: cuts from the rib section

Chuck: sometimes called patio steak; derived from the neck and shoulder-blade areas

Crown roast: rib bones of a lamb or pork loin tied into a circle

Filet mignon: thick (two to three inch), tender steaks cut from the long, cylindrical beef tenderloin

Flank: large, thin, flat steak that is flavorful and chewy

Flat iron: Also called top blade, it's cut from the chuck and sold as steak.

Hangar: thin cut of flavorful, chewy beef from the hindquarter, below the short loin; tastes great marinated

Porterhouse: This huge cut has portions of the tenderloin and top loin and contains the T-bone.

Ribeye: Cut from a standing rib roast or prime rib, ribeye is boneless, flavorful, well-marbled, and tender.

Round: from the hind section

Shank: from the front leg of a cow, pig, or lamb; used for osso buco

Short loin: area located in the center of the back between the rib cage and the sirloin

Sirloin: tender cut of meat located near the rear section of the back, behind the short loin

Sirloin (bone in): usually one-inch-thick cuts of sirloin; best marinated and grilled

Sirloin (double): usually two to three inches thick

Skirt: comes from the diaphragm muscle, has lots of flavor, and can be a bit tough; often used in fajitas

Strip: also called a New York steak, New York strip, or shell steak; part of the top loin with bone removed

T-bone: tender, bone-in steak similar to but not as large as the Porterhouse, and containing less of the tenderloin

Tenderloin: Filet mignon comes from the tenderloin, the rear portion of the loin in beef and pork.

Top loin: front part of the short loin, yielding Delmonico, Kansas City, and New York strip steaks

Tri-tip: cut from the bottom cap of the sirloin butt; moderately chewy and very flavorful

LOBEL'S PRIME MEATS
1096 Madison Ave (bet 82nd and 83rd St)   212/737-1373
Mon-Sat: 9-6: closed Sat in summer   www.lobels.com

Lobel's runs periodic sales on some of the best cuts of meat (poultry and veal, too). Because of their excellent service and reasonable prices, few carnivores in Manhattan *haven't* heard of the shop. The staff has published seven cookbooks, and they are always willing to explain the best use for each cut. It's hard to go wrong, since Lobel carries only the best. They will ship all over the country. Great hamburgers, too!

L. SIMCHICK
944 First Ave (at 52nd St)   212/888-2299
Mon-Fri: 8-7; Sat: 8-6

One and a half centuries in business have made these folks famous! You'll find wild game, prime meats, poultry products, wonderful homemade sausage, and a good selection of prepared foods. Free delivery is provided on the East Side.

OPPENHEIMER PRIME MEATS
2606 Broadway (bet 98th and 99th St)   212/662-0246
Mon-Fri: 8-7; Sat: 8-6

Reliable and trustworthy, Oppenheimer is a first-rate source for prime meats in New York. Under the ownership of Robert Pence, an experienced butcher and chef, the traditions of Harry Oppenheimer have been carried forward. It's an old-fashioned butcher shop, offering the kind of service and quality you would never find at a supermarket. Prime dry-aged beef, milk-fed veal, free-range poultry, and game are all sold at competitive prices. Delivery is available throughout Manhattan.

OTTOMANELLI'S MEAT MARKET
285 Bleecker St (bet Seventh Ave and Jones St)   212/675-4217
Mon-Fri: 8:30-6:30; Sat: 8-6   www.wildgamemeatsrus.com

Looking for the unusual? Ottomanelli's stock-in-trade is rare gourmet fare. Among the weekly offerings are boar's head, whole baby lambs, game, rabbits, and pheasant. They also stock buffalo, ostrich, rattlesnake, alligator meat, suckling pig, and quail. Quality is good, but service from the right person can make the difference between a good cut and an excellent one. They gained their reputation by offering full butcher services and a top-notch selection of prime meats, game, prime-aged steaks, and milk-fed veal. The latter is cut into Italian roasts, chops, and steaks, and their preparation by Ottomanelli's is unique. Best of all, they will sell it by the piece for a quick meal at home.

PARK EAST KOSHER BUTCHER & FINE FOODS
1623 Second Ave (bet 84th and 85th St)   212/737-9800
Mon-Wed: 7-7; Thurs: 7 a.m.-9 p.m.; Fri: 5:30 a.m. till two hours before sunset; Sun: 9-6   www.parkeastkosher.com
(closed Sun in July and Aug)

This is one-stop kosher shopping: butcher items, cooked foods, packaged meats, bakery goods, candy, sauces and dressings, pickled products, salads and dips, frozen food, vegetables, fruits, cheese, and sushi. Park East carries over 700 items in all! They promise delivery within three hours throughout Manhattan. **Park East Grill** (1564 Second Ave, 212/717-8400) is their restaurant, offering fine kosher items.

PREMIER VEAL
555 West St (off West Side Hwy, two blocks south of 14th St)
Mon-Fri: 3:30 a.m.-1 p.m.   212/243-3170
                                                        www.premierveal.com

Premier Veal offers veal and lamb stew, Italian cutlets, shoulder and leg roasts, rabbit, and veal pockets for stuffing, all at wholesale prices with no minimum order. Of course, if you're trekking to West Street, it might be economical to make the order as large as possible. Three or four friends could go in together on a few loins. A loin weighing 26 pounds breaks down to 16 or 24 steaks and chops, and the price is a fraction of what a butcher shop charges.

SCHALLER & WEBER
1654 Second Ave (bet 85th and 86th St)   212/879-3047
Mon-Fri: 9-6; Sat: 8-6   www.schallerweber.com

Once you've been in this store, the image will stay with you because of the sheer magnitude of cold cuts on display. Schaller & Weber is *Babes in Toyland* for delicatessen lovers, and there is nary a wall or nook that is not covered with deli meats. Besides offering a complete line of deli items, Schaller & Weber stocks game and poultry. Try the sausage and pork, which they will bake, prepare, smoke, or roll.

Don't miss the sausage sandwiches on crusty, fresh-baked rolls with your choice of toppings and corn fritters at **Mandler's: The Original Sausage Co.** (26 E 17th St, 212/255-8999). They make poultry, seafood, and vegetable sandwiches, too!

TARTARE
653 Ninth Ave (at 46th St)   212/333-5300
Mon-Fri: 7:30 a.m.-9 p.m.; Sat: 9:30-8

Tartare is an offshoot of Piccinini Brothers, a well-known meat purveyor for many years. This shop offers great prepared meats to go, a number of side dishes, imported foods and oils, chicken, filet mignon, and much more. A butcher shop is on the premises, and even the desserts are first-class. Catering is also offered. This is a real find!

YORKVILLE PACKING HOUSE
1560 Second Ave (at 81st St)   212/628-5147
Mon-Sat: 8-6; Sun: 9-5

Yorkville used to be a bastion of Eastern European ethnicity and culture before becoming the Upper East Side's swinging singles playground. Here and there, remnants of Old World society remain. Yorkville Packing House is patronized by Hungarian-speaking old ladies in black, as well as some of the city's greatest gourmands. The reason is simple: these prepared meats are available nowhere else in the city and possibly on the continent. The shop offers a vast variety of sausages and salami. Smoked meats include pork shoulder and tenderloin. Goose is a mainstay of Hungarian cuisine, so goose liverwurst, smoked goose, and goose liver are staples here. Fried bacon bits and bacon fried with paprika (a favorite Hungarian spice) are other popular offerings, and there's more: preserves, jams, spices, ground nuts, jellies, prepared delicacies, head cheese, breads, and takeout meals. And it is all authentic!

Pickles

GUSS' PICKLES
85-87 Orchard St (bet Broome and Grand St)
Sun-Thurs: 9:30-6; Fri: 9:30-4

Guss' is *the* pickle outfit in Manhattan! In their famous huge barrels outside and in the refrigerator inside, you'll find half-sour, sour, and hot pickles; sweet peppers; pickled tomatoes; sweetkraut and sauerkraut; olives; relishes; and much more. There is no other place like this!

Seafood

CATALANO'S FRESH FISH MARKET
Vinegar Factory
431 E 91st St (bet York and First Ave)   212/987-0885
Mon-Sun: 7 a.m.-9 p.m.

Joe Catalano is that rare blend of knowledge and helpfulness. Catalano's customers, including many local restaurants, rely on him to select the best items for their dinner menus. This he does with a careful eye toward health, price, and preparation. Catalano's at the Vinegar Factory also has a good selection of poached fish, plus crawfish and soft-shell crabs in season. On cold winter days, don't miss the Manhattan clam chowder.

CENTRAL FISH COMPANY
527 Ninth Ave (bet 39th and 40th St)   212/279-2317
Mon-Fri: 8-6:30; Sat: 8-5:30

Central Fish doesn't look like much from the outside, but the stock is so vast that it's easier to list what is *not* available than what *is*. They have 35 fish species in stock at any given time, including imported sardines from Portugal. Assisting customers through this whale of a selection are friendly and knowledgeable salespeople. Louis and Anthony Riccoborno and Calogero Olivri are skillful guides who stock all manner of fresh and frozen fish and seafood products. That includes fish that even the most devoted seafood lover might have trouble identifying. Prices are reasonable.

DOWNEAST SEAFOOD
402 W 13th St (bet Ninth Ave and Hudson St)
Mon-Fri: 8-3; Sat: 10-2   212/243-5639

Two excellent reasons to shop here: They have just about any seafood-related item you could possibly want, and their prices are usually about 30% to 40% below retail. They also offer free delivery in Manhattan with orders of $75 or more. A good catch!

LEONARD'S SEAFOOD AND PRIME MEATS
1385 Third Ave (bet 78th and 79th St)   212/744-2600
Mon-Fri: 8-7; Sat: 8-6; Sun: 11-6

Leonard's, a family-owned business since 1910, has expanded its inventory. You'll find oysters, crabs, striped bass, halibut, salmon, live lobsters, and squid. In addition, there are farm-fresh vegetables and organic dairy products. Their takeout seafood department sells codfish cakes and crab cakes; hand-sliced Norwegian, Scottish, and Irish smoked salmon; lobsters; and some of the best Manhattan clam chowder in Manhattan! Barbecued poultry, cooked and prepared foods, and aged prime meats (beef, lamb, and veal) round out Leonard's selection. Their homemade seafood chili, turkey chili, and beef stew are customer favorites. They also make beautiful platters of boiled shrimp, crabmeat, and smoked salmon for parties. This service-oriented establishment provides fast, free delivery.

LOBSTER PLACE
Chelsea Market   212/255-5672
75 Ninth Ave (bet 15th and 16th St)   www.lobsterplace.com
Mon-Fri: 9:30-8; Sat: 9:30-7; Sun: 10-6

Imagine distributing one million pounds of lobster every year! The Lobster Place does just that, and they have a full line of fish, shrimp, and shellfish, too. Top hotels and restaurants take advantage of their buying power, so you are assured of quality, freshness, and value.

If you can put up with periodic poor service at **Pisacane Midtown Seafood** (940 First Ave, 212/752-7560), this wholesale and retail seafood operation is worth a visit.

MURRAY'S STURGEON SHOP
2429 Broadway (bet 89th and 90th St)   212/724-2650
Sun-Fri; 8-7; Sat: 8-8

Murray's is *the* stop for fancy smoked fish, fine appetizers, and caviar. Choose from sturgeon, Eastern and Norwegian salmon, whitefish, kippered salmon, sable, pickled herring, and schmaltz. The quality is excellent, and prices are fair. Murray's also offers kosher cold cuts, dried fruits, and nuts.

WILD EDIBLES
535 Third Ave (bet 35th and 36th St)   212/213-8552
Mon-Fri: 11-9; Sat: 1-8; Sun: 11-7   www.wildedibles.com

You can't beat these folks for fresh, high-quality seafood, some of it unique and imported. Many of the same foods served at Manhattan's top restaurants are sold here. Delivery is available throughout the city, and a catering menu boasts that seafood caught anywhere in the world can be put on your home or office table! Kosher (uncertified) and health foods also are stocked.

Spices

ANGELICA'S HERBAL AND NUTRITIONAL HYGIENE
147 First Ave (at 9th St)   212/677-1549
Food shop hours: Sun-Thurs: 11:30-10; Fri, Sat: 11:30 a.m.-midnight
Herb shop hours: Fri-Wed: 1:30 p.m.-6:30 p.m.

Angelica's carries medicinal herbs, spices, and essential oils, and they offer health counseling by appointment. The delicatessen and confectionery offer freshly prepared meals (cooked and raw) and snacks, juices, smoothies, desserts, pastries, and candies. All are organic, vegan, tasty, and available for eat-in or takeout. Certified organic fresh fruits and vegetables and other bulk foods are also sold.

APHRODISIA
264 Bleecker St (bet Ave of the Americas and Seventh Ave)
Mon-Sat: 11:30-7; Sun: 12:30-5   212/989-6440

Aphrodisia is stocked from floor to ceiling with nearly every herb and spice imaginable—800 of them, which are neatly displayed in glass jars. Some of the teas, potpourri, dried flowers, and oils (200 of them!) are really not what one might expect. The general accent is on folk remedies, but most every ingredient for ethnic cooking can be found as well. Aphrodisia also conducts a mail-order business.

V. Where to Find It:
New York's Best Services

One of the many reasons I love New York is that you can find someone —and usually *several* someones—for every need imaginable. Whether you need a chair re-caned, a doll repaired, a party planned, or stained glass restored, I can recommend an expert who will take care of you with great skill and quality service. I can also direct you to places to rent formal wear, televisions, and even a personal assistant. On top of it all, I can point you to the right hotel at a good price.

Air Conditioning

AIR-WAVE AIR CONDITIONING COMPANY
2421 Jerome Ave (at Fordham Road), The Bronx   212/545-1122
Mon-Fri: 9-5 (Sat in spring and summer)   www.airwaveac.com

If the dog days are getting you down or you want to plan ahead to make sure that they don't, give these folks a call. Air-Wave has been in business for half a century and comes highly recommended. They have sold tens of thousands of units over the years: top brands like Friedrich, Carrier, West-inghouse, and Panasonic. They offer same-day delivery and installation.

Animal Adoptions

**AMERICAN SOCIETY FOR THE PREVENTION
OF CRUELTY TO ANIMALS**
424 E 92nd St (bet First and York Ave)   212/876-7700, ext. 4120
Mon-Sat: 11-7; Sun: 11-5   www.aspca.org

This is one of the oldest animal protection organizations in the world, and these folks take pet adoptions very seriously. You'll need to fill out an appli-cation, go through an interview, bring two pieces of identification (at least one with a photograph), provide two references that the ASPCA staff can call, and offer proof of employment. The whole process sometimes takes longer than you might wish—but then *they're* sure that *you're* serious, and you can go home with a good pet that needs a loving home. Adoption fees for dogs and cats start at $75; puppies and kittens are higher. The fee includes a veteri-narian's exam, vaccinations, and spaying or neutering. ASPCA also enforces animal cruelty laws and has an on-site animal hospital.

Animal Services

ANIMAL MEDICAL CENTER
510 E 62nd St (bet FDR Dr and York Ave)   212/838-8100
Daily: 24 hours   www.amcny.org

If your pet becomes ill in New York, try the Animal Medical Center first. This nonprofit organization does all kinds of veterinary work reasonably and competently. They handle over 60,000 cases a year and have more than 80 veterinarians on staff. The care is among the best offered in the city. They suggest calling for an appointment first; emergency care costs more.

BISCUITS & BATH
1535 First Ave (at 80th St)   212/419-2500
701 Second Ave (at 38th St)
41 W 13th St (at Fifth Ave)
Mon-Fri: 7 a.m.-10 p.m.; Sat, Sun: 8 a.m.-10 p.m.
                                          www.biscuitsandbath.com

One could refer to these places as Doggy City! They offer grooming, training, workshops and seminars, vet care, dog walking, day and overnight care, swimming, and even Sunday brunches. The place is pocketbook-friendly.

CAROLE WILBOURN
299 W 12th St (bet Eighth and Ninth Ave)   212/741-0397
Mon-Sat: 9-6   www.thecattherapist.com

Do you want to talk to the author of *Total Cat, Cats on the Couch*, and *Cat Talk*? Perhaps you need a fascinating speaker? Carole Wilbourn is an internationally known cat therapist who has the answer to most cat problems. Carole makes house calls from coast to coast and can take care of many feline issues with just one session and a follow-up phone call. She does international consultations, takes on-site appointments at Westside Veterinary Center, and is available for speaking engagements.

DOGGIE DO AND PUSSYCATS, TOO!
567 Third Ave (bet 37th and 38th St)   212/661-9111
Mon-Fri: 7-7; Sat: 9-6   www.doggiedo.com

You will find top-notch grooming facilities, an exclusive collection of custom-tailored coats and sweaters, European-designed collars, and much more. Doggie measurements are kept on file.

EAST VILLAGE VETERINARIAN
241 Eldridge St (at Houston St)   212/674-8640
Daily: 9-3:30 (Wed, Sat till noon)

This is the only practicing homeopathic veterinary clinic in New York City. It features a complete homeopathic dispensary, with over a thousand remedies in stock. It is also a full-service animal hospital with an emphasis on prevention.

FIELDSTON PETS   718/796-4541
Mon-Sat: 9-7   www.pawsacrossamerica.com

Bash Dibra is a warm, friendly man who speaks dog language. Known as the "dog trainer to the stars," Bash is an animal behaviorist. If your dog has bad manners, Bash will teach it to behave. He believes in "tandem training"—training owners to train their dogs—because it's the owner who'll be in charge. Bash's experience in training a pet wolf gave him unique insight into the minds of dogs, and his success in bringing the most difficult pets to heel has made him a regular on the talk-show circuit. In addition to training sessions, dog and cat grooming is available.

LE CHIEN
Trump Plaza
1044 Third Ave (bet 61st and 62nd St)   212/752-2120
Mon-Sat: 8-6 (Thurs till 7)   www.lechiennyc.com

Occupying two floors of Trump Plaza, Le Chien is a luxurious pet day spa offering grooming and attentive boarding services. A boutique carries a fabulous selection of custom imported accessories, as well as Le Chien's own fragrance lines. They sell puppies directly from show breeders.

NEW YORK DOG SPA & HOTEL
145 W 18th St (bet Ave of the Americas and Seventh Ave)
32 W 25th St (bet Ave of the Americas and Broadway)
                              212/243-1199 (both locations)
                              www.dogspa.com

This is a full-service hotel for dogs, offering boarding, day care, massage, training, vet services, and more.

PET CARE NETWORK
Daily: 9-6 and by appointment   212/580-6004
                                   www.petscarenetwork.com

Pet Care Network, a kennel alternative established in 1985, offers all the comforts of home to pets (dogs, cats, birds) in 35 separate New York apartments. Your pet will receive individual attention from caring "dog people" or "cat people." There are no cages. One or two weeks notice is preferred. These folks are bonded and insured.

SUTTON DOG PARLOUR
311 E 60th St (bet First and Second Ave)   212/355-2850
Mon-Fri: 8-7; Sat: 8-6; Sun: 9-6   www.suttonpets.com

Sutton has been around for over four decades, so you know it is a responsible establishment. You will find dog grooming, boarding and day care, and supplies for dogs, cats, and birds. There's even a private outdoor park for your beloved pooch to enjoy. Sutton also boards birds, with each housed in its own large cage. A radio in the bird room keeps them up-to-date on world affairs—a necessity, of course!

WOOFSPA AND RESORT
678 Hudson St (bet 13th and 14th St)   212/229-WOOF
Daily: 6:30 a.m.-11 p.m. (overnight care available, too)
                                     www.woofspa.com

Quite a place! In a clean environment, you'll find most everything you need for your animal companion. Services include day and overnight care (both in-store and in-home), grooming, training, dog walking, photography, retail, car service pickup and return, special events, and doggy parties. If you are traveling and a hotel won't take your pet, call these folks.

> Sometimes it is handy and even necessary to have a vet make a house call. One of the best is **Dr. Amy Attas** (212/581-7387).

Antique Repair

MICHAEL J. DOTZEL AND SON
402 E 63rd St (at York Ave)   212/838-2890
Mon-Fri: 8-4:30

Dotzel specializes in the repair and maintenance of antiques and precious heirlooms. They won't touch modern pieces or inferior antiques, but if your older piece is made out of metal and needs repair, this is the place for the job. They pay close attention to detail and will hand-forge or hammer metal work, including brass. If an item has lost a part or if you want a duplication of an antique, it can be re-created. Dotzel also does stripping and replating, but since it isn't always good for an antique, they may try to talk you out of it.

SANO STUDIO
767 Lexington Ave (at 60th St), Room 403   212/759-6131
Mon-Fri: 10-5 (by appointment; closed Aug)

Jadwiga Baran presides over this fourth-floor antique repair shop, and she has an eye for excellence. That eye is focused on the quality of the workmanship and goods to be repaired. Both must be the best. Baran is a specialist who limits herself to repairing porcelain, pottery, ivory, and tortoise-shell works and antiques. She has many loyal adherents.

> Someone broke your prized piece of glassware? Don't worry—just call **Gus Jochec** (1597 York Ave, 212/517-3287).

Appliance Repair

AUDIOVISION
1386 Second Ave (bet 71st and 72nd St)   212/639-1733
Mon-Fri: 9:30-6:30; Sat: 9:30-4:30

Audiovision has been in business for two decades, providing top-quality radio and TV repairs (guaranteed for three months) on all major brands. Pickup and delivery, installation, and hookup are also offered.

Art Appraisals

ABIGAIL HARTMANN ASSOCIATES
415 Central Park W (at 101st St)   212/316-5406
Mon-Fri: 9-6 (by appointment); also available on weekends
                                              www.ah-haa.com

This firm specializes in fine and decorative art appraisals for insurance, donation, or other reasons. Their highly principled and experienced staff does not buy, sell, or receive kickbacks. (This can be a common practice with some auction houses, insurance companies, and galleries.) Fees are by the hour, consultations are available, and the friendly personnel can also provide restoration, framing, shipping, and storage contacts.

Art Services

A.I. FRIEDMAN
44 W 18th St (bet Fifth Ave and Ave of the Americas)   212/243-9000
Mon-Fri: 9-7; Sat: 10-7; Sun: 11-6   www.aifriedman.com

Those who want to frame it themselves can take advantage of one of the largest stocks of ready-made frames in the city at A.I. Friedman. Nearly all are sold at discount. In addition to fully assembled frames, they sell do-it-yourself frames that come equipped with glass and/or mats. Custom framing is also available.

If you need a painting restored, call the **American Institute for Conservation of Historic and Artistic Works** in Washington, D.C. (202/452-9545). They can direct you to legitimate conservators in New York City.

ELI WILNER & COMPANY
1525 York Ave (bet 80th and 81st St)   212/744-6521
Mon-Fri: 9:30-5:30   www.eliwilner.com

Eli Wilner's primary business is period frames and mirrors. He keeps over 3,300 19th- and early 20th-century American and European frames in stock and can locate any size or style. Wilner can create an exact replica of a frame in his inventory to your specifications. His staff of over 25 skilled craftsmen also does expert restoration of frames. Boasting such clients as the Metropolitan Museum of Art and the White House, Wilner's expertise speaks for itself.

GUTTMANN PICTURE FRAME ASSOCIATES
180 E 73rd St (bet Lexington and Third Ave)   212/744-8600
Mon-Thurs: 9-5

Though the Guttmanns have worked on frames for some of the nation's finest museums, including the Metropolitan, they stand apart from other first-class artisans in that they are not snobby or picky about the work they will accept. They will restore, regild, or replace any type of picture frame. They are masters at working with masterpieces but are equally at home restoring or framing a snapshot. Even better, they are among the few experts who don't price themselves out of the market. Bring a broken or worn-out frame, and they will graciously tell you exactly what it will cost to fix it.

J. POCKER & SON
135 E 63rd St (bet Park and Lexington Aye)   212/838-5488
Mon-Fri: 9-5:30; Sat: 10-5:30 (closed Sat in summer)
                                            www.jpocker.com

Three generations of this family have been in the custom framing business, so rest assured that you will receive expert advice from a superbly trained staff. As a sidelight, Pocker offers a gallery specializing in English sporting and botanical prints. Pickup and delivery are offered.

JINPRA NEW YORK PICTURE FRAMING
1208 Lexington Ave (at 82nd St)   212/988-3903
Tues-Fri: 11-6; Sat: 11-5

The proprietor of Jinpra is Wellington Chiang, and his service is as unique as his name. Jinpra provides art services (cleaning and gilding) in general and picture framing in particular. Chiang makes the high-quality frames himself; his artistry is evident in every piece he creates, including his murals.

JULIUS LOWY FRAME AND RESTORING COMPANY
223 E 80th St (bet Second and Third Ave)   212/861-8585
Mon-Fri: 9-5:30   www.lowyonline.com

Serving New York City since 1907, Lowy is the nation's oldest, largest, and most highly regarded firm for the conservation and framing of fine art. Lowy's services include painting and paper conservation, professional photography, conservation framing, and curatorial work. They sell antique frames (the largest inventory in the U.S.) and authentic reproduction frames (the best selection anywhere). In addition, Lowy provides complete conservation work, mat-making, and fitting services. Their client base includes art dealers, private collectors, auction houses, corporate collections, institutions, and museums.

LEITH RUTHERFURD TALAMO
By appointment only   212/396-0399

Did movers mishandle a treasured painting? Has the masterpiece that hung over the fireplace darkened with age? Do you need help hanging or lighting a collection? All of these services—plus cleaning, relining, painting, and polishing frames—are done with expertise and class by Leith Rutherfurd Talamo.

Babysitters

BABY SITTERS' GUILD
60 E 42nd St (bet Madison and Park Ave), Suite 912   212/682-0227
Daily: 9-9   www.babysittersguild.com

Established in 1940, the Baby Sitters' Guild charges high rates, but their professional reputation commends them. All guild sitters have passed rigorous scrutiny, and only the most capable are sent out on jobs. Believe it or not, the sitters can speak 16 languages between them. They enforce a four-hour minimum and add on any travel expenses.

BARNARD BABYSITTING SERVICE
Millbank Hall
3009 Broadway (at 120th St), Room 11   212/854-2035
Call for hours   www.barnard.edu

Barnard Babysitting Service is a nonprofit organization run by students at the undergraduate women's college affiliated with Columbia University.

The service provides affordable child care in the New York metropolitan area. At the same time, it allows students to seek convenient employment. Live-in help is also available. A minimum registration fee is required.

Nannies (all highly recommended)
Basic Trust (212/222-6602): day care
Fox Agency (212/753-2686): good record
Pavillion Agency (212/889-6609): very reliable

Beauty Services

Botox Treatment
Verve Laser and Medical Spa (216 E 50th St, 212/888-3003)

Cellulite Treatment
Wellpath (1100 Madison Ave, 212/737-9604): up-to-date equipment

Cosmetic Surgeons and Consultants
Denise Thomas (212/734-0233)
Dr. Amiya Prasad (50 E 78th St, 212/265-8877): cosmetic eyelid plastic surgeon
Dr. Neil Sadick (772 Park Ave, 212/712-7242): Polaris anti-aging treatment

Eyebrow Styling
Eliza Petrescu at Avon Centre (725 Fifth Ave, 212/755-2866): very popular
Robin Narvaez at Borja Color Studio (118 E 57th St, 212/308-3232)
Showha Threading (594 Broadway, Suite 403, 212/931-8363): shaping

Home Services
Eastside Massage Therapy Center (212/249-2927)
Joseph Martin (212/838-3150): hair coloring, nails, pedicure
Lady Barber (Kathleen Giordano, 212/826-8616): will come to offices
Lori Klein (212/996-9390): makeup
Trish McEvoy (212/758-7790): makeup

Liposuction
Taranow Plastic Surgery (169 E 69th St, 212/772-2100)

Makeup
Kimara Ahnert Makeup Studio (1113 Madison Ave, 212/452-4252)
Makeup Center (150 W 55th St, 212/977-9494): good value
Makeup Shop (131 W 21st St, 212/807-0447)

Men's Grooming
Greenhouse Spa (127 E 57th St, 212/644-4449): manicure, pedicure
John Allan's Men's Club (95 Trinity Pl, 212/406-3000): men's full-service
Kiehl's (109 Third Ave, 212/677-3171): toiletries
Mezzanine Spa at La Boîte à Coupe (18 W 55th St, 212/246-2097)
Pierre Michel (131 E 57th St, 212/593-1460): manicure
Salon A.K.S. (694 Madison Ave, 212/888-0707): hair coloring
SkinCareLab (568 Broadway, Suite 403, 212/334-3142): manicure
Soho Integrative Health (62 Crosby St, 212/431-1600): pedicure
Warren Tricomi (Sports Club LA, 45 Rockefeller Plaza, 212/218-8650): pedicure

Yasmine Djerradine (30 E 60th St, 212/588-1771): men's facials

Nails and Pedicures
Angel Nails (151 E 71st St, 212/535-5333): nail wrapping, massage, body waxing
Christine Valmy School (437 Fifth Ave, 2nd floor, 212/779-7800): inexpensive
Jin Soon Natural Hand & Foot Spa (56 E 4th St, 212/473-2047 and 23 Jones St, 212/229-1070): Jin Soon herself is at the Jones Street location.
Karen Wu (1377 Third Ave, 212/585-2044)
Paul Labrecque Salon and Spa (Reebok Sports Club/NY, 160 Columbus Ave, 212/595-0099)
Pierre Michel (131 E 57th St, 212/593-1460): old-school
Rescue Beauty Lounge (34 Gansevoort St, 212/206-6409)
Sweet Lily (222 West Broadway, 212/925-5441): "natural" nail spa and boutique

Skin Care
Advanced Skin Care Day Spa (532 Madison Ave, 3rd floor, 212/758-8867)
Aida Bicaj (629 Park Ave, 212/772-6968): lifting facial
Alla Katkov (Miano Viel, 16 E 52nd St, 2nd floor, 212/980-3222): great facials
D. Esse Spa (350 Hudson St, 212/206-1655)
GK Salon (501 Madison Ave, 212/838-3200)
Glow Skin Spa (30 E 60th St, Suite 808, 212/319-6654): skin transformation
Joean Skin Care (163 Hester St, 212/966-3668): Chinese-style
Lia Schorr (686 Lexington Ave, 212/486-9670)
Ling Skin Care Salons (105 W 77th St, 212/877-2883; 12 E 16th St, 212/989-8833; and 191 Prince St, 212/982-8833): great skin care
Oasis on Park (1 Park Ave, 212/254-7722): Facials are a specialty.
Paul Labrecque Salon and Spa East (171 E 65th St, 212/595-0099): Regina Viotto is a great facialist.
Shizuka New York (133 E 58th St, Suite 512, 212/644-7400): anti-aging facial with intense pulsed light
Tracie Martyn (59 Fifth Ave, Suite 1, 212/206-9333): resculpting facial

Tanning
Brazil Bronze (580 Broadway, 212/431-0077): bronzing formula spray
Spa at Equinox (205 E 85th St, 212/396-9611): body bronzing
Times Square Tanning (136 W 46th St, 212/354-8266): tanning beds and stand-up units

Tattoos and Body Piercing
LiteTouch Medical Cosmetology (1775 Broadway, Suite 433, 866/837-1390): tattoo removal
Timeless Image Aesthetics (580 Broadway, Suite 905, 212/226-8399): permanent makeup, artistic tattoos, body piercing

Teeth Whitening
Dr. Jan Linhart (230 Park Ave, 212/682-5180)
Dr. Frederick Solomon (Tribeca Smiles, 44 Lispenards St, 212/473-4444)

DAY SPAS (by area)

Chelsea
Azure Day Spa and Laser Center (227 W 29th St, Suite 9F, 212/563-5365): ear-candling therapy to relieve allergies, migraines, and sinus infections
Graceful Spa (205 W 14th St, 2nd floor, 212/675-5145): budget friendly
Nickel Spa (77 Eighth Ave, 212/242-3203): men's retreat
Spa at Chelsea Piers (Sports Center, Chelsea Piers, 60 Twelfth Ave, 2nd floor, 212/336-6780)

East Village
Great Jones Spa (29 Great Jones St, 212/505-3185): new spa
Mezzanine Spa at Soho Integrative Health (62 Crosby St, 212/431-1600): medical spa

Flatiron District
Carapan Urban Spa and Store (5 W 16th St, 212/633-6220): Santa Fe spirituality
Completely Bare (103 Fifth Ave, 212/366-6060): one of the best laser treatments in town; dewrinkling
Just Calm Down (32 W 22nd St, 212/337-0032): "Peelin' Groovy" facials
Longevity Spa (166 Fifth Ave, 2nd floor, 212/675-9355): hydrotherapy treatments
Shija Day Spa (37 Union Sq W, 212/366-0706): packages for couples, friends, and mother/daughter occasions
Spa Sun (26 W 20th St, 212/337-0020)

Gramercy Park
Oasis Day Spa (108 E 16th St, 212/254-7722)
Olive Leaf Wholeness Center (145 E 23rd St, 212/477-0405): sound therapy

Greenwich Village
Acqua Beauty Bar (7 E 14th St, 212/620-4329): Indonesian flavor, pedicures
Silk Day Spa (47 W 13th St, 212/255-6457): "Silk Supreme Eastern Indulgence Body Scrub and Polish"

Kips Bay
Oasis Day Spa (1 Park Ave, 212/254-7722)
Essential Therapy (122 E 25th St, 212/777-2325): new spa whose services have a healing bent

Midtown
Avon Salon & Spa (725 Fifth Ave, 212/755-2866): eyebrow sculpting, reflexology
Bliss 57 (19 E 57th St, 212/219-8970)
Cornelia Day Resort (663 Fifth Ave, 212/871-3050)
Elizabeth Arden Red Door Salon (611 Fifth Ave, 212/940-4000 and 691 Fifth Ave, 212/546-0200)
Faina European Skin Care Center and Day Spa (315 W 57th St, 212/245-6557): acupuncture rejuvenation facial
Frederic Fekkai Beauté de Provence (15 E 57th St, 212/753-9500): the ultimate
Ido Holistic Center (9 E 45th St, 8th floor, 212/599-5300): immune-system boost

La Beaute Salon & Spa (805 Third Ave, 212/752-9664): hair removal
La Prairie at the Ritz-Carlton Spa (50 Central Park S, 212/521-6135): top-drawer
Lia Schorr (686 Lexington Ave, 212/486-9670): efficient, reasonable
Metamorphosis (127 E 56th St, 212/751-6051): small but good; men welcome
Peninsula New York Spa and Health Club (The Peninsula New York Hotel, 700 Fifth Ave, 212/903-3910)
Repéchage (115 E 57th St, 212/751-2500): European-style spa; men welcome
Salon de Tokyo (200 W 57th St, Room 1308, 212/757-2187): Shiatsu parlor
Spa at the Four Seasons Hotel New York (57 E 57th St, 212/350-6420): new spa
Susan Ciminelli Day Spa (Bergdorf Goodman, 754 Fifth Ave, 9th floor, 212/872-2650): highly recommended; the ultra spa package for men … if you have to ask the price …
Warren Tricomi (Sports Club LA, 45 Rockefeller Plaza, 212/218-8650): chair massage

Midtown South
Avalon Day Spa (40-A E 33rd St, 212/213-2000): honey-almond pedicure
Gua Sha (245 Fifth Ave, 646/935-2220): Chinese healing process
Juvenex (25 W 32nd St, 646/733-1330): Jade and more, 24-hour Korean oasis
Yi Pak (10 W 32nd St, 2nd floor, 212/594-1025)

Murray Hill
Ella Baché Day Spa (8 W 36th St, 212/279-8562)
Oasis Day Spa (150 E 34th St, 212/254-7722)
Murray Hill Skin Care (567 Third Ave, 212/661-0777): "backcial"—a facial for the back

Queens
Oasis Day Spa (Jet Blue Terminal 6, JFK Airport, 212/254-7722)

Soho
Aveda Institute (233 Spring St, 212/807-1492)
Bliss Spa (568 Broadway, 2nd floor, 212/219-8970): oxygen facial
Erbe (196 Prince St, 212/966-1445)
Haven (150 Mercer St, 212/343-3515): calm and refreshing
SkinCareLab (568 Broadway, Suite 403, 212/334-3142): body treatments, facials
Soho Sanctuary (119 Mercer St, 212/334-5550)

Tribeca
Euphoria (18 Harrison St, 2nd floor, 212/925-5925): "Fresh Air Facial"
Ula (8 Harrison St, 212/343-2376)

Upper East Side
Ajune (1294 Third Ave, 212/628-0044): full-service, Botox, superb facials
Bliss 49 (W New York, 541 Lexington Ave, 212/755-1200)
Completely Bare (764 Madison Ave, 212/717-9300): sunspot removal
Dr. Howard Sobel Skin and Spa (960-A Park Ave, 212/288-0060): medical personnel on the premises

Equinox Wellness Spa (140 E 63rd St, 212/750-4671): facials, sports massage
Gloss Day Spa (51 E 73rd St, Suite 2B, 212/249-2100): fruit facial masks
Institute Beauté/Foot and Wellness Spa (885 Park Ave, 212/535-0229): foot facial
Paul Labrecque Salon and Spa East (171 E 65th St, 212/595-0099): Thai massages, facials
Skin N.Y. (655 Park Ave, 212/794-3900): Dr. Wells' anti-aging procedure
Yasmine Djerradine (30 E 60th St, 212/588-1771): Djerradine's famous facial

Upper West Side
Dorit Baxter Skin Care, Beauty & Health Spa (47 W 57th St, 3rd floor, 212/371-4542): salt scrub
Ettia Holistic Day Spa (239 W 72nd St, 212/362-7109)
Natural Alternative Center (269 W 72nd St, 212/580-3333)
Paul Labrecque Salon and Spa (Reebok Sports Club/NY, 160 Columbus Ave, 212/595-0099): Thai massages, facials
Prenatal Massage Center of Manhattan (123 W 79th St, 212/330-6846): new spa
Spa at Mandarin Oriental New York (Time Warner Center, 80 Columbus Circle, 35th floor, 212/805-8880): "Lomi Lomi," a deep tissue massage

HAIR CARE (by area)

Chelsea
Antonio Prieto (127 W 20th St, 212/255-3741): popular styling for the average woman

East Village
Astor Place Hair Stylists (2 Astor Pl, 212/475-9854): one of the world's largest barber shops; very inexpensive
Salon Zoia (448 E 13th St, 212/614-1898)

Flatiron District
Sacha and Oliver (6 W 18th St, 212/255-1100): very French
Salon 02 (20 W 22nd St, 212/675-7274)

Greenwich Village
Gemini Salon and Spa (547 Hudson St, 212/675-4546): "Opti-Smooth" straightening treatment

Lower Manhattan
Laicale Salon (129 Grand St, 212/219-2424): no attitude

Midtown
Bumble & Bumble (146 E 56th St, 212/521-6500): no-nonsense establishment
Color and Cut Salon (331 Madison Ave, 212/557-3123): straight ironed hair
Kenneth's (Waldorf-Astoria Hotel, 301 Park Ave, lobby level, 212/752-1800): full service with an able staff, but a long wait for Kenneth himself
Nardi Salon (111 E 56th St, 212/421-4810): long-hair specialists

Ouidad Hair Salon (37 W 57th St, 4th floor, 212/888-3288): curly- and frizzy-hair specialists
Pierre Michel (131 E 57th St, 212/593-1460): J.F. Lazartigue treatment products
Salon Ishi (70 E 55th St, 212/888-4744): scalp massages for men and women
Stephen Knoll (625 Madison Ave, 212/421-0100): highly recommended

---

Inexpensive prices on grooming are available if you are willing to try training schools. Here are some of the better ones:

Dentistry: **New York University College of Dentistry** (345 E 24th St, 212/998-9800): initial visit, X-rays and all, for $90!

Facials and manicures: **Christine Valmy School** (437 Fifth Ave, 2nd floor, 212/779-7800): facials for $27

Haircut (blow dry): **Jean Louis David** (10 E 41st St, 212/779-3555): $36

Haircut: **Mark Garrison Salon** (108 E 60th St, 212/570-2455): training price—$40!

Hairstyling and manicures: **LTBS** (22 W 34th St, 212/695-4555): an old-fashioned learning institute; perms for $22, color rinse for $11, and manicure for $4

Hairstyling: **Bumble & Bumble** (146 E 56th St and 415 W 13th St, 212/521-6500): good deals

Massage: **Swedish Institute** (226 W 26th St, 212/924-5900): six one-hour Swedish-shiatsu massages for $125

Men's haircuts: **Atlas Barber School** (32 Third Ave, 212/475-1360 and 80 E 10th St, 212/475-5699): haircuts for $5; women welcome, too

---

Soho
John Masters (77 Sullivan St, 212/343-9590): all-organic
Oscar Bond Salon (42 Wooster St, 212/334-3777)
Privé (310 West Broadway, 212/274-8888): all hair services, with shampoos a specialty at this trendy spot; open Sunday

Upper East Side
Elizabeth Arden Red Door Salon (Saks Fifth Avenue, 611 Fifth Ave, concourse level, 212/940-4000): top-grade, full-service
Frederic Fekkai Beauté de Provence (15 E 57th St, 212/753-9500): elegant
Garren New York (Henri Bendel, 712 Fifth Ave, 3rd floor atrium, 212/841-9400): personally customized services
John Barrett Salon (Bergdorf Goodman, 754 Fifth Ave, penthouse, 212/872-2700): top cut
John Frieda (797 Madison Ave, 212/879-1000): very "in"
Josephine Beauty Retreat (200 E 62nd St, 212/223-7157): Curls, curls, curls!
Julian Farel Salon (605 Madison Ave, 2nd floor, 212/888-8988): upscale, computers available, private hair parties
Mark Garrison Salon (108 E 60th St, 212/570-2455): popular
Peter Coppola (746 Madison Ave, 212/988-9404): reliable

Salon A.K.S. (694 Madison Ave, 212/888-0707): former stylists from Frederic Fekkai

Vidal Sassoon (730 Fifth Ave, 212/535-9200): popular with men and women

Yves Durif (130 E 65th St, 212/452-0954): reliable

Upper West Side
Salon Above (2641 Broadway, 212/665-7149): salon, spa

HAIR SERVICES

Discount Haircuts
Dandie (100 Stanton St, 212/598-4490): free cuts Wed and Thurs, 12-5

Mingle Salon (16 W 55th St, 2nd floor, 212/459-3320): free cuts Wed, 7 p.m.- 9 p.m.

Parlor (102 Ave B, 212/673-5520): free cuts Thurs, 11a.m.-1 p.m.; $15 color Tues, 11 a.m.-1 p.m.

Family Haircuts
Snip 'n Sip (204 Waverly Place, 212/242-3880)

Hair Blowout
Jean Louis David (locations throughout the city): good work at reasonable prices

Salon A.K.S. (694 Madison Ave, 212/888-0707): Mika Rummo; also does house calls

Warren Tricomi (16 W 57th St, 212/262-8899): for work that lasts

Hair Coloring
Alexis Antonellis at A.K.S. (694 Madison Ave, 212/888-0707)
Borja Color Studio (118 E 57th St, 212/308-3232)
Linda Tam Beauty Salon (680 Fifth Ave, 7th floor, 212/757-2555)
Louis Licari Salon (693 Fifth Ave, 212/758-2090)
Q Hair (19 Bleecker St, 212/614-8729): brunettes
Warren Tricomi (16 W 57th St, 4th floor, 212/262-8899)

Hair Loss Treatment
Le Metric Hair Center for Women (124 E 40th St, Suite 601, 212/986-5620)

Hair Removal
J. Sisters Salon (35 W 57th St, 212/750-2485): waxing
Verve Laser and Medical Spa (216 E 50th St, 212/888-3003)

Men's Hairstylist
Chelsea Barber (465 W 23rd St, 212/741-2254): inexpensive

Toupees
Bob Kelly (151 W 46th St, 212/819-0030)
Ira Senz (13 E 47th St, 212/752-6800)

Close shave? One of the few places left where a fellow can get a straight-edged razor shave is **Pole Mole** (1031 Lexington Ave, 212/535-8461). Cost? A whopping $30!

DASHING DIVA SALON & NAIL BOUTIQUE
41 E 8th St (at University Place and Broadway)   212/673-9000
Sun-Wed: 10-8; Thurs-Sat: 9-9   www.dashingdiva.com

The owner of Dashing Diva is said to be the largest manufacturer of artificial nails in the world. These folks claim that virtual nails are quicker and healthier than regular wraps or tips. This place is also the first eyelash bar in Manhattan.

NINA'S EUROPEAN SPA FOR MEN & WOMEN
5 W 35th St (bet Fifth Ave and Ave of the Americas)   212/594-9610
Mon-Fri: 10-8; Sat, Sun: 10-7   www.ninasskincare.com

Nina has been in the skin-care field for nearly four decades, so you can be assured that she and her staff know the business inside out. You will find just about everything at this spa: facial treatments, body treatments, body-fat reduction, body wraps, micro-dermabrasion, electrolysis, massages, waxing, nail care, tanning, exfoliation, reflexology, and more. It's a worldly place, too: the expertise is Russian, the atmosphere French, and the technology American. I'm intrigued by their "chocolate treatments"!

Bookbinding

TALAS
20 W 20th St (bet Fifth Ave and Ave of the Americas), 5th floor
Mon-Fri: 9-5:30   212/219-0770, www.talasonline.com

Jake and Marjorie Salik preside over this outlet, which offers tools, supplies, and books for artists, restorers, collectors, bookbinders, museums, archives, libraries, calligraphers, and retail customers. Expanded inventories feature custom boxes and portfolios, a wide variety of photo storage, and display items, and archival papers. They are also distributors of conservation supplies.

WEITZ, WEITZ & COLEMAN
1377 Lexington Ave (bet 90th and 91st St)   212/831-2213
Mon-Thurs: 9-7; Fri: 9-5; Sat: 12-5 (Sun and evenings by appointment)
www.weitzcoleman.com

Weitz is a highly respected name in the rare-book field. Leo Weitz began a rare-book business in New York in 1909 and has done work for the Rockefellers, DuPonts, Firestones, three presidents (Ford, Reagan, and Bush), and other famous families. Today, Herbert Weitz (his son) and partner Elspeth Coleman continue the tradition of fine bookbinding. Weitz and Coleman restore and rebind books and family heirlooms. They also design and create leather photo albums, guest books, archival boxes, presentation folders, and special gift books. Coleman's specialty is custom-designing to clients' specifications. Weitz and Coleman buy and sell rare books, too.

Cabinetry

HARMONY WOODWORKING
153 W 27th St (bet Ave of the Americas and Seventh Ave), Room 902
Daily: by appointment   212/366-7221

Expert woodworker Jerry Gerber devotes his time to doing custom projects, especially bookcases, wall units, entertainment centers, desks, and tables.

JIM NICKEL
Call for appointment   718/963-2138

Jim Nickel, who lives in Brooklyn, is an expert in projects that use wood: cabinets, bookcases, wall sculptures, and much more. He prefers small- to medium-sized jobs and can do an entire project—from consultation and design to installation—all by himself. He has decades of practical experience and is very budget conscious. Call Jim in the afternoon or evening for an appointment.

Carpentry

Finding a reliable carpenter is not easy. In my opinion, the best outfit to call is **R&N Construction** (914/699-0292). These folks do quality work, and they are reasonably priced and nice to deal with. Ask for Nick Alpino.

If you are interested in cabinetry, call Joe Lonigro at **European Woodworking** (914/969-5724). His custom millwork is outstanding, and believe it or not, some folks actually claim that he "tends to undercharge"!

An idea for an unusual party and/or some serious exercise: **Extra Vertical Climbing Center** (Harmony Atrium, 61 W 62nd St, 212/586-5718, www.extravertical.com). This indoor climbing gym features a 30-foot indoor wall and a 50-foot outdoor climbing wall. Lessons, lockers, and a changing room are available.

Carriages

CHATEAU STABLES/CHATEAU THEATRICAL ANIMALS/
CHATEAU WEDDING CARRIAGES
Call for reservations   212/246-0520
Mon-Fri: 8:30-6:30   www.chateaustables.net
                                        www.chateauweddingcarriages.com

There is nothing quite as romantic as a ride in an authentic hansom cab. If you would like to arrive at your next dinner party in a horse-drawn carriage, Chateau is the place to call. They have the largest working collection of horse-drawn vehicles in the U.S. and have been a family business for over 40 years. Although they prefer advance notice, requests for weddings, group rides, tours, movies, and overseas visitors can be handled at any time.

Cars for Hire

AAMCAR CAR RENTALS
315 W 96th St (bet West End Ave and Riverside Dr)
Mon-Fri: 7:30-7:30; Sat, Sun: 9-5   212/222-8500, 800/722-6923

506 W 181st St (at Amsterdam Ave)   212/927-7000
Mon-Fri: 9-7; Sat: 9-1   www.aamcar.com

This independent car rental company has a full line of cars, vans, and sport utility vehicles. AAMCAR has been around for several decades and offers over 200 cars.

CAREY LIMOUSINE NY
212/599-1122 (reservations), 718/898-1000 (office), 800/336-4646
24 hours   www.ecarey.com

Carey is the grandfather of car-for-hire services. They provide chauffeur-driven limousines and sedans and will take clients anywhere, at any time, in almost any kind of weather. Last-minute reservations are accepted on an as-available basis. Discuss rates before making a commitment.

CARMEL CAR SERVICE
2642 Broadway (at 100th St)   212/666-6666, 800/9CARMEL
24 hours   www.carmellimo.com

These people are highly commended for good service and fair prices. Full-size and luxury sedans, minivans, passenger vans, and limos are available. Prices for limos begin at $65 per hour.

COMPANY II LIMOUSINE SERVICE
24 hours   718/430-6482

Steve Betancourt provides responsible, efficient service at reasonable prices. I can personally vouch that his reputation for reliability is well earned.

Stretch limos are big in more ways than one! If you want to impress someone or take a carload of friends or kids out for a fun time, try **Dav-El Chauffeured Transportation Network** (800/922-0343).

Casting

SCULPTURE HOUSE CASTING
155 W 26th St (bet Ave of the Americas and Seventh Ave)
Mon-Fri: 8-5 (Sat by appointment)   212/645-9430, 888/374-8665
                                                www.sculptshop.com

Sculpture House has been a family-owned business since 1918, making it one of the city's oldest casting firms. A full-service casting foundry, it specializes in classical plaster reproductions, mold-making, and casting in all mediums and sizes. Sculpting tools and supplies and ornamental plastering are also available.

Chair Caning

VETERAN'S CHAIR CANING AND REPAIR SHOP
442 Tenth Ave (bet 34th and 35th St)   212/564-4560
Mon-Thurs: 7:30-4:30; Fri: 7:30-4; Sat: 8-1

John Bausert, a third-generation chair caner, has written a book about his craft. Certainly, his prices and craftsmanship are among the best in town. Bausert believes in passing along his knowledge, encouraging customers to repair their own chairs. The procedure is outlined in Bausert's book, and necessary materials are sold in the shop. If you don't want to try it yourself, Veteran's will repair your chair. For a charge, they'll even pick it up from your home. In addition to caning, Veteran's stocks materials for chair and furniture repair, does wicker repair, and repairs and reglues wooden chairs.

China and Glassware Repair

CENTER ART STUDIO
307 W 38th St (bet Eighth and Ninth Ave), Room 1315 212/247-3550
Mon-Thurs: 9-6; Fri: 9-5 (by appointment only) www.centerart.com

"Fine art restoration and display since 1919" is the motto here. The word *fine* should be emphasized, as owners of really good crystal, porcelain, china, and bronze art have made Center Art Studio *the* place to go for repairs. The house specialty is antiques restoration. They will restore or repair scagliola, lacquer, porcelain, terra cotta, shells, and precious stones. Their craftsmen will also restore antique furniture and decorative objects, using original materials whenever possible. They'll even design and install display bases and cases. Among the oldest and most diverse art restoration studios in the city, Center Art offers a multitude of special services, like designs and sketches by fax and multilingual personnel for overseas shoppers. Owner Lansing Moore has a superbly talented staff that has worked on furniture designed by the likes of Frank Lloyd Wright.

GLASS RESTORATIONS
1597 York Ave (bet 84th and 85th St) 212/517-3287
Mon-Fri: 9:30-5

Did you chip your prize Lalique glass treasure? Glass Restorations restores all manner of crystal, including pieces by Steuben, Baccarat, Daum, and Waterford, as well as antique art glass. This place is a find, as too few quality restorers are left in the country. Ask for Gus!

HESS RESTORATIONS
200 Park Ave S (at 17th St), Room 1514
Mon-Fri: 11-4, and by appointment 212/260-2255, 212/979-1143

Hess has been in business since 1945, providing a restoration service so professional that previous damage is usually unnoticeable. Repair and restoration of silver and crystal are available. Their emphasis is on fine European porcelains, ivory, tortoise shell, sculptures, and objets d'art. They are recommended by leading museums, auction houses, and galleries in Manhattan. The replacement of blue glass liners for antique silver salt dishes is unique. Hess accepts insured shipments of items to be repaired and will send an estimate for restoration work.

Clock and Watch Repair

FANELLI ANTIQUE TIMEPIECES
790 Madison Ave (bet 66th and 67th St), Suite 202 212/517-2300
Mon-Fri: 10-6; Sat: 11-5

In a beautiful clock gallery, Cindy Fanelli specializes in the care of high-quality "investment-type" timepieces, especially carriage clocks. Her store has one of the nation's largest collections of rare and unusual Early American grandfather clocks and vintage wristwatches. They do sales and restoration, make house calls, give free estimates, rent timepieces, and purchase single pieces or entire collections.

J&P TIMEPIECES
1057 Second Ave (at 56th St)   212/980-1099
Mon-Fri: 10-5; Sat: 11-4   www.jptimepieces.com

In Europe, fine-watch repairing is a family tradition, but this craft is slowly being forgotten in our country. Fortunately for Manhattan, the Fossners have passed along this talent from father to son for four generations. You can be confident in their work on any kind of mechanical watch. They guarantee repairs for six months and will generally turn around jobs within ten days.

SUTTON CLOCK SHOP
139 E 61st St (at Lexington Ave)   212/758-2260
Tues-Fri: 11-4 (Sat by appointment)

Sutton's forte is selling and acquiring unusual timepieces, but they are equally interested in the maintenance and repair of antique clocks. Some of the timepieces they sell—even the contemporary ones—are truly outstanding, and numerous satisfied customers endorse their repair work. They sell and repair barometers as well.

TIME PIECES REPAIRED
115 Greenwich Ave (at 13th St)   212/929-8011
Tues-Fri: 10:30-6:30; Sat: 9-5; Mon by appointment
                                                www.timepiecesrepaired.com

Grace Szuwala services, restores, repairs, and sells antique timepieces. Her European training has made her an expert on antique watches and clocks. She has a strong sensitivity for pieces that have more sentimental than real value. She has been doing business on Greenwich Avenue since 1978.

Clothing Repair

FRENCH-AMERICAN REWEAVING COMPANY
119 W 57th St (bet Ave of the Americas and Seventh Ave), Room 1406
Mon-Fri: 10:30-5:30; Sat: 11-2   212/765-4670

Has a tear, burn, or other catastrophe ruined your favorite outfit? These folks will work on almost any garment for men or women in nearly every fabric. Often a damaged item will look just like new!

Need a quick repair? Go straight to **Ban Custom Tailor Shop** (1544 First Ave, 212/570-0444), and they will take care of you right away.

Computer Service and Instruction

ABC COMPUTER SERVICES
375 Fifth Ave (bet 35th and 36th St), 2nd floor   212/725-3511
Mon-Fri: 9-5   www.abccomputerservices.com

ABC provides sales, service, and supplies for desktop and notebook computers, as well as all kinds of printers. They'll work on Apple, Microsoft, and Novell-based systems, and they are an authorized Hewlett-Packard service center. Computer instruction is offered in your home or office. They have been around for over a decade, which is a good recommendation in itself.

For computer rentals, try **Business Equipment Rental** (250 W 49th St, 212/582-2020). Prices are reasonable; pickup and delivery are available. These are the best shops in town for computer repair:
Data Vision (445 Fifth Ave, 212/689-1111)
Machattan (175 Fifth Ave, 212/242-9393): Mac only
RCS Computer Experience (575 Madison Ave, 212/949-6935)

TEKSERVE
119 W 23rd St (bet Ave of the Americas and Seventh Ave)
Mon-Fri: 9-7; Sat: 10-6; Sun: 12-5 (sales, pick-up, and drop-off only)
212/929-3645, www.tekserve.com

For Apple Computer sales and service, you can't do better than this outfit. Tekserve carries a huge inventory of computers and peripherals, and the firm is noted for excellent customer care. A full range of services, including data recovery, is available.

If you need some special part for your computer, copier, fax machine, or printer, call **E.T. Computer Supplies & Services** (659 Washington Ave, Suite 3, Brooklyn, 718/789-2973). Same-day service is available.

WEB2ZONE CYBER CENTER
54 Cooper Square (at Astor Place)   212/614-7300
Mon-Fri: 9 a.m.–midnight; Sat: 10 a.m.–midnight; Sun: 12-10
www.web2zone.com

web2zone has been named one of the best cyber centers in the nation, and with good reason. You'll find high-speed Internet access; a laptop area; PC and iMac stations; fax, copy, CD burning, and scanning facilities; and game-zone PCs and consoles (xBox and PS2). Prices are reasonable, the personnel are knowledgeable, and the atmosphere is clean and pleasant. Located in the East Village, this popular cyber center is owned by Samsung. Birthday parties are big in the game-zone area!

Delivery, Courier, Messenger Services

AIRLINE DELIVERY SERVICES
60 E 42nd St (bet Park and Madison Ave)   212/687-5145
Daily: 24 hours   www.airlinedelivery.com

Even before the big guys got in the business, this outfit was doing round-the-clock local and long-distance deliveries. If you have time-sensitive material, give them a call. They'll promptly pick up your item, even in the middle of the night or a snowstorm. There are several branches throughout the city.

KANGAROO COURIER
150 E 23rd St (bet Lexington and Third Ave), 3rd floor
Mon-Fri: 8:15-7   212/684-2233
                                          www.kangaroocourier.com

Kangaroo is set up to provide any and all courier services. They can handle everything from a crosstown rush letter (delivery completed within an hour) to delivering a box in the tri-state area.

Detectives

DECISION STRATEGIES
33 E 33rd St (bet Madison and Park Ave), 4th floor   212/935-4040
Daily: 9-5   www.vanceglobal.com

Do you need to launch a corporate investigation? Are you suspecting infidelity? Do you want assistance with fraud prevention? This company has more than a dozen top-notch investigators, and their experience in nearly every field can save you headaches—and maybe a lot of cash. They also do online forensics.

Doll Repair

NEW YORK DOLL HOSPITAL
787 Lexington Ave (bet 61st and 62nd St), 2nd floor   212/838-7527
Mon-Sat: 10-6

New York Doll Hospital has been fixing, mending, and restoring dolls to health since 1900. Owner Irving Chais has operated in this cramped two-room "hospital" since 1947. That was the year he took over from his father, who had begun fixing dolls for his clients' children in his hair salon. Chais has replaced antique fingers, reconstructed china heads and German rag dolls, and authentically restored antique dolls. Additional services include appraisals, made-to-order dolls, and buying and selling antique dolls and toys. He will also work on teddy bears and other stuffed animals, and he can even fix talking dolls that have computer chips.

Dry Cleaners, Laundries

CLEANTEX
2335 Twelfth Ave (at 133rd St)   212/283-1200
Mon-Fri: 8-4

In business since 1928, Cleantex specializes in cleaning draperies, furniture, balloon and Roman shades, vertical blinds, and Oriental and area rugs. They provide free estimates, pickup, and delivery. Museums, churches, and rug dealers are among their satisfied clients.

HALLAK CLEANERS
1232 Second Ave (at 65th St)   212/879-4694
Mon-Fri: 7-6:30; Sat: 8-3   www.hallak.com

Hallak has been a family business for nearly 40 years. Joseph Hallak, Sr., a native of France, instilled his work ethic and dedication to detail into sons John-Claude and Joseph, Jr. This no doubt accounts for the pride and personal service they offer customers. Much of their work comes from referrals by such famed boutiques as Armani and Ferragamo. Hallak does all work in their state-of-the-art plant. They will clean shirts, linens, suede, leather, and draperies. Their specialty is museum-quality cleaning and preservation of wedding gowns. For those (like your author) who have trouble with stains on ties, Hallak is the place to go. Their skilled work takes time, though rush service is available at no additional cost.

LEATHERCRAFT PROCESS OF AMERICA
Call for locations   212/564-8980
Mon-Fri: 8-5:30

Leathercraft will clean, re-dye, re-line, repair, and lengthen or shorten any suede or leather garment. That includes boots, gloves, clothing, and handbags, as well as odd leather items. Because leather is extremely difficult to clean, the process can be painfully expensive. However, Leathercraft has a reputation dating back to 1938, and their prices remain competitive.

If you need a really good dry cleaner, there is none better than **Chris French Cleaners** (57 Fourth Ave, 212/475-5444), in the East Village.

MADAME PAULETTE CUSTOM COUTURE CLEANERS
1255 Second Ave (bet 65th and 66th St)
Mon-Fri: 7:30-7; Sat: 8-5   212/838-6827, 877/COUTURE
                                                  www.madamepaulette.com

What a clientele: Christian Dior, Vera Wang, Chanel, Givenchy, Saks, Burberry, and Henri Bendel. This full-service establishment has been in business for nearly 40 years. They do dry cleaning (including knits, suedes, and leathers), tailoring (including reweaving and alterations), laundry, and household and rug cleaning. They provide fur and box storage. Taking care of wedding dresses is a specialty, and they do superior hand-cleaning of cashmere, making sure each item's shape is maintained. Their experts can repair garments damaged by water, bleach, and fire, do wet cleaning, and handclean upholstery and tapestry. Madame Paulette offers free pickup and delivery throughout Manhattan, will set up charge accounts, and can do one-day service upon request.

MEURICE GARMENT CARE
31 University Pl (bet 8th and 9th St)   212/475-2778
Mon-Fri: 7:30-6 (Wed till 7); Sat: 9-6; Sun: 10-3
                                                  www.garmentcare.com
245 E 57th St (bet Second and Third Ave)   212/759-9057
Mon-Fri: 8-6:30; Sat: 9-3

Meurice specializes in cleaning and restoring fine garments. They handle each piece individually, taking care of details like loose buttons and tears. Special services: exquisite hand-finishing, expert stain removal, museumquality preservation, cleaning and restoration of wedding gowns, special handling of ultra fragile and chemically sensitive garments, and on-site leather cleaning and repairs. Another special service is smoke, fire, and water restoration. Delivery and shipping are available.

MIDNIGHT EXPRESS CLEANERS
Mon-Fri: 7-5   718/392-9200
                                      www.midnightexpressny.com

Midnight Express does dry cleaning, shirt laundering, leather and suede cleaning and repair, and bulk laundering. Best of all, they will pick up and deliver. Prompt return is assured. They specialize in dry-cleaning restoration of smoke, fire, and water-damaged goods. This is Manhattan's only OSHA-compliant laundry service. Be sure to keep their number handy!

It is not necessary to pay big bucks for good alterations. Try Hong Kong-trained Angela Gong at **G-G Cleaners** (30 Grand St, 212/966-9813). Her work is professional, and the price is right! This specialty tailor is legendary among fashion editors and boutique owners.

NEW YORK'S FINEST FRENCH CLEANERS & TAILORS
154 Reade St (bet Hudson and Greenwich St)   212/431-4010
Mon-Fri: 7-7; Sat: 7-5

Three generations of the same family have operated this quality business, featuring pickup, delivery, and one-day service. Tailoring and storage are available, as is care for fine silks and leathers.

TIECRAFTERS
252 W 29th St (bet Seventh and Eighth Ave)   212/629-5800
Mon-Fri: 9-5   www.tiecrafters.com

Old ties never fade away at Tiecrafters. Instead, they're dyed, widened, narrowed, straightened, and cleaned. They believe that a well-made tie can live forever, and they provide services to make longevity possible. In addition to converting tie widths, they restore soiled or stained ties and clean and repair all kinds of neckwear. Owner Andy Tarshis will give pointers on tie maintenance. (Hint: if you hang a tie at night, wrinkles will be gone by morning.) Tiecrafters offers several pamphlets on the subject, including one that tells how to remove spots at home. Their cleaning charge is reasonable, and they also make custom neckwear, bow ties, braces, scarves, vests, and cummerbunds.

VILLAGE TAILOR & CLEANERS
125 Sullivan St (at Prince St)   212/925-9667
Mon-Fri: 7-7; Sat: 8-6   www.villagetailor.com

Village Tailor specializes in cleaning and repairing leather and suede garments. Shoe repair, shirt service, and laundry are also available. They have been in business since the early 1930s and can provide overnight service.

Electricians

ALTMAN ELECTRIC
283 W 11th St (at Bleecker St)   212/924-0400, 800/287-7774
Daily: 24 hours   www.altmanelectric.com

The licensed crew at this reliable outfit is available day and night. They will do small or large jobs at home or office, and rates are reasonable. Altman has been in business for over half a century.

Embroidery

JONATHAN EMBROIDERY PLUS
256 W 38th St (bet Seventh and Eighth Ave)   212/398-3538
Mon-Fri: 8:30-6:30   www.jeplus.com

Any kind of custom embroidery work can be done at this classy workshop. Bring a photo or sketch, or just give them an idea, and they will produce a design that you can then amend or approve.

> The newest twist (make that *stitch*) in the knitting and crocheting craze is the knitting cafe. At **Knit New York** (307 E 14th St, 212/387-0707, www.knitnewyork) you can enjoy stitching, chatting, pastries and coffee, and first-rate instruction.

Exterminators

ACME EXTERMINATING
460 Ninth Ave (bet 35th and 36th St)   212/594-9230
Mon-Fri: 8-5   www.acmeexterminating.com

Acme is expert at debugging homes, offices, stores, museums, and hospitals. They employ state-of-the-art integrated pest-management technology.

Eyeglass Repair

E.B. MEYROWITZ AND DELL OPTICIANS
19 W 44th St (at Fifth Ave)   212/575-1686
Mon-Fri: 9-6 (till 5:30 in July, Aug); Sat: 9-3 (closed Sat in July, Aug)

If you desperately need E.B. Meyrowitz and Dell Opticians, you probably can't read this. No need to worry, as they do on-the-spot emergency repair of eyeglasses. This is *the* place to go for optical emergencies in the city. There is a large frame selection, from 18-karat gold to buffalo horn. They also repair binoculars. You're welcome to stop by for regular optical needs, too.

Fashion Schools

FASHION INSTITUTE OF TECHNOLOGY
Seventh Ave at 27th St   212/217-7675 (admissions)
212/217-7999 (general information)
www.fitnyc.edu

The Fashion Institute of Technology (FIT), a branch of the State University of New York, is the fashion industry's premier educational facility. The school was founded almost 60 years ago. Its graduate roster reads like a "who's who" of the fashion world, including Jhane Barnes, Calvin Klein, and Norma Kamali. The school offers a multitude of majors: accessories, advertising, display and exhibit, toy design, illustration, photography, fine arts, fashion buying and merchandising, marketing, apparel production, management, patternmaking, and jewelry, interior, textile, and fashion design. FIT also maintains a student placement service. All students are top-caliber. The

Museum at FIT is the world's largest repository of fashion, with over a million articles of clothing. Call 212/217-5800 for information about exhibits and shows.

Formal Wear

A.T. HARRIS FORMALWEAR
11 E 44th St (bet Madison and Fifth Ave), 2nd floor   212/682-6325
Mon-Fri: 9-6 (Thurs till 7)   www.atharris.com
Sat: 10-5 (by appointment)

Ten U.S. presidents have been fitted for formal attire at this store! A.T. Harris has been in business since 1892, selling and renting formal wear of the highest quality. You will find cutaways, tails, tuxedos, shoes, top hats, stud and cuff-link sets, and kid and suede gloves.

BALDWIN FORMALS
1156 Ave of the Americas (at 45th St)   212/245-8190, 800/427-0072
Mon-Fri: 9-7; Sat: 10-5   www.nyctuxedos.com

If you are invited to some upscale function, Baldwin will take care of the dressing details. They rent and sell all types of formal attire: suits, overcoats, top hats, shoes, and more. They will pick up and deliver for free in midtown and for a slight charge to other addresses. Same-day service is guaranteed for rental orders received by early afternoon. Rapid alteration service (two or three days) is available on sale merchandise.

Funeral Service

FRANK E. CAMPBELL FUNERAL CHAPEL
1076 Madison Ave (at 81st St)   212/288-3500
Daily: 24 hours   www.frankecampbell.com

In time of need, it is good to know of a highly professional funeral home. These folks have been providing superior service since 1898.

Furniture Rental

CHURCHILL CORPORATE SERVICES
245 W 17th St (bet Seventh and Eighth Ave)
Mon-Thurs: 9-6; Fri: 9-5; Sun: 11-5   212/686-0444, 800/658-7366
                                         www.furnishedhousing.com

Mention Churchill and you think of staid old England, right? Well, *this* Churchill is starkly contemporary, as well as traditional. They can fill any size order for a business or residence, and they offer free interior-decorating advice and a lease-purchase plan. A customer simply selects what is needed from stock or borrows from the loaner program until special orders are processed. Churchill also offers a comprehensive package, including house-wares and appliances. They specialize in executive relocations and will rent out anything from a single chair to an entire home. Churchill offers corporate apartments and housing on a short- or long-term basis. Their clients include team-sports managers, executives on temporary assignment, and actors on short-term contracts.

CORT FURNITURE RENTAL
711 Third Ave (bet 44th and 45th St)   212/867-2800
Mon-Fri: 9-6; Sat: 10-5   www.cort1.com

Cort rents furnishings for a single room, entire apartment, or office. They show accessories as well. All furnishings (including electronics and housewares) are available for rental with an option to purchase. An apartment location service is offered, free professional decorating is available, and a multilingual staff is at your service. Working with Japanese clients is a specialty. The stock is large, delivery and setup can often be done within 48 hours. All styles of furniture and accessories are shown in their 12,000-square-foot showroom, conveniently located near Grand Central Station.

Furniture Repair

JOSEPH BIUNNO LTD
129 W 29th St (bet Ave of the Americas and Seventh Ave), 2nd floor
Mon-Fri: 9-5   212/629-5630

Joseph is a really nice guy! You will enjoy working with him. He restores and reproduces furniture and does metal work. There are also carvers, turners, gold leafers, finishers, and painters in his shop. Joseph is a third-generation restorer and craftsman.

Gardening

**COUNCIL ON THE ENVIRONMENT OF
NEW YORK CITY (CENYC)**
51 Chambers St (bet Broadway and Centre St), Room 228
Mon-Fri: 9-5   212/788-7900, www.cenyc.org

It is a little-known fact that the city will loan tools to groups involved in community-sponsored open-space greening projects. Loans are limited to one week, but the waiting period is not long and the price (nothing!) is right. You can borrow the same tools several times a season. A group can be as few as four people. CENYC also runs Greenmarket—weekly farmers markets in 33 locations, including Union Square. They carry a number of interesting free publications.

Where to Get Things Fixed
Ceramics: **Ceramic Restorations** (224 W 29th St, 12th floor, 212/564-8669; by appointment)
Clocks: **Sid Shapiro** (212/925-1994)
Furniture: **Joseph Biunno** (129 W 29th St, 212/629-5630)
Glassware: **Glass Restorations** (1597 York Ave, 212/517-3287)
Jewelry: **Murrey's Jewelers** (1395 Third Ave, 212/879-3690)
Lamps and appliances: **AABCO A/C, TV, and Vacuum Repairs** (307 E 85th St, 212/585-2431)
Leather restoration: **Robert Falotico** (315 E 91st St, 212/369-1217)
Silver: **Thome Silversmiths** (49 W 37th St, 212/764-5426)

Gift Baskets

CORPORATE AMENITIES INTERNATIONAL
134 W 29th St (bet Ave of the Americas and Seventh Ave), Suite 606
Mon-Fri: 9-6   866/643-7364
                                                       www.caigifts.com

For over a quarter of a century, this firm has been putting a distinct touch on baskets or any kind of gift you might want to send. The sky is the limit: newborn twins, a sales seminar for 500 people, a 50-year wedding anniversary—you name it, and they will respond with a stylish and unique gift. The best part is that they are reliable, imaginative, and reasonably priced. Baskets start as low as $29.95.

Haircuts

Children

COZY'S CUTS FOR KIDS

1125 Madison Ave (at 84th St)	212/744-1716
448 Amsterdam Ave (at 81st St)	212/579-2600
1416 Second Ave (at 74th St)	212/585-COZY (2699)

Mon-Sat: 10-6; Sun: 11-5 (Madison Ave only)

www.cozyscutsforkids.com

Cozy's takes care of kids of all ages, including the offspring of famous personalities. What an experience: videos and videogames, themed barber chairs, balloons, candy, and free toys. They issue a "first-time" diploma with a keepsake lock of hair! Besides providing professional styling services, Cozy's is a toy boutique. There are "glamour parties" for girls, makeup and glamour art projects, and mini-manicures. Their own "So Cozy" hair-care products for children are available in-shop and online. Adults are well taken care of, too!

Family

ASTOR PLACE HAIR STYLISTS

2 Astor Pl (at Broadway)   212/475-9854
Tues-Fri: 8 a.m.-10:30 p.m.; Sat: 8-8; Sun: 9-6

The personnel inside of what was once a modest neighborhood barbershop give some of New York's trendiest and most far-out haircuts. It all started when the Vezza brothers inherited a barbershop from their father in the East Village at a time when "not even cops were getting haircuts." Enrico took note of the newly gentrified neighborhood's young trendies and their sleek haircuts and changed the name of the shop to "Astor Place Hair Stylists." Now, the shop is staffed with a resident manager, a doorman, and an ever-increasing number of barbers.

ATLAS BARBER SCHOOL

32 Third Ave (bet 9th and 10th St)   212/475-1360
Mon-Fri: 9-7:30; Sat: 9-6

Atlas Barber School teaches general barbering and shaving techniques. They've been at it for 55 years. High style it isn't; great value it is!

FEATURE TRIM

1108 Lexington Ave (bet 77th and 78th St)   212/650-9746
Tues-Sat: 11-6

This neighborhood establishment maintains its standard of basic hair care for men, women, and children. Low maintenance is the key to Feature Trim's haircuts. Easy care, reasonable prices, friendly faces, and more than 50 years of combined experience keep an impressive clientele asking for proprietors Victor and Joe. Appointments are encouraged, but walk-ins are welcome.

PAUL MOLE FAMILY BARBERSHOP
1031 Lexington Ave (at 74th St)   212/535-8461
Mon-Fri: 7:30-6:30; Sat: 7:30-5:30; Sun: 9-3:30

As the name says, this is a family business. They will trim the heads of both dad and the kids, with customer-friendly hours and pocketbook-friendly prices. The place is packed after school and on weekends, so appointments are suggested.

Health and Fitness Clubs

I have listed the most popular highly recommended health clubs in Manhattan by area. Note that special membership offers appear regularly in local newspapers. For visitors, reciprocal memberships are available at some clubs, and one- or two-day passes may be obtained. Most Manhattan hotels have some kind of fitness equipment. Don't be afraid to check out the location to see if staff, cleanliness, and equipment meet your needs.

Clubs by Area

Chelsea
David Barton (215 W 23rd St, 212/414-2022)
New York Sports Club (270 Eighth Ave, 212/243-3400 and 128 Eighth Ave, 212/627-0065)
Phoenix Fitness (127 W 25th St, 212/206-7011)
Sports Center at Chelsea Piers (Pier 60, 23rd St at Hudson River, 212/336-6000)
24/7 Fitness Club (47 W 14th St, 212/206-1504)
YMCA (125 W 14th St, 212/741-9210)

Downtown
Battery Park Swim & Fitness (375 South End Ave, 212/321-1117)
Church Street Boxing (25 Park Pl, 212/571-1333)
Complete Body John Street (80 John St, 212/248-3030)
Crunch (25 Broadway, 212/269-1067 and 152 Christopher St, 212/366-3725)
Equinox (14 Wall St, 212/964-6688)
Lucille Roberts (143 Fulton St, 212/267-3730)
New York Health and Racquet Club (39 Whitehall St, 212/269-9800)
New York Sports Club (217 Broadway, 212/791-9555; 160 Water St, 212/363-4600; and 30 Wall St, 212/482-4800)
Trinity Boxing Club (110 Greenwich St, 212/374-9393)

East Village
Dolphin Fitness (18 Ave B, 212/777-1001; 94 E 4th St, 212/387-9500; and 242 E 14th St, 212/614-0390)

Flatiron District
Equinox (897 Broadway, 212/780-9300)
New York Health and Racquet Club (60 W 23rd St, 212/989-2300)
New York Sports Club (34 W 14th St, 212/337-9900)

Gramercy Park
Crunch (554 Second Ave, 212/545-9757)

14th Street Y (344 E 14th St, 212/780-0800)
New York Sports Club (4-10 Irving Place, 212/477-1800 and 113 E 23rd St, 212/982-4400)

Greenwich Village
Aerospace (336 W 13th St, 212/929-1640)
Clay (25 W 14th St, 212/206-9200)
Crunch (623 Broadway, 212/420-0507; 404 Lafayette St, 212/614-0120; and 54 E 13th St, 212/475-2018)
Equinox (97 Greenwich Ave, 212/620-0103)
Hanson Fitness (826 Broadway, 212/982-2233 and 132 Perry St, 212/741-2000)
Lucille Roberts (80 Fifth Ave, 212/255-3999)
New York Health and Racquet Club (24 E 13th St, 212/924-4600)
New York Sports Club (125 Seventh Ave S, 212/206-1500 and 232 Mercer St, 212/780-7407)
Printing House Fitness and Racquet Club (421 Hudson St, 212/243-7600)

Harlem
New York Sports Club (2311 Frederick Douglass Blvd, 212/316-2500)

Kips Bay
New York Sports Club (614 Second Ave, 212/213-5999 and 131 E 31st St, 212/213-1408)

Midtown
Athletic & Swim Club (Equitable Center, 787 Seventh Ave, 212/265-3490)
Bally Sports Club (335 Madison Ave, 212/983-5320 and 350 W 50th St, 212/265-9400)
Bally Total Fitness (641 Ave of the Americas, 212/645-4565; 139 W 32nd St, 212/465-1750; and 45 E 55th St, 212/688-6630)
Crunch (144 W 38th St, 212/869-7788; 555 W 42nd St, 212/594-8050; and 1109 Second Ave, 212/758-3434)
E at Equinox (59 Columbus Circle, 212/871-3001)
Equinox (10 Columbus Circle, 212/871-0425; 250 E 54th St, 212/277-5400; 1633 Broadway, 212/541-7000; 420 Lexington Ave, 212/953-2499; and 521 Fifth Ave, 212/972-8000)
Excelsior Athletic (301 E 57th St, 212/688-5280)
Exhale Spa (150 Central Park S, 212/561-7400)
Gold's Gym (250 W 54th St, 212/307-7760)
Lucille Roberts (300 W 40th St, 212/268-4199)
Manhattan Plaza Health Club (482 W 43rd St, 212/563-7001)
Mid City Gym (244 W 49th St, 212/582-8924)
New York Health and Racquet Club (132 E 45th St, 212/986-3100; 20 E 50th St, 212/593-1500; 110 W 56th St, 212/541-7200; and 115 E 57th St, 212/826-9650)
New York Sports Club (502 Park Ave, 212/308-1010; 575 Lexington Ave, 212/317-9400; 1601 Broadway, 15th floor, 212/977-8880; 1221 Ave of the Americas, 212/840-8240; 200 Park Ave, 212/682-4440; 19 W 44th St, 212/768-3535; 230 W 41st St, 646/366-9400; 1372 Broadway, 212/575-4500; 200 Madison Ave, 212/686-1144; and 50 W 34th St, 212/868-0820)
Plus One Fitness (Waldorf-Astoria Hotel, 301 Park Ave, 212/872-4970)

Sports Club/LA (45 Rockefeller Plaza, 212/218-8600)
Strive Fitness (330 E 59th St, 212/486-6966)
YWCA (610 Lexington Ave, 212/755-4500)

Murray Hill
New York Sports Club (633 Third Ave, 212/661-8500 and 3 Park Ave, 212/686-1085)

Northern Manhattan
Lucille Roberts (1387 St. Nicholas Ave, 212/927-8376)

Soho
Hanson Fitness (963 Greene St, 212/431-7682)
New York Sports Club (503-511 Broadway, 212/925-6600)
Plus One Fitness (106 Crosby St, 212/334-1116)

Staten Island
Johnny Lats Gym (1775 South Ave, 718/698-1121)

Tribeca
Eastern Athletic (80 Leonard St, 212/966-5432)
Equinox (54 Murray St, 212/566-6555)
24/7 Fitness Club (107 Chambers St, 212/267-7949)
New York Sports Club (151 Reade St, 212/571-1000 and 102 North End Ave, 212/945-3535)

Upper East Side
Asphalt Green (555 E 90th St, 212/369-8890)
Bally Total Fitness (1915 Third Ave, 212/369-3063 and 144-146 E 86th St, 212/722-7371)
Casa Spa & Fitness (The Regency, 540 Park Ave, 212/223-9280)
David Barton (30 E 85th St, 212/517-7577)
Equinox (205 E 85th St, 212/439-8500 and 140 E 63rd St, 212/750-4900)
Exhale Spa (980 Madison Ave, 212/561-6400)
Liberty Fitness (244 E 84th St, 212/585-4245)
New York Health and Racquet Club (1433 York Ave, 212/737-6666)
New York Sports Club (1637 Third Ave, 212/987-7200; 151 E 86th St, 212/860-8630; and 349 E 76th St, 212/288-5700)
92nd Street Y (1395 Lexington Ave, 212/415-5700)
Sports Club/LA (330 E 61st St, 212/355-5100)

Upper West Side
All Star Fitness Center (75 West End Ave, 212/265-8200)
Crunch (162 W 83rd St, 212/875-1902)
Equinox (2465 Broadway, 212/799-1818 and 344 Amsterdam Ave, 212/721-4200)
Lucille Roberts (505 W 125th St, 212/222-2522)
New York Sports Club (2527 Broadway, 212/665-0009; 248 W 80th St, 212/873-1500; 2162 Broadway, 212/496-2444; 23 W 73rd St, 212/496-6300; 61 W 62nd St, 212/265-0995; and 1657 Broadway, 212/307-9400)
Paris Health Club (752 West End Ave, 212/749-3500)
Reebok Sports Club/NY (160 Columbus Ave, 212/362-6800)
West Side YMCA (5 W 63rd St, 212/875-4100)

Clubs with Childcare

Crunch (1109 Second Ave, 212/758-3434)
Equinox (54 Murray St, 212/566-6555)
New York Health and Racquet Club (all locations)
Paris Health Club (752 West End Ave, 212/749-3500)
Sports Club/LA (330 E 61st St, 212/355-5100)

Health Specialties

Personal Trainers
Bodysmith (212/249-1824): women only
Casa Specialized Private Fitness (212/223-9280)
Christa Bache (646/279-5926)
David Kirsch (212/683-1836)
Dorit Baxter (212/371-4542)
Jean-Pierre Cusin (212/727-9637)
Joe Massiello (212/319-3816)
La Palestra Center for Preventive Medicine (212/799-8900)
Mike Creamer (212/353-8834)
Nathaniel Oliver (917/867-0606)
Patricia Durbin-Ruiz (646/643-8369): prenatal
Salvatore Fichera (212/687-1646, www.forzafitness.com): With two decades of experience, he is one of the very best.
Shelby Grayson (212/362-3543): clinical exercise
Timothy Callaghan (212/585-4245)

Pilates
Alycea Ungaro (Tribeca Bodyworks, 212/625-0777)
RE:AB (33 Bleecker St, 212/420-9111)
Soho Sanctuary (119 Mercer St, 212/334-5550)

Private training, pilates, massage, and yoga
Sal Anthony's Movement Salon (190 Third Ave and 119 E 17th St, 212/420-7242, www.movementsalon.com): a real exercise salon with no membership fees

Registered male nurse and masseur
John Percik (212/924-7684)

Yoga
Integral Yoga Institute (227 W 13th St, 212/929-0585)
Integral Yoga Uptown Center (200 W 72nd St, 212/721-4000)
Jivamukti Yoga Center (404 Lafayette St, 212/353-0214)
Now Yoga (377 Park Ave, 2nd floor, 212/447-9642)
Om Yoga (826 Broadway, 6th floor, 212/254-9642)

Kevin Coulthard (917/515-8039) is a top experienced professional in the specialties of massage and personal training.

Hotels

The Manhattan hotel scene has changed a great deal in recent years. A number of new operations have arrived in both luxury and budget categories. Small boutique hotels have become very popular, especially for the single traveler. Some of the best names in the industry have opened multiple units in the city. Hotel dining has improved immeasurably over the past decade (see "Hotel Dining"). Practically every hotel now has some kind of athletic facility. The new ones have large, elaborate setups, while the old-time hotels have been converting space for this much asked-for amenity. Spas are increasingly popular. Kids' programs are featured by a number of hotels that cater to families.

The best hotel rates can still be found by calling a hotel directly, many times at the last minute. Be careful of high charges for in-room bars, telephone calls, room service, laundry service, and use of business centers. New York has many fine hotels in every price category. Your choice should take into account the type of accommodations you desire and the area of the city that will be the most convenient. Several older hotels are being converted, in part or in whole, into condominiums.

Checklist

If any of these features particularly matter to you, ask about them when making reservations. It might make the difference between a pleasurable stay and a disappointing one.

- adjustable thermostat
- good reading lights
- good quality towels in adequate supply
- comfortable in-room sitting area
- on-site dining facilities
- on-site parking
- conveniently located ice machines
- direct-dial phones
- nonsmoking rooms
- late checkout
- shuttle service to and from airports
- hotel drugstore or newsstand
- windows that open
- express checkout
- free morning paper
- evening turndown service
- concierge
- 24-hour room service
- health club facilities
- removable closet hangers
- in-room safe
- reliable message service
- umbrellas available for loan
- well-marked fire escapes

Special Hotel Classifications

Extended Stays

If you are planning to stay awhile in Manhattan, check out these extended stay facilities. Some require a 30-day minimum stay. Washers and dryers are available.

Bristol Plaza (210 E 65th St, 212/753-7900): kitchens, daily maid service, health club, concierge

Phillips Club (155 W 66th St, 212/835-8800): kitchens, daily maid service, computer-friendly, business center, concierge

Hostels

Big Apple Hostel (119 W 45th St, 212/302-2603, www.bigapplehostel.com): midtown location; dorms and private rooms; reservations made online

Central Park Hostel (19 W 103rd St, 212/678-0491): dorm-style rooms with shared baths ($26 and up); lockers; private rooms ($75 and up)

Chelsea International Hostel (251 W 20th St, 212/647-0010): dormitory rooms ($28 and up) and private rooms ($70 and up)

Chelsea Star Hostel (300 W 30th St, 212/244-7827): hotel ($75 and up) and hostel ($35 and up)

Hostelling International New York (891 Amsterdam Ave, 212/932-2300, www.hinewyork.org): one of the world's largest; prices start at $29

Times Square Roommates (356 W 40th St, 2nd floor, 212/216-0642): dorms and private rooms with shared baths and lockers

Inexpensive

Carlton Arms (160 E 25th St, 212/679-0680)
Edison (228 W 47th St, 212/840-5000)
Excelsior Hotel (45 W 81st St, 212/362-9200)
59th Street Bridge Apartments (351 E 60th St, 212/754-9388)
Hostelling International New York (891 Amsterdam Ave, 212/932-2300)
Hotel 31 (120 E 31st St, 212/685-3060)
Hotel 57 (130 E 57th St, 212/753-8841)
Hotel Wolcott (4 W 31st St, 212/268-2900)
Larchmont (27 W 11th St, 212/989-9333)
Manhattan (273 W 38th St, 212/921-9791)
The Milburn Hotel (242 W 76th St, 212/362-1006)
Murray Hill Inn (143 E 30th St, 212/545-0879)
Off Soho Suites (11 Rivington St, 212/353-0860)
Portland Square Hotel (132 W 47th St, 212/382-0600)
Ramada Inn Eastside (161 Lexington Ave, 212/545-1800)
Stanford Hotel (43 W 32nd St, 212/563-1481)
Super 8 Times Square (59 W 46th St, 212/719-2300)
Union Square Inn (209 E 14th St, 212/614-0500)
Washington Square Hotel (103 Waverly Pl, 212/777-9515)
Webster Apartments (419 W 34th St, 212/967-9000): women only
Westside Inn (237 W 107th St, 212/866-0061)

Small Luxury Hotels

Fitzpatrick Manhattan Hotel (687 Lexington Ave, 212/355-0100)
Hotel Chandler (12 E 31st St, 212/889-6363)
Hotel Elysee (60 E 54th St, 212/753-1066)
Inn at Irving Place (56 Irving Pl, 212/533-4600)

Lowell Hotel (28 E 63rd St, 212/838-1400)
The Mark Hotel (25 E 77th St, 212/744-4300)

Time Shares
Manhattan Club (200 W 56th St, 212/489-8488)

Kid-Friendly Hotels
Doubletree Guest Suites Times Square (1568 Broadway, 212/719-1600): kids' playroom
Le Parker Meridien Hotel (118 W 57th St, 212/245-5000): in-elevator videos
Novotel New York (226 W 52nd St, 212/315-0100): kids' corner with entertainment
Ritz-Carlton New York, Battery Park (2 West St, 212/344-0800): "Ritz Kids" program, with exciting perks
The Westin New York Times Square (270 W 43rd St, 212/921-9575): kids' club with amenities

Pet-Friendly Hotels
Affinia 50 (155 E 50th St, 212/751-5710)
Beekman Tower (3 Mitchell Pl, 212/355-7300)
The Benjamin (125 E 50th St, 212/715-2500)
The Carlyle Hotel (35 E 76th St, 212/744-1600)
Eastgate Tower (222 E 39th St, 212/687-8000)
Essex House, a Westin Hotel (160 Central Park S, 212/247-0300)
Hilton New York (1335 Ave of the Americas, 212/586-7000)
Le Parker Meridien Hotel (118 W 57th St, 212/245-5000)
Millennium Broadway Hotel New York (145 W 44th St, 212/768-4400)
New York Helmsley Hotel (212 E 42nd St, 212/490-8900)
New York Marriott Marquis (1535 Broadway, 212/398-1900)
New York Palace Hotel (455 Madison Ave, 212/888-7000)
New York Park Lane (36 Central Park S, 212/371-4000)
New York's Hotel Pennsylvania (401 Seventh Ave, 212/736-5000)
The Peninsula New York Hotel (700 Fifth Ave, 212/956-2888)
The Regency (540 Park Ave, 212/759-4100)
RIHGA Royal New York (151 W 54th St, 212/307-5000)
Ritz-Carlton New York, Battery Park (2 West St, 212/344-0800)
Ritz-Carlton New York, Central Park (50 Central Park S, 212/308-9100)
St. Regis New York (2 E 55th St, 212/753-4500)
Shelburne Murray Hill (303 Lexington Ave, 212/689-5200)
Sheraton Manhattan Hotel (790 Seventh Ave, 212/581-3300)
Sheraton New York Hotel and Towers (811 Seventh Ave, 212/581-1000)
The Shoreham Hotel (33 W 55th St, 212/247-6700)
Southgate Tower Hotel (371 Seventh Ave, 212/563-1800)
Surrey Hotel (20 E 76th St, 212/288-3700)
Swissôtel New York—The Drake (440 Park Ave, 212/421-0900)
Trump International Hotel and Tower (1 Central Park W, 212/299-1000)
W New York—The Tuscany (120 E 39th St, 212/686-1600)
W New York—Times Square (1567 Broadway, 212/930-7400)
W New York—Union Square (201 Park Ave S, 212/253-9119)
The Waldorf Towers (100 E 50th St, 212/355-3100)
The Westin New York at Times Square (270 W 43rd St, 212/921-9575)

Hotel Concierge

A concierge is the handiest person in a hotel if you want special services or advice. There is no charge for this help, but tipping is expected. Ten dollars is about right for an average service, more if a request takes an unusual amount of time or trouble. For requests above and beyond the call of duty, 15% of the value of the service is a good guideline. If you are a regular guest, it is wise to cultivate a good relationship with these helpful folks.

A few services a concierge can help arrange: babysitting, couriers, emergency medical services, escorts, flowers, gifts, health and beauty care, kennels, massage, notary public, party venues, pet services, photographers, rental cars, restaurants, secretarial services, tickets for events, shows, transportation, tours, translators, and videos.

In other words, a concierge can be almost as helpful as this book!

Hotel Lingo

Hotel consolidator: clearinghouse for unsold hotel rooms
Limited-service hotels: oversized rooms with work spaces but no restaurant and few amenities; rates about one-third less than full-service hotels
Modified American Plan: room rate includes breakfast and dinner
Rack rate: full retail price of a room as listed on rate cards and brochures
Service charge: fixed percentage automatically added to room and meal bills

Hotels Near Airports

The following are conveniently located, provide airport transportation, have restaurants, and are reasonably priced (ask for corporate rates). Some have recreational facilities, such as fitness rooms and pools.

John F. Kennedy International: **Anchor Motor Inn** (66 rooms, Bayside, 718/428-8000), **Courtyard by Marriott** (166 rooms, Jamaica, Queens, 718/848-2121), **Crowne Plaza JFK** (184 rooms, Jamaica, Queens, 718/489-1000), **Golden Gate Motor Inn** (145 rooms, Brooklyn, 718/743-4000), **Hampton Inn** (216 Rooms, Jamaica, Queens, 718/322-7500), **Holiday Inn** (360 rooms, Jamaica Queens, 718/659-0200), **Radisson** (386 rooms, Jamaica, Queens, 718/322-2300), and **Ramada Plaza Hotel-JFK** (478 rooms, Jamaica, Queens, 718/995-9000)

LaGuardia: **Best Western City View Inn** (71 rooms, Long Island City, 718/392-8400), **Clarion Hotel at LaGuardia** (170 rooms, East Elmhurst, Queens, 718/335-1200), **Comfort Inn** (50 rooms, Flushing, Queens, 718/939-5000), **Courtyard by Marriott** (288 rooms, East Elmhurst, Queens, 718/446-4800), **Crowne Plaza New York-LaGuardia** (358 rooms, East Elmhurst, Queens, 718/457-6300), **Marriott LaGuardia Airport** (437 rooms, East Elmhurst, Queens, 718/565-8900), **Sheraton LaGuardia East** (173 rooms, Flushing, Queens, 718/460-6666), and **Wyndham Garden Hotel** (229 rooms, East Elmhurst, Queens, 718/426-1500)

Newark International: **Four Points by Sheraton** (260 rooms, Elizabeth, NJ, 908/527-1600), **Hilton Newark Airport** (378 rooms, Elizabeth, NJ, 908/351-3900), **Hilton Newark Gateway** (253 rooms, Newark, NJ, 973/622-5000), **Holiday Inn** (412 rooms, Newark, NJ, 973/589-1000), **Marriott Newark** (596 rooms, Newark, NJ, 973/623-0006), **Ramada Newark Airport** (347 rooms, Newark, NJ, 973/824-4000), and **Sheraton Newark Airport** (504 rooms, Newark, NJ, 973/690-5500)

New and Remodeled Hotels

Affinia 50 (155 E 50th St, 212/751-5710): formerly Plaza Fifty; executive club suite hotel; midtown

Alex Hotel (205 E 45 St, 212/867-5100): extended stay; midtown

The Blakely New York (136 W 55th St, 212/245-1800): formerly The Gorham; large rooms; moderate; midtown

Blue Moon Hotel (100 Orchard St, 212/533-9080): 22-room guesthouse within a 19th century tenement; Lower East Side

Comfort Inn (129 W 46th St, 212/221-2609): entirely smoke-free; midtown

Dream Hotel (210 W 55th St, 212/247-2000, 866/437-3266): surrealist; moderate; midtown

Four Points by Sheraton Manhattan (160 W 25th St, 212/627-1888): Chelsea

Hotel 41 at Times Square (26 W 41st St, 212/703-8600): boutique; Times Square

Hotel on Rivington (107 Rivington St, 212/475-2600): boutique; Lower East Side

Hotel QT (125 W 45th St, 212/354-2323): bunk beds; inexpensive; midtown

LaQuinta Manhattan (17 W 32nd St, 212/736-1600): great value; Chelsea

Marriott Courtyard (125th St and Park Ave): Harlem

Marriott Residence Inn—Bryant Park Tower (1033 Ave of the Americas, 212/768-0007): midtown

The Melrose Hotel (140 E 63rd St, 212/838-5700): formerly Barbizon; Upper East Side

Millenium Hilton (55 Church Place, 212/693-2001): business hotel; Lower Manhattan

Pioneer of Soho Hotel (341 Broome St, 212/226-1482): budget from $79; Soho

Premier (boutique) and **Millennium Broadway Hotel New York** (145 W 44th St, 212/768-4400): 750 rooms; good banquet facilities; midtown

Radio City Apartments (142 W 49th St, 877/921-9321, 212/730-0728): studio from $145; one-bedroom suite with full kitchen, $195; two-bedroom, $250; midtown

Ramada Inn Eastside (161 Lexington Ave, 212/545-1800): Murray Hill

Red Roof Inn Manhattan (6 W 32nd St, 212/643-7100); midtown south

San Carlos Hotel (150 E 50th St, 212/755-1800): luxury boutique; midtown

70 Park Avenue Hotel (70 Park Ave, 212/973-2400): formerly Doral Park Avenue; boutique; Murray Hill

Solita Soho Clarion (159 Grand St, 212/925-3600): a "Clarion Collection" hotel; Soho

Super 8 Times Square (59 W 46th St, 212/719-2300): inexpensive; midtown

W Hotel Harlem (233 W 125th St): under discussion at the time this book went to press

Hotel Restaurants

The Carlyle Hotel, **Dumonet** (35 E 76th St, 212/744-1600): French

Casablanca, **Tony's Di Napoli** (147 W 43rd St, 212/221-0100): Italian

Chambers, **Town** (15 W 56th St, 212/582-4445): American

Fitzpatrick Manhattan Hotel, **Fitzer's** (687 Lexington Ave, 212/355-0100): Irish-American

Four Seasons Hotel New York, **Fifty Seven Fifty Seven** (57 E 57th St, 212/758-5757): American

Hilton New York, **Etrusca** (1335 Ave of the Americas, 212/261-5750): Italian

Hotel Gansevoort, **Ono** (18 Ninth Ave, 212/660-6766): Japanese

Hotel Plaza Athenee New York, **Arabelle** (37 E 64th St, 212/606-4647): French

Hudson Hotel, **Hudson Cafeteria** (356 W 58th St, 212/554-6000): American

Inn at Irving Place, **Lady Mendl's Tea Salon** (56 Irving Pl, 212/533-4466): high tea

Iroquois, **Triomphe** (49 W 44th St, 212/453-4233): Continental

Kimberly Hotel, **George O'Neill's of New York** (145 E 50th St, 212/888-1220): seafood and chophouse

Le Parker Meridien Hotel, **Seppi's** (123 W 57th St, 212/708-7444): French; and **Norma's** (212/708-7460): American; breakfast is a specialty

Library Hotel, **Branzini** (299 Madison Ave, 212/557-3340): Mediterranean

Lowell Hotel, **Post House** (28 E 63rd St, 212/935-2888): steakhouse

The Lucerne Hotel, **Nice Matin** (201 W 79th St, 212/873-6423): Niçoise

Mandarin Oriental New York, **Asiate** (80 Columbus Circle, 212/805-8881): French-Japanese

The Maritime Hotel, **La Bottega** (363 W 16th St, 212/243-8400): Italian

The Mark Hotel, **Mark's Restaurant** (25 E 77th St, 212/879-1864): Continental

The Melrose Hotel, **Landmark** (140 E 63rd St, 212/838-5700): American

Mercer Hotel, **Mercer Kitchen** (99 Prince St, 212/966-5454): American-Asian

Millennium Broadway Hotel New York, **Charlotte** (145 W 44th St, 212/768-4400): New American

New York Marriott Financial Center, **Roy's** (130 Washington St, 212/266-6262): Hawaiian fusion

Omni Berkshire Place, **Kokachin** (21 E 52nd St, 212/754-5043): American

The Peninsula New York Hotel, **Fives** (700 Fifth Ave, 212/903-3918): Atlantic Rim

The Pierre Hotel, **Cafe Pierre** (2 E 61st St, 212/940-8195): French-American

The Regency, **540 Park** (540 Park Ave, 212/339-4050): American

RIHGA Royal New York, **Prime 54** (151 W 54th St, 212/468-8888): Tuscan steakhouse

Ritz-Carlton New York, Battery Park, **2 West** (2 West St, 917/790-2525): American

St. Regis New York, **Astor Court** (2 E 55th St, 212/245-4500): Continental

Shelburne Murray Hill, **Rare** (303 Lexington Ave, 212/481-1999): American

Sheraton Manhattan Hotel, **Russo's Steak & Pasta** (790 Seventh Ave, 212/621-8537): American

60 Thompson, **Kittichai** (60 Thompson St, 212/219-2000): Thai

Soho Grand Hotel, **The Gallery** (310 West Broadway, 212/965-3588): American

Surrey Hotel, **Cafe Boulud** (20 E 76th St, 212/772-2600): French-American

Swissôtel New York—The Drake, **Q56** (65 E 56th St, 212/756-3800): American-International

Tribeca Grand Hotel, **Church Lounge & Trinity** (2 Ave of the Americas, 212/519-6677): International

Trump International Hotel and Tower, **Jean Georges** (1 Central Park W, 212/299-3900): French-Asian

W New York, **Heartbeat** (541 Lexington Ave, 212/407-2900): American
W New York—Union Square, **Olives New York** (201 Park Ave S, 212/353-8345): Mediterranean
Wales Hotel, **Sarabeth's Kitchen** (1295 Madison Ave, 212/410-7335): Continental

Hotels with Swimming Pools

Crowne Plaza Times Square (1605 Broadway): for exercise buffs
Hotel Gansevoort (18 Ninth Ave): underwater music
Le Parker Meridien Hotel (118 W 57th St): visibly exciting
Mandarin Oriental New York (80 Columbus Circle): 75-foot pool
Millenium Hilton (55 Church St): gorgeous
The Peninsula New York Hotel (700 Fifth Ave): very classy
Sheraton Manhattan Hotel (790 Seventh Ave): kid-friendly
Trump International Hotel and Tower (1 Central Park W): magnificent

New York's Finest Hotels

Bearing in mind that this *is* New York, I have categorized hotels by room tariff per night (without taxes) as follows:

- Inexpensive: $199 and under
- Moderate: $200 to $399
- Expensive: $400 and up
- Very Expensive: $500 and up

AFFINIA HOSPITALITY

Affinia Dumont, 150 E 34th St (bet Third and Lexington Ave)	
	212/481-7600
Affinia 50, 155 E 50th St (at Third Ave)	212/751-5710
Beekman Tower, 3 Mitchell Pl (at 49th St)	212/355-7300
The Benjamin, 125 E 50th St (at Lexington Ave)	212/715-2500
Eastgate Tower, 222 E 39th St (bet Second and Third Ave)	
	212/687-8000
Lyden Gardens, 215 E 64th St (bet Second and Third Ave)	
	212/355-1230
Shelburne Murray Hill, 303 Lexington Ave (at 37th St)	
	212/689-5200
Southgate Tower, 371 Seventh Ave (at 31st St)	212/563-1800
Surrey Hotel, 20 E 76th St (bet Madison and Fifth Ave)	
	212/288-3700
Moderate to moderately expensive	www.affinia.com

Looking for style and value? These all-suites hotels are among the most reasonably priced and conveniently located in New York. Each features 24-hour attendants and modern kitchens. Over 2,000 suites in all—studio, junior, and one- or two-bedroom suites—are available at very attractive daily, weekly, or monthly rates. These are particularly convenient for long-term corporate visitors and traveling families who can economize by having the kids sleep on pull-out couches and by using the fully equipped kitchens. Fitness centers are available at most properties. Food facilities vary. The famous Cafe Boulud can be found at the Surrey. Women especially like these accommodations when they travel and dine alone.

ALGONQUIN HOTEL
59 W 44th St (bet Fifth Ave and Ave of the Americas)
Moderately expensive   212/840-6800, 888/304-2047
www.algonquinhotel.com

A $3.5 million facelift has made this hotel even more attractive! The legendary Algonquin was designated a historic landmark by the city of New York in 1987. This home of the famous Roundtable—where Dorothy Parker, Alexander Woollcott, Harpo Marx, Tallulah Bankhead, Robert Benchley, and other literary wits sparred and dined regularly—now exudes the same charm and character as it did in the Roaring Twenties! There are 174 rooms, including 23 suites (some named after well-known personalities), and the atmosphere is intimate and friendly. The remodeled lobby is the best place in the city for people-watching, and the Oak Room is arguably the best cabaret venue in New York.

CASABLANCA
147 W 43rd St (bet Broadway and Ave of the Americas)
Moderate   212/869-1212
www.casablancahotel.com

Now that the Times Square area has been cleaned up, you might consider staying at Casablanca, an attractive, safe, and clean boutique hotel with a Moroccan flavor. It's small (48 rooms and suites), newly renovated, and family-owned. It offers complimentary amenities and comfortable rates, and the atmosphere is friendly. Special attractions: free continental breakfast, passes to the New York Sports Club, Internet browsing on the lounge computer, and bottled water, iced tea, and chocolates in the rooms. High-speed Internet access is available in all guest rooms. Best of all, you are right in the center of the action!

The best travel agents for New York and other big cities:
Barbara Galley, Linden Travel Bureau, 212/421-3320
Jody Bear, Bear & Bear/VWT, 212/532-3400
Valerie Ann Wilson, Valerie Wilson Travel, 212/532-3400

CITY CLUB HOTEL
55 W 44th St (bet Fifth Ave and Ave of the Americas)   212/921-5500
Moderate   www.cityclubhotel.com

City Club is a small luxury hotel that features Frette linens, feather beds, high-speed Internet access, in-room electronic safes, guest privileges at the nearby New York Sports Club, large marble bathrooms, and Daniel Boulud's DB Bistro Moderne on-premises. This excellent restaurant also provides room service for the hotel. On the second level you'll find Tracy Stern SALONTEA.

ESSEX HOUSE, A WESTIN HOTEL
160 Central Park S (bet Ave of the Americas and Seventh Ave)
Moderately expensive to expensive   212/247-0300
www.essexhouse.com

Central Park is at your door! A friend of mine who travels all over the world claims that this is the best hotel she has ever stayed at. The Essex House has been restored to its original art deco grandeur, and it is a beauty. The restaurants—Cafe Botanica on the Park and Alain Ducasse—offer top French cuisine. Guest rooms feature classic art-deco decor, and many have spectacular views of Central Park. The all-marble bathrooms come with robes, scale, hair dryer, and superb toiletries. A business center and health spa are added features. Great weekend getaway packages are available through the reservations department. You can't do better!

FOUR SEASONS HOTEL NEW YORK
57 E 57th St (bet Madison and Park Ave) 212/758-5700
Expensive www.fourseasons.com

In the hotel world, fewer names elicit higher praise or win more awards than Four Seasons. They are considered one of the best in the business. Upscale visitors to the Big Apple have an elegant, 52-story Four Seasons to call their home away from home. Designed by I. M. Pei and Frank Williams, the Four Seasons provides 364 oversized rooms and suites (some with terraces), and several fine eating places, including the top-notch Fifty Seven Fifty Seven and a lobby lounge for light snacks and tea. There's also a fully equipped business center, complete with freestanding computer terminals and modem hookups; a $3.5 million, 6,000-square-foot fitness center and spa with all the latest equipment; and numerous meeting rooms. The principal appeal, however, is the size of the guest rooms, which average 600 square feet, offer spectacular views of the city, and feature huge, luxurious marble bathrooms with separate dressing areas. A classy staff makes this another award-winning Four Seasons property.

HILTON NEW YORK
1335 Ave of the Americas (bet 53rd and 54th St) 212/586-7000
Moderate to moderately expensive www.newyorktowers.hilton.com

This Hilton flagship at Rockefeller Center has benefited from a $148 million renovation and redesign. The Hilton New York features two restaurants: New York Marketplace, an all-day dining facility, and Etrusca, an intimate Italian room featuring Tuscan foods and wines. Special features include an outstanding art collection, upscale executive floors with private lounge and large luxury suites, dozens of rooms equipped for the disabled, a highly trained international staff, and an 8,000-square-foot state-of-the-art fitness club and spa. A popular business and convention hotel, the Hilton outfits its rooms with the most up-to-date communications equipment. For those leisure travelers interested in shopping, theater, Radio City Music Hall, and other midtown attractions, this location is highly desirable.

HOTEL ELYSEE
60 E 54th St (bet Park and Madison Ave) 212/753-1066
Moderate www.elyseehotel.com

The Hotel Elysee is a gracious, European-style boutique hotel in the heart of midtown Manhattan. The 101 spacious guest rooms feature such amenities as robes, in-room safe, minibar, wireless Internet access, two-line phones, voice mail, and marble baths. Rates include complimentary continental breakfast, afternoon tea or coffee with cookies, and wine and hors d'oeuvres each weekday evening in the second-floor Club Room. The on-premises Steakhouse at Monkey Bar is one of New York's hottest sipping and dining spots.

HOTEL GANSEVOORT
18 Ninth Ave (bet 13th and Gansevoort St)   212/206-6700
Moderate to moderately expensive   www.hotelgansevoort.com

A classy hotel in the Meatpacking District? Yes, Hotel Gansevoort is a 12-story beauty with dramatic outdoor lighting. Its 187 rooms offer many creature comforts but are not overdone. Ceilings are high, the beds and linens are first-class, and many rooms have good views of the Hudson River. A top-floor lounge with a retractable glass roof is an exciting place to gather—and there's a swimming pool up there, as well! A large Japanese restaurant, Ono, is an additional attraction, as is a modern new spa.

HOTEL PLAZA ATHENEE NEW YORK
37 E 64th St (bet Park and Madison Ave)   212/734-9100
Expensive   www.plaza-athenee.com

This European-style hotel ranks with New York's best in several cate-gories, including service. Most of the rooms have been renovated, and all have marble bathrooms. Some of the suites on the higher floors feature solar-iums and roof terraces. Additional amenities include a workout facility, CD players in every room, high-speed Internet access, twice-daily maid serv-ice, 24-hour room service, and the outstanding Arabelle restaurant. Check out Bar Seine, their trendy lounge.

HOTEL WOLCOTT
4 W 31st St (bet Fifth Ave and Broadway)   212/268-2900
Inexpensive   www.wolcott.com

One of Manhattan's better hotel bargains, Hotel Wolcott offers a good location (just south of midtown), refurbished rooms with private baths, good security, direct-dial phones, TVs with in-room movies and videogames, and fitness and business centers. No wonder students, foreign travelers, and savvy business people are regular patrons! Free coffee and muffins are served each morning.

HUDSON HOTEL
356 W 58th St (bet Eighth and Ninth Ave)   212/554-6000
Inexpensive to moderate   www.hudsonhotel.com

Ian Schrager has done something special with this property. He has opened an affordable hotel in an often unaffordable area. A lushly landscaped courtyard garden is open to the sky. You will find abundant amenities plus a reasonably priced restaurant and busy bars. There are 1,000 guest rooms with minimal decor and furniture, but given the reasonable prices you won't worry too much about that. There are, in fact, some nice decorative touches, such as the attractive wood paneling. But the scene is really the big thing here, especially the fabulous Library Bar.

KIMBERLY HOTEL
145 E 50th St (bet Lexington and Third Ave)   212/755-0400
Moderate   www.kimberlyhotel.com

If big hotels turn you off, then the Kimberly may be just what you are looking for. This charming and hospitable boutique hotel in the center of Manhattan offers guests the kind of personal attention that is a rarity in today's commercial world. There are 185 luxury guest rooms, marble bathrooms, in-room safes, one- and two-bedroom suites with fully equipped kitchens, and private terraces with most suites. There is eating at George O'Neill's of New York (a steakhouse), or enjoy the scene at VUE, a popular supper club. Access to the New York Health and Racquet Club is complimentary, and room service is available.

LE PARKER MERIDIEN HOTEL
118 W 57th St (bet Ave of the Americas and Seventh Ave)
Moderate to moderately expensive   212/245-5000
www.parkermeridien.com

This large midtown hotel has a lot going for it: great location, ergonomically designed rooms, good eateries, excellent health club, penthouse pool, free high-speed Internet access, CD and DVD players, junior suites with separate sitting areas, and more! They even boast of having baths and showers big enough for two. *Viva la France*! Norma's is one of New York's top breakfast rooms. You won't find better burgers in town than at Le Parker's well-hidden, street-level burger joint, or if you prefer French, try the classic bistro, Seppi's. This hotel can even help plan your visit through their "New York Smart Aleck" program. It's a lot less expensive than going to Paris! Note: The entrance to Le Parker Meridien for those with a car is on 56th Street.

LIBRARY HOTEL
299 Madison Ave (at 41st St)   212/983-4500
Moderate   www.libraryhotel.com

For the avid reader, check out the Library! Rooms are individually appointed with artwork and books relating to a specific theme. Guests can also enjoy the Poetry Terrace, which houses volumes of verse by assorted authors. Breakfast and an afternoon wine-and-cheese reception are included in the rate. The 60 rooms are wired for high-speed Internet access. A unique feature: room numbers are based on the Dewey decimal system of book classification.

LOWELL HOTEL
28 E 63rd St (bet Park and Madison Ave)   212/838-1400
Moderately expensive   www.lowellhotel.com

Like an attractive English townhouse, this classy, well-located hotel features 47 suites and 21 deluxe rooms. Amenities include a 24-hour multilingual concierge service, at least two phones per room, fax machine with a dedicated line, VCRs and outlets for personal computers, marble bathrooms, complimentary shoeshines, and a fitness center. Most suites have wood-burning fireplaces and ten have private terraces. The "Hollywood Suite" has all the latest entertainment amenities, plus a fully equipped kitchen.

MANDARIN ORIENTAL NEW YORK
80 Columbus Circle (at 60th St)   212/805-8800
Expensive to very expensive   www.mandarinoriental.com

From a spectacular location at Columbus Circle in the Time Warner Center, the Mandarin Oriental boasts great views of Central Park from the rooms on the 38th floor and upwards. In its usual classy (and pricey) style, the Mandarin Oriental offers New York visitors 203 deluxe rooms and 48 suites, all beautifully furnished and equipped with the latest entertainment technology. Magnificent art pieces dot the public spaces. Asiate (see restaurant reviews) features French-Japanese fare, the 35th-floor Mobar is a popular spot for drinks, a beautiful ballroom is available, and a two-story spa features "holistic rejuvenation." A 75-foot lap pool has a spectacular setting.

THE MARITIME HOTEL
363 W 16th St (at Ninth Ave)   212/242-4300
Moderate   www.themaritimehotel.com

The Maritime is located in an area with few modern hotels, making it convenient for those doing business in Chelsea. Amenities include Italian and Japanese restaurants (La Bottega and Matsuri), a fitness center, flat-screen TVs, and wireless Internet service. In good weather, you can dine and drink alfresco. Rooms and bathrooms are small.

THE MARK HOTEL
25 E 77th St (bet Fifth and Madison Ave)   212/744-4300
Moderately expensive   www.themarkhotel.com

An older residency building (the Hyde Park, built in 1926) has been converted into one of the most charming hotels in New York. There are 125 guest rooms and 60 suites done in English-Italian style, all decorated in comfy traditional decor, and every room has cable TV, high-speed Internet access, two-line phones, and most have pantries. I strongly recommend the suites, which contain separate vanities and marble baths. Some even have libraries, wet bars, and terraces. The location is terrific, and the personnel (including a multilingual concierge) are extremely accommodating. Mark's Restaurant, an excellent restaurant just off the lobby, serves all meals, plus tea and brunch. Guests get Frette linens, heated towel racks, down pillows, umbrellas, and Molton Brown of London soaps. The bar is sensational!

THE MARMARA-MANHATTAN
301 E 94th St (at Second Ave)   212/427-3100, 800/621-9029
Moderate   www.marmara-manhattan.com

The conveniently located Marmara-Manhattan is an extended-stay hotel that provides turn-key living for folks who need temporary quarters. They offer flexible lease terms for stays beyond 30 days. Suites with up to three bedrooms, as well as studio apartments, are available. Choose from sleek and sophisticated to more traditional, "comfy" rooms. Amenities include modern kitchens with cooking and serving utensils, daily housekeeping, 24-hour concierge and doorman services, spacious bathrooms, terraces, and an exercise room. There are over a hundred custom-decorated suites, many with sensational views.

Try a hotel consolidator like **Quikbook** (800/789-9887, www.quikbook.com), **Hotels.com** (800/964-6835, www.hotels.com), or **Priceline** (www.priceline.com). They buy excess rooms and pass on savings.

MILFORD PLAZA
270 W 45th St (at Eighth Ave)   212/869-3600, 800/221-2690
Moderate   www.milfordplaza.com

Value is the key word here. The Milford Plaza, located at the edge of the Theater District, offers reasonable rates that are partially offset by its location. Rest assured the hotel has extremely tight security. The 1,300 guest rooms are small but clean, late-night dining is available, and there is a state-of-the-art fitness center. Very attractive rates are available on weekends and for groups.

MUSE HOTEL
130 W 46th St (bet Ave of the Americas and Seventh Ave)
Moderate   212/485-2400
                                                       www.themusehotel.com

Guests at the Muse appreciate the large rooms (181 "dream rooms," 19 suites), the excellent restaurant District, and the busy lounge. Rates are very comfortable, and there is no charge for local calls (an unusual perk for New York hotels). A free *New York Times* is delivered daily, and wireless 'net access is available in public areas. Feather beds and duvets ensure a restful stay.

Good news! After decades of revolving-door ownership and neglectful management, the **Plaza Hotel** (59th St and Fifth Ave) has closed for modernization, Although this grand old hotel will be partially converted to high-end condos, the great public rooms will be saved and nightly guests will be able to enjoy approximately 350 rooms on the Fifth Avenue and 58th Street sides.

NEW YORK MARRIOTT FINANCIAL CENTER
85 West St (at Battery Park)   212/385-4900
Moderate   www.nymarriottfinancialcenter.com

For those doing business in the Wall Street area, this 500-room hotel is ideal. It has two restaurants, including a branch of the famous Roy's chain, a popular lobby lounge, restful beds with down comforters, good Internet connections throughout, and a great fitness center and swimming pool.

NEW YORK MARRIOTT MARQUIS
1535 Broadway (bet 45th and 46th St)   212/398-1900
Moderate to moderately expensive   www.nymarriottmarquis.com

Recently renovated at a cost of over $150 million, the New York Marriott Marquis has over 2,000 guest rooms and suites, sizable meeting and convention facilities, and one of the largest hotel atriums in the world. Guests can enjoy a 232-seat two-story revolving restaurant and lounge atop the building. In addition, a legitimate Broadway theater, a fully equipped health club, six restaurants and lounges, and a special concierge level are on the property.

NEW YORK PALACE HOTEL
455 Madison Ave (bet 50th and 51st St)   212/888-7000
Expensive   www.newyorkpalace.com

Located close to Saks Fifth Avenue, the 896-room New York Palace offers commanding views of the city skyline, which is particularly enchanting in the evening. The public rooms encompass the 120-year-old Villard Houses, a legendary New York landmark. Rooms feature high-speed Internet access, fax machines, and safes. A comprehensive renovation added such facilities as an expansive fitness center, an executive lounge, and the two-floor Villard Center (with meeting and function rooms). The casually elegant Mediterranean restaurant Istana offers New American cuisine. Don't miss the Villard Bar and Lounge, whose Tiffany windows are worth a visit in themselves. A complimentary shuttle is offered to Wall Street and the Theater District.

OFF SOHO SUITES
11 Rivington St (at Second Ave)   212/979-9815, 800/633-7646
Moderate   www.offsoho.com

Looking for a downtown location? Off Soho is a European-style hotel located two blocks south of Houston Street. It offers a number of conveniences that add up to good value: exercise room, cafe, two phones with Internet access, full kitchen with cookware, special rates for extended stays, self-service laundry, and large marble baths in some suites.

THE PENINSULA NEW YORK HOTEL
700 Fifth Ave (at 55th St)   212/956-2888
Expensive   www.newyork.peninsula.com

When the name Peninsula is mentioned, the words *quality* and *class* immediately come to mind. This is especially true in Manhattan, where a $45 million facelift made the property even more luxurious. The building is a 1902 landmark with 185 rooms and 54 suites, including the palatial Peninsula Suite (more than 3,000 square feet at $10,000 per night!). Room features include oversized marble bathrooms, in-room fax machines, large work desks, audiovisual systems with cable, and numerous bathroom amenities. Features of the 21st-floor Peninsula New York Spa and Health Club include an indoor pool, jacuzzi, sun decks, modern fitness equipment, and spa services. Spa menu, too!

The best rates for Manhattan hotel rooms can be obtained at **www.nycvisit.com** (click on "Book Your Hotel"). Remember that prices change from day to day and even hour to hour.

THE PIERRE HOTEL
2 E 61st St (at Fifth Ave)   212/838-8000
Expensive   www.fourseasons.com/pierre

Combine the Pierre's name with the Four Seasons' reputation and you're bound to get top quality. Overlooking Central Park, this property provides 201 elegant rooms and suites with 1930s detailing, a magnificent lobby, the Rotunda (famous for afternoon tea and light meals), and Cafe Pierre (offering continental cuisine for breakfast, lunch, and dinner). Function rooms are the site of many of Manhattan's glitziest events. A fitness center, outfitted with Italian marble, provides the latest in cardiovascular equipment. With a staff of over 650, you can be assured of highly personalized service.

THE REGENCY
540 Park Ave (at 61st St)   212/759-4100
Moderately expensive to expensive   www.loewshotels.com

With an outstanding location on Park Avenue and renovations that have created a more contemporary and relaxed feeling, this Loews hotel offers 351 spacious guest rooms and 86 outstanding suites, including 12 grand suites that have housed many of the entertainment world's greats. The one-bedroom suites feature two bathrooms. Rooms contain business conveniences such as two-line phones and data ports; fax machines and printers are provided on request. Use of the fitness center and overnight shoeshine service are complimentary. Two excellent restaurants—the classy 540 Park and The Library, an intimate, residential-style lounge—offer daily meal service. Feinstein's at the Regency is a classy nightclub. Power breakfasts at the Regency are legendary. More than 70% of the hotel's guests are repeat visitors!

Nostalgic visitors and history buffs will love the refurbished **Roosevelt Hotel** (45 E 45th St, 212/661-9600, www.theroosevelthotel.com). Prices are moderate, the lobby is classic, and service is excellent.

RIHGA ROYAL NEW YORK
151 W 54th St (bet Ave of the Americas and Seventh Ave)
Moderately expensive   212/307-5000
                                                   www.rihgaroyalny.com

In a very handy midtown location, the RIHGA Royal New York, a JW Marriott Hotel, is a luxury residential-style all-suites hotel that is great for both domestic and international travelers. Between them, the staff speaks 15 languages! The hotel offers a fully equipped 24-hour business center, fitness center, and complimentary newspapers. Guests of their "Pinnacle" suites receive complimentary Town Car service from New York area airports. The on-site restaurant, Prime 54, is a very good Tuscan steakhouse.

RITZ-CARLTON NEW YORK, BATTERY PARK
2 West St (at Battery Park)   212/344-0800
Expensive

RITZ-CARLTON NEW YORK, CENTRAL PARK
50 Central Park S (at Ave of the Americas)   212/308-9100
Expensive   www.ritzcarlton.com

These two relatively new arrivals have added luster to the Manhattan hotel scene, providing all the usual amenities and outstanding service identified with this brand name. You'll find great views, top-grade lobby-level restaurants, gym and spa services, luxurious rooms and bathrooms, and business centers. Club-level guests get special treatment. The Battery Park location offers a 14th-floor bar that can be described as a very romantic hideaway.

ST. REGIS NEW YORK
2 E 55th St (at Fifth Ave)   212/753-4500
Expensive   www.stregis.com

The St. Regis, a historic landmark in the heart of Manhattan, is one of the crown jewels of Starwood Hotels, and for good reason. With 315 oversized (and overpriced) deluxe rooms and 91 suites, the hotel provides luxurious accommodations. Some rooms are being converted to condominiums. Each room has marble baths. Round-the-clock butler service is provided (including free pressing of two garments upon arrival), and 24-hour room service is available. Outstanding restaurants are a feature here: Astor Court (breakfast, lunch, afternoon tea, and dinner) and the King Cole Bar (great Bloody Marys). The St. Regis' Roof—the only hotel-rooftop ballroom in the city—is available for private functions.

SALISBURY HOTEL
123 W 57th St (bet Ave of the Americas and Seventh Ave)
Moderate   212/246-1300
                                                www.nycsalisbury.com

I highly recommend this place to price-savvy travelers. The Salisbury, capably run by Edward Oliva, has nearly 200 rooms and suites, most of which have been redecorated. Many are outfitted with butler's pantries and refrigerators. Suites are large, comfortable, and reasonably priced. The thick walls are really soundproof! If you want to be near Carnegie Hall and other midtown attractions, the Salisbury is for you. If you've waited until the last minute for reservations, the Salisbury is a good place to call. Since it is not well-known among out-of-towners, rooms are usually available.

If you are looking for a hotel with a really cool bar, check out the **Time Hotel** (224 W 49th St, 212/320-2900) and its appropriately named lounge, **La Gazelle**.

SHERATON MANHATTAN HOTEL
790 Seventh Ave (at 52nd St)   212/581-3300, 800/325-3535
Moderate   www.starwood.com

With a convenient location, this 650-room hotel is ideal for both families and business travelers. It is within easy walking distance of Manhattan's best stores, theaters, and restaurants. The Sheraton Manhattan features a 50-foot indoor swimming pool (a rarity in midtown), a first-rate health club, an excellent restaurant (Russo's Steak & Pasta), and 24-hour room service.

SHERATON NEW YORK HOTEL AND TOWERS
811 Seventh Ave (at 52nd St)   212/581-1000, 800/325-3535
Moderate to moderately expensive   www.starwood.com

An outstanding location in central Manhattan and a wide selection of restaurants and lounges (Hudson's Sports Bar & Grill, Streeter's New York Cafe, and Lobby Court Lounge) make the Sheraton New York an excellent choice for tourists and business travelers. Sheraton Towers—the more luxurious upper floors—offer exclusive digs that include butler service. "Corporate Club" rooms come equipped with office amenities. A wide selection of package deals and seasonal specials are available.

SOHO GRAND HOTEL
310 West Broadway (at Grand St)   212/965-3000
Moderately expensive   www.sohogrand.com

If business or pleasure takes you to Soho, this facility may be for you
... but at a price. The custom-designed rooms will not appeal to traditionalists, though yuppies will love them. Two penthouse suites with outdoor terraces are special. A fitness center, business amenities, 24-hour room service,
and valet parking are available. The on-premises Grand Bar & Lounge offers
cocktail cuisine.

SWISSÔTEL NEW YORK—THE DRAKE
440 Park Ave (at 56th St)   212/421-0900
Moderate   www.swissotel-newyork.com

The refurbished Drake offers 495 rooms and 108 suites that are operated
with typical Swiss efficiency. It has a multilingual concierge staff, spa, valet
parking, a good central location, fully equipped guest rooms, and 12 meeting
rooms for receptions and events. Q56, a fashionable and attractive room with
good food, and a branch of the French *patisserie*, Fauchon, are on-premises.

TRIBECA GRAND HOTEL
2 Ave of the Americas (bet Walker and White St)
Moderate   212/519-6600, 877/519-6600
                                                   www.tribecagrand.com

When visiting this vibrant part of Manhattan, you might consider the
Tribeca Grand. With over 200 guest rooms, custom-designed meeting spaces,
luxurious in-room amenities, built-in bathroom television sets, a fitness center, and valet parking, guests enjoy every comfort and convenience.

If you need a short-term rental, try **Affordable New York City** (21
E 10th St, 212/533-4001, www.affordablenewyorkcity.com). Ask for
Susan Freschel.

TRUMP INTERNATIONAL HOTEL AND TOWER
1 Central Park W (at 60th St)   212/299-1000
Expensive   www.trumpintl.com

Trump International is everything you would expect from a place with
Donald's name attached. There are special amenities (fresh flowers, umbrellas, telescopes, and garment bags), 24-hour room service, complete office
facilities, entertainment centers in every room, a state-of-the-art fitness
center, swimming pool, and marble bathrooms. One of Manhattan's best (and
most expensive) restaurants, Jean Georges, will pamper your taste buds.

W NEW YORK
541 Lexington Ave (bet 49th and 50th St)   212/755-1200
Moderately expensive   www.whotels.com

Located in midtown, this Starwood property has 691 rooms (including 59
spacious suites), a large ballroom, a full-service spa and health club, 24-hour
room service, and two-line telephones with data ports in every room. The

look is strictly modern, right down to the black staff uniforms. Health-food addicts will love the Heartbeat, and the hip Oasis Bar is right off the lobby.

W NEW YORK—TIMES SQUARE
1567 Broadway (at 47th St)   212/930-7400
Moderately expensive   www.whotels.com

With over 500 rooms in the heart of Times Square, this 57-story W flagship offers the Blue Fin restaurant (seafood), a classy retail store, a fitness room and spa, 24-hour room service, and other quality amenities. Ask to stay on the highest floor possible, as the views are dramatic. The Whiskey Bar is an underground watering hole and screening room with a coed bathroom!

THE WALDORF-ASTORIA
301 Park Ave (at 50th St)   212/355-3000
Moderately expensive   www.waldorfastoria.com

Hilton has invested more than $200 million restoring their flagship property. The Royal Suite alone—used by the late Duke and Duchess of Windsor —was restored at a cost of $10 million! The work shows, and renovations are ongoing. The rich, impressive lobby is bedecked with magnificent mahogany wall panels, hand-woven carpets, and a 148,000-tile mosaic floor. The management has created larger spaces by reducing the number of units. Oversize executive business rooms are available. All-marble bathrooms have been installed in some suites. There is a fitness center, several restaurants, and deluxe rooms and suites in the Waldorf Towers/A Conrad Hotel. An event at the Waldorf is sure to be something special. Junior League members have access to rooms at substantial savings. Sign up for a behind-the-scenes tour of the Waldorf.

HOTEL TIPPING GUIDE

Doorman	$1 or $2 per bag $1 or $2 for hailing a taxi
Bellhop	$1 or $2 per bag, depending on size and weight $1 or $2 for every delivery to your room
Concierge	$5 to $10 for special services like securing hard-to-get theater tickets and restaurant reservations
Housekeeper	$1 or $2 a night If you ask the housekeeper for any extra service, tip an additional $1 or $2
Room service	15% to 18% of the bill before taxes; be aware that tip is often figured into the bill!

THE WESTIN NEW YORK AT TIMES SQUARE
270 W 43rd St (at Eighth Ave)   212/201-2700
Moderate to moderately expensive   www.westinnewyork.com

With an exciting multicolored exterior and much-talked-about atrium lobby, the Westin New York has brought a new look to midtown Manhattan. The hotel is a 45-story, $300 million marvel, with 863 rooms and suites, high-speed Internet access, Westin's trademark "Heavenly" beds, a Don Shula steakhouse, and all the other amenities associated with Westin.

WYNDHAM HOTEL
42 W 58th St (at Fifth Ave)   212/753-3500
Moderate

John Mados has created a winner! This charming hotel is more like a large home in which rooms are rented out. Many guests regularly make the Wyndham their Manhattan headquarters. Advantages are numerous: great location, uniquely decorated rooms and suites, complete privacy, individual attention, and no business conventions. On the other hand, the hotel is always busy, and reservations may be difficult for newcomers. There is a restaurant (no room service), and suites have pantries with refrigerators.

Alternative Housing

ABINGDON GUEST HOUSE
13 Eighth Ave (bet 12th and Jane St)   212/243-5384
Moderate   www.abingdonguesthouse.com

A charming bed and breakfast located in Greenwich Village, Abingdon Guest House consists of two landmark 1850s Federal-style townhouses, with fine examples of period architecture. The Brewbar Coffee Bar is available for continental breakfast and lunch. All rooms are smoke-free, and each has a private bath and distinctive decor. Abingdon offers its guests many amenities, including daily maid service.

ABODE
P.O. Box 20022, New York, NY 10021   212/472-2000
Mon-Fri: 9-5   800/835-8880 (outside tri-state area)
Moderate to moderately expensive   www.abodenyc.com

Do you have your heart set on staying in a delightful old brownstone? How about a contemporary luxury apartment in the heart of Manhattan? Abode selects apartments with great care, and all homes are personally inspected to ensure the highest standards of cleanliness, attractiveness, and hospitality. All are nicely furnished. Nightly rates begin at $135 for a studio and rise to $400 for a two-bedroom apartment. Extended stays of a month or longer receive discount rates. There is a minimum stay of four nights.

BED AND BREAKFAST NETWORK OF N.Y.
130 Barrow St (bet Washington and West St), Room 508
Mon-Fri: 8-6   212/645-8134
Moderate   800/900-8134
                                            www.bedandbreakfastnetny.com

At Bed and Breakfast Network of N.Y. you have your choice of over

200 hosted and unhosted accommodations in Manhattan. The hosted rate runs from $80 to $150 a night for single or double occupancy. The weekly rate varies from $500 to $1,000. For unhosted apartments of up to three bedrooms, the fee ranges from $130 to $400 a night and from $900 to $2,500 a week. Monthly rates are also available. Leslie Goldberg has been in business since 1986, and this is a very reliable outfit.

BROADWAY BED & BREAKFAST INN
264 W 46th St (at Eighth Ave)   212/997-9200, 800/826-6300
Moderate   www.broadwayinn.com

This is the only European country-style inn in New York City. The 41 rooms are immaculate, the atmosphere is homey, the location in the Theater District is safe, and the operation is family-owned and affordable. Additional amenities include a free continental breakfast, a library stocked with newspapers, and Internet access. The facility, built as a hotel in 1907, has been fully restored. Ask about discounted tickets for Broadway shows!

HOSTELLING INTERNATIONAL NEW YORK
891 Amsterdam Ave (at 103rd St)   212/932-2300
Inexpensive   www.hinewyork.org

Visitors of all ages are welcome (although those under 18 must be accompanied by an adult). The hostel provides over 646 beds in a newly renovated, century-old landmark. They offer meeting spaces, cafeteria, coffee bar, airport shuttle, catering, tours, self-service kitchens, and laundry facilities to individuals and groups. Best of all, the price is right!

INN NEW YORK CITY
266 W 71st St (bet West End and Broadway)   212/580-1900
Moderately expensive   www.innnewyorkcity.com

Situated in a restored, 19th-century townhouse, Inn New York City offers four suites behind a discreet exterior. Depending on which suite you choose, you may find a double Jacuzzi, extensive library, leaded glass skylights, fireplaces, baby grand piano, private terrace, or fully equipped kitchen stocked with hearty delights. Additional services include high-speed Internet access, cable TV, VCR, DVD, daily newspapers, maid service, and a 24-hour concierge.

INTERNATIONAL HOUSE
500 Riverside Dr (at 122nd St)   212/316-8436 (admissions)
Moderate   212/316-8473 (guest rooms and suites)
                                               www.ihouse-nyc.org

International House is a community of over 700 graduate students, interns, trainees, and visiting scholars from nearly 100 countries. Occupants spend anywhere from a day to a few years in New York City. It is located on the Upper West Side near Columbia University and the Manhattan School of Music. Special features include a low-budget cafeteria, pub, gymnasium, and self-service laundry. Free programs for residents include ballroom dancing, lectures, a practice room for musicians, computer lab, films, recitals, and organized sports. During the summer, single-room occupancy (for periods of one to ten days) with shared bath runs $50 per night. The rate drops to $45 per night for stays of 10-20 days. Rates are less still by the semester.

Reasonably priced guest suites ($105-$130 per night) with private bath, air conditioning, daily maid service, and cable television are also available.

IVY TERRACE B&B
230 E 58th St (bet Second and Third Ave)   516/662-6862
Moderate   www.ivyterrace.com

There are three guest apartments in this century-old townhouse, two with outdoor terraces. Kitchens are stocked with breakfast goodies. Hostess Vinessa (a professional actress) promises special care, including the possibility of tickets to TV-show tapings. The Ivy Terrace is gay-friendly. Weekly rates are available.

> Roommates can help bring down the cost of housing in Manhattan. Try **Rainbow Roommates** (212/982-6265).

METRO HOME
515 Madison Ave (at 53rd St), 25th floor   212/813-2244, 800/987-1235
Moderate   www.metro-home.com

If you are looking for a reasonably priced, full-service, short-term furnished apartment in Soho, midtown, Murray Hill, Upper East Side, Upper West Side, Greenwich Village, Chelsea, or the Theater District, this is a good number to call. They have over 200 apartments in their inventory and feature discounts for extended stays.

92ND STREET Y (DE HIRSCH RESIDENCE)
1395 Lexington Ave (at 92nd St)   212/415-5650
Mon-Thurs: 9-7; Fri: 9-5; Sun: 10-5   800-858-4692
Inexpensive   www.dehirsch.com

The De Hirsch Residence offers convenient, inexpensive, and secure dormitory housing for men and women between the ages of 18 and 30. Special discounts for Y health-club memberships and single and double rooms are available. Lengths of stay can range from 30 days to one year. Admission is by application.

PHILLIPS CLUB
Lincoln Square
155 W 66th St (at Broadway)   212/835-8800
Moderate to moderately expensive   www.phillipsclub.com

This 174-unit residential hotel near Lincoln Center is designed for long-term visitors but will also take nightly customers. Suites come with fully equipped kitchens, direct-dial phone numbers, and stereo systems. Other impressive features include a 24-hour business center and concierge, laundry and valet service, in-room safes, a handy conference room, and preferential membership at the nearby Reebok Sports Club NY.

SOLDIERS', SAILORS', MARINES', AND AIRMEN'S CLUB
283 Lexington Ave (bet 36th and 37th St)   212/683-4353
Inexpensive   www.ssmaclub.org

Here is a great find in the Murray Hill area of Manhattan for American and allied servicemen and women—active, retired, veterans, reservists, military cadets, and Coast Guard personnel alike! Rates are extremely low (with no tax), and the hotel has 29 comfortable rooms and club-style facilities to enjoy. There are several lounges, TVs with VCRs, and a lobby canteen with refrigerator, microwave, and coffee.

WEBSTER APARTMENTS
419 W 34th St (at Ninth Ave)   212/967-9000
Inexpensive   www.websterapartments.org

This is one of the best deals in the city for working women with moderate incomes. It is not a transient hotel but operates on a policy developed by Charles B. Webster, a first cousin of Rowland Macy (of the department store family). Webster left the bulk of his estate to found these apartments, which opened in 1923. Residents include college students, designers, actresses, secretaries, and other business and professional women. Facilities include diningrooms, recreation areas, a library, and lounges. The Webster also has private gardens for its guests, and meals can be taken outdoors in good weather. Rates are $175-$230 per week, which includes two meals a day and maid service. The Webster is a secret find known mainly to residents and readers of this book.

Interior Designers

AERO STUDIOS
419 Broome St (bet Lafayette and Crosby St)   212/966-4700
Mon-Fri: 11-6; Sat: 12-5   www.aerostudios.com

Whether it is a major commercial design project or a minor residential one, Aero Studios' staff is well equipped to handle the task. Be sure to visit their store, and you'll no doubt come away with some special ideas.

If your room needs a good *trompe l'oeil* (mural), call Agnes Liptak at **Fresco Decorative Painting** (324 Lafayette St, 5th floor, 212/966-0676). You can also request decorative stucco, faux finishing, and leafing ($8 to $50 per square foot).

ALEX CHANNING
250 W 19th St (bet Seventh and Eighth Ave), Suite 11C
By appointment   212/366-4800
                                          www.alexchanning.com

Licensed interior designer Alex Channing has built a reputation as one of Manhattan's young up-and-comers. He does furniture design and custom-made furnishings, and he'll help with site selection, move-ins, and installations. Channing does both commercial and residential work.

DESIGNER PREVIEWS
36 Gramercy Park E (bet 20th and 21st St)   212/777-2966
By appointment only   www.designerpreviews.com

Having problems finding the right decorator? Designer Previews keeps tabs on over 300 of the most trustworthy and talented designers, architects, and landscaping experts in Manhattan and elsewhere. They will help you select the best, based on your style and personal requirements, through consultation or online presentation. Karen Fisher, the genius behind this handy service, is a former design editor for *Woman's Wear Daily* and *Esquire*.

MARTIN ALBERT INTERIORS
9 E 19th St (bet Broadway and Fifth Ave)
Mon-Fri: 9-5   212/673-8000, 800/525-4637

Martin Albert specializes in window treatments. They measure and install their product line at prices that are considerably lower than most decorators. Martin Albert offers 250,000 fabric samples, ranging from $8 to $400 a yard. Custom upholstery and slipcovers, a furniture shop, and a large selection of drapery hardware are also available, and they'll deliver to all 50 states.

PARSONS SCHOOL OF DESIGN
66 Fifth Ave (at 13th St)   212/229-5424
Mon-Fri: 9-5   www.parsons.edu

Parsons, a division of the New School University, is one of the top two schools in the city for interior design. Those who call for design assistance will get their request posted on the school's career services board, and every effort is made to match clients with student decorators. Individual negotiations determine the price and length of a job, but it will be considerably less than what a practicing professional charges. Most of these students don't yet have a decorator's card, but this is a good place to contact if you just want a consultation.

Looking for an architect or decorator? The best of the best:

Bilhuber (330 E 59th St, 6th floor, 212/308-4888): Jeffrey Bilhuber has contemporary ideas.

David Netto Design (270 Lafayette St, Suite 806, 212/343-7415): David Netto is a master of innovation.

Glenn Gissler Design (36 E 22nd St, 8th floor, 212/228-9880): Glenn Gissler works well with art.

Miles Redd (77 Bleecker St, Room C-111, 212/674-0902): color expert

MR Architecture & Decor (150 W 28th St, Suite 1102, 212/989-9300): David Mann is very practical.

Ruby (41 Union Square W, Studio 1036, 212/741-3380): Alysa Weinstein and Bella Zakarian are mindful of budgets.

Shamir Shah Design (10 Greene St, 212/274-7476): Shamir Shah's designs are modern and clean.

Specht Harpman (338 W 39th St, 10th floor, 212/239-1150): Scott Specht and Louise Harpman are pocketbook-conscious.

S.R. Gambrel (270 Lafayette St, 212/925-3380): You can't beat Steven Gambrel for detailing.

Steven Holl Architects (450 W 31st St, 11th floor, 212/629-7262): Homes are a specialty.

RICHARD'S INTERIOR DESIGN
1390 Lexington Ave (bet 91st and 92nd St)   212/831-9000
Mon-Fri: 10-6; Sat: 10-4   www.richardsinteriordesign.com

Here you will find over 10,000 decorator fabrics, including tapestries, damasks, stripes, plaids, silks, velvets, and floral chintzes. These are all first-quality goods at competitive prices. The fabrics are imported from the same European mills used by Kravet, Lee Jofa, Robert Allen, Brunswig & Fils, and Clarence House. Richard's does upholstery, furniture, reupholstery, slip-covers, draperies, top treatments, shades, bedroom ensembles, and wall coverings. Design services, in-home consultation, and installation are available.

Pearl stringing is a real art. Perhaps the best practitioner in the city is Doris Kahn at **Murrey's Jewelers** (1395 Third Ave, 212/875-3690).

Jewelry Services

GEM APPRAISERS & CONSULTANTS
608 Fifth Ave (at 49th St), Suite 602   212/333-3122
Mon-Fri: 9-5, by appointment   www.robaretz.com

Robert C. Aretz, who owns Gem Appraisers & Consultants, is a graduate gemologist and director of the Appraisers Association of America. He is entrusted with appraisals for major insurance companies, banks, and retail jewelry stores. His specialty is antique jewelry, precious colored stones, diamonds, and natural pearls. Aretz will do appraisals and/or consultations for estate, insurance, tax, equitable distribution, and other purposes.

RISSIN'S JEWELRY CLINIC
4 W 47th St (at Fifth Ave)   212/575-1098
Mon, Tues, Thurs: 9:30-5; closed first two weeks of July

Rissin's is indeed a clinic! The assortment of services is staggering: jewelry repair and design, antique repair, museum restorations, supplying diamonds and other stones, eyeglass repair, pearl and bead stringing, restringing of old necklaces, stone identification, and appraisals. The patent for the Rissins' "Earquilizer" (an earring stabilizer), has been approved, and you can try it at the store. (Bring your own earrings.) Joe and Toby Rissin run the place. Joe's father was a master engraver, so the family tradition has been passed along. *Honesty* and *quality* are their bywords. Estimates are gladly given, and all work is guaranteed.

Yes, there is a reliable pawnshop in Manhattan: **New York Pawnbrokers** (177 Rivington St, 212/228-7177).

ZDK COMPANY
48 W 48th St (bet Fifth Ave and Ave of the Americas), Suite 1410
By appointment only   212/575-1262

Zohrab David Krikorian has created original pieces for neighbors in the Diamond District, and he will also do professional work for individuals in his free time. In addition to making jewelry, ZDK mends and fixes broken jewelry as only a professional craftsman and artist can. He makes complicated repairs look easy and has yet to encounter a job he can't handle. If he can't match the stones in an antique earring or other piece of jewelry, he'll redo the whole item so that it looks even better than before. He loves creating contemporary designs from traditional materials, and his prices are reasonable.

Lamp Repair

THE LAMP SURGEON
Mon-Sat: 8 a.m.-10 p.m.   917/414-0426

Roy and Lois Schneit do lamp repairs and rewiring at customers' homes, offices, and apartments. Services include work on table and floor lamps, chandeliers, wall sconces, and antiques. Roy has over 30 years experience in this business.

Leather Repair

CARNEGIE LUGGAGE
1392 Ave of the Americas (bet 56th and 57th St)   212/586-8210
Mon-Sat: 9-6; Sun: 11-5

It's a pleasure to do business with these people. Carnegie Luggage is handy to most major midtown and Central Park hotels. Rush service is possible if you let them know you're in a hurry. Expert repair is done on-premises. They offer reliable work at competitive prices. Their complete line of top-brand luggage and travel accessories includes Delsey and Samsonite.

MODERN LEATHER GOODS
2 W 32nd St (bet Fifth Ave and Broadway), 4th floor   212/279-3263
Mon-Fri: 8:30-5; Sat: 8-1:30

Is a briefcase, suitcase, or handbag looking beaten up? Some people regard signs of wear on leather as a mark of class, but I like to see things looking good. Modern Leather Goods, a family business for over 60 years, is the place to go for repairs. Ask for owner Tony Pecorella. They also do needlepoint mounting, reglaze alligator bags, and clean leather and suede.

SUPERIOR REPAIR CENTER
141 Lexington Ave (at 29th St)   212/967-0554
Mon-Fri: 10-6; Sat: 10-3   www.superiorleathernyc.com

Do you own a fine leather garment that's been damaged? Leather repair is the highlight of the service at Superior. Many major stores in the city use them for luggage and handbag work. They are experts at cleaning leather (suede and shearling are specialties) and repairing or replacing zippers on leather items. They will also work on sporting equipment, such as tents and backpacks. Superior has the answer to all leather problems. Just ask Gucci, Calvin Klein, Chanel, Escada, St. John, Bergdorf Goodman, and Prada!

Locksmiths

AAA LOCKSMITHS
44 W 46th St (at Ave of the Americas)   212/840-3939
Mon-Thurs: 8-5:30; Fri: 8-5   www.aaahardware.com

You can learn a lot from trying to find a locksmith in New York. For one thing, as a profession it probably has the most full-page ads in the Manhattan Yellow Pages. For another, this particular "AAA" is *not* the place to call about an automobile emergency. However, in an industry that does not often inspire loyalty or recommendations, AAA Locksmiths has been a family business for over 60 years, and that says a lot right there.

LOCKWORKS LOCKSMITHS
By appointment   212/736-3740

Lock problems? Give Joel at Lockworks a call. He has been in the locksmith trade for over two decades, and there isn't anything he can't do. This gentleman does not advertise, but he is highly regarded by some of the top businesses in Manhattan.

NIGHT AND DAY LOCKSMITH
1335 Lexington Ave (at 89th St)   212/722-1017
Mon-Fri: 9-6; Sat: 10-5 (24 hours for emergencies)

Carry Night and Day's number in case you're ever locked out! Locksmiths must stay ahead of the burglar's latest expertise and offer fast, on-the-spot service for a variety of devices designed to keep criminals out. (After all, no apartment has just *one* lock.) Mena Safer, Night and Day's owner, fulfills these rigid requirements. The company answers its phone 24 hours a day; posted hours are for the sale and installation of locks, window gates, intercoms, car alarms, safes, and keys. Inside and outside welding is a specialty.

Marble Works

PUCCIO MARBLE AND ONYX
661 Driggs Ave, Brooklyn (warehouse showroom)
                                    718/387-9778, 800/778-2246
                                                www.puccio.info

Work of the highest quality is a tradition with Puccio. The sculpture and furniture designs range from traditional to sleekly modern. John and Paul Puccio show dining and cocktail tables, chairs, chests of drawers, buffets, desks, consoles, and pedestals. Custom-designed installations include foyer floors, bathrooms, kitchens, bars, staircases, fountains, and fireplaces. Retail orders are accepted. They are the largest distributor and fabricator of onyx in the country.

Matchmaking

FIELD'S EXCLUSIVE SERVICE
50 E 42nd St, Suite 805   212/391-2233, 800/264-7539
Daily; by appointment   www.fieldsdatingservice.com

Living up to the motto "New York lives by this book!" is a big challenge. In an attempt to be comprehensive, I've even included a matchmaking service. Dan Field's company has been playing Cupid for three quarters of a century. If Dan is successful for you, how about a testimonial for *Where to Find It, Buy It, Eat It in New York*—the Romance Edition, of course!

An afterhours dental emergency can be very inconvenient. Here are some numbers you can call to get relief:

Metropolitan Dental Associates (225 Broadway, 212/732-7400): Saturday 9 to 5; across from City Hall

Stuyvesant Dental Associates (430 E 20th St, 212/473-4151): alternating Saturdays

Dr. Sadettin Sun (246 E 46th St, 212/697-2813): weekends to 7 p.m.

Medical Services

LEAGUE FOR THE HARD OF HEARING

50 Broadway (bet Morris St and Exchange Pl)   917/305-7700
Mon-Fri: by appointment   www.lhh.org

People of all ages who have hearing disabilities are customers of this not-for-profit organization. They dispense hearing aids, sponsor classes, and work with patients and families to find alternatives to help the hearing impaired. They come highly recommended, and their services are a real value.

Some special pharmacies:

Anatole Pharmacy (650 First Ave, 212/481-0909): foreign prescriptions

Brodwin-Sosa Chemists (1344 First Ave, 212/879-9050): pharmaceutical information

J. Leon Lascoff & Sons, Inc. (1209 Lexington Ave, 212/288-9500): the very best pharmacy services

Meadowsweet Herbal Apothecary (77 E 4th St, 212/254-2870): herbal medicines

Medicine Shoppe (306 Eighth Ave, 212/255-9111): hard-to-find medications and compounded prescriptions

Village Apothecary (346 Bleecker St, 212/807-7566): HIV/AIDS drugs and alternative medicine

N.Y. HOTEL URGENT MEDICAL SERVICES   212/737-1212
www.travelmd.com

This is one of the most valuable contacts in Manhattan! Dr. Ronald Primas, the CEO and medical director of this outfit, is tops in his field. This service is locally based and has been in operation for over a decade. All manner of healthcare is available on a 24-hour, seven-days-a-week basis: internists, pediatricians, obstetricians, surgeons, dentists, chiropractors, and more. Doctors will come to your hotel or apartment, arrange for tests, prescribe medications, admit patients to hospitals, and even provide nurses. They can provide travel immunizations and consultations, and they are an official WHO-designated yellow-fever vaccination site. The urgent care center is also available around the clock by appointment for patients not requiring a house call. Payment is expected at the time of service; credit cards are accepted. All physicians are board-certified and have an exemplary bedside manner.

STATSCRIPT PHARMACY
197 Eighth Ave (at 20th St)   212/691-9050
Mon-Fri: 9-9; Sat: 9-5:30   www.chronimed.com

Statscript Pharmacy provides home delivery of prescription medications, comprehensive claims management, and links to community resources and national support networks. Their specialties include prescriptions for patients with HIV or transplants. All pharmaceuticals are available, as is an extensive line of vitamins and homeopathic and holistic products. Many hard-to-find items can be provided with one-day service. They will bill insurance companies directly so that customers need not pay up front. Nationwide shipping is available.

When it becomes necessary to look into long-term home healthcare, call **Priority Home Care** (212/401-1700).

Metal Work

ATLANTIC RETINNING AND METAL REFINISHING
549 W 26th St (at Tenth Ave)   973/848-0700
Mon-Fri: 9-6   www.retinning.com

Jamie Gibbons has taken over a long-established Manhattan business whose specialty is retinning (which is basically tin plating). Drawing upon many years of experience, Gibbons restores brass and copper antiques, designs and creates new copperware, sells restored copper pieces, and restores lamps, chandeliers, and brass beds.

Movers

BIG APPLE MOVING & STORAGE
83 Third Ave (bet Bergen and Dean St), Brooklyn
Mon-Fri: 9-5; Sat: 9-12   212/505-1861, 718/625-1424
                                    www.bigapplemoving.com

This is a handy number to have for moving and storage. Even though Big Apple Moving & Storage is located in downtown Brooklyn, they do 80% of their moving business in Manhattan. They can handle antiques, art, and high-end moves, yet manage to keep their rates reasonable. Call them for a free "no surprises" estimate. They stock every size of box and will build wood crates if needed. They also have bubble pack, plate dividers, custom paper, Styrofoam peanuts, and "French wraps" for crystal and delicate breakables. Many of the expert packers have been with Big Apple since they opened in 1979. You can save up to 50% on moving supplies by shopping at their "do-it-yourself" moving store; large orders are delivered for free. For those who need overnight or short-term storage, Big Apple offers something rare in New York: they will keep your entire truckload of furniture inside their high-security heated warehouse. When they move, every item of furniture is fully wrapped and padded before leaving your residence. Big Apple is also equipped to handle an interstate move.

BROWNSTONE BROS. MOVING
321 Rider Ave (at 140th St), The Bronx   718/665-5000
Mon-Fri: 9:30-5   www.brownstonebros.com

Since 1977 Brownstone Bros. has been offering moving and storage services with a very personal touch by head man Bill Gross. They are highly rated by customers.

MOVING RIGHT ALONG
101-21 101st St   718/738-2468
Ozone Park, NY   www.movingrightalong.com
Mon-Fri: 8:30-6; Sat: 9-2

Nearly three decades of service and a top-quality reputation speak well of Moving Right Along. Moving, storage, packing, and crating are offered, plus a handy cleanout service that will allow your residence to be ready for occupancy quickly. They will also sell your pre-owned furniture. Owner Jim Rueda is a hands-on manager whose work has won accolades from numerous satisfied customers.

A few hints on movers:
- Make sure the mover is licensed.
- Check the Better Business Bureau for complaints.
- Be wary of estimates that are far below competitors'.
- Confirm the mover's address.
- Find out how long they've been in business.
- Beware of someone "trashing the competition."
- Ask for references and referrals.

WEST SIDE MOVERS
644 Amsterdam Ave (bet 91st and 92nd St)   212/874-3800
Mon-Fri: 8-6; Sat: 9-4; Sun: 9-3   www.westsidemovers.com

The late Steve Fiore started West Side Movers in the kitchen of his studio apartment more than three decades ago. From its expanded location on Amsterdam Avenue, West Side Movers continues to offer dependable residential and office moving, specializing in fine art and antiques. Close attention is paid to efficiency, promptness, care, and courtesy. Packing consultants will help do-it-yourselfers select moving boxes and other supplies. Their boxes come in a multitude of sizes, including four specifically for mirrors. West Side Movers also rents and sells dollies and moving pads.

Office Services

PURGATORY PIE PRESS
19 Hudson St (bet Duane and Reade St), Room 403   212/274-8228
Mon-Fri: by appointment only   www.purgatorypiepress.com

Purgatory Pie Press is ideal for small printing jobs. They do typography designs, hand letterpress printing, die-cutting, and hand bookbinding. They'll also craft handmade envelopes, do logos and other identity designs, and provide handmade paper with uniquely designed watermarks. Specialties include printing and calligraphy for weddings and parties. They also carry limited-edition postcards and artists' books. Private lessons and small group classes are offered in letterpress printing and artist books.

WORLD-WIDE BUSINESS CENTRES
575 Madison Ave (at 57th St)   212/605-0200, 800/296-9922
Mon-Fri: 9-5:30   www.wwbcn.com

Alan Bain, a transplanted English lawyer, has created a business that caters to executives who need more than a hotel room and companies that need a fully-equipped, furnished, and staffed office in New York on short notice. The operation grew out of Bain's personal frustration in trying to put together a makeshift office. On-premises administrative, word-processing, clerical, and mail-room services are available. So are high-quality voice and data communications capabilities, including high-speed Internet access and video conferencing. Desk space, private offices, and conference rooms may be rented on a daily, weekly, monthly, or quarterly basis. The daily rate includes a private office, telephone answering, and receptionists.

Painting

BERNARD GARVEY PAINTING   718/894-8272
By appointment

I am constantly asked to recommend an outstanding and reliable painter who can also do plastering and decorative finishes. Bernard Garvey Painting services residential clients, and his customers tout his reasonable prices and terrific work.

Other reliable painters:
Robert Star Painting (212/737-8855)
Roth Painting (212/758-2170)

GOTHAM PAINTING COMPANY
123 E 90th St (at Lexington Ave)   212/427-5752
Mon-Fri: 8-5

If you need interior paint or wallpaper for your home, Gotham is a handy resource. They do spray work, restoration, faux painting, and plastering, with over 50 full-time painters, all fully licensed and bonded. They have been in business for nearly two decades.

Parenting Resources

PARENTING CENTER AT THE 92ND STREET Y
1395 Lexington Ave (at 92nd St)   212/415-5611
Mon-Fri: 9-5 (office hours)   www.92y.org

Just about everything the 92nd Street Y does is impressive, and its Parenting Center is no exception. It offers every kind of class you can imagine: a newborn-care class for expectant parents, a baby massage class for new parents and their infants, a cooking class for preschoolers, and so on. As this Y is a Jewish institution, Shabbat get-togethers and a Jewish heritage class for preschoolers are offered, along with workshops and seminars on a wide range of topics, from potty training to raising an only child. They provide babysitting for various parenting classes (as well as unrelated Y classes) and host new parent get-togethers. Perhaps most important, they act as a resource and support center for members. Membership costs $175 a year, and benefits include discounts and priority sign-up. Non-members are welcome to take classes, too.

PARENTS LEAGUE
115 E 82nd St (bet Lexington and Park Ave)   212/737-7385
Mon-Thurs: 9-4 (Tues till 6); Fri: 9-12   www.parentsleague.org

This nonprofit organization is a goldmine for parents in New York. In addition to putting together a calendar of events for children of all ages, the Parents League maintains extensive files on babysitters, birthday party places, tutors, summer camps, early childhood programs, and independent schools throughout the city. For a membership fee of $100 per academic year, you can access those files and attend workshops and other events. If you are the parent of a small child, you also get a copy of *The Toddler Book,* an invaluable list of more than 275 activities in New York for little ones.

SOHO PARENTING CENTER
568 Broadway (at Prince St)   212/334-3744
www.sohoparenting.com

Soho Parenting Center is dedicated to the notion that parenting ought to be talked about and shared. It conducts workshops and group discussions for parents of newborns, toddlers, and even older children. It offers play groups for children while parents talk about their experiences and challenges. Individual parent counseling is available.

Party Services

AMERICAN FOLIAGE & DESIGN
122 W 22nd St (bet Ave of the Americas and Seventh Ave)
Mon-Fri: 8-5   212/741-5555

For events of all kinds, American Foliage & Design can be a great help. They provide items for television, movie, and commercial production design, plus silk lanterns, terrace designs, and anything to do with gardens and exteriors. Full service is provided, including trucking and installation. Both sales and rentals are offered.

If you're in need of party items, I have two suggestions:
- **Triserve Party Rentals** (770 Lexington Ave, 212/688-8808; by appointment) stocks top-quality tents, tables, chairs, platters, china place settings, linens, and more.
- **AAA Best Chair Rentals** (212/929-8888) offers excellent prices on chair rentals, china, and silverware.

BALOOMS
147 Sullivan St (bet Prince and Houston St)   212/673-4007
Mon-Fri: 10-6; Sat: 12-6; Sun: available for parties

Balooms is a small balloon store that encourages browsing. In addition to balloon bouquets, they offer party decorating and custom-designed bouquets with names and logos. Delivery is available in Manhattan and the boroughs. The store also rents helium tanks. As befits this lighthearted business, owner Marlyne Berger is delightful.

BLAIR McMILLEN   917/334-6488
www.blairmcmillen.com

Look no further if you are seeking top-notch piano entertainment. Blair McMillen is an extremely talented and personable concert pianist, having performed for President Clinton, Mikhail Gorbachev, and the Japanese Royal family. McMillen, a Julliard School graduate, will work with other musicians. Flexible in style, he is adept at Broadway, pop, New Age, Latin, and jazz standards, although classical piano is his first love.

BUBBY GRAM
60 E 8th St (at Broadway)   212/353-3886
Daily (by phone): 10-9   www.bubbygram.com

If creating fun and laughter is on your mind, call this number. These folks have outrageous and humorous acts that run from simple singing telegrams to complete shows for parties or business meetings. They'll provide celebrity impersonators, magicians, psychics, bellydancers, and entertainment for kids.

ECLECTIC ENCORE
620 W 26th St (at Eleventh Ave)   212/645-8880
Mon-Fri: 9-5   www.eclecticprops.com

Their name says it all. Eclectic Encore specializes in hard-to-find props for a party at home, a set for motion pictures or television, or a novel product announcement. They have been in business since 1986 and are known for an extensive collection of 18th-, 19th- and 20th-century furniture and accessories. You can find everything from an armoire to a zebra—even one of those cakes from which a scantily clad lady pops out.

EXPRESSWAY MUSIC & EVENTS
104 E 40th St (bet Park and Lexington Ave), Suite 106   212/953-9367
By appointment   www.expresswaymusic.com

If you are interested in entertainment for any kind of personal or business event, give these folks a call. Their artists include the Expressway Music Jazz Trio (modern jazz), and the Professionals (a six-piece band that plays 1970s disco, rock, dance music, swing, jazz, and more). Other ensembles include chamber music, duets, trios, and quartets (for weddings, cocktail hours, and other events) and a steel drum band with up to seven pieces. David Swirsky is the director.

HIGHLY EVENTFUL
11 Fifth Ave (at 8th St), Suite 7C   212/777-3565
Daily: 10-6   www.highlyeventful.com

Since 1994, Highly Eventful has been arranging events in New York and throughout the world. These folks take charge of everything, including food, liquor, equipment rentals, tents, flowers, lighting, music, and trained personnel. They will secure prime locations, such as grand ballrooms, churches (like the Cathedral Church of St. John the Divine), museums (like the Metropolitan), and yachts.

LINDA KAYE'S BIRTHDAYBAKERS, PARTYMAKERS
195 E 76th St (bet Lexington and Third Ave)   212/288-7112
Mon-Fri: 9:30-6; parties can be scheduled for any day
                                                   www.partymakers.com

Linda Kaye offers children's birthday parties at two of Manhattan's most desirable locations: the Central Park Wildlife Center and the American Museum of Natural History. Wildlife Center parties are for children from one to ten years old. Themes include Animal Alphabet Safari, Animal Olympics, Safari Treasure Hunt, and Mystery Movie Making. The Natural History parties are for children four and up, with such themes as Dinosaur Discovery, Cosmic Blast-Off, Underwater Treasure, and Safari Adventure. Linda Kaye's website serves as a resource and shopping site for birthday party needs, listing entertainers and party locations. Partymakers also specializes in creative custom cakes (including a pop-out cake) and unique corporate events.

Are you tired of cooking or perhaps planning a big party? Here are some of the best personal chefs in New York:

Belinda Clarke (212/253-6408)
Bill Feldman (212/983-2952)
Jayson Grossberg (917/414-1947)
Michael Yang (718/380-1149)

The **United States Personal Chef Association** (800/995-2138, www.uspca.com) can provide more names.

MARCY BLUM ASSOCIATES
259 W 11th St (bet 4th and Bleecker St)   212/929-9814
By appointment only

What a great lady! Marcy is so well organized that no matter what the event—wedding, reception, birthday party, bar mitzvah, or dinner for the boss—she will execute it to perfection. As anyone knows, it's the details that count, and Marcy is superb at the nitty-gritty. She has organized many celebrity weddings.

PARTY POOPERS
98-100 Greenwich St (bet Carlisle and Rector St), 4th floor
Call ahead   212/274-9955 (party planning)
                                           212/587-0734 (supplies)
                                           www.partypoopers.com

Party Poopers is a group of entertainers who never throw the same party twice. Offering some of the best private party rooms in New York, they handle setup, clean-up, and entertainment, allowing parents to sit back and relax. Themes include fairytales, superheroes, game shows, dance parties, murder mysteries, or anything else you can dream up. They also have costume characters, magicians, and other party entertainers. The online store carries favors, paper goods, balloons, theme packs, and gifts.

PROPS FOR TODAY
330 W 34th St (bet Eighth and Ninth Ave)   212/244-9600
Mon-Fri: 8:30-5   www.propsfortoday.com

This is the handiest place in town when you are planning a party. Props for Today has the largest rental inventory of home decorations in New York, allowing you to distinguish your events with unique decor. Whether you want everyday china and silver or unique antiques, they've got the goods. There are platters, vases, tablecloths, and much more. They have a Christmas section, children's items, books, fireplace equipment, artwork, garden furniture, foreign items, and ordinary kitchenware. Over a million items are available! Phone orders are taken, but I'd recommend checking out the three floors of inventory for yourself.

Pen and Lighter Repair

AUTHORIZED REPAIR SERVICE
30 W 57th St (bet Fifth Ave and Ave of the Americas), 2nd floor
Mon-Fri: 8:30-5 (Wed till 6); Sat: 10-3:30   212/586-0947
www.shavers.com, www.vintagelighters.com

After more than four decades, this outfit remains incredibly busy, perhaps because it is almost without competition. Those who use fountain pens or are interested in vintage pens or lighters (vintage and new) are devoted customers. Authorized Repair services nearly every brand and is the national service center for Alfred Dunhill, Ltd. They repair electric shavers, too! Numerous lines of pens and lighters are sold at discount. Travelers headed overseas can pick up 220-volt appliances and adapter plugs. The polite and helpful staff is well versed in the fine points of each brand.

FOUNTAIN PEN HOSPITAL
10 Warren St (bet Broadway and Church St)
Mon-Fri: 8-6   212/964-0580, 800/253-7367
www.fountainpenhospital.com

Located across from City Hall, this experienced establishment sells and repairs fountain pens of all types. It also carries one of the world's largest selections of modern and vintage writing tools.

Personal Services

A. E. JOHNSON EMPLOYMENT AGENCY
380 Lexington Ave (at 42nd St), Suite 3810   212/644-0990
Mon-Fri: 9-5   www.aejohnsonagency.com

Dating from 1890, Johnson is the oldest licensed employment agency in the U.S. dealing exclusively with household help. They specialize in providing affluent clients with highly qualified butlers, cooks, housekeepers, chauffeurs, bodyguards, nannies, personal assistants, valets, maids, and couples. Both temporary and permanent workers are available, many on a moment's notice. Employment references, criminal records, and drivers' licenses are checked by an independent firm.

AL MARTINO'S CHEFS INTERNATIONAL
60 E 42nd St (bet Park and Madison Ave), Suite 2227
Mon-Fri: 9-5   212/867-1910
www.chefinternational.com

Since 1972 this outfit has been providing top-notch help, including butlers and personal assistants. They can also send out highly qualified chefs, sous chefs, cooks, and bartenders for private homes or businesses. Yes, they are a bit pricey, but it is worth it to have good people.

Here is a first-class way to see this great city! James Smythe's **My Kind of Town New York** (212/754-4500, www.mykindoftownny.com) offers private and personalized custom tours of the area in a Mercedes-Benz sedan for one to four guests. Special arrangements can be made for larger groups.

BIG APPLE GREETER
1 Centre St (at Chambers St)   212/669-8159
Office: Mon-Fri: 9-5
By appointment (available daily)   www.bigapplegreeter.org

Big Apple Greeter volunteers from all five boroughs meet families or individuals—up to six people in all—to show them New York City through the eyes of a native. On visits of two to four hours, Greeters use public transportation or travel on foot to see neighborhoods and the city's hidden treasures. There are more than 350 volunteer Greeters, and they speak over 30 languages between them. They are matched with visitors by language, interest, and neighborhoods requested by the visitor. This service is free of charge, and tipping is not permitted. Three to four weeks advance notice is required. It is like having a new friend show you the wonders of the city!

CELEBRITIES STAFFING SERVICES
198 Broadway (bet John and Fulton St), Suite 706   212/227-3877
Mon-Fri: 9-6   www.celebrities-staffing.com

This is a handy firm to know about! They have a good track record for finding the best baby nurses, nannies, "mannies" (male nannies), housekeepers, ladies' maids, butlers and housemen, chefs, couples, house managers, personal assistants, personal shoppers, chauffeurs, caregivers, and other types of personnel. Not surprisingly, bodyguards are one of the more popular service categories.

COLUMBIA BARTENDING AGENCY
70-74 Morningside Dr (bet 116th and 117th St)   212/854-4537
Mon-Fri: 10-4   www.columbia.edu/cu/ccs/bartending

Columbia Bartending Agency (part of the Columbia University School of

Mixology) uses students who are so expert at bartending that one wonders what profession they could possibly do as well after college. The service has been around a long time, and there is none better. They'll advise you on liquor, mixers, garnishes, and recipes for your party. Columbia also supplies waiters, waitresses, and coat checkers.

CROSS IT OFF YOUR LIST
915 Broadway (at 21st St)   212/725-0122
Mon-Fri: 9-7 (or by appointment)   www.crossitoffyourlist.com

Cross It Off Your List can help you do just that! These folks will do just about anything to help busy people: Organize closets and file cabinets, manage a move, help with daily chores, plan trips, pack bags, and take care of mail.

DOMESTICITY
307 Ave of the Americas (at 2nd St), Room 2R
Brooklyn   718/768-3040
Daily: 9-9

You will want to become friends with owner Katherine Hammond. Her design and organizing team will help improve your home environment. They can do just about anything associated with in-home styling and decorating, including such chores as putting up a Christmas tree and wrapping gifts. Stylists can locate anything you desire, do home designs, and create a "scene" for a special occasion.

EMILY CHO
By appointment   201/816-8530

Emily Cho's job is to make her clients "look and feel terrific!" She has been a clothing psychologist for nearly three decades. The process begins with an in-depth interview at your home or hotel, where your wardrobe is reviewed. She will organize your existing wardrobe, do extensive research for ideal new additions, and then escort you on a fun personal shopping spree. Emily finds new resources every year, and she promises to stay within a client's budget. Corporate services and an intensive two-day course in personal image consulting are also available. This talented professional has written four books and appeared several times on *Oprah*.

ETIQUETTE PROFESSIONNELLE
337 E 54th St (bet Second and First Ave)   212/751-1653
Call for appointment

Did you know that showing the sole of your shoe while crossing your legs is an insult in the Middle East? You'll learn this and much more from Jacqueline Baertschi, who teaches the fine points of manners and comportment in the international business community. Classes are available for children and members of the hospitality industry.

> Have you grown tired of that closet? **California Closets** (1625 York Ave, 212/517-7877) will reorganize that dreary space and even paint it!

FASHION UPDATE

Mon-Fri: 9-5   718/377-8873, 888/447-2846
                                               www.fashionupdate.com

Sarah Gardner is a mother of three who wants the most value for every clothing dollar spent. Gardner found she could buy apparel for her family at wholesale prices from some manufacturers, so she decided to share her discoveries. She started *Fashion Update,* a quarterly publication that uncovers over 250 bargains per season in women's, men's, and children's designer clothing, accessories, and jewelry. Furniture, home accessories, and restaurants, too! She conducts shopping expeditions to designer showrooms at $175 per person for 2½ hours.

FLATIRON CLEANING COMPANY

230 E 93rd St (at Second Ave)   212/876-1000
Mon-Fri: 7:30-4:30   www.flatironcleaning.com

Can you imagine how many homes and apartments these people have cleaned since opening for business in 1893? Expert services include residential house and window cleaning, installing and refinishing wood floors, and maid service. You might call the Rockefellers for references!

FLOOD'S CLOSET

By appointment   212/348-7257

Want to be pampered? Barbara Flood will shop for or with you. She can even bring items to consider to your home. To top it off, she'll also help with closets, clothes, jewelry, decor, and other time-consuming chores.

IN TOWN RUN-A-ROUND

Mon-Fri: 9-6:30; Sat: by appointment   917/359-6688
                                               www.intownrunaround.com

Owner Henry Goldstein is the man to contact if you don't have the time or desire to bring back a piece of jewelry from Rome, shop for groceries, or find a venue for your parents' 50th anniversary. These pleasant, efficient, and reliable folks will even wait in your apartment for a repairman!

INTREPID NEW YORKER

220 E 57th St (bet Second and Third Ave), Room 2D
Mon-Fri: 9-5   212/750-0400
                                               www.intrepidny.com

Like your author, Tory Masters delights in helping folks unravel the hassles and confusion of this great city. She provides one of the most complete services in this area and is available at any time. A corporate relocation service for people moving within a 75-mile radius is available.

LET MILLIE DO IT!

By appointment   212/535-1539

Millie Emory is a real problem solver! She has worked for decades as a professional organizer, saving people time, money, and stress. Millie especially likes working for theatrical folks, but she can help anyone with a broad variety of tasks. She will organize and unclutter apartments, desks, files, closets, libraries, attics, basements, garages, and storage rooms. She will also pay bills, balance checkbooks, and get papers in order for a tax accountant or IRS audit. She can help with paper flow, time management, and space problems. Millie is also good at finding antiques and out-of-print books and records. She assists seniors in dismantling their homes before entering nursing facilities. When a loved one dies, Millie will handle estate liquidations, sales, and donations, leaving the space "broom clean."

LIGHTEN UP! FREE YOURSELF FROM CLUTTER
Call for appointment   877/373-3376
www.freefromclutter.com, www.estateresolutionservices.com

Michelle Passoff, the genius behind this operation, calls New York City "the clutter capital of the world." Lighten Up is a service for people who want to free themselves from all the clutter in their lives and develop new habits. Being very much an "unclutterer" myself, I think Michelle offers a useful service in handling trash flow and all that goes with it. She offers private consultations, classes, workshops, training, lectures for organizations and corporations, and an instructional program on tape and DVD. A new program called "Estate Organization and Resolution Service" provides assistance to heirs, executors, and attorneys in organizing the estate of the deceased.

Make room in your BlackBerry or Rolodex for Linda Siegal at **New York Concierge** (212/751-8591). Dinner reservations, theater tickets, events for groups from 50 to 500—Linda can get it all done!

NEW YORK CELEBRITY ASSISTANTS (NYCA)
459 Columbus Ave, Suite 216   212/803-5444
New York, NY 10024 (mailing address only)
www.nycelebrityassistants.org

Are you in need of a professional assistant? This outfit is comprised of current and former assistants to top celebrities in film, TV, theater, music, sports, philanthropy, fashion, business, and politics. NYCA provides educational forums, networking opportunities, and employment referrals.

NEW YORK'S LITTLE ELVES
151 First Ave, Suite 204   212/673-5507
New York, NY 10017
Office: Daily: 7:30-6
Call for appointment

Just finish a construction or remodeling job? Is the place a mess? If you need some elves to clean up, this is the outfit to call. They provide estimates, employ screened personnel, carry liability insurance, are fully bonded, and have an outstanding reputation. The "elves" will also help set up for a party and return afterwards to put your home or apartment back in shape.

PAVILLION AGENCY
15 E 40th St (bet Fifth and Madison Ave), Suite 400   212/889-6609
Mon-Fri: 9-5   www.pavillionagency.com

Pavillion has been a family-owned and -operated business for 40 years. If you are in need of nannies, housekeepers, laundresses, couples, butlers, major-domos, chefs, chauffeurs, security personnel, caretakers, gardeners, property managers, or personal assistants, call and ask for Keith or Clifford Greenhouse. Applicants are screened by a private investigation firm.

RED BALL
221 E 85th St (bet Second and Third Ave)   212/861-7686
Mon-Fri: 8-5:30

These people have cleaned a lot of windows since opening in 1928! Still a family business, they specialize in residential and commercial window cleaning. The higher the windows, the happier they are.

If you are interested in astrology, the lady to contact is **Susan Miller** (917/833-2480). Business consulting and strategizing are specialties.

SAVED BY THE BELL
11 Riverside Dr (bet 73rd and 74th St)   212/874-5457
Mon-Fri: 9-7 (or by appointment)

Susan Bell's goal is to take the worry out of planning and carrying out virtually any type of job for people who are too busy or need help. Bell says "doing the impossible is our specialty," and you can believe her. Specialties include weddings, fundraising and charity benefits, party planning, tag sales, relocations, shopping, delivery arrangements, and service referrals.

SMARTSTART
334 W 86th St (bet West End Ave and Riverside Dr)   212/580-7365
By appointment only

There is always someone in New York to fill a special niche or need. Such a person is Susan Weinberg. She learned from experience that many expectant mothers and fathers are too busy to plan for the arrival of their little bundle of joy. So she started Smartstart, a consulting service to aid parents in pulling everything together. Her service helps provide the basic things a newborn will need, as well as interior design, storage creation, gifts, and personal shopping. In addition, Susan sells hand-painted children's furniture—everything from table and chair sets to coat hooks and toy chests. Custom cabinet work is a specialty. She is truly the stork's number-one assistant!

TALKPOWER
333 E 23rd St (bet First and Second Ave)   212/684-1711
Mon-Fri: 9-5   www.talkpowerinc.com

Do you know that speaking in front of a group is the single most feared experience? If you suffer from this phobia, give these folks a call. They are true professionals who train clients to make public appearances. Personal or group sessions are available for intensive weekends. They now offer a "Golf Power" program to enhance golfers' concentration.

UNAME IT ORGANIZERS
226 E 10th St (bet First and Second Ave), Suite 222   212/598-9868
Daily: 24 hours   www.masterorganizers.com

Eleni Marudis claims, "As long as it is legal, we will do it!" They perform more than 200 personal services, from uncluttering your home or office to finding a soulmate. They locate apartments and can even track down a plumber on Christmas Eve. In the crowded field of organizers, uName It has been in business for nearly two decades, which means they're doing something right.

Oreck Clean Home Center (2003 Broadway, 212/875-0002) is devoted entirely to keeping your abode clean and healthy. We're not just talking vacuum cleaners, either!

WHITE GLOVE ELITE
39 W 32nd St (bet Fifth Avenue and Broadway), Room 900
Mon-Fri: 8-8; Sat: 9-3; Sun: 10-2 (cleaners available anytime)
212/684-4460
www.whitegloveelite.com

Actors Sarah and Jim Ireland started this business as an adjunct to their stage careers. They provide trained cleaners for apartments in Manhattan, the Bronx, Brooklyn, and Queens. About half of their cleaners are also actors between jobs.

ZOE INTERNATIONAL
198 Broadway (bet John and Fulton St), Suite 706   212/227-3880
Mon-Fri: 9-5; 24-hour emergency service   www.zoehomecare.com

This agency specializes in the placement of nurses and nurses' aides, home health and personal care aides, companions, and housekeepers to work for the elderly, sick, and chronically ill. They work closely with doctors, hospitals, health-care organizations, family members, friends, attorneys, estate planners, and others involved in a patient's life. Caregivers are available for live-in or live-out and can work day or night shifts or provide 24-hour service. Specially priced packages are available for families on fixed incomes. This is a valuable service to consider.

Dirty windows? Call **Frank's Window Cleaning Company** (212/288-4631).

Photographic Services

DEMETRIAD CREATIVE MEDIA
1674 Broadway (at 52nd St), 4th floor   212/315-3400
Mon-Fri: 9-7   www.demetriad.com

These folks were trained as commercial photographers and have parlayed their expertise into portrait and head-shot photography, as well as digital and document system imaging and restoration of old and damaged photographs. They are pros at retouching, making a copy negative when the original is missing, and doing quantity work at special prices. Developing and processing are hand-done.

HAND HELD FILMS
315 W 36th St (bet Eighth and Ninth Ave), Room 2E   212/502-0900
Mon-Fri: 9-6   www.handheldfilms.com

Hand Held Films rents motion picture equipment for feature films, commercials, music videos, and documentaries. Avid media composers and digital video cameras are also available. You can be assured of finding the latest equipment, lenses, and "toys," including lighting and digital editing.

Relatives coming to visit? Need pictures framed today? One-hour framing service is available at **O.J. Art Gallery** (920 Third Ave, 212/754-0123; Mon-Sat: 10-7; Sun: 12-5).

PHOTOGRAPHICS UNLIMITED / DIAL-A-DARKROOM
17 W 17th St (bet Fifth Ave and Ave of the Americas), 4th floor
Mon-Thurs: 9 a.m.-l0 p.m.; Fri, Sat: 9-7; Sun: noon-7
212/255-9678

Here's another only-in-New York idea. Photographics Unlimited offers photographers a full range of darkroom equipment and rental workspace. The shop has everything from the simplest equipment to an 8x10 Saltzman enlarger, as well as a lab for developing black-and-white and color photographs. They carry all kinds of printing paper and film supplies, and they also do custom processing and printing. Ed Lee claims his center is equipped to meet the needs of amateurs and advanced professional photographers alike. A hotline is available to answer technical questions. Digital camera work is a small part of their operation.

VISKO HATFIELD
Mon-Fri: 9-5   212/979-9322, 917/544-9300
                                          www.vhpictures.com

Visko offers an opportunity to have a truly one-of-a-kind portrait done by a talented photographer. He has captured images of celebrities from the literary, fashion, art, and sports scenes. You could be next!

Plumbing and Heating

KAPNAG HEATING AND PLUMBING
150 W 28th St (at Seventh Ave), Suite 501   212/929-7111

When a reliable plumber and/or heating expert is needed, you can't do better than this outfit. They handle plumbing renovations for kitchens and bathrooms, replace toilets, repair pipes and heating equipment, and more. Two dozen highly qualified workers have kept Kapnag at the top since 1935.

Portraits

CATHERINE STOCK
Mid-October through mid-May by appointment   212/534-8941
                                                   www.catherinestock.com

Catherine Stock has quite a life, dividing her time between France and

New York. She is one of the best children's portrait artists. Stock usually paints in watercolor, requiring just one sitting. Stock's portraits are represented at **Magic Windows** (1186 Madison Ave, 212/289-0028), a children's boutique.

Relocation

BROWN HARRIS STEVENS
Numerous locations   917/825-4195
Call for appointment   www.brownharrisstevens.com/agent

If you want action and expertise in the real estate world, call relocation expert Shelley Saxton, who specializes in sales and high-end leasing. She is helpful with a wide array of properties, and rental clients swear by her. Shelley is a member of both the Real Estate Board of New York and also RELO, the largest network of independent residential real estate firms.

Scissors and Knife Sharpening

HENRY WESTPFAL CO, INC.
107 W 30th St (bet Ave of the Americas and Seventh Ave)
Mon-Fri: 9:30-6:30   212/563-5990

The same family has been running Henry Westpfal since 1874. They do all kinds of sharpening and repair, from barber scissors and pruning shears to cuticle scissors. They'll also work on light tools. Tools for leather workers, cutlery, shears, and scissors are sold here. They even sell lefthanded scissors!

Shipping and Packaging

THE UPS STORE
800/Pick-UPS (information and nearest location)
www.theupsstore.com

The UPS Store has over 40 locations in New York, offering professional packaging and shipping jobs. Handy services—not all of them available at every location—include copying and printing, faxing, private mailboxes, mail forwarding, business cards, office stationery, notary and secretarial work, passport photos, laminating, rubber stamps, engraving, key duplication, computer-generated letters, and money transfers. They also sell stamps, office supplies, boxes, and packing supplies.

THE PADDED WAGON
1431 York Ave (bet 75th and 76st St)   212/327-0822
Mon-Fri: 9-7; Sat: 9-4

1569 Second Ave (bet 81st and 82nd St)   212/570-5500
Mon-Fri: 9-7; Sat: 9-4; Sun: 12-5

For giftwrapping help, these are the places to visit. The Padded Wagon carries all sizes of boxes and paper, moving supplies, and tape, and they provide UPS and FedEx service. They also offer moving and storage service.

UNITED SHIPPING & PACKAGING
200 E 10th St (at Second Ave)   212/475-2214
Mon-Fri: 10:30-8; Sat: 11-6   www.uspnyc.com

United Shipping will send anything anywhere in the world! They also sell
packaging supplies and boxes. Additional services include faxing, mailboxes,
office supplies, messenger services, and small moves within the city.

For a place to store art, furniture, records, or whatever, try **Sofia
Storage Centers** (475 Amsterdam Ave, 139 Franklin St, and 4396
Broadway; 212/873-0700). They have been family owned since 1910.

Shoe Repair

B. NELSON SHOE CORPORATION
1221 Ave of the Americas (at 49th St), Level C-2
Mon-Fri: 7:30-5   212/869-3552, 800/750-7669
                                                        www.bnelsonshoes.com

B. Nelson is very good at repairing high-grade dress, leisure, and athletic
shoes. They have performed factory-method resoling for over a century. If
your Birkenstocks need repair, this is the place. Prices are excellent and over-
the-counter prices are even cheaper than online. Service is terrific, and their
client list is tops.

JIM'S SHOE REPAIR
50 E 59th St (bet Madison and Park Ave)   212/355-8259
Mon-Fri: 8-6; Sat: 9-4; closed Sat in summer

This operation offers first-rate shoe repair, shoeshine, and shoe supplies.
The shoe repair field is rapidly losing its craftsmen, and this is one of the few
shops that upholds the tradition. Owner Joseph A. Rocco specializes in ortho-
pedic shoe and boot alterations.

TOP SERVICE
845 Seventh Ave (bet 54th and 55th St)   212/765-3190
Mon-Fri: 8-6; Sat: 9-3

Shoe repair is the main business at Top Service, but there is much more.
Dance shoes are a specialty, and this source is used by many Broadway theater groups. In addition, they will cut keys, engrave anything, do luggage and
handbag repair, clean suede, and dye and clean shoes. This is a great place to
keep in mind for last minute emergencies.

Silver Repair

BRANDT & OPIS
46 W 46th St (bet Fifth Ave and Ave of the Americas), 5th floor
Mon-Thurs: 8-5; Fri: 8-2   212/302-0294

If it has to do with silver, Roland Markowitz at Brandt & Opis can handle
it. This includes silver repair and polishing, buying and selling estate silver,
repairing and replating silver-plated items, and fixing silver tea and coffee

services. They restore combs and brushes (dresser sets), and replace old knife blades. Other services include gold-plating, lamp restoration, and plating antique bath and door hardware. In short, Brandt & Opis are complete metal restoration specialists.

THOME SILVERSMITHS
49 W 37th St (bet Fifth Ave and Ave of the Americas), 4th floor
Wed, Thurs: 10-5   212/764-5426

Thome cleans, repairs, and replates silver. They also buy and sell some magnificent pieces. They have a real appreciation for the material, and it shows in everything they do. They will restore antique silver and objets d'art, repair and polish brass and copper, and repair and clean pewter. Thome can do silver- and gold-plating. They'll even restore the velvet backs of picture frames and velvet box linings.

Stained Glass Restoration

VICTOR ROTHMAN FOR STAINED GLASS
57 Nepperhan Ave (at Lake Ave), Yonkers
                                    212/255-2551, 914/969-0919

With over 30 years experience, this studio specializes in museum-quality stained-glass restoration, from residences to churches and public buildings. Consultation is provided, and specification reports are prepared for professional and private use. Stained-glass windows can be designed and fabricated.

Custom tailoring is a luxury few can afford. If you want to splurge, here are several of the best in Manhattan:

Bruno Cosentino (711 Fifth Ave, 212/753-9292): English-Italian style
William Fioravanti (45 W 57th St, 212/355-1540)
John Green (24 E 71st St, 212/861-9611): The fit is magnificent.
Lianna Lee (828 Lexington Ave, 212/588-9289): British power suits by a woman
Leonard Logsdail (9 E 53rd St, 212/752-5030)
Tony Maurizio (18 E 53rd St, 5th floor, 212/759-3230)
Domenico Spano (Saks Fifth Avenue, 611 Fifth Ave, 6th floor, 212/940-2676): "Mimmo" is a legend, just like the store.
Domenico Vacca (781 Fifth Ave, 212/759-6333): He will do good things for your figure.

Tailors

BHAMBI'S CUSTOM TAILORS
14 E 60th St (bet Fifth and Madison Ave), Room 610   212/935-5379
Mon-Sat: 9-7   www.bhambis.com

With notice, this firm can cut suits in as little as two weeks. They have been in business for over 35 years and have developed an excellent reputation. Next-day alterations and hand-stitching on suits are specialties.

Choose from hundreds of bolts of cloth by such makers as Ermengildo Zenga, Cerruti, Dormeuil, Holland & Sherry, Loro Piana, and more.

If you have seen some sensational garment modeled on a fashion runway but cannot afford the exorbitant designer prices, here are some suggestions on where to go for copies. These houses usually quote prices from 20% to 60% less than the originals! Call for appointments.

Atelier Eva Devecsery (201 E 61st St, 212/751-6091): alterations and custom work

Dynasty Custom Tailor (6 E 38th St, 212/679-1075)

Euroco (247 W 30th St, 212/629-9665): Much of their work is for Broadway shows.

Ghost Tailor (153 W 27th St, 11th floor, 212/253-9727)

PEPPINO TAILORS
780 Lexington Ave (at 60th St)   212/832-3844
Mon-Fri: 9-6:30; Sat: 9-4

Joseph Peppino is a fine craftsman who has been in the tailoring field for over a quarter of a century. All types of garments, including evening wear, receive his expert attention for alterations. Delivery is offered.

SEBASTIAN TAILORS
767 Lexington Ave (at 60th St), Room 404   212/688-1244
Mon-Fri: 8:30-5:30; Sat 9-4

Tailors are a vanishing breed in New York. In a city that is the home of the garment industry, most professionals who repair garments call themselves "custom alteration and design specialists," or else they're dry cleaners who mend bedraggled outfits that have been brought in for cleaning. Sebastian Tailors is one of the few true tailor shops left in the city. Custom alterations for men and women are quick, neat, and reasonable. Sebastian also does reweaving. Best of all, everything is accomplished without the usual ballyhoo most such establishments seem to regard as their due.

We all know about those unfortunate spills on the carpet. No worry, just call **ID Carpet Cleaners** (212/645-8027, www.idcleaners.com). They will even treat floor coverings with flame retardant.

Translation Services

BOWNE GLOBAL SOLUTIONS
132 W 31st St (bet Ave of the Americas and Seventh Ave), 12th floor
Mon-Fri: 9-5   917/339-4700, 800/608-6088
                                              www.boglobal.com

For translations (both verbal and written) and technical writing, this is *the* place. Bowne Global Solutions can be of major help with foreign languages, including localization—i.e., creating multiple language versions of a product.

Travel Services

PASSPORT PLUS.NET
20 E 49th St (bet Fifth and Madison Ave), 3rd floor
Mon-Fri: 9:30-5   212/759-5540, 800/367-1818
                                                   www.passportplus.net

Sometimes getting a passport and the proper visas can be a real pain in the neck. Passport Plus.Net takes care of these tedious chores by securing business and tourist travel documents; renewing and amending U.S. passports; obtaining duplicate birth, death, and marriage certificates; and obtaining international driver's licenses. They work closely with the U.S. Passport Agency and Foreign Consulates and Embassies. Passport Plus.Net offers aid in the case of lost or stolen passports. These folks serve customers all over the country.

To save time and money, log onto these useful travel websites:

Expedia (800/397-3342; www.expedia.com)
Hotwire (www.hotwire.com)
Orbitz (www.orbitz.com)
Priceline (www.priceline.com)
Travelocity (888/709-5983; www.travelocity.com)

Uniform and Costume Rentals

I. BUSS-ALLAN UNIFORM RENTAL SERVICE
121 E 24th St (bet Lexington and Park Ave), 7th floor   212/529-4655
Mon-Fri: 9-5   www.ibuss-allan.com

Because most costumes are used only once, it is far less expensive to rent than buy. At this establishment you can rent any number of costumes: contemporary, period, animal, Santa Claus, and more. They also provide uniform rentals and retail.

Upholstering

RAY MURRAY
143 W 29th St (bet Ave of Americas and Seventh Ave) 212/838-3752
Mon-Fri: 9-5

Ray Murray is an Old World shop that does things the old-fashioned way. It is a very fine and expensive drapery workroom that also does upholstery. They specialize in creating classic custom-made furniture and can copy any design you want, including heirloom pieces.

VI. Where to Buy It: New York's Best Stores

Gerry's Tips for Saving When Shopping

The retail business is highly competitive these days. You'll find some good money-saving hints here:

- **Attire yourself for flea-market shopping**—Dress down.
- **Pay cash, if possible**—Better prices might be available if you do.
- **Tell the shop owner you came because of this book**—If he or she is on the ball, you might just get a special discount!
- **Price-check**—Know prices, if possible, before going to a store.
- **Comparison shop**—There can be wide price differences.
- **Read ads carefully**—Sometimes the fine print is misleading.
- **Look beyond brand names**—Many items without fancy labels are just as good.
- **Color-coordinate**—Buy outfits that can be mixed and matched.
- **Budget your dollars**—Know exactly what you can afford to spend.
- **Frequent thrift shops**—Some excellent values can be found at second-hand stores.
- **Beware of garage sales**—Be very selective, as there can be lots of junk.
- **Shop alone**—Don't let peer pressure influence you.
- **Approach price tags warily**—Be leery of a series of markdown prices, as the merchandise might be undesirable.
- **Keep receipts**—Returns are much easier.
- **Avoid seasonal buying**—Buy in the off-season, when items are less expensive.
- **Avoid impulse buying**—You may regret it later.
- **Use coupons**—They can save you big bucks.
- **Check out store shopping programs**—Good discounts for regular customers can be had.
- **Barter**—Believe it or not, haggling is still possible in many stores!

The Best Places to Shop for Specific Items in New York: An Exclusive List

Things for the Person (Men, Women, Children)

Accessories, fashion (1890-2000): **Eye Candy** (329 Lafayette St, 212/343-4275)

Accessories, women's: **Marc Jacobs Accessories** (385 Bleecker St, 212/924-6126)

Backpacks: **Bag House** (797 Broadway, 212/260-0940)

Bags, antique: **Sylvia Pines Uniquities** (1102-B Lexington Ave, 212/744-5141)

Boots, comfort and fashion: **Lord John's Bootery** (428 Third Ave, 212/532-2579)

Boots and shoes, men's handmade: **E. Vogel Boots and Shoes** (19 Howard St, 212/925-2460)

Boutique, men's: **Odin** (328 E 11th St, 212/475-0666)

Bras: **Bra Smyth** (905 Madison Ave, 212/772-9400)

Bridal gowns and accessories (expensive): **Vera Wang** (991 Madison Ave, 212/628-3400; by appointment)

Bridal gowns, used: **Michael's** (1041 Madison Ave, 212/737-7273)

Bridal wear, nontraditional: **Jane Wilson-Marquis** (130 E 82nd St, 212/452-5335; appointments preferred)

Briefcases: **Per Tutti** (37 Greenwich Ave, 212/675-0113)

Buttons: **Tender Buttons** (143 E 62nd St, 212/758-7004)

Clothing, children's (basics): **Lester's** (1534 Second Ave, 212/734-9292), **Marsha D.D.** (1574 Third Ave, 212/831-2422), and **Morris Bros.** (2322 Broadway, 212/724-0107)

Clothing, children's classic: **flora and henri** (943 Madison Ave, 212/249-1695)

Clothing, children's French: **Jacadi** (787 Madison Ave, 212/535-3200 and 1296 Madison Ave, 212/369-1616)

Clothing, children's (funky and fun): **Space Kiddets** (46 E 21st St, 212/420-9878) and **Peanutbutter & Jane** (617 Hudson St, 212/620-7952)

Clothing, children's (pricey and "Frenchy"): **Catimini** (1125 Madison Ave, 212/987-0688)

Clothing, children's, party dresses and suits: **Prince and Princess** (41 E 78th St, 212/879-8989)

Clothing, children's resale: **Jane's Exchange** (207 Ave A, 212/674-6268)

Clothing, denim: **G-Star** (270 Lafayette St, 212/219-2744)

Clothing, designer, resale: **Ina** (101 Thompson St, 212/941-4757)

Clothing, designer, sample sale: **Showroom Seven** (498 Seventh Ave, 212/643-4810; February, May, September, and December)

Clothing, hip-hop: **Mr. Joe** (500 Eighth Ave, 212/279-1090)

Clothing, imported designer: **India Cottage Emporium** (1150 Broadway, 212/685-6943)

Clothing, infants' (traditional): **Wicker Garden's Baby** (1327 Madison Ave, 212/410-7001)

Clothing, men's and boys, traditional: **Jay Kos** (986 Lexington Ave, 212/327-2382)

Clothing, men's brand-name (discounted): **L.S. Men's Clothing** (49 W 45th St, 3rd floor, 212/575-0933) and **Century 21** (22 Cortlandt St, 212/227-9092)

Clothing, men's classic: **Peter Elliot** (1070 Madison Ave, 212/570-2300)

Clothing, men's European suits: **Jodamo International** (321 Grand St, 212/219-0552)

Clothing, men's shirts, custom-made: **Arthur Gluck Shirtmaker** (47 W 57th St, 212/755-8165)

Clothing, men's shirts and suits, custom-made: **Ascot Chang** (7 W 57th St, 212/759-3333)

Clothing, men's shirts, Italian (great prices): **Acorn Shirts** (54 W 21st St, 4th floor, 212/366-1185; call ahead)

Clothing, men's tuxedo shirts and accessories (discounted): **Ted's Fine Clothing** (83 Orchard St, 212/966-2029)

Clothing, men's and women's cashmere sweaters: **Best of Scotland** (581 Fifth Ave, 212/644-0415)

Clothing, men's and women's custom-made: **Alan Flusser** (3 E 48th St, 212/888-4500)

Clothing, men's and women's custom-made (good value): **Saint Laurie Merchant Tailors** (22 W 32nd St, 5th floor, 212/643-1916)

Clothing, men's and women's designer: **Outlet Seven** (117 E 7th St, 212/529-0766)

Clothing, men's and women's raingear: **Paul & Shark** (772 Madison Ave, 212/452-9868)

Clothing, sportswear, name-brand: **Atrium** (644 Broadway, 212/473-9200)

Clothing, suits and dresses: **Blue** (137 Ave A, 212/228-7744)

Clothing, T-shirts: **Eisner Bros.** (75 Essex St, 212/475-6868)

Clothing, "tween" girls: **Betwixt** (245 W 10th St, 212/243-8590) and **Space Kiddets** (46 E 21st St, 212/614-3235)

Clothing, unusual: **Gallery of Wearable Art** (34 E 67th St, 212/425-5379)

Clothing, vintage: **Bobby 2000** (104 E 7th St, 212/674-7649), **Ellen Christine** (255 W 18th St, 212/242-2457), **Reminiscence** (50 W 23rd St, 212/243-2292), and **Resurrection Vintage Clothing** (217 Mott St, 212/625-1374)

Clothing, women's: **TG-170** (170 Ludlow St, 212/995-8660)

Clothing, women's (be careful of pricing): **S&W** (287 Seventh Ave, 718/431-2800)

Clothing, women's (funky): **Lingo** (257 W 19th St, 212/929-4676)

Clothing, women's (good prices): **Miriam Rigler** (14 W 55th St, 212/581-5519)

Clothing, women's (trendy): **Betsey Johnson** (248 Columbus Ave, 212/362-3364; 251 E 60th St, 212/319-7699; 1060 Madison Ave, 212/734-1257; and 138 Wooster St, 212/995-5048)

Clothing, women's (vintage fabrics): **D.L. Cerney** (13 E 7th St, 212/673-7033)

Clothing, women's active evening wear: **Ashley Tyler** (112 Greene St, 212-965-1110)

Clothing, women's bridal and evening wear: **Reem Acra** (14 E 60th St, 212/308-8760)

Clothing, women's classic (superior): **Yigal Azrouël** (408 W 14th St, 212/929-7525)

Clothing, women's designer (resale): **Kavanagh's** (146 E 49th St, 212/702-0152) and **New & Almost New** (166 Elizabeth St, 212/226-6677)

Clothing, women's designer sportswear (discounted): **Giselle** (143 Orchard St, 212/673-1900)

Clothing, women's dresses, evening and wedding (made-to-order): **Jane Wilson-Marquis** (130 E 82nd St, 212/452-5335)

Clothing, women's maternity (stylish): **Liz Lange Maternity** (958 Madison Ave, 212/879-2191)

Clothing, women's pants: **Theory** (230 Columbus Ave, 212/362-3676)

Clothing, women's party and wedding dresses: **Mary Adams** (138 Ludlow St, 212/473-0237)

Clothing, women's post-breast surgery: **Underneath It All** (444 E 75th St, 212/717-1976 and 160 E 34th St, 212/779-2517)

Clothing, women's sportswear (good prices): **Giselle** (143 Orchard St, 212/673-1900)

Condoms: **Condomania** (351 Bleecker St, 212/691-9442)

Cuff links: **J. Mavec** (20 E 76th St, 212/517-7665; by appointment), **Links of London** (402 West Broadway, 212/343-8024; 535 Madison Ave, 212/588-1177; and 200 Park Ave, 212/867-2580), and **Missing Link** (40 W 25th St, Room 108, basement, 212/645-6928)

Cuff links, vintage: **Deco Jewels** (131 Thompson St, 212/253-1222)

Denim, vintage: **What Comes Around Goes Around** (351 West Broadway, 212/343-9303)

Earrings: **Ted Muehling** (27 Howard St, 212/431-3825)

Eyewear (discounted): **Quality Optical** (169 E 92nd St, 212/289-2020)

Eyewear, elegant: **Vision Fashion Eyewear** (2 W 47th St, 212/421-3750) and **Morgenthal-Frederics Opticians** (944 Madison Ave, 212/744-9444; 399 West Broadway, 212/966-0099; and 699 Madison Ave, 212/838-3090)

Fabrics, decorator and upholstery: **Beckenstein Home Fabrics** (4 W 20th St, 212/475-4887)

Fabrics, decorator (discounted): **Harry Zarin** (318 Grand St, 212/925-6112)

Fabrics, designer (discounted): **B&J Fabrics** (525 Seventh Ave, 212/354-8150)

Fabrics, men's: **Beckenstein Men's Fabrics** (257 W 39th St, 212/475-6666)

Fabrics, Oriental: **New Age Designer** (38 Mott St, 212/349-0818)

Fragrances, custom-blended: **Creed** (9 Bond St, 212/228-1732; 680 Madison Ave, 212/838-2780; and 897 Madison Ave, 212/794-4480)

Furs: **G. Michael Hennessy Furs** (345 Seventh Ave, 5th floor, 212/695-7991)

Furs, fashion: **Zamir Furs** (90 W Houston St, 212/677-2332)

Gloves, custom and readymade: **La Crasia** (15 W 28th St, 4th floor, 212/803-1600)

Handbags (good value): **Fine and Klein** (119 Orchard St, 212/674-6720) and **RAFE New York** (1 Bleecker St, 212/780-9739)

Handbags (magnificent and very expensive): **Judith Leiber** (680 Madison Ave, 212/223-2999)

Handbags, custom: **Roberto Vascon** (140 W 72nd St, 212/787-9050)

Handbags, vintage: **Chelsea Girl** (63 Thompson St, 212/343-1658)

Hats: **Dae Sung** (65 W 8th St, 212/420-9745)

Hats, custom-made fur: **Lenore Marshall** (231 W 29th St, 212/947-5945)

Hats, high-end: **Eugenia Kim** (203 E 4th St, 212/674-1345)

Hats, men's: **Arnold Hatters** (535 Eighth Ave, 212/768-3781), **J.J. Hat Center** (310 Fifth Ave, 212/239-4368), **Rod Keenan** (202 W 122nd St, Suite 1, 212/678-9275), and **Young's Hat Store** (139 Nassau St, 212/964-5693)

Hats, men's (discounted): **Makin's Hats** (212 W 35th St, 212/594-6666)

Jackets, casual: **P.J. Huntsman** (36 W 44th St, 212/302-2463)

Jackets, leather: **Arizona** (91 Spring St, 212/941-7022)

Jackets, leather bomber: **Avirex** (652 Broadway, 212/254-4000)

Jeans, discounted: **O.M.G. Inc.** (546 Broadway, 212/925-9513; 476 Broadway, 212/343-1164; and 428 Broadway, 212/925-5190)

Jeans, men's and women's good quality (Dutch): **G-Star** (270 Lafayette St, 212/219-2744)

Jeans, one-of-a-kind: **Jean Shop** (435 W 14th St, 212/366-5326)

Jewelry: **Fortunoff** (681 Fifth Ave, 212/758-6660)

Jewelry, costume and travel: **Lanciani** (992 Madison Ave, 212/717-2759; 510 Madison Ave, 212/644-2852; and 826 Lexington Ave, 212/832-2092)

Jewelry, custom-designed: **Sheri Miller** (578 Fifth Ave, 212/944-2153)

Jewelry, fine: **Stuart Moore** (128 Prince St, 212/941-1023)

Jewelry, handmade: **Ten Thousand Things** (423 W 14th St, 212/352-1333)

Jewelry, Victorian: **Antique Source** (212/681-9142; by appointment)

Jewelry, vintage costume: **Deco Jewels** (131 Thompson St, 212/253-1222)

Jewels, rare and historic: **Edith Weber & Associates** (994 Madison Ave, 212/570-9668)

Leather, jackets and wallets, men's and women's: **M0851** (115 Mercer St, 212/431-3069)

Leather goods: **Dooney & Bourke** (20 E 60th St, 212/223-7444), **Il Bisonte** (120 Sullivan St, 212/966-8773), and **René Collection** (1007 Madison Ave, 212/327-3912)

Leather goods, personally tailored: **The Leather Man** (11 Christopher St, 212/243-5339)

Lingerie (discounted): **Orchard Corset** (157 Orchard St, 212/674-0786) and **Howard Sportswear** (85 Orchard St, 212/226-4307)

Lingerie, fantasy: **Agent Provocateur** (133 Mercer St, 212/965-0229)

Lingerie, fine: **Bra Smyth** (905 Madison Ave, 212/772-9400) and **37=1** (37 Crosby St, 212/226-0067)

Lingerie, sexy: **Victoria's Secret** (34 E 57th St, 212/758-5592; 1240 Third Ave, 212/717-7035; 115 Fifth Ave, 212/477-4118; 565 Broadway, 212/274-9519; and other locations)

Massage oils: **Fragrance Shop** (21 E 7th St, 212/254-8950)

Millinery, one-of-a-kind: **Kelly Christy** (212/965-0686; by appointment)

Outdoor wear: **Eastern Mountain Sports** (20 W 61st St, 212/397-4860)

Pearls: **Sanko Cultured Pearls & J. Haas, Inc** (45 W 47th St, 212/819-0585; by appointment, Mon-Fri: 9-5)

Perfume (discounted): **R.S.V. Trading** (34 W 27th St, 212/481-8651)

Perfume copies: **Essential Products** (90 Water St, 212/344-4288)

Prescriptions: **J. Leon Lascoff & Sons** (1209 Lexington Ave, 212/288-9500)

Purses, men's: **Longchamp Paris** (713 Madison Ave, 212/223-1500)

Sandals, handmade: **Jutta Neumann** (158 Allen St, 212/982-7048)

Secondhand items, unusual: **Out of the Closet Thrift Shop** (220 E 81st St, 212/472-3573)

Sewing patterns: **P&S Fabrics** (355 Broadway, 212/226-1534)

Shaving products: **The Art of Shaving** (141 E 62nd St, 212/317-8436; 373 Madison Ave, 212/986-2905; and other locations)

Shoes, adult comfort and fashion: **David Z** (655 Ave of the Americas, 212/807-8595; 556 Broadway, 212/431-5450; 384 Fifth Ave, 917/351-1484; and other locations)

Shoes, big sizes: **Tall Size Shoes** (3 W 35th St, 212/736-2060)

Shoes, bridal: **Peter Fox Shoes** (105 Thompson St, 212/431-7426)

Shoes, children's party (discounted): **Trevi Shoes** (141 Orchard St, 212/505-0293)

Shoes, children's upscale: **East Side Kids** (1298 Madison Ave, 212/360-5000), **Harry's Shoes** (2299 Broadway, 212/874-2035), and **Shoofly** (42 Hudson St, 212/406-3270)

Shoes (discounted): **DSW** (40 E 14th St, 212/674-2146) and **Stapleton Shoe Company** (68 Trinity Pl, 212/964-6329)

Shoes, men's and women's (good value): **Co-Pilot** (654 Broadway, 212/475-1592)

Shoes, men's and women's custom-made: **Oberle Custom Shoes/Mathias Bootmaker** (1502 First Ave, 212/717-4023)

Shoes, men's and women's sneakers (discounted): **Shoe City** (120 Nassau St, 212/732-3889)

Shoes, non-leather: **MooShoes** (152 Allen St, 212/254-6512)

Shoes, sneakers, limited edition: **Alife Rivington Club** (158 Rivington St, 212/375-8128)

Shoes, walking: **Hogan** (134 Spring St, 212/343-7905)

Shoes, women's small sizes: **Giordano's** (1150 Second Ave, 212/688-7195)

Soaps: **Fresh** (57 Spring St, 212/925-0099)

Swimwear, men's and boys': **Vilebrequin** (1070 Madison Ave, 212/650-0353 and 436 West Broadway, 212/431-0673)

Swimwear, women's: **Eres** (621 Madison Ave, 212/223-3550 and 98 Wooster St, 212/431-7300), **Malia Mills Swimwear** (199 Mulberry St, 212/625-2311; 1031 Lexington Ave, 212/517-7485; and 220 Columbus Ave, 212/874-7200), and **Wolford** (122 Greene St, 212/343-0808)

Ties, custom-made and limited edition: **Seigo** (1248 Madison Ave, 212/987-0191)

Umbrellas: **Brella Bar** (248 Elizabeth St, 212/625-3133)

Uniforms, medical and housekeeping: **Ja-Mil Uniforms** (92 Orchard St, 212/677-8190)

Watchbands: **George Paul Jewelers** (1023 Third Ave, 212/838-7660)

Watches: **G. Wrublin Co.** (134 W 25th St, 212/929-8100), **Movado** (610 Fifth Ave, 212/218-7555), and **Swatch** (640 Broadway, 212/777-1002)

Watches (discounted): **Yaeger Watch** (578 Fifth Ave, 212/819-0088) and **Foto Electric Supply/Etronics** (37 Essex St, 212/673-5222)

Watches, Swiss Army: **Swiss Army Soho** (136 Prince St, 212/965-5714)

Wedding rings: **Wedding Ring Originals** (674 Lexington Ave, 212/751-3940)

Wigs: **Theresa Wigs and Eyelashes** (217 E 60th St, 212/486-1693)

Yard goods: **P&S Fabrics** (355 Broadway, 212/226-1534)

Yarns, luxury: **String** (1015 Madison Ave, 212/288-9276)

Zippers: **Feibusch** (27 Allen St, 212/226-3964)

Things for the Home

Accessories (high end): **Etro** (720 Madison Ave, 212/317-9096)

Air conditioners: **Elgot Sales** (937 Lexington Ave, 212/879-1200)

Appliances (discounted): **Bloom and Krup** (504 E 14th St, 212/673-2760), **Kaufman Electrical Appliances** (365 Grand St, 212/475-8313), **Price Watchers** (800/336-6694), and **LVT Price Quote Hotline** (888/225-5588 and 631/234-8884)

Appliances (for use abroad): **Appliances & Video Overseas** (246 Eighth Ave, 3rd floor, 212/924-2604)

Appliances, kitchen: **Gringer & Sons** (29 First Ave, 212/475-0600) and **Zabar's** (2245 Broadway, 212/787-2000)

Art (great prices): **Miriam Rigler** (14 W 55th St, 212/581-5519)

Art, American Indian: **Common Ground** (113 W 10th St, 212/989-4178 and 55 W 16th St, 212/620-3122)

Art, ancient Greek, Roman, and Near Eastern: **Royal Athena Galleries** (153 E 57th St, 212/355-2033)

Art, antique Oriental: **Imperial Oriental Art** (790 Madison Ave, 212/717-5383)

Art deco, French: **Maison Gerard** (53 E 10th St, 212/674-7611)

Art, decorative: **Susan P. Meisel Decorative Arts** (141 Prince St, 212/254-0137)

Art, erotic: **Erotics Gallery** (41 Union Sq W, Suite 1011, 212/633-2241; by appointment)

Art, 19th- and 20th-century Western: **J.N. Bartfield Galleries** (30 W 57th St, 212/245-8890)

Art, pop: **Pop Shop** (292 Lafayette St, 212/219-2784)

Art, pre-Columbian: **Lands Beyond** (1218 Lexington Ave, 212/249-6275)

Art, 20th-century American and European: **Timothy Baum** (212/879-4512)

Artifacts: **Jacques Carcanagues** (21 Greene St, 212/925-8110)

Bakeware (discounted): **Broadway Panhandler** (477 Broome St, 212/966-3434)

Baking supplies: **New York Cake & Baking Distributor** (56 W 22nd St, 212/675-2253)

Baskets: **Bill's Flower Market** (816 Ave of the Americas, 212/889-8154)

Baskets, fruit: **Macres** (41 W 58th St, 212/832-9800 and 30 E 30th St, 212/246-1600)

Bath and bed items: **Bed Bath & Beyond** (620 Ave of the Americas, 212/255-3550 and 410 E 61st St, 646/215-4702)

Bath fixtures (expensive): **Boffi** (31½ Greene St, 212/431-8282)

Beds: **Charles P. Rogers** (55 W 17th St, 212/675-4400)

Beds, Murphy: **Murphy Bed Center** (20 W 23rd St, 2nd floor, 212/645-7079)

Beds, sofa: **Avery-Boardman** (979 Third Ave, 212/688-6611)

Boxes, wooden: **An American Craftsman Galleries** (60 W 50th St, 212/307-7161)

Candles: **Candle Shop** (118 Christopher St, 212/989-0148)

Carpets, antique: **Art Treasury** (212/722-1235; by appointment)

Chairs, luxury massage: **Family Inada** (7 W 56th St, 212/582-8787)

Chandeliers, vintage Italian: **The Lively Set** (33 Bedford St, 212/807-8417)

China, Amari: **Bardith** (901 Madison Ave, 212/737-3775)

China, bargain pieces: **Fishs Eddy** (889 Broadway, 212/420-9020 and 2176 Broadway, 212/873-8819)

Christmas decor: **Christmas Cottage** (871 Seventh Ave, 212/333-7380)

Christmas decorations (discounted): **Kurt Adler's Santa World** (1107 Broadway, 212/924-0900; open after Thanksgiving for two weeks)

Christmas ornaments: **Matt McGhee** (22 Christopher St, 212/741-3138)

Clocks, cuckoo: **Alfry** (48 W 46th St, 5th floor, 212/575-9444) and **Time Pieces Repaired** (115 Greenwich Ave, 212/929-8011)

Closet fixtures: **Hold Everything** (1309-11 Second Ave, 212/879-1450 and 104 Seventh Ave, 212/633-1674)

Closet items (bargain): **Creative Closets** (364 Amsterdam Ave, 212/496-2473)

Cookbooks, used: **Joanne Hendricks Cookbooks** (488 Greenwich St, 212/226-5731)

Cookware: **Bed Bath & Beyond** (620 Ave of the Americas, 212/255-3550 and 410 E 61st St, 646/215-4702)

Crystal, imported: **Clio** (92 Thompson St, 212/966-8991)

Dinnerware: **Bed Bath & Beyond** (620 Ave of the Americas, 212/255-3550 and 410 E 61st St, 646/215-4702)

Dinnerware, Fiesta (individual pieces): **Mood Indigo** (181 Prince St, 212/254-1176)

Dinnerware, porcelain: **Bernardaud** (499 Park Ave, 212/371-4300)

Displays, jewelry: **Premier Display** (31 W 46th St, 212/719-5151)

Domestics: **Harris Levy** (98 Forsyth St, 212/226-3102)

Doorknobs: **Simon's Hardware & Bath** (421 Third Ave, 212/532-9220)

Electronics, VCRs (discounted): **Sound City** (58 W 45th St, 212/575-1060)

Electronics, vintage: **Waves** (251 W 30th St, 212/273-9616)

Fire merchandise: **Fire Zone** (34 W 51st St, 212/698-4529)

Fixtures, antique: **Olde Good Things** (124 W 24th St, 212/989-8401 and 19 Greenwich Ave, 212/229-0850)

Floor coverings: **ABC Carpet & Home** (888 Broadway, 212/473-3000)

Floral arrangements, imported dried-flower: **Melonie de France** (41 E 60th St, 212/935-4343)

Floral designs: **Country Gardens** (1160 Lexington Ave, 212/966-2015)

Flower bouquets, fresh: **Posies** (150 Seventh Ave S, 212/675-6190)

Flower bulbs: **Van Bourgondien's** (800/622-9997)

Flowers, fresh-cut, from Europe: **VSF** (204 W 10th St, 212/206-7236)

Flowers, silk: **Pany Silk Flowers** (146 W 28th St, 212/645-9526)

Foliage, live and artificial: **American Foliage & Design** (122 W 22nd St, 212/741-5555)

Frames, picture: **A.I. Friedman** (44 W 18th St, 212/243-9000) and **Framed on Madison** (740 Madison Ave, 212/734-4680)

Furnishings, classic hand-carved: **Devon Shops** (111 E 27th St, 212/686-1760)

Furniture: **Design Within Reach** (142 Wooster St, 212/475-0001 and 408 W 14th St, 212/242-9449)

Furniture and mattresses, foam: **Dixie Foam** (113 W 25th St, 212/645-8999)

Furniture, antique: **H.M. Luther Antiques** (35 E 76th St, 212/439-7919 and 61 E 11th St, 212/505-1485)

Furniture, Asian: **Jacques Carcanagues** (106 Spring St, 212/925-8110)

Furniture, baby accessories: **Albee Baby Carriage** (715 Amsterdam Ave, 212/662-5740) and **Schneider's Juvenile Furniture** (41 W 25th St, 212/228-3540)

Furniture, children's (basic): **Chelsea Kids Quarters** (33 W 17th St, 212/627-5524) and **Kids' Supply Company** (1343 Madison Ave, 212/426-1200)

Furniture (discounted): **Knoll** (76 Ninth Ave, 11th floor, 212/343-4000)

Furniture, handcrafted (expensive): **Thomas Moser Cabinetmakers** (699 Madison Ave, 2nd floor, 212/753-7005)

Furniture, handcrafted, 18th-century American reproductions: **Barton-Sharpe** (200 Lexington Ave, 646/935-1500)

Furniture, hardwood: **Pompanoosuc** (124 Hudson St, 212/226-5960)

Furniture, leather: **Sofa So Good** (27 Mercer St, 212/219-8860)

Furniture, modern design (pricey): **Cassina USA** (155 E 56th St, 212/245-2121)

Furniture, rental: **Props for Today** (330 W 34th St, 12th floor, 212/244-9600)

Furniture, summer: **Smith & Hawken** (394 West Broadway, 212/925-0687)

Furniture, Swedish antique: **Eileen Lane Antiques** (150 Thompson St, 212/475-2988)

Gadgets: **Brookstone** (18 Fulton St, 212/344-8108)

Garden items: **Lexington Gardens** (1011 Lexington Ave, 212/861-4390)

Glass: **Simon Pearce** (120 Wooster St, 212/334-2393 and 500 Park Ave, 212/421-8801)

Glass, Venetian: **Gardner & Barr** (213 E 60th St, 212/752-0555)

Glassware and tableware: **Avventura** (463 Amsterdam Ave, 212/769-2510) and **67th Street Wines & Spirits** (179 Columbus Ave, 212/724-6767)

Glassware, Steuben (used): **Lillian Nassau** (220 E 57th St, 212/759-6062)

Glassware, vintage: **Mood Indigo** (181 Prince St, 212/254-1176)

Home accessories: **Carole Stupell** (29 E 22nd St, 212/260-3100)

Home furnishings, primitive: **Andrianna Shamaris** (121 Greene St, 212/388-9898)

Housewares: **Dinosaur Designs** (250 Mott St, 212/680-3523) and **Gracious Home** (1217 and 1220 Third Ave, 212/517-6300 and 1992 Broadway, 212/231-7800)

Housewares, upscale: **Lancelotti** (66 Ave A, 212/475-6851)

Ice buckets, vintage: **Mood Indigo** (181 Prince St, 212/254-1176)

Kitchen gadgets: **Bed Bath & Beyond** (620 Ave of the Americas, 212/255-3550 and 410 E 61st St, 646/215-4702) and **J.B. Prince** (36 E 31st St, 212/683-3553)

Kitchenware, professional: **Hung Chong Imports** (14 Bowery St, 212/349-3392) and **J.B. Prince** (36 E 31st St, 212/683-3553)

Knives: **Roger & Sons** (268 Bowery, 212/226-4734)

Lampshades: **Just Shades** (21 Spring St, 212/966-2757)

Lampshades, custom-made: **Oriental Lampshade Co.** (223 W 79th St, 212/873-0812 and 816 Lexington Ave, 212/832-8190) and **Unique Custom Lamp Shades** (247 E 77th St, 212/472-1140)

Lightbulbs: **Just Bulbs** (5 E 16th St, 212/228-7820)

Lighting, custom and antique: **Lampworks** (231 E 58th St, 212/750-1500)

Lighting fixtures: **City Knickerbocker** (665 Eleventh Ave, 212/586-3939) and **Lighting by Gregory** (158 Bowery, 212/219-2271)

Linens: **Bed Bath & Beyond** (620 Ave of the Americas, 212/255-3550 and 410 E 61st St, 646/215-4702) and **Nancy Koltes at Home** (31 Spring St, 212/219-2271)

Linens, antique: **Jana Starr** (236 E 80th St, 212/861-8256)

Linens, Indian: **Pondicherri** (454 Columbus Ave, 212/875-1609)

Linens, vintage: **Geminola** (41 Perry St, 212/675-1994)

Linoleum, vintage: **Second Hand Rose** (138 Duane St, 212/393-9002)

Locks: **Lacka Lock and Safe** (253 W 46th St, 212/391-5625)

Mattresses (good value): **Town Bedding & Upholstery** (205 Eighth Ave, 212/243-0426)

Movie star photos: **Movie Star News** (134 W 18th St, 212/620-8160)

Perfume bottles, vintage: **Gallery 47** (1050 Second Ave, 212/888-0165)

Pianos, decorative grand: **Maximiliaan's House of Grand Pianos** (305 Second Ave, Suite 322, 212/689-2177; by appointment)

Plumbing fixtures: **Blackman** (85 Fifth Ave, 2nd floor, 212/337-1000) and **George Taylor Specialties** (76 Franklin St, 212/226-5369)

Poster originals, 1880 to present: **Philip Williams** (85 West Broadway, 212/513-0313)

Posters (best selection): **Carrandi Gallery** (138 W 18th St, 212/242-0710)

Posters, international movie: **Jerry Ohlinger's Movie Material Store** (253 W 35th St, 212/989-0869)

Posters, Broadway theater: **Triton Gallery** (323 W 45th St, 212/765-2472)

Posters, vintage: **La Belle Epoque Vintage Posters** (280 Columbus Ave, 212/362-1770)

Pottery, handmade and paint-your-own: **Mugi Pottery** (993 Amsterdam Ave, 212/866-6202) and **Our Name Is Mud** (1566 Second Ave, 212/570-6868)

Prints, botanical: **W. Graham Arader** (29 E 72nd St, 212/628-3668 and 1016 Madison Ave, 212/628-7625)

Quilts: **Down and Quilt Shop** (518 Columbus Ave, 212/496-8980 and 1225 Madison Ave, 212/423-9358) and **J. Schachter's** (5 Cook St, Brooklyn, 718/384-2732)

Rugs, antique: **Doris Leslie Blau** (306 E 61st St, 212/586-5511; by appointment)

Safes: **Empire Safe** (6 E 39th St, 212/684-2255)

Screens, shoji: **Miya Shoji** (109 W 17th St, 212/243-6774)

Shelves: **Shelf Shop II** (1295 First Ave, 212/988-7246)

Silver, unusual: **Jean's Silversmiths** (16 W 45th St, 212/575-0723)

Silverware and holloware (good values): **Eastern Silver** (4901 Sixteenth Ave, Brooklyn, 718/854-5600)

Sofas: **Classic Sofa** (5 W 22nd St, 212/620-0485)

Sofas, vintage: **Regeneration Furniture** (38 Renwick St, 212/741-2102)

Stairs and rails, replacement: **Stairbuilders by B&A** (516/432-1201)

Stationery, personalized: **Jamie Ostrow** (876 Madison Ave and 54 W 21st St, 212/734-8890)

Stone pieces: **Modern Stone Age** (54 Greene St, 212/219-0383)

Strollers and other baby equipment: **Schneider's Juvenile Furniture** (41 W 25th St, 212/228-3540)

Tabletop merchandise: **Clio** (92 Thompson St, 212/966-8991) and **April Cornell** (487 Columbus Ave, 212/799-4342)

Tapestries: **Lovelia Enterprises** (356 E 41st St, 212/490-0930; by appointment) and **Saint-Remy** (818 Lexington Ave, 212/486-2018)

Teaware: **Ito En** (822 Madison Ave, 212/988-7111)

Textiles: **Design in Textiles by Mary Jaeger** (51 Spring St, 212/941-5877)

Tiles: **Mosaic House** (62 W 22nd St, 212/414-2525)

Tiles, ceramic and marble: **Quarry Tiles, Marble & Granite** (132 Lexington Ave, 212/679-8889) and **Complete Tile Collection** (42 W 15th St, 212/255-4450)

Trays: **Extraordinary** (251 E 57th St, 212/223-9151)

Vacuum cleaners: **Desco** (131 W 14th St, 212/989-1800)

Venetian glass: **End of History** (548½ Hudson St, 212/647-7598)

Wallpaper, antique: **Second Hand Rose** (138 Duane St, 212/393-9002)

Wallpaper (discounted): **Janovic Plaza** (136 Church St, 212/349-0001 and other locations)

Wrought-iron items: **Morgik Metal Design** (145 Hudson St, 212/463-0304)

Things for Leisure Time

Accordions: **Main Squeeze** (19 Essex St, 212/614-3109)

Art supplies: **Pearl Paint Company** (308 Canal St, 212/431-7932)

Athletic gear: **Modell's** (55 Chambers St, 212/732-8484 and other locations)

Athletic gear, team: **Yankee Clubhouse** (110 E 59th St, 212/758-7844 and 393 Fifth Ave, 212/685-4693) and **New York Mets Clubhouse** (143 E 54th St, 212/888-7508)

Beads: **Beads of Paradise** (16 E 17th St, 212/620-0642) and **Beads World** (1384 Broadway, 212/302-1199)

Bicycles: **Bicycle Habitat** (244 Lafayette St, 212/625-1347)

Binoculars: **Clairmont-Nichols** (1016 First Ave, 212/758-2346)

Books (good deals): **Bargain Books** (34 Carmine St, 212/229-0079)

Books, academic: **Labyrinth Books** (536 W 112th St, 212/865-1588)

Books, art: **Strand Book Store** (828 Broadway, 212/473-1452)

Books, astrology: **New York Astrology Center** (370 Lexington Ave, Suite 416, 212/949-7211)

Books, children's and parents': **Bank Street Bookstore** (610 W 112th St, 212/678-1654)

Books, exam-study and science-fiction: **Civil Service Book Shop** (89 Worth St, 212/226-9506)

Books, fashion design: **Fashion Design Bookstore** (250 W 27th St, 212/633-9646)

Books, Japanese: **Zakka** (147 Grand St, 212/431-3961)

Books, metaphysical and religious: **Quest Bookshop** (240 E 53rd St, 212/758-5521)

Books, mystery: **Black Orchid Bookshop** (303 E 81st St, 212/734-5980), **Murder Ink** (2486 Broadway, 212/362-8905), and **Partners & Crime** (44 Greenwich Ave, 212/243-0440)

Books, plate (lithographs): **George D. Glazer** (28 E 72nd St, Room 3A, 212/327-2598)

Books, progressive political: **Revolution Books** (9 W 19th St, 212/691-3345)

Books, rare: **Imperial Fine Books** (790 Madison Ave, 2nd floor, 212/861-6620), **J.N. Bartfield Galleries** (30 W 57th St, 212/245-8890), **Martayan Lan** (70 E 55th St, 212/308-0018), and **Strand Book Store** (828 Broadway, 212/473-1452)

Books, used and review copies: **Strand Book Store** (828 Broadway, 212/473-1452)

Chess sets: **Chess Forum** (219 Thompson St, 212/475-2369)

Cigarettes, luxury: **Nat Sherman International** (500 Fifth Ave, 212/764-5000)

Cigars: **Davidoff of Geneva** (535 Madison Ave, 212/751-9060) and **J.R. Cigars** (562 Fifth Ave, 212/997-2227)

Cigars, hand-rolled: **PB Cuban Cigars** (137 W 22nd St, 212/367-8949)

Comic books: **Village Comics** (214 Sullivan St, 212/777-2770)

Comic books, vintage: **Metropolis Collectibles** (873 Broadway, Suite 201, 212/260-4147)

Compact discs, records, tapes, DVDs (discounted): **Disc-O-Rama** (40 Union Sq E, 212/260-8616; 146 W 4th St, 212/477-9410; and 186 W 4th St, 212/206-8417; records only at 4th St location)

Compact discs, used: **NYCD** (173 W 81st St, 212/724-4466) and **St. Mark's Sounds** (20 St. Marks Pl, 212/677-3444)

Computers, Apple products: **The Apple Store** (103 Prince St, 212/226-3126)

Computers, hand-held: **RCS Computer Experience** (575 Madison Ave, 212/949-6935)

Costumes and makeup: **Halloween Adventure** (104 Fourth Ave, 212/673-4546)

Dance-related items: **World Tone Dance** (230 Seventh Ave, 212/691-1934)

Dolls, vintage: **Manhattan Dollhouse** (428 Second Ave, 212/725-4520)

Dollhouses: **Tiny Doll House** (1179 Lexington Ave, 212/744-3719)

Drums: **Drummer's World** (151 W 46th St, 3rd floor, 212/840-3057)

Embroidery, custom-designed: **Jonathan Embroidery Plus** (256 W 38th St, 212/398-3538)

Filofax (discounted): **Altman Luggage** (135 Orchard St, 212/254-7275)

Fishing tackle: **Orvis** (522 Fifth Ave, 212/827-0698)

Games, war: **Compleat Strategist** (11 E 33rd St, 212/685-3880)

Games, *Warhammer*: **Games Workshop** (54 E 8th St, 212/982-6314)

Gifts: **Mxyplyzyk** (125 Greenwich Ave, 212/989-4300)

Gifts, pop-culture curiosities: **Exit 9** (64 Avenue A, 212/228-0145)

Globes, antique world and celestial: **George D. Glazer** (28 E 72nd St, Room 3A, 212/327-2598)

Golf equipment (best selection): **New York Golf Center** (131 W 35th St, 212/564-2255)

Guitars: **Carmine Street Guitars** (42 Carmine St, 212/691-8400), **Dan's Chelsea Guitars** (220 W 23rd St, 212/675-4993), **Guitar Salon** (45 Grove St, 212/675-3236; by appointment), **Ludlow Guitars** (164 Ludlow St, 212/353-1775), **Manny's Music** (156 W 48th St, 212/819-0576), **Matt Umanov Guitars** (273 Bleecker St, 212/675-2157), and **Rogue Music** (251 W 30th St, 10th floor, 212/629-5073)

Guns: **Beretta Gallery** (718 Madison Ave, 212/319-3235) and **Holland & Holland** (10 E 40th St, 212/752-7755)

Handicrafts and art, imported: **Sam's Souk** (979 Lexington Ave, 212/535-7210)

Harley-Davidson gear: **Harley-Davidson of New York** (686 Lexington Ave, 212/355-3003)

Holographs: **Holographic Studio** (240 E 26th St, 212/686-9397)

Home Entertainment: **J&R Music & Computer World** (23 Park Row, 212/238-9000)

Horseback riding equipment: **Copperfield's New York** (117 E 24th St, 212/673-1400)

Luggage, soft: **Bag House** (797 Broadway, 212/260-0940)

Magazines: **DINA Magazines** (72nd and Broadway, 212/875-8824), **Eastern Newsstand** (many locations), and **Universal News** (977 Eighth Ave, 212/459-0932 and 676 Lexington Ave, 212/750-1855), **Union Square Magazine Shop** (200 Park Ave S, 212/598-9406)

Magic tricks: **Tannen's Magic** (45 W 34th St, 212/929-4500)

Maps: **Hagstrom Map and Travel Center** (51 W 43rd St, 212/398-1222)

Maps, rare, vintage: **Richard B. Arkway** (59 E 54th St, 6th floor, 212/751-8135)

Maps and prints, antiquarian: **Argosy Book Store** (116 E 59th St, 212/753-4455)

Marine supplies: **West Marine** (12 W 37th St, 212/594-6065)

Music collections, mp3 format (for iPods): **Hungrypod** (307 Seventh Ave, 212/741-5080)

Musical gifts and souvenirs: **Backstage Memories** (1638 Broadway, 212/582-5996)

Musical instruments: **Manny's Music** (156 W 48th St, 212/819-0576), **Music Inn World Instruments** (169 W 4th St, 212/243-5715), and **Sam Ash Music Store** (160 W 48th St, 212/719-2299)

Needlecraft, knitting: **Yarn Company** (2274 Broadway, 212/787-7878)

New York memorabilia: **Museum of the City of New York** (1220 Fifth Ave, 212/534-1170)

Newspapers, out-of-town: **Hotalings News Agency** (212/974-9419)

Novelties (5,000 kinds!): **Gordon Novelty** (52 W 29th St, 212/696-9664)

Outdoor gear: **Tent and Trails** (21 Park Pl, 212/227-1760)

Paper items (huge selection): **PaperPresentation.com** (23 W 18th St, 212/463-7035)

Papers, elegant: **Il Papiro** (1021 Lexington Ave, 212/288-9330)

Pens, antique and new: **Arthur Brown & Brother** (2 W 46th St, 212/575-5555)

Pet supplies (discounted): **Petland Discounts** (312 W 23rd St, 212/366-0512, and other numerous locations)

Pets: **Pets-on-Lex** (1271 Lexington Ave, 212/426-0766)

Photographic supplies: **Ben Ness Photo** (111 University Pl, 212/253-2313) and **Calumet Photographic** (16 W 19th St, 212/989-8500)

Pipes: **Connoisseur Pipe Shop** (1285 Ave of the Americas, concourse level, 212/247-6054)

Pool tables: **Blatt Billiards** (809 Broadway, 212/674-8855)

Quilting supplies: **City Quilter** (133 W 25th St, 212/807-0390)

Records: **Tower Records and Video** (692 Broadway, 212/505-1500; 1961 Broadway, 212/799-2500; and 725 Fifth Ave, 212/838-8110)

Records, Broadway shows: **Footlight Records** (113 E 12th St, 212/533-1572)

Records, out-of-print: **House of Oldies** (35 Carmine St, 212/243-0500)

Records, vintage rock and roll: **Strider Records** (22 Jones St, 212/675-3040)

Science fiction: **Forbidden Planet** (840 Broadway, 212/473-1576)

Scuba diving and snorkeling equipment: **Pan Aqua Diving** (460 W 43rd St, 212/736-3463) and **Scuba Network** (669 Lexington Ave, 212/750-9160 and 655 Ave of the Americas, 212/243-2988)

Skateboards: **Supreme** (274 Lafayette St, 212/966-7799)

Skating equipment: **Blades Board & Skate** (120 W 72nd St, 212/787-3911; 659 Broadway, 212/477-7074; 901 Ave of the Americas, 646/733-2738; and other locations)

Soccer supplies: **Soccer Sport Supply** (1745 First Ave, 212/427-6050)

Software, computer: **J&R Music & Computer World** (15 Park Row, 212/238-9000)

Soldiers, toy: **Classic Toys** (218 Sullivan St, 212/674-4434) and **Second Childhood** (283 Bleecker St, 212/989-6140)

Sports cards: **Alex's MVP Cards** (256 E 89th St, 212/831-2273)

Sports videos: **Famous Sports Video** (32 W 39th St, 212/398-6690)

Stationery: **Kate's Paperie** (561 Broadway, 212/941-9816; 1282 Third Ave,

212/396-3670; 8 W 13th St, 212/633-0570; and 140 W 57th St, 212/459-0700)

Theatrical items: **One Shubert Alley** (1 Shubert Alley, 212/944-4133)

Toys (good overall selection): **Kidding Around** (60 W 15th St, 212/645-6337)

Toys, high-quality imports: **Geppetto's Toy Box** (10 Christopher St, 212/620-7511)

Toys, Japanese imports: **Image Anime** (103 W 30th St, 212/631-0966)

Toys, museum-quality (1900-1950): **Bizarre Bazaar** (130¼ E 65th St, 212/517-2100; appointment suggested)

Toys, novelties and party supplies: **E.A.T. Gifts** (1062 Madison Ave, 212/861-2544)

Toys, vintage: **Alphaville** (226 W Houston St, 212/675-6850) and **Darrow's Fun Antiques** (212/838-0730; by appointment)

Toys, young adult: **Kidrobot** (126 Prince St, 212/966-6688)

Videogames: **EB Games** (1217 Third Ave, 212/879-9544; 901 Ave of the Americas, 212/564-4156; and 687 Broadway, 212/473-6571)

Videotapes and DVDs, rare and foreign (for sale or rent): **Evergreen Video** (37 Carmine St, 212/691-7362) and **Mondo Kim's** (6 St Mark's Pl, 212/598-9985)

Violins: **Universal Musical Instrument** (732 Broadway, 212/254-6917)

Woodwinds: **Roberto's Woodwind Repair Shop** (146 W 46th St, 212/391-1315)

Writing instruments (great selection): **Rebecca Moss** (510 Madison Ave, 212/832-7671)

Yarns, luxury: **Gotta Knit!** (498 Ave of the Americas, 212/989-3030)

Things from Far Away

British imports: **99X** (84 E 10th St, 212/460-8599)

Buddhas: **Leekan Designs** (93 Mercer St, 212/925-8575)

Chinese dinnerware: **Wing On Wo & Co.** (26 Mott St, 212/962-3577)

Chinese goods: **Pearl River Emporium** (477 Broadway, 212/431-4770) and **Chinese American Trading Company** (91 Mulberry St, 212/267-5224)

European pottery: **La Terrine** (1024 Lexington Ave, 212/988-3366)

Himalayan craft items: **Himalayan Crafts** (2007 Broadway, 212/787-8500)

Indian imports: **Sarajo** (130 Greene St, 212/966-6156)

Indian rugs, shawls, and more: **Kashmir** (157 E 64th St, 212/861-6464)

Italian clothing and shoes: **Cellini Uomo** (59 Orchard St, 212/219-8657)

Japanese gift items: **Katagiri** (224 E 59th St, 212/755-3566)

Japanese kimonos: **Kimono House** (131 Thompson St, 212/505-0232) and **Old Japan** (382 Bleecker St, 212/633-0922)

Lampshades, Oriental: **Oriental Lampshade Co.** (223 W 79th St, 212/873-0812)

Leather items, imported: **Il Bisonte** (120 Sullivan St, 212/966-8773)

Mexican imports: **Pan American Phoenix** (857 Lexington Ave, 212/570-0300) and **Quinto Sol** (937 Madison Ave, 212/734-5653)

Moroccan gifts: **Gates of Morocco** (8 Prince St, 212/925-2650)

Scandinavian imports: **Antik** (104 Franklin St, 212/343-0471)

Southeast Asian furniture and accessories: **Thunder Bay, Ltd.** (134 W 24th St, 212/633-8138)

Tibetan treasures: **Do Kham** (51 Prince St, 212/966-2404 and 304 E 5th St, 212/358-1010), **Tibet Bazaar** (473 Amsterdam Ave, 212/595-8487),

Tibet (144 Sullivan St, 212/529-4344), and **Vision of Tibet** (167 Thompson St, 212/995-9276)

Turkish carpets: **Beyond the Bosphorus** (79 Sullivan St, 212/219-8257)

Miscellaneous Other Things

Butterflies: **Mariposa, the Butterfly Gallery** (South Street Seaport, Pier 17, 2nd floor, 212/233-3221)

Cat memorabilia: **Just Cats** (244 E 60th St, 212/888-2287)

Firefighting memorabilia: **New York Firefighters' Friend** (263 Lafayette St, 212/226-3142)

Fish, tropical: **New World Aquarium** (204 E 38th St, 646/865-9604)

Flags and banners: **Art Flag Co.** (8 Jay St, 212/334-1890)

Judaica: **Eichler's** (62 W 45th St, 212/719-1918)

Office furniture (good prices): **Discount Office Furniture** (132 W 24th St, 212/691-5625)

Office supplies, Muji: **MoMA Design Store** (81 Spring St, 646/613-1367)

Optical instruments: **Clairmont-Nichols** (1016 First Ave, 212/758-2346)

Plexiglas and Lucite items: **Plexi-Craft Quality Products** (514 W 24th St, 212/924-3244)

Portfolios, custom: **House of Portfolios** (52 W 21st St, 212/206-7323)

Store fixtures: **Liberty Display & Supply** (138 W 25th St, 212/929-2777)

Travel items: **Flight 001** (96 Greenwich St, 212/691-1001)

Typewriter ribbons: **Abalon Business Machines** (60 E 42nd St, 212/682-1653)

A money-saving guide to outlet malls
- Beware of items that were never sold in retail stores.
- Carefully examine garments for quality.
- Be sure to save merchandise tags for possible returns.
- Don't assume that all outlet stores have bargain prices.
- Ask for a volume discount from store managers.
- Sign up for your favorite store's mailing list.
- Request coupon books from your favorite outlet mall.
- Go to www.outletbound.com before you shop and request a free VIP voucher.

Factory Outlet Centers in the Tri-State Area

Connecticut

Clinton Crossing Premium Outlets (20 Killingsworth Turnpike, Clinton, CT; 860/664-0700): 70 outlet stores, including Anne Klein, Barneys New York, Brooks Brothers, The Gap, Liz Claiborne, Nautica, Off 5th (Saks outlet), Polo/Ralph Lauren, Waterford/Wedgewood, and more

New Jersey

Flemington area:

Flemington Cut Glass (156 Main St, Flemington, NJ; 908/782-3017): Flemington Cut Glass, Framing Gallery, Main Street Antiques, and more

Heritage Place (Route 31 at Church St, Flemington, NJ; 908/782-3413): Jockey, Levi's, Reebok, Rockport, and Springmaid/Wamsutta

Liberty Village Premium Outlets (1 Church St, Flemington, NJ; 908/782-8550): Over 60 outlet stores, including Anne Klein, Brooks Brothers, Geoffrey Beene, Izod, Liz Claiborne, L.L. Bean, Polo/Ralph Lauren, Villeroy & Boch, and more

Secaucus Area:

Designer Outlet Gallery (55 Hartz Way, Secaucus, NJ; 201/223-5999): Donna Karan, DKNY Jeans, Jones New York, Jones NY Country, OshKosh B'Gosh, and more

Harmon Cove Outlet Center (20 Enterprise Ave N, Secaucus, NJ; 201/348-4780): Carter's Childrenswear, Decor Home Furnishings, Geoffrey Beene, Bass, London Fog, Perry Ellis, and more

Other New Jersey areas:

Circle Factory Outlets (Route 35 at Manasquan Circle, Wall Township, NJ; 732/223-2300): Bass Shoes, Carter's Childrenswear, Harry and David, Izod, Jones NY, Mikasa, Samsonite, and more

Jackson Outlet Village (537 Monmouth Rd, Jackson, NJ; 732/833-0503): Banana Republic, Brooks Brothers, Casual Corner, Claire's Accessories, Conair, Dress Barn, Sunglass Hut, Timberland, and more

Jersey Gardens (651 Kapkowski Rd, Elizabeth, NJ; 908/354-5900): 200 outlets, including Banana Republic, Brooks Brothers, The Gap, Kenneth Cole, Nautica, Pacific Sunwear, Perry Ellis, and more

Marketplace I (Route 34, Matawan, NJ; 732/583-8700): Bernina Sewing Center, Calico Corners, Cinderella Bridal, Dress Barn, Lighting for Less, Nine West, Van Heusen, Wholesale for Kids, and more

Marketplace II (Route 34, Matawan, NJ; 732/583-8700): Bon Worth, Carter's Childrenswear, L'eggs/Hanes/Bali, and more

Olde Lafayette Village (Route 15 at Route 94, Lafayette, NJ; 973/383-8323): Bass, Geoffrey Beene, Izod, Marty's Shoes, Van Heusen, and more

Princeton Forrestal Village Factory Outlet Stores (Route 1 at College Rd W, Princeton, NJ; 609/799-7400): Bass, Dansk, Izod, Van Heusen, and more

New York

Outlets at Bellport (10 Farber Dr, Bellport, NY; 631/286-4952): Dress Barn, The Gap, Liz Claiborne, Pfaltzgraff, Springmaid/Wamsutta, and more

Woodbury Common Premium Outlets (498 Red Apple Court, Central Valley, NY; 845/928-4000): 220 outlet stores, including Adidas, Banana Republic, Coach, Donna Karan, The Gap, Geoffrey Beene, Neiman Marcus Last Call, Off 5th (Saks outlet), Polo/Ralph Lauren, Reebok, Rockport, and more

Pennsylvania

Franklin Mills (1455 Franklin Mills Circle, Philadelphia, PA: 800/336-MALL): 200 outlet stores, including BCBG, Guess, Nautica, Off 5th (Saks outlet), and more

Well-Known Names in Retailing

A La Vielle Russie (781 Fifth Ave, 212/752-1727): antiques
A. Testoni (665 Fifth Ave, 212/223-0909): luxury leather goods

Abercrombie & Fitch (199 Water St, 212/809-9000): preppy men's and women's clothing and accessories

Alfred Dunhill (711 Fifth Ave, 212/753-9292): men's fashions and accessories

Ann Taylor (645 Madison Ave, 212/832-2010 and other locations): women's clothing and accessories

Asprey (723 Fifth Ave, 212/688-1811): luxury jewelry and clothing

Baccarat (625 Madison Ave, 212/826-4100): crystal

Bang & Olufsen (927 Broadway, 212/388-9792; 330 Columbus Ave, 212/501-0926; and 952 Madison Ave, 212/879-6161): home entertainment equipment

Bernardaud (499 Park Ave, 212/371-4300): elegant tableware and furniture

Bottega Veneta (699 Fifth Ave, 212/371-5511): fashions

Botticelli (666 Fifth Ave, 212/586-7421; 620 Fifth Ave, 212/582-6313; and 522 Fifth Ave, 212/768-1430): leather goods

Brioni (55 E 52nd St, 212/355-1940 and 57 E 57th St, 212/376-5777): apparel for men and women

Brooks Brothers (666 Fifth Ave, 212/261-9440 and 346 Madison Ave, 212/682-8800): traditional fashions for men, women, and boys

Buccellati (46 E 57th St, 212/308-2900): silver flatware and jewelry

Bulgari (730 Fifth Ave, 212/315-9000): jewelry, watches

Burberry (131 Spring St, 212/925-9300 and 9 E 57th St, 212/407-7100): plaid everything and more

Calvin Klein (654 Madison Ave, 212/292-9000): fashions for the body and home

Carolina Herrara (954 Madison Ave, 212/249-6552): wedding gowns and fine attire

Cartier (653 Fifth Ave, 212/308-0843): jewelry

Caswell-Massey (518 Lexington Ave, 212/755-2254): beauty and skin-care extravagances

Chanel (15 E 57th St, 212/355-5050 and 139 Spring St, 212/334-0055): classic apparel and accessories

Chopard (725 Madison Ave, 212/218-7222): jewelry and watches

Christian Dior (21 E 57th St, 212/207-8448): clothing and accessories

Christofle (680 Madison Ave, 212/308-9390): silver, crystal, and porcelain

Coach (3 W 57th St, 212/754-0041): leather goods and shoes

Crate & Barrel (650 Madison Ave, 212/308-0011 and 611 Broadway, 212/308-0011): housewares and furniture

Crouch & Fitzgerald (400 Madison Ave, 212/755-5888): luggage and leather accessories

Daum (694 Madison Ave, 212/355-2060): crystal

Dolce & Gabbana (825 Madison Ave, 212/249-4100): clothing and sunglasses

Donna Karan (819 Madison Ave, 212/861-1001): clothing and home furnishings

Emanuel Ungaro (792 Madison Ave, 212/249-4090): clothing

Emilio Pucci (24 E 64th St, 212/752-8957 and 701 Fifth Ave, 212/230-1135): retro clothing

Ermenegildo Zegna (663 Fifth Ave, 212/421-4488): haberdashery and women's clothing

Escada (715 Fifth Ave, 212/755-2200): women's fashions

Etro (720 Madison Ave, 212/317-9096): men's and women's clothing and home fashions

Façonnable (636 Fifth Ave, 212/319-0111): styles for men and women
Fendi (627 Fifth Ave, 212/767-0100): women's fashions
Fortunoff (681 Fifth Ave, 212/758-6660): jewelry and watches
Frette (799 Madison Ave, 212/988-5221): bedding and accessories
Georg Jensen (685 Madison Ave, 212/759-6457 and 125 Wooster St, 212/343-9000): silver home accessories and gifts, jewelry and sunglasses
Gianfranco Ferré (870 Madison Ave, 212/717-5430): fragrances, men's and women's clothing, and accessories
Giorgio Armani (760 Madison Ave, 212/988-9191): men's and women's couture
Givenchy (710 Madison Ave, 212/688-4338): classic clothes
Gucci (685 Fifth Ave, 212/826-2600 and 840 Madison Ave, 212/717-2619): sportswear, leather goods, and accessories
Harry Winston (718 Fifth Ave, 212/245-2000): serious jewelry
Hermés (691 Madison Ave, 212/751-3181): scarves, ties, and fragrances
Hickey Freeman (666 Fifth Ave, 212/586-6481): menswear
Hugo Boss (717 Fifth Ave, 212/485-1800): men's and women's clothing
Issey Miyake (119 Hudson St, 212/226-0100 and 992 Madison Ave, 212/439-7822): innovative apparel
Jack of Diamonds (52 W 47th St, 212/869-7272): diamonds, of course
Jean Paul Gaultier (759 Madison Ave, 212/249-0235): fashions for men and women
Jil Sander (11 E 57th St, 212/838-6100): ladies' clothing and accessories
Jonathan Adler (47 Greene St, 212/941-8950): pottery and home furnishings
Judith Leiber (680 Madison Ave, 212/223-2999): luxury handbags and accessories
Kiehl's (109 Third Ave, 212/677-3171): skin care and toiletries
Lacoste (608 Fifth Ave, 212/459-2300 and 575 Madison Ave, 212/750-8115): polo shirts
Lalique (712 Madison Ave, 212/355-6550): crystal, jewelry, and leather goods
Leron (804 Madison Ave, 212/753-6700): linens for the home and lingerie
Lladro U.S.A. (43 W 57th St, 212/838-9356): porcelain figurines
Loro Piana (821 Madison Ave, 212/980-7961): men's and women's clothing
Louis Vuitton (1 E 57th St, 212/758-8877 and 116 Greene St, 212/274-9090): leather goods, fashions, and accessories
Malo (814 Madison Ave, 212/396-4721): cashmere clothing
Manolo Blahnik (31 W 54th St, 212/582-3007): sexy shoes for women
Mexx (650 Fifth Ave, 212/956-6506 and 500 Broadway, 212/343-7954): family fashions
Michael C. Fina (545 Fifth Ave, 212/557-2500): silver, china, crystal, giftware, and jewelry
Michael Kors (974 Madison Ave, 212/452-4685): women's sportswear
Missoni (1009 Madison Ave, 212/517-9339): men's and women's knit items
Montblanc-Madison (598 Madison Ave, 212/223-8888): writing instruments
Nicole Miller (780 Madison Ave, 212/288-9779): women's clothing and evening gowns
Niketown New York (6 E 57th St, 212/891-6453): athletic wear, gear, and shoes

Oscar de la Renta (772 Madison Ave, 212/288-5810): fashions for men and women
Peter Elliot (1070 Madison Ave, 212/570-2300): tailored clothing and sportswear for men and women
Piaget (730 Fifth Ave, 212/246-5555): luxury watches and snazzy jewelry
Porthault (18 E 69th St, 212/688-1660): luxurious linens and gifts
Prada (575 Broadway, 212/334-8888; 724 Fifth Ave, 212/664-0010; and 841 Madison Ave, 212/327-4200): clothing, shoes, and accessories
Pratesi (829 Madison Ave, 212/288-2315): linens, towels, and bathrobes
Ralph Lauren (867 Madison Ave, 212/606-2100 and 380 Bleecker St, 212/625-1660): fashions and accessories for the family and home
Roberto Vascon (140 W 72nd St, 212/787-9050): handbags
Salvatore Ferragamo (655 Fifth Ave, 212/759-3822): shoes and clothing
Shanghai Tang (714 Madison Ave, 212/888-0111): Oriental-influenced family clothing and home fashions
St. John (665 Fifth Ave, 212/755-5252): women's wear
Steuben (667 Madison Ave, 212/752-1441): fine glassware
Swarovski (625 Madison Ave, 212/308-1710): crystal jewelry, miniatures, and figurines
Thomas Pink (520 Madison Ave, 212/838-1928 and 1155 Ave of the Americas, 212/840-9663): shirts and accessories
Tiffany & Co. (727 Fifth Ave, 212/755-8000): luxurious jewelry and gifts
Tourneau (12 E 57th St, 212/758-7300): exquisite timepieces
Turnbull & Asser (42 E 57th St, 212/752-5700): custom- and ready-made classic shirts and clothes for men and women
Valentino (747 Madison Ave, 212/772-6969): formalwear and accessories
Van Cleef & Arpels (744 Fifth Ave, 212/644-9500): jewelry
Wempe (700 Fifth Ave, 212/397-9000): jewelry and watches
Yves St. Laurent Rive Gauche (855 Madison Ave, 212/472-5299): clothing and accessories

---

New York's most popular radio personality, **Joan Hamburg**, can be heard on WOR Radio (710 AM). Joan has been sharing her encyclopedic knowledge about the city—shopping, eating, touring—for over three decades. You'll love her! Tune in 9 to 11 a.m. Monday through Friday and 10 a.m. to noon on Saturday.

New York Stores: The Best of the Lot
Anatomical Supplies

EVOLUTION
120 Spring St (bet Greene and Mercer St)   212/343-1114
Daily: 11-7   www.evolutionstore.com

Evolution is one of the most unique stores in Manhattan. This Soho emporium offers mounted butterflies and beetles, seashells, fossils, skulls and skeletons, horns, feathers, jewelry, books, and more. You've got to see it to believe it!

MAXILLA & MANDIBLE, LTD.
451 Columbus Ave (bet 81st and 82nd St)   212/724-6173
Mon-Sat: 11-7; Sun: 1-5 (call ahead; closed some days seasonally)
www.maxillamandible.com

Henry Galiano grew up in Spanish Harlem. On the days his parents weren't running their beauty parlor, the family often went to the American Museum of Natural History. His interest in things skeletal increased when he got a job at the museum as a curator's assistant. He soon started his own collection of skeletons and bones. That, in turn, led to his opening Maxilla & Mandible (the scientific names for upper and lower jaw, respectively), which is the first and only such store in the world. How many people need complete skeletons—or even a single maxilla? More than you might think! The shop started by supplying museum-quality preparations of skulls, skeletons, bones, teeth, horns, skins, butterflies, beetles, seashells, fossils, meteorites, minerals, taxidermy mounts, and anatomical charts and models to artists, sculptors, painters, interior decorators, jewelry manufacturers, propmasters, medical personnel, scientists, and educators. They also carry bronze dinosaur models and scientific equipment.

One big difference between "uptown" and "downtown" stores is their hours. While those in midtown and on the East Side and West Side often open at 9 or 10 in the morning, many stores in Greenwich Village, Soho, and Tribeca don't open until 11 or noon. The same is often true of museums.

Animals, Fish, and Accessories

PACIFIC AQUARIUM & PET
46 Delancey St (bet Forsyth and Eldridge St)   212/995-5895
Daily: 10-7:30

Goldfish are the specialty of the house, but Pacific Aquarium & Pet also carries all types of freshwater and saltwater fish, parakeets and finches, and every kind of aquarium and supply you could imagine. They will even come to your home and maintain an aquarium while you're away.

PETCO
147-149 E 86th St (at Lexington Ave)   212/831-8001
560 Second Ave (at 30th St)   212/779-4550
860 Broadway (at Union Square W)   212/358-0692
2475 Broadway (at 92nd St)   212/877-1270
Mon-Sat: 9 a.m.-10 p.m.; Sun: 10-6   www.petco.com

With a selection of over 10,000 items—including food, toys, treats, and pet-care products—this store is a pet owner's treasure trove. There are sections for cats, dogs, birds, fish, and even reptiles! Services include low-cost vaccine clinics, pet photography, dog training, and grooming.

PETLAND DISCOUNTS
85 Delancey St (at Orchard St)   212/477-6293
132 Nassau St (bet Beekman and John St)   212/964-1821
530 E 14th St (at Ave B)   212/228-1363

312 W 23rd St (bet Eighth and Ninth Ave)	212/366-0512
137 W 72nd St (bet Columbus and Amsterdam Ave)	212/875-9785
404 Third Ave (bet 28th and 29th St)	212/447-0739
976 Second Ave (bet 51st and 52nd St)	212/755-7228
389 Ave of the Americas (bet 8th St and Waverly Pl)	212/741-1913
734 Ninth Ave (at 50th St)	212/459-9562
2708 Broadway (at 104th St)	212/222-8851
304 E 86th St (bet First and Second Ave)	212/472-1655
56 W 117th St (bet Malcolm X Blvd and Fifth Ave)	212/427-2700
167 E 125th St (bet Ave of the Americas and Lexington Ave)	
	212/426-7193
1954 Third Ave (bet 107th and 108th St)	212/987-6714
Hours vary from store to store	www.petlanddiscounts.com

The folks at the New York Aquarium recommend this chain for fish and aquarium accessories. Petland also carries birds and discount food and accessories for dogs, cats, reptiles, and other pets.

You'll find excellent antique Americana at **Susan Parrish** (390 Bleecker St, 212/645-5020, www.susanparrishantiques.com). Susan has been in business since 1973, and she puts her heart and soul into her selections: 19th-century furniture, textiles, quilts, homespun blankets, tablecloths, paintings, hooked rugs, and more.

Animation
ANIMAZING GALLERY—SOHO
461 Broome St (bet Greene and Mercer St) 212/226-7374
Mon-Sat: 10-7; Sun: 11-6 www.animazing.com

No one is better at showing animation than Animazing Gallery. They are New York City's largest authorized Disney art gallery. They showcase the *Peanuts* pop art of Tom Everhart (friend of the late Charles Schultz), and exclusively offer the work of Dr. Seuss and many other artists. Vintage and contemporary cels and drawings from all major studios are featured. Specialties include appraisals, consignments, searches, and autographed books. Monthly gala events, shows, and sales are also featured. Their expanded space now includes 3D work by master American craftspeople, new sculpture glass art, Wild Home furnishings, and Art to Wear jewelry.

Antiques
Bleecker Street

Les Pierre Antiques (369 Bleecker St, 212/243-7740): French Country
Susan Parrish (390 Bleecker St, 212/645-5020): quilts

Chelsea

Upstairs Downstairs Antiques (12 W 19th St, 212/989-8715): eclectic and full-service

Greenwich Village

Agostino Antiques, Ltd. (979 Third Ave, 212/421-8820): English and French 17th-, 18th-, and 19th-century furniture

Donzella (17 White St, 212/965-8919): 1930s, 1940s, and 1950s furnishings
End of History (548½ Hudson St, 212/647-7598): vintage hand-blown glass
Howard Kaplan Antiques & Bath Shop (827 Broadway, 212/674-1000):
French and English Country furniture
Hyde Park Antiques (836 Broadway, 212/477-0033): English furniture
Karl Kemp & Associates (34 E 10th St, 212/254-1877): furniture
Kentshire Galleries (37 E 12th St, 212/673-6644): English antiques
L'Epoque (30 E 10th St, 212/353-0972): 18th- and 19th-century French
and continental furniture
Little Antique Shop (44 E 11th St, 212/673-5173): eclectic
Maison Gerard (53 E 10th St, 212/674-7611): French art deco
Ritter-Antik (35 E 10th St, 212/673-2213): early first-period Beidermeier

Lexington Avenue

Hayko (857 Lexington Ave, 212/717-5400): kilims
L'Art de Viere (978 Lexington Ave, 212/734-3510): early 20th-century
Nancy Brous Antiques (1008 Lexington Ave, 212/772-7515): bamboo
Sam's Souk (979 Lexington Ave, 212/535-7210): chests and accessories
Sara (952 Lexington Ave, 212/772-3243): Japanese pottery and porcelain
Sylvia Pines Uniquities (1102 Lexington Ave, 212/744-5141): diverse

Lower East Side

Billy's Antiques & Props (76 E Houston St, 917/576-6980): fun antiques

Madison Avenue

Alexander Gallery (942 Madison Ave, 212/517-4400): English 18th- and
19th-century paintings
Antiquarium (948 Madison Ave, 212/734-9776): jewelry and antiquities
Art of the Past (1242 Madison Ave, 212/860-7070): South and Southeast
Asia
Bernard & S. Dean Levy (24 E 84th St, 212/628-7088): American furniture
and silver
Cora Ginsburg (19 E 74th St, 212/744-1352): antique textiles
DeLorenzo (956 Madison Ave, 212/249-7575): art deco
Didier Aaron (32 E 67th St, 212/988-5248): 17th-, 18th-, and 19th-century
pieces
Edith Weber & Associates (994 Madison Ave, 212/570-9668): rare and his-
toric jewels
Fanelli Antique Timepieces (790 Madison Ave, Suite 202, 212/517-2300):
antique timepieces
Florian Papp (962 Madison Ave, 212/288-6770): furniture
Friedman & Vallois (27 E 67th St, 212/517-3820): high-end French art deco
George D. Glazer (28 E 72nd St, 212/535-5706): maps, globes
Guild Antiques II (1089 Madison Ave, 212/717-1810): English formal
J.J. Lally (41 E 57th St, 212/371-3380): Chinese art
L'Antiquaire & the Connoisseur (36 E 73rd St, 212/517-9176): French and
Italian furniture
Linda Horn Antiques (1015 Madison Ave, 212/772-1122): late 19th-cen-
tury English & French
Macklowe Gallery & Modernism (667 Madison Ave, 212/644-6400):
Tiffany
Time Will Tell (212/787-8848; by appointment): vintage watches

Ursus Books and Prints (981 Madison Ave, 212/772-8787): books
W. Graham Arader (29 E 72nd St, 212/628-3668): rare prints

Meatpacking District

Lars Bolander N.Y. (72 Gansevoort St, 212/924-1000): 17th- and 18th-century Swedish and French reproductions

Midtown

A La Vielle Russie (781 Fifth Ave, 212/752-1727): Russian art
Chameleon (223 E 59th St, 212/355-6300): lighting
Dalva Brothers (44 E 57th St, 212/758-2297): French furniture
Doris Leslie Blau (360 E 61st St, 212/586-5511): rugs
Eric Originals & Antiques (4 W 47th St, 212/819-9595): antique diamond jewelry
Gardner & Barr (213 E 60th St, 212/752-0555): Murano glass
George N. Antiques (227 E 59th St, 212/935-4005): mirrors
Gotta Have It! (153 E 57th St, 212/750-7900): celebrity memorabilia
Gray Boone (32 W 47th St, 212/719-4698): vintage engagement rings
Hugo, Ltd. (233 E 59th St, 212/750-6877): 19th-century lighting and decorative arts
James Robinson (480 Park Ave, 212/752-6166): silver flatware
Leo Kaplan, Ltd. (114 E 57th, 212/249-6766): ceramics and glass
Manhattan Art & Antiques Center (1050 Second Ave, 212/355-4400): 100 galleries
Martayan Lan (70 E 55th, 6th floor, 212/308-0018): 16th- and 17th-century maps and prints
Mary Finkelstein Antique Jewelry (50 W 47th St, 212/719-1708): antique jewelry
Naga Antiques (145 E 61st St, 212/593-2788): antique Japanese screens
Nesle (151 E 57th St, 212/755-0515): lighting only
Newel Art Galleries (425 E 53rd St, 212/758-1970): all styles and periods
Paris to Province (207 E 60th St, 212/750-0037): French and English furniture
Philip Colleck (311 E 58th St, 212/486-7600): 18th- and early 19th-century English furniture
Ralph M. Chait Galleries (724 Fifth Ave, 10th floor, 212/758-0937): Chinese art
S.J. Shrubsole (104 E 57th St, 212/753-8920): English silver
Stephen Herdemian (78 W 47th St and 73 W 47th St, 212/944-2534): antique jewelry
T&K French Antiques (200 Lexington Ave, Room 901, 212/213-2470): French furniture

Soho/Tribeca

Alan Moss (436 Lafayette St, 212/473-1310): 20th-century furniture
Alice's of Soho (72 Greene St, 212/966-6867): iron beds
Art & Industrial Design Shop (50 Great Jones St, 212/477-0116): items from the 1940s, 1950s, and 1960s
Beyond the Bosphorus (79 Sullivan St, 212/219-8257): Turkish kilims and pillows
Bikini Bar (148 Duane St, 212/571-6737): Hawaiian, vintage rattan, surfboards

David Stypmann (190 Ave of the Americas, 212/226-5717): eclectic, pottery, mirrors

Eileen Lane Antiques (150 Thompson St, 212/475-2988): Swedish art deco and Beidermeier

Gill & Lagodich Fine Period Frames (108 Reade St, 212/619-0631; by appointment): frames

Greene Street Antiques (65 Greene St, 212/274-1076): Scandinavian and Beidermeier

Lost City Arts (18 Cooper Square, 212/375-0500): furniture, fixtures

Second Hand Rose (138 Duane St, 212/393-9002): 19th-century Moorish antiques

Urban Archaeology (143 Franklin St, 212/431-4646): architectural antiques

WaterMoon Gallery (110 Duane St, 212/925-5556, by appointment): Chinese antiques and works of art

Wyeth (315 Spring St, 212/243-3661; by appointment): early-to-mid-20th-century antiques and custom furniture

Upper East Side

Bizarre Bazaar (130¼ E 65th St, 212/517-2100): 20th-century industrial design

Evergreen Antiques (1249 Third Ave, 212/744-5664): furniture

Leigh Keno American Antiques (127 E 69th St, 212/734-2381): 16th-, 17th-, and early 18th-century American furniture

Upper West Side

La Belle Epoque Vintage Posters (280 Columbus Ave, 212/362-1770): advertising posters

Art Supplies

LEE'S ART SHOP
220 W 57th St (at Broadway)   212/247-0110
Mon-Sat: 9-7:30; Sun: 11-6

Lee's offers an expanded stock of materials for amateur and professional artists and kids. There are architectural and drafting supplies, lamps, silk screens, art brushes, paper goods, stationery, pens, cards, gifts, and much more. Same-day on-premises framing is available, along with catalog ordering. Ask for Ricky, the very able boss.

NEW YORK CENTRAL ART SUPPLY
62 Third Ave (at 11th St)   212/473-7705
Mon-Sat: 8:30-6:15   www.nycentralart.com

Since 1905 artists have looked to this firm for fine art materials, especially unique and custom-made items. There are two floors of fine art papers, including one-of-a-kind decorative papers and over a thousand Oriental papers from Bhutan, China, India, Japan, Thailand, Taiwan, and Nepal. Amateur and skilled artisans will find a full range of decorative paints and painting materials. This firm specializes in custom priming and stretching of artists' canvas. The canvas collection includes Belgian linens and cottons in widths from 54" to 197". Their selection of brushes is outstanding.

PEARL PAINT COMPANY
308 Canal St (bet Broadway and Church St)   212/431-7932
Mon-Fri: 9-7; Sat: 10-6:30; Sun: 10-6   800/221-6845
www.pearlpaint.com

Thirteen retail floors contain a vast selection of arts, graphics, and crafts merchandise, plus lighting and furniture. Selections and services include fabric paint, silk-screening and gold-leaf items, drafting and architectural goods, a fine writing department, and custom framing. They provide fine-art supplies at some of the best prices in town and can ship overseas. Their **Custom Frame Factory** (56 Lispenard St, 212/431-7932, ext. 6966) sells frames at discount prices. Three other affiliated stores are **NYC Craft Center** (42 Lispenard St, 212/431-7932 ext. 3717), **NYC Home Design Center** (58 Lispenard St, 212/431-7932, ext. 4530), and **School of Visual Arts** (207 E 23rd St, 212/592-2179).

The Showplace (40 W 25th St, 212/633-6063, www.nyshowplace.com) is the largest antique center in New York, with 135 quality galleries on three floors selling jewelry, art glass, art nouveau, art deco, bronze, pottery, paintings, furniture, silver, and more. There is even a silversmith on-premises. They are open from 10 to 6 on weekdays and 8:30 to 5:30 on weekends.

SAM FLAX
900 Third Ave (bet 54th and 55th St)   212/813-6666
12 W 20th St (bet Fifth Ave and Ave of the Americas)
Mon-Fri: 9-7; Sat: 10-6; Sun: 11-6   212/620-3000
www.samflaxny.com

Sam Flax is one of the biggest and best art supply houses in the business. The stock is enormous, the service special, and the prices competitive. They carry a full range of art and drafting supplies, organization and archival storage items, gifts, pens, classic and modern furniture and home decor items, and photographic products. Framing services are offered at both stores.

UTRECHT ART AND DRAFTING SUPPLIES
111 Fourth Ave (at 11th St)   212/777-5353
Mon-Sat: 9-7; Sun: 11-6

237 W 23rd St (bet Seventh and Eighth Ave)   212/675-8699
Mon-Sat: 9-8; Sun: 12-6   www.utrecht.com

Utrecht is a major manufacturer of paint, art, and drafting supplies, with a large factory in Brooklyn. At this retail store, factory-fresh supplies are sold at discount, and both quality and prices are superb. Utrecht also carries other manufacturers' lines at impressive discounts.

Autographs

JAMES LOWE AUTOGRAPHS
30 E 60th St (bet Madison and Park Ave), Suite 304   212/759-0775
By appointment only

James Lowe is one of the nation's most established autograph houses. Regularly updated catalogs make visiting the gallery unnecessary, but in-person inspections are fascinating and invariably whet the appetite of autograph collectors. The gallery shows whatever superior items are in stock, including historic, literary, and musical autographs, manuscripts, documents, and 19th-century photographs (both signed and unsigned). The offerings range from autographed pictures of Buffalo Bill to three bars of an operatic score by Puccini.

KENNETH W. RENDELL GALLERY
989 Madison Ave (at 77th St)   212/717-1776
Mon-Sat: 10-6 or by appointment   www.kwrendell.com

Kenneth Rendell has been in the business for over 40 years. He offers a fine collection of pieces from famous figures in literature, arts, politics, and science. Rendell shows autographed letters, manuscripts, documents, books, and photographs. All are authenticated, attractively presented, and priced according to rarity. Rendell also evaluates collections for possible purchase.

Bathroom Accessories

A.F. SUPPLY CORPORATION
22 W 21st St (bet Fifth Ave and Ave of the Americas), 5th floor
Mon-Fri: 8-5 and by appointment   212/243-5400
www.afsupply.com

A.F. Supply offers a great selection of luxury bath fixtures, whirlpools, faucets, bath accessories, door and cabinet hardware, saunas, steam showers, shower doors, medicine cabinets, and spas from top suppliers.

For bathroom and kitchen fix-ups, several firms stand out. **Krup's Kitchen & Bath** (11 W 18th St, 212/243-5787) is a good spot to go for appliances. For tiles, try **Get Real Surfaces** (37 W 20th St, 212/414-1620). Interesting furnishings are shown at **Wyeth** (315 Spring St, 212/243-3661). The best selection of specialty glass can be found at **Bendheim** (122 Hudson St, 212/226-6370). You can't do better than **George Taylor Specialties** (76 Franklin St, 212/226-5369) for all manner of plumbing supplies. **Simon's Hardware & Bath** (421 Third Ave, 212/532-9220) carries practically everything you could possibly want for your bathroom.

HOWARD KAPLAN ANTIQUES & BATH SHOP
827 Broadway (bet 12th and 13th St)   212/674-1000
Mon-Fri: 9-5   www.howardkaplanantiques.com

Howard Kaplan presents the largest assortment of top-quality antique bath items (1890–1940) in the country. Even the setting—an 1870 Napoleon III building—is special. You will definitely want to inspect the unusual French, English, and American merchandise, including fine reproduction bathroom accessories.

SHERLE WAGNER INTERNATIONAL
60 E 57th St (at Park Ave)   212/758-3300
Mon-Fri: 9:30-5:30   www.sherlewagner.com

Sherle Wagner takes the often-skirted topic of the bathroom and places it in the most elegant location in the city, where it rubs elbows with silversmiths, art galleries, and exclusive antique shops. The luxurious hardware and bathroom fixtures, bed and bath items, and general home furniture are deserving of their 57th Street location. Fixtures come in a variety of materials, some so striking that they warrant being exhibited in a glass case. Prices are high, as might be expected. The displays are on the lower level, and what seems like the world's slowest elevator may leave you feeling claustrophobic.

Beads

BRUCE FRANK BEADS & FINE ETHNOGRAPHIC ART
215 W 83rd St (bet Broadway and Amsterdam Ave)   212/595-3746
Daily: 11-7:30   www.brucefrankbeads.com

You'll find one of the area's best selections of beads at this store, including semiprecious stones, sterling silver, gold-plated Czech and Japanese seed beads, brass beads, contemporary glass beads, and much more. Besides the selection of vintage and antique beads from all over the world, the store carries a large stock of supplies and findings. There's weekly beading classes, re-stringing, and repair, too! Volume discounts are available.

GAMPEL SUPPLY
11 W 37th St (bet Fifth Ave and Ave of the Americas)   212/575-0767
Mon-Fri: 8:30-5   www.elveerosenberg.com

This is the kind of esoteric business New York does best. Request a particular kind of bead, and Gampel will invariably have it—at a cheap price, too. While single beads go for a dollar each at a department store one block away, Gampel sells them in bulk for a fraction of that price. Though they prefer to deal with wholesalers, individual customers are treated as courteously as institutions, and wholesale prices are offered to all. As for the stock—well, a visit to Gampel is an education. Pearlized beads alone come in over 20 different guises and are used for everything from bathroom curtains to earrings and flowers. Since many of its customers are craftspeople, Gampel also sells supplies for bead-related crafts. They stock needles, cartwheels, cords (in colors to match each bead), threads, chains, adhesives, jewelry tools, jewelry findings, and costume jewelry parts and pieces.

Books

The book business has changed drastically in recent years, and superstores are now the name of the game in many areas. Unless a small dealer has a special location or niche in book marketing, times are not easy. One exception is **Coliseum Books**, one of New York's outstanding, long-time book operations. You don't want to miss a visit to Coliseum (11 W 42nd St, bet Fifth and Sixth Aves, 212/803-5890; Mon-Fri: 8 a.m.-8:30 p.m., Sat: 11-8:30; Sun: noon-7; www.coliseum books.com). You will find exceptional selection and service and a bookstore that shows that an individual operation can make it in a highly competitive market. Coliseum is especially helpful with special orders.

Antiquarian

COMPLETE TRAVELLER ANTIQUARIAN BOOKSTORE
199 Madison Ave (at 35th St)   212/685-9007
Mon-Fri: 10-7; Sat: 10-6; Sun: 11-5

www.completetravellerbooks.com

The largest collection of Baedeker Handbooks is but one feature of this store, which deals exclusively in rare, antiquarian, and out-of-print books pertaining to travel. The 8,000-book collection includes volumes on polar expeditions, adventure travel, literature, first editions, children's books, and 18th- and 19th-century maps. Books on New York are also available.

Architecture

URBAN CENTER BOOKS
457 Madison Ave (bet 50th and 51st St)   212/935-3595
Mon-Thurs: 10-7; Fri: 10-6; Sat: 10-5:30

www.urbancenterbooks.com

The Municipal Art Society is a nonprofit organization dedicated to urban planning and historic preservation. Although best known for exceptionally diverse and well-conceived walking tours, the organization also runs a gallery and bookstore at its headquarters in the north end of the elegant Villard Houses. The bookstore is among the best sources in the country for books, magazines, and journals on such topics as urban and land-use planning, architecture, and interior design. It also carries a wide selection of guidebooks to New York City.

Art

PRINTED MATTER
535 W 22nd St (bet Tenth and Eleventh Ave)   212/925-0325
Tues-Fri: 12-6; Sat: 11-7   www.printedmatter.org

The name Printed Matter is a misnomer since this store is one of a few in the world devoted exclusively to artists' books—a trade term for a portfolio of artwork in book form. They stock 24,000 titles by over 3,500 artists. The result is inexpensive, accessible art that can span an artist's entire career or focus on a particular period or theme. The idea is carried further with a selection of periodicals and audiotapes in a similar vein. Nearly all featured artists are contemporary (from 1960), so just browsing the store will bring you up-to-date on what is happening in the art world. They sell wholesale and retail, and you can browse their catalog online.

Biography

BIOGRAPHY BOOKSHOP
400 Bleecker St (at 11th St)   212/807-8655
Sun-Thurs: 11-10; Fri, Sat: 11-11

This shop specializes in books of a biographical nature. If you are researching a particular person or have an interest in someone's life story, this is the place to find it. There are biographies, books of letters, autobiographies, diaries, journals, and biographies for children. They have broadened their scope into other areas, but the emphasis remains on bios.

Children's

BANK STREET BOOKSTORE
2879 Broadway (at 112th St)   212/678-1654
800/439-1486 (outside New York State)
Mon-Thurs: 11-7; Fri-Sat: 10-6; Sun: 12-6
www.bankstreetbooks.com

Adjacent to the Bank Street College of Education—a progressive graduate school for teachers and lab school for children—this store is a marvelous
source of books for children, as well as books about children, education, and
parenting. It also has a great selection of tapes, videos, and CDs, plus an
expanded section of educational toys and teacher's supplies. While the store
is a little cramped even when it isn't crowded, the staff really knows its stock
and cares enormously about quality children's literature. Make sure to check
online for readings and other special children's events.

BOOKS OF WONDER
18 W 18th St (bet Fifth Ave and Ave of the Americas)   212/989-3270
Mon-Sat: 10-7; Sun: 11-6   www.booksofwonder.com

Books of Wonder is an enchanting place. In addition to the largest selection of Oz (as in *The Wizard of*) books in the world, this store is known for
frequent "Meet the Author" events, beautiful used and often signed children's classics, a newsletter, and a story hour for young children on Sunday
mornings. Look for gift-wrapping in the back of the store.

SCHOLASTIC STORE
557 West Broadway (bet Prince and Spring St)
Mon-Sat: 10-7; Sun: 12-6   212/343-6166, 877/286-0137
www.scholastic.com/sohostore

The Scholastic Store is the world's only retail store of this educational
publishing giant. It's a bright, cheerful space full of familiar titles and characters. In addition to children's books, the store stocks a range of toys, puzzles, software, videos, and Klutz products, as well as a tremendous selection
of parent/teacher resource books on the second floor. Ask for a calendar of
events, which lists readings, workshops, and performances.

Comics

ACTION COMICS
337 E 81st St (bet First and Second Ave)   212/639-1976
Wed-Fri: 1:30-8; Sat: 2-7

Action Comics presents the best selection of comic books in the city.
There are new comics from all publishers, collectors' comics from the 1930s
to the present, new and collectors' sports (and non-sports) cards, new and old
collectors' action figures, magic cards, T-shirts, and collecting supplies. They
will evaluate collections and even buy them.

METROPOLIS COLLECTIBLES
873 Broadway (at 18th St), Suite 201   212/260-4147
Mon-Fri: 10-6 (by appointment only)   www.metropoliscomics.com

Metropolis specializes in vintage comic books from the turn of the century through the 1960s, with over 100,000 vintage titles in stock. It is the largest dealer of vintage comic books in the world, with a private showroom where fabulous one-of-a-kind books and horror movie posters are displayed. Ask to see the Boris Karloff poster from the 1931 movie *Frankenstein*.

ST. MARK'S COMICS
11 St. Mark's Pl (bet Second and Third Ave)   212/598-9439
Mon, Tues: 10 a.m.-11 p.m.; Wed-Sat: 10 a.m.-1 a.m.; Sun: 11-11

This unique store carries mainstream and licensed products, as well as hard-to-find small-press and underground comics. They have a large selection of back issues and claim, "If it's published, we carry it." The folks here are very service-oriented and will hold selections for you. Comic-related toys, T-shirts, statues, posters, and cards are stocked. They also carry TV- and movie-related products.

Here is a very useful service! **Anything on Earth** (800/928-7179) is one of the oldest and most experienced full-service custom acquisition firms in the country. They will help locate and acquire any item, product, or service in a professional and cost-effective manner. A free consultation is followed by a free preliminary investigation to estimate the cost and time required to locate what you want. The final fee is based on time spent, a percentage of the purchase price, or a combination of both, plus applicable expenses.

VILLAGE COMICS & COLLECTIBLES
214 Sullivan St (bet Bleecker and 3rd St)   212/777-2770
Mon, Tues: 10:30-7:30; Wed-Sat: 10-8:30; Sun: 11-7
www.villagecomics.com

You will find just about everything for most tastes and age groups at Village Comics & Collectibles. There are collectors items, old and new books, limited editions, graphic novels, collectors' cards, a large and varied adult section, a large selection of videos, hard-to-find items, toys, and model kits of comic and horror figures in resin, vinyl, and plastic. Some discounts are available.

Cookbooks

KITCHEN ARTS & LETTERS
1435 Lexington Ave (at 94th St)   212/876-5550
Mon: 1-6; Tues-Fri: 10-6:30; Sat: 11-6; closed Sat in July and Aug

Cookbooks traditionally are strong sellers, and with all the interest in health, fitness, and natural foods, they are selling better than ever. It should come as no surprise that Nachum Waxman's Kitchen Arts & Letters found immediate success as a store specializing in food- and wine-related books and literature. Imported books are a specialty. Waxman claims his store is the only one like it in the city and that there are fewer than ten in the entire country. He is a former editor at Harper & Row and Crown publishers, where he supervised cookbook projects. Bitten with the urge to start a specialty bookshop, he identified a huge demand for out-of-print cookbooks. So while the tiny shop stocks more than 10,000 current titles, much of the business consists of finding deleted and want-listed books.

Foreign

LIBRAIRE DE FRANCE/LIBRERIA HISPANICA
Dictionary Store/Learn-a-Language Store
Rockefeller Center
610 Fifth Ave (bet 49th and 50th St)   212/581-8810
Mon-Sat: 10-6 (call ahead to see if open on Sun)
                                                    www.frencheuropean.com

A short stroll through Rockefeller Center Promenade takes you to this
unique foreign-language bookstore, which has occupied the same location
since 1934. Inside you will find an interesting collection of French magazines and newspapers, children's books, cookbooks, best sellers, greeting
cards, and recorded French music. It is on the lower level, however, where
most of the treasures are found. French books are available on almost every
topic. There is a Spanish bookstore, as well as French and Spanish films on
video, books on cassette, a multimedia section, books and recordings for
learning more than a hundred languages, and a specialized foreign-language
dictionary section covering engineering, medicine, business, law, and dozens
of other fields.

NEW YORK KINOKUNIYA BOOKSTORE
10 W 49th St (at Fifth Ave)   212/765-7766
Daily: 10-7:30   www.kinokuniya.com

Kinokuniya is Japan's largest and most esteemed bookstore chain. An
American branch, located in Rockefeller Plaza, has two floors of books about
Japan. It is the largest collection of Japanese books in the city. The atmosphere is the closest thing to Tokyo in New York. On the first floor are 20,000
English-language books on all aspects of Japanese culture: art, cooking,
travel, language, literature, history, business, economics, martial arts, comic
books, and more. The rest of the floor is rounded out with Japanese-language
books on the same subjects. Japanese stationery is sold on the second floor.

General

BARNES & NOBLE
Numerous locations throughout Manhattan, including:
600 Fifth Ave (Rockefeller Center)	212/765-0592
160 E 54th St (at Third Ave)	212/750-8033
1972 Broadway (at 66th St)	212/595-6859
675 Ave of the Americas (at 22nd St)	212/727-1227
33 E 17th St (bet Broadway and Park Ave)	212/253-0810
2289 Broadway (at 82nd St)	212/362-8835
1280 Lexington Ave (at 86th St)	212/423-9900
240 E 86th St (at Second Ave)	212/794-1962
396 Ave of the Americas (at 8th St)	212/674-8780
4 Astor Pl (bet Broadway and Lafayette St)	212/420-1322
Hours vary by store	www.bnnewyork.com

For value and selection, you can't beat Barnes & Noble. Their stores are
beloved by book buyers and browsers in virtually every area of the city.
Generations of New York students have purchased textbooks at the main
store (105 Fifth Avenue, 212/675-5500). Barnes & Noble has opened a number of superstores with enormous stocks of books (including bargain-priced

remainders), comfortable shopping conveniences (including cafes), and a large selection of magazines. Best of all, they continue to offer deep discounts on best sellers and other popular titles.

BORDERS BOOKS AND MUSIC
461 Park Ave (at 57th St)   212/980-6785
Mon-Fri: 9 a.m.-10 p.m.; Sat: 10-8; Sun: 11-8

576 Second Ave (at 32nd St)   212/685-3938
Mon-Sat: 9 a.m.-11 p.m.; Sun: 10-10

100 Broadway (bet Pine and Wall St)   212/964-1988
Mon-Fri: 7:30 a.m.-8 p.m.; Sat: 10-8; Sun: 11-8

10 Columbus Circle (Time Warner Building)   212/823-9775
Mon-Fri: 8 a.m.-10 p.m.; Sat: 10-10; Sun: 11-8

www.borders.com

Borders is one of the major national bookstore chains, offering books, CDs, periodicals, reading areas, and a cafe. The stock at Borders is wide and deep. There is plenty of well-informed help, and in-person author events draw crowds. Customer kiosks allow access to their extensive inventory via computerized searches by author, title, and keyword.

GOTHAM BOOK MART
16 E 46th St (bet Fifth and Madison Ave)   212/719-4448
Mon-Fri: 9:30-6:30; Sat: 9:30-6

The Gotham is a legend in Manhattan. Opened in 1920, it's still providing a marvelous selection of books on literature and the arts more than 80 years later. You'll find new, used, and out-of-print volumes, along with very knowledgeable personnel.

MCNALLY ROBINSON BOOKSELLERS
50 Prince St (bet Lafayette and Mulberry St)   212/274-1160
Daily: 10-10   www.mcnallyrobinsonnyc.com

Sarah McNally is a brave lady. "Brave" because opening an independent bookstore these days is a daring endeavor! But she has been successful. The store is chock full of titles in every category. Author appearances are frequent, there is a teahouse for resting between shopping and reading, and personal, informed service will help lead you to the right book.

RIZZOLI
31 W 57th St (bet Fifth Ave and Ave of the Americas)   212/759-2424
Mon-Fri: 10-7:30; Sat: 10:30-7; Sun: 11-7   www.rizzoliusa.com

When you talk about class in the book business, Rizzoli tops the list. They have maintained an elegant atmosphere that makes patrons feel as if they are browsing a European library rather than a midtown Manhattan bookstore. The emphasis is on art, architecture, literature, photography, fashion, and interior design. There is a good selection of paperbacks. Upstairs you will find Italian books, a music department, and children's books.

STRAND BOOK STORE
828 Broadway (at 12th St)   212/473-1452
Mon-Sat: 9:30 a.m.-10:30 p.m.; Sun: 11-10:30

Strand Book Annex
95 Fulton St (at Gold St) 212/732-6070
Mon-Fri: 9:30-9; Sat, Sun: 11-8 www.strandbooks.com

Would you believe the Strand now has air conditioning and an elevator? For book lovers, no trip to New York is complete without a visit to the Strand. Family-owned for over three-quarters of a century, this fabulous institution is the largest used bookstore (over 2.5 million volumes) in the world. For New Yorkers, the Strand is the place to start looking for that volume you must have. The store's 18 miles of books are tagged at up to 85% off list price. This enormous bookstore houses secondhand, out-of-print, and rare books at heavily discounted prices. In addition, the Strand offers thousands of new books at 50% off publisher's list price, plus a huge stock of quality remainders. In the rare book department, located on the third floor, individual titles are priced up to $125,000. There is also a fine selection of more moderately priced collectibles, including 20th-century first editions, limited signed editions, fine bindings, and a huge selection of art books. The store imports English remainders, sells to libraries, sells books by the foot (supplying decorators, TV networks, and hotels), and does a booming mail-order business. Strand Book Annex, located three blocks east of Broadway, has 15,000 square feet of books and is surprisingly sunny and organized. There's even a children's reading room. Owner Fred Bass and daughter Nancy are two of the nicest and brightest individuals in the book business.

THREE LIVES & CO.
154 W 10th St (at Waverly Pl) 212/741-2069
Mon-Tues: 12-8; Wed-Sat: 11-8:30; Sun: 12-7 www.threelives.com

Three Lives is one of the best remaining independent bookstores. Founded in 1978, they specialize in literary fiction and nonfiction, with good sections on poetry, art, New York, cooking, and gardening. Best of all, the staff is super-friendly and knowledgeable.

Music
JUILLIARD BOOKSTORE
60 Lincoln Center Plaza (65th St at Broadway), plaza level
Mon-Thurs: 9:30-7:30; Fri, Sat: 10-6 212/799-5000, ext 237
www.bookstore.juilliard.edu

With over 20,000 sheet music titles and scores in stock, this bookstore claims to carry every classical music book in print! And there is more: imprinted stationery and apparel, conductors' batons, metronomes, historic recordings, and music software.

Mystery
BLACK ORCHID BOOKSHOP
303 E 81st St (bet First and Second Ave) 212/734-5980
Tues-Fri: 12-7; Sat: 11-6:30; Sun: 12-5 (closed Sun in July and Aug)
www.ageneralstore.com

The Black Orchid caters to all kinds of mystery readers, stocking current titles and out-of-print books. A number of signed titles are available.

MURDER INK®
2486 Broadway (bet 92nd and 93rd St)   212/362-8905
Mon-Sat: 10-9; Sun: 11-7   www.murderink.com

For the diehard Sherlock Holmes fan, this is the place! They have a great selection of rare mystery books, as well as signed first editions of current mysteries. Its sister store, **Ivy's Books** (2488 Broadway, 212/362-8905), carries new and used literature, rare and collectible titles, kids' books, and volumes on New York.

MYSTERIOUS BOOKSHOP
129 W 56th St (bet Ave of the Americas and Seventh Ave)
Mon-Sat: 11-7   212/765-0900
www.mysteriousbookshop.com

Otto Penzler is a Baker Street Irregular, a Sherlock Holmes fan extraordinaire (an elementary deduction!), and the Mysterious Bookshop's owner. As you might expect, the shop is friendly, and spontaneous conversation among customers is the norm. Mysterious stocks new hardcover and paperback books that deal with all types of mystery. Upstairs, via a winding staircase, the store branches out to the width of two buildings and is stocked floor-to-ceiling with out-of-print, used, and rare books. Amazingly, the staff seem to know exactly what is in stock. If it is not on the shelves, they will order it. There is as much talk as business conducted here, and you can continue the conversation with authors who sign their works from time to time in the back room. Mysterious carries thousands of autographed books and several store-sponsored book clubs provide autographed first editions to members.

New York

CITYSTORE
1 Centre St (Municipal Bldg at Chambers St), north plaza
Mon-Fri: 9-4:30   212/669-8246
www.nyc.gov/citystore

This city government bookstore has access to more than 120 official publications, all of which are dedicated to helping New Yorkers cope with their complex lives. *The Green Book* is the official directory of the city of New York, listing phone numbers and addresses of more than 900 government agencies and 6,000 officials. It includes state, federal, and international listings, as well as courts and a section on licenses. There is also a unique collection of New York memorabilia: city-seal ties, pins, and more.

Out-of-Print and Rare

ALABASTER BOOKSHOP
122 Fourth Ave (bet 12th and 13th St)   212/982-3550
Mon-Sat: 10-8; Sun: 11-8

There was a time when Fourth Avenue was known as "Bookshop Row." Back then, it was *the* place for used books in Manhattan. All that has changed with the advent of superstores and the demise of smaller entrepreneurs. Well, Steve Crowley has bucked the trend, offering a great selection of used and rare books in all categories, ranging from $2 paperbacks to a $1,000 first edition. Specialities include New York City, photography, and modern first editions.

ARGOSY BOOK STORE
116 E 59th St (bet Park and Lexington Ave)   212/753-4455
Mon-Fri: 10-6; Sat: 10-5 (closed Sat in summer)
www.argosybooks.com

Argosy is the largest out-of-print, secondhand, and rare volume book-store in New York. The six-story building houses a stock of books from the 16th through the 20th centuries, including modern first editions and regional American-history volumes, as well as others on art, science, and medicine. A separate autograph section includes items from a number of well-known personalities. Their print department is famous for its large collection of antique maps from all over the world, prints of every conceivable subject, and vintage posters.

BAUMAN RARE BOOKS
535 Madison Ave (bet 54th and 55th St)   212/751-0011
Mon-Sat: 10-6   www.baumanrarebooks.com

Bauman offers a fine collection of books and autographs dating from the 15th through the 20th centuries. Included are works of literature, history, economics, law, science, medicine, nature, travel, and exploration. They also provide services from designing and furnishing libraries to locating books for customers.

IMPERIAL FINE BOOKS
790 Madison Ave (bet 66th and 67th St), 2nd floor   212/861-6620
Mon-Sat: 10:30-6   www.imperialfinebooks.com

If you are in the market for books that look as great as they read, Imperial is the place to visit. You will find fine leather bindings, illustrated books, vintage children's books, unique first editions, and magnificent sets of prized volumes. Their inventory includes literary giants like Twain, Dickens, Brontë, and Shakespeare. There is also an outstanding Oriental art gallery, featuring Chinese, Japanese, and Korean ceramics and antiques. (They will purchase fine pieces.) Services include complete restoration and binding of damaged or aged books. A search office will locate titles and make appraisals.

J.N. BARTFIELD GALLERIES AND FINE BOOKS
30 W 57th St (bet Fifth Ave and Ave of the Americas), 3rd floor
Mon-Fri: 10-5; Sat: 10-3 (closed Sat in summer)   212/245-8890

This shop is a spectacular hunting ground for lovers of fine paintings and rare books. Since 1937 they have specialized in masters of the American West and 19th- and 20th-century American paintings and sculptures. I have purchased outstanding collections of leatherbound books from them and can vouch for their expertise. First editions, sporting books, and high-quality antiquarian books are featured. Who wouldn't be excited to browse elegantly bound volumes that once graced the shelves of old family libraries?

PAGEANT BOOKS AND PRINT SHOP
By appointment   212/674-5296
www.pageantbooks.com

Give these folks a call for a great selection of antiquarian books, maps, prints, etchings, rare volumes, and first editions from the 15th to the 20th centuries. Pageant is one of the last outfits in Manhattan to carry a really wonderful inventory in all of these categories.

Religious

CHRISTIAN PUBLICATIONS BOOK STORE
315 W 43rd St (bet Eighth and Ninth Ave)   212/582-4311
Mon-Sat: 9-9   www.christianpub.com

With over 20,000 titles in stock, this is the largest Christian bookstore in the metropolitan area. It also stocks religious CDs, tapes, videos, and church and school supplies. A large number of these items are available in Spanish, as befits the Latino neighborhood.

J. LEVINE BOOKS & JUDAICA
5 W 30th St (bet Fifth Ave and Broadway)   212/695-6888
                                        800/5-JEWISH (outside New York City)
Mon-Wed: 9-6; Thurs: 9-7; Fri: 9-2; Sun: 10-5 (closed Sun in July)
                                                www.levinejudaica.com

The history of the Lower East Side is reflected in this store. Started back in 1905 on Eldridge Street, it was a fixture in the area for many years. Now J. Levine operates uptown, just off Fifth Avenue. Being one of the oldest Jewish bookstores in the city, Levine is a leader in the Jewish-book marketplace. Though the emphasis is still on the written word, they have expanded the store with many gift items, tapes, coffee table books, and thousands of items of Judaica. A 100-page catalog is available.

ST. PATRICK'S CATHEDRAL GIFT STORE
15 E 51st St (bet Fifth and Madison Ave)   212/355-2749, ext 400
Daily: 10-6

This store is an oasis of calm in midtown. Lovely music plays in the background as you browse books on Catholicism, displays of rosary beads, statues of saints, and related items. Proceeds of every sale benefit the cathedral.

Theater

DRAMA BOOK SHOP
250 W 40th St (bet Seventh and Eighth Ave)
Mon-Sat: 10-8; Sun: 12-6   212/944-0595, 800/322-0595
                                                www.dramabookshop.com

Since 1923 this shop has been providing a valuable service to the performing arts community. Its stock includes publications dealing with theater, film, dance, music, puppetry, magic, design, costumes, and more. The Drama Book Shop is known for courteous and knowledgeable service, both in-store and by mail.

RICHARD STODDARD—PERFORMING ARTS BOOKS
By appointment   212/598-9421
                                                www.richardstoddard.com

Richard Stoddard runs a one-man operation dedicated to rare, out-of-print, and used books, and to memorabilia relating to the performing arts. Equipped with a Ph.D. from Yale in theater history and three decades of experience as a dealer and appraiser of performing arts materials, Stoddard offers a broad range of items. He has the largest collection of New York playbills (about 20,000) for sale in the U.S., as well as books, autographs, souvenir programs, and original stage designs. He is the sole agent for the estate of Jo Mielziner, an esteemed Broadway designer, and he also offers designs by a half-dozen other set designers.

Used

HOUSING WORKS USED BOOK CAFE
126 Crosby St (bet Houston and Prince St)   212/334-3324
Mon-Fri: 10-9; Sat: 12-9; Sun: 12-7
www.housingworks.org/usedbookcafe

You'll find it all: used books, collectibles, out-of-print titles, first editions, DVDs, and audio books. The cafe features baked goods, seasonal soups, summer sandwiches, soft drinks, and beer and wine. Proceeds go to programs for homeless people with AIDs, providing supportive housing, medical care, and job training.

Butterflies

MARIPOSA, THE BUTTERFLY GALLERY
South Street Seaport (at Fulton St), Pier 17   212/233-3221
Mon-Sat: 10-9; Sun: 11-8

At Mariposa, butterflies are regarded as art. Marshall Hill is a renowned designer in this unusual medium. Butterflies are unique, and Mariposa (the Spanish word for butterfly) displays them separately, in panels, and in groups. Butterfly farms breed and raise butterflies, which live their full one-month life spans under ideal conditions for creating this art.

Buttons

TENDER BUTTONS
143 E 62nd St (bet Lexington and Third Ave)   212/758-7004
Mon-Fri: 10:30-6; Sat: 10:30-5:30

Millicent Safro's retail button store is complete in variety as well as size. One antique wooden display cabinet shows off Tender Buttons' selection of original buttons, many imported or made exclusively for the store. There are buttons of pearl, wood, horn, Navajo silver, leather, ceramics, bone, ivory, pewter, and semiprecious stones. Many are antiques. Some are as highly valued as artwork; a French enamel button, for instance, can cost almost as much as a painting! Unique pieces can be made into special cuff links—real conversation pieces for the lucky owner. Blazer buttons are a specialty. They also have a fine collection of antique and period cuff links and men's stud sets. I am a cuff links buff and have purchased some of my best pieces from this shop. They also have wonderful small antiques.

Candles

CANDLE SHOP
118 Christopher St (bet Bleecker and Hudson St)   212/989-0148
Mon-Sat: 12-8; Sun: 1-7   www.candlexpress.com

Thomas Alva Edison's inventions haven't made a flicker of an imprint on the folks at the Candle Shop, the oldest specialty candle store in New York. They have assembled a collection of beeswax, paraffin, and stearin candles in an assortment of sizes and colors. It's positively illuminating to learn that candles are available in so many configurations! They will fulfill custom requests. The shop also carries candle holders and accessories, oil lamps, and incense.

OTHER WORLDLY WAXES
131 E 7th St (bet First Ave and Ave A)   212/260-9188
Tues-Sun: 2-9
                    www.candletherapy.com, www.otherworldlywaxes.com

In this interesting store you'll find scented candles, aromatherapy products, hand-blended oils, and incense. They also offer spiritual advice, promising that their candles "merge psychological goals with whatever spiritual framework you have." Here's a sampling of the properties associated with their oils and incense: "Cleopatra" (balm of Gilead) is a secret weapon of seduction, while "Vavoom" (coconut) promises big-time sex appeal and flair. Who knows? A visit here might change your life! Ask for Catherine Riggs-Bergesen, who is a practicing clinical psychologist. Candles are prepared as you wait, and readings are by appointment.

China, Glassware

CRATE & BARREL
650 Madison Ave (at 59th St)   212/308-0011
Mon-Fri: 10-8; Sat: 10-7; Sun: 12-6

611 Broadway (at Houston St)   212/780-0004
Mon-Sat: 10-9; Sun: 12-7   www.crateandbarrel.com

Crate & Barrel is a must-see! Even if you aren't in the market for china, glassware, bedroom furnishings, or casual furniture, the displays will make shopping hard to resist. First, the place is loaded with attractive, quality merchandise at sensible prices. Second, it is fixtured magnificently, with every item shown to best advantage. Third, the lighting and signing are masterfully done. Finally, the store layout and number of checkout stands make for quick work in completing a sale. These folks are professional merchants in the best sense of the word.

FISHS EDDY
889 Broadway (at 19th St)   212/420-9020
2176 Broadway (at 77th St)   212/873-8819
Hours vary by store   www.fishseddy.com

Besides being treasure troves for bargain hunters, these shops are fun to browse for some of the most unusual industrial-strength china and glassware items available anywhere. Nearly everything is made in America, and the stock changes on a regular basis. For young people setting up a new residence or a business looking for unique pieces, try Fishs Eddy first.

Clothing and Accessories

Antique and Vintage

THE FAMILY JEWELS
130 W 23rd St (bet Ave of the Americas and Seventh Ave)
212/633-6020
Sun-Wed: 11-7; Thurs-Sat: 11-8   www.familyjewelsnyc.com

Family Jewels is *the* place for vintage clothing and accessories, from the Victorian era through the 1970s. The stock is well organized, the selections are huge, the service is excellent, and shopping is fun! Even the decor is 1940s, and appropriately, retro music plays. Prices are reasonable. A costume and styling service is available.

FROM AROUND THE WORLD
209 W 38th St (bet Seventh and Eighth Ave), Suite 1201
Mon-Fri: 9:30-5:30 (by appointment only)   212/354-6536

This is a vintage clothing archive, wardrobe lending library, and retail outlet specializing in unique, high-quality vintage apparel and accessories from all over the world. The continually replenished selection of designer, ethnic, military, Western, Hawaiian, work, and athletic wear, includes collectible and never-worn dead-stock items.

REMINISCENCE
50 W 23rd St (bet Fifth Ave and Ave of the Americas)   212/243-2292
Mon-Sat: 11-7:30; Sun: 12-7   www.reminiscence.com

It's fun to revisit the 1960s and 1970s at this hip emporium, created by Stewart Richer on lower Fifth Avenue. Although he is a child of this era, most of Richer's customers are between the ages of 13 and 30. The finds are unusual and wearable, with large selections of colorful vintage clothing and attractive displays of jewelry, hats, gifts, and accessories. Richer's goods, although vintage in style, are mostly new, and the company has become a manufacturer that sells to outlets all over the world. Because of its vast distribution, Richer is able to produce large quantities and sell at low prices.

SCREAMING MIMI'S
382 Lafayette St (bet 4th and Great Jones St)   212/677-6464
Mon-Fri: 12-8; Sat: 12-8; Sun: 1-7   www.screamingmimis.com

Everyone agrees this is a fun place to shop! Laura Wills presides over Screaming Mimi's, which features accessories for men and women from the 1940s through the 1980s, as well as contemporary merchandise. There is an excellent showing of handbags, shoes, jewelry, sunglasses, and lingerie, plus a good selection of sportswear. A newer department features designer and vintage couture.

TRASH & VAUDEVILLE
4 St. Mark's Pl (bet Second and Third Ave)   212/982-3590
Mon-Thurs: 12-8; Fri: 11:30-8:30; Sat: 11:30-9; Sun: 1-7:30

This place is hard to pin down, since the stock changes constantly and seems to have no boundaries. Trash & Vaudeville describes its stock as punk clothing, accessories, and original designs. "Punk clothing" means rock and roll styles from the 1950s to the present, including outrageous footwear. They also carry new clothing from Europe.

VINTAGE DESIGNS/WHAT COMES AROUND GOES AROUND
351 West Broadway (bet Broome and Grand St)   212/343-9303
Mon-Sat: 11-8; Sun: 12-7   www.nyvintage.com

If vintage clothing is your thing, then don't miss this place. It claims to be one of the largest vintage outlets in the world, with over 60,000 items in stock. Many of the labels are familiar, and the prices are right. Denim and military wear are especially well represented.

Bridal

HERE COMES THE BRIDESMAID . . .
238 W 14th St (bet Seventh and Eighth Ave)   212/647-9686
Tues-Thurs: 11-8; Fri, Sat: 11-5 (by appointment)
www.bridesmaids.com

After walking down the aisle as a bridesmaid in 13 weddings, Stephanie Harper decided it was time that bridesmaids had a store of their own. Her establishment carries gowns from Siri, Lazzaro, Jim Hjelm, and others. She also features gowns that can be hemmed and worn again to occasions other than weddings. Weekend hours make Here Comes the Bridesmaid especially convenient for working women. Call ahead for an appointment.

KLEINFELD
110 W 20th St (at Ave of the Americas)   718/765-8500
Tues, Thurs: 12:30-9; Fri, Sun: 10-6; Sat: 9:30-6
By appointment   www.kleinfeldbridal.com

The bridal business has changed a great deal in recent years. Yet little has changed at Kleinfeld, other than a new location in Manhattan. They are absolutely number one in the business. Some specialty stores carry very limited collections of bridal wear, but not this bridal complex, which stocks up to 1,250 styles of bridal gowns. The mother of the bride will find a special section called Kleinfeld's P.M., which specializes in evening wear. Kleinfeld carries every major name in bridal wear and accessories, including Amsale, Carolina Herrera, Reem Acra, and Monique Lhuillier. One quarter of the collection is of international origin. The store operates by appointment and can handle over a hundred customers a day. This is the place to come when wedding bells will soon be ringing.

Brides, here is a money-saving hint! **Bridal Garden** (54 W 21st St, Suite 907, 212/252-0116, www.bridalgarden.org) has hundreds of sample wedding gowns from leading designers. Bargains range from $400 to $3,000, and all proceeds go to charity. It's in the Flatiron District, and appointments are necessary.

VERA WANG
991 Madison Ave (at 77th St)   212/628-3400
Mon-Sat: 9:30-6 (Thurs: 10:30-7)   www.verawang.com

Vera Wang is one of the top bridal designers in the world, and this is her only salon. Be prepared for beautiful styles that are priced accordingly. Wedding gowns are in the $3,000 to $20,000 range. Exclusive evening-wear designs may be purchased off the rack. A special store for bridesmaids, **Vera Wang Maids** (980 Madison Avenue, 212/628-9898), is on the third floor across the street.

Children's

Before describing what I consider to be the best children's clothing stores in New York, let me be clear about what I'm not including: big chains and the haughty "just so" boutiques that line Madison Avenue. That is not to say some of the chains don't have great stores here. Baby Gap and Gap Kids, The Children's Place, Gymboree, OshKosh B'Gosh, and even Europe's Oilily all have good selections, as does the cavernous "big-box" buybuy Baby. But unlike the stores listed below, they sell very little that you can't buy in any other city in America. As for the haughty boutiques, I see no reason to patronize these wildly overpriced and unwelcoming places.

BETWIXT
245 W 10th St (at Hudson St)   212/243-8590
Mon-Fri: 11:30-6:30; Sat: 11-6; Sun: 12-5

The latest rage among marketers is the "tween" set, that group of children who aren't really little anymore but aren't quite teenagers either. This airy, well-designed clothing store in the West Village—complete with a logo that will remind Baby Boomer parents of the old *Bewitched* television show—caters to "tween" girls. Cool, sophisticated clothing, shoes, and accessories line the shelves, while cool, sophisticated girls and petite women fill the store.

BU AND THE DUCK
106 Franklin St (bet Church St and West Broadway)   212/431-9226
Mon-Sat: 10-7; Sun: 12-6   www.buandtheduck.com

Ask owner-designer Susan Lane-Camacho about the unusual store name! *Quality* is the byword here. Come to Bu and the Duck for outstanding hand-made sweaters, clothing, shoes, and accessories for infants to eight-year olds. All designs are original.

LESTER'S
1522 Second Ave (at 79th St)   212/734-9292
Mon-Fri: 10-7; Sat: 10-6; Sun: 12-5

If you're looking for basic clothes, shoes, campwear, and/or accessories for children and don't want to leave the East Side, Lester's is your best bet. It is large and inviting, including a downstairs section dedicated entirely to boys. In fact, you can clothe everyone from infants to teenagers here. You can even find a good selection of shoes. While its stock might not win any fashion awards, Lester's is just stylish enough to keep East Side moms and kids coming back.

LILLIPUT
265 Lafayette St (bet Spring and Prince St)   212/965-9567
Mon: 12-6; Tues-Sat: 11-7   www.lilliputsoho.com

Children's clothing stores in New York's hot shopping neighborhoods have multiplied in recent years, and a lot of them start to look alike after awhile. Sometimes a good buyer with a sharp eye can set a store apart, however. In certain respects Lilliput resembles a lot of other relatively upscale children's stores, and some of what you'll find here is neither unusual nor well-priced. But look a little closer and you'll see certain items, including a wide selection from Lili Gaufreete, that make a trip here worthwhile. In addition to a wide and varied selection of infant clothes, Lilliput has a great shoe selection, unusual accessories, a few toys, and a diverse range of clothes for young children to size 8. A sister store, **Lilliput Soho Kids** (240 Lafayette St, 212/965-9201), offers clothes for girls to size 16. It's right down the block and keeps the same hours.

MARSHA D.D.
1574 Third Ave (bet 88th and 89th St)   212/831-2422
Mon-Sat: 10-6; Sun: 12-5:30

Featuring backpacks, stylish clothing, and accessories galore, this friendly East Side institution is a hot spot for "tweens" and their younger siblings. Owner Marsha Drogin Dayan has a really good feel for what's "in," particularly among the private-school set, and she makes everyone feel welcome. Unlike the separate girls' and boys' stores she maintained for years, this spot is comfortable and spacious.

MORRIS BROS.
2322 Broadway (at 84th St)   212/724-9000
Mon-Sat: 9:30-6:30; Sun: 12-5:30

You can't be a parent or kid on the Upper West Side and not know about Morris Bros. Whether you're looking for a backpack, hat, tights, pajamas, jeans, underwear, or clothes for gym class and camp, this is the place to go for basic kids' clothing and accessories at decent prices. One negative: the selection for girls is significantly smaller than that for boys. In fact, while Morris Bros. carries sizes 4 through 20 for boys, it carries only sizes 7 through 14 for girls.

PEANUTBUTTER & JANE
617 Hudson St (at 12th St)   212/620-7952
Mon-Sat: 10:30-7; Sun: 11-6

A friend describes this store as "very Village." In addition to a varied and fun selection of clothing, it carries funky things like ruby slippers for children, leather jackets for toddlers, and wonderfully imaginative dress-up clothes. Indeed, almost everything is unique to the store. Unlike a lot of children's clothing stores in which older children wouldn't be caught dead, Peanutbutter & Jane appeals both to teenagers and their younger siblings. You'll find some fun toys and novelties as well.

SPACE KIDDETS
46 E 21st St (bet Park Ave S and Broadway)   212/420-9878
Mon, Tues, Fri, Sat: 10:30-6; Wed, Thurs: 10:30-7
www.spacekiddets.com

This cheerful store is overflowing with funky children's clothes, shoes, and accessories. It has been around for a long time but somehow always feels fresh and fun. The prices may seem a bit high if you're from out-of-town, but they're reasonable compared to some of the boutiques in trendier neighborhoods. Moreover, the sales staff is welcoming and helpful. Clothing for little boys and girls can be found on street level in the main store, while clothing for preteens is located upstairs through a separate entrance.

Costumes

ABRACADABRA
19 W 21st St (bet Fifth Ave and Ave of the Americas) 212/627-5194
Mon-Sat: 11-7   www.abracadabrasuperstore.com

Abracadabra can transform you into almost anything! They rent and sell costumes and costume accessories, magician's supplies, theatrical makeup, and stock props for magic tricks. It is a gagster's heaven! Free magic shows are given on Saturday afternoon.

HALLOWEEN ADVENTURE
104 Fourth Ave (bet 11th and 12th St)   212/673-4546
Mon-Sat: 11-8; Sun: 12-7 (extended hours at Halloween time)
                                        www.newyorkcostumes.com

Your kids will be the talk of the neighborhood after a visit here. You'll find wigs, costumes for adults and kids, hats, gags, magic items, props, and all manner of games and novelties. In addition, a professional makeup artist is on hand most of the time.

PARAMOUNT
52 W 29th St (bet Broadway and Ave of the Americas) 212/696-9664
Mon-Fri: 9-5

Crowns, tiaras, headpieces, false teeth, wigs, beards, eyepatches, eyelashes, swords, fake blood—name the prop or theatrical accessory, and chances are good this fading old store sells it either singly or by the dozen. The collection of masks is extensive.

Furs

FURS BY DIMITRIOS
130 W 30th St (bet Ave of the Americas and Seventh Ave)
Mon-Fri: 9-6; Sat: 10-4; Sun: 10-4 (winter only)   212/695-8469

This store is the best source for men's fur coats at wholesale prices. The racks are shaggy with furs of all descriptions and sizes for both genders. Prices are wholesale but go up slightly if the garment has to be specially ordered. This shouldn't be necessary, though, since the high-quality off-the-rack selection is the most extensive in the city.

G. MICHAEL HENNESSY FURS
345 Seventh Ave (bet 29th and 30th St), 5th floor   212/695-7991
Mon-Fri: 9:30-5; Sat by appointment

You'll find an abundance of beautiful, affordable furs here! Fur lovers should get to know Michael Hennessy and his wife, Rubye, a former fashion editor. Hennessy furs are famous worldwide. The label assures you of superior pelts, great designs, and the lowest possible prices. Their showroom in the wholesale fur district stocks hundreds of furs, ranging from highly coveted minks and sables to sporty boutique furs and shearlings. You'll find all the newest fashion looks, colors, shapes, and techniques. A spectacular Italian fur collection is exclusive to Hennessy. Today's fur technology is evident in skillfully executed sheared and grooved minks, "double-face" reversible styles, and furs that weigh next to nothing but still keep you warm. No wonder the Hennessys command such a large international following. They have a huge remodeling business, turning furs that are a few years old into brand-new styles. That classic mink you've worn for years can have a second life as a sheared swingcoat or *blouson*. While this is a sizable company, Michael or Rubye is always on hand to assist you.

GOODMAN COUTURE FURS
224 W 30th St (bet Seventh and Eighth Ave), Suite 902   212/244-7422
Mon-Fri: 10-6; Sat by appointment   www.buonuomo.com

Since 1918, the Goodmans have been creating fine fur styles. Father Gus and son David are continuing the family tradition, offering a quality collection of fur-lined and reversible fur coats and jackets for men and women. You may choose from an array of furs, including mink, sheared mink, and fine sables. Your out-of-date or unused fur coats can be brought back to life with a new all-weather design. The Goodmans offer a custom cashmere knit collection under the label Buonuomo ("good man"), made in an Italian cashmere factory and trimmed with luxurious furs. Additionally, they have developed an innovative line of fur accessories, including scarves, collars, and handbags. A full-time staff designer specializes in custom designs. Their hottest new items are feather-weight, fur-lined, reversible coats.

HARRY KIRSHNER AND SON
307 Seventh Ave (bet 27th and 28th St)   212/243-4847
Mon-Fri: 9-6; Sat: 10-5

Kirshner should be one of your first stops for any kind of fur product, from throw pillows to full-length mink coats. They re-line, clean, alter, and store any fur at rock bottom prices. They are neither pushy nor snobbish. Harry Kirshner offers tours of the factory. If nothing appeals to a customer, a staff member will design a coat to specifications. Often, however, the factory offers a collection of restored secondhand furs in perfect and fashionable condition. Many customers come in for a new fur and walk out with a slightly worn one for a fraction of what they expected to spend.

LIBRA LEATHER
259 W 30th St (bet Seventh and Eighth Ave)   212/695-3114
Mon-Fri: 9-5:30   www.libraleather.com

For over a half century this family-owned business has been the ultimate source for fashion fur and leather skins. You'll find leather, suede, and shearling skins for home furnishings, women's and men's better clothing, and accessory items such as bags, belts, and shoes. The inventory is enormous—with quality skins from Italy, France, and Spain—and the staff is multilingual.

RITZ FURS
107 W 57th St (bet Ave of the Americas and Seventh Ave)
Mon-Sat: 9-6 (closed Sat in July); Sun: 11-5 (Nov-Jan)   212/265-4559
www.ritzfurs.com

For luxurious furs at affordable prices, no one beats the Ritz! Famous for great prices for over fifty years, the Ritz is New York's department store for fur. Styles run from contemporary to classic, up to funky, and include mink, sable, fox, lynx, and more. They offer an ever-changing variety of one-of-a-kind designer furs, luxurious shearlings, and fur-lined and fur-trimmed outerwear. In addition, the Ritz has one of New York's largest selections of previously owned luxury furs at good savings. The Ritz takes gently used furs on consignment and occasionally buys them outright. The experienced, multilingual staff offers personal service.

Hosiery

FOGAL
510 Madison Ave (at 53rd St)   212/355-3254
Mon-Sat: 10-6:30   www.fogal.com

Before Fogal came to New York from Switzerland, the thought of a Madison Avenue boutique devoted to hosiery was, well, foreign. But since opening in 1982, it's hard to imagine Manhattan without it. If it's fashionable and different leg wear you're after, Fogal has it. Plain hosiery comes in nearly 100 hues, at last count; the designs and patterns make the number of choices almost incalculable. You might say that Fogal has a leg up on the competition! Fogal also carries lingerie, bodywear, and men's socks.

Leather

BARBARA SHAUM
60 E 4th St (bet Bowery and Second Ave)   212/254-4250
Wed-Sat: 1-6

Barbara Shaum has done magical things with leather since 1963. She's a wonder with sandals, bags, sterling-silver buckles, belts (with handmade brass, nickel-silver, inlaid wood, and copper buckles), jewelry, attaché cases, and briefcases. Everything is designed in the shop, and Shaum meticulously crafts each item using only the finest materials. She is regularly featured in leading fashion magazines.

Men's and Women's—General

AVIREX
652 Broadway (bet Bleecker and Bond St)   212/254-4000
Mon-Sat: 11-7; Sun: 12-6   www.avirex.com

This is a fascinating store for folks who travel. A fabulous collection of flight jackets, flight suits, varsity leather jackets, motorcycle jackets, T-shirts, coveralls, sweaters, insignias, watches, bags, and gift items is available.

CHRISTOPHER FISCHER
80 Wooster St (bet Broome and Spring St)   212/965-9009
Mon-Sat: 11-7; Sun: 11-6   www.christopherfischer.com

Fischer carries luxurious cashmere goods for men and women, including sweaters, blankets, shawls, and cushions. Accessories from Henry Beguelin are also available

DAFFY'S

111 Fifth Ave (at 18th St)	212/529-4477
Mon-Sat: 10-9; Sun: 12-7	
335 Madison Ave (at 44th St)	212/557-4422
Mon-Fri: 8-8; Sat, Sun: 10-6:30	
1311 Broadway (at 34th St)	212/736-4477
Mon-Fri: 10-9; Sat: 10-8; Sun: 11-6	
462 Broadway (at Grand St)	212/334-7444
Mon-Fri: 11-8; Sat: 11-9; Sun: 12-6	
125 E 57th St (bet Lexington and Park Ave)	212/376-4477
Mon-Fri: 10-8; Sat: 10-7; Sun: 12-6	
1775 Broadway (at 57th St)	212/294-4477
Mon-Fri: 9-8:30; Sat: 10-7; Sun: 11-6	
50 Broadway (bet Exchange Pl and Beaver St)	212/422-4477
Mon-Fri: 8-8; Sat: 10-6; Sun: 12-6	www.daffys.com

Daffy's describes itself as a bargain clothing outlet for millionaires. Since a lot of folks got to be millionaires by saving money, perhaps Daffy's has something going for it! Great bargains can be found in better clothing (including unusual European imports) for men, women, and children. Fine leather items are a specialty. This is not your usual "off-price" store, as they have done things with a bit of flair.

FILENE'S BASEMENT

2222 Broadway (at 79th St)	212/873-8000
Mon-Sat: 9:30-9; Sun: 11-7	
620 Ave of the Americas (at 18th St)	212/620-3100
Mon-Sat: 9:30-9; Sun: 11-7	
4 Union Square S (at 14th St and University Pl)	212/358-0169
Mon-Sat: 9:30 a.m.-10 p.m.; Sun: 11-8	www.filenesbasement.com

Anyone who has shopped in Boston knows the name Filene's Basement, which is recognized for outstanding bargains. Well, Filene's is also in New York, offering great bargains in brand-name goods for misses and men. The store claims 30% to 60% savings. Sometimes it's more and sometimes less, but you can always depend on the quality. The store is easy to shop in, and there are huge stocks of merchandise in every category.

Watch for the opening of **Ecko Unlimited** (217 W 42nd St), a trendy clothing and lifestyle outlet, sometime in 2006. Located in the former Times Square Theater, the store will feature clothing, art, videogames, electronics, and collectibles. As the last of eight historic theaters on 42nd street to be reborn, the building will retain many of its architectural features.

H&M
Several locations throughout Manhattan, including:
640 Fifth Ave (at 51st St)   212/489-0390
558 Broadway (bet Prince and Spring St)   212/343-2722
Hours vary by store   www.hm.com

From the day it opened, H&M has been packing them in, and it's no secret why! In a convivial atmosphere, up-to-date clothing and accessories for the young, as well as those who want to remember their carefree days, can be found at very reasonable prices. Don't come here for pricey labels; what you will find are knockoffs of merchandise that sells for much more at boutiques and department stores. The Swedes learned quickly that American yuppies like nothing better than to fill their closets with clothing that doesn't cost very much. This is the place to get it!

HARLEM UNDERGROUND
2027 Fifth Ave (at 125th St)   212/987-9385
Mon-Thurs: 10-7; Fri, Sat: 10-8   www.harlemunderground.com

This is a good stop for comfortable, reasonably priced, and "cool" urban wear. The merchandise has the feel of the historic area it represents. Personal or corporate embroidery is available for denim shirts and jackets, T-shirts, sweats, and caps.

Jeans . . . jeans . . . jeans . . . they come in all manner of styles, colors, fabrics, prices, and comfort levels. For the very best selection, here are some recommended outlets:

Anik (1122 Madison Ave, 212/249-2417 and 1355 Third Ave, 212/861-9840)
Atrium (644 Broadway, 212/473-9200)
Bloomingdale's (1000 Third Ave, 212/705-2000 and 504 Broadway, 212/729-5900)
Calvin Klein (654 Madison Ave, 212/292-9000)
Levi's Store (750 Lexington Ave, 212/826-5957 and 536 Broadway, 646/613-1847)
Saks Fifth Avenue (611 Fifth Ave, 212/753-4000)
Scoop (532 Broadway, 212/925-2886; 861 Washington St, 212/691-1905; and 1275 Third Ave, 212/535-5577)

HOUSE OF MAURIZIO
18 E 53rd St (bet Fifth and Madison Ave), 5th floor   212/759-3230
Mon-Fri: 9-5

Tony Maurizio caters to men and women who like the functional and fashionable tailored look of suits. Although almost any kind of garment can be copied, this house is known for coats, two- to four-piece suits, and mix-and-match combinations. This look is favored by busy executives, artists, and journalists who have to look well-dressed but don't have hours to spend dressing. House of Maurizio's tailors create blazers or suits in a range of 2,000 fabrics, and those in silk, linen, cotton, and solid virgin wool are sensational. In addition to women's garments, they design and create coats and suits for men in the same broad range of fabrics. Tony promises fast service, expert tailoring, and moderate prices.

JEFFREY—NEW YORK
449 W 14th St (bet Ninth and Tenth Ave)   212/206-1272
Mon-Fri: 10-8 (Thurs till 9); Sat: 10-7; Sun: 12:30-6

You wouldn't expect to find a store like Jeffrey Kalinsky's in Manhattan's Meatpacking District! It offers men's and women's clothing and accessories (with a big emphasis on shoes). His Atlanta operation has been successful, and now he's brought such fashion names as Pucci, Prada, Gucci, Manolo Blahnik, and Yves St. Laurent to downtown Manhattan.

LOUIS VUITTON
1 E 57th St (at Fifth Ave)   212/758-8877
Mon-Sat: 10-7 (Thurs till 8); Sun: 12-6   www.vuitton.com

In spectacular new quarters at 57th and Fifth, Louis Vuitton is nearly everything you might expect: a dramatic exterior, compelling windows, tasteful assortments of merchandise, snobby service, and inflated prices. Designer Marc Jacobs has certainly polished the label. If the LV signature is important to you, then this is the place to shop. But be warned: you are paying for four floors of very expensive real estate when you shop here.

MEXX
650 Fifth Ave (at 52nd St)   212/956-6506
500 Broadway (bet Broome and Spring St)   212/343-7954
Mon-Wed: 10-8; Thurs-Sat: 10-9; Sun: 11-7   www.mexx.com

Mexx is a global lifestyle brand with a modern European edge. For shoppers who want current styles at good prices, it is a popular destination. They have stores around the world and are quick to capitalize on hot items.

Here is a novel one. **Nom de Guerre** (640 Broadway, 212/253-2891) can only be reached by going underground! Once there you will find unusual T-shirts, sweatshirts, jeans, and sneakers. It's worth a visit.

POLO—RALPH LAUREN
867 Madison Ave (at 72nd St)   212/606-2100
878 Madison Ave (at 72nd St)   212/606-3376
379 West Broadway (bet Spring and Broome St)   212/625-1660
380 Bleecker St (bet Charles and Perry St)   212/645-5513
381 Bleecker St (bet Charles and Perry St)   646/638-0684
Hours vary by store   www.polo.com

Ralph Lauren has probably done as much as anyone to bring a classic look to American fashion and furnishings. That little monogrammed horse says something about your taste and lifestyle! His Manhattan showcase store, housed in the magnificent Rhinelander mansion, is fabulous. Four floors of merchandise for men, women, and home are beautifully displayed and expertly accessorized. You will see a much larger selection here than in the many specialty Polo boutiques in department stores. There are several things to be aware of, however. One is the haughty way some of the staff greet customers who don't look like they have big bucks. Moreover, although the clothes and furnishings are classy, one can find items of equal or better quality elsewhere at considerably lower prices. The purple-label merchandise is grossly overpriced. But shopping here means you can carry out your purchase in one of those popular green bags, if that matters to you. Across the street, **Polo Sport** (888 Madison Ave, 212/606-2100), is also done with class and flair.

REPLAY STORE
109 Prince St (at Greene St)   212/673-6300
Mon-Sat: 11-7; Sun: 11-6

This very attractive Soho store carries dozens of different washings and fits in jeans and a variety of shirt styles. Outdoor clothing is featured. This is one of the more well-stocked stores in the area, and prices are as comfortable as the merchandise.

Folks often ask where they can buy French cuffed shirts and a good selection of links. Here is my answer:
Links of London (535 Madison Ave, 212/588-1177)
Missing Link (40 W 25th St, Room 10B, 212/645-6928)
Thomas Pink (520 Madison Ave, 212/838-1928; 1155 Ave of the Americas, 212/840-9663; and 10 Columbus Circle, 212/812-9650): Ask for Michael Rodriguez.

STEVEN ALAN
103 Franklin St (bet Church St and West Broadway)   212/343-0692
465 Amsterdam Ave (bet 82nd and 83rd St)   212/595-8451
Daily: 11:30-7 (Thurs till 8)   www.stevenalan.com

Steven Alan is a real find for men and women who have difficulty finding small or large sizes in designer merchandise. They also stock accessories, outerwear, and toiletries.

Men's Formal Wear

DANTE ZELLER TUXEDOS
201 E 23rd St (at Third Ave), 2nd floor   212/532-7320
459 Lexington Ave (at 45th St), 3rd floor   212/286-9786
1010 Third Ave (at 60th St)   212/688-0100
421 Seventh Ave (at 33rd St), 2nd floor   212/290-0217
Mon-Fri: 9-7; Sat: 10-6; Sun: 10-6 (Third Ave location only)

Dante Zeller Tuxedos is Manhattan's largest locally owned formal-wear specialist, offering over 75 years of experience. Their wide selection includes the newest styles and colors from Calvin Klein, Ralph Lauren, Hugo Boss, Tallia Uomo, and others.

JACK AND COMPANY FORMAL WEAR
128 E 86th St (bet Lexington and Park Ave), 2nd floor
Mon-Fri: 10-7; Sat: 10-4   212/722-4609
                           www.jacktuxedos.com

Jack and Company rents and sells men's formal wear. They carry an excellent selection of sizes and names (After Six and Lord West), and they've had a good reputation for service since 1925. In sales or rentals, Jack's can supply head-to-toe formal wear. The staff is excellent at matching outfits to customers, as well as knowing exactly what is socially required for any occasion. Same-day service is available, and the full rental price will be applied toward purchase!

Men's—General

CAMOUFLAGE
141 Eighth Ave (at 17th St)   212/741-9118
Mon-Fri: 12-7; Sat: 11:30-6:30; Sun: 12-6

At Camouflage you'll find men's branded clothing, plus private label trousers, shirts, ties, and accessories. Considering some of the designer names, prices range from reasonable to good. Camouflage can attire customers with a dignified but unique look. You definitely won't blend into the wallpaper!

Gentlemen! Do you want to add some real excitement to your appearance? I suggest a visit to **Duncan Quinn** (8 Spring St, 212/226-7030, www.duncanquinn.com). You'll find the ultimate in British class in their superb suits and furnishings. Be sure to tell him I sent you!

EISENBERG AND EISENBERG
16 W 17th St (bet Fifth Ave and Ave of the Americas)   212/627-1290
Mon-Fri: 9-6 (Thurs till 7); Sat: 9-5; Sun: 10-4
www.eisenbergandeisenberg.com

The Eisenberg and Eisenberg style is a classic that dates from 1898. E&E consistently offers top quality and good prices on suits, tuxedos, coats, and sportswear. They also stock outerwear, slacks, raincoats, cashmere sport jackets, and 100% silk jackets. All are sold at considerable discounts, and alterations are available. London Fog coats are featured, and no label is better known for wet-weather needs.

FACONNABLE
636 Fifth Ave (at 51st St)   212/319-0111
Mon-Sat: 10-7 (Thurs till 8); Sun: 12-6   www.faconnable.com

Facconable (a French outfit) has made a name for itself in the fashion world with clothes that appeal to conservative dressers. Their New York store—which admittedly does not match the class or selection of the Beverly Hills operation—carries a good showing of men's and women's sportswear, tailored clothing, watches, suits, and shoes.

J. PRESS
7 E 44th St (bet Fifth and Madison Ave)   212/687-7642
Mon-Sat: 9-6   www.jpressonline.com

As one of New York's classic conservative men's stores, J. Press takes pride in its sense of timelessness. Its salespeople, customers, and attitude have changed little from the time of the founder. Styles are impeccable and distinguished. Blazers are blue, and shirts are button-down and straight. Even when button-down collars were out, they never went away at J. Press.

JOHN VARVATOS
149 Mercer St (bet Houston and Prince St)   212/965-0700
Mon-Sat: 11-7; Sun: 12-6   www.johnvarvatos.com

Elegance is the tradition at John Varvatos, with an outstanding collection of leather and shearling outerwear, sportswear, accessories, and skin-care and fragrance items. Men of all ages will feel comfortable with the Old World detailing of a line that exudes class.

L.S. MEN'S CLOTHING
49 W 45th St (bet Fifth Ave and Ave of the Americas), 3rd floor
Mon-Thurs: 9-7; Fri: 9-3; Sun: 10-4   212/575-0933
                                              www.lsmensclothing.com

L.S. Men's Clothing bills itself as "*the* executive discount shop," but I would go further and call them a must for fashion-minded businessmen. For one thing, the expanded midtown location means one needn't trek down to Fifth Avenue in the teens, which is the main area for men's discount clothing. Better still, as owner Israel Zuber puts it, "There are many stores selling $400 suits at discount, but we are one of the few in mid-Manhattan that discount the $550 to $1,500 range of suits." The main attraction, though, is the tremendous selection of executive-class styles. Within that category, a man could outfit himself almost entirely at L.S. Men's. Natural, soft-shoulder suits by name designers are available in all sizes. A custom-order department is available, with over 2,500 bolts of Italian and English goods in stock. Custom-made suits take four to six weeks and sell for around $595; sport coats are priced at $445. This is one of the very best spots for top-drawer names.

PAUL STUART
Madison Ave at 45th St   212/682-0320
Mon-Fri: 8-6:30 (Thurs till 7); Sat: 9-6; Sun: 12-5
                                              www.paulstuart.com

This is *the* store for shoppers who don't really know what they want, have trouble putting things together to make a "look," and worry about quality. You would be hard-pressed to find a better selection of men's and women's fine apparel and accessories. One drawback: there is little excitement here, either in the presentation or merchandise. Nonetheless, the men's suits, ties, and sport jackets are first-class, as is the collection of handmade English shoes.

ROTHMAN'S
200 Park Ave S (at 17th St)   212/777-7400
Mon-Fri: 10-7 (Thurs till 8); Sat: 9:30-6; Sun: 12-6
                                              www.rothmansny.com

Forget your image of the old Harry Rothman operation. Harry's grandson, Ken Giddon, runs this classy men's store, which offers a huge selection of quality clothes at discounts of up to 40% in a contemporary and comfortable atmosphere. He carries top names like Canali, Hickey-Freeman, Corneliani, Joseph Aboud, Calvin Klein, Zegna, and Hugo Boss. Sizes at

Rothman's range from 36 to 50 in regular, short, long, and extra long. Rain-coats, slacks, sport jackets, and accessories are also sold at attractive prices.

SAINT LAURIE MERCHANT TAILORS
22 W 32nd St (bet Fifth Ave and Ave of the Americas), 5th floor
Mon-Fri: 9-6; Sat: 9-5:30   212/643-1916
                                                    www.saintlaurie.com

Saint Laurie has been in business since 1913—that's four generations!—offering good-looking, made-to-measure clothing for men and women at rack prices. A laser body scanner ensures accurate measurements. Accessories like ties and cuff links are also available. The firm buys directly from the weavers, resulting in price savings. In addition, the showroom is located where the clothing is made, shortening delivery time. An interesting note: Saint Laurie produces goods for Broadway shows and films.

For gentlemen who don't want to pay uptown prices or don't like the haughty airs of some uptown salesmen, here are several downtown alternatives.

Memes (3 Great Jones St, 212/420-9955): cool and casual clothes
Seize Sur Vingt (243 Elizabeth St, 212/343-0476): ritzy, custom-made suits, shirts, and sweaters in beautiful fabrics from Scotland and Italy
Stussy (140 Wooster St, 212/995-8787): for the hip set
Urns (226 Elizabeth St, 212/431-5533): colorful sweaters
Vice (252 Lafayette St, 212/219-7788): shoes and shirts in an intimate, attitude-free setting

---

Men's Hats

J.J. HAT CENTER
310 Fifth Ave (at 32nd St)   212/239-4368, 800/622-1911
Mon-Fri: 9-6; Sat: 9:30-5:30   www.jjhatcenter.com

This outfit stocks over 15,000 brand-name hats and caps (to size 8) from all over the world. Founded in 1911, it is New York's oldest hat shop. Special services include free brush-up, hat stretching or tightening, custom orders, and a free catalog.

Men's Shirts

MARK CHRISTOPHER
55 W 26th St (bet Broadway and Ave of the Americas), 35th floor
Mon-Fri: 11-8; Sat: 12-7; Sun: 12-6 (by appointment)   212/686-9190
                                        www.markchristophercustomshirts.com

When it comes to custom-making shirts for well-dressed executives or upwardly mobile types, owner Mark Lingley is the guy to see. The classy shirts at Mark Christopher are made of fine cotton and hand-cut with superb tailoring. You pay for such special merchandise, but the service (they will make office calls) and care (the typical shirt requires about 20 measurements for a fitting) are worth the extra bucks. Shirts are the foundation of the operation, but suits and ties are also available.

SHIRT STORE
51 E 44th St (bet Vanderbilt and Madison Ave)   212/557-8040
Mon-Fri: 8-6:30; Sat: 10-5   www.shirtstore.com

The attraction here is that you buy directly from the manufacturer, so there's no middle man to increase the price. The Shirt Store offers all-cotton shirts for men in sizes from 14x32 to 18½x37. Although the ready-made stock is great, they will also do custom work and even come to your office with swatches. Additional services include mail order, alterations, and monogramming.

STATS
331 W 57th St (bet Eighth and Ninth Ave), Suite 280   212/262-5844
Mon-Fri: 8-7; weekends by appointment

What does STATS stand for? Shirts, Ties, and Terrific Service, of course! Julie Manis sells custom dress and casual shirts, neckwear, braces, and accessories in the convenience of one's office or home. She carries tailoring tools and fabrics, and can special-order fabrics not in stock. Appointments can be made to suit your busy schedule. She also takes the extra step of a sample shirt fitting.

Men's Ties

GOIDEL NECKWEAR
138 Allen St (bet Rivington and Delancey St)   212/475-7332
Sun-Fri: 9:30-3

Since 1935 this has been *the* place for bargains on ties, cummerbunds, men's jewelry, and accessories. They triple as manufacturers, wholesalers, and retailers, so savings are passed on to customers. Special note to groups: these folks will match most items brought in, usually within a week or two.

Men's Underwear

UNDER WARES
210 E 58th St (bet Second and Third Ave)   212/838-1200
Mon-Fri: 10-7; Sat: 10-6; Sun: 12-5   800/237-8641
                                                www.underwaresforhim.com

Not so long ago, the average fellow couldn't tell you what kind of underwear he wore and probably didn't buy it himself. All that changed when ads began featuring celebrity jocks. These days men's underwear makes a fashion statement. Under Wares sells over a hundred styles of briefs and boxer shorts. They stock the largest selection of men's undergarments in the world, carrying many top labels. There are also T-shirts, hosiery, robes, pajamas, workout wear, swimwear, and gift items. You can browse and order from their website, too.

Resale Clothing

ALLAN & SUZI
416 Amsterdam Ave (at 80th St)   212/724-7445
Mon-Sun: 12-7   www.allanandsuzi.net

This "retro clothing store" is quite an operation! Under one roof you'll find current designer and vintage clothing for men and women, old and new shoes, and accessories. There are big names (like Galliano, Lacroix, Ungaro, and Versace) and ones so new you probably haven't heard of them yet. Some outfits are discounted. They are proud of the fact that they dress a number of Hollywood and TV personalities. Ask for Allan Pollack or Suzi Kandel.

DESIGNER RESALE
324 E 81st St (bet First and Second Ave)   212/734-3639
Mon-Fri: 11-7 (Thurs till 8); Sat: 10-6; Sun: 12-5
                                                    www.resaleclothing.net

"Gently worn" is the byword here! Designer Resale offers previously owned ladies' designer clothing and accessories at moderate prices. Most major fashion names are represented. You might find Chanel, Armani, Hermes, or Valentino garments on the racks. If items do not sell, prices are marked down further. Call to ask about the latest bargains.

ENCORE
1132 Madison Ave (bet 84th and 85th St), upstairs   212/879-2850
Mon-Fri: 10:30-6:30 (Thurs till 7:30); Sat: 10:30-6;
Sun: 12-6 (closed Sun in July, Aug)   www.encoreresale.com

Founded in 1954, Encore can honestly be billed as a "resale shop of gently worn clothing of designer/couture quality." When you see the merchandise and clientele, you'll know why. For one thing, it is a consignment boutique, not a charity thrift shop. Its donors receive a portion of the sales price, and according to owner Carole Selig, many of the donors are socialites and other luminaries who don't want to be seen in the same outfit twice. Selig can afford to be picky, and so can you. The fashions are up-to-date and are sold at 50% to 70% off of original retail prices. There are over 6,000 items in stock. Prices range from reasonable to astronomical—but just think how much they sold for originally!

GENTLEMEN'S RESALE
322 E 81st St (bet First and Second Ave)   212/734-2739
Mon-Fri: 11-7; Sat: 10-6; Sun: 12-5   www.resaleclothing.org

Gentlemen interested in top-quality designer suits, jackets, and sportswear can save a bundle at this resale operation. Shopping here is like a treasure hunt, and that is half the fun. Imagine picking up a $1,000 Armani suit for $200! You might also earn a few extra bucks by consigning some of your own wardrobe.

KAVANAGH'S
146 E 49th St (bet Third and Lexington Ave)   212/702-0152
Tues-Fri: 11-6; Sat: 11-4

I can vouch highly for this designer resale shop. It is owned by Mary Kavanagh, formerly of Bergdorf Goodman. She has superb taste! As that store's director of personal shopping, she had access to the finest labels in the world. At Kavanagh's she carries many of those same labels: Chanel, Versace, Valentino, Ungaro, Armani, Galanos, Beene, Bill Blass, Oscar de la Renta, and many more. Chanel clothes and accessories are a specialty. Mary describes her store as a "sunny, happy spot filled with attractive antiques." It is a classy shopping haven where customers come first. Moreover, she will open early, stay late, or open on Sunday for special groups.

MICHAEL'S, THE CONSIGNMENT SHOP FOR WOMEN

1041 Madison Ave (at 79th St)   212/737-7273
Mon-Sat: 9:30-6 (Thurs till 8)   www.michaelsconsignment.com

Is your mouth watering for one of those gowns you have seen in the papers or on TV? Want to dress up like one of the stars? Here's the place to come for pieces from top designers like Chanel, Prada, Gucci, Hermes, YSL, Dolce and Gabanna, Armani, and others. However, evening wear is just a small part of their stock. You'll also find pant sets, skirts, suits, bags, shoes, and more. Personal attention is assured, and prices are right.

Consignment and Thrift Shops

Chelsea

Fisch for the Hip (153 W 18th St, 212/633-9053)
Goodwill Superstore (103 W 25th St, 646/638-1725)
Housing Works Thrift Shop (143 W 17th St, 212/366-0820)

East 20s

City Opera Thrift Shop (222 E 23rd St, 212/684-5344)
Goodwill Superstore (220 E 23rd St, 212/447-7270)
Marble Thrift Shop (382 Third Ave, 212/532-5136)
Housing Works Thrift Shop (157 E 23rd St, 212/529-5955)
Salvation Army Thrift Store (212 E 23rd St, 212/532-8115)
St. George's Thrift Shop (61 Gramercy Park N, 212/475-2674)

Upper East Side

Arthritis Foundation Thrift Shop (1383 Third Ave, 212/772-8816)
Bis Designer Resale (1134 Madison Ave, 2nd floor, 212/396-2760)
Cancer Care Thrift Shop (1480 Third Ave, 212/879-9868)
Council Thrift Shop (246 E 84th St, 212/439-8373)
Housing Works Thrift Shop (202 E 77th St, 212/772-8461)
Kavanagh's (146 E 49th St, 212/702-0152)
Memorial Sloan-Kettering Thrift Shop (1440 Third Ave, 212/535-1250)
Michael's (1041 Madison Ave, 212/737-7273)
Out of the Closet Thrift Shop (220 E 81st St, 212/472-3573)
Spence-Chapin Thrift Shop (1473 Third Ave, 212/737-8448)
Stuyvesant Square Thrift Shop (1704 Second Ave, 212/831-1830)

Upper West Side

Goodwill Superstore (217 W 79th St, 212/874-5050)
Housing Works Thrift Shop (306 Columbus Ave, 212/579-7566)

TATIANA

767 Lexington Ave (bet 60th and 61st St)   212/755-7744
Mon-Sat: 11-7; Sun: 12-5   www.tatianas.com

This is a unique designer consignment boutique outlet. For consigners, Tatiana offers free estimates and pickup service. For retail customers, she will try to find whatever outfit they may want. The stock is top-grade, with clothing, jewelry, bags, shoes, hats, and furs bearing top names like Chanel, Gucci, Valentino, Armani, YSL, Versace, and Bill Blass.

Shoes—Children's

EAST SIDE KIDS
1298 Madison Ave (bet 92nd and 93rd St)   212/360-5000
Mon-Fri: 9:30-6; Sat: 9-6

East Side Kids stocks footwear items up to a woman's size 10 and a man's size 9. They can accommodate older children and juniors, plus adults with small to average-sized feet. Of course, there is also a great selection of children's shoes in both domestic and imported styles. Frequent-buyer cards are kept on file for special discounts. The store is known for helpful service.

SHOOFLY
42 Hudson St (bet Reade and Chambers St)   212/406-3270
Mon-Sat: 10-7; Sun: 12-6   www.shooflynyc.com

Shoofly carries attractive and reasonably priced imported shoes for infants to 14-year-olds. Women with tiny feet will appreciate their chic selection of footwear as well. Shoofly will take care of your shoewear needs with styles both funky and classic. The selection of tights and socks is great, too!

Some interesting new stores you might want to visit:
Archipelago (38 Walker St, 212/334-9460): home accessories
Darling (1 Horatio St, 646/336-6966): clothing
Lingo (257 W 19th St, 212/929-9872): clothing
Ro (150 W 28th St, 212/477-1595): shoes and accessories
Sydney's Playground (66 White St, 212/431-9125): children's goods

---

Shoes—Family

E. VOGEL BOOTS AND SHOES
19 Howard St (one block north of Canal St, bet Broadway and
   Lafayette St)   212/925-2460
Mon-Fri: 8-4; Sat: 8-1:30 (closed Sat in summer and first two weeks
   of July)   www.vogelboots.com, www.vogelshoes.com

Hank and Dean Vogel and Jack Lynch are the third- and fourth-generation family members to join this business since 1879. They will happily fit and supply made-to-measure boots and shoes for any adult or child who can find the store. Howard is one of those streets that even native New Yorkers don't know exists. Still, many beat a path to Vogel for top-quality shoes and boots (including equestrian boots). While not inexpensive, prices are reasonable for the service involved. Amazingly, made-to-measure shoes do not always fit properly, but they do at Vogel. Moreover, once your pattern is on record, they can make new shoes without a personal visit. For craftsmanship, this spot is top-drawer. There are more than 500 Vogel dealers throughout the world, but this is the original store, and the people here are super.

KENNETH COLE
597 Broadway (at Houston St)   212/965-0283
353 Columbus Ave (bet 76th and 77th St)   212/873-2061
95 Fifth Ave (at 17th St)   212/675-2550

107 E 42nd St (bet Vanderbilt and Park Ave)   212/949-8079
130 E 57th St (at Lexington Ave)   212/688-1670
Hours vary by store   www.kennethcole.com

In addition to signs that induce hearty laughter at the expense of some well-known personalities, Kenneth Cole offers quality shoes, belts, scarves, watches, outerwear, and accessories at sensible prices.

LORD JOHN'S BOOTERY
428 Third Ave (bet 29th and 30th St)   212/532-2579
Mon-Fri: 10-8; Sat: 10-7   www.lordjohnsbootery.com

Lord John's Bootery has been family-owned and operated for three generations, spanning over half a century. The store has been renovated and expanded and now carries one of the largest selection of dress, casual, and comfort shoes in the area. They offer footwear for men and women from such manufacturers as Ecco, Mephisto, Paul Green, Rockport, Sebago, Birkenstock, Merrell, Camper, Kenneth Cole, Santana, and Dansko.

SHOE MANIA
853 Broadway (bet 14th St and Union Square)   212/253-8744
331 Madison Ave (bet 42nd and 43rd St)   212/557-6627
30 E 14th St (bet University St and Fifth Ave)   212/627-0420
11 W 34th St (bet Fifth Ave and Ave of the Americas) 212/564-7319
Hours vary by store   www.shoemania.com

Shoe Mania carries men's and women's shoes for fashion, comfort, and sport at great prices. Most major brands—Hugo Boss, Adidas, Birkenstock, Converse, Kenneth Cole, Mephisto, New Balance, Rockport, Steve Madden, Via Spiga, and more—are stocked in a broad range of sizes (women's 5 to 12, men's sizes 7 to 14). What more could you ask for?

T.O. DEY CUSTOM SHOE MAKERS
9 E 38th St (bet Fifth and Madison Ave), 7th floor   212/683-6300
Mon-Fri: 9-5; Sat: 9-12:30   www.todeyshoes.com

T.O. Dey is a solid jack-of-all-trades operation. Though their specialty is custom-made shoes, they can also repair any kind of shoe. These folks will create men's or women's shoes based on a plaster mold of a customer's feet. Their styles are limited only by a client's imagination. They make arch supports, cover shoes to match a garment, and sell athletic shoes for football, basketball, cross-country, hockey, boxing, and running.

Shoes—Men's
CHURCH ENGLISH SHOES
689 Madison Ave (at 62nd St)   212/758-5200
Mon-Sat: 10-6   www.churchshoes.com

Anglophiles feel right at home here, not only because of the *veddy* English atmosphere but also for the pure artistry and "Englishness" of the shoes. Church has been selling English shoes for men since 1873 and is known for classic styles, superior workmanship, and fine leathers. The styles basically remain unchanged year after year, although new designs are occasionally added as a concession to fashion. All shoes are custom-fitted, and if a style or size does not feel right, they will special order a pair that does.

STAPLETON SHOE COMPANY

68 Trinity Pl (at Rector St)	212/964-6329
1 Rector St (bet Broadway and Trinity Pl)	212/425-5260

Mon-Thurs: 8:30-5:30; Fri: 8:30-5

Their motto is "better shoes for less," but that doesn't begin to describe this superlative operation. Gentlemen, these stores offer Bally, Alden, Allen-Edmonds, Cole-Haan, Timberland, Rockport, Johnston & Murphy, and a slew of other top names at discount. There isn't a better source for quality shoes. They are size specialists, carrying men's sizes 5-18 in widths A-EEE.

Shoes—Women's

ANBAR SHOES

60 Reade St (bet Church St and Broadway)	212/227-0253

Mon-Fri: 9-6:20; Sat: 11-5:45

Bargain hunters, rejoice! Anbar customers can find great deals on brand-name styles at discounts up to 80%. This is a good place to save money.

GIORDANO'S SHOES

1150 Second Ave (at 60th St)	212/688-7195
Mon-Fri: 11-7; Sat: 11-6	www.petiteshoes.com

Susan Giordano has a very special clientele. Her store stocks a fine selection of women's designer shoes in small sizes (a range that is virtually non-existent in regular shoe stores). If you're a woman who wears shoes in the 4 to 5½ medium range, you are probably used to shopping in children's shoe departments or having shoes custom-made, either of which can cramp your style. For these women, Giordano's is a godsend. Brands carried include Anne Klein, Stuart Weitzman, Donald Pliner, Via Spiga, Rangoni, and more.

PETER FOX SHOES

105 Thompson St (bet Prince and Spring St)	212/431-7426
Mon-Sat: 11-7; Sun: 12-6	www.peterfox.com

Peter Fox has been *the* downtown trailblazer for women's shoes. His shop carries only exclusive, limited-edition designer footwear. Perhaps because of the Soho location, Fox's designs are more adventurous than those of its competitors; the look is younger and more casual. If you're looking for shoes to be seen in, this is the place to go.

TALL SIZE SHOES

3 W 35th St (at Fifth Ave)	212/736-2060

Mon-Sat: 9:30-6 (Thurs till 7)

Finding comfortable shoes if you are a "tall size" is not easy. This store can solve the problem, as they carry a broad selection of shoes to size 14 in widths from AA to extra-wide. There are custom-made shoes and designer names to choose from: Naturalizer, Trotters, Franco Sarto, Via Spiga, Vanelli, Sesto Meucci, Moda Spana, Costa Blanca, and many more. They also have a Cinderella department with a wide selection of shoes from size 4 on up. They will take phone orders and ship anywhere.

Sportswear

FOOTACTION USA
430 Seventh Ave (at 34th St)   646/473-1945
Mon-Sat: 8 a.m.-10 p.m.; Sun: 10-9

Major sports clothing and accessories may be found here! A nice selection of athletic shoes (like Michael Jordan's Nike line) and NBA fan gear is also available.

If you have large feet, these outfits have shoes that will fit them.
Johnston & Murphy (345 Madison Ave, 212/697-9375 and 520 Madison Ave, 212/527-2342): men's to size 15
Stapleton Shoe Company (68 Trinity Pl, 212/964-6329): men's to size 18
Tall Size Shoes (3 W 35th St, 212/736-2060): women's to size 14

GERRY COSBY AND COMPANY
2 Pennsylvania Plaza (32nd St at Seventh Ave)   212/563-6464
Mon-Fri: 9:30-7:30; Sat: 9:30-6; Sun: 12-5   877/563-6464
                                                        www.cosbysports.com

There's a lot to like about this company. Located in the famous Madison Square Garden lobby, they are a professional business in an appropriate venue for "team sportswear"—that is, what athletes wear. They remain open for a half-hour after Rangers and Knicks home games. Gerry Cosby designs and markets protective equipment and is a top supplier of professionally licensed products. The protective equipment and bags are designed for pros but are available to the general public as well. They accept mail and phone orders for everything, including personalized jerseys and jackets.

HOWARD SPORTSWEAR
85 Orchard St (at Grand St)   212/226-4307
Sun-Fri: 9-5:30

Howard transformed itself from a typical Lower East Side shop into a fashionable boutique without sacrificing the bargain prices. They carry an excellent selection of women's underwear, including top names like Hanes, Bali, Vanity Fair, Warners, Maidenform, Wacoal, Olga, Lilyette, and Jockey.

NBA STORE
666 Fifth Ave (at 52nd St)   212/515-6270
Mon-Sat: 10-7; Sun: 11-6

The National Basketball Association does a tremendous job of marketing itself. (I wish I could say the same for all of the NBA players!) This two-story store, occupying a prime tourist location on Fifth Avenue, is always busy with people buying team jerseys and equipment, and watching NBA videos.

NIKETOWN NEW YORK
6 E 57th St (bet Fifth and Madison Ave)   212/891-6453
Mon-Sat: 10-8; Sun: 11-7   www.niketown.com

Product innovation and Nike's sports heritage are the foundations of

Niketown New York. They offer a huge selection of Nike products, including footwear, apparel (not their strongest category), items for timing and vision, and hot new tech-lab products. If you don't see your favorite athletes on the giant 36' by 22' video screen, you might find them shopping next to you.

Surplus

KAUFMAN'S ARMY & NAVY
319 W 42nd St (bet Eighth and Ninth Ave)   212/757-5670
Mon-Fri: 11-6 (Thurs till 7); Sat: 12-6
www.kaufmansarmynavy.com

Kaufman's has long been a favorite among New Yorkers and visitors alike for its extensive selection of genuine military surplus from around the globe. Over the last half-century, Kaufman's has outfitted dozens of Broadway and TV shows and supplied a number of major motion pictures with military garb. The store is a treasure trove of military collectibles, hats, helmets, uniforms, and insignias. Over a thousand military pins, patches, and medals from armies the world over are on display.

NOM DE GUERRE
640 Broadway (at Bleecker St), lower level   212/253-2891
Mon-Sat: 12-6; Sun: 12-7   www.nomdeguerre.net

Unique is the word here. Located in a multilevel subterranean space that's hidden from the street, the store features merchandise that reflects Manhattan's many cultures. It has the look of a high-end Army surplus store with an emphasis on utilitarian and street-wear clothes. Features include denim, cult designers, limited-edition clothing, accessories, and footwear.

UNCLE SAM'S ARMY NAVY OUTFITTERS
37 W 8th St (bet Fifth Ave and Ave of the Americas)   212/674-2222
Mon-Wed: 10-9; Thurs-Sat: 10-10; Sun: 11-8
www.iamunclesam.com

There are a lot of Army-Navy surplus stores, but this is the only outlet in the city that gets it stock straight from the U.S. government. The quality at Uncle Sam's is very good. You'll find an excellent selection of pants, shirts, tank tops, flight jackets, watches, flags, pins, patches, and more. They will also loan out goods for a 48-hour period for various production needs —even school plays and church groups – at no cost.

Sweaters

BEST OF SCOTLAND
581 Fifth Ave (bet 47th and 48th St), penthouse
Mon-Fri: 9:30-6; Sat: 10-4   212/644-0403, 800/215-3864
www.cashmerenyc.com

Cashmere is big these days, and these folks are among the very best purveyors of cashmere goods. There is a big difference in the quality of cashmere from Scotland and the Far East. At Best of Scotland you will find luxurious sweaters, baby blankets, ladies' capes, scarves, mufflers, and throws. Don't worry about sizes: you'll find ladies' sweaters up to size 48 and gentlemen's to size 59. In addition to their beautiful classic styles, you'll find superfine cashmere for spring and summer wear, and fitted sweaters for ladies. Nice people, too!

GRANNY-MADE
381 Amsterdam Ave (bet 78th and 79th St)   212/496-1222
Mon-Fri: 11-7; Sat: 10-6; Sun: 12-5   www.granny-made.com

Michael Rosenberg (grandson of Bert Levy, the namesake "Granny") has assembled an extensive collection of sweaters for infants, young people, and adults. These include handmade sweaters from all over the world, as well as ones hand-loomed right here at home. The selection of women's sweaters, knitwear, dresses, skirts, slacks, soft items, and accessories is unique, as are the men's sweaters. They have an extensive selection of infant and toddler clothing, hats, and accessories. Granny-Made has an extremely service-oriented, knowledgeable staff. They also sell "Moon and Star" cookies, made from a recipe passed down three generations!

> Check the labels on your cashmere clothing! Items from Scotland, Italy, and Japan are best.

T-Shirts

EISNER BROS.
75 Essex St (bet Grand and Delancey St)   212/475-6868
Mon-Thurs: 8:30-6:30; Fri: 8:30-3; Sun: 8:30-4:30   800/426-7700
                                                  www.eisnerbros.com

Eisner Bros. carries a full line of licensed NBA, NFL, NHL, MLB, collegiate, and other sports, character, and novelty T-shirts and sweat shirts. Major quantity discounts are offered. You will also find police, fire, and emergency department logos, as well as Disney and Harley-Davidson. Personalizing is featured on all items. They are the largest source in the area for blank, printable corporate sportswear, T-shirts, sweat shirts, caps, jackets, work clothing, uniforms, reflective vests, tote bags, towels, aprons, umbrellas, gym and exercise equipment, team uniforms, and much more.

Uniforms

JA-MIL UNIFORMS
92 Orchard St (at Delancey St)   212/677-8190
Mon-Thurs: 10-5 or by appointment

This is *the* bargain spot for those who must wear uniforms but do not want to spend a fortune on work clothes. There are outfits for doctors, nurses, and technicians, as well as the finest domestic uniforms and chef's apparel. Dansko clogs, Nurse Mates, and SAS shoes are available in white and colors. Mail orders are accepted.

Western Wear

BILLY MARTIN'S
220 E 60th St (bet Second and Third Ave)   212/861-3100
Mon-Fri: 11-7; Sat: 11-5:30; Sun: 1-5   www.billymartin.com

If Western wear is on your shopping list, then head to Billy Martin's! They have a great selection of deerskin jackets, shirts, riding pants, skirts, hats, and parkas. They also boast one of the best collections of cowboy boots in the city for men and women. Great accessory items like bandannas, jewelry, sterling silver buckles, and belt straps complete the outfit. The items are well-tooled, well-designed, and priced accordingly.

Women's Accessories

BLUE BAG
266 Elizabeth St (bet Prince and Houston St)   212/966-8566
Daily: 11-7 (Mon-Sat: 12-8; Sun: 12-7 in summer)

Every month you'll find a different stock of small designer bags from all over the world at Blue Bag. You probably won't see these bags in any other stores, and Blue Bag never reorders the same bag. Prices range from $75 to $400 for suedes, leathers, and other materials.

EUROSPORT BAG
39 W 29th St (bet Broadway and Ave of the Americas)   212/685-5226
Mon-Thurs: 7:30-6; Fri: 7:30-5; Sat: 7:30-1
(first Sunday of each month: 8:30-3)

Kim Hyuk, Jr., runs an importing company exclusively devoted to handbags. Importing and wholesaling companies are common in this area. What is uncommon is the courtesy and selection Kim gives individual retail customers. He has a knack for making everyone feel like a valued customer and does not take offense when a finicky lady picks through the entire stock in search of the perfect handbag. Besides, it shouldn't be too hard to find, within certain guidelines. "Imported" here usually refers to origins from points west rather than east. Hyuk imports vinyl, canvas, and nylon handbags. School backpacks are a specialty. Most of this is average, serviceable stuff, but there are a few stars in the line. Prices border on magnificent. Minimum purchase is 12 pieces.

FINE AND KLEIN
119 Orchard St (at Delancey St)   212/674-6720
Sun-Thurs: 9-4:30; Fri: 9-3

The finest handbag store for value and selection is not in Rome, Paris, or London. It is not even on Fifth Avenue in New York. It is on the Lower East Side, and the name is Fine and Klein. What a selection! There is a bag for every purpose, any time of day, in every fabric. Top labels are sold for a fraction of what you would pay uptown. In addition, shopping at Fine and Klein is fun. At times the crowds, especially on Sundays and holidays, are so large that the number allowed to enter must be controlled! My good friends Julius Fine and Murray Klein are the epitome of old-time merchants, and you will be delighted with their service. Tell them I sent you!

JIMMY CHOO
716 Madison Ave (bet 63rd and 64th St)   212/759-7078
Mon-Sat: 10-6 (Thurs till 7); Sun: 12-5   www.jimmychoo.com

Follow the celebrities to Jimmy Choo's, where you can find classic boots, daytime and evening bags, small leather goods, fabulous designer footwear, and jeweled sandals. Bring along your goldest credit card!

MARY JAEGER

51 Spring St (bet Mulberry and Lafayette St)   212/941-5877
Mon-Fri: 12:30-6:30; Sat: 12 -7; Sun: 12-5   www.maryjaeger.com

Mary Jaeger's shop carries an excellent collection of fashionable women's accessories, interior accessories (like pillows and throws), and things for babies. Custom-designed decorative pillows made from vintage fabrics are a specialty. A couture and custom-design studio in Tribeca is an unusual feature, allowing Mary to complete special orders quickly.

RAFE NEW YORK

1 Bleecker St (at Bowery St)   212/780-9739
Mon-Sat: 12-7 (Fri till 8); Sun: 12-6   www.rafe.com

When you need a lift, this is a good store to visit. The selection of bags, shoes, and accessories is outstanding. Unusual items designed for both men and women are manufactured all over the world. The large shop is owned by designer Ramon Totengco, better known as "Rafe." If you want to see merchandise that is on the cutting edge of cool, this is the place!

SUAREZ

450 Park Ave (bet 56th and 57th St)   212/753-3758
Mon-Sat: 10-6; Sun: 11-5   www.suarezny.com

Suarez has been in business for more than a half-century (three generations). In that time, they have cultivated a reputation for quality merchandise, good service, excellent selection, and reasonable prices. For years the Suarez name has been whispered by women-in-the-know as a resource for fine leather goods. They offer a great selection of exotic skin bags in a wide variety of colors.

No need to buy an around-the-world airplane ticket. Just take a ride (or stroll) to **Roberta Freymann** (153 E 70th St, 212/585-3767). Roberta will tell you all about the clothes and accessories she has assembled for her boutique. It reads like a United Nation's tour!

Women's—General

BETSEY JOHNSON

248 Columbus Ave (bet 71st and 72nd St)   212/362-3364
138 Wooster St (bet Prince and Houston St)   212/995-5048
251 E 60th St (at Second Ave)   212/319-7699
1060 Madison Ave (at 80th St)   212/734-1257
Hours vary by store   www.betseyjohnson.com

In the 1960s and 1970s, Betsey Johnson was *the* fashion designer. Her designs appeared everywhere, as did Betsey herself. As an outlet for those designs not sold to exclusive boutiques, Betsey co-founded Betsey Bunky Nini, but her own pursuits led to more designing and ultimately a store in Soho. The store proved so successful that Betsey moved to larger quarters and then up and across town, as well as into such department stores as Bloomingdale's. While her style has always managed to be avant-garde, it has never been too far out. Johnson believes in making her own statement, and each store seems unique, despite the fact that she has over 40 of them across the country and internationally. Prices, particularly at the Soho store (which started as an outlet), are bearable. Incidentally, it's hard to overlook the shops: pink with neon accents, yellow floral with gold accents, great windows, and funky, personable staff.

BEVERLY M. LTD.
By appointment   212/744-3726

Beverly Madden will design and make skirts in a selection of unusual and pure fabrics just for you. Sizing adjustment is done at no extra cost. Delivery takes three to four weeks, depending on fabric availability.

EILEEN FISHER
314 E 9th St (bet First and Second Ave)	212/529-5715
521 Madison Ave (bet 53rd and 54th St)	212/759-9888
341 Columbus Ave (bet 76th and 77th St)	212/362-3000
166 Fifth Ave (bet 21st and 22nd St)	212/924-4777
1039 Madison Ave (at 79th St)	212/879-7799
395 West Broadway (bet Spring and Broome St)	212/431-4567
Hours vary by store	www.eileenfisher.com

For the lady who likes her clothes cool, loose, and casual, look no further than Eileen Fisher. This talented designer has put together a collection of easy-care, mostly washable natural-fiber outfits that travel well and are admired for their simple and attractive lines. The colors are earthy. From a small start in the East Village to six units all over Manhattan and space in some of the top stores, Eileen has produced a winner. The East Village store features discounted merchandise and first-quality goods.

ELENY
18 W 56th St (at Fifth Ave), 5th floor   212/245-0001
Mon-Sat: 10-6 (by appointment)   www.eleny.com

Have you dreamed about designing a dress for yourself? Well, at Eleny, this is possible. The customer-oriented personnel enjoy receiving input from their clients, and you can rest assured your gown will not be seen anywhere else. They will send sketches and finished gowns anywhere, and Eleny (who has been designing clothes for over two decades) gives each client her undivided attention. All fabrics are imported from Europe.

ELIZABETH CHARLES
639½ Hudson St (bet Gansevoort and Horatio St)   212/243-3201
Tues-Sat: 12-7:30; Sun: 12-6:30   www.elizabeth-charles.com

Flirty original designer clothes for all occasions from Australia and New Zealand make this a very special shop. You can even bring your boyfriend along, as the shop provides a great antique couch for patient partners!

FORMAN'S
82 Orchard St (bet Broome and Grand St)   212/228-2500
Sun-Wed: 9-6; Thurs: 9-7; Fri: 9-4

560 Fifth Ave (bet 45th and 46th St)   212/719-1000
Mon-Thurs: 8-8; Fri: 8-5; Sun: 10-7

Forman's has a well-deserved reputation for being the "fashion oasis of the Lower East Side." You'll find trendy discounted sportswear, separates, and outerwear from such famous houses as Evan Piccone, Jones NY, Kasper, and Liz Claiborne in sizes that will satisfy petites, normal figures, and plus-size women. The stock changes rapidly, so periodic visits are in order.

GALLERY OF WEARABLE ART
34 E 67th St (bet Madison and Park Ave)   212/425-5379
Tues-Sat: 10:30-6   www.galleryofwearableart.com

The best phrase to describe this innovative business is "anti-trendy." The Gallery of Wearable Art carries New York's largest collection of unusual clothing, jewelry, and accessories from all over the world. It is primarily a cottage industry with a specialty in creating and designing special occasion and bridal wear. Make this your destination if you are looking for unusual evening gowns, cocktail suits, bridal alternatives for nontraditional weddings, attractive jewelry, one-of-a-kind art jackets in antique textiles, and lace collage ensembles. You can even create your own gown. One thing is guaranteed: you won't see similar apparel on a friend or relative!

GEMINOLA
41 Perry St (bet Seventh Ave and 4th St)   212/675-1994
Tues-Sun: 12-7   www.geminola.com

Geminola has an eclectic assortment of styles for the home and self. All of their clothing is made from vintage pieces, and the original designs are adapted to customer specifications.

GISELLE
143 Orchard St (bet Delancey and Rivington St)   212/673-1900
Sun-Thurs: 9-6; Fri: 9-3   www.giselleny.com

Women's designer sportswear, current-season goods, a large selection (sizes 4 to 20), and discount prices are among the reasons Giselle is one of the more popular shopping spots on the Lower East Side. All merchandise is first-quality. Factor in excellent service, and Giselle is well worth a trip.

LEA'S DESIGNER FASHIONS
119 Orchard St (near Delancey St), mezzanine level   212/677-2043
Mon-Fri: 9:30-5; Sun: 9-5

You don't have to pay full price for your Louis Feraud, Valentino, or various European designer clothes. Lea's, a popular Lower East Side outlet, discounts her merchandise up to 30% and sells the previous season's styles for 50% to 60% off. Don't expect much in the way of amenities, but you'll save enough to afford a special dinner to show off your new outfit!

MIRIAM RIGLER
14 W 55th St (at Fifth Ave)   212/581-5519
Mon-Sat: 10-6 (Thurs: 10-7)   www.miriamrigler.com

Miriam Rigler is the quintessential ladies' dress shop. They have it all: personal attention, expert alterations, wardrobe coordination, custom designing (including bridal), and a large selection of sportswear, knits, and evening gowns in sizes 4 to 20. Also featured: custom headpieces, traditional and nontraditional bridal gowns, mother-of-the-bride ensembles, and debutante dresses. A subdivision now shows original paintings described as "gently priced." Despite the location, all items are discounted, including special orders. Don't miss the costume jewelry!

PALMA
521 Broome St (at Thompson St)   212/966-1722
Tues-Sat: 11-7; Sun: 12-6

Palma has remained in business in Soho for three decades, and that is a tribute to sound retailing. This store carries designs for men and women from American, English, Italian, Canadian, French, and Spanish designers. They also provide personal wardrobe consultations.

REALLY GREAT THINGS
284 Columbus Ave (bet 72nd and 73rd St)   212/787-5354
300 Columbus Ave (at 73rd St)   212/787-5868
Mon-Sat: 11-7; Sun: 1-6

There are not many stores on the Upper East Side like these! The store at 284 Columbus Avenue is filled with high couture merchandise, while the shop at 300 Columbus Avenue has a more casual feel and lower prices. The stores are indeed full of really great things: clothing, bags, and accessories from the hottest European designers.

S&W
165 W 26th St (at Seventh Ave)   718/431-2800
Mon-Thurs: 10-6:30; Fri: 10-3; Sun: 10-6

S&W is one of the best places in the city for ladies' designer coats, dresses, shoes, and bags. Unlike so many other discount boutiques, S&W maintains a consistent level of quality. On the down side, they would hardly win any "service with a smile" awards.

SAN FRANCISCO CLOTHING
975 Lexington Ave (at 71st St)   212/472-8740
Mon-Sat: 11-6   www.sanfranciscoclothing.com

The women's and children's clothing at San Francisco Clothing is just right for a casual weekend. Their merchandise is comfortable, colorful, and classy. The mature woman will find an especially good selection. Separates to go with your evening clothes are also a specialty.

SPITZER'S
101 Rivington St (at Ludlow St)   212/477-4088
Sun-Thurs: 9:30-5; Fri: 9:30-2:30   www.spitzersclothing.com

Spitzer's on Rivington is a Lower East Side landmark. There are two good reasons for shopping here: an excellent selection of designer clothing and discount prices. On the down side, you have to put up with less than helpful salespeople, unmarked merchandise, and three rooms jammed with goods. A bit of haggling may be necessary, but you should be able to get some great bargains and have a memorable shopping experience to boot.

TEMPERLEY LONDON

453 Broome St (at Mercer St)   212/219-2929
Daily: 10-6 by appointment   www.temperleylondon.com

Only one client at a time is seen in this distinctive shop, created by London fashion designer Alice Temperley. Lots of big names shop here for hand-beaded women's ready-to-wear bridal dresses, as well as leather and suede goods. And what would you expect from a classy shop like this? Champagne, wine, and more, of course! If you want to splurge, then this is a good place to start. Ask for Halleh Amiralai.

TG-170

170 Ludlow St (bet Houston and Stanton St)   212/995-8660
Mon-Sun: 12-8   www.tg170.com

You won't see the clothes carried here in any other store. That is because most of the merchandise is made in small quantities especially for this store. TG-170 started as a studio where baseball hats and T-shirts were made but has graduated into a retail showroom that displays unique items from young, emerging designers and some well-known ones. Freitag bags, too!

Women's—Maternity

Readers interested in maternity clothes ought to visit such national chains as Mimi Maternity and Pea in the Pod, both of which have well-stocked Manhattan locations. The stores I list here are unique to New York.

LIZ LANGE MATERNITY

958 Madison Ave (bet 75th and 76th St)   212/879-2191
Mon-Fri: 10-7; Sat: 10-6; Sun: 12-5   www.lizlange.com

This boutique carries its own line of very stylish maternity clothes. The prices are about what you would expect, given the location and high-end clothes, but the salespeople are friendly and the clothes well-made.

MATERNITY WORKS

16 W 57th St (bet Fifth Ave and Ave of the Americas), 3rd floor
                                                 212/399-9840
Mon-Wed: 10-7; Thurs: 10-8; Fri, Sat: 10-6; Sun: 12-6
                                          www.maternitymall.com

The building is grubby and the elevator to the third floor is incredibly cramped, but the bargains on maternity basics are well worth the trip. This is an outlet of sorts, selling both Mimi Maternity (which has branches throughout Manhattan and across the U.S.) and Motherwork clothes and related items at sometimes significant discounts.

Women's Millinery

BARBARA FEINMAN MILLINERY

66 E 7th St (bet First and Second Ave)   212/358-7092
Mon-Sat: 12:30-8; Sun: 1-7 (open later on weekends in summer)
                                  www.barbarafeinmanmillinery.com

Although accessories are carried here, the big draw is the hats, made on-premises from original designs. If you are looking for something really funky—or, by contrast, very classy—try this spot first. Costume jewelry is also a specialty.

THE HAT SHOP
120 Thompson St (at Prince St)   212/219-1445
Mon-Sat: 12-7; Sun: 1-6 (closed Mon in summer)

Owner Linda Pagan has quite a background. Formerly a Wall Street broker, then a bartender and world traveler, she's now boss at the Hat Shop. The stock reflects that diverse history, with showings from some 20 local milliners. Sewn and knit hats are priced from $20 to $125; blocked hats run from $125 to $400. For those who cannot visit the shop, Linda will send photos to help choose the right look! Custom orders are welcome.

MANNY'S MILLINERY SUPPLY COMPANY
26 W 38th St (bet Fifth Ave and Ave of the Americas) 212/840-2235
Mon-Fri: 9:30-5:30; Sat: 10-4

To say that Manny's carries millinery supplies is an understatement. Row after row of drawers are dedicated to particular aspects of head adornment. The section for ladies' hatbands alone takes up almost a hundred boxes and runs the gamut from thin pearl lines to wide Western-style leather belts. They have rhinestone banding and an enormous selection of artificial flowers and feathers. The center of the store is lined with tables displaying odds and ends, as well as several bins bulging with larger items that don't fit in the wall drawers. At the front, hat forms adorn stands, and sample hats are displayed in no particular order. Manny's will help accessorize any hat with interchangeable decorations. They also sell completed hats, close-outs, and samples. They will even re-create an old hat!

Women's Undergarments

A.W. KAUFMAN
73 Orchard St (bet Broome and Grand St)
Sun-Thurs: 10:30-5; Fri: 10:30-2   212/226-1629

Trying to find a gift for that special someone? A.W. Kaufman offers imported underwear, socks, robes, and pajamas—even nightshirts for men! For four generations, Kaufman has combined excellent merchandise with quality customer service. Among the many outstanding labels are Hanro, Diamond Tea, Chantelle, Pluto, Zimmerli, and Oscar de la Renta.

> The well-known words "you can find anything in New York" hold true if you are looking for fashion-forward millinery or women's shoes. Head to **Eugenia Kim** (203 E 4th St, 212/673-9787) for special selections of both.

IMKAR COMPANY (M. KARFIOL AND SON)
294 Grand St (bet Allen and Eldridge St)   212/925-2459
Mon-Thurs: 10-5; Fri: 9:30-2; Sun: 10-5 (till 3 in summer)

Imkar carries pajamas, underwear, and shifts for women at roughly a third off retail prices. A full line of Carter's infants' and children's wear is also available at good prices. The store has a fine line of women's lingerie, including dusters and gowns. Featured names include Model's Coat, Vanity Fair, Arrow, Jockey, Lollipop, and Munsingwear. Gold Toe hosiery and Arrow and Van Heusen shirts for men are also stocked.

LA PETITE COQUETTE

51 University Pl (bet 9th and 10th St)   212/473-2478
Mon-Sat: 11-7 (Thurs till 8); Sun: 12-6   www.thelittleflirt.com

Interested in a male-friendly lingerie store that will take care of your gift needs? La Petite Coquette offers a large, eclectic mix of lingerie from around the world in a diverse price range. I like their description of the atmosphere: "Flirtatious!" You'll find everything from classic La Perla to edgy designers like Ingwa Melero and Aubade. There are also old standbys like Cosabella, Hanky Panky, Mary Green, On Gossamer, Only Hearts, Eberjey, and La Cosa.

SCHACHNER FASHIONS

95 Delancey St (bet Orchard and Ludlow St)   212/677-0700
Sun-Fri: 9-5

Schachner is a Lower East Side institution that's been selling brandname robes, sleepwear, underwear, and loungewear at discount prices for more than 40 years. Special orders are the norm.

UNDERNEATH IT ALL

444 E 75th St (at York Ave)   212/717-1976
Mon-Thurs: 10-6

160 E 34th St (at Lexington Ave), 4th floor   212/779-2517
Mon-Fri: 9-5   www.underneathitallnyc.com

Underneath It All is a one-stop shopping service for women who have had breast cancer or are undergoing chemotherapy. You can be assured of attentive, informed, and personal service from the staff, some of whom are breast cancer survivors. The store carries a large selection of breast forms in light and dark skin tones and in a variety of shapes, sizes, and contours. There is also a complete line of mastectomy bras and name-brand bras; mastectomy and designer swimwear; sleepwear, loungewear, and body suits; and wigs and fashionable head accessories. They also have lymph edema sleeves at the 34th Street location. They accept insurance coverage from Medicare, Medicaid, Empire Blue Cross Blue Shield, and Aetna.

VICTORIA'S SECRET

565 Broadway (at Prince St)	212/274-9519
19 Fulton St (South Street Seaport)	212/962-8122
115 Fifth Ave (bet 18th and 19th St)	212/477-4118
1328 Broadway (at 34th St)	212/356-8380
34 E 57th St (bet Park and Madison Ave)	212/758-5592
1981 Broadway (at 67th St)	646/505-2280
1240 Third Ave (at 72nd St)	212/717-7035
165 E 86th St (bet Lexington and Third Ave)	646/672-9183
Hours vary by store	www.victoriassecret.com

These are some of the sexiest stores in the world! The beautiful lingerie and bedroom garb, bridal peignoirs, exclusive silks, and accessories are displayed against the most alluring backdrops. The personnel are absolutely charming as well.

Coins, Stamps

H.R. HARMER
3 E 28th St (bet Madison and Fifth Ave), 7th floor   212/532-3700
Mon-Fri: 9:30-5:30   www.hrharmer.com

If you think you own a stamp that will make you a millionaire, then talk to these people. The same family has run this business since 1918. They will appraise your rare stamps and autographs. You can stay informed about their stamp auctions via catalogs, brochures, and online.

STACK'S RARE COINS
123 W 57th St (at Ave of the Americas)   212/582-2580
Mon-Fri: 10-5   www.stacks.com

Established in 1858, Stack's is the country's oldest and largest rare-coin dealer. Moreover, it is still a family operation. Specializing in coins, medals, and paper money of interest to collectors, Stack's has a solid reputation for individual service, integrity, and knowledge of the field. In addition to walk-in business, Stack's conducts 11 public auctions a year. Both neophytes and experienced numismatists will do well at Stack's.

Computers
(See also "Electronics")

COMPUSA
420 Fifth Ave (bet 37th and 38th St)   212/764-6224
1775 Broadway (at 57th St)   212/262-9711
Mon-Fri: 8:30-8; Sat: 10-7; Sun: 11-6   www.compusa.com

There are over 5,000 computer products in stock at these computer superstores, from modern desktop models to sophisticated software. The best part of the operation, besides the selection and competitive pricing, is the service. Even though these CompUSA franchises are incredibly big and busy, the courteous sales staff will answer even the simplest questions.

RCS COMPUTER EXPERIENCE
575 Madison Ave (at 56th St)   212/949-6935
Daily: 9-8   www.rcsnet.com

This is the best name to know for computers, phones and accessories, radios, and all the latest gadgets. The personnel are well-informed, the selections are vast, and the gift possibilities are endless. Customers enjoy the hassle-free environment. For those who like high-tech toys for adults (like your author), RCS is heaven!

TEKSERVE
119 W 23rd St (bet Ave of the Americas and Seventh Ave)
Mon-Fri: 9-7; Sat: 10-5; Sun: 12-5   212/929-3645
www.tekserve.com

Tekserve sells and services Macintosh computers and other Apple products. They also have a pro audio and video department, and sell all kinds of Mac accessories. On-site service and equipment rentals are offered. In business since 1987, their interest in individual customers is evidenced by the fact that Tekserve is very busy all the time.

Cosmetics, Drugs, Perfumes

BOYD'S MADISON AVENUE DEPARTMENT STORE
655 Madison Ave (at 60th St)   212/838-6558
Mon-Fri: 8:30-7:30; Sat: 9:30-7; Sun: 12-6   www.boydsnyc.com

Boyd's is a drugstore in a city full of drugstores, so it has to have something special to be worthy of mention. In addition to a prescription service, Boyd's carries a complete line of cosmetics, magnifying mirrors, soaps, jewelry, and brushes. The latter range from common to esoteric: i.e., nail brushes and mustache combs in a variety of sizes and shapes. Boyd's has one of the city's most complete selections of drugs, cosmetics, and sundries. A boutique department carries handbags, lingerie, hats, scarves, gloves, jackets, and hair accessories. However, service by unfriendly salespeople can be very frustrating.

> For a large selection of perfumes and fragrances at really good discounts, head to **Columbus Perfumery** (274 Columbus Ave, 212/496-4160).

ESSENTIAL PRODUCTS
90 Water St (bet Wall St and Hanover Sq)   212/344-4288
Mon-Fri: 9-5

Essential Products has been manufacturing flavors and fragrances for over a century. Knowing that advertising and packaging drive up the price of name-brand colognes and perfumes, they set out to see how closely they could duplicate expensive scents at low prices. They describe their fragrances as "elegant interpretations" of designer names, sold at a fraction of the designer price. Essential features 50 perfumes and 23 men's colognes, and they offer a money-back guarantee. If you send a self-addressed stamped envelope, they will return scented cards and ordering information.

KIEHL'S
109 Third Ave (bet 13th and 14th St)   212/677-3171, 800/543-4571
Mon-Sat: 10-7; Sun: 12-6   www.kiehls.com
Kiehl's has been a New York institution since 1851. Their special treatments and preparations are made by hand and distributed internationally. Natural ingredients are used in their full lines of cleansers, scrubs, toners, moisturizers, eye-area preparations, men's creams, masks, body moisturizers, bath and shower products, sports items, ladies' leg-grooming formulations, shampoos, conditioners, and treatments. Express interest in a particular product and you'll leave with a decent-size sample and extensive advice. Customers will also enjoy the unusual collection of memorabilia related to aviation and motorcycles. A branch is located on the street floor of Bloomingdale's.

Crafts

ALLCRAFT JEWELRY & ENAMELING CENTER
135 W 29th St (bet Ave of the Americas and Seventh Ave), Room 205
Mon-Fri: 9-5   212/279-7077, 800/645-7124
                                    www.allcraftonline.com

Allcraft is *the* jewelry-making supply store. Their catalog includes a complete line of tools and supplies for jewelry making, silver- and metalsmithing, lost-wax casting, and much more. Out-of-towners usually order from their catalog, but New Yorkers shouldn't miss an opportunity to visit this gleaming cornucopia. Call for a catalog or browse it online.

CITY QUILTER
133 W 25th St (bet Ave of the Americas and Seventh Ave)
Tues-Fri: 11-7; Sat: 10-6; Sun: 11-5   212/807-0390
                                                www.cityquilter.com

This is the only shop in Manhattan that's completely devoted to quilting. They serve everyone from beginners to professionals with classes, books, notions, thread, gifts, and 2,000 bolts of all-cotton fabrics.

CLAYWORKS POTTERY
332 E 9th St (bet First and Second Ave)   212/677-8311
Tues-Thurs: 3-7; Fri: 3-8:30; Sat: 1-8:30; Sun: 2-8:30
(call ahead, as hours can vary)   www.clayworkspottery.com

For three decades, talented Helaine Sorgen has been at work here. If you are interested in stoneware and porcelain, Clayworks has a wide range for tabletop or home decor. All of Clayworks' pottery is lead-free and dishwasher- and microwave-safe. Small classes in wheel-throwing are given for adults. Everything is individually produced, from teapots to casseroles, mugs, and sake sets. One-of-a-kind decorative pieces include honey pots, garlic jars, pitchers, cream and sugar sets, vases, goblets, platters, and bowls.

GOTTA KNIT!
498 Ave of the Americas (bet 12th and 13th St), 2nd floor
Mon-Fri: 11-6 (Thurs till 8); Sat, Sun: 11-4   212/989-3030
                                                 www.gottaknit.net

At Gotta Knit! you will find luxury yarns for hand-knitting, crocheting, and custom pattern-writing for unique garments, as well as a selection of accessories, books, and buttons. Individual instructions and classes are offered.

LOVELIA ENTERPRISES
356 E 41st St (in Tudor City Place)   212/490-0930, 800/843-8438
Mon-Fri: 9:30-5 (by appointment)

Lovelia F. Albright's establishment is one of New York's great finds. From a shop overlooking the United Nations at Tudor City Place, she dispenses the finest European Gobelin, Aubuisson, and Beauvais machine-woven tapestries at prices that are often one-third that of other places. The tapestries are exquisite. Some depict the ubiquitous unicorns cavorting in medieval scenes, while others are more modern. They come in all sizes. The latest additions include tapestries for upholstery, wool-pile miniature rugs for use as mats under objets d'art, and an extensive line of tapestry-woven borders. They're designed by Albright and made exclusively for her in Austria and France.

WOOLGATHERING
318-B 84th St (bet First and Second Ave)   212/734-4747
Tues-Fri: 10:30-6; Sat: 10:30-5; Sun: 12-5

Woolgathering is a unique oasis dedicated to the fine art of knitting. You'll find a big selection of quality European woolen, cotton, and novelty yarns. They carry many exclusive classic and contemporary designs, a complete library of knitting magazines and books, and European-made knitting implements and gadgets. They also provide very professional finishing services, as well as crocheting and needlepoint. They will even help with your project if purchases are made at the store.

Dance Items

CAPEZIO DANCE THEATRE SHOP
1650 Broadway (at 51st St), 2nd floor   212/245-2130
www.capeziodance.com

CAPEZIO 57TH STREET
1776 Broadway (at 57th St)   212/586-5140

CAPEZIO EAST
136 E 61st St (at Lexington Ave)   212/758-8833

CAPEZIO EAST UPTOWN (children's)
1651 Third Ave (bet 92nd and 93rd St), 3rd floor   212/348-7210

ON STAGE WITH CAPEZIO (premier dancewear)
197 Madison Ave (bet 34th and 35th St)   212/725-1174
www.onstagedancewear.com

Known for service and selection, Capezio stores offer one-stop shopping for all your dance, theater, and fitness needs. Capezio Dance Theatre Shop is the largest dance and theater retail store in the world, with specialized sections for men, Flamenco, Skatewear, and a wide variety of shoes. Capezio East reflects the fashion-conscious East Side neighborhood. On Stage serves professional ballet and theater companies across the world, including the New York City Ballet. Individuals are welcome, too!

Department Stores

The heyday of the great locally owned complete department stores is over. Don't expect New York stores to be different than those anywhere else. The only difference may be the size of the store. You'll find huge cosmetics departments (because they are so profitable); sporadic and uninformed service (because personnel are moved about); fewer services (like free gift wrapping); sale after sale (beware, as merchandise is marked up many times only to be reduced); and eliminated departments (like white goods, books, notions, sporting goods, and the like).

Of course, there are exceptions. Saks Fifth Avenue and Bergdorf Goodman have huge selections of quality merchandise. Century 21 offers some great bargains. Lord & Taylor is trying desperately to regain its former cachet. Barneys is still overpriced but service has improved. Macy's is wonderful if you want to see vast showings of merchandise. Bloomingdale's is not what it used to be, but shopping here is still an *experience*.

BARNEYS NEW YORK
660 Madison Ave (bet 60th and 61st St)   212/826-8900
Mon-Fri: 9-8; Sat: 10-7; Sun: 11-6   www.barneys.com

Barney Pressman founded this store—originally for men's and boys' discounted wear—in 1923. Through the years there has been much turmoil (family and otherwise), and today's Barneys (and Barneys Co-op) are a far cry from the humble beginnings. The merchandise mix is lately more appealing than it has been, although it is still priced on the high side. The best deals are found in their twice-yearly sales events. And the store—both the layout and sometimes snobby service—is not customer friendly. Fred's restaurant on the ninth floor is a pleasant place to relax and enjoy good food.

For the latest hip fashions, try one of the **Barneys Co-op** stores. They offer young designer clothes, denim, T-shirts, shoes, and handbags. Prices at the following are considerably lower than at Barneys uptown.
- 236 W 18th St (bet Seventh and Eighth Ave, 212/593-7800)
- 116 Wooster St (bet Prince and Spring St, 212/965-9964): women's merchandise only
- 2151 Broadway (at 75th St, 646/335-0978)

BERGDORF GOODMAN
754 Fifth Ave (at 58th St)   212/753-7300
BERGDORF GOODMAN MEN
745 Fifth Ave (at 58th St)   212/753-7300
Mon-Sat: 10-7 (Thurs till 8); Sun: 12-6

Bergdorf Goodman is the epitome of style. The store has broadened its appeal, reaching out to young and affluent customers. Lines have been expanded, and practically every major fashion name in the world is represented. Dollar sales per square foot are among the highest in the nation. Bergdorf Goodman emphasizes top fashion names in all departments, and many of the styles are found exclusively in this store. Their windows usually display a fine selection of this apparel. The seventh floor presents an exciting array of home-accessory merchandise, carefully selected and beautifully displayed. Downstairs, an impressive cosmetics department is one of the busiest in the store. Personnel are great if they know you; if not, don't appear in your grubbies. You'll find top names and prices to match at Bergdorf Goodman Men, across the street. If you're looking for a special men's gift or are intent on attiring yourself in the best-of-the-best, this is the place to go.

If you get hunger pangs after spending big bucks at Bergdorf's, get refreshed for another spree at **Goodman's Cafe**. Located in a corner on the lower level, it is cozy, crowded, and has good food.

BLOOMINGDALE'S
1000 Third Ave (at 59th St)   212/705-2000
Mon-Fri: 10-8:30; Sat: 10-7; Sun: 11-7   www.bloomingdales.com

Although this store is still the destination for thousands of local and visiting shoppers, one will not find the unique merchandise that once was the operation's hallmark. However, several standouts remain. The first floor cosmetics department is like no other in the world. Kiehl's, the famous New York pharmacy, has an outlet on the main floor. The "Main Course" home furnishings area is superb. The fashion departments appeal particularly to the working woman. Chocolates at Martine's (on the sixth floor) are some of the best in the city. The chocolate yogurt served at Forty Carrots (downstairs) is worth a trip in itself. What was once an outstanding furniture department, with great model rooms, is now very mundane. The men's departments can't hold a candle to Saks, Bergdorf Goodman, and Macy's (although the latter is under the same ownership). Service can be very frustrating, as part-timers often have little knowledge of the merchandise.

BLOOMINGDALE'S SOHO
504 Broadway (bet Broome and Spring St)   212/729-5900
Mon-Fri: 10-9; Sat: 10-8; Sun: 11-7

This smaller sister store has enlivened the Soho area. The young Soho crowd enjoys the fine showing of up-and-coming designers. Bloom is one of several in-store eating spots.

CENTURY 21
22 Cortlandt St (bet Broadway and Church St)   212/227-9092
Mon-Fri: 7:45 a.m.-8 p.m.; Sat: 10-8; Sun: 11-7

www.c21stores.com

Century 21 has become a destination in itself! Ask anyone who works in the Wall Street area where they most like to shop, and most will say Century 21. Why? Because the 16 departments in this bargain palace carry an amazing selection of quality merchandise for men, women, children, and the home at discounts that run from 25% to 75%. Outstanding departments include housewares, women's shoes, and children's apparel, where brand names are tops and prices comfortable. Don't expect fancy fitting rooms and special amenities. However, service is informed and courteous, and you will not be disappointed.

HENRI BENDEL
712 Fifth Ave (bet 55th and 56th St)   212/247-1100
Mon-Sat: 10-8; Sun: 12-7   www.henribendel.com

Founded in 1896 as a millinery store, Bendel's was a fixture on 57th Street for years. In a boutique setting, the store catered to high-fashion women's apparel for the upwardly mobile New Yorker. The present store, in the former Coty Building, keeps the same boutique atmosphere, appealing to a younger audience. Wood is used prominently throughout, and the magnificent original windows by Rene Lalique have been incorporated into the store design. Bendel's "stylists" can take you from boutique to boutique via oval staircases. Unfortunately, the store does not have the class it once did, although the restrooms are nice.

LORD & TAYLOR
424 Fifth Ave (at 39th St)   212/391-3344
Mon-Fri: 10-8:30; Sat: 10-7:30; Sun: 11-7   www.lordandtaylor.com

Lord & Taylor is making a heroic effort to regain some of its lost glamour. Merchandise and advertising tout "the Signature of American Style," especially in women's wear. Shoppers will find ten floors of famous-name options for everyone—from fashions to gifts for the home, plus special-size shops for petites and larger women. The traditional Soup Bar on the sixth floor is popular. During December, Lord & Taylor's award-winning Christmas windows are one of New York's most popular attractions. On the down side, service is uneven and the men's sections leave much to be desired.

MACY'S
151 W 34th St (Herald Square, bet Broadway and Seventh Ave)
Mon-Sat: 10-9; Sun: 11-8   212/695-4400
                                                                 www.macys.com

The Macy's name has become a national brand, but it all started here in Manhattan! Macy's New York is billed as "the world's largest department store," and I doubt anyone would dispute that! Changes in the retail field have had a profound impact on this store, which has renewed sparkle, more inventory, better service, and an increased showing of top names in clothing and accessories. The downstairs, housewares-filled "Cellar" is a highlight. The Cellar's food market is colorful and busy. In the rest of the store, you'll find a great selection of items for kids, an outstanding home furnishings section, and several fun places to rest and grab a snack. At Easter time, Macy's flower show is magnificent.

SAKS FIFTH AVENUE
611 Fifth Ave (at 50th St)   212/753-4000
Mon-Sat: 10-7 (Thurs till 8); Sun: 12-6   www.saksfifthavenue.com

What a great store! Saks Fifth Avenue demonstrates an ongoing commitment to quality and excellence in fashion merchandising and service. In a prime location on Fifth Avenue at Rockefeller Center, this store continues to be a favorite shopping place for overseas visitors, tourists, and local residents. The Evening Boutique on the third floor is *the* shopping place for women who want to dress with flair for a special occasion. The men's sections offer the top names in the country. The professional woman will find timeless fashions in clothing and accessories. Cafe S.F.A., with gourmet lunches and light fare, is a delightful eighth-floor resting place with a great view. There is much more: outstanding departments for infants and young people, a beauty salon, and multilingual sales help for foreign visitors. Saks' premium credit-card program, "SaksFirst," rewards loyal shoppers with a bevy of bonuses and perks.

There's a little bit of Saigon in Manhattan! You can buy art objects, fashion accessories, and items for your home at **Saigoniste** (186½ Spring St, 212/925-4610, www.saigoniste.com). Merchandise at this classy Soho emporium comes from hip Vietnamese sources!

TAKASHIMAYA
693 Fifth Ave (bet 54th and 55th St)   212/350-0100
Mon-Sat: 10-7; Sun: 12-5   www.takashimaya.com

This store is as much a museum and gallery as it is a retail establishment. It certainly is different from most American department stores. Upstairs you'll find beautiful Japanese-made clothing and accessory items, home furnishings, and gifts. The top floor is an oasis for beauty addicts, with fragrances, hair-care products, makeup—all top-end merchandise. Gorgeous flower arrangements are featured on the first floor. The downstairs Tea Box is a restful Japanese cafe where teas and related accessories are sold.

Domestics

BED BATH & BEYOND
620 Ave of the Americas (bet 18th and 19th St)   212/255-3550
410 E 61st St (at First Ave)   646/215-4702
1932 Broadway (at 65th St)   917/441-9391
Daily: 9 a.m.-10 p.m.   www.bedbathandbeyond.com

As a former retail merchant, I am always impressed with a store that does things in a big way while still making every customer feel important. Bed Bath & Beyond is just that kind of place. The selections are huge. The quality is unquestioned. The service is prompt and informed. The store on the Avenue of the Americas has over 103,000 square feet of sheets, blankets, rugs, kitchen gadgets, hangers, towels, dinnerware, hampers, furniture, cookware, kiddie items, pillows, paper goods, appliances, and much more. The store on 61st Street has three levels jam-packed with great merchandise. The layout of the newest store on Broadway makes it a shopper's paradise. Prices are discounted.

D. PORTHAULT
18 E 69th St (bet Madison and Fifth Ave)   212/688-1660
Mon-Fri: 10-6; Sat: 10-5:30   www.dporthault.fr

Porthault, the French queen of linens, needs no introduction. Custom-made linens are available in a range of 600 designs, scores of colors, and weaves of luxurious density. Wherever the name Porthault appears—for instance, on the linens at some fancy hotels—you know you're at a top-notch operation. Their printed sheets seem to last forever and are handed down from one generation to another. Porthault can handle custom work of an intricate nature for odd-sized beds, baths, and showers. Specialties include signature prints, printed terry towels, unusual gift items, and decorative accessories like trays, wastebaskets, tissue-box covers, and room sprays.

HARRIS LEVY
98 Forsyth St (bet Grand and Broome St)   212/226-3102
Sun-Fri: 9-5   www.harrislevy.com

Over a century old, Harris Levy has moved into a space that was originally a premier downtown catering hall called "Pearl's Mansion," built in 1900. The building has been completely renovated, and this outstanding retailer of luxury home furnishings now includes all manner of quilts, pillows, bed linens, table accessories, bath products, candles, and fragrances —even stuffed animals for the kids. Harris Levy is a must-visit for those who want to outfit their home or apartment with goods at sensible prices.

440   STORES

Where to Shop for Bargains in New York!

Bed Bath & Beyond (410 E 61st St, 646/215-4702 and 620 Ave of the Americas, 212/255-3550): one-stop home furnishings

B&H Photo-Video-Pro Audio (420 Ninth Ave, 212/444-6600): camera, audio, and video superstore

Bis Designer Resale (1134 Madison Ave, 212/396-2760): upscale clothing, shoes, accessories

Broadway Panhandler (477 Broome St, 212/966-3434): kitchenware

Century 21 (22 Cortlandt St, 212/227-9092): discount department store

Crate & Barrel (611 Broadway, 212/780-0004 and 650 Madison Ave, 212/308-0011): housewares and furniture

H&M (1328 Broadway, 646/473-1164; 558 Broadway, 212/343-2722; 640 Fifth Ave, 212/489-0390; 435 Seventh Ave, 212/643-6955; and 125 W 125th St, 212/665-8300): family clothing

Jam Paper & Envelope (135 Third Ave, 212/473-6666 and 611 Ave of the Americas, 212/255-4593): specialty stationery and office products

M&J Trimming (1010 Ave of the Americas, 212/391-9072): fine sewing and upholstering notions

Old Navy (150 W 34th St, 212/594-0115; 610 Ave of the Americas, 212/645-0663; and 503-511 Broadway, 212/226-0838): clothing

Pearl River Mart (477 Broadway, 212/431-4770 and 200 Grand St, 212/966-1010): Asian emporium

Pier 1 Imports (71 Fifth Ave, 212/206-1911 and 1550 Third Ave, 212/987-1746): imports, gifts

Super Runners Shop (360 Amsterdam Ave, 212/787-7665; Grand Central Station, 42nd St at Vanderbilt Ave, 646/487-1120; 1337 Lexington Ave, 212/369-6010; and 1246 Third Ave, 212/249-2133): shoes, apparel, and accessories

SYMS (400 Park Ave, 212/317-8200 and 42 Trinity Pl, 212/797-1199): family fashions

Zara (580 Broadway, 212/343-1725; 101 Fifth Ave, 212/741-0555; 750 Lexington Ave, 212/754-1120; and 39 W 34th St, 212/868-6551): men's and women's clothing from Spain

---

J. SCHACHTER'S
5 Cook St (at Manhattan St), Brooklyn   718/384-2732, 800/INTOBED
Mon-Thurs: 10-5

J. Schachter's is the foremost purveyor of quilts in the New York area and perhaps on the entire continent. It is the oldest quilting firm in New York. Quilts are available in white goose down, polyester, lamb's wool, and cotton. The talented staff can make a quilt in any size and in 20 different quilting patterns from any fabric. They can also do outline quilting for bedspreads. Baby ensembles are a specialty. Schachter's has a complete line of custom-order linens as well. Some of their bed linens come from Europe and are offered at guaranteed lowest prices. Custom pillows can be made while you wait. Entire bedrooms and bathrooms—from rugs to ceiling and wall coverings—can be coordinated. The experts at Schachter's refurbish down pillows, comforters, and sofa cushions, as well as window treatments and balloon and Venetian shades.

LA MAISON MARINA
345 West Broadway (bet Broome and Grand St)   212/343-9911
Daily: 11-7

This shop specializes in French linens and antiques. Their linens are woven exclusively for them in the Basque country. You'll find some very attractive unbleached Egyptian cotton bath towels, robes, and slippers. They carry French personal-care products, olive oils and vinegars from Italy and Greece, as well as dishes, glasses, and baby gifts. Custom monogramming and embroidery are also available.

NANCY KOLTES AT HOME
31 Spring St (bet Mott and Mulberry St)   212/219-2271
Mon-Sat: 11-7; Sun: 12-6   www.nancykoltes.com

Visit Nancy Koltes if you are interested in quality luxury home products, including beautiful bed and table linens made of the finest Italian yarns. There is a wholesale division also.

PONDICHERRI
454 Columbus Ave (at 82nd St)   212/875-1609
Daily: 11-8   www.pondicherrionline.com

The beautiful window displays might make you think you could never afford anything inside Pondicherri. However, if you like exotic cotton prints and are looking for pillows, pillowcases, bags, handicrafts and furniture from India, silks, tablecloths, quilts, curtains, bags, clothing, and the like, by all means go in. Both selection and prices are excellent! You'll find items from Tibet, India, Africa, Morocco, and other exotic spots. Because the selection is large and most items are folded on shelves, you might want to ask for help.

PORTICO BED & BATH
903 Broadway (at 21st St)   212/473-6662
72 Spring St (bet Crosby and Lafayette St)   212/941-7800
Chelsea Market, 75 Ninth Ave (bet 15th and 16th St)   212/243-8515
Hours vary by store   www.porticohome.com

Portico is known for its highly unusual collection of bath and body-care products, fine furniture, imported luxury linens, and home accessories. This is not a store for bargain hunters; rather, Portico is for discerning shoppers who take pride in making their home a very special place.

PRATESI
829 Madison Ave (at 69th St)   212/288-2315
Mon-Sat: 10-6   www.pratesi.com

Pratesi says it carries the best linens the world has to offer, and they're right. Families hand them down for generations. Customers who don't have affluent ancestors will wish to avail themselves of the new collections that come out in spring and fall. The Pratesi staff is unsurpassed in coordinating linens to decor or creating a custom look. This three-story store has a garden that sets the mood for perusing the luxurious linens. Towels are made exclusively for Pratesi in Italy and are of a quality and thickness that must be felt to be believed. Bathrobes are magnificent, plush, and quietly understated. (So are the price tags.) Cashmere pillows, throws, and blankets are available, and there is also a baby boutique.

Eco-Friendly

IIKH
458 W 17th St (at Tenth Ave)   212/675-9400
Tues-Sat: 11-7 (Thurs till 9); Sun: 12-5 (Mon by appointment)
www.twokh.com

A team of former fashion executives have opened a store with products that are chic and eco-friendly. Mara Kloiber, Jim Kloiber, and Erin Hawker (thus the name IIKH) have a passion for the environment. You'll find items for the home, bath, body, and gourmet. Same-day delivery is offered within the city, and they have complimentary gift wrapping. Free shipping is offered for online orders of $50 or more.

Electronics and Appliances

DALE PRO AUDIO
22 W 19th St (bet Fifth Ave and Ave of the Americas)   212/475-1124
Mon-Fri: 9:30-5:30   www.daleproaudio.com

A family business for nearly half a century, this professional audio dealership carries a large inventory of Sony and Panasonic replacement parts, as well as merchandise for the recording, broadcast, DJ, and sound-contracting community. They know their stuff and are respected by customers.

GRINGER & SONS
29 First Ave (at 2nd St)   212/475-0600
Mon-Fri: 8-5:30 (Wed till 7:30 in Summer); Sat: 8-4:30
www.gringerandsons.com

Come to Gringer & Sons for brand-name major appliances at good prices. Gringer's informed personnel sell all major appliances—including refrigerators, microwaves, and ranges—to residential and commercial customers.

HARVEY ELECTRONICS
2 W 45th St (at Fifth Ave)   212/575-5000
Mon-Fri: 10-7 (Thurs till 8); Sat: 10-6; Sun: 12-5
www.harveyonline.com

Not everyone understands the fine points of the new technologies flooding the market. For those who need professional advice and individual attention, Harvey's is the place to shop. They offer state-of-the-art audio/video components, with home theater flat-screen and high-definition televisions being their specialty. Harvey has an in-home design and installation division that integrates audio and video systems into new or existing residences.

J&R MUSIC & COMPUTER WORLD
15 and 23 Park Row (across from City Hall)   212/238-9000
Mon-Sat: 9-7:30; Sun: 10:30-6:30   www.jr.com

These folks pride themselves on being one of the nation's most complete computer, electronics, and home-entertaimnent department stores. They carry cameras, radios, televisions, speaker systems, VCRs, DVDs, cassette and CD players, personal electronics, compact discs, computer systems, telephones and answering machines, PDAs, kitchen essentials, personal-care items, and much more. The place is well organized, though it can get rather hectic at times. Prices are competitive and merchandise is guaranteed. Another J&R store a few doors down at 27 Park Row carries kitchenware—including items like blenders, coffee makers, toasters, and juicers—at prices competitive with some discounters.

BlackBerry fans! Now you have your own store at **BreakThrough Wireless** (109 W 39th St, 212/596-4060).

LYRIC HIGH FIDELITY
1221 Lexington Ave (bet 82nd and 83rd St)   212/439-1900
Mon-Sat: 10-6

Lyric is a favorite among audiophiles, catering to those with a passion for recorded music and the cash to indulge their wildest audio fantasies. You can buy a basic music system at Lyric for under $1,000, but you can also part with a six-figure sum for an exotic component ensemble. They sell audio equipment to people who want the best, and they are very particular about the lines they carry. Custom installations and whole-house integration of electronic equipment are specialties.

P.C. RICHARD & SON
120 E 14th St (bet Third and Fourth Ave)   212/979-2600
205 E 86th St (bet Second and Third Ave)   212/289-1700
2372 Broadway (at 86th St)   212/579-5200
53 W 23rd St (bet Ave of the Americas and Seventh Ave)
Mon-Fri: 9 a.m.-9:30 p.m.; Sat: 9-9; Sun: 10-7   212/924-0200
                                                            www.pcrichard.com

For nearly a century this family-owned and -operated appliance, electronics, and computer store has been providing superior service to customers. They offer a large inventory, good prices, delivery seven days a week, and an in-house service center. The store started as a hardware outfit, and unlike many other family operations, the genius of personalized service has been successfully passed from one generation to the next.

SHARPER IMAGE
10 W 57th St (at Fifth Ave)   212/265-2550
Mon-Fri: 10-8; Sat: 10-7; Sun: 12-6

50 Rockefeller Plaza (bet Fifth Ave and Ave of the Americas)
Mon-Sat: 10-8; Sun: 10-7   646/557-0861
Pier 17, South Street Seaport   212/693-0477
Mon-Sat: 10-9; Sun: 11-8
900 Madison Ave (at 73rd St)   212/794-4974
Mon-Sat: 10-7; Sun: 12-6
98 Greene St (bet Prince and Spring St)   917/237-0221
Mon-Fri: 10-7; Sat: 10-8; Sun: 11-6   www.sharperimage.com

If you are a gadget freak like me, you'll go wild at this fascinating emporium. This is truly a grown-up's toy store! The latest electronic gadgets, household helpers, sports items, games, novelties, and clothing make browsing the Sharper Image a unique experience.

SONY STYLE
550 Madison Ave (bet 55th and 56th St)   212/833-8800
Mon-Sat: 10-7; Sun: 11-6   www.sonystyle.com

You'll delight at this mixture of two Sony retail stores and a consumer-friendly atrium. Sony is often on the cutting-edge of new developments in consumer electronics, so periodic visits here will keep you up to date with the latest in radios, televisions, audio equipment, home theater systems, cameras, clocks, and more. Sony's sales personnel are patient and knowledgeable. However, their phone service is unbelievably bad, and special orders are not always handled professionally.

STEREO EXCHANGE
627 Broadway (at Houston St)   212/505-1111
Mon-Fri: 11-7:30; Sat: 10:30-7; Sun: 11-6   www.stereoexchange.com

For high-end audio-video products, you can't do better than this outfit! They carry top names like Marantz, Macintosh, and B&W, and can handle customer installation. Moreover, the personnel really seem to care about their products.

WAVES
251 W 30th St (bet Seventh and Eighth Ave)   212/273-9616
Mon-Sat: 11-6   www.wavesllc.com

Bruce and Charlotte Mager are trying to make the past last forever with their collection of vintage record players, radios, receivers, and televisions. They have scorned the electronics age in favor of the age of radio. Their shop is a virtual shrine to the 1930s and before. At Waves you'll find the earliest radios (still operative!) and artifacts. There are promotional pieces, such as a radio-shaped cigarette lighter. Gramophones and anything dealing with the radio age are available. Waves also rents phonographs, telephones, and neon clocks. They make appraisals and will answer questions about repairs, sales, and rentals.

Eyewear and Accessories

THE EYE MAN
2264 Broadway (bet 81st and 82nd St)   212/873-4114
Mon, Wed: 10-7; Tues, Thurs: 10-7:30; Fri, Sat: 10-6;
Sun: 12-5 (closed Sun in summer)

Dozens of stores in Manhattan carry eyeglasses, but few take special care with children. The Eye Man carries a great selection of frames for young people, as well as specialty eyewear for grownups.

GRUEN OPTIKA
599 Lexington Ave (bet 52nd and 53rd St)   212/688-3580
1076 Third Ave (bet 63rd and 64th St)   212/751-6177
740 Madison Ave (at 64th St)   212/988-5832
2009 Broadway (at 69th St)   212/874-8749
1225 Lexington Ave (bet 82nd and 83rd St)   212/628-2493
2382 Broadway (at 87th St)   212/724-0850
Mon-Fri: 10-7; Sat: 10-5:30

The same faces and quality care can be found at Gruen Optika year after year. The firm enjoys a reputation for excellent service. They can do emergency fittings and one-day turnaround, and they carry a superb selection of specialty eyewear. Their sunglasses, theater glasses, sports spectacles, and party eyewear are noteworthy.

JOEL NAME OPTIQUE DE PARIS

65 W Houston St (at Wooster St)	212/777-5888
Mon-Fri: 11-7; Sat: 11-6	
448 West Broadway (at Prince St)	212/260-1701
Mon: 11-5; Tues-Sat: 11-7; Sun: 12-6	

Service is the name of the game at Lyric. Owner Joel Nommick and his crew of professionals stock some of the most fashionable specs in town.

LIGHTHOUSE STORE

111 E 59th St (bet Park and Lexington Ave)	212/821-9384
Mon-Fri: 10-6; Sat: 10-5	www.lighthouse.org

This is a wonderful place for people who are blind or partially sighted. Their vast selection includes glare-free lighting, magnifying mirrors, talking products, watches, clocks, computer software, and cellular phones. Open houses and hands-on demonstrations allow customers to learn about state-of-the-art technology and talk with product manufacturers and vision-rehabilitation professionals.

MORGENTHAL-FREDERICS OPTICIANS

699 Madison Ave (bet 62nd and 63rd St)	212/838-3090
Mon-Fri: 9-7; Sat: 10-6; Sun: 12-6	
944 Madison Ave (bet 74th and 75th St)	212/744-9444
Mon-Fri: 10-7; Sat: 10-6; Sun: 12-6	
399 West Broadway (at Spring St)	212/966-0099
Mon-Fri: 11-8; Sat: 11-7; Sun: 12-6	
Bergdorf Goodman, 754 Fifth Ave (at 58th St)	212/872-2526
Mon-Sat: 10-7	
10 Columbus Circle	212/956-6402
Mon-Fri: 10-7; Sat: 10-6; Sun: 12-6	www.morgenthalfrederics.com

If you're looking for unique eyewear and accessories, Morgenthal-Frederics is one of the places of choice. Owner Richard Morgenthal displays a well-conceived collection of innovative styles, including exclusive designs. With Morgenthal-Frederics' various locations and attentive staff, clients are truly well serviced. They'll even make appointments with some of New York's best ophthalmologists.

20/20 EYEWEAR

150 E 86th St (bet Third and Lexington Ave)	212/876-7676
57 E 8th St (bet Broadway and University Pl)	212/228-2192
Mon-Fri: 10-7:30; Sat: 10-6; Sun: hours vary	

www.twentytwentyeyewear.com

Whether you see glasses as a simple necessity, a statement of style, or both, the large selection at 20/20 will suit your needs. For over two decades 20/20 has offered trendsetting eyewear in a casual, appealing atmosphere. They provide overnight delivery, eye exams, and prescription fulfillment.

Fabrics, Trimmings

A.A. FEATHER COMPANY
(GETTINGER FEATHER CORPORATION)
16 W 36th St (bet Fifth Ave and Ave of the Americas), 8th floor
Mon-Thurs: 9-6; Fri: 9-3   212/695-9470
www.gettingerfeather.com

Do you need an ostrich plume, feather fan, or feather boa for your latest ensemble, or have you made a quilt that you'd like to stuff with feathers? Well, you're in luck with A.A. Feather (a.k.a. Gettinger Feather Corporation). The Gettingers have been in business since 1915, and first grandson Dan Gettinger runs it today. There aren't many family-owned businesses left, and there are almost no other sources for fine-quality feathers. This is a find!

A. FEIBUSCH—ZIPPERS & THREADS
27 Allen St (bet Canal and Hester St)   212/226-3964
Mon-Fri: 9-5; Sun: 9:30-1 (closed Sun in summer)
www.zipperstop.com

A. Feibusch boasts of having "one of the biggest selections of zippers in the U.S.A," as if they really believe there are zipper stores throughout the country! They stock zippers in every size, style, and color (hundreds of them), and can make zippers to order. I saw one woman purchasing tiny zippers for doll clothes. Feibusch carries matching threads to sew in a zipper, webbing, ribbons, and other sewing supplies. Eddie Feibusch assures me that no purchase is too small or large, and he gives each customer prompt, personal service.

ALMAR FABRICS
255 W 36th St (bet Seventh and Eighth Ave), Room 401
Mon-Fri: 9-5   212/869-9616

Almar Fabrics specializes in bridal, mother-of-the bride, bridesmaids, and other special-occasion fabrics at reasonable prices. Almar is also known for imported high-end woolens (super 80s, super 160s) at discount.

B&J FABRICS
525 Seventh Ave (at 38th St), 2nd floor   212/354-8150
Mon-Fri: 8-5:45; Sat: 9-4:45   www.bandjfabrics.com

B&J started in the fabric business in 1940 and is now run by the second and third generations of the Cohen family. They carry fashion fabrics, many imported directly from Europe. Specialties of the house: natural fibers, designer fabrics, bridal fabrics, ultra-suede, Liberty of London, and silk prints (over a thousand in stock!). Swatches are sent free of charge by specific request. You will also find a wonderful selection of hand-dyed batiks.

BECKENSTEIN MEN'S FABRICS
257 W 39th St (bet Seventh and Eighth Ave)   212/475-6666
Mon-Sat: 9-6   800/221-2727

Beckenstein is the finest men's fabric store in the nation. Proprietor Neal Boyarsky and his son Jonathan have been called "the fabric czars of the U.S." These folks sell to a majority of custom tailors in the country and to many top manufacturers of men's clothing, so you know the goods are best-quality. Their customer list reads like a who's who of politicians, film stars, and sports figures. You will find every kind of fabric, from goods selling for $10 a yard to fabulous pieces at $1,000 a yard. There are pure cashmeres, fine English suitings, silks, camel hair, and more.

HANDLOOM BATIK
214 Mulberry St (at Spring St)   212/925-9542
Thurs-Sat: 12-8; Sun: 1-6   www.handloombatik.com

At Handloom you'll find one of the largest and best collections of batik outside of a crafts museum. Carol Berlin runs Handloom Batik with reverence for her merchandise. All fabrics are handmade, and she is quick to show how each can be set off to best advantage. Hand-woven and hand-batiked fabrics (primarily from India and Indonesia) are sold by the yard as fabric or as finished clothing, napkins, tablecloths, and handiwork. In addition, a gift selection features handicrafts of wood, stone, brass, and paper from the aforementioned countries. Pillows, bed covers, curtains, and napkins can be custom-made from the store's cotton ikat and batik.

HYMAN HENDLER AND SONS
67 W 38th St (bet Fifth Ave and Ave of the Americas)   212/840-8393
Mon-Fri: 9-5   www.hymanhendler.com

Although Hyman Hendler has passed away, the store that proudly bears his name is in the capable hands of his son-in-law. In the middle of the trimmings center of the world, it is one of the oldest businesses (established in 1900) and the crown head of the ribbon field. This organization manufactures, wholesales, imports, and acts as a jobber for every kind of ribbon. It's hard to believe as many variations exist as are jammed into this store.

LONG ISLAND FABRIC WAREHOUSE
406 Broadway (bet Canal and Walker St)   212/431-9510
Daily: 9-7

Long Island Fabric Warehouse has one huge floor of every imaginable kind of fabric and trimming. Since all are sold at discount, it's one of the best places to buy fabrics. Some of the attractions include an extensive wool collection and such dressy fabrics as chiffon, crepe, silk, and satin. Most amazing are the bargain spots, where remnants and odd pieces go for so little it's laughable. They sell an excellent selection of patterns, notions, trimmings, and dollar-a-yard fabrics.

M&J TRIMMING/M&J BUTTONS
1006 and 1008 Ave of the Americas (bet 37th and 38th St)
Mon-Fri: 9-6; Sat: 10-5   212/391-9072
                 www.mjtrim.com

These folks claim to have the largest selection of trims at one location, and I'm inclined to believe them! You will find imported trims, buttons, decorator trims, and various fashion accessories. One store specializes in clothing and fashion trims, and the other features interior decor trim. They have over a half century of experience in this business.

MARGOLA IMPORT CORP.
48 W 37th St (bet Fifth Ave and Ave of the Americas)
Mon-Fri: 8:30-6; Sat: 10-4 (closed Sat in summer)   212/564-2929
www.margola.com

You'll find an outstanding showing of beads and rhinestones at Margola —one of the best in Manhattan. They will help with any phase of beading.

PARON WEST
206 W 40th St (at Seventh Ave)   212/768-3266
Mon-Sat: 8:30-5:30 (Thurs till 7)   www.paronfabrics.com

Paron carries an excellent selection of contemporary designer fabrics at discount prices. Many of the goods are available only in their store. This is a family operation, so personal attention is assured. Paron Annex, their half-price outlet, adjoins Paron West.

PIERRE DEUX FRENCH COUNTRY
625 Madison Ave (bet 58th and 59th St)   212/521-8012
Mon-Sat: 10-6 (Thurs till 7); Sun: 12-5   www.pierredeux.com

Pierre Deux, the French Country home-furnishings company, specializes in authentic handcrafted products from the provinces of France. Everything from 18th-century antique and reproduction furniture to fabrics, brightly colored pillows, handbags, faience, pewter, lighting, wallpaper, table linens, glassware, and gourmet specialties from Le Cordon Bleu can be found here. Services include a personalized bridal registry and custom orders.

SILK SURPLUS/BARANZELLI HOME
942 Third Ave (bet 56th and 57th St)   212/753-6511
Mon-Fri: 10-6; Sat: 10-5

Silk Surplus is the exclusive outlet for Scalamandre close-outs of fine fabrics, trimmings, and wallpaper, as well as Baranzelli's own line of imported and domestic informal fabrics and trimmings. Scalamandre sells for half of retail, and a choice selection of other luxurious fabrics is offered at similar savings. There are periodic sales, even on already discounted fabrics, at this elegant fabric store. They also have custom workrooms for upholstery, drapery, pillows, and custom furniture.

TINSEL TRADING
47 W 38th St (bet Fifth Ave and Ave of the Americas)   212/730-1030
Mon-Fri: 10-5:30; Sat: hours vary   www.tinseltrading.com

Tinsel Trading claims to be the only firm in the United States specializing in antique gold and silver metallics from the 1900s. They have everything from gold thread to lamé fabrics. Tinsel Trading offers an amazing array of tinsel threads, braids, fringes, cords, tassels, gimps, medallions, edging, banding, gauze lamés, bullions, fabrics, soutache, trims, and galloons. All are genuine antiques, and many customers buy them for accenting modern clothing. The collection of military gold braids, sword knots, and epaulets is unsurpassed. Visit their new ribbon emporium, **The Store Across the Street** (64 W 38th St, 212/354-1242), where you'll find vintage and new ribbons galore in a beautiful setting.

TOHO SHOJI
990 Ave of the Americas (at 36th St)　　　　212/868-7466
Mon-Fri: 9-7; Sat: 10-6; Sun: 10-5

Ever hear of a bead and trimmings supermarket? Only in New York will you find an establishment like Toho Shoji, which stocks all manner of items to design and make custom jewelry: earring parts, metal findings, chains, and every kind of jewelry component. Items are well displayed for easy selection.

THE YARN COMPANY
2274 Broadway (bet 81st and 82nd St), Room 1C　　212/787-7878
Tues-Sat: 12-6 (Wed till 8)　　　　www.theyarnco.com

The largest selection of unique high-end knitting yarns in the city can be found here. You'll find cashmeres, merino wools, silk, linen, rayon, and more. The best part of this second-floor operation is the personal interest shown by the owners, who have written two knitting books. There are many samples to look at, and these folks are up to date on new yarns and designs. Workshops and classes are available.

ZARIN FABRIC WAREHOUSE
318 Grand St (at Allen and Orchard St)　　　212/925-6112
Sun-Thurs: 9-6; Fri: 9-5; Sat: 10-6　　　www.zarinfabrics.com

Founded in 1936, Zarin is the largest and oldest drapery and upholstery fabric warehouse in Manhattan (or so the folks here claim). This "fabric heaven" occupies an entire city block stocked with thousands of designer fabrics and trim at below wholesale prices. With the largest selection of designer fabrics in New York, Zarin is a favorite inside source for decorators, set designers, and celebrity clientele. Remodeled in 2003, Zarin now carries some of the finest ready-made collections of window panels, custom lampshades, lamps, and other home furnishings. Another worthy Zarin operation is **BZI Distributors** (318 Grand St, 212/966-6690), which sells trimmings, fringe, and drapery and upholstery hardware.

Fans

SUPERIOR LIGHT & FAN
5 E 16th St (at Union Square West)　　　　212/677-9191
Mon-Sat: 9-6 (Tues, Thurs till 8); Sun: 12-6　　www.superiorlf.com

Superior is a 5,000-square-foot showroom of contemporary lighting and ceiling fans. They are certified specialists for lighting installation and repair.

Fireplace Accessories

DANNY ALESSANDRO
308 E 59th St (bet First and Second Ave)　　　212/421-1928
Mon-Fri: 9-5 (open weekends by appointment)

New Yorkers have a thing for fireplaces, and Danny Alessandro caters to that infatuation. Alessandro has been in business for more than four decades. Just as New York fireplaces run the gamut from antique brownstone to ultramodern blackstone, Alessandro's fireplaces and accessories range from antique pieces to a shiny new set of chrome tools. The shop also stocks antique marble and sandstone mantelpieces, andirons, and an incredible display of screens and tool kits. In the Victorian era, paper fans and screens were popular for blocking fireplaces when not in use. The surviving pieces stocked at Alessandro are great for modern decorating. They will also custom-order mantels, mantelpieces, and fireplace accessories. They do not repair or clean fireplaces.

WILLIAM H. JACKSON COMPANY
210 E 58th St (bet Second and Third Ave)   212/753-9400
Mon-Thurs: 9:30-5; Fri: 9:30-4   www.wmhj.com

In the real-estate ads "wbfp" stands for "wood-burning fireplace," and they are the rage in New York. In business since 1827, William H. Jackson is familiar with the various types of fireplaces in the city. In fact, they orginally installed many of those fireplaces. Jackson has hundreds of mantels on display in its showroom. They range from antiques and reproductions (in wood or marble combinations) to starkly modern pieces. There are also andirons, fire sets, screens, and excellent advice on enjoying your fireplace. Jackson does repair work (removing and installing mantels is a specialty), but they're better known for selling fireplace accessories. Handy item: a reversible sign that reads "Damper Is Open"/"Damper Is Closed."

Flags

ACE BANNER FLAG AND GRAPHICS
107 W 27th St (at Ave of the Americas)   212/620-9111
Mon-Fri: 7:30-4   www.acebanner.com

If you need a flag, Ace is the right place. Established in 1916, Ace prides itself on carrying the flags of every nation, as well as New York City and New York State flags in all sizes. Other kinds of flags can be made to order. They range in size from 4" by 6" desk flags to bridge-spanning banners. Ace also manufactures custom banners, from podium to building size. If you're running for any kind of office, campaign paraphernalia can be ordered with a promise of quick delivery. They will ship anywhere. Outfitting grand openings and personalizing equipment with such items as boat flags accounts for much of Ace's business. Ask for owner Carl Calo!

Floor Coverings

BEYOND THE BOSPHORUS
79 Sullivan St (bet Spring and Broome St)   212/219-8257
Tues-Sun: 11-7

Ismail Basbag, the owner of this establishment, was a kilim dealer for 12 years in Istanbul's grand bazaar before opening his shop in Soho in 1985. Anyone who could survive at that colorful, crowded, and noisy marketplace can certainly do business in Manhattan! Here you will find hand-woven Turkish kilim rugs and pillows in a variety of sizes, patterns, and colors. A new line of Turkish bolsters is available. Basbag travels to Turkey several times a year in order to fill customers' special requests. Rug cleaning and repair are available.

COUNTRY FLOORS
15 E 16th St (bet Fifth Ave and Union Square W)   212/627-8300
Mon-Fri: 9-6; Sat: 9-5   www.countryfloors.com

Country Floors is one of New York's biggest retail success stories, no doubt because they offer a magnificent product. Begun in 1964 in a tiny, cramped basement under the owner's photography studio, Country Floors has grown to include huge stores in New York and Los Angeles, with nearly 60 affiliates worldwide, including Canada and Australia. Customers from across the country have learned that Country Floors carries the finest in floor and wall tiles—stone, glass, and terra cotta tiles. Their sources include artisans from all over the world. A visit—or at least a look at their catalogs—is necessary to appreciate the quality and intricacy of each design. Even the simplest solid-color tiles are beautiful.

ELIZABETH EAKINS
21 E 65th St (bet Fifth and Madison Ave)   212/628-1950
Mon-Fri: 10-5:30   www.elizabetheakins.com

Elizabeth Eakins is a first-class source for wool and cotton rugs. She custom designs and makes hand-woven and hand-hooked rugs in standard and hand-dyed colors.

JANOS P. SPITZER FLOORING
131 W 24th St (bet Ave of the Americas and Seventh Ave)
Mon-Fri: 8-4:30   212/627-1818
                                                   www.janosspitzerflooring.com

This is top-notch flooring headquarters! Spitzer features installation of high-end (read: pricey) residential wooden floors, as well as expert restoration and repair. You'll find many unusual finishes here. These are highly reliable and experienced craftspeople who stock only the finest products. For large buildings, they will help with purchasing products, hiring workers, and follow-up work to insure specifications have been met. Janos Spitzer, a Hungarian craftsman, has over four decades of experience.

LOOM & WEAVE
1 E 28th St (bet Fifth and Madison Ave), 5th floor   212/779-7373
Mon-Fri: 10-5 (by appointment)

Loom & Weave stocks one of the largest collections of antique and semi-antique Oriental rugs in the city—over 2,000 in all sizes are available. The current owners come from a family tradition of five decades in the rug business. Modern premises provide an attractive setting for rugs offered at good discounts.

MOMENI INTERNATIONAL
36 E 31st St (bet Park and Madison Ave), 2nd floor   212/532-9577
Mon-Fri: 9-5   www.momeni.com

These people will tell you they are wholesale only, but don't let that scare you away. Those who visit their expanded showroom will be rewarded by one of the best sources for Oriental rugs in the city. Since they don't officially serve individual retail customers, their prices reflect wholesale rather than retail business. That doesn't make them cheap (good Oriental rugs never are), but it does assure top quality at a fair price.

NEMATI COLLECTION
Art and Design Building
1059 Third Ave (bet 62nd and 63rd St), 3rd floor
Mon-Fri: 9-6; Sat: 10-4 (or by appointment)   212/486-6900
                                              www.nematicollection.com

The Nemati Collection was founded by Parviz Nemati, author of *The Splendor of Antique Rugs and Tapestries*. He has been dealing in antique Oriental rugs and tapestries for four decades. The tradition is now carried on by his son, Darius Nemati. In addition to an extensive collection of antique Oriental rugs and period tapestries, the gallery also features modernist and contemporary rugs, as well as an exclusive collection of custom carpeting and natural-fiber flooring. Services includes a full restoration and conservation department, consulting, insurance appraisals, and professional cleaning.

PASARGAD CARPETS
180 Madison Ave (bet 33rd and 34th St)   212/684-4477
Mon-Fri: 9-6; Sat: 10-6; Sun: 11-5   www.pasargadcarpets.com

Pasargad is a fifth-generation family business established in 1904. They know everything about antique, semiantique, and new Persian and Oriental rugs. They have one of the largest collections in the country, and they provide decorating advice, repair and cleaning, and pickup and delivery service. Pasargad will also buy or trade quality antique rugs.

Shopping in Harlem

Books: **Hue-Man Bookstore** (2319 Frederick Douglass Blvd, 212/665-7400)

Clothing and accessories: **Grandview** (2531 Frederick Douglass Blvd, 212/694-7324)

Housewares: **Xukuma** (183 Malcolm X Blvd, 212/222-0490)

SAFAVIEH CARPETS
153 Madison Ave (at 32nd St)   212/683-8399
238 E 59th St (at Second Ave)   212/888-0626
Mon-Fri: 9-6; Sun: 12-6
902 Broadway   212/477-1234
Mon-Sat: 10-7; Sun: 11-6   www.safavieh.com

There was a time when it was possible to visit the teeming markets of Tehran and find some real rug bargains. At Safavieh one is still able to see a vast selection of these beautiful works of art, even if the setting is a little less glamorous. Safavieh has one of the finest collections of Persian, Indian, Pakistani, and Chinese rugs in this country. They're displayed in a showroom spacious enough for customers to visualize how the prized pieces would look in their home or place of business. These rugs are truly heirlooms, and you will want to spend time hearing about their exotic origins. Prices, although certainly not inexpensive, are competitive for the superior quality represented. It doesn't hurt to do a little haggling.

Flowers, Plants, and Gardening Items

CHELSEA GARDEN CENTER HOME
499 Tenth Ave (at 38th St)   212/727-7100
Mon-Sat: 9-6; Sun: 10-6   www.chelseagardencenter.com

These folks have combined their home store and outdoor garden center into one large operation. For the urban gardener this place is a dream, offering a wide selection of plants and flowers, soil, fertilizers, containers, fountains, tabletop items, lighting, candles, holiday decor, tools, indoor and outdoor furniture, garden books, and much more.

COUNTRY GARDENS
1160 Lexington Ave (at 80th St)   212/966-2015
Mon-Fri: 9-6; Sat: 10-3 (closed July and Aug in summer)

The service at Country Garden is highly personalized, and they show a great selection of cut flowers and plants. They arrange everything to order and will deliver all over Manhattan.

SIMPSON & COMPANY FLORISTS
852 Tenth Ave (at 56th St)   212/772-6670
Mon-Fri: 9-6; Sat: 10-3   www.simpsonflowers.com

Simpson specializes in unusual baskets, cut flowers, plants, and orchids. These folks will decorate for gatherings of all sizes, and their prices are very competitive.

TREILLAGE
418 E 75th St (at York Ave)   212/535-2288
Mon-Fri: 10-6; Sat: 10-5 (closed weekends in July and Aug)
                                            www.treillageonline.com

New Yorkers have gardens, too, although they are small. Many times they are just patios, but still they add a special dimension of charm to city living. Treillage can help make an ordinary plot of outside living into something special. There are all sorts of garden items, including furniture and accessories for indoors and outdoors, with a great selection of unusual pieces that will set your place apart. They sell everything except plants and flowers! Prices are not inexpensive, but why not splurge to enhance your little corner of the great outdoors?

VSF
204 W 10th St (bet 4th and Bleecker St)   212/206-7236
Mon-Fri: 8-5; Sat: 11-4

If you want a special look when it comes to fresh-cut flowers or dried creations, you can't do better than this outfit. They have a top-drawer list of clients who take advantage of their talents for weddings and other special events. Ask for owners Jack Follmer or Todd Rigby.

ZEZÉ FLOWERS
398 E 52nd St (bet First Ave and East River)   212/753-7767
Mon-Fri: 8-6 (also open holiday weekends)

Zezé came to New York several decades ago from Rio de Janeiro, a city known for its dramatic setting, and he brought a bit of that drama to the flower business in Manhattan. Zezé's windows reflect his unique talent. The exotic orchid selection is outstanding. You'll find premium fresh-cut flowers, topiaries, unique ceramics and glassware, gift items, and antiques. They offer the ultimate in personalized service, including same-day deliveries and special requests.

Frames

HOUSE OF HEYDENRYK
601 W 26th St (bet Eleventh and Twelfth Ave), Suite 305
Mon-Fri: 9:30-5; Sat: 9:30-3 (closed Sat in summer)   212/206-9611
www.heydenryk.com

These folks have been doing frame reproductions of the highest quality since 1845 in Europe (and since 1936 in Manhattan). They stock over 3,000 antique and reproduction frames, many of them Georgian-era English and American folk art. Indeed, theirs is one of the largest collections of period frames in the country!

Furniture, Mattresses

General

CHARLES P. ROGERS
55 W 17th St (bet Fifth Ave and Ave of the Americas)   800/561-0467
Mon-Fri: 9-8; Sat: 10-7; Sun: 12-6   www.charlesprogers.com

Rogers has been allowing folks to sleep comfortably since 1885! Their brass beds are made from heavy-gauge brass tubing with solid brass castings. Iron beds are hand-forged, making them exceptionally heavy and sturdy. Wooden beds are available, too. A leather headboard collection is now available. Rogers stocks bed linens made from the finest materials, including European linen, Egyptian, and Prima cotton. All are machine washable.

Shopping in Tribeca
Beauty products: **Lafco New York** (285 Lafayette St, 212/925-0001)
Bikes: **Gotham Bikes** (112 West Broadway, 212/732-2453)
Clothing: **Sorelle Firenze** (139½ Reade St, 212/528-7816) and **Tribeca Issey Miyake** (119 Hudson St, 212/226-0100)
Furniture: **Dune** (88 Franklin St, 212/925-6171)
Home furnishings: **Baker Tribeca** (129 Hudson St, 212/343-2956)

FLOU
42 Greene St (bet Broome and Grand St)   212/941-9101
Mon-Fri: 10-6; Sat: 11-7   www.flou.it

In its U.S. flagship store, Flou shows everything for the bedroom, from designer beds, mattresses, and furniture to sleepwear. This outfit is well known in Europe and Japan, where they tout the brand as promoting "the art of sleeping."

FOREMOST FURNITURE SHOWROOMS

8 W 30th St (at Fifth Ave), 5th floor   212/889-6347
Mon-Fri: 10-6 (Thurs till 7); Sat: 10-5; Sun: 11-5

www.foremostfurniture.com

Foremost provides professional design service at no cost to their customers. There are five full floors of furniture with about 250 lines represented. The personnel are friendly and helpful, making this an excellent source. The values are indeed very good, so shop around and then make this one of your last stops.

GRANGE

200 Lexington Ave (at 32nd St), 2nd floor   212/685-9057
Mon-Fri: 9-6   www.grange.fr

French furniture and accessories fill this stylish showroom. The pieces range from classic period design to exotic and contemporary. All, however, emphasize form, function, and comfort.

KENTSHIRE GALLERIES

37 E 12th St (bet University Pl and Broadway)   212/673-6644
Mon-Fri: 9-5   www.kentshire.com

Kentshire presents eight floors of English furniture and accessories, circa 1690–1870, with a particular emphasis on the Georgian and Regency periods. This gallery has an excellent international reputation, and the displays are a delight to see, even if the price tags are a bit high. There is also a collection of 18th- and 19th-century English jewelry. A Kentshire boutique at Bergdorf Goodman features antique jewelry.

LOST CITY ARTS

18 Cooper Square (Bowery at 5th St)   212/375-0500
Mon-Fri: 10-6; Sat, Sun: 12-6   www.lostcityarts.com

Lost City Arts shows mid 20th-century (1950s and 1960s) furniture and lighting fixtures, plus many more vintage items.

NORTH CAROLINA FURNITURE SHOWROOM

12 W 21st St (at Fifth Ave), 5th floor   212/645-2524
Mon-Sat: 10-6 (Thurs till 8); Sun: 12-5   www.ncarolinafurniture.com

You'll find over 400 famous name brands at this showroom, and most everything is discounted. There are items for livingrooms and bedrooms, diningroom tables and chairs, sofa beds, recliners, platform beds and bedding, and furniture for children's rooms. For New Yorkers, who must make every square inch of apartment space count, this place is a must-visit.

OFFICE FURNITURE HEAVEN

22 W 19th St (bet Fifth Ave and Ave of the Amercas), 7th floor
Mon-Fri: 9-6   212/989-8600

www.officefurnitureheaven.com

Has opening a new office nearly exhausted your budget? Relax. This place has bargains in first-quality contemporary pieces. Some are manufacturers' close-outs, while others are discontinued or used items that have been refurbished to look almost new. You'll find such names as Knoll, Herman Miller, and Steelcase. There are conference tables, chairs, bookcases, file cabinets, accessories, and much more.

PHILIP ENGEL
205 Lexington Ave (at 32nd St)	212/684-7555
Mon-Fri: 10-7; Sat: 10-6; Sun: 12-5	www.philipengel.com

They like to call themselves the "world's greatest leather store." Indeed, Philip Engel features outstanding pieces of furniture in leather and microfiber: sofas, diningroom tables and chairs, sectionals, sofa beds, and reclining chairs from all over the world. The company has been in business since 1967. Prices are reasonable, delivery is quick, pieces may be custom-ordered, and a free in-store design service is available.

SLEEPY'S
Several locations throughout Manhattan, including:
176 Ave of the Americas (at Spring St)	212/966-7002
874 Broadway (at 18th St)	212/995-0044
Hours vary by store	www.sleepys.com

Sleepy's specializes in bedding sold below department store prices. The byword is *discount*. Sleepy's features mattresses from Stearns & Foster, Sealy, Simmons, Serta, Kingsdown, and more. They claim to beat competitors prices by 20%.

Infants and Children

ALBEE BABY CARRIAGE
715 Amsterdam Ave (at 95th St)	212/662-5740
Mon-Sat: 9-5:30 (Thurs till 7)	www.albeebaby.com

As a longtime retailer, I get crazy when I set foot into this place. Albee has one of the city's best selections of basics for infants and toddlers—everything from strollers and car seats to cribs and rocking chairs—and the staff can be very helpful. Organizationally it's a disaster area, and it is sometimes hard to get anyone's attention in the chaos, particularly on weekends. That said, Albee Baby Carriage is very popular with Manhattan parents (and grandparents), and it's worth a visit if you're expecting.

Burlington Coat Factory (707 Ave of the Americas, 212/229-2247) is the sort of place that has many New Yorkers bemoaning the "malling" of their city. But if you need basic baby furniture and equipment and know what you want, the prices at the "Baby Depot" on the third floor are often the best in town—that is, if you can find someone to help you.

Another one-stop option for new parents is **buybuy Baby** (270 Seventh Ave, 917/344-1555), a cavernous Bed Bath & Beyond relative. The sales help and selection are better than at Burlington Coat Factory, but most prices aren't nearly as good.

CHELSEA KIDS QUARTERS
33 W 17th St (bet Fifth Ave and Ave of the Americas)	
Mon-Sat: 10-6:30; Sun: 11-5:30	212/627-5524
	www.chelseakidsquarters.com

There is nothing fancy about this relative newcomer to the children's furniture scene, but the selection of beds (including lots of bunk beds), desks, dressers, and other children's room basics is good, prices are reasonable, and the salespeople are friendly. If you're turning a nursery into a child's room and don't want to break the bank, Chelsea Kids Quarters merits a look.

GRANNY'S RENTALS
231 E 88th St (bet Second and Third Ave), Suite 4W   212/876-4310
By appointment   www.grannysrental.com

Whether you're a new parent wanting to try out a particular item or a visitor who needs a stroller for a week, this is a great spot to know about! Granny's Rentals has all sorts of equipment and furniture for babies and children, including strollers, cribs, breast pumps, and car seats. They also rent tables and chairs for children's parties. The minimum rental is for one week, and they'll deliver directly to you from their warehouse in the Bronx.

LAURA BETH'S BABY COLLECTION
321 E 75th St (bet First and Second Ave)   212/717-2559
By appointment

Laura Beth, who spent nearly a decade as the senior buyer for Barney's fashionable baby department, offers one-stop shopping for moms-to-be to create the perfect nursery, right down to crib linens, gliders, and decorative accessories. Shopping here is like perusing a private boutique, with Laura Beth on hand to provide expert guidance. Once the room is complete, she can help choose your birth announcement from a wide selection of the finest stationery at prices that are better than retail.

PLAIN JANE
525 Amsterdam Ave (bet 85th and 86th St)   212/595-6916
Mon-Sat: 11-6   www.plainjanekids.com

What a pleasure it is to discover a store brimming with quality merchandise and a friendly, knowledgeable staff! This welcome addition to the baby and small child home furnishing scene offers unique furniture, bedding, and accessories. Prices are higher than you'd pay straight off the shelf, but you're receiving excellent personal service and terrific style at Plain Jane. If you're having a baby or know somebody who is, stop in and look around.

SCHNEIDER'S JUVENILE FURNITURE
41 W 25th St (bet Broadway and Ave of the Americas)
Mon-Sat: 10-6   212/228-3540
                                          www.schneidersbaby.com

This Chelsea store is a find for those interested in furniture for children between infancy and teenhood, and at very comfortable prices. You'll also find cribs, car seats, strollers, diaper bags, backpacks, and most everything else for this age group.

WICKER GARDEN'S BABY
1300 Madison Avenue (bet 92nd and 93rd St)   212/410-7000
Call for hours   www.wickergarden.com

Pamela Scurry has a great sense of style. If you like wicker furniture, handpainted detail, and unusual, often whimsical designs, you'll love the baby and juvenile furniture on the second floor of this East Side institution. Moms-to-be take note: the selection of nice-looking and comfortable gliders is the best in the city.

Games—Adult

COMPLEAT STRATEGIST
11 E 33rd St (at Fifth Ave)   212/685-3880, 800/225-4344
Mon-Sat: 10:30-6 (Thurs till 9)   www.thecompleatstrategist.com

The Compleat Strategist was established over a quarter of a century ago as an armory of sorts for military games and equipment. As the only such place in the city, it was soon overrun with military strategists. As time went on, the store branched into science fiction, fantasy, and murder-mystery games, as well as adventure games and books. Today people who are fighting the Civil War all over again can browse alongside Dragon Masters. The stock is more than ample, and the personnel are knowledgeable and friendly. For more cerebral sorts, they have chess and backgammon sets—even good old Monopoly! Free shipping is offered on mail orders. There are special events for gamers every Saturday; call for schedules.

VILLAGE CHESS SHOP
230 Thompson St (bet Bleecker and 3rd St)   212/475-9580
Daily: noon-midnight   www.chess-shop.com

People who enjoy chess can play at the Village Chess Shop for a small price. Those searching for unique chess pieces should patronize this shop as well. Chess sets are available in pewter, brass, ebony, onyx, and more. Village Chess has outstanding backgammon sets, too. In short, this should be your first stop if you're planning on moving chess pieces—either from one square to another or from this store to your home!

Gifts, Accessories

ADRIEN LINFORD
927 Madison Ave (bet 73rd and 74th St)   212/628-4500
1339 Madison Ave (at 93rd St)   212/426-1500
Daily: 11-7

At Adrien Linford you will find an eclectic mixture of gifts, decorative accessories for the home, occasional furniture, lighting, jewelry, and whatever else Gary Yee finds interesting and exciting. The atmosphere and price tags are definitely upscale; you'll be suitably impressed with the tasteful stock.

BESPECKLED TROUT
422 Hudson St (at St. Luke's Pl)   212/255-1421
Mon-Sat: 7-10; Sat, Sun: 8-8

This turn-of-the-century general store features unique items for fishermen and anyone else with good taste. There is folk art, tea-related antiques, and handmade chocolates, plus Bill Craig's collection of angling antiquities and eccentricities. An old-fashioned soda fountain of early 20th-century vintage serves egg creams, cherry-lime rickeys, malts, lemonade, and more.

Craig and Charlotte Hero's grandfather owned the shop's original fixtures. You can try homemade American pies on what used to be a real fishing ground. Yes, Bespeckled Trout occupies the former site of Minetta Creek, which still flows under the Village.

BIZARRE BAZAAR
130¼ E 65th St (bet Lexington and Park Ave)   212/517-2100
Mon-Sat: 12-6 (call for appointment)   www.bizarrebazaarltd.com

Some people collect baseball cards while others find political buttons fascinating. I collect "Do Not Disturb" signs from hotels where I have stayed. For the discerning and serious collector, Bizarre Bazaar offers antique toys, aviation and automotive memorabilia, vintage Louis Vuitton luggage, enamel glassware, French perfume bottles, Lalique pieces, artists' mannequins, architectural miniatures, and much more of good quality.

CAROLE STUPELL
29 E 22nd St (bet Park Ave and Broadway)   212/260-3100
Mon-Sat: 12-6   www.carolestupell.com

In my opinion, Carole Stupell is the finest home-accessories store in the country. The taste and thought that has gone into the selection of merchandise is simply unmatched. Keith Stupell, a second-generation chip-off-the-old-block, has assembled a fabulous array of china, glassware, silver, tabletop, and imported gift treasures designed solely for this store, and he displays them in spectacular settings. In addition, there is a large selection of china and glassware replacement patterns that date back over 30 years. Prices are not in the bargain range, but the quality is unequaled.

The relatively new **Time Warner Center** (10 Columbus Circle 212/823-6300) is a brave experiment in a city that has not taken kindly to vertical malls. In a dramatic setting, on the corner of Central Park West and Central Park South, the complex offers much for well-heeled shoppers, diners, and lodgers. The shops represent some of the finest names in American retailing: **Coach, Cole Haan, Hugo Boss, Joseph Abboud, Thomas Pink** (*really* British), **Williams-Sonoma**, and more.

The **Whole Foods Market** in the downstairs area can only be described as stupendous. It has comfortably wide aisles lined with magnificent selections of food, and there are numerous checkout stations. **Borders Books** is a dream-like bookstore, with vast, efficiently displayed selections. The lower concourse houses a complete **Equinox Fitness Club**.

On the upper floors, a selection of fine (and expensive) restaurants offer a variety of dining experiences (see Restaurants). And the magnificent **Mandarin Oriental New York** (see Services) is a deluxe place to rest your head. All of this luxury comes at a price, and only time will tell whether New Yorkers will support the various venues. One thing is for sure: no expense has been spared in bringing a mall to Manhattan that compares with the very best found in any suburban area.

EXTRAORDINARY
251 E 57th St (bet Second and Third Ave)   212/223-9151
Daily: 11-10

An international gift selection is the draw at Extraordinary. Owner J.R. Sanders has a background as a museum exhibition designer, and it shows. You'll find boxes, bowls, trays, candleholders, lamps, jewelry, and other items for the home. The round-the-world theme includes merchandise from the Philippines, Japan, Thailand, China, Vietnam, India, Morocco, Ghana, Peru, and other stops. Quite a unique jewel!

FEDERICO DE VERA
1 Crosby St (at Howard St)   212/625-0838
Tues-Sat: 11-7

Many folks would love to own a store that sells only things that they like, but few are able to do so. An exception is Federico, who travels the world purchasing whatever catches his eye. The result is a unique operation, with decorative arts, antiques, Asian lacquerware, Venetian glass, and more. There's an emphasis on jewelry (vintage, one-of-a-kind, and some even designed by Federico!). You see he is a craftsman as well as a merchant, and he does wonders with the most unusual items. Perhaps this place should be listed in the Museums section as well!

FELISSIMO DESIGN HOUSE
10 W 56th St (bet Fifth Ave and Ave of the Americas)   212/247-5656
Mon-Sat: 11-6 (Fri till 8)   www.felissimo.com

Constructed with the senses in mind, Felissimo Design House is a venue for "design experiences in everyday life." They sell not just products but "space, inspiration, experience, and opportunity." The first four floors showcase the latest in everyday product design, while the fifth floor is an ever-changing exhibition space.

FLIGHTS OF FANCY
1502 First Ave (bet 78th and 79th St)   212/772-1302
Mon-Fri: 11-7 (Wed till 8); Sat: 10-7; Sun: 12-5

www.flightsoffancynyc.com

Flights of Fancy exudes charm, presenting soft music and an array of American treasures in a Victorian parlor setting beckoning passers-by. Many of the gifts are handmade and exclusive to the shop. Certain items are so unusual and special that orders pour in from around the country. Prices range from $2 to $2,000, so there is something for every gift-giving budget. A handmade American theme runs through the ever-changing stock.

GLOBAL TABLE
107 Sullivan St (bet Prince and Spring St)   212/431-5839
Mon-Sat: 12-7; Sun: 12-6   www.globaltable.com

Affordable. Different. Fun. Worldwide in scope. These all describe the stock at this crowded tabletop and accessory store, where you will find pottery, ceramic, wood, and plastic gifts. You might find a thoughtful surprise for mom or the perfect gift to take to your next dinner party.

IT'S A MOD, MOD WORLD
85 First Ave (bet 5th and 6th St)   212/460-8004
Mon-Thurs: noon-10; Fri, Sat: noon-11; Sun: noon-8
www.modworldnyc.com

Weird is the operative concept here. In a highly unique atmosphere, you will find all manner of whimsical and unusual items, like appliquéd clocks and altered Barbie dolls. If you feel inventive, they will even design special items (clocks, candles, votives, etc.) to your specifications. Don't miss the amazing floor lamps.

KIRNA ZABÊTE
96 Greene St (bet Prince and Spring St)   212/941-9656
Mon-Sat: 11-7; Sun: 12-6   www.kirnazabete.com

If you're looking for something different, Kirna Zabête surely qualifies. Here is a mixture of high-end designer items, candy (at $3 a bag), dog accessories, and much more, with *color* and *imagination* being the bywords!

MAYA SCHAPER CHEESE & ANTIQUES
106 W 69th St (at Columbus Ave)   212/873-2100
Mon-Sat: 10-8; Sun: 12-7

Maya Schaper is one of those special personalities who knows what she likes and wants to share her interest in cheese and food-related antiques. Granted, this is an unusual combination. But Maya is an unusual person. You'll find interesting gifts, gift baskets, dried flower arrangements from France, country antiques, and painted furniture. Schaper will locate special items for customers. An interesting note: Scenes from the movie *You've Got Mail*, starring Tom Hanks and Meg Ryan, were filmed in this shop.

MICHAEL C. FINA
545 Fifth Ave (at 45th St)   212/557-2500, 800/BUY-FINA
Mon-Thurs: 11-8; Fri: 10-7, Sat: 10-6; Sun: 12-6
www.michaelcfina.com

A New York tradition for over 60 years, Michael C. Fina is a popular bridal registry firm with an extensive selection of sterling silver, china, crystal, jewelry, brand-name watches, and housewares. Prices are attractive, quality is top-notch, and the store is well organized.

Some say the 99-cent store is a relic of the past. Not so! Try **Jack's World** (110 W 32nd St, 212/268-9962; 45 W 45th St, 212/354-6888; and 16 E 40th St, 212/696-5767).

ONLY HEARTS
386 Columbus Ave (bet 78th and 79th St)   212/724-5608
230 Mott St (bet Prince and Spring St)   212/431-3694
Mon-Sat: 11-7; Sun: 12-6   www.onlyhearts.com

At this "heart"-themed boutique, Helena Stuart offers romantics an extraordinary collection of European designer accessories, posh scents, soaps, and candles. She also shows a beguiling array of intimate apparel, lingerie, and women's wear.

WORKS GALLERY
1250 Madison Ave (bet 89th and 90th St)   212/996-0300
Mon-Sat: 12-6; Sun: 12-5 (closed Sun in summer)
www.worksgallery.com

Sometimes we all need a unique gift for a special person or occasion. At Works Gallery you will find one-of-a-kind jewelry and art-glass items hand-made by talented artists. You can even have a personal piece made from your own stones. They have been in business for two decades.

YELLOW DOOR
1308 Avenue M (bet 13th and 14th St), Brooklyn   718/998-7382
Mon-Thurs: 10-5:45; Fri: 10-4; Sun: 11-5   www.theyellowdoor.com

One of the best things about Brooklyn is a discount gift store on Avenue M in Flatbush, off the promenade of Ocean Parkway. It is run by entrepreneur Luna Zemmol. For over 30 years the Yellow Door has been providing "Madison Avenue style at Brooklyn prices." The store carries an unparalleled selection of the finest name brands (Lalique, MacKenzie-Childs, Waterford, Baccarat, Lenox, Orrefors, Alessi, Towle) in gold jewelry, gifts, china, table accessories, and bath items. Services include free local delivery, a bridal registry, and phone orders.

Greeting Cards

UNICEF CARD & GIFT SHOP
3 United Nations Plaza (44th St bet First and Second Ave)
Mon-Sat: 10-6   212/326-7054
www.unicefusa.org

For nearly 60 years the United Nations Children's Emergency Fund (UNICEF) has been improving the lives of the world's children. One way this tremendous organization raises money for its life-saving projects and programs is through the sale of cards and gifts. If you've never seen UNICEF products before, then you're in for a treat at this well-planned and friendly store, which carries greeting cards, stationery, books and games for children, apparel, and a fascinating assortment of Nepalese paper products. It also sells cards chosen for sale in Asia, Africa, Europe, and South America. In fact, it's the only store in the U.S. that sells these exotic cards!

UNTITLED
159 Prince St (at West Broadway)   212/982-2088
Daily: 10-8 (Fri, Sat till 9)

The Metropolitan Museum of Art and the Louvre each have approximately 1,500 art cards for sale. Untitled, by contrast, has 4,000-plus cards in stock at any given moment. Those cards include modern art postcards, greeting cards, and note cards. The postcards are filed either as pre- or post-1945, and they're further ordered within those classifications by artist. There are also postcards featuring famous photos and depictions of every possible type of art. Some of these items are good for gags, while others are suitable for framing. Untitled also sells design magazines, boxed cards, and books on art, design, typography, architecture, and photography.

Hearing Aids

EMPIRE STATE HEARING AID BUREAU
25 W 43rd St (bet Fifth Ave and Ave of the Americas)   212/921-1666
Mon-Thurs: 9-5:30; Fri: 9-5   www.empirestatehearingaid.com

The late President Reagan set a shining example by not being ashamed to wear a hearing aid. The latest hearing aids are so small that most people cannot even tell they're being worn. Their products are up-to-date and state-of-the-art. Empire State has been in the business for over 50 years and carries the top names in the field: Siemens, Starkey, Oticon, and GN ReSound. Skilled personnel will test and fit quality hearing aids in a quiet, unhurried atmosphere.

Hobbies

AMERICA'S HOBBY CENTER
263 W 30th St (bet Seventh and Eighth Ave)   212/675-8922
Mon-Fri: 9-5:30; Sat: 9-3:30   www.ahc1931.com

While hobbies and models are serious business here, there's also a light-hearted touch evident in the shop. Marshall Winston introduces himself as the "known authority on vehicular hobbies," which include model airplanes, boats, ships, trains, cars, radio-controlled objects, model books, helicopters, model rocketry, tools, and everything for model builders. They also sell by mail order and conduct an export business. Ask for a catalog to see what they have in your field of interest.

JAN'S HOBBY SHOP
1435 Lexington Ave (bet 93rd and 94th St)   212/987-4765
Mon-Sat: 10-7; Sun: 12-5

Jan's is one of my favorite examples of New York retailing! When Fred Hutchins was young, he was obsessed with building models and dioramas, particularly on historical themes. Eventually, his parents bought his favorite source of supply. Now he runs the shop, keeping Jan's stocked with every-thing a serious model builder could possibly want. The store has a superb stock of plastic scale models, model war games, paints, books, brushes and all kinds of model cars, trains, planes, ships, and tanks. It also carries remote-controlled planes, sailboats, ships, and tanks. Fred himself creates models and dioramas to order for television, advertising, and private customers. He is noted for accurate historical detail and can provide information from his vast library of military subjects. There is yet another business: showcase building. Because any hobbyist likes to show his wares, Fred custom-makes wood, plexiglass, glass, and mahogany showcases.

The lady in the harbor is 101 feet tall from base to torch and 305 feet tall from pedestal foundation to torch. She has a 35-foot waist, an 8-foot index finger, and she weighs 450,000 pounds.

Home Furnishings

ABC CARPET & HOME
888 Broadway (at 19th St)   212/473-3000
Mon-Fri: 10-8; Sat: 10-7; Sun: 11-6:30   www.abchome.com

If you can visit only one home furnishings store in Manhattan, ABC should be it! What started in 1897 as a pushcart business has grown and expanded into one of the city's most unique, exciting, and well-merchandised emporiums. (It's actually two buildings located across the street from each other.) ABC is the Bergdorf Goodman of home furnishings. There are floors of great-looking furniture, dinnerware, linens, gifts, accessories, antiques, and more. You will see many one-of-a-kind pieces as you explore corner after corner. There is an entire floor of fabrics by the yard and an extensive carpet and rug selection at great prices. Don't miss their pan-Latin restaurant, **Lucy Latin Kitchen** (212/475-LUCY). The barbecued lamb is a winner! An ABC outlet store is located in the Bronx (1055 Bronx River Ave, 718/842-8772).

It used to be that only those with designer's cards were admitted to some trade buildings. Now, however, a number of design outfits will take care of individual customers, even if the signs on their doors say "Trade Only." Listed below are some of the buildings in New York to check out; each has a multitude of shops where you can find just about anything you want to fix up an apartment or home.
Architects & Designers Building (150 E 58th St, 212/644-2766; Mon-Fri: 9-5)
Decoration & Design Building (979 Third Ave, 212/759-5408; Mon-Fri: 9-5): It's a good idea to bring a decorator along with you.
Fine Arts Building (232 E 59th St, 212/980-5077; Mon-Fri: 9-5)
Manhattan Art & Antiques Center (1050 Second Ave, 212/355-4400; Mon-Sat: 10:30-6; Sun: 12-6)

AUTO
805 Washington St (bet Gansevoort and Horatio St)   212/229-2292
Mon-Sat: 12-7; Sun: 12-6   www.thisisauto.com

Stock at Auto includes specially designed and sometimes hard-to-find home furnishings such as pillows, ceramics, glassware, and throws, plus some accessories. Most are handmade and one-of-kind. It's worth a visit!

BEDFORD & CO.
995 Lexington Ave (bet 71st and 72nd St)   212/772-7000
Mon-Fri: 10:30-6; Sat: 11-5 (closed Sat in July and Aug)

Donna D'Urso has assembled a fascinating collection of home furnishings and accessories, all selected with good taste and priced reasonably. For unusual vases, trays, pillows, and framed artwork, this is a good place.

BELLORA
156 Wooster St (bet Houston and Prince St)   212/228-6651
Mon-Sat: 11-7; Sun: 12-6

At Bellora the boat (or plane) has just arrived from Italy! What a superb showing of quality linens for the home, tabletop items like dishes and flatware, body and bath products, robes, and window treatments. Bellora will come to your home or office, and they offer expanded hours for designers. On-site alterations are available.

HOME DEPOT
980 Third Ave (bet 58th and 59th St)	212/888-1512
28-40 W 23rd St (bet Fifth Ave and Ave of the Americas)	
Mon-Sat: 7 a.m.-9 p.m.; Sun: 8-7	212/929-9571
	www.home.depot.com

It was bound to happen. Home Depot has set up two stores in Manhattan, and they are huge. Modern, too: flat-panel touch screens will display inventories and print out product lists and how-to instructions. Expert salespeople can customize products for small spaces in Manhattan apartments. You'll find kitchen and bath items, appliances, window treatments and moldings, lighting fixtures, phones and accessories, paints, cleaning supplies, lumber and building materials, tools, plants and patio furniture (seasonal), and more. Same-day and next-day delivery are offered.

KARKULA
68 Gansevoort St (bet Greenwich and Washington St)	212/645-2216
Mon-Sat: 11-7	www.karkula.com

Sexy urban contemporary furniture and home furnishings with an American and European flair are shown to advantage at this hip outfit. A lot of up-and-coming designers get their start here. Designs feature such materials as bronze, wood, leather, and felt. You'll also find contemporary sculpture and jewelry.

SURPRISE! SURPRISE!
91 Third Ave (bet 12th and 13th St)	212/777-0990
Mon-Sat: 10-7; Sun: 11-6	www.surprisesurprise.com

Surprise! Surprise! offers a complete line of reasonably priced items for the home. They claim to possess the stock and know-how to make your new apartment look like a home the same day you move in! You'll find a large selection of kitchenware, furnishings, patio furniture, and lamps.

Don't miss **Helen Wang's** new outlet for home furnishings and clothes for both men and women (69 Mercer St, 212/997-4180).

Housewares, Hardware

BRIDGE KITCHENWARE
214 E 52nd St (bet Second and Third Ave)	212/688-4220
Mon-Fri: 9-5:30; Sat: 10-4:30	www.bridgekitchenware.com

Bridge Kitchenware is a unique-to-New York store that supplies almost every restaurant within 500 miles. Named for founder Fred Bridge, the store carries bar equipment, cutlery, pastry equipment, molds, copperware, ironware, woodenware, stoneware, and kitchen gadgets. All goods are professional quality and excellent for home gourmets. Be sure to see the lines of imported French copperware, professional knives, and baking pans. After cooking with them, people use no other. Call for a catalog.

BROADWAY PANHANDLER
477 Broome St (at Wooster St)   212/966-3434, 866/266-5927
Mon-Sat: 11-7; Sun: 11-6   www.broadwaypanhandler.com

These folks are a pleasure to deal with. Thousands of cutlery, bakeware, tabletop items, and cookware pieces are available at sizable savings. Guest chefs make periodic appearances, and a fine selection of professional items is offered to walk-in customers and restaurant and hotel buyers.

DOMUS
413 W 44th St (at Ninth Ave)   212/581-8099
Tues-Sat: 12-8; Sun: 12-7 (closed Sun in Aug)

What fun it is shopping at this eclectic Hell's Kitchen housewares store! Luisa Cerutti and Nicki Lindheimer have excellent taste and have picked out one-of-a-kind European imports like pottery, tabletop, vintage glassware, linens, china, furniture, and unusual pieces that will catch everyone's attention. This is a super place to shop for wedding gifts. Free gift wrapping and delivery in Manhattan are available.

Top Button
PO Box 3423
Church Street Station   212/269-7253
New York, NY 10008   www.topbutton.com

Top Button is a web-based company that informs consumers about sample, warehouse, outlet, clearance, and promotional sales. Categories include apparel, housewares, and accessories. Information can be accessed by company name, product type, and date. The service is free.

GARBER HARDWARE
710 Greenwich St (bet 10th and Charles St)   212/929-3030
Mon, Thurs: 8-6; Tues, Wed: 8-7; Fri, Sat: 8-5; Sun: 10-4
                                       www.garberhardware.com

This unique family business has become a New York institution. The Garbers have been operating since 1884 at the same location with the appealing motto "Either we have it or we can get it for you." You will find a complete inventory of paints, hardware, home and garden, plumbing and electrical supplies, housewares, locks, tools, and building materials. Custom window shades, lamp repair, key-cutting, and pipe-cutting are among the many handy services offered.

GARRETT WADE
161 Ave of the Americas (at Spring St) 212/807-1155, 800/221-2942
Mon-Fri: 9-5:30; Sat: 10-3   www.garrettwade.com

The Garrett Wade customer appreciates fine woodworking tools, as the store prides itself on offering the highest-quality tools from all over the world. The main business is mail-order, and the catalog is all-encompassing.

It lists every imaginable woodworking aid, explaining each piece's function. It reads like a how-to guide! Garrett Wade assumes that anyone can put together a rocker or, at the very least, appreciate the function of a lightweight spokeshave. After a visit here, you may become a believer, too!

GEORGE TAYLOR SPECIALTIES
76 Franklin St (bet Church St and Broadway)   212/226-5369
Mon-Thurs: 7:30-5; Fri: 7:30-4

Taylor stocks plumbing replacement parts to fit all faucets, and custom faucets can be fabricated via special order. They also offer reproduction faucets and custom designs of fittings for unique installations. Antique-style towel bars, bath accessories, and pedestal sinks are a specialty. Founded in 1869, Taylor remains a family-run operation. Ask for father Chris, daughter Valerie, or son John.

Remodelers and builders, take note! For lumber, plywood, masonite, bricks, cork, paint, and more, **Metropolitan Lumber and Hardware** (175 Spring St, 212/966-3466 and 617 Eleventh Ave, 212/246-9090) is a good name to remember.

GRACIOUS HOME
1217 and 1220 Third Ave (bet 70th and 71st St)   212/517-6300
Mon-Fri: 8-7; Sat: 9-7; Sun: 10-6
1992 Broadway (at 67th St)   212/231-7800
Mon-Sat: 9-9; Sun: 10-7   www.gracioushome.com

A great store! For over four decades Gracious Home has been a popular shopping spot for savvy New Yorkers. It is a must-visit for anyone interested in fixing up their home, establishing a new one, looking for gifts, or just browsing a store that typifies the New York lifestyle. The style, expertise, and service are outstanding. You'll find appliances, wall coverings, gifts, hardware, decorative bath accessories, lighting, china, casual furniture, bedding, shelving, pots and pans, and heaven knows what else! They install window coverings, large appliances, and countertops; offer tool rental and repair services; provide a special-order department; and will deliver in Manhattan for free.

LEESAM KITCHEN AND BATH CENTER
124 Seventh Ave (at 17th St)   212/243-6482
Mon-Fri: 10-6; Sat: 11-5   www.leesamkitchens.com

Since 1934 these folks have been fixing up kitchens and bathrooms. Whether you're shopping for medicine cabinets, kitchen cabinets, faucets, shower enclosures, or counters, you will see large selections of top brands from domestic suppliers. There's no excuse not to remodel your cluttered, dysfunctional old kitchen using one of their computer-designed plans.

P.E. GUERIN
23 Jane St (bet Greenwich and Eighth Ave)   212/243-5270
Mon-Fri: 9-5:30 (by appointment)   www.peguerin.com

Andrew Ward, P.E. Guerin's current president, is the fourth generation to run the oldest decorative hardware firm in the country and the only foundry in the city. It was founded in 1957 and has been on Jane Street since 1892. In that time, the firm has grown into an impressive worldwide operation. The main foundry is now in Valencia, Spain (although work continues at the Village location), and there are branches and showrooms across the country and in Puerto Rico. The Jane Street location is still headquarters for manufacturing and importing decorative hardware and bath accessories. Much of it is done in brass or bronze, and the foundry can make virtually anything from those materials, including copies and reproductions. The Gueridon table has garnered design and production awards and enjoys an international reputation. No job is too small for this firm, which operates like the hometown industry it thinks it is. They offer free estimates and help with any hardware problems.

The famous French purveyor of high-quality kitchen and tableware, **Sur la Table** (75 Spring St, 212/966-3375), has opened a 5,000-square-foot store in Soho. It's in the space formerly occupied by George Smith, a British luxury furniture retailer. Passionate foodies will love this place.

RESTORATION HARDWARE
935 Broadway (at 22nd St)   212/260-9479
Mon-Sat: 10-8; Sun: 11-7   www.restorationhardware.com

Do you prefer a classic, quality look? Then this is your store! You'll find a large selection of furniture, bed and bath items, drapery, lighting, bathware, and hardware. A good selection of cleaning and maintenance supplies, too! These people are among the best in their field.

S. FELDMAN HOUSEWARES
1304 Madison Ave (at 92nd St)   212/289-7367
Mon-Sat: 9-6; Sun: 11-5   www.wares2u.com

Keep this name and address on your refrigerator door! Founded in 1929, Feldman was originally a five-and-dime store. Over the years it has changed dramatically, but it still is family-owned and -operated. You'll find housewares, cookware, home decor, gifts, tabletop items, appliances, toys, and more. Customer service is a big plus; they even offer free espresso. With over 12,000 in-store items to choose from, this can be a true one-stop shopping spot for you and your family. They also repair vacuum cleaners.

SIMON'S HARDWARE & BATH
421 Third Ave (bet 29th and 30th St)   212/532-9220
Mon-Fri: 8-5:30 (Thurs till 7); Sat: 10-6 www.simons-hardware.com

This is really a hardware supermarket. Simon's offers one of the city's finest selections of quality decorative hardware items and bath and kitchen fixtures and accessories. The personnel are patient, even if you just need something to fix a broken handle on a chest of drawers.

WILLIAMS-SONOMA

1175 Madison Ave (at 86th St)	212/289-6832
110 Seventh Ave (at 17th St)	212/633-2203
121 E 59 St (bet Park and Lexington Ave)	917/369-1131
10 Columbus Circle (Time Warner Building)	212/823-9750
Hours vary by store	www.williams-sonoma.com

From humble beginnings in the wine country of Sonoma County, California, Williams-Sonoma has expanded across the nation and is now referred to as the "Tiffany of cookware stores." The serious cook will find a vast display of quality cookware, bakeware, cutlery, kitchen linens, specialty foods, cookbooks, small appliances, kitchen furniture, glassware, and tableware. The stores also offer a gift and bridal registry service, cooking demonstrations, free recipes, gift baskets, and shopping assistance for corporations or individuals. Especially at holiday time, their candy assortment is first-class. Ask for their attractive catalog, which includes a number of excellent recipes.

The Best of British!

British sweets: **Carry On Tea & Sympathy** (110 Greenwich Ave, 212/807-8329)

Clothes and housewares: **Eskandar** (Bergdorf Goodman, 754 Fifth Ave, 3rd floor, 212/872-8659)

Fashion designer: **Alexander McQueen** (417 W 14th St, 212/645-1797)

Paper goods: **Smythson of Bond Street** (4 W 57th St, 212/265-4573)

Purses, shoes, umbrellas, socks: **Lulu Guinness** (394 Bleecker St, 212/367-2120)

Imports

Afghan

NUSRATY AFGHAN IMPORTS

215 W 10th St (at Bleecker St)	212/691-1012
Daily: 1-9	

Abdul Nusraty has transformed a corner of the Village into a vision of Afghanistan that is fascinating (and, thankfully, free of political strife). Nusraty is one of the best sources of Afghan goods on the continent. There are magnificently embroidered native dresses and shirts displayed alongside semiprecious stones mounted in jewelry or shown individually. One area of the store features carpets and rugs, while another displays antique silver and jewelry. Nusraty has an unerring eye; all of his stock is of the highest quality and is often unique as well. The business operates on both a wholesale and retail level.

Chinese

CHINESE PORCELAIN COMPANY

475 Park Ave (at 58th St)   212/838-7744
Mon-Fri: 10-6; Sat: 11-5 (closed Sat in summer)
www.chineseporcelainco.com

Look here for Chinese ceramics and works of art. There are Chinese, Tibetan, Indian, Khymer, and Vietnamese sculptures, as well as French and continental furniture.

WING-ON TRADING
145 Essex St (bet Delancey and Houston St)   212/477-1450
Mon-Sat: 9-6

There's no need to go to Hong Kong to get your Chinese porcelain or earthenware. Even though it is located on the ramshackle Lower East Side, Wing-On has a complete and well-organized stock of household goods. One of their specialties is Chinese teas at low prices.

Eskimo/Native American
ALASKA ON MADISON
937 Madison Ave (bet 74th and 75th St)   212/879-1782
Tues-Sat: 11:30-6 (or by appointment)   www.alaskaonmadison.com

This gallery is New York's most complete source for Eskimo art. Rare antiquities and artifacts of centuries-old Arctic cultures are displayed next to sculptures of Indians of the Northwest. Periodic shows highlight aspects of these cultures. A number of contemporary artists whose works have been shown here have gained international acclaim.

General
JACQUES CARCANAGUES
21 Greene St (bet Grand and Canal St)   212/925-8110
Tues-Sun: 11:30-7   www.jacquescarcanagues.com

After a stint in the diplomatic service, Frenchman Jacques Carcanagues decided to assemble and sell the finest artifacts he had encountered in his world travels. So while the store is mostly Southeast Asian, it is, in Jacques own words, "a complete ethnic department store, not a museum." Yet the stock is all of museum quality. Textiles and *tansus* (dressers) are everywhere, as are jewelry and lacquerware. It is also very appealing to Soho shoppers, who can choose among Indian, Burmese, and Thai sculptures of many periods and unusual household objects not seen elsewhere in New York. The overall effect is that of an Eastern bazaar.

KATINKA
303 E 9th St (at Second Ave)   212/677-7897
Tues-Sat: 4-7 (call ahead, as hours can vary)

This is an import paradise, with jewelry, natural-fiber clothing, shoes, scarves, belts, hats, musical instruments, incense, and artifacts from India, Thailand, Pakistan, Afghanistan, and South America. The most popular items are colorful shoes and embroidered silk skirts from India. The place is small, and prices are reasonable. Jane Williams and Billy Lyles make customers feel like they have embarked on a worldwide shopping expedition!

PIER 1 IMPORTS
71 Fifth Ave (at 15th St)   212/206-1911
1550 Third Ave (at 87th St)   212/987-1746
Mon-Sat: 10-9; Sun: 11-7   www.pier1.com

Pier 1 is one of my very favorite stores! There's no need to spend your time or money running off to distant places. At Pier 1, you will find imported diningroom sets, occasional furniture, bathroom accessories, picture frames, brassware, china and glassware, floor coverings, bedding, pillows, and much more. The goods come from exotic lands throughout Asia and the rest of the world. The selections are inviting, the prices are right, and the stores are fun to visit. Besides, the chain's head honcho, Marvin Girouard, is one of the best merchants in the business!

SHEHERAZADE IMPORTS
121 Orchard St (bet Delancey and Rivington St)   212/539-1771
Daily: 11-7   www.sheherazadenyc.com

Sheherazade features handcrafted merchandise from a number of countries, all imported directly. You'll find home furnishings from North Africa, the Middle East, and Asia, including antique and contemporary furniture, carpets, tapestries, chandeliers, lanterns, jewelry, and gifts. Custom-made furniture can be ordered.

Indian

INDIA COTTAGE EMPORIUM
1150 Broadway (at 27th St)   212/685-6943
Mon-Fri: 9-6:30; Sat: 9-5

India Cottage features clothing, jewelry, handicrafts, and gifts imported directly from India. Moti R. Chani has a sharp eye for the finest details; the Indian clothing he sells reflects his taste and expertise. The clothing is prized by Indian nationals and neighborhood residents for its sheer beauty. The garments are made of cotton and feature unique madras patterns. Pay particular attention to the leather bags.

Japanese

SARA
952 Lexington Ave (bet 69th and 70th St)   212/772-3243
Mon-Fri: 11-7; Sat: 12-6   www.saranyc.com

Looking for something with a Japanese flair? Sara is the place to go for modern Japanese ceramics, glassware, tableware, and gifts.

THINGS JAPANESE
800 Lexington Ave (bet 61st and 62nd St), 2nd floor   212/371-4661
Mon-Sat: 11-5   www.thingsjapanese.com

Things Japanese believes that the Japanese "things" most in demand are prints. So while there are all sorts of Japanese artworks and crafts, prints highlight the selection. They know the field well and will help would-be collectors establish a grouping or assist decorators in finding pieces to round out decor. There are also original 18th- to 20th-century Japanese woodblock prints, porcelains, baskets, chests, lacquers, and books. Prices range from ten to several thousand dollars, and every piece is accompanied by a certificate of authenticity. Things Japanese claims that you need to appreciate both the subject matter and the artistry in the works it sells, and that is not a difficult or unpleasant task at all.

Japanese designer Nigo has created a new destination store, **Bathing Ape** (91 Greene St, 212/925-0222), for lovers of things Japanese. Offerings include unusual clothing, toys, home accessories, and shoes. Fans of rock-concert-style will be blown away by the merchandise.

Middle Eastern

PERSIAN SHOP
534 Madison Ave (bet 54th and 55th St)   212/355-4643
Mon-Sat: 10-6

This outfit has been in business since 1940, featuring unusual Middle Eastern items: end tables, chairs, frames, mirrors, and brocades sold by the yard or made into magnificent neckties for men. The jewelry selection is especially noteworthy. You'll find precious and semiprecious items, silver and gold cuff links, rings, earrings, bracelets, necklaces, and heirloom pieces. There are also Chinese vases, Russian and Greek icons, and planters that will add a special air of interest to any setting.

Ukrainian

SURMA (THE UKRAINIAN SHOP)
11 E 7th St (at Third Ave)   212/477-0729
Mon-Fri: 11-6; Sat: 11-4   www.surmastore.com

Since 1918, Surma has conducted business as the "general store of the Slavic community in New York City." Quite honestly, it seems capable of serving the entire hemisphere. Surma is a bastion of Ukrainianism. Once inside, it is difficult to believe you're still in New York. The clothing is pure ethnic opulence. There are dresses, vests, shirts, blouses, hand-tooled and soft-soled leather dancing shoes, and accessories. All are hand-embroidered with authentic detailing. For the home, there are accent pieces (including an entire section devoted to Ukrainian Easter egg decorating), brocaded linens, and Surma's own Ukrainian-style honey (different and very good). Above all, Surma is known for its educational tapes and books. Pay particular attention to the paintings and stationery, which feature modern-day depictions of ancient Ukrainian glass paintings.

Jewelry

BILL SCHIFRIN & HERMAN ROTENBERG
National Jewelers Exchange
4 W 47th St (bet Fifth Ave and Ave of the Americas), Booth 86
Mon-Fri: 10-5:30   212/944-1713, 800/877-3874
                                      www.unusualweddingrings.com

From a booth in the National Jewelers Exchange—better known for its collection of gold, platinum, and diamond wedding and engagement rings —Bill Schifrin and son-in-law Herman Rotenberg preside over a collection of over 2,000 unusual wedding rings. Prices range from under $100 to several thousand dollars, depending upon the work's complexity, metal, and stones. Bill has been doing this for over 50 years and knows the story behind each ring.

CHROME HEARTS
159 E 64th St (bet Lexington and Third Ave)   212/327-0707
Mon-Sat: 11-7   www.chromehearts.com

Chrome Hearts shows a broad selection of handmade jewelry in sterling silver, 22-karat gold and platinum, and precious stones; clothing in leather and fabric; gadgets for people who think they have everything; handcrafted furniture in exotic woods; great-looking eyewear; and much more. All merchandise is of a nontraditional nature. If you're looking for unique accessories, this is a good place.

DIAMONDS BY RENNIE ELLEN
15 W 47th St (bet Fifth Ave and Ave of the Americas), Room 503
Mon-Fri: 10-4:30 (by appointment)   212/869-5525
                                                  www.rennieellen.com

Rennie Ellen is a wholesaler offering the sort of discounts for which the city's wholesale businesses are famous. She was the first female diamond dealer in the male-dominated Diamond District. Rennie personally spent so much time and effort keeping the district straight and honest that she earned the title "Mayor of 47th Street." In other words, Ellen's reputation is impeccable. Her diamond-cutting factory deals exclusively in diamond jewelry. There are pendants, wedding bands, engagement rings, and diamonds to fit all sizes, shapes, and budgets. All sales are made under Ellen's personal supervision and are strictly confidential. Call for her $3 mail-order catalog.

FORTUNOFF
681 Fifth Ave (at 54th St)   212/758-6660
Mon-Sat: 10-6 (Thurs till 7); Sun: 12-5   www.fortunoff.com

This is one of the best stores in Manhattan devoted to quality merchandise. Prices on all items are competitive. There is a crystal and clock department, but it is in the jewelry area (especially antique silver) that the store really shines. A jeweler is on duty at all times. Fortunoff shows one of the largest and finest collections of 14- and 18-karat gold jewelry in the city, as well as a fine selection of precious and semiprecious stones, brand-name watches, and flatware.

See How the Other Half Lives!

Just for kicks (unless your last name is Trump, Rockefeller, or Gates) drop into **Graff** (721 Madison Ave, 212/355-9292) and gaze upon some of the most spectacular and expensive jewelry this side of London.

While you are strolling around this area, drop by **Alessandro Dell'Acqua** (818 Madison Ave, 212/253-6861, www.alessandro dellacqua.com) for a look at their beautiful, top-grade, and pricey designer clothes for men and women.

JENNIFER MILLER JEWELRY
972 Lexington Ave (bet 70th and 71st St)   212/734-8199
Mon-Sat: 10-5:30   www.jewelsbyjen.com

Jennifer Miller specializes in slightly altered versions of contemporary, classic, and estate jewelry. The varied assortment of fine and faux jewels changes almost daily, and everyone is sure to find something they can't live without. Well-priced resin rings ($75 to $195) and silver and faux-diamond bangles ($25) are popular. At the other extreme, you'll find a vintage-style long diamond chain for $61,000 or a 14-karat faux version for $1,800. (Hardly anyone will be able to tell the difference.) Handbags, shoes, and decorative home items round out the mix.

MAX NASS
118 E 28th St (bet Park Ave S and Lexington Ave)   212/679-8154
Mon-Fri: 9:30-6; Sat: 9:30-4

The Shah family members are jewelry artisans. Araceli is the designer and Parimal ("Perry") is the company president. Together they make and sell handmade jewelry, service and repair clocks and watches, and restore antique jewelry. They deal in virtually every type of jewelry: antique (or merely old), silver and gold, as well as semiprecious stones. Two special sales each year bring Max Nass's already low prices down even further. One is held the last three weeks in January (33% discount), and the other runs for two weeks in July (25% discount). In between, Araceli will design pieces on a whim or commission. His one-of-a-kind necklaces are particularly impressive. The store also restrings, restores, and redesigns necklaces.

MURREY'S JEWELERS
1395 Third Ave (bet 79th and 80th St)   212/879-3690
Mon-Sat: 9:30-6

I heartily recommend this shop! Family jewelers since 1936, Murrey's sells fine jewelry, watches, and giftware. In the service area, they do fine-jewelry repair, expert special-order design and manufacturing, European clock repair, engraving, pearl stringing, and watch repair. The talented staff includes three goldsmiths, three watchmaker/clockmakers (including one of the world's best), one stringer, and one setter.

MYRON TOBACK
25 W 47th St (bet Fifth Ave and Ave of the Americas)   212/398-8300
Mon-Fri: 8-4   www.myrontoback.com

Myron Toback is ostensibly a refiner of precious metals with a specialty in findings, plate, and wire. Not very useful to the average customer, you might think, but note the address. Toback is not only in the heart of the Diamond District but is also the landlord of an arcade crammed full of wholesale artisans of the jewelry trade. Taking their cue from Toback, they are open and friendly to individual retail customers. So bookmark Toback as a source of gold, gold-filled, and silver chains sold by the foot at wholesale prices. And don't overlook the gold and silver earrings, beads, and other jewelry items sold at prices that are laughably less than those at establishments around the corner on Fifth Avenue. Tools and other materials for stringing beads and pearls are also carried. Though most customers are professional jewelers or wholesale organizations, Toback is simply charming to do-it-yourselfers, schools, and hobbyists. His son and daughter have joined him in the business.

PEDRO BOREGAARD
636 Broadway (bet Houston and Bleecker St), Suite 1022
By appointment   212/826-3660
                                                    www.boregaard.com

Unusual rings, earrings, brooches, chains, and bracelets—all handmade and each a true work of art—are hallmarks of this very talented designer, who features items for men and women. Pieces may combine rubies, sapphires, and diamonds shaded in colors from champagne to cognac, and pink, white, or yellow gold. Boregaard's credentials are impressive: apprenticeship and professional work in Germany, a jewelry workshop in England, and work with Tiffany for designers such as Angela Cummings, Elsa Peretti, and Paloma Picasso.

Ladders

PUTNAM ROLLING LADDER COMPANY
32 Howard St (bet Lafayette St and Broadway)   212/226-5147
Mon-Fri: 8:30-4:30   www.putnamrollingladder.com

Putnam is an esoteric shop on an esoteric street! Why, you might ask, would anyone in New York need those magnificent rolling ladders traditionally used in formal libraries? Could there possibly be enough business to keep a place like this going since 1905? The answer is that clever New Yorkers turn to Putnam to improve access to their lofts (especially sleeping lofts). Here's a partial list of ladders, which come in many hardwoods: rolling ladders (custom-made, if necessary), rolling work platforms, telephone ladders, portable automatic ladders, scaffold ladders, pulpit ladders, folding library ladders, library stools, aerial platforms, library carts with steps, steel warehouse ladders, safety ladders, electric stepladders for industrial use, and mechanics' stepladders.

Lighting Fixtures and Accessories

CITY KNICKERBOCKER
665 Eleventh Ave (at 48th St), 2nd floor   212/586-3939
Mon-Fri: 8:30-5   www.cityknickerbocker.com

The fourth generation of the Liroff family operates this outfit, which has been in business since 1906. These folks are completely reliable when it comes to all aspects of lighting, including quality antique reproductions, glassware, and first-rate repair. In addition to a large sales inventory, which includes contemporary art-glass lamps, rentals are available.

JUST BULBS
5 E 16th St (near Union Square W)   212/228-7820
Mon-Sat: 9-6 (Tues, Thurs till 8); Sun: 12-6   www.justbulbs.net

This store stocks almost 25,000 types of bulbs, including some that can be found nowhere else. In addition to all the standard sizes, Just Bulbs has lightbulbs for use in old fixtures. The shop looks like an oversized backstage dressing-room mirror. Everywhere you turn there are bulbs connected to switches that customers are invited to flick on and off. They also refresh light fixtures, changing the bulb and cleaning fixtures at home or office.

JUST SHADES
21 Spring St (at Elizabeth St)   212/966-2757
Tues-Sat: 9:30-4

Just Shades specializes in lampshades. They are experts at matching shades to lamps and willingly share their knowledge with retail customers. They have lampshades of silk, hide, parchment, and other materials. Their biggest peeve is customers who don't remove the protective cellophane from their shades. When left on, the cellophane actually collects ruinous dust.

LAMPWORKS
231 E 58th St (bet Second and Third Ave)   212/750-1500
Mon-Fri: 9-6   www.lampworksinc.com

You will find an extensive selection of table lamps, antiques, imports, custom lampshades, and exterior lighting fixtures at Lampworks. Over 45 lines are available, and they specialize in custom lighting.

LIGHTING BY GREGORY
158 Bowery (bet Delancey and Broome St)   212/226-1276
Mon-Fri: 8:30-5:30; Sat, Sun: 9-5:30   www.lightingbygregory.com

No false modesty here! This full-service discount lighting store claims to be the most technically knowledgeable outfit in the country. They are major dealers of Lightolier, Tech Lighting, and Casablanca ceiling fans, as well as experts in track lighting.

LIGHTING PLUS
680 Broadway (bet 2nd and 3rd St)   212/979-2000
Mon-Sat: 10-6:45; Sun: 11-6:45

Do you need an electrical gadget or replacement part to fix a lamp or ceiling fan? Save yourself a lot of running around and go straight to Lighting Plus. In this well-organized store, you can find just about anything related to ceiling fixtures, and the personnel are eager to help.

TUDOR ELECTRICAL SUPPLY
222-226 E 46th St (bet Second and Third Ave)   212/867-7550
Mon-Thurs: 8:30-5; Fri: 8:30-4:30

At first glance you may feel like you need an engineering degree to patronize Tudor Electrical. However, the staff is trained to explain everything in stock. Lightbulbs are the store's forte. They are cataloged by wattage, color, and application by a staff who can quickly locate the right bulb for your needs. Some basic knowledge: quartz, tungsten, and halogen bulbs offer undistorted light, while incandescent and fluorescent lamps are best for desk work. Tudor discounts by at least 20%.

Luggage and Other Leather Goods

DEAN LEATHER
822 Third Ave (at 50th St)   212/583-0461
877 Seventh Ave (at 56th St)   212/581-5228
Mon-Fri: 8:30-7:30; Sat: 8:30-7; Sun: 9-6

If it is leather, you probably can find it here: briefcases, wallets, luggage, watches, and gift items. The prices are right and repair of luggage and leather goods is offered. Dean's carries many top names like Hartmann, Swiss Army, Samsonite, Briggs & Riley, Bosca, Mont Blanc, and more.

LEXINGTON LUGGAGE
793 Lexington Ave (bet 61st and 62nd St)   800/822-0404
Daily: 9-6   www.lexingtonluggage.com

If you are in the market for luggage, don't miss this place! They carry nearly every major brand at nearly wholesale prices. Luggage and handbag repairs can be done the same day. Other pluses: free same-day delivery, free monograms, and friendly personnel. You'll also find leather goods, briefcases, attaché cases, pens, poker sets, trunks, and a nice gift selection.

ORIGINAL LEATHER STORE
176 Spring St (bet Thompson St and West Broadway)   212/219-8210
Daily: 11:30-7:30   www.originalleather.com

This store is a must for leather lovers, trendsetters, and the fashion elite. Original Leather offers just what the name says: one-of-a-kind coats, leather pants, stylish shearlings, and jackets in every leather, length, and size. They also carry handbags, classy briefcases, and travel bags. Most garments are designed and made in-house from leather, suede, and exotic skins imported from France, Italy, and Spain. There is a stylish selection of modern classics, boasting funky and functional designs at competitive prices.

T. ANTHONY
445 Park Ave (at 56th St)   212/750-9797, 800/722-2406
Mon-Fri: 9:30-6; Sat: 10-6   www.tanthony.com

T. Anthony handles luxurious luggage of distinction. Anything purchased here will stand out in a crowd. Luggage ranges in size from small overnight bags to massive pieces like steamer trunks. Their briefcases, jewelry boxes, desk sets, albums, key cases, and billfolds make terrific gifts, individually or in matched sets. Don't come looking for discount prices; however, their high quality and courteous service are well-established New York traditions. Exclusive T. Anthony products are also available through the store's catalog.

Magic

TANNEN'S MAGIC
45 W 34th St (bet Fifth Ave and Ave of the Americas), Suite 608
Mon-Fri: 10-5 (Thurs till 7); Sat: 10-4   212/929-4500
                                               www.tannens.com

Tannen is the world's largest supplier of magician items, stocking more than 8,000 magic tricks, books, and DVDs. They have all that a magician of any level could possibly need. Tannen's showroom is patronized by the finest magicians in the country. The floor demonstrators are some of the best in the business—always friendly, helpful, and eager to share their knowledge with those willing to study the art of magic. Tannen also runs a "Magic Summer Camp" for boys and girls age 12 to 18; it has spawned some of today's greatest working magicians.

Maps

HAGSTROM MAP AND TRAVEL CENTER
51 W 43rd St (at Ave of the Americas)   212/398-1222
Mon-Fri: 8:30-6; Sat: 10:30-4:30   www.hagstrom.com

Hagstrom is the only complete map and chart dealer in the city, highlighting the maps of major manufacturers and three branches of government. There are also nautical, hiking, global, and travel guides, plus globes, atlases, and foreign-language phrase books. The staff are experts when it comes to

---

Where to Buy New York City Theme Merchandise

CityStore (New York Convention & Visitors Bureau, 810 Seventh Ave, 212/484-1222, www.nycvisit.com): official City of New York merchandise

FDNY Fire Zone (34 W 51st St, 212/698-4520, www.fdnyfirezone. com): officially licensed FDNY products

Harlem Underground (2027 Fifth Ave, 212/987-9385, www.harlem underground.com): sleek sportswear with Harlem logo and uptown attitude

Metropolitan Museum of Art (Fifth Ave at 82nd St, 212/535-7100, www.metmuseum.org): posters of recent art exhibits

Museum of the City of New York (1220 Fifth Ave, 212/534-1672, www.mcny.org): ties, scarves, and umbrellas with New York-themed designs

New York City Police Museum (100 Old Slip, 212/480-3100, www. nycpolicemuseum.org): gift items include stuffed bears, coloring books, and books

New-York Historical Society (2 W 77th St, 212/873-3400, www. nyhistory.org): posters, prints, and holiday cards featuring scenes of old New York

Our Name Is Mud (59 Greenwich Ave, 212/647-7899, www.our nameismud.com): creative dinnerware with a New York theme

Statue of Liberty (212/363-3180, www.nps.gov/stli): mini statues, books, postcards, glassware, and holiday ornaments

Steuben (667 Madison Ave, 212/752-1441, www.steuben.com): gorgeous crystal apple and the Manhattan skyline etched in crystal

Tiffany & Co. (727 Fifth Ave, 212/755-8000, www.tiffany.com): apple-themed items, including an apple key ring and Elsa Perettidesigned silver apple earrings, necklaces, and bracelets

---

maps and travel information.

Memorabilia

CBS STORE
1691 Broadway (at 53rd St)   212/975-8600
Mon-Sat: 10-8; Sun: 12-5   www.cbs.com

Just down the street from the Ed Sullivan Theater (where *The Late Show with David Letterman* is filmed), this store stocks T-shirts, mugs, and other merchandise with the CBS logo or images from the network's shows, such as *CSI* and *Survivor.*

GOTTA HAVE IT! COLLECTIBLES
153 E 57th St (bet Lexington and Third Ave)   212/750-7900
Mon-Fri: 10-6; Sat: 11-5   www.gottahaveit.com

Do you have a favorite sports star, Hollywood personality, musical entertainer, or political figure? If you are a collector or are looking for a gift for someone who is, Gotta Have It features original and unique products in these categories. There are signed photos, musical instruments, baseball bats, used sports uniforms, documents, and movie props. All items are fully authenticated and guaranteed for life.

MOVIE STAR NEWS
134 W 18th St (bet Ave of the Americas and Seventh Ave)
Mon-Fri: 10-6; Sat: 10-3   212/620-8160
www.moviestarnews.com

Movie Star News may be the closest thing to Hollywood on the East Coast! It claims to have the world's largest collection of movie photos. Stars past and present shine brightly in this shop, which offers posters and other movie memorabilia. The store is laid out like a library. Ira Kramer, who runs the shop, does a lot of research for magazines, newspapers, and other media.

NBC EXPERIENCE STORE
30 Rockefeller Plaza (49th St bet Fifth Ave and Ave of the Americas)
Mon-Sat: 8-7; Sun: 9-6   212/664-3700
www.shopnbc.com/nbcstore

The NBC Experience Store offers walking tours that take visitors behind the scenes of NBC's studios and around one of New York's most recognizable landmarks, Rockefeller Center. The 20,000-square-foot facility is located directly across from Studio 1A, home of the *Today Show*. It stocks T-shirts, mugs, keychains, and other merchandise with the NBC logo or images from its television shows.

NEW YORK FIREFIGHTERS' FRIEND
263 Lafayette St (bet Prince and Spring St)   212/226-3142
Mon-Sat: 10-6; Sun: 12-5   www.nyfirestore.com

Firemen, kids, and firefighting buffs from all over the world find this the most fascinating store in Manhattan! New York Firefighters' Friend carries patches, T-shirts, toys, turnout coats, work shirts, FDNY memorial shirts, and related items. Firefighter jackets for kids are a big hit!

NEW YORK 911
263½ Lafayette St (bet Prince and Spring St)   212/219-3907
Mon-Sat: 10-6; Sun: 12-5   www.ny911.com

For police buffs, this place is fascinating! Cops and just plain folks can find police T-shirts, caps, pins, shirts, kids' clothes, gifts, and toys. New York 911 is truly a one-stop cop shop!

ONE SHUBERT ALLEY
1 Shubert Alley (45th St bet Broadway and Eighth Ave)
212/944-4133, 800/223-1320 (mail order only)

Mon-Thurs: 12-8; Fri, Sat: 12-11; Sun: 12-6:30

www.broadwaynewyork.com

Shubert Alley is often used as a shortcut between Broadway theaters. One Shubert Alley is the only retail establishment in the alley. It's a fascinating place to browse for T-shirts, posters, recordings, buttons, and other paraphernalia from current shows on and off-Broadway.

Mirrors

SUNDIAL-SCHWARTZ
159 E 118th St (bet Lexington and Third Ave)
Mon-Fri: 8-4   800/876-4776, 212/289-4969
www.antiquemirror.net

The people at Sundial supply "decorative treatments of distinction." Anyone who has ever seen a cramped New York apartment suddenly appear to expand with the strategic placement of mirrors will understand that claim. Sundial deals with professional decorators and do-it-yourselfers, and both benefit from the staff's years of experience. They carry tabletop glass, shower doors, and mirrors for the home, office, and showroom. In addition, Sundial will remodel, re-silver, and antique mirrors. Sundial also custom-designs window treatments, blinds, shades, and draperies.

Museum and Library Shops

As anybody on a mailing list knows, scores of museums across the country produce catalogs that allow people to browse their gift shops from a great distance. In New York, however, you can browse in person at more than four dozen museums. Even at museums that charge an admission fee, you need not pay if you're there to shop. Rather than simply list all the museum gift shops in New York, I've chosen particularly large or unique ones. Indeed, whether you're looking for a one-of-a-kind gift or unusual books and posters, I highly recommend shopping in the following places. Instead of Empire State Building salt-and-pepper shakers, expect to find classy, artistic, well-made items. In most cases, at least some of the wares relate directly to current and past exhibits or the museum's permanent collection. You might save money by becoming a member and taking advantage of discounts.

AMERICAN FOLK ART MUSEUM
45 W 53rd St (bet Fifth Ave and Ave of the Americas)
Daily: 10-6 (Fri till 8)   212/265-1040
1 Lincoln Square (Columbus Ave bet 65th and 66th St)
Tues-Sun: 11-7:30   212/595-9533
www.americanfolkart.com/store

Both at its beautiful new home on 53rd Street and its homey branch location across from Lincoln Center, the American Folk Art Museum runs great gift shops stocked with lots of unusual handcrafted items in various price ranges. The Lincoln Square location has a particularly good selection of books about quilting, and both stores are excellent sources for books on folk and decorative arts. Children's toys and books are also available at both locations.

AMERICAN MUSEUM OF NATURAL HISTORY
Central Park West bet 77th and 81st St   800/671-7035
Daily: 10-5:45 (Fri till 7:45)   www.amnh.org

The museum's triplex shop features a wide selection of unusual merchandise related to the natural world, diverse cultures, and exploration and discovery. Jewelry, books, videos, toys, ceramics, gifts, posters, and some great T-shirts are among the many offerings. The main shop is accessible through the rotunda inside the museum's Central Park West entrance. Five smaller satellite shops throughout the museum offer children's toys, space-themed merchandise, and dinosaur-related items. Temporary shops are also set up to accompany some of the museum's special exhibits.

ASIASTORE
725 Park Ave (at 70th St)   212/327-9217
Daily: 11-6 (Fri till 9)   www.asiasociety.org/asiastore

Offerings at the Asia Society and Museum's AsiaStore include hundreds of unique items from Asia, including a wide selection of jewelry, fashion accessories, home accents, stationery, gifts, and novelty items. A selection of books on Asia includes scores of titles on art, culture, politics, and religion. AsiaStore strives to showcase the best in Asian design.

THE CLOISTERS
Fort Tryon Park   212/650-2277
Tues-Sun: 9:30-5 (till 4:15 in winter)   www.metmuseum.org/store

The Cloisters gift shop is stocked with items related to the museum's medieval collection. The shop closes a bit earlier than the museum.

COOPER-HEWITT NATIONAL DESIGN MUSEUM
2 E 91st St (bet Fifth and Madison Ave)   212/849-8355
Tues-Thurs: 10-5; Fri: 10-9; Sat: 10-6; Sun: 12-6
                                                    www.ndm.si.edu/shop

Housed in the enchanting library of Andrew Carnegie's incredible mansion, this terrific store offers an eclectic mix of items that relate to the museum's extensive collection and reflect its dedication to design excellence and innovation. Whether you're looking for pens or other office items, tea cups, jewelry, clocks, vases, lamps, plates, or an unusual wedding present, this is a good place. The store also has a pretty good collection of books and toys for children, as well as an extensive offering of books relating to the museum's collection. Be sure to look around at the room (and the ceiling!) as you browse. The shop closes 15 minutes earlier than the museum.

EL MUSEO DEL BARRIO
1230 Fifth Ave (at 105th St)   212/831-7272
Wed-Sun: 11-5   www.elmuseo.org

This unique museum gift shop was added to the museum during its 1994 renovation. In addition to housing a small collection of books about such topics as Latin American art, Caribbean culture, and the Puerto Rican experience in New York, the shop sells children's books in English and Spanish.

It also sells carnival masks made in Puerto Rico and a variety of crafts from throughout the Caribbean and Latin America.

FRICK COLLECTION
1 E 70th St (bet Fifth and Madison Ave)   212/288-0700
Tues-Sat: 10-5:45 (Fri till 8:45); Sun: 1-5:45   www.frick.org

The Frick's gift shop makes the most of its small space by concentrating on exquisite cards, stationery, maps, guidebooks, and art books. The shop closes 15 minutes earlier than the museum.

GUGGENHEIM MUSEUM STORE
1071 Fifth Ave (bet 88th and 89th St)   212/423-3615
Daily: 10-6 (Fri till 8)   www.guggenheimstore.org

Although much that's for sale here is ordinary—including scarves, T-shirts, prints and posters, tote bags, umbrellas, note cards and stationery, jewelry, and children's toys—the design and craftsmanship are anything but. If you're looking for an unusual clock, a great wedding present, or the right pair of earrings to set you apart from the crowd, try this store. Just be aware that prices are often through the roof. Of course, the store also carries books on modern art and exhibition catalogs. Note that the store is open on Thursday, but the museum itself is not.

INTERNATIONAL CENTER OF PHOTOGRAPHY
1133 Ave of the Americas (at 43rd St)   212/857-9725
Tues-Thurs: 10-6; Fri: 10-8   www.icpmuseumstore.org

Located just inside the entrance to the International Center of Photography's midtown gallery, this store is definitely worth a look if you're shopping for a photography buff with high-quality gifts in mind. It has an excellent collection of books about the history and technology of photography and photojournalism. You can also find coffee-table books of collected works by photographers, as well as prints, picture frames, and unusual postcards.

INTREPID SEA-AIR-SPACE MUSEUM
Pier 86 (46th St at Hudson River)   212/245-0072
Daily: 10-5 (weekends till 7 in summer)
                          www.intrepidmuseum.org/intrepid/store/

Intrepid's two-floor gift shop has huge volumes of touristy junk for youngsters, but it's also a great source for books on military history, space exploration, and aircraft and weapon systems for both adults and children. It is a good place to look for model airplanes, ships, and action figures, too.

JEWISH MUSEUM
1109 Fifth Ave (at 92nd St)   212/423-3211
Sun-Wed: 11-5:45; Thurs: 11-8; Fri: 11-3
                               www.thejewishmuseum.org

This relatively large store is an excellent source for Jewish literature, decorative art, and Judaica. Its selection of menorahs is among the classiest in the city. The store also sells cards, coffee-table books, and a wide selection of children's books with Jewish themes and characters. Celebrations, the Jewish Museum's Design Shop, is housed in a brownstone next to the museum. It is worth a look if you're interested in very high-quality ceremonial objects, jewelry, and things for the home. Note the abbreviated

Friday hours.

METROPOLITAN MUSEUM OF ART
1000 Fifth Ave (bet 80th and 84th St)   212/570-3894
Tues-Sun: 9:30-5:15 (Fri, Sat till 8:45)
Macy's (Herald Square, 34th St at Ave of the Americas), mezzanine
212/268-7266
Rockefeller Center (15 W 49th St, bet Fifth Ave and Ave of the Americas)
212/332-1360
Soho (113 Prince St, bet Wooster and Greene St)   212/614-3000
The Cloisters (Fort Tryon Park)   212/923-3700
Hours vary by store   www.metmuseum.org

The two-floor store inside the Metropolitan Museum of Art is the grand-father of all museum gift shops. It specializes in reproductions of paintings and other pieces in the Met's incredible collection, as well as museum collections around the world. You can find jewelry, statues, vases, scarves, ties, porcelains, prints, rugs, napkins, silver serving dishes, and scores of other beautiful gift ideas. They also carry books relating to special exhibits and the museum's extensive holdings, as well as umbrellas, tote bags, and other items with the Metropolitan's name emblazoned on them. There's even a bridal registry department! Prices range from reasonable to wildly expensive, and the salespeople are usually patient and helpful. Satellite gift shops are located inside the museum itself (a beautiful one across the main entrance hall specializes in jewelry) and throughout Manhattan. Hours at the satellite shops vary. The second floor of the main store in the Met and the satellite shop in Rockefeller Center have particularly good children's sections.

METROPOLITAN OPERA SHOP
Metropolitan Opera House   212/580-4090
Lincoln Center (Columbus Ave at 65th St)   www.metoperashop.org
Mon-Sat: 10 a.m. to end of second intermission; Sun: 12-6

Opera lovers will be in opera heaven. In addition to operas on video, compact discs, and other media, you'll find books, mugs, umbrellas, stationery, T-shirts, and pillows for the opera buff. Be sure to check out the Performing Arts Shop on the lower concourse, too. And if you're looking for posters and prints from various seasons, visit The Gallery, also on the lower concourse.

MUSEUM OF AMERICAN FINANCIAL HISTORY
28 Broadway (bet Morris St and Battery Pl)   212/908-4613
Tues-Sat: 10-4

A small but unusual find in the basement of John D. Rockefeller's old Standard Oil headquarters, this may be the only museum shop in the country dedicated to financial memorabilia and art. Wonderful bronze bull and bear bookends, unique "nest egg" sculptures, and even some antique stock certificates are among the eclectic items.

MUSEUM OF THE CITY OF NEW YORK
1220 Fifth Ave (bet 103rd and 104th St)   212/534-1672, ext 3330
Mon: 12-5; Tues-Sun: 10-5   www.mcny.org

Thanks to the efforts of a store manager who really cares about New York and this museum, this is an exciting place to shop. You will find black-and-white prints from the museum's extensive archives, videos on such subjects as the construction of the subway system, books on the outer boroughs, imaginative children's toys and books, and selections relating to the museum's exhibitions.

MUSEUM OF JEWISH HERITAGE
36 Battery Pl (in Battery Park City)   646/437-4200
Sun-Thurs: 10-5:45 (Wed till 8); Fri: 10-3   www.mjhnyc.org

This store is a fitting companion to the museum in its celebration of Jewish art, crafts, and culture. The selection of items, many of which are related to the museum's collection, is diverse. Everything is high-quality and much of it is quite unusual. A carefully chosen section includes books and gifts for children of various ages. Elegant jewelry and Judaica are also available. The prices are remarkably good. Note that the store and the museum are closed on all major Jewish holidays.

MUSEUM OF MODERN ART DESIGN AND BOOK STORE
44 W 53rd St (bet Fifth Ave and Ave of the Americas)   212/767-1050
Daily: 10-6:30 (Fri till 8)   www.momastore.org

SOHO DESIGN TOO
81 Spring St (at Crosby St)   646/613-1367
Mon-Sat: 11-8; Sun: 11-7

These magnificent stores—the main one across the street from the Museum of Modern Art and a satellite shop in Soho—are dedicated to what the curators consider the very best in modern design. Furniture, textiles, vases, ties, kitchen gadgets, silverware, frames, watches, lamps, and toys and books for children are just a few things you'll find. These items are not cheap, and I've found some of the salespeople at the midtown location to be disinterested, but the selection is really exceptional. You'll find books and furniture on the lower level of the Soho store.

NATIONAL MUSEUM OF THE AMERICAN INDIAN
1 Bowling Green (at the foot of Broadway)
Museum Shop   212/514-3766
The Gallery   212/514-3767
Daily: 10-5

Like everything else about the National Museum of the American Indian, its two gift shops are classy operations. The Gallery—located on the main floor to the right of the entrance—has a wide selection of books and high-quality Native American weavings, jewelry, and other handicrafts. The Museum Shop—down the grand marble staircase from the main entrance— is more focused on kids and families. Children's books, videos, toys, craft kits, and the obligatory arrowheads are for sale, along with T-shirts and some moderately priced jewelry. Because the museum is part of the Smithsonian Institution, both stores offer discounts to Smithsonian Associates.

THE NEUE GALERIE BOOKSTORE AND DESIGN SHOP
1048 Fifth Ave (at 86th St)   212/628-6200

Mon, Wed-Sun: 11-6 (Fri till 9)   www.neuegalerie.org

The Neue Galerie Bookstore is clearly *the* source for books on art, architecture, and cultural life in Germany, Austria, and even Central Europe in the 19th and 20th centuries. The Design Shop has a small but well-chosen selection of beautiful high-end jewelry, tableware, textiles, and other decorative arts by modern German and Austrian designers. Both stores are immediately to the left of the museum's entrance.

NEW YORK PUBLIC LIBRARY SHOP
Fifth Ave bet 41st and 42nd St   212/930-0641
Tues, Wed: 1-6; Thurs-Sat: 10-6; Sun: 1-5   www.thelibraryshop.org

If ever there was a perfect gift shop for intellectuals, this is it. Located just off the main lobby of the New York Public Library's main branch, it features everything from magnets with sayings like "I Think, Therefore I'm Dangerous" and "Think for Yourself, Not for Me" to books about the library's history. In addition to stocking a high-quality selection of unusual merchandise, the staff is particularly pleasant and helpful.

NEW YORK TRANSIT MUSEUM
Grand Central Station (42nd St at Vanderbilt Ave)   212/878-0106
Mon-Fri: 8-8; Sat, Sun: 10-4   www.mta.info

Run by the Metropolitan Transportation Authority, this little shop makes train and subway buffs downright giddy. Items for sale include books, conductor's caps, clever T-shirts, replicas of old station signs, banks for children in the shape of city buses, giant chocolate subway tokens, jewelry made from old tokens, and very classy mirrors made by one of the artists restoring the subway system's mosaics. Bus and subway maps, as well as other MTA information, are also available. Note that this shop is a branch of the much larger main store at the **New York Transit Museum** in Brooklyn (Boerum Place at Schermerhorn Street, 718/694-5100).

PERFORMING ARTS SHOP
Metropolitan Opera House
Lincoln Center (Columbus Ave at 65th St), lower concourse
Mon-Sat: 10 a.m. until first intermission; Sun: 12-6   917/441-1195

This store is lots of fun for anyone interested in opera, classical music, and ballet. Much like the Metropolitan Opera Shop on the floor above, the Performing Arts Shop also has a wide selection of music, books, instruments, and toys for children, plus an even wider selection of recordings and various ballet-related items. It stays open weekdays and Saturdays until the end of the second intermission. If you're interested in prints and posters from past seasons, walk a little farther down the hall and visit The Gallery.

THE SHOP AT SCANDINAVIA HOUSE
58 Park Ave (bet 37th and 38th St)   212/847-9737
Tues-Sat: 12-5:45

Tucked into the back of the first floor behind Cafe AQ, this little gem is a tribute to Scandinavian design and good taste. Household items—including vases, tableware, and glasses—are featured, as are beautiful pieces of jewelry and a small selection of children's items.

THE STORE AT THE MUSEUM OF ARTS AND DESIGN
40 W 53rd St (bet Fifth Ave and Ave of the Americas)
Daily: 10-6 (Thurs till 8)   212/956-3535, ext. 157
                                              www.madmuseum.com

Though the name is a mouthful—thanks in part to the renaming of the American Craft Museum—this well-conceived shop is a great complement to the other museum shops on West 53rd Street. Showcasing the work of exceptional artists from around the United States, the recently redesigned store offers jewelry, textiles, housewares, and unusual handmade objects.

STUDIO MUSEUM
144 W 125th St (bet Malcolm X and Adam Clayton Powell, Jr. Blvd)
Wed-Fri: 12-5:45; Sat, Sun: 10-5:45   212/864-0014
                                              www.studiomuseum.org/store

Located just inside the museum's entrance on the right, this store sells a wide and generally high-quality selection of jewelry, textiles, crafts, note cards, and calendars created by African and African-American artists. It also sells an unusually broad selection of cookbooks, fiction, biographies, and children's books by and about Africans and African-Americans. The store closes 15 minutes before the museum.

UKRAINIAN MUSEUM
222 E 6th St (bet Second and Third Ave)   212/228-0110
Wed-Sun: 1-5   www.ukrainianmuseum.org

As this book went to press, the museum and store were in the process of moving to their new location. The stock will remain the same, and it's well worth a visit if you want to find Ukrainian Easter eggs (already made and kits for do-it-yourselfers), embroidery, and other handicrafts. Be sure to ask about holiday baking, embroidery, beading, and Easter egg classes.

UNITED NATIONS
First Ave bet 45th and 46th St   212/963-4475
Mon-Fri: 9-5; Sat, Sun: 10-5 (closed weekends in Jan, Feb)

On the lower level of the main UN building is a bookstore, post office (a real treat for stamp collectors), small UNICEF shop, and an even smaller shop run by the UN Women's Guild. That's in addition to the main gift shop, also on the lower level. The bookstore features calendars, postcards with the flags of member nations, holiday cards in dozens of languages, and a wide variety of books about the UN and related subjects. The main gift shop features a wonderful array of carvings, jewelry, scarves, dolls, and other items from all over the world. The better imports can get pricey, but it's definitely going to a good cause! One final thought: if you are interested in UNICEF cards and gifts but find the selection at the UN itself rather thin, then visit the store in the lobby of the nearby **UNICEF House** (3 United Nations Plaza, 44th St bet First and Second Ave, 212/326-7054).

Music

ACADEMY RECORDS & CDs
12 W 18th St (at Fifth Ave)   212/242-3000

Mon-Sat: 11:30-8; Sun: 11-7   www.academy-records.com

Academy Records & CDs has Manhattan's largest stock of used, out-of-print, and rare classical LPs and CDs. Emphasizing opera, contemporary classical, and early music (the Baroque period and before), Academy boasts an international reputation. Prices are fair. The rock and jazz holdings, while less extensive, continue to grow.

BLEECKER BOB'S GOLDEN OLDIES RECORD SHOP
118 W 3rd St (bet MacDougal St and Ave of the Americas)
Sun-Thurs: 11 a.m.-1 a.m.; Fri, Sat: 11 a.m.-3 a.m.   212/475-9617
www.bleeckerbobs.com

Let us sing the praises of Bleecker Bob, who is nothing if not perverse. (Name another store that's open till 3 a.m. on Christmas Day!) For one thing, although there is a real Bob (Plotnik, the owner), the store isn't on Bleecker Street. For another, Bleecker Bob is an institution to generations of New Yorkers who have sifted through his vast selection of rock, punk, and heavy-metal recordings. They stock vintage rock and soul records (plus some rare jazz), hold autograph parties for rock stars, and boast that they can fill any wish list. Bleecker Bob's is also the gathering place in the wee hours of the morning in the Village. Above all, it's a great source for out-of-print, obscure, and imported compact discs, and rare music DVDs.

FOOTLIGHT RECORDS
113 E 12th St (bet Third and Fourth Ave)   212/533-1572
Mon-Fri: 11-7   www.footlight.com

In keeping with this outfit's passion for rare and unusual records and compact discs, the emphasis is on show tunes, film soundtracks, and jazz. Their prices are among the best around, and many of their records just aren't available anywhere else. If there's an original cast album of a Broadway show, you can bet Footlight has it. They stock one of the most comprehensive collections of film scores in the country. They also carry an impressive showing of European and Japanese imports in related fields, a large selection of big band and early jazz recordings, and rock LPs.

FRANK MUSIC
244 W 54th St (bet Broadway and Eighth Ave), 10th floor
Mon-Fri: 10-5   212/582-1999
www.frankmusiccompany.com

Founded in 1938, this professional business has never advertised, relying instead on word of mouth. They sell classical sheet music from European and American publishers. There is an aisle for voice and violin, another for piano, and so on. Frank Music gladly fills mail orders. Ask for Heidi Rogers, the helpful owner, or Dean Streit, her assistant.

JAZZ RECORD CENTER
236 W 26th St (bet Seventh and Eighth Ave), Room 804   212/675-4480
Tues-Sat: 10-6 (Sept-May); Mon-Fri: 10-6 (June-Aug)
www.jazzrecordcenter.com

This is the only jazz specialty store in the city. They deal in out-of-print and new jazz records, CDs, videos, books, posters, photos, periodicals, postcards, and T-shirts. The store buys collections, fills mail orders, and offers appraisals. They regularly auction jazz rarities on eBay. Jazz Record Center is run by Frederick Cohen, a charming guy who really knows his business.

JOSEPH PATELSON MUSIC HOUSE

160 W 56th St (at Seventh Ave)   212/582-5840
Mon-Sat: 9-6   www.patelson.com

Located behind Carnegie Hall, Joseph Patelson is known to every student of music in the city. From little first graders to artists from Carnegie Hall, everyone stops here first because of the fabulous selection and excellent prices. The stock includes music scores, sheet music, music books, and orchestral and opera scores. All are neatly cataloged and displayed in open cabinets. One can easily browse a given section of interest—be it piano music, chamber music, orchestral scores, opera scores, concerts, ethnic scores, or instrumental solos. Sheet music is filed in bins the way records are elsewhere. There are also musical accessories like metronomes and pitch pipes. Patelson is an unofficial meeting place for the city's young musicians. Word goes out that "we're looking for a violinist," and meetings are often arranged in the store. Mail and phone orders are accepted.

OTHER MUSIC

15 E 4th St (bet Broadway and Lafayette St)   212/477-8150
Mon-Fri: 12-9; Sat: 12-8; Sun: 12-7   www.othermusic.com

If you can't find it elsewhere, try Other Music. They have CDs and vinyl, hard-to-find releases, jazz, modern compositions, and a wide variety of imports. They will purchase or give store credit for used CDs and records, but only in person.

TOWER RECORDS AND VIDEO

692 Broadway (at 4th St)   212/505-1500
Trump Tower, 725 Fifth Ave (bet 56th and 57th St)   212/838-8110
Lincoln Center, 1961 Broadway (at 66th St)   212/799-2500
20 E 4th St (at Lafayette St)   212/505-1166
Hours vary by store   www.towerrecords.com

These stores feature different categories by location. Stock includes records, tapes, CDs, videos, and DVDs. The Lafayette Street location focuses on video sales and rentals, and it also has an upstairs outlet with discounted merchandise. The Lincoln Center location on Broadway has a Ticketmaster outlet.

VINYL MANIA RECORDS

60 Carmine St (at Bedord St)   212/924-7223
Mon-Wed: 11-8; Thurs-Sat: 11-9   www.vinylmania.com

For over 25 years Vinyl Mania has been New York's specialty shop for DJs. Its business is 80% vinyl, as they cater to the dance, hip-hop, and rap audiences. They also carry a choice selection of imported and domestic CDs.

WESTSIDER RARE BOOKS AND RECORDS

233 W 72nd St (at Broadway)   212/874-1588
Daily: 11-8
2246 Broadway (bet 80th and 81st St)   212/362-0706
Daily: 10 a.m.-12 a.m.   www.westsiderbooks.com

Westsider remains one of the few stores specializing in rare and out-of-print LPs. Compact discs have been added to the stock of 80,000 LPs. You'll also find printed music and books on the performing arts, fine arts, photography, fiction, and poetry. Raymond Donnell will guide customers through his classical DVD, jazz, rock, pop, and spoken-word holdings.

Musical Instruments

DRUMMER'S WORLD
151 W 46th St (bet Ave of the Americas and Seventh Ave), 3rd floor
Mon-Fri: 10-6; Sat: 10-4   212/840-3057
www.drummersworld.com

This is a great place, unless the patron is your teenager or an upstairs neighbor! Barry Greenspon and his staff take pride in guiding students and professionals through one of the best percussion stores in the country. Inside this drummer's paradise is everything from commonplace equipment to one-of-a-kind antiques and imports. All of the instruments are high-quality symphonic percussion items, and customers receive the same attention whether they are members of an orchestra, rock band, or rap act. The store also offers instructors and how-to books. There are esoteric ethnic instruments for virtuosos who want to experiment. Drummers World has a catalog and will ship anywhere in the country.

GUITAR SALON
45 Grove St (at Sheridan Sq)   212/675-3236
By appointment only   www.theguitarsalon.com

Beverly Maher's Guitar Salon NY is a unique one-person operation located in a historic brownstone in Greenwich Village. You will find handmade classical and flamenco guitars for students, professionals, and collectors. Outstanding personal service is provided by Beverly, whose salon specializes in 19th- and 20th-century vintage instruments. Appraisals are available, and lessons are given on all styles of guitars. Even the Rolling Stones have been known to shop here!

MANNY'S MUSIC
156 W 48th St (bet Ave of the Americas and Seventh Ave)
Mon-Sat: 10-7; Sun: 12-6   212/819-0576
www.mannysmusic.com

Manny's is a huge discount department store for musical instruments. "Everything for the Musician" is their motto, and it is borne out by a collection of musical equipment so extensive that each department has its own salespeople. The emphasis is on modern music, as evidenced by the hundreds of autographed pictures of popular musicians on the walls and the huge collection of electronic instruments. All of the instruments, equipment, accessories, and supplies are sold at discount. They also have a large computer department for musical software needs.

RITA FORD MUSIC BOXES
19 E 65th St (at Madison Ave)   212/535-6717
Mon-Sat: 9-5   www.ritaford.com

Gerry and Nancy Wright and Joseph and Diane Tenore collect antique music boxes and have become experts in all aspects of the business. Stock consists of valuable antique and new music boxes. The main stock-in-trade is expertise; having been in business for half a century, these folks know all there is to know about music boxes. They are experts on music box scores, workings, and outer casings. Some pieces are rare antiques that are priced accordingly. Contemporary reproductions are more modestly priced. The store also does repairs.

Photographic Equipment and Supplies

ADORAMA CAMERA
42 W 18th St (bet Fifth Ave and Ave of the Americas)   212/741-0052
Mon-Thurs: 9-6:15; Fri: 9-1:15; Sun: 9:30-5:15

www.adorama.com

These people operate one of the largest photographic mail-order houses in the country. They carry a huge stock of photographic equipment and supplies, telescopes, video paraphernalia, and digital equipment, all sold at discount.

ALKIT PRO CAMERAS
820 Third Ave (at 50th St)	212/832-2101
222 Park Ave S (at 18th St)	212/674-1515
830 Seventh Ave (at 53rd St)	212/262-2424
Hours vary by store	www.alkit.com

If you want to shop where photographers of the Elite and Ford modeling agencies go, Alkit is the place. You don't have to be a professional to visit, however. While most establishments that deal with the pros have little time for amateurs, nothing gives Alkit's employees more pleasure than introducing the world of photography to neophytes. Alkit maintains a full line of digital and film cameras, film, and equipment. They have a one-hour processing lab on-premises. The shop repairs and rents photographic equipment, and it also publishes an informative catalog full of praise and gripes about particular models.

B&H PHOTO-VIDEO-PRO AUDIO
420 Ninth Ave (bet 33rd and 34th St)   212/444-6600
Mon-Thurs: 9-7; Fri: 9-2; Sun: 10-5   www.bhphotovideo.com

This is quite a store! You'll find professional and nonprofessional departments for video, pro audio, pro lighting, darkroom, film and film processing, books, used equipment, and more. Trade-ins are welcome, and used equipment is sold. The store has been in operation since 1974 and is staffed by knowledgeable personnel. Inventory levels are high, prices are reasonable, and hands-on demo areas make browsing easy. A catalog is available.

CALUMET PHOTOGRAPHIC
16 W 19th St (bet Fifth Ave and Ave of the Americas)   212/989-8500
Mon-Sat: 8:30-5:30   www.calumetphoto.com

In business for over 60 years, this firm provides start-to-finish photographic service. Professional camera equipment, film, digital cameras and accessories, printers, and scanners are all available at good prices.

LAUMONT DIGITAL
333 W 52nd St (bet Eighth and Ninth Ave)   212/245-2113
Mon-Fri: 9-5:30 (evenings and weekends by appointment)
www.laumont.com

Whether you're a professional or amateur, Laumont can take care of your photographic needs. They do excellent work producing exhibition-quality Cibachrome, Fuji, Lambda, Lightjet, Iris, and pigment prints. They are patient and understanding with those who need advice. Laumont's staff are also experienced digital retouchers and duplicators, and they can repair damaged originals or create brand-new images on state-of-the-art computers. Lamination and print mounting are done on-premises.

WILLOUGHBY'S KONICA IMAGING CENTER
298 Fifth Ave (at 31st St)   212/564-1600, 800/378-1898
Mon-Thurs: 9-7:30; Fri: 9-2; Sun: 11-6:30   www.willoughbys.com

Established in 1898, this is New York's oldest camera store. Willoughby's has a huge stock, an extensive clientele, and a solid reputation. They can handle almost any kind of camera order, either in person or by mail order. They service cameras, supply photographic equipment, and recycle used cameras. Moreover, they sell computers, video cameras, cellular phones, and other high-tech equipment.

Pictures, Posters, and Prints

CARRANDI GALLERY
138 W 18th St (bet Ave of the Americas and Seventh Ave)
Tues-Sat: 12-6   212/242-0710
www.carrandigallery.com

You've never seen a poster gallery like this one! Carrandi Gallery (formerly Poster America) features original posters from 1880 to 1970, nearly all of which are lithographs. One of the oldest galleries in the country devoted to vintage poster art, it is set in a former stable and carriage house that used to serve the department stores on Ladies' Mile in the 1880s. The magnificent mahogany-and-glass storefront still catches the eyes of passersby, luring them into a huge, well-appointed gallery. The shop is known for brilliant graphics and the magnitude of rare and unusual posters, including vintage circus and magic posters.

JERRY OHLINGER'S MOVIE MATERIAL STORE
253 W 35th St (bet Seventh and Eighth Ave)   212/989-0869
Mon-Sat: 11-7   www.moviematerials.com

Jerry Ohlinger has a huge selection of movie posters and photographs from film and TV. He also researches these items and will gladly provide a catalog.

OLD PRINT SHOP
150 Lexington Ave (bet 29th and 30th St)   212/683-3950
Tues-Fri: 9-5; Sat: 9-4   www.oldprintshop.com

Established in 1898, the Old Print Shop exudes an old-fashioned charm, and its stock only reinforces the impression of timelessness. Kenneth M. Newman specializes in Americana, including original prints, town views, Currier and Ives prints, and original maps that reflect America as it used to be. Most of the nostalgic bicentennial pictures that adorned calendars and stationery were copies of prints found here. Amateur and professional historians have a field day in this shop. Newman also does "correct period framing," and prints housed in his custom frames are striking. Everything bought and sold here is original, and Newman purchases estate and single items.

TRITON GALLERY
323 W 45th St (bet Eighth and Ninth Ave)   212/765-2472
Mon-Sat: 10-6; Sun: 1-6   www.tritongallery.com

Theater posters are presented at Triton like nowhere else. The posters of current Broadway shows are but a small part of what's available. There is also a broad range of older show posters from here and abroad. Show cards —which are the most readily available items—are the standard 14" x 22" size. Posters range in size from 23" x 46" to 42" x 84" and are priced according to rarity, age, and demand. The collection is not limited to Broadway or even American plays, and some of the more interesting pieces come from other times. Triton also does custom framing. Much of the business is conducted via mail and phone.

Plastic Goods

PLEXI-CRAFT QUALITY PRODUCTS
514 W 24rd St (bet Tenth and Eleventh Ave)   212/924-3244
Mon-Fri: 9:30-5   www.plexi-craft.com

Plexi-Craft offers anything made of Lucite and Plexiglas at wholesale prices. If you can't find what you want among the pedestals, tables, chairs, shelves, racks, stands, and cubes shown here, they will make it for you. A catalog is available for $2.

Rubber Goods

CANAL RUBBER SUPPLY COMPANY
329 Canal St (at Greene St)   212/226-7339
Mon-Fri: 9-5; Sat: 9-4   wwwcanalrubber.com

"If It's Made of Rubber, We Have It" is the motto at this wholesale-retail operation. There are foam mattresses, bolsters, cushions, pads cut to size, hydraulic hoses, rubber tubing, vacuum hoses, floor matting, tiles, stair treads, sheet-rubber products, and much more.

Safes

EMPIRE SAFE
6 E 39th St (bet Fifth and Madison Ave)   212/684-2255, 800/543-5412
Mon-Fri: 9-5   www.empiresafe.com

Empire shows one of the city's largest and most complete selections of safes. Their products are used in residences and businesses, with delivery and installation offered. Also on display are rare antique and art-deco safes, memorabilia, old photos, and historical documents. Whether you want to protect documents in a small apartment or huge office building, these folks are able to help.

Sexual Paraphernalia

COME AGAIN
353 E 53rd St (at First Ave)   212/308-9394
Mon-Fri: 11-7; Sat: 11-6

Come Again is a large shopping center for sexual paraphernalia. There's exotic lingerie for men and women to size 4XL, adult books and magazines, "how-to" DVDs and videos, oils and lotions, gift baskets, party gifts, and toys and equipment of a decidedly prurient nature. They offer a 20% discount for readers of this book!

CONDOMANIA
351 Bleecker St (bet 10th and Charles St)   212/691-9442
Sun-Thurs: 11-11; Fri, Sat: 11 a.m.-midnight   www.condomania.com

Condomania specializes in all shapes, sizes, and colors of condoms. Mixed in are bachelor and bachelorette gift items, mood enhancers, and the like. Reflecting the liberated times, Condomania is as popular with ladies as gentlemen.

EVE'S GARDEN INTERNATIONAL
119 W 57th St (bet Ave of the Americas and Seventh Ave), Suite 1201
Mon-Sat: 11-6:45   800/848-3837
                                            www.evesgarden.com

This is not your usual sex shop; it is particularly geared to women who wish to shop in a pleasant atmosphere. Eve's Garden is a pleasure chest of games, books, and videos to seduce the mind. A vast array of sensuous massage oils, candles, and incense will help realize your wildest fantasies. Mail orders are welcome.

Signs

LET THERE BE NEON
38 White St (bet Broadway and Church St)   212/226-4883
Mon-Fri: 9-5   www.lettherebeneon.com

Though the image of neon is modern, it harks back to 1915, when Georges Claudes captured it from oxygen. While the flashing neon sign has become the ultimate urban cliché, here it is rendered as artistic fine art. Let There Be Neon operates as a gallery with a variety of sizes, shapes, functions, and designs to entice the browser. Almost all of their sales are custom pieces. Even a rough sketch is enough for them to create a literal or abstract neon sculpture. Some vintage pieces are available.

Silver

GRAND STERLING SILVER COMPANY
345 Grand St (bet Essex and Ludlow St)   212/674-6450
Sun-Thurs: 10:30-5:30   www.grandsterlingusa.com

Since 1963 Grand Sterling has been both a wholesale and retail destination. Ring the bell and you will be admitted to a stunning collection of silver religious art pieces. You'll also find almost anything from silver toothpick holders to baroque candelabras over six feet tall. Grand Sterling will repair holders to baroque candelabras over six feet tall. Grand Sterling will repair or polish any item, religious or secular. They are manufacturers and importers of fine sterling holloware. Silver is revered with unmatched dedication here!

JEAN'S SILVERSMITHS
16 W 45th St (at Fifth Ave)   212/575-0723
Mon-Fri: 9-4:45   www.jeanssilversmiths.com

Having a problem replacing a fork that went down the disposal? Proceed directly to Jean's, where you will find over a thousand discontinued, obsolete, and current flatware patterns. They specialize in antique and second-hand silver, gold, and diamond jewelry, and they also sell watches.

ROGERS AND ROSENTHAL
2337 Lemoine Ave, Suite 101
Fort Lee, NJ 07024
Mon-Fri: 10-4   201/346-1862 (mail order)

Rogers and Rosenthal is one of the very best sources for silver, china, and crystal. Nearly all of their business is done by mail. They feature major brand names and offer a minimum 25% discount on every piece. They will send price lists upon request, and what isn't in stock can be ordered.

TIFFANY & CO.
727 Fifth Ave (at 57th St)   212/755-8000
Mon-Fri: 10-7; Sat: 10-6; Sun: 12-5   www.tiffany.com

Despite the fact that Tiffany has appeared in plays, movies, books, and songs, this legendary store really isn't that formidable or forbidding, and it can be an exciting place to shop. Yes, there really is a Tiffany diamond, and it can be viewed on the first floor. That floor also houses the watch and jewelry departments. While browsing is welcome, salespeople are quick to approach loiterers. The store carries clocks, silver jewelry, sterling silver, bar accessories, centerpieces, leather accessories, fragrances, knickknacks, china, crystal, glassware, flatware, and engraved stationery. The real surprise is that Tiffany carries an excellent selection of reasonably priced items. Many are emblazoned with the Tiffany name and wrapped in the famed blue box.

Sporting Goods

Bicycles and Accessories

BICYCLE RENAISSANCE
430 Columbus Ave (at 81st St)   212/724-2350
Mon-Fri: 10-7:30; Sat, Sun: 10-5

Biking is a way of life at Bicycle Renaissance. Services include custom-building bikes and bicycle repair, and the mechanics aim for same-day service on all makes and models. They carry racing and mountain bikes by Trek, Cannondale, and Specialized, as well as custom frames for Seven, Shimano, and others. Prices are on par with so-called discount shops.

LARRY & JEFF'S SECOND AVENUE BICYCLES PLUS
1690 Second Ave (at 87th St)   212/722-2201
Daily: 10-8

Larry started fixing bicycles at age 15, so you can bet he knows all about them. He then taught the art to Jeff, and together they have been operating this unique shop since 1977. Bikes range in price from $200 to $5,000, and plenty of parts and accessories are stocked, too. Special services include a lifetime of free tune-ups with the purchase of a new bicycle, bike rentals for rides through Central Park, and free delivery.

Billiards
BLATT BILLIARDS
809 Broadway (bet 11th and 12th St)   212/674-8855
Mon-Fri: 9-6:30; Sat: 10-5   www.blattbilliards.com

Blatt's six floors are outfitted from top to bottom with everything for billiards. You can also get friendly pointers from a staff that seems, at first glance, to be all business.

Exercise Equipment
GYM SOURCE
40 E 52nd St (bet Park and Madison Ave)   212/688-4222
Mon-Fri: 9-7; Sat: 10-6   www.gymsource.com

This is the largest exercise equipment dealer in the Northeast. They carry treadmills, bikes, stair-steppers, weight machines, rowers, and more. Over 300 top brands are available at good prices, and Gym Source's skilled technicians provide competent service. They also rent equipment and will even provide items for use in Manhattan hotel rooms.

Fishing
CAPITOL FISHING TACKLE COMPANY
218 W 23rd St (at Seventh Ave)   212/929-6132
Mon-Fri: 10-6 (Thurs till 7:30); Sat: 10-5

Where else but in New York could you find a fishing store so totally land-locked that a subway roars beneath it, and yet it offers bargains unmatched at seaport fishing stores? Set amid the hustle and bustle of Chelsea, where it shares an address with the Chelsea Hotel, Capitol features a complete range of fishing tackle. They carry such brand names as Penn, Shimano, Garcia, and Daiwa at low prices. There is a constantly changing selection of specials and close-outs. Capitol buys surplus inventories, bankrupt dealers, and liquidations, then passes the savings on to customers.

URBAN ANGLER
206 Fifth Ave (bet 25th and 26th St), 3rd floor
Mon-Fri: 10-6 (Wed till 7); Sat: 10-5   212/689-6400
                                                   www.urbanangler.com

Urban Angler is the only pro fly-fishing shop in Manhattan. You'll find fly-fishing tackle, high-end spin and surf tackle, and travel clothing. They offer casting and fly-tying lessons, and they can even plan fishing trips locally and around the world.

General

EASTERN MOUNTAIN SPORTS (EMS)
20 W 61st St (bet Broadway and Columbus Ave)   212/397-4860
Mon-Fri: 10-9; Sat: 10-8; Sun: 12-6   www.ems.com

EMS is *the* place for outdoor clothing and gear. Although prices can be bettered elsewhere, it's an excellent source for one-stop shopping and the merchandise is of a higher quality than that carried in department stores. EMS covers virtually all outdoor sports, including mountain climbing, backpacking, skiing, hiking, tenting, kayaking, and camping.

G&S SPORTING GOODS
43 Essex St (at Grand St)   212/777-7590, 800/215-3947
Sun-Fri: 9:30-6   www.gandsboxinggear.com

If you are looking for a place to buy a birthday or Christmas gift for a sports buff, I recommend G&S. They have a large selection of brand-name sneakers, in-line skates, boxing equipment, balls, gloves, toys, games, sports clothing, and accessory items. Prices reflect a 20% to 25% discount.

MODELL'S
1535 Third Ave (bet 86th and 87th St)   212/996-3800
51 E 42nd St (bet Madison and Vanderbilt Ave)   212/661-4242
606 W 181st St (at St. Nicholas Ave)   212/568-3000
300 W 125th St (at Eighth Ave)   212/280-9100
55 Chambers St (at Broadway)   212/732-8484
1293 Broadway (at 34th St)   212/244-4544
234 W 42nd St (bet Seventh and Eighth Ave)   212/764-7030
Hours vary by store   www.modells.com

You can't beat this outfit for quality and value! Founded in 1889, Modell's is America's oldest family-owned and -operated sporting goods chain. The stores specialize in sporting goods, footwear, and a large selection of apparel for men, women, and children. Make note of Modell's low price guarantee.

NBA STORE
666 Fifth Ave (at 52nd St)   212/515-NBA1
Mon-Sat: 10-7; Sun: 11-6   www.nba.com/nycstore

You'll find the largest assortment of NBA and WNBA merchandise in the nation at this attractive and well-laid-out store. A winding ramp allows full exposure to areas featuring apparel and accessories, jewelry, watches, photographs, collectibles, headwear, practice gear, basketballs, and more. The store also features multimedia presentations of game action and highlights of historic moments. A basketball half-court surrounded by bleachers is a popular spot for the store's more athletic shoppers. Hang Time Cafe, on the lower level, is a great place to score a quick bite to eat.

PARAGON SPORTS
867 Broadway (at 18th St)   212/255-8036
Mon-Sat: 10-8; Sun: 11-6:30   www.paragonsports.com

Paragon is truly a sporting goods department store, with over 100,000 square feet of specialty shops devoted to all kinds of sports and fitness equipment and apparel. There are separate departments for team equipment, athletic footwear, skateboards, ice skates, in-line skates, racquet sports, aerobics, swimming, golf, skiing and snowboarding, hiking, camping, diving, biking, sailing, and anything else that can be done in the great outdoors. They also carry gift items, and the stock is arranged for easy shopping.

Golf

NEW YORK GOLF CENTER
131 W 35th St (bet Seventh Ave and Broadway)   212/564-2255
Mon-Fri: 10-8; Sat: 10-7; Sun: 11-6   888/465-7890
www.nygolfcenter.com

This shop is the ultimate hole-in-one for golfers! New York Golf Center, the Big Apple's only golf superstore, offers goods at prices that average 20% below list. There are clubs, bags, clothing, shoes, accessories, and novelties . . . everything except one's own hard-won expertise. They carry pro-line equipment such as Callaway, Taylor Made, Cleveland, Titleist, Ping, and Nike. Employees couldn't be nicer or more helpful. Mention this book and receive a free sleeve of golf balls with any $20 purchase.

Guns

JOHN JOVINO GUN SHOP
183 Grand St (at Mulberry St)   212/925-4881
Mon-Fri: 9:30-5:30; Sat: 9:30-3:30   www.johnjovinogunshop.com

These folks have been in business since 1911 and are recognized leaders in the field. They carry all major brands of handguns, rifles, and shotguns, as well as ammunition, holsters, bulletproof vests, knives, and scopes. Major brands include Smith & Wesson, Colt, Ruger, Beretta, Browning, Remington, Walther, Glock, Winchester, and Sig Sauer. Jovino is an authorized warranty repair station for gun manufacturers, with a licensed gunsmith on-site.

Marine

WEST MARINE
12 W 37th St (at Fifth Ave)   212/594-6065
Mon-Fri: 9-6; Sat, Sun: 9-4   www.westmarine.com

West sells marine supplies as if it were situated in the middle of a New England seaport rather than the heart of Manhattan. The staff sometimes looks like a ship's crew on leave in the Big Apple, and they actually are that knowledgeable. They carry marine electronics, sailboat fittings, big-game fishing tackle, lifesaving gear, ropes, anchors, compasses, clothing, clocks, barometers, and books. You'll also find foul-weather suits and a line of clothing for yacht owners.

Outdoor Equipment

TENT AND TRAILS
21 Park Pl (bet Broadway and Church St)   212/227-1760
Mon-Sat: 9:30-6 (Thurs, Fri till 7); Sun: 12-6   800/237-1760
www.tenttrails.com

Whether you are outfitting yourself for a weekend camping trip or an ascent of Mt. Everest, Tent and Trails is the place to go! In the urban canyons near City Hall, this 6,000-square-foot store is devoted to camping. The staff is experienced and knowledgeable. There are boots from Asolo, Garmont, Lowa, Merrell, Vasque, Hi Tee, Scarpa Footwear, and Nike. They carry camping gear from Patagonia, Camp Trails, Moonstone, JanSport, Gregory Packs, Mountainsmith Packs, Osprey, Lowe Alpine, Eureka Tent, Mountain Hardwear, Coleman, Moss Tent, Timberland, and NorthFace. You'll find backpacks, sleeping bags, tents, down clothing, and much more. Tent and Trails also rents camping equipment.

Running

ATHLETIC STYLE PROMOTIONS
118 E 59th St (bet Park and Lexington Ave)	212/838-2564
Mon-Fri: 9-5	www.athleticstyle.com

Athletic Style is one of the top outlets in the city in terms of quality, value, and service. The store has evolved into a custom outlet offering personalization in print, embroidery, and laser engraving. Owners Vic and Dave are always on the job. Footwear includes many famous names. They also carry a good stock of clothing, including logo merchandise and personalized T-shirts, caps, and sweats.

SUPER RUNNERS SHOP
1337 Lexington Ave (at 89th St)	212/369-6010
360 Amsterdam Ave (at 77th St)	212/787-7665
1246 Third Ave (bet 71st and 72nd St)	212/249-2133
Grand Central Station (42nd St at Vanderbilt Ave)	646/487-1120
Hours vary by store	www.superrunnersshop.com

Co-owner Gary Muhrcke was the winner of the first New York City Marathon in 1970, and his passion has become his livelihood. The stock includes a superb selection of men's and women's running and racing shoes, as well as performance running clothes. The informed staff, who are themselves runners, believe that each person should be fitted individually in terms of sizing and need. Entry blanks for local races are available in the stores.

Skating

BLADES BOARD & SKATE
120 W 72nd St (bet Broadway and Columbus Ave)	212/787-3911
659 Broadway (at Bleecker St)	212/477-7350
Manhattan Mall, 901 Ave of the Americas	
(at 33rd St), Level C2	646/733-2738
Mon-Sat: 11-9 (Sun hours vary by store)	www.blades.com

Founded in 1990 by Jeff Kabat, Blades Board & Skate has become the largest action-sports retail company in the nation. There are a number of reasons for this: a great selection of equipment for snowboarding, skateboarding, and in-line skating; a good stock of lifestyle apparel; informed service; and a 30-day price guarantee.

Skiing

SCANDINAVIAN SKI AND SPORT SHOP
16 E 55th St (bet Madison and Fifth Ave)   212/757-8524
Mon, Tues, Fri, Sat: 10-6; Wed: 10-6:30; Thurs: 10-7; Sun: 11-5
www.skishop.com

Despite its name, this shop is really an all-around sporting goods store. They stock a full range of goods, from skis and skiwear to bikes and skates. They offer repairs and advice, and can outfit customers for ski and bike trips.

Soccer

SOCCER SPORT SUPPLY
1745 First Ave (bet 90th and 91st St)   212/427-6050, 800/223-1010
Mon-Fri: 10-6; Sat: 10-4   www.homeofsoccer.com

Hermann and Jeff Doss, the proprietors of this 70-year-old soccer and rugby supply company, claim that half their business involves importing and exporting equipment around the world. Visitors to the store have the advantage of seeing the selection in person, as well as receiving guidance from a staff that knows the field (pardon the pun) completely.

Tennis

MASON'S TENNIS MART
56 E 53rd St (bet Park and Madison Ave)   212/755-5805
Mon-Fri: 10-7; Sat: 10-6; Sun: 11-5

Mason's is the only tennis specialty store left in Manhattan. Mark Mason offers a superb collection of clothing with all the best brand names: Fila, Polo, Tail, LBH, Nike, Wimbledon, Lacoste, Ralph Lauren, and more. U.S. Open products are carried from May to December. You will also find ball machines, bags, and other tennis paraphernalia. They will match any authorized dealer on racquet prices and special order any tennis product. Same-day stringing is offered. A yearly half-price clothing sale (excluding children's wear) takes place in mid-January.

Stationery

JAM PAPER & ENVELOPE
135 Third Ave (bet 14th and 15th St)   212/473-6666
611 Ave of the Americas (at 18th St)   212/255-4593, 800/8010-JAM
Mon-Fri: 8:30-7; Sat, Sun: 10-6   www.jampaper.com

This outfit has become the largest paper and envelope store in the city and perhaps the world! They stock over 150 kinds of paper, with matching card stock and envelopes. They have a vast selection of presentation folders, plastic portfolios, plastic envelopes and folders, cello sleeves, translucents, bags, tissue, and raffia—all in matching colors. Close-outs and discounted items provide excellent bargains. Ask for their free catalog!

JAMIE OSTROW
54 W 21st St (bet Fifth Ave and Ave of the Americas), 2nd floor
Mon-Thurs: 11-6 (Fri and evenings by appointment)   212/734-8890

For contemporary personalized stationery and invitations, you can't do better than Jamie Ostrow. Items are designed and manufactured to customers' specifications. Crane stationery and wedding invitations are carried. A good selection of boxed Christmas and holiday cards is shown, and personalized Christmas cards are a specialty.

KATE'S PAPERIE

561 Broadway (bet Prince and Spring St)   212/941-9816
Mon-Fri: 10-7:30; Sat: 10-7; Sun: 11-7

8 W 13th St (at Fifth Ave)   212/633-0570
Mon-Fri: 10-7:30; Sat: 10-6; Sun: 12-6

140 W 57th St (bet Ave of the Americas and Seventh Ave)
Mon-Fri: 9-8; Sat: 10-7; Sun: 10-6   212/459-0700

1282 Third Ave (bet 73rd and 74th St)   212/396-3670
Mon-Fri: 10-7; Sat, Sun: 11-6   www.katespaperie.com

Here you will find one of the largest selections of decorative and exotic papers in the country. Kate's has thousands of kinds of papers, including papyrus, hand-marbled Italian, Japanese lace, recycled papers from Zimbabwe, and just about anything else you can think of. But that isn't all. There are leatherbound photo albums and journals, classic and exotic stationery, boxes, wax seals, rubber stamps, pens, and desk accessories. They will do custom printing and engraving, personal and business embossing, and custom and corporate gift selection and gift wrapping.

MRS. JOHN L. STRONG

699 Madison Ave (bet 62nd and 63rd St), 5th floor   212/838-3848
Mon-Fri: 10-5 and by appointment

Several barriers must be crossed to reach this high-end stationery establishment in a fifth-floor room. First, a claustrophobic elevator. Then a locked door. When you are buzzed in, the atmosphere is strictly high-altitude, as are the noses of some of the salesladies. Strong sells very high-quality papers, invitations, and announcements—with very high prices to match. If you are looking for the best, this is the place to splurge.

PAPERPRESENTATION.COM

23 W 18th St (bet Fifth Ave and Ave of the Americas)   212/463-7035
Mon-Fri: 9-7; Sat: 11-6; Sun: 11-6   www.paperpresentation.com

If it is made of paper, this is the place to go for huge selections and quality merchandise. Business cards, writing paper, invitations, brochures, postcards, envelopes, folders, Oriental laser paper, bags, labels, and more are shown in quantity. Certificate plaques are also available.

PAPIVORE

233 Elizabeth St (bet Prince and Houston St)   212/334-4330
Mon-Sat: 11-7; Sun: 12-6

Unusual notepads, writing papers, notebooks, photo albums, and correspondence cards from Europe and the Americas are featured at Papivore. They also specialize in custom printing.

PURGATORY PIE PRESS

19 Hudson St (bet Duane and Reade St), Room 403   212/274-8228
Mon-Fri: by appointment   www.purgatorypiepress.com

The name may be strange, but the people at Purgatory Pie know what they are doing. They do letterpress printing from hand-set metal and wood type. In addition, they do book production, albums, custom hand bookbinding, yearly datebooks, invitations, coasters, artists' books, and handmade paper with uniquely designed watermarks. Classes are taught in handmaking books and typography.

The name **Papyrus** is synonymous with upscale paper stores. In all of their outlets you will find an attractive and friendly environment, superior service, custom printing, stationery, gift wrap, gift products, and a great selection of greeting cards. Here are their Manhattan outlets:

852 Lexington Ave (bet 64th and 65th St), 212/717-0002
1270 Third Ave (at 73rd St), 212/717-1060
Grand Central Station, 42nd St at Vanderbilt Ave, 212/490-9894 and 212/682-9359
2157 Broadway (bet 75th and 76th St), 212/501-0102
1250 Ave of the Americas (at 50th St), Suite 1, 212/265-9003

REBECCA MOSS
510 Madison Ave (at 53rd St)   212/832-7671, 800/INK-PENS
Mon-Sat: 10-6   www.rebeccamoss.com

If you are in the market for pens, this is the place! Moss carries a fine selection of their exclusive brand of pens, and they offer refills for most other big names. You'll also find leather goods like purses, travel bags, and portfolios. Moreover, the personnel are informed and friendly. It is a family-owned business, and customers are treated as part of the clan. The late Rebecca Moss would be pleased at the job her grandson is doing!

Tiles

BISAZZA MOSAICO
43 Greene St (bet Broome and Grand St)   212/334-7130
Tues-Sat: 11-7   www.bisazzausa.com

Bisazza Mosaico says it is the world's leading glass mosaic company. They have large stocks of glass mosaic tile, custom mosaics, and tiles for residential, commercial, indoor, and outdoor use. They have been in business for over a half-century and carry recognized quality products.

COMPLETE TILE COLLECTION
42 W 15th St (bet Fifth Ave and Ave of the Americas)   212/255-4450
Mon-Fri: 10-6:30; Sat: 11-6

Try Complete Tile when you are shopping for quality tiles. They carry American art tiles, glass, ceramic, concrete, metal, slate, granite, molded tiles, marble and limestone mosaics, glass tiles, and a large assortment of handmade tiles. Design services are available, and the selection is tops. They now fabricate stone countertops, too!

IDEAL TILE
405 E 51st St (at First Ave)   212/759-2339
Mon-Fri: 9-5; Sat: 10-3

Ideal Tile imports ceramics, porcelain, marble, granite, and terra cotta from Italy, Spain, and Brazil. They have absolutely magnificent hand-painted Italian ceramic pottery as well. This outfit guarantees installation of tiles by skilled craftsmen. They also offer marble and granite fabrication for fireplaces, countertops, windowsills, and tables.

Tobacco and Accessories

BARCLAY-REX
75 Broad St (bet Beaver and William St)   212/962-3355
Mon-Fri: 8-6:30
70 E 42nd St (bet Madison and Park Ave)   212/692-9680
Mon-Fri: 8-6:30; Sat: 9:30-5:30
570 Lexington Ave (at 51st St)   212/888-1015
Mon-Fri: 8-7:30; Sat: 9:30-5:30
3 World Financial Center (at Winter Garden)   212/385-4632
Mon-Fri: 8-7; Sat: 11-5; Sun: 12-5   www.barclayrex.com

Established in 1910, Barclay-Rex is the product of three generations of the Nastri family. The shop caters to devotees of fine cigars, pipes, tobaccos, and smoking-related gifts and accessories. They have one of the city's best selections of pipes. Their shops are stocked with more than 200 brands of imported and domestic tobaccos. The finest tobaccos from all over the world are hand-blended and packaged under the Barclay-Rex label, and custom blending is one of their specialties. Cigars are housed in walk-in humidors at controlled temperatures.

> Gentlemen! Tired of searching in vain for a place where cigar smoking is not only allowed but encouraged? Well, I have found a spot where you can enjoy your stogie, a cup of coffee, and good conversation, too. **De La Concha** (1390 Ave of the Americas, 212/757-3167) sells high-quality imported and domestic cigars, cigarettes, pipes, and tobacco.

CONNOISSEUR PIPE SHOP
1285 Ave of the Americas (bet 51st and 52nd St), concourse level
Mon-Fri: 10:15-5:30   212/247-6054

Edward Burak has assembled a beautiful collection of hand-carved pipes that range in price from $47 to over $6,000. His store features natural unvarnished pipes, custom-made pipes, custom-blended tobacco, and expert repair. Burak will also do appraisals for insurance purposes. If your pipe came from Connoisseur, you will get admiring glances from those who know quality.

J.R. CIGARS
562 Fifth Ave (at 46th St)   212/997-2227, 800/JR-CIGAR
Mon-Fri: 9-7; Sat: 10-5; Sun: 11-4   www.jrcigars.com

For years Lew Rothman has claimed to offer the world's largest selection of cigars and pipe tobacco at the lowest prices. Over 3,000 styles and 300 brands of cigars are stocked. Prices are 20% to 70% off retail.

OK CIGARS
383 West Broadway (bet Spring and Broome St)   212/965-9065
Sun-Wed: 11-9; Thurs: 11-10; Fri, Sat: 11 a.m.-midnight
(call for winter hours)   www.okcigars.com

Looking for a really good cigar? Len Brunson promises some of the best in a pleasant atmosphere. Unique accessories are available, including some of the finest and most peculiar antique tobacciana to be found.

Toys and Children's Items
General

CHILDREN'S GENERAL STORE
Grand Central Station (42nd Street at Lexington Passage)
Mon-Fri: 8-8; Sat: 10-6; Sun: 11-5   212-682-0004

Along the Lexington Avenue Passage to Grand Central Station, this is a terrific all-purpose toy store. The emphasis is less on space-age wizardry and battery-operated gizmos than on basic, well-made toys designed to encourage creative and imaginative play. The diverse stock is chosen by people who clearly know and love children.

CLASSIC TOYS
218 Sullivan St (bet Bleecker and 3rd St)   212/674-4434
Sun-Tues: 11-7; Wed-Sat: 10:30-8   www.classictoysnyc.com

Classic carries old and new toys that have proven popular with generations of youngsters. It is also a haven for collectors and those (like your author) who just like to browse toy shops. Here you will find the largest selection of die-cast vehicles in New York, with pieces of old Matchbox, Dinky, and Corgi that go back to the 1930s. Over a hundred years of toy soldiers are on display, as well as other miniatures, stuffed animals, and a great selection of antiques that will charm parents and children. They even maintain a list of stores for shoppers who can't find what they want here!

DINOSAUR HILL
306 E 9th St (bet First and Second Ave)   212/473-5850
Daily: 11-7   www.dinosaurhill.com

At Dinosaur Hill you can travel the world through toys! There are marbles from England, tin windups from China, papier-maché masks from Venice, wooden pull toys from France, and solid wood blocks made right here in the U.S. In addition, there is handmade clothing in natural-fiber fabrics for infants through four years and a wonderful assortment of hats, music boxes, monkeys, moons, and mermaids! They also keep a birthday book.

ENCHANTED FOREST
85 Mercer St (bet Spring and Broome St)   212/925-6677
Mon-Sat: 11-7; Sun: 12-6

The Enchanted Forest physically and philosophically lives up to its name. Owners David Wallace and Peggy Sloane hired theatrical set designer Matthew Jacobs to create an enchanted forest backdrop for a collection of toys, whimsies, and artwork. The shop purports to be a "gallery of beasts, books, and handmade toys celebrating the spirit of the animals, the old stories, and the child within." The emphasis is on the gallery aspect, so it really isn't suitable for restless small children. Featured items include a fine selection of fairy tales and myths, puppets, kaleidoscopes, baskets brimming with unusual little treasures, and various eclectic gems. This place truly is enchanted!

EXOTICAR MODEL CO.
280 Park Ave (at 48th St) 212/573-9537
Mon-Sat: 10-6; Sun: 11-5 www.exoticar.com

For the automobile buff, Exoticar is a must-visit place! You'll find all manner of collectibles, apparel, books, magazines, and accessories. Ask to see the Munster Coach, which is worth a visit in itself!

F.A.O. SCHWARZ
767 Fifth Ave (at 58th St) 212/644-9400
Mon-Sat: 10-7; Sun: 11-6 www.fao.com

Shopping here is still a special experience! In the competitive (and sometimes unprofitable) field of toy retailing, the flagship F.A.O. store has had its problems. Now the store has been made over. Shopping is a bit easier and prices are somewhat more comfortable. You'll see some merchandise that is not readily available elsewhere, and the mere fact that your purchase came from this store makes it special for many youngsters (and adults), too!

A good place to start the young ones on a chocolate craze is at the **F.A.O. Schwarz** snack bar, where a Volcano is not inexpensive but certainly is delicious! Contents: chocolate and ice cream, candy boulders and chocolate caramel lava (serves four). The menu also includes an edible chocolate toy chest with candy and ice cream.

GEPPETTO'S TOY BOX
10 Christopher St (bet Ave of the Americas and Seventh Ave)
Mon-Fri: 11-7; Sat: 10:30-6:30; Sun: 12:30-6 212/620-7511
www.nyctoys.com

The owners of this West Village toy store are clearly consumer-savvy, stocking trendy favorites. Yet the heart of this store is its exceptionally high-quality teddy bears, jack-in-the-boxes, snow globes, marionettes, and other whimsical toys and games. Moreover, it's obviously run with great passion and care. You'll also find a variety of interesting items made by local artists and a small but carefully chosen selection of books. If you're a toy collector, have a child in your life, or simply like a kid's store that's run with class and grace, make a visit to Geppetto's a top priority. If you're visiting in the winter, be sure to call ahead, as hours are shortened.

GOOD-BYES
230 E 78th St (bet Second and Third Ave) 212/794-2301
Mon-Fri: 11-6; Sun: 12-5

Owner Carla Freeland has renovated and remade this former consignment store into a treasure trove of toys for the toddler and preschool set. You won't find big-name plastic toys here. Instead it is brimming with a wide selection of classic wooden puzzles, building sets, and musical toys chosen with love and thought. Look for colorful, creative items that can be personalized. With prices that are unusually reasonable for this neighborhood, the reborn Good-Byes is a pleasure to visit!

KID O
123 W 10th St (at Ave of the Americas)   212/366-KIDO
Mon-Sat: 11-7; Sun: 12-6   www.kidonyc.com

Lisa Mahar has gathered products that have both a design and educational focus. She believes such items can accelerate children's development. You'll find play objects, kids' furniture, artwork, nursery items, and books. Educational materials include Montessori and Froebel gifts.

KIDDING AROUND
60 W 15th St (bet Fifth Ave and Ave of the Americas)
Mon-Sat: 10-7; Sun: 11-6   212/645-6337

This bright, spacious emporium in the heart of Greenwich Village is arguably the city's best toy store. Books, toys, puzzles, balls, games, craft supplies, birthday party favors—you name it, they've got it. In addition to a wide selection of Playmobil, Brio, and Corrole dolls, Kidding Around stocks an amazing assortment of quality wooden toys for riding, building, and just having fun. The store's collection of clothing is small but well chosen, and the dress-up clothes are great, too. An affiliated location in Montclair, NJ, features a more extensive clothing selection.

MARY ARNOLD TOYS
1010 Lexington Ave (at 72nd St)   212/744-8510
Mon-Fri: 9-6; Sat: 10-5

You won't find any great bargains and likely won't see anything you haven't seen before, but Mary Arnold Toys is a spacious, well-organized, and well-stocked source for the basics. There are separate sections for games, puzzles, books, stuffed animals, craft kits and supplies, Playmobil, videos, and Madame Alexander dolls. The dress-up collection deserves a close look.

TOYS 'R' US
1514 Broadway (at 44th St)   800/869-7787
Mon-Sat: 10-10; Sun: 11-8   www.toysrus.com

No family trip to Manhattan is complete without a visit to Toys 'R' Us—the toy store to beat all toy stores! Set in the heart of the city, this $32 million marvel features a huge stage set with a giant Animatronic dinosaur and a 60-foot tall ferris wheel in the atrium, with each car modeled after a different toy. Seemingly every square inch of this busy store is devoted to showing merchandise. You have to see it to believe it!

ZITTLES
969 Madison Ave (at 76th St), 3rd floor   212/737-2040
Mon-Fri: 9-8; Sat: 9-7; Sun: 10-6   www.zittles.com

Housed on the third floor of Zitomer—Madison Avenue's often amusingly snobby drugstore-cum-department-store—Zittles has one of the most extensive selections of toys, games, stuffed animals, dolls, books, software, and videos for children in the city. There are neither bargains nor much imagination shown here, but there is a lot of space, and every inch of it is filled with all the basics and more. On your way up the elevator, which is back by the 76th Street entrance, look on the second floor for an extensive selection of children's clothing and accessories.

Gifts and Accessories

LITTLE EXTRAS
676 Amsterdam Ave (at 93rd St)   212/721-6161
Mon-Fri: 10:30-6:30 (Thurs till 7); Sat: 10:30-6; Sun: 11-5
(closed Sun in summer)

Whether you're looking for a personalized bathrobe, the perfect picture frame, a baby present, or hand-painted furniture, this cheerful store is teeming with gifts and accessories for infants and children. Owner Terry Siegel's great taste shows in everything. Make sure to look up at the mobiles hanging from the ceiling! An added bonus: Little Extras offers a wide selection of birth announcements, thank-you notes, and party invitations at a discount.

Specialty and Novelty

ALPHABETS
115 Ave A (bet 7th and 8th St)   212/475-7250
Sun-Thurs: 12-8; Fri, Sat: 12-10
47 Greenwich Ave (bet Charles and Perry St)   212/229-2966
Daily: 12-7
2284 Broadway (near 82nd St)   212/579-5702
Mon: 12-8; Tues-Fri: 11-9; Sat: 10-9; Sun: 11-7
                                               www.alphabetsnyc.com

These crowded little spaces are a combination toy store, novelty shop, and stroll down memory lane for baby boomers. If you're looking for a Desi Arnaz wristwatch, a Gumby and Pokey piggy bank, kitschy ceramics, or a T-shirt with the Velveeta logo on it, this is the place to come. They also carry offbeat New York souvenirs. The Upper West Side location is a somewhat tamer version of the other two.

BALLOON CENTER OF NEW YORK
5 Tudor City Pl (bet First and Second Ave)   212/682-3803
Mon-Fri: 10-4:30 or by appointment

The Balloon Center of New York sells balloons individually or in quantities of up to 50,000. There are graduations in diameter, thickness, style, and type (including Mylar balloons). Sizes range from peewees to blimps and extra-long shapes. Helium, ribbon, balloon clips, and balloon imprinting are available. Most of this whimsical business is done for advertising campaigns and corporate and special events. I recommend calling first to check hours.

DISNEY STORE
711 Fifth Ave (at 55th St)   212/702-0702
Mon-Sat: 10-8; Sun: 11-6   www.disneystore.com

If the "malling" of New York hasn't gotten you down, this store can be a fun place to shop. Unlike the staff at a lot of the huge stores that have popped up all over New York, these folks really know their stock and are personable to boot. If you don't have a Disney Store back home and are looking for kids' luggage with Mickey Mouse on it, backpacks in the shape of Winnie the Pooh, or other Disney-related items, visit this store.

Once one of the most famous areas of Manhattan, "Ladies' Mile," is again on the itineraries of wise shoppers. There are some great stores grouped on Avenue of the Americas between 18th and 19th streets:

Bed Bath & Beyond: a wonderful store, with huge selections of bed, bath, and home furnishings at good prices

Filene's Basement: famous for clothing bargains

Old Navy: very "in," especially with the young and anti-yuppie set; clothing is fashionable and priced right

T.J. Maxx: values in clothing and accessories for the family

E.A.T. GIFTS
1062 Madison Ave (bet 80th and 81st St)　　　　212/861-2544
Mon-Sat: 10-6; Sun: 12-5　　　　www.elizabar.com

It's impossible to sum up what this store offers in a few sentences. E.A.T. Gifts is a wonderland of imaginative party favors and stocking stuffers that must be seen to be believed. From tiny tea sets, party supplies, and invitations to the pinatas on the ceiling and seasonal holiday items, you'll want to inspect every square foot of this store. Indeed, it's the kind of place where you inevitably spot one more thing as the salesperson is totaling up your purchases! The focus is mostly on kids and items you'll remember from childhood, but there is something for just about everyone at this wonderful store. The Madison Avenue address is a tipoff there's nothing inexpensive here, and sometimes the whines of overprivileged children can be a bit tiresome. But if you want to put together a special party bag, holiday stocking, or gift basket, this is the place to go.

FORBIDDEN PLANET
840 Broadway (at 13th St)　　　　212/473-1576
Mon-Sat: 10-10; Sun: 11-8

Mike Luckman's unique shop is a shrine of science-fiction artifacts. Forbidden Planet stocks sci-fi comic books and publications, videos, posters, T-shirts, cards, toys, and games.

IMAGE ANIME
103 W 30th St (at Ave of the Americas)　　　　212/631-0966
Mon-Fri: 11-7; Sat: 12-6　　　　www.imageanime.com

Image Anime specializes in imported Japanese toys and collectibles. If that category is of interest to you—and there are a great many children and adults who are almost fanatically devoted to it—then this packed little store will thrill you. Lines include Gundam, Pokémon, Transformers, Robotech, Anime, and just about every other popular Japanese line.

LOVE SAVES THE DAY
119 Second Ave (at 7th St)   212/228-3802
Daily: 1-9

As Starbucks and The Gap slowly take over the East Village, stores like Love Saves the Day are a welcome relief. The floor-to-ceiling merchandise ranges from vintage clothing and accessories (including really great go-go boots) to *Star Wars* action figures and more Pez dispensers than I've ever seen. If you're nostalgic for the 1960s and 1970s or just want to hang out with some funky folks, you're really going to groove on this place. Oddly enough, there's a branch in New Hope, PA, as well.

MANHATTAN DOLLHOUSE
428 Second Ave (bet 24th and 25th St)   212/253-9549
Mon-Fri: 11-6; Sat: 1-5   www.manhattandollhouse.com

Edwin Jacobowitz operates the Manhattan Dollhouse, which boasts the city's largest collection of dolls (including Madame Alexander), dollhouses, and related furniture and paraphernalia. The store is also a hospital where injured dolls can be made well again.

RED CABOOSE
23 W 45th St (bet Fifth Ave and Ave of the Americas), basement
Mon-Fri: 11-7; Sat: 11-5:30   212/575-0155
                                                www.theredcaboose.com

Owner-operator Allan J. Spitz will tell you that 99% of his customers are not wide-eyed children but sharp-eyed adults who are dead serious about model railroads. If you happen to be a train buff, this is your spot. The Red Caboose claims to have 100,000 items on hand, including a line of 300 hand-finished, imported brass locomotives. Spitz claims that the five basic sizes—1:22, 1:48, 1:87, 1:161, and 1:220, in a ratio of scale to life size—will allow a model railroader to build layouts sized to fit everywhere from a desk drawer to a basement. They carry an extensive line of plastic kits, paints, tools, and model supplies. Adapting to the changing market, Red Caboose has expanded its range of products to include die-cast airplanes (military and commercial), autos, and military vehicles that are factory-finished and affordable.

Travel Items

FLIGHT 001
96 Greenwich Ave (bet Jane and 12th St)   212/691-1001
Mon-Sat: 11-8:30; Sun: 12-6   877/FLIGHT1
                                                   www.flight001.com

Traveling these days isn't always fun, but a trip to Flight 001 will make it more bearable. You will find novel and useful travel aids, including cosmetics, bags, guidebooks, stationery, luggage, and more.

Videotapes

EVERGREEN VIDEO
37 Carmine St (at Bleecker St)   212/691-7362
Mon-Thurs: 10-10; Fri: 10-11; Sat: 12-11; Sun: 12-10

Evergreen has more than 10,000 titles, including New York's largest rental collection of silent films; films of the 1930s, 1940s, and 1950s; foreign-language titles and documentaries; and 8,000 DVDs for sale or rent. This store is particularly popular with folks in the arts and media.

VIDEO ROOM
1487 Third Ave (at 84th St)   212/879-5333
300 Rector Pl (South End Ave at Thames St)   212/962-6400
Mon-Fri: 12-11; Sat: 11-11; Sun: 12-10   www.videoroom.net
Video Room stocks a large selection of foreign films and classics. Their highly competent staff of film students is motivated to help inquiring customers. There is also an in-depth selection of new releases, home pickup and delivery service ($89 per year), and a special-order department for hard-to-find films.

Watches

TEMPVS FVGIT AT THE SHOWPLACE
40 W 25th St (bet Ave of the Americas and Broadway) 212/633-6063
Thurs, Fri: 10-5:30; Sat, Sun: 8:30-5; and by appointment
                                 www.tempvsfvgit.com

If you're looking for a vintage Rolex, this is the place. They carry other top brands and watchbands, all at considerable savings. Watch repair is also available.

YAEGER WATCH
578 Fifth Ave (at 47th St)   212/819-0088
Mon-Fri: 10-5; Sat: 10-3 (closed Sat in summer)
                               www.yaegerwatch.com

Over 2,000 discounted watches are carried at Yaegar Watch. Choose from name brands retailing from $100 to $150,000 in a store that has been owned by the same family since 1970. Watch repair and warranties are offered, and prices are quoted over the phone.

New York watch stores include **Cellini Fine Jewelry** (509 Madison Ave, 212/888-0505), **Kenjo** (40 W 57th St, 212/333-7220), **Tourneau** (500 Madison Ave, 212/758-6098; 12 E 57th St, 212/758-7300; and 200 W 34th St, 212/563-6880), and **Wempe** (700 Fifth Ave, 212/397-9000).

VII. Where to "Extras"

As I research each new edition of this book, I'm always struck by how much information doesn't fit neatly into any of the other chapters. That's why I came up with this chapter of "Extras": where to go dancing, take kids, spend a romantic evening, and host a special event. Those are just several of the subjects this chapter addresses.

WHEN TO GO
Annual Events

While stores, museums, restaurants, and the like are open all year, some special events are held only during certain seasons or once a year. The "For More Resources" section at the end of this chapter offers suggestions about how to find out what's happening in New York at any given time. *Time Out New York* is a tremendous source of up-to-date information, as are *New York* magazine and *The New Yorker.*

JANUARY
Polar Bear Club New Year's Dip (Coney Island)
Ice skating (Rockefeller Center and Central Park)
Winter Antiques Show (Seventh Regiment Armory)
Chinese New Year (January or February)

FEBRUARY
Westminster Kennel Club Dog Show (Madison Square Garden)
Empire State Run-Up (Empire State Building)
National Antiques Show (Madison Square Garden)
Kids' Night on Broadway
Valentine's Day wedding ceremony (Empire State Building)
Winter Festival (Great Lawn, Central Park)
Art Dealers Association exhibition (Seventh Regiment Armory)

MARCH
St. Patrick's Day Parade (Fifth Avenue)

International Cat Show (Madison Square Garden)
Spring Armory Antiques Show (Seventh Regiment Armory)
Big East and NIT college basketball tournaments (Madison Square
   Garden)
New York Flower Show (Pier 92, Twelfth Ave at 52nd St)
Macy's Spring Flower Show
Radio City Easter Show (Radio City Music Hall)

APRIL
International Auto Show (Jacob K. Javits Convention Center)
Baseball season opens (Yankee Stadium and Shea Stadium)
New York Antiquarian Book Fair (Seventh Regiment Armory)

MAY
International Food Festival (Ninth Avenue)
Ukrainian Festival (East 7th Street)
Fleet Week (week before Memorial Day)
Lower East Side Jewish Festival
Washington Square Outdoor Art Exhibit

JUNE
Salute to Israel Parade (Fifth Avenue)
Free concerts and performances (Central Park and other city parks)
Museum Mile Festival (Fifth Avenue)
Feast of St. Anthony of Padua (Little Italy)
Summer restaurant "sale" (throughout Manhattan)
Lower Manhattan Cultural Council's Buskers Fair
Jazz festivals (Bryant Park, Carnegie Hall, and other locations)

JULY
Free concerts and performances (Central Park and other city parks)
Free movies (Bryant Park and other locations)
Fourth of July fireworks (East River and other locations)
American Crafts Festival (Lincoln Center)
Mostly Mozart (Avery Fisher Hall)
Midsummer's Night Swing (Lincoln Center)

AUGUST
Free concerts and performances (Central Park and other city parks)
Free movies (Bryant Park and other locations)
New York City Triathlon
Lincoln Center Out-of-Doors Festival (Lincoln Center)
Festival Latino (Public Theater and other locations)
U.S. Open begins (National Tennis Center)

SEPTEMBER
Autumn Crafts Festival (Lincoln Center)
Third Avenue Festival
Feast of San Gennaro (Little Italy)
New York Film Festival (Lincoln Center)
Broadway Cares/Equity Fights AIDS flea market and auction (Shubert
   Alley)

OCTOBER
Columbus Day Parade (Fifth Avenue)
Basketball season opens (Madison Square Garden)
Soho Arts Festival
Fall Antiques Show (Pier 92, Twelfth Ave at 52nd St)
Halloween Parade (Greenwich Village)
New York Marathon (late October or early November)

NOVEMBER
Home Show (Jacob K. Javits Convention Center)
Margaret Meade Film Festival (American Museum of Natural History)
Macy's Thanksgiving Day Parade (Central Park West and Broadway)
Christmas tree lighting (Rockefeller Plaza)

DECEMBER
Christmas windows (Saks Fifth Avenue, Macy's, and other locations)
Messiah Singalong (Avery Fisher Hall)
Radio City Christmas Show (Radio City Music Hall)
Holiday bazaar (Grand Central Station)
Menorah lighting (Grand Army Plaza)
Christmas Day walking tour (Big Onion Walking Tours)
New Year's Eve celebrations (Times Square and other locations)
First Night celebrations (Grand Central Station, Central Park, and other
    locations)

Holidays

Whether or not you celebrate given holidays, it is important to know when
they occur because they not only affect traffic, store sales, and museum hours
in New York, but also might mean there's a great parade to watch.

2006

January 1	New Year's Day
January 16	Martin Luther King, Jr. Day
February 14	Valentine's Day
February 20	Presidents Day
March 17	St. Patrick's Day
April 13	Passover begins (eight days)
April 14	Good Friday
April 16	Easter
May 14	Mother's Day
May 29	Memorial Day
June 18	Father's Day
July 4	Independence Day
September 4	Labor Day
September 23	Rosh Hashana (two days)
September 24	Ramadan begins (one month)
October 2	Yom Kippur
October 9	Columbus Day
October 31	Halloween
November 10	Veterans Day (observed)
November 23	Thanksgiving Day

| December 16 | Hanukkah begins (eight days) |
| December 25 | Christmas Day |

2007

January 1	New Year's Day
January 15	Martin Luther King, Jr. Day
February 14	Valentine's Day
February 19	Presidents Day
March 17	St. Patrick's Day
April 3	Passover begins (eight days)
April 6	Good Friday
April 8	Easter
May 13	Mother's Day
May 28	Memorial Day
June 17	Father's Day
July 4	Independence Day
September 3	Labor Day
September 13	Rosh Hashana (two days)
	Ramadan begins (one month)
September 22	Yom Kippur
October 8	Columbus Day
October 31	Halloween
November 12	Veterans Day (observed)
November 22	Thanksgiving Day
December 25	Christmas Day
	Hannukkah begins (eight days)

WHERE TO SIT
Parks

As hard as it may be to believe when you're standing amid the skyscrapers of midtown, Manhattan has almost 2,600 acres of parkland. That means almost 20% of the city is grass, trees, rocks, lakes, playgrounds, and walking trails. Spanning 843 acres in the middle of the island, Central Park is the biggest and certainly the most famous. Smaller ones like Carl Schurz Park on the Upper East Side and Lighthouse Park on Roosevelt Island can be more peaceful, however, because fewer people know about them. Inwood Hill Park and Fort Tryon Park on Manhattan's northern tip are so wooded and hilly that you won't believe you're in New York. You might even spot a bald eagle!

Unless you are going to a scheduled event such as a play or concert, you probably don't want to walk around in any park late at night. (It is worth noting, however, that the Central Park police precinct is the safest in Manhattan.) If you are by yourself, stay away from isolated and densely vegetated areas even during the day. That said, the parks are real treasures to explore and enjoy. They offer a wonderful respite from the concrete and chaos, and thanks to a concerted effort to clean and refurbish them, the city's parks are looking better than at any time since I began visiting New York a half century ago.

The following is an annotated listing of some of the city's biggest parks, as well as some personal favorites among the lesser known ones.

BATTERY PARK
southern tip of Manhattan below State St and Battery Pl

This 23-acre park was named for the gun battery built along its old shore-line during the War of 1812. It's the site of Castle Clinton, a National Monument originally built as a fort during the War of 1812 and now the place to buy tickets for the Statue of Liberty and Ellis Island. One of the last remaining kiosks for the original subway system is in Battery Park, too. The Staten Island Ferry's beautiful new Whitehall Terminal is adjacent to the park's eastern edge. The marvelous National Museum of the American Indian is directly north of the park, and the Museum of Jewish Heritage is on the park's northwest edge. You'll find lots of benches and pathways, as well as an excellent view of New York Harbor.

> Artwork valued at more than $100 million, including public pieces as well as items in private collections, was destroyed in the September 11, 2001, attack on the World Trade Center. *The Sphere*—a sculpture that once stood in the World Trade Center plaza—survived, battered but intact, and now sits in Battery Park.

BRYANT PARK
Ave of the Americas bet 40th and 42nd St

Located behind the stately main branch of the New York Public Library, this was the site of the 1853 World's Fair, where Isaac Singer unveiled the sewing machine and Elisha Otis introduced the elevator. After years of neglect, the park underwent a multimillion-dollar renovation a decade ago and is now a real gem. The benches are great resting spots, and you'll find lots of vendors and a fine garden in the spring and summer. You'll also find games like checkers and Scrabble for rent, toy boats to rent and sail in the fountain, a wonderful new carousel in warmer months, and free movies on Monday nights in summer. Imagine 10,000 people watching *The Wizard of Oz* and singing "Somewhere Over the Rainbow"! Bryant Park even has clean and safe public restrooms (just off 42nd Street, behind the library), complete with attendants and fresh flowers in the ladies' room.

CENTRAL PARK
Fifth Ave to Central Park W bet 59th and 110th St

Designed in 1858 by Frederick Law Olmsted, the same landscape architect who designed the U.S. Capitol Grounds in Washington, D.C., this is the ultimate urban park. The 843-acre park has two ice-skating rinks (in winter), lakes, ponds, a marvelous wildlife conservation center, theaters, jogging tracks, a reservoir, baseball diamonds and other playing fields, playgrounds, tennis courts, a miniature golf course (in summer), and a castle. You can even find a wonderful restaurant (Park View at the Boathouse, near 72nd Street on the east side), a more downscale cafe (near 65th Street on the west side), and two warm-weather Italian sidewalk cafes (inside the Columbus Circle entrance). There's lots of open space and 58 miles of paths. Thanks to the Central Park Conservancy, the park has undergone a major facelift, with updates and renovations of everything from the Great Lawn to the pond near the park's southwest entrance. In summer, Central Park is home to a wide variety of cultural events, including Shakespeare in the Park, various concerts on the "Summer Stage," and free concerts by the New York Philharmonic and the Metropolitan Opera.

For maps and a schedule of current events, stop by the Visitor Information Center at The Dairy, just behind Wollman Rink at what would be 65th Street and Avenue of the Americas (if those roads went into the park); the Henry Luce Nature Observatory, in Belvedere Castle at mid-park near 79th Street; or at the Charles A. Dana Discovery Center, in the park's northeast corner, near 110th Street and Fifth Avenue. You can also go to www.nycgovparks.org and click "Things to Do." If you ever get lost in the park, remember that the first digits of the number plate on the lampposts correspond to the nearest cross street.

Adopt-a-Bench

Central Park has almost 9,000 benches, and roughly a quarter of them have been "adopted." For $7,500, all of which goes to the Central Park Conservancy, anyone can get a brief message inscribed on a bench. "To the world, you were one person," reads one dedicated to a victim of the terrorist attacks of September 11, 2001. "To me, you were the world."

FORT TRYON PARK
Riverside Dr to Broadway bet 192nd and Dyckman St

This 66-acre gift from John D. Rockefeller, Jr., is a hilly and wooded treasure with magnificent views of the Hudson River and the Palisades. Make sure to visit the beautiful but little known Heather Garden, the largest public garden in Manhattan, as well as The Cloisters. Take a friend along, however, if you plan on exploring off the beaten path.

INWOOD HILL PARK
northwest tip of Manhattan

The second largest park in Manhattan, Inwood Hill Park is bordered by the Harlem River to the north and the Hudson River on the west. These rugged 200 acres are home to a marsh, caves once used by Algonquin Indians, and the island's last remaining stands of virgin timber. (Most of the original forests were cut down by British troops during the Revolutionary War.) Hiking and climbing enthusiasts will love its relatively unspoiled wilderness, but travel in groups for safety's sake. Drop by the Urban Ecology Center (inside the park at 218th St) for information on nature walks and other scheduled events.

LIGHTHOUSE PARK
northern tip of Roosevelt Island

If you really want to get away but only have a little time, take a short ride out to this magical place on the northern tip of Roosevelt Island in the middle of the East River. The view of the Manhattan skyline from the west side of the park is among the best in the city. A tram to Roosevelt Island leaves frequently from its own station on Second Avenue between 59th and 60th streets. It costs $2 each way, and the bus that takes you from the tram station to the northern end of the island costs just one thin dime.

MADISON PARK
Madison Ave to Fifth Ave bet 23rd and 26th St

Thanks to a tremendous restoration, you can transport yourself back to 19th century New York in this swath of greenspace in Lower Manhattan. Yes, this was the site of the original Madison Square Garden, as well as P.T. Barnum's Hippodrome. But no, that's not James Madison—or even Abraham Lincoln, whom it really resembles—in the park's southeast corner. It's actually U.S. Senator and Secretary of State William Seward. The fountains at the park's south end are particularly impressive.

What Are Those Flags Flying All Over New York?

The presence of the United Nations means that flags of many countries fly in New York. However, two flags flown over the city can't be found in any world atlas. The white one with the green maple leaf is the New York City Parks and Recreation Department's flag, while the blue, white, and orange one is the official flag of New York City.

ROBERT WAGNER, JR. PARK, BATTERY PARK ESPLANADE, and NELSON A. ROCKEFELLER PARK
southwest edge of Manhattan

These are a series of relatively new and expanding parks marching their way up the west side of the island. As you head north through Battery Park City and up toward TriBeCa, you'll find open spaces, walkways, benches, playgrounds, and lots of New Yorkers reveling in the reclaimed waterfront. For a real treat, start your walk at Chambers Street and head south along the river for some of the most sweeping views in the city. The views of Ellis Island and the Statue of Liberty are particularly spectacular from Robert Wagner, Jr. Park, just above Battery Park at the south end of Battery Park City.

RIVERSIDE PARK
Riverside Dr to Hudson River bet 72nd and 159th St

Like Central Park, this is another of Frederick Law Olmsted's creations. In addition to playgrounds, great paths for walking, jogging, and bicycling; popular clay tennis courts at 92nd Street; and a terrific view of the Hudson River, the park is home to the Eleanor Roosevelt statue (at 72nd Street), the 79th Street Boat Basin, the Soldiers and Sailors Monument (at 89th Street), and Grant's Tomb (at 122nd Street). People used to complain about erosion and vandalism in the park, but those who live around it now take responsibility for its upkeep.

UNION SQUARE PARK
Broadway to Park Ave S bet 14th and 17th St

Known largely for its drug scene a generation ago, this old park has really come back to life. It stretches between Broadway (called Union Square

West here) and Park Avenue South (Union Square East) and is home to the city's most popular Greenmarket. You'll also find playgrounds, picnic benches, and, in warmer months, an outdoor bar and cafe near the Abraham Lincoln statue at the park's north end. The George Washington statue at the south end was erected in 1856 to commemorate the 80th anniversary of the signing of the Declaration of Independence, while a statue of the late Indian leader Mohatma Ghandi graces the park's southwest corner.

WASHINGTON SQUARE PARK
foot of Fifth Ave below 8th St

Long considered the emotional if not the geographic center of Greenwich Village, this park sits at the foot of Fifth Avenue and is best known for the Washington Memorial Arch. The park was constructed in 1827, but the marble arch was not dedicated until 1895. (It replaced a wooden one.) The park is near New York University, and its chess tables, playgrounds, and other amenities are much used by students and neighborhood residents.

For information about any of the parks in Manhattan, call the city's information hotline at 311 or go to www.nycgovparks.org.

WHERE TO PLAY
Nightlife

Whether you want an evening of elegant dining and dancing, rocking and rolling till the wee hours, dropping in on a set of jazz, or catching some stand-up comedy, New York's club scene offers endless choices. For descriptions of places to go and information about who is playing, look under "Night Life" in the front of *The New Yorker* or under specific listings in the back of *New York* magazine and throughout *Time Out New York*. I've listed several popular places in each category to get you started. Most levy a cover charge, many offer at least a light menu, and a very few require reservations and jackets for men. (Don't worry if you don't have one, as they'll have "loaners.") As with so many other things, it is wise to call in advance.

Cabaret Rooms

Bemelmans Bar, Carlyle Hotel (35 E 76th St, 212/744-1600)
Danny's Skylight Room (346 W 46th St, 212/265-8133)
Don't Tell Mama (343 W 46th St, 212/757-0788)
Feinstein's at the Regency, Regency Hotel (540 Park Ave, 212/339-4095)
Firebird (363 W 46th St, 212/586-0244)
Oak Room, Algonquin Hotel (59 W 44th St, 212/840-6800)

Comedy Clubs

Caroline's on Broadway (1626 Broadway, 212/757-4100)
Comedy Cellar (117 MacDougal St, 212/254-3480)
Dangerfield's (1118 First Ave, 212/593-1650)
Gotham Comedy Club (34 W 22nd St, 212/367-9000)
Stand-Up New York (236 W 78th St, 212/595-0850)

Dancing

China Club (268 W 47th St, 212/398-3800): live music and DJs on weekends

Rainbow Room (30 Rockefeller Plaza, 65th floor, 212/632-5100)

SOB (204 Varick St, 212/243-4940): Latin and Caribbean beats

Supper Club (240 W 47th St, 212/921-1940): weekend ballroom dinner dances

---

Do you want to hear Woody Allen (yes, *that* Woody Allen) tooting the clarinet in a Dixieland jazz band? He plays most Monday nights at **Cafe Carlyle**, in the Carlyle Hotel (35 E 76th St, 212/570-7189), but call ahead to be sure.

Gay and Lesbian Clubs

Boiler Room (86 E 4th St, 212/254-7536): gay

G Lounge (225 W 19th St, 212/929-1085): gay

Monster (80 Grove St, 212/924-3557): gay

Rubyfruit Bar and Grill (531 Hudson St, 212/929-3343): lesbian

Jazz Clubs

Birdland (315 W 44th St, 212/581-3080)

Blue Note (131 W 3rd St, 212/475-0049)

Cotton Club (656 W 125th St, 212/663-7980)

Iridium (1650 Broadway, 212/582-2121)

Jazz Standard (116 E 27th St, 212/576-2232)

Showman's Cafe (375 W 125th St, 212/864-8941)

Smoke (2751 Broadway, 212/864-6662)

Village Vanguard (178 Seventh Ave S, 212/255-4037)

Rock and Folk Clubs

Bitter End (147 Bleecker St, 212/673-7030): one of the original Greenwich Village folk clubs, now with rock and blues as well

CBGB (315 Bowery, 212/982-4052): the birthplace of punk-rock

"Let's Have a Drink"

Aquavit (65 W 55th St, 212/307-7311)

Campbell Apartment (Grand Central Station, 42nd St at Vanderbilt Ave, 212/953-0409)

Fifty Seven Fifty Seven, Four Seasons Hotel (57 E 57th St, 212/758-5757)

Grand Bar, Soho Grand Hotel (310 West Broadway, 212/965-3000)

Mark's Bar, The Mark Hotel (25 E 77th St, 212/606-4500)

21 Club (21 W 52nd St, 212/582-7200)

Villard Bar and Lounge, New York Palace Hotel (24 E 51st St, 212/888-7000)

Music in the Museums

Brooklyn Museum (200 Eastern Parkway, Brooklyn, 718/638-5000): music and dancing on the first Saturday evening of every month between 5 and 11

Frick Collection (1 E 70th St, 212/288-8700): chamber music some Sundays at 5

Guggenheim Museum (1071 Fifth Ave, 212/423-3500): live jazz on Friday and Saturday evening in the warmer months

Metropolitan Museum of Art (Fifth Ave bet 80th and 84th St, 212/535-7710): classical music on Friday and Saturday from 5 to 8

Rose Center for Earth and Space (81st bet Columbus Ave and Central Park West, 212/769-5100): jazz on Friday night

---

Some theater productions close almost as soon as they open and others run for only a couple months. But one has been going on since 1987: **Tony 'n' Tina's Wedding**. It's theater with a twist: you follow the couple from their wedding (St. Luke's Church, 308 W 48th St) to the reception (Edison Hotel, 221 W 46th St), complete with a pasta dinner, champagne, and wedding cake. Intrigued? Call 212/352-3101 or go to www.tonylovestina.com for more information.

Recreation

Visitors sometimes see Manhattan as nothing but concrete and can't imagine what those who live here do for exercise other than walking. The people who live here, however, know that you can do just about anything in New York that can be done anywhere else—and then some! Whether it's a batting cage, tennis, horseback riding, or driving range, chances are that New York has it if you just know where to look.

Something for Everyone in City Parks!
New York's city parks and recreation centers are likely going to be your best and often by far your least expensive recreation bets. For more information about what's available, go to www.nycgovparks.org, then click on "Things to Do" and "Park Activities and Facilities." What an amazing list! Use of a particular space may require a permit, but information about permits and how to get them is on the website.

Baseball
Baseball Center NYC (202 W 74th St, 212/362-0344)
Field House at Chelsea Piers (Hudson River bet 17th and 23rd St, 212/336-6500)

Basketball
BasketBall City (Pier 63 at W 23rd St and the Hudson River, 212/924-4040)
Field House at Chelsea Piers (Hudson River bet 17th and 23rd St, 212/336-6500)

Billiards
Billiard Club (344 Amsterdam Ave, 212/496-8180)
Slate Billiards (54 W 21st St, 212/989-0096)

Bowling

AMF Chelsea Piers Bowling (bet Piers 59 and 60, 23rd St at Hudson River, 212/835-2695)
Bowlmor Lanes (110 University Pl, 212/255-8188)
Leisure Time Bowling (Port Authority Bus Terminal, 42nd Street at Eighth Ave, 212/268-6909)

Chess, Checkers, and Backgammon

Bryant Park (42nd St bet Fifth Ave and Ave of the Americas)
Chess Shop (230 Thompson St, 212/475-9580)
Washington Square Park (foot of Fifth Ave below 8th St)

Climbing

Extra Vertical Climbing Center (61 W 62nd St, 212/586-5718)
Field House at Chelsea Piers (Hudson River bet 17th and 23rd St, 212/336-6500)
North Meadow Recreation Center (Central Park at 97th St, 212/348-4867)

Golf

Golf Academy at Chelsea Piers (driving range at Hudson River bet 17th and 23rd St, 212/336-6400)
Split Rock (public course in The Bronx, 718/885-1258)

Horseback Riding

Claremont Stables (175 W 89th St, 212/724-5100)

Ice Skating

Lasker Rink (Central Park at 107th St, 917/492-3856)
Rockefeller Plaza (Fifth Ave bet 49th and 50th St, 212/632-3975)
Sky Rink at Chelsea Piers (Hudson River at 23rd St, 212/336-6100)
Wollman Rink (Central Park at 63rd St, 212/439-6900)

If you have your heart set on ice skating at Rockefeller Plaza, I suggest going on a weekday morning. There's no wait and relatively few people will be watching in case you hit the ice!

Roller Skating

Chelsea Piers Roller Rink (Hudson River at 23rd St, 212/336-6100)

Soccer

Field House at Chelsea Piers (Hudson River at 23rd St, 212/336-6500)

Swimming

All-Star Fitness Center (75 West End Ave, 212/265-8200)
Asphalt Green (1750 York Ave, 212/369-8890)
Carmine Street Recreation Center (1 Clarkson St, 212/242-5418)
Vanderbilt YMCA (224 E 47th St, 212/756-9600)

Tennis

Columbus Avenue Tennis Club (795 Columbus Ave, 212/662-8367)

Sutton East Tennis Center (488 E 60th St, 212/751-3453)
Tennis Club at Grand Central (Grand Central Station, 42nd St at Vander-
bilt Ave, 212/687-3841)
USTA National Tennis Center (Forest Hills, Queens, 718/760-6200)

Want to Rent a Bike?
   New York's parks are full of bike paths, including a 6.2-mile loop in
Central Park and a 5.5-mile route that runs along the Hudson River down
to Battery Park. Go to www.transalt.org/calendar/century/rental for an
extensive list of places that rent bikes by the hour and day.

Spectator Sports

   Some people associate New York with fine food and expensive stores,
while others link the city with the Yankees, the Mets, the Knicks, the Rangers,
and other professional sports teams. The New York area is home to more than
half a dozen professional sports teams—although only basketball's Knicks
and hockey's Rangers actually play in Manhattan. (Home field for the city's
two pro football teams, the Jets and the Giants, is across across the river
in New Jersey, although there's been a lot of talk about building a stadium
for the Jets in Manhattan.) Diagrams of all area stadiums appear near the
front of the Manhattan Yellow Pages.
   Tickets for regular-season baseball games can often be purchased as late
as game day. Tickets for football's Giants and Jets, however, are almost
impossible to find unless you have a generous friend with season tickets.
Even Knicks tickets are hard to come by. If you're planning a trip to New
York, it's worth finding out which team is in town and who they're playing.
   A word of warning: New York sports fans are like no others. They are loud,
rude, and typically very knowledgeable about their teams and sports in general. If you're cheering against the home team, keep your voice down—and
your head, too!

Baseball

NEW YORK METS
Shea Stadium (Queens)   718/507-8499, www.mets.com

   The easiest ways to get to Shea stadium from Manhattan are by subway
(take the 7 line from Times Square or Grand Central Station to the Willets
Point/Shea Stadium stop) or boat (call New York Waterway at 800/533-3779
for game-day sailings and fare information). Tickets are easy to get and relatively inexpensive. The regular season runs from April through September.

NEW YORK YANKEES
Yankee Stadium (The Bronx)   212/307-1212
                                                www.newyorkyankees.com

   Although the Yankees may eventually move to a new stadium in Manhattan, the so-called House that Ruth Built (because Babe Ruth played here for
many years) is a great place to watch a baseball game. It's also an easy subway ride (take the C or D line from Manhattan's West Side or the 4 line on

the East Side to the 161st Street/Yankee Stadium stop) or boat trip (call New York Waterway at 800/533-3779 for game-day sailings and fare information). Tickets usually remain plentiful until the playoffs. The regular season runs from April through September.

Baseball Has Returned to Brooklyn!
Almost a half century after the Brooklyn Dodgers moved west, baseball is again being played in Brooklyn. The Cyclones, a minor league farm team of the New York Mets, play on Coney Island. For more information, call 718/449-8497 or go to www.brooklyncyclones.com.

Basketball

NEW YORK KNICKS
Madison Square Garden   212/465-6741, www.nba.com/knicks

The Knicks play at Madison Square Garden, directly above Penn Station in the heart of Manhattan. The better the Knicks are doing, the harder tickets are to come by. And be forewarned: tickets are expensive. The season runs from late October through April.

NEW YORK LIBERTY
Madison Square Garden   212/564-9622, www.wnba.com/liberty

The Liberty are a perennial powerhouse in the Women's National Basketball Association. These tickets are a great deal: they are easy to get, not very expensive, and buy a terrific evening of basketball. Their season runs from late May through August.

What a Deal!
For $75 a year (just $10 for senior citizens over 55 and free for children under 18), you can join the city's wonderful recreation centers, use their often excellent facilities, and sign up for all sorts of classes. For more information go to www.nycgovparks.org and then click on "Things to Do" and "Recreation Centers" for detailed descriptions of each center and its offerings.

Football

NEW YORK GIANTS
The Meadowlands (New Jersey)   201/935-8111, www.giants.com

Getting tickets to a Giants game is virtually impossible. In case you do land tickets, buses run between Port Authority Bus Terminal and Giants Stadium in the Meadowlands. The season runs from September through December.

NEW YORK JETS
The Meadowlands (New Jersey)   516/560-8200
                                                     www.newyorkjets.com

Tickets for Jets games are almost as hard to get as for the Giants, but you can always try. Buses run between Port Authority Bus Terminal and Giants Stadium in the Meadowlands. The season runs from September through December.

Football in Manhattan?
Plans are in the works to build a 75,000-seat stadium on the far west side of Manhattan, near the Jacob Javits Convention Center, as part of a massive redevelopment plan for the area. Whether or not it will happen is anyone's guess, in part because there are strong and vocal opponents of the plan, but it could be that the New York Jets will really play in New York sometime soon.

Hockey

NEW YORK RANGERS
Madison Square Garden   212/465-6741, www.newyorkrangers.com

Everything I said at the outset about New York sports fans goes double for the Rangers. These games are loud and tough. Getting tickets is tough, too. Assuming the league hasn't folded because of the season-ending 2004–05 strike, the season runs from October through April.

Tennis

U.S. OPEN
National Tennis Center (Forest Hills, Queens)   718/760-6200
www.usta.com

One of four Grand Slam tournaments in professional tennis, the U.S. Open is held at summer's end. Finals are played over Labor Day weekend. Tickets to the finals and semifinals sell out as soon as they go on sale, but tickets for earlier rounds can usually be purchased in the weeks leading up to the tournament.

WHAT TO EXPECT

Safety

There are more crimes committed in New York than any other American city, because more people live here. But New York is not nearly as dangerous as people think. In fact, per capita crime in New York is lower than in any other major U.S. city. The violent crime rate has plummeted and continues to fall, and security is probably tighter here than in any U.S. city other than Washington, D.C.

The percentages are definitely with you, especially if you observe a few commonsense "don'ts":

- Don't display big wads of money or flashy watches and jewelry. In fact, avoid taking them with you. Leave most of your cash and all of your valuables at home or in the hotel safe.
- Don't open your wallet in public.
- Don't use ATMs when no one else is around.
- Don't leave ATMs until you've put your money in a wallet and then put the wallet in your pocket or purse.

- Don't keep your wallet in your back pocket unless it's buttoned. Better yet, carry your wallet in a front pocket, along with keys and other important items.
- Don't wear your purse slung over one shoulder. Instead, put the strap over your head and keep your purse in front of you or to the side.
- Don't doze off on the subway or bus.
- Don't take the subway late at night or very early in the morning.
- Don't walk down empty streets or enter empty subway stations.
- Don't jog in Central Park or anywhere else after dark.
- Don't let yourself believe that staying in "good" neighborhoods protects you from crime. The only time I was ever mugged was on Park Avenue at 62nd Street, and you can't find a better neighborhood than that!
- Don't let anybody in your hotel room, even if they claim to work for the hotel, unless you've specifically asked them to come or have checked with the front desk to verify their authenticity.
- Don't talk to strangers who try to strike up a conversation unless you're sure of their motivation.
- Don't ever leave bags unattended. If you're going to put a bag or backpack on the floor at a restaurant or bathroom stall, put your foot or a leg of your chair through the strap.
- Don't hang your purse or anything else on the back of the door in a public bathroom stall.
- Don't walk around with your mouth open, camera slung over your shoulder and map visible, while saying things like, "Gee, honey, we sure don't have buildings this tall back home!"
- Don't be afraid to cross the street if a situation doesn't feel right. Shout for help if somebody is bothering you.
- Move away from any unattended packages and immediately report any suspicious items or behavior to authorities.

A final word of warning: watch where you walk. Manhattan has an incredible amount of traffic, and the struggle among cars, taxis, trucks, buses, and pedestrians is constant. The city has tried with limited success to erect pedestrian barriers at some of the most dangerous intersections. Particularly troublesome spots include Park Avenue at 33rd Street, Avenue of the Americas and Broadway at 33rd and 34th streets (Herald Square), and 42nd Street and Eighth Avenue at Port Authority Bus Terminal. It may sound silly to repeat a warning from childhood, but look both ways before stepping into the street, wherever you are.

If you're traveling with a group or family, it's always a good idea to plan a meeting place in case you get separated, If there's an emergency, don't hesitate to call 911.

Tipping and Other Expenses

Be forewarned: New York is expensive. *Really* expensive. The city's hotels are among the most expensive in the country, often costing upwards of $300 per night for a basic double room. The average dinner at a decent restaurant can easily run upwards of $50 per person, most theater and opera tickets are just plain outrageous, and even a quick lunch under $10 is increasingly hard to find. Everybody expects a tip, too. It's up to you, of course, but $1 per bag to the bellman, between 15% and 20% of your fare to the cab driver, and between 15% and 20% of your pre-tax restaurant bill (double the tax—it's 8.25% on just about everything) to your waiter is typical. Most people also tip wine stewards (10% of the wine bill), parking valets ($2), private tour guides (at least $5 a day), and doormen who hail cabs ($1), among others.

The good news is that prices have not risen much in recent years. With a little effort, you can find cheaper hotels, less expensive restaurants, good deals, and even some free events and activities. You can also try to make wise choices. The difference between buying a single bagel through room service at one midtown hotel and a deli a block away, for instance, is more than $10! However, in general my advice is be prepared to spend money—and lots of it—if you're here for a special visit. Don't nickel-and-dime yourself out of enjoying a priceless experience!

Checklists

If you're planning a trip to New York, think ahead about what you want to do and read the relevant sections of this book carefully. Pay special attention to things that require advance planning, like tickets to certain events, Broadway shows, television show tapings, and tours. Special sales or events require that you visit at certain times of year. Weather is always a consideration. Average temperatures range from highs in the 30s and 40s in December, January, and February (with snow always a possibility) to highs in the 80s and 90s in June, July, and August (when the humidity can wilt even the sturdiest among us). Whenever you come and whatever you plan to do, I recommend packing these key items:

- comfortable walking shoes
- umbrella and raincoat (or warm coat, scarf, and boots)
- jacket and tie (still required in a few places) or nice dress
- opera glasses
- address book and postcard stamps
- prescriptions and an extra pair of glasses (in case you lose them)
- fanny pack or money belt
- tickets (airplane and others)
- AARP and/or Medicare card if you qualify for a senior discount
- student ID card if you qualify for a student discount
- a picture ID card

All the little items that you may want in your hotel room or when you're out and about cost a lot less at home than in New York. Most hotels will supply small sewing kits, many now have in-room coffeemakers, and some will let you borrow an umbrella or hair dryer for free. But consider packing film, aspirin, snacks, and gum. Plan what you're going to need for the day before leaving the hotel room. Put a couple of credit cards, driver's license, and some money in a secure pocket, fanny pack, or money belt and then stash everything else in a shoulder bag so there's no worrying about a stolen purse or wallet. Leave your room key at the front desk for the same reason. Depending on the time of year, here's a list of things I recommend taking with you for a day of exploring:

- addresses and phone numbers of places you plan to visit and details about how to get there
- address and phone number of your hotel
- bus and subway maps
- tissues
- list of public bathrooms in the areas you'll be going
- umbrella
- coat or sweater
- unlimited-use MetroCard (for subways and buses)
- loose change and small bills

    Finally, don't forget this book!

Cool Ideas for Teens and "Tweens"

If you're traveling with older children or teenagers, check out the recommendations on the city's official website. Go to www.nycvisit. com and click on "Visitors," "Things to See," and "Teen Scene."

WHERE TO GO WITH CHILDREN

When I first began writing this book, I did so from the perspective of an adult who comes to New York without children. I quickly learned, however, that many people bring kids to New York, whether they're coming for business or pleasure. That's even more true now than ever before. The number of kids living in New York has also increased dramatically over the years. Restaurants, hotels, museums, theaters, and other tourist venues have noted this trend and adjusted their offerings to this growing audience. Always ask about special deals and events for children and families.

Remember that New York can be totally overwhelming for children. (The same is true for adults!) Don't push too hard and retreat to the quiet spaces from time to time. Remember, too, that New York can be a wonderland for all ages, if you know where to go. The "Kids" pages in the back of *New York* magazine and *Time Out New York* are great places to look for children's events and activities. Look inside toy stores and bookstores for seasonal calendars, and get hold of *Big Apple Parent* or one of the other free parenting magazines published in New York. A couple of good websites for families and children in New York are:

- www.parentsknow.com
- www.NewYorkKids.net
- www.ny.com/kids

I've listed some suggestions for things to do with kids in several categories: entertainment, museums, and sights; restaurants; and toy and bookstores. In many cases, these places are described in detail in other parts of this book, and I've noted them with an asterisk (*). Of course children's interests can vary dramatically, so I've inevitably included places that one child will love and another might find boring. I'll let you be the judge of that! I also recommend looking under Children's Books, Children's Clothing Stores, and Toy Stores in Chapter III.

Entertainment, Museums, and Sights

Busy Little Ones

Central Park Carousel (behind The Arsenal in Central Park at 64th St)
*Central Park Zoo (behind The Arsenal in Central Park at 64th St, 212/439-6500)
*Children's Museum of the Arts (182 Lafayette St, 212/941-9198)
Helmbold Family Children's Learning Center (Scandinavia House, 58 Park Ave, 212/879-9779)
92nd Street Y (Parenting Center, 1395 Lexington Ave, 212/427-6000)

A Day in the Park

For a list of dozens of great public playgrounds in New York, go to www.nycparkgov.org and click "Things to Do," "Activities & Facilities," and "Playgrounds." My personal favorites are the playground outside the Metropolitan Museum of Art in Central Park, the one by the Hudson River in Battery Park City, and those scattered throughout Riverside Park.

Museums with a Family Focus

*American Museum of Natural History (Central Park West bet 77th and 81st St, 212/769-5100)
*Children's Museum of Manhattan (212 W 83rd St, 212/721-1234)
*Dyckman Farmhouse Museum (4881 Broadway, 212/304-9422)
*Fraunces Tavern Museum (54 Pearl St, 212/425-1778)
Liberty Science Center (Liberty State Park, Jersey City, NJ, 201/200-1000)
*Lower East Side Tenement Museum (90 Orchard St, 212/431-0233)
*Madame Toussaud's (234 W 46th St, 212/512-9600)
*Museum of the City of New York (1220 Fifth Ave, 212/534-1672)
*New York City Fire Museum (278 Spring St, 212/691-1303)
*New York City Police Museum (100 Old Slip, 212/480-3100)
*Sony Wonder Technology Lab (550 Madison Ave, 212/833-8100)
*South Street Seaport Museum (east end of Fulton St, 212/732-7678)

New York Classics

Bronx Zoo (The Bronx, 718/367-1010)
*Ellis Island (New York Harbor, 212/363-7620)
*Empire State Building (Fifth Ave bet 33rd and 34th St, 212/736-3100)
New York Hall of Science (4701 111th St, Queens, 718/699-0005)
*Statue of Liberty (New York Harbor, 212/363-3200)
*United Nations (First Ave bet 45th and 46th St, 212/963-7713)
*Yankee Stadium (The Bronx, 212/307-1212)

Plays, Books, Movies, and TV

Donnell Library Children's Center (20 W 53rd St, 212/621-0636)
IMAX Theater (American Museum of Natural History, 212/769-5034)
Kaye Playhouse (Hunter College, 68th St at Lexington Ave, 212/772-4448)
*Museum of Television and Radio (25 W 52nd St, 212/621-6600)
*NBC Experience Studio Tour (50th St bet Fifth Ave and Ave of the Americas, 212/664-7174)
*New Amsterdam Theater/The Lion King (214 W 42nd St, 212/282-2900)

Trains, Boats, and Other Transportation
*Circle Line Sightseeing Tours (Pier 83, Hudson River at 43rd St, 212/563-3200)
*Intrepid Sea-Air-Space Museum (Pier 86, Hudson River at 46th St, 212/245-0072)
*New York Transit Museum (Boerum Pl at Schermerhorn St, Brooklyn, 718/243-3060)
*Roosevelt Island Tram (Second Ave bet 59th and 60th St)
*Staten Island Ferry (Whitehall Terminal, south end of Manhattan)

Hi Art!
   Cyndie Bellen-Berthezene offers young children—even very young ones—and their families innovative exposure to art, dance, and music through museum and gallery visits, studio workshops, and classes. For more information, call 212/362-8190 or go to www.hiartkids.com.

Restaurants

Good for Grownups, Too
Shake Shack (Madison Square Park, Madison Ave at 23rd St)
*Tavern on the Green (Central Park W at 67th St, 212/873-3200)
*Union Square Cafe (215 E 16th St, 212/243-4020)

Great Basics
EJ's Luncheonette (447 Amsterdam Ave, 212/873-3444 and other locations)
*Jackson Hole Burgers (232 E 64th St, 212/371-7187 and other locations)
*John's Pizzeria (278 Bleecker St, 212/243-1680 and other locations)
Lombardi's (32 Spring St, 212/941-7994)
Two Boots Pizza (37 Avenue A, 212/505-2276 and other locations)

For Young Athletes
   If you have a child who wants to climb a wall, take batting practice, or kick a soccer ball around, there's only one place to go: the **Field House at Chelsea Piers**. Located on the far west side of Manhattan between 17th and 23rd streets, this remarkable complex has it all. Call 212/336-6500 or go to www.chelseapiers.com for more information.

Great Desserts
*Blue Smoke (116 E 27th St, 212/447-7733)
Bubby's (120 Hudson St, 212/219-0666)
*Cafe Lalo (201 W 83rd St, 212/496-6031)
Peanut Butter & Co. (240 Sullivan St, 212/677-3995)
*Piece of Cake (1370 Lexington Ave, 212/987-1700)
*Serendipity 3 (225 E 60th St, 212/838-3531)

Theme Restaurants
Barking Dog Luncheonette (1678 Third Ave, 212/831-1800 and other locations)

*Brooklyn Diner USA (212 W 57th St, 212/977-1957)
 ESPN Zone (1472 Broadway, 212/921-3776)
 Hard Rock Cafe (1501 Broadway, 212/489-6565)
 Jekyll & Hyde (1409 Ave of the Americas, 212/541-9505, and other locations)
 Mars 2112 (Broadway at 51st St, 212/582-2112)
 Planet Hollywood (1540 Broadway, 212/333-7827)

Toy Stores and Bookstores

Bookstores

*Bank Street Bookstore (2875 Broadway, 212/678-1654)
*Books of Wonder (16 W 18th St, 212/989-3270)
*Scholastic Store (557 Broadway, 212/343-6166)

Toy Stores

*E.A.T. Gifts (1062 Madison Ave, 212/861-2544)
*F.A.O. Schwarz (767 Fifth Ave, 212/644-9400)
*Kid O (123 W 10th St, 212/366-KIDO)
*Kidding Around (60 W 15th St, 212/645-6337)
 West Side Kids (498 Amsterdam Ave, 212/496-7282)

Take My Money . . . Please!

American Girl Doll Place (609 Fifth Ave, at 49th St) is a restaurant, theater, store, and giant credit-card bill all wrapped up into one. A relative newcomer, you'll know it by the line of dressed-up little girls coming and going. If you're familiar with the American Girl Doll phenomenon, I need explain no more. If you're not, you don't want to know! A whole-day dream package starts at $270 for one child over six and an accompanying adult. Call 877/247-5223 or go to www.americangirl.com for more information.

Just as some things are fun to do with kids, there are others that you should *not* do with them. A few museums—such as the Frick Collection, the Neue Galerie, and the Grolier Club's gallery—are not places to bring small children. Indeed, children under 16 are not allowed on the tour of the Federal Reserve Bank, children under 12 are not welcome at the Neue Galerie; under 10 are not allowed in the Frick; under 6 can't go on the NBC Studio Tour; under 5 are not welcome on the tour of the United Nations; and under 4 are not allowed in most Broadway theaters. If you're going shopping at a perpetually crowded place like Zabar's or Fairway, don't take kids or keep a firm grip on their hands if you do. The latter holds true just about everywhere in New York—it's easy for a young one to get lost in a crowd! And remember that kids tire more quickly than adults. Chances are you'll be doing a lot of walking, and they're taking two or three steps for every one of yours! As the *New York Times* once put it, "Baby miles are like dog years."

Finally, a word of warning: It's a real challenge to tote an infant or toddler in New York. While hundreds of thousands of children are born and raised in the city, visitors who are accustomed to carting their children through malls in strollers and around town in car seats may have trouble here. Many places, including the subway system, are not exactly stroller-accessible, and the United Nations, the Forbes Magazine Galleries, the Metropolitan Museum of Art (on Sundays), and the Museum of Jewish Heritage ban them altogether. (However, the Museum of Jewish Heritage offers free backpacks and Snugglies during your visit.) Taxis with functioning seatbelts have become much easier to find in recent years, but ones with car seats are a rarity. Only a few public restrooms have changing tables, and I've yet to hear of a store that has followed the Nordstrom chain's example and set aside space for nursing mothers. The good news is that up to three children under 44 inches tall ride free with a fare-paying adult on buses and subways.

> More than a decade ago, The Gap arrived in Manhattan and seemingly overnight there were Gap franchises on every corner. Next, it was Starbucks. Then it was **Duane Reade**, the 24-hour drugstore. If you need to pick up some toiletries or have a prescription filled in the middle of the night, just look down the street: once just a small chain among many, there are Duane Reade stores on practically every corner!

WHERE TO GO
In the Middle of the Night

New York bills itself as "the city that never sleeps," and many who live here are night people. They include not only actors and artists but also those who clean and maintain the huge office buildings, work for answering services, put together morning newspapers and newscasts, work the night shift at hospitals and other businesses that never close, and secretaries, transcribers, and editors who must make sure paperwork is ready overnight.

In general, stores and restaurants in Soho, Tribeca, and Greenwich Village stay open later than those in the rest of the city. The restaurants and mom-and-pop operations along Broadway on the Upper West Side and on Lexington and Third avenues on the Upper East Side also tend to keep late hours. As with everything else, call before setting out to make sure they are still keeping late hours.

> **Up Late and Looking for Something to Do?**
> **Barnes & Noble** (2289 Broadway, 212/362-8835 and other locations)
> **Bowlmor Lanes** (110 University Pl, 212/255-8188)
> **Chess Shop** (230 Thompson St, 212/475-9580)
> **Crunch Fitness** (404 Lafayette St, 212/614-0120)
> **Slate Billiards** (54 W 21st St, 212/989-0096)
> **Tower Records** (692 Broadway, 212/505-1500 and 1961 Broadway, 212/799-2500)
> **Tower Video** (20 E 4th St, 212/505-1166)
> **Virgin Records Megastore** (1540 Broadway, 212/921-1020)
>
> **Need Help in the Middle of the Night?**
> **Animal Medical Center** (212/838-8100)
> **Doctors on Call** (212/737-2333)
> **Moonlight Courier** (212/473-2246)

For Free

There's no way to get around it: New York is expensive. Even the most frugal and resourceful visitors often feel as if they're bleeding money. ("Didn't we just get $200 out of the cash machine!?") Still, you can find some good deals and do a lot of sightseeing for free. Look in *Time Out New York*'s tremendous weekly listings of events for boxes noting free ones. You can also go to www.nycvisit.com and click "Visitors," "Things to Do," and "NYC for Free."

New York Pass

If you're planning to visit certain prime tourist spots in New York and want to save a little money, consider getting a **New York Pass**. You can buy one, two, three, or seven day passes that allow free admission to dozens of museums and tours, including the American Museum of Natural History, the NBC Studio Experience Tour, and Madame Tussaud's Wax Museum. It also gives you discounts at such restaurants and stores as the Hard Rock Cafe and Planet Hollywood. Prices start at $49 for adults and $39 for children between 2 and 12. Call 877/714-1999 or go to www.newyorkpass.com for more information.

Museums and Sights

The Museum of Modern Art recently broke the $20 ceiling for admission to museums, and other places are approaching fees that high. Still, you can find some free museums and sights in New York. They include:

Cathedral Church of St. John the Divine
General Grant National Monument
Hispanic Society of America
National Museum of the American Indian
New York Public Library
Sony Wonder Technology Lab
Transit Museum Gallery (Grand Central Station)
Trinity Church
Whitney Gallery and Sculpture Court at Altria

It used to be that all the museums along Museum Mile on Fifth Avenue offered free admission one night a week. Unfortunately, that tradition lives on only one night a year in late June. Still, some museums do offer pay-as-you-wish admission on certain evenings. They include:

Guggenheim Museum: Friday from 6 to 8
International Center of Photography: Friday from 5 to 8
Jewish Museum: Thursday from 5 to 8
Museum of Arts and Design: Thursday from 6 to 8
Museum of Modern Art: Friday from 4 to 8
New Museum of Contemporary Art: Thursday from 6 to 8
Studio Museum: first Saturday of every month
Whitney Museum of American Art: Friday from 6 to 9

Children under 12 are admitted to a lot of places for free. Active duty military personnel are admitted free to the Intrepid Sea-Air-Space Museum, military personnel in uniform are admitted free to the Empire State Building, and Smithsonian Associates are admitted free to the Cooper-Hewitt. Although it definitely isn't free, you can tour both The Cloisters and the Metropolitan Museum of Art on the same day for one admission price. You can also get a discount on admission to the Jewish Museum if you show a ticket stub from the Museum of Jewish Heritage (and vice versa).

Note: If you're interested in visiting any of the places listed here, you will find addresses, phone numbers, and more information in Chapter III.

Tours

Like the admission prices at various museums in the city, the cost of some tours has gone through the roof. However, some of them will still only cost you nothing but time. They include:

Central Park
Federal Reserve Bank
Grand Central Station
Lower East Side
New York Public Library
Schomburg Center for Research in Black Culture

Views

While it does cost to take in the view from the top of the Empire State Building, most of the best views in New York are free. Some of my favorites include:

Battery Park Esplanade (Chambers Street to Battery Park)
Brooklyn Bridge
Staten Island Ferry
Fort Tryon Park
Wave Hill in Brooklyn

Although it costs $2 each way to take the tram to Roosevelt Island, the view of the Manhattan skyline from that remarkable oasis is spectacular.

New York has scores of 24-hour food shops where you can get a decent meal for relatively cheap. My favorite in midtown is **Longwood Gourmet** (500 Lexington Ave, 212/980-3644). It has hot and cold salad bars, a deli, and sushi. Open daily 24 hours, 7 days a week, Longwood Gourmet is always clean and bright. Tables for eat-in are available.

For a Romantic Interlude

Whether you're falling in love for the first time or celebrating a wedding anniversary, New York can be one of the most romantic places in the world. If you're in the mood for love or want to create a mood that's just right for romance, try the following:

- Drinks by the fireplace followed by dinner at **One if by Land, Two if by Sea** (17 Barrow St).
- A summertime dinner in the garden at **Barbetta** (321 W 46th St).
- Dinner at the discreet and classy **Le Périgord** (405 E 52nd St).

- Dinner at **Tavern on the Green**'s sparkling Crystal Room (in Central Park off 67th St).
- Drinks in the **Campbell Apartment**, an elegant spot tucked away in Grand Central Station (just east of Vanderbilt Avenue).
- A late-night visit to the **Empire State Building Observation Deck** (Fifth Ave between 33rd and 34th St).
- A walk across the **Brooklyn Bridge** is a must!
- Watching the sun rise from the **Brooklyn Bridge**, the **Battery Park Esplanade**, **Lighthouse Park** on Roosevelt Island, or the deck of the **Staten Island Ferry**.
- A visit to the restored **Winter Garden** (World Financial Center).
- A teatime interlude at **Payard Patisserie** (1032 Lexington Ave).
- A picnic lunch looking out over the Hudson River from **The Cloisters**.
- A stroll through the splendid lobby of the **Waldorf-Astoria Hotel**.
- An early evening spent listening to classical music from the balcony of the **Metropolitan Museum of Art**'s Great Hall or jazz at the **Guggenheim Museum**.
- A rowboat or gondola ride on **Central Park Lake** or a nighttime sail around Manhattan.
- An evening carriage ride through **Central Park** after a fresh snow has fallen or a springtime stroll on some of the park's less traveled paths.

For Parties and Special Events

If you're looking for the perfect spot to hold a wedding reception, bar mitzvah, or gala event for thousands, New York inevitably has the right place . . . and the people to put it together for you. The trick, of course, is finding them. The other trick is paying for them!

Note that you will not find museums, restaurants, or hotels in the following list. Many museum spaces, including the **Mount Vernon Hotel Museum & Garden**, the **Cooper-Hewitt National Design Museum**, and the **Roosevelt Rotunda** at the **American Museum of Natural History** (complete with its dinosaur display) can be rented for parties and other events. Many restaurants have spaces for private parties, as do most hotels.

Some of my favorite private party rooms in New York are at **Barbetta** (321 W 46th St), **Firebird** (365 W 46th St), **Four Seasons** (99 E 52nd St), **Gramercy Tavern** (42 E 20th St), **Hard Rock Cafe** (1501 Broadway), the **Hudson River Club** (World Financial Center), **Le Périgord** (405 E 52nd St), **Lutèce** (249 E 50th St), **Montrachet** (239 Broadway), **One if by Land, Two if by Sea** (17 Barrow St), **Primavera** (1578 First Ave), **Serendipity 3** (225 E 60th St), **Tavern on the Green** (Central Park W at 67th St), **The Terrace** (400 W 119th St), **The Tonic** (108 W 18th St), and **Tribeca Grill** (375 Greenwich St). If you want to throw a party at your favorite museum, restaurant, hotel, or bar, by all means ask.

Some venues available for special events take care of all the catering, while others simply provide the space. Among the former are the **Art Club** (100 Reade St), the **Burden Mansion** (7 E 91st St), **New York Public Library** (Fifth Ave at 41st St), the **Puck Building** (Lafayette St at Houston St), and **Studio 450** (450 W 31st St). Among the latter are **Astra** (979 Third Ave), **The Boathouse** (in Central Park), **Glorious Foods** (522 E 74th St), the **Museum Club at Bridgewaters** (South Street Seaport), **Pier 60** (at Chelsea Piers), and **Upper Crust 91** (91 Horatio St). Catering is optional at the **New**

York Botanical Garden (in the Bronx) and the **Pratt Mansion** (1026 Fifth Ave). This list should give you an idea of the breadth of spaces available.

Before you forge ahead with planning a party in New York, be forewarned that it's going to cost a great deal of money. I'm talking *really* big bucks. You can save money by avoiding Saturday evening, holding your numbers down, and throwing your party in the off months of July and August or between January and early April. Some places and services will negotiate on price. But don't expect any great or even particularly good deals. And make your reservations at least two months and as far as two years in advance. The **Landmarks Conservancy** has a website (www.nylandmarks.org) with details on more than two dozen potential gathering spots and the cost of renting them.

Do-It-Yourself Decorations

If you're planning a special event and trying not to break the bank, I have a tip for easy, inexpensive decorations. Stop by the **Flower District** (28th St bet Fifth Ave and Ave of the Americas) to pick up the flowers you need. Let the vendors know that you are buying in bulk (a couple hundred stems at least), bring cash, and go early.

For Restrooms

Nothing can ruin a trek around New York more quickly than not being able to find a bathroom when one is needed. By law, public buildings are required to have public restrooms. They are not, however, required to be clean and safe.

Following is a list of bathrooms that meet at least a minimum standard of safety and cleanliness. You may need to ask for directions or a key at some of them, but all are free to the public. As a general rule, try hotel lobbies, department stores, schools, theaters, municipal goverment buildings, churches, libraries, and even hospitals. **Barnes & Noble** and **Starbucks** locations throughout the city are also good bets. Of course, if you have small children in tow, just about any store or restaurant will likely take pity.

Wherever you end up, be sure to follow a few safety tips. Leaving anything on the floor in a public restroom is a mistake, as purses, packages, and everything else have a bad habit of disappearing while you're occupied! The same is true of items left hanging on the back of a stall door. Of course, it's also a good idea to stay away from deserted bathrooms. No matter how badly you need to go, avoid bathrooms in parks (except the ones listed below) and most subway stations.

Below 14th Street

- **Castle Clinton** (inside Battery Park)
- **National Museum of the American Indian** (1 Bowling Green)
- **World Financial Center**
- **Trinity Church** (Broad St at Wall St)
- **Federal Hall National Memorial** (Wall St at Nassau St)
- **South Street Seaport** (Fulton at Water St)
- **City Hall** (Broadway at Chambers St)
- **New York City Fire Museum** (289 Spring St, bet Hudson and Varick St)
- **Kmart** (Lafayette at 8th St)
- **Strand Book Store** (Broadway at 12th St)

Between 14th and 42nd streets
- **Loehmann's** (Seventh Ave and 17th St)
- **ABC Carpet & Home** (Broadway at 19th St)
- **Supreme Court of the State of New York** (25th St bet Madison and Park Ave)
- **Macy's** (Herald Square, Broadway at 34th St)
- **Science, Industry, and Business Library** (Madison Ave at 34th St)
- **Sheraton Park Avenue Hotel** (Park Ave and 37th St)
- **New York Public Library** (Fifth Ave bet 40th and 42nd St)
- **Bryant Park** (42nd St bet Fifth Ave and Ave of the Americas)
- **Grand Hyatt Hotel** (42nd St bet Park and Lexington Ave)

Comfort Station

New York's Parks Department has placed more than 600 "comfort stations" (in all five boroughs) inside its parks. While many languish in disrepair, several dozen have been significantly improved in recent years, thanks in part to revenue from selling advertising space in some of them. By far the nicest is in Bryant Park, behind the main branch of the New York Public Library.

Midtown
- **United Nations** (First Ave bet 45th and 46th St)
- **Waldorf-Astoria Hotel** (Park Ave at 50th St)
- **Saks Fifth Avenue** (611 Fifth Ave, bet 49th and 50th St)
- **Rockefeller Center** (bet Fifth Ave and Ave of the Americas from 49th to 51st St)
- **Olympic Tower** (bet Fifth and Madison Ave from 51st to 52nd St)
- **Park Avenue Plaza** (55 E 52nd St)
- **Trump Tower** (Fifth Ave bet 55th and 56th St)
- **Henri Bendel** (712 Fifth Ave)
- **Omni Park Central** (870 Seventh Ave)
- **Sony Wonder Technology Lab** (56th St at Madison Ave)

Upper East Side
- **McDonald's** (Third Ave bet 57th and 58th St)
- **Bloomingdale's** (1000 Third Ave, at 59th St)
- **Asia Society** (725 Park Ave, at 70th St)
- **Ralph Lauren** (867 Madison Ave, at 72nd St)
- **92nd Street Y** (1395 Lexington Ave, at 92nd St)
- **Museum of the City of New York** (Fifth Ave bet 103rd and 104th St)
- **Charles A. Dana Discovery Center** (in Central Park, Fifth Ave at 110th St)

Upper West Side
- **Avery Fisher Hall** (Lincoln Center, 64th St at Broadway)
- **New York Public Library for the Performing Arts** (Lincoln Center, 65th St at Broadway)
- **Barnes & Noble** (Broadway at 82nd St)
- **Cathedral Church of St. John the Divine** (Amsterdam Ave at 112th St)

For More Information

I suggest doing a few things before packing your bags for New York. Contact **NYC & Company** (800/692-8474, 212/484-1222, or www.nycvisit. com), the city's marketing arm, to request a free copy of the official **NYC Guide**. (For a $5.95 shipping and handling fee, they'll send you the guide, a map, and a lot of brochures, but the guide is sufficient for most people.) Second, look through both the "Tours" and "Tickets" sections of Chapter III to find out which things you want to do that require advance reservations. Third, write the **New York City Transit Authority** (Attention: Customer Services, 370 John Jay Street, Brooklyn, NY 11201) for maps and brochures about the public transportation system so you can hit the ground (or subway) running.

Whether you're planning in advance or already sitting in your hotel room, get copies of *The New Yorker*, *New York* magazine, *Time Out New York*, and the *New York Times*. All but *Time Out New York* are generally available throughout the country (although the various out-of-town editions of the *New York Times* are abridged). The *New Yorker* (in the front), *New York* magazine (in the back), and *Time Out New York* (throughout) carry detailed information about current theater productions, movies, gallery and museum exhibitions, concerts, dance, and New York nightlife. Be forewarned that the free magazines in hotel rooms are paid for by advertisers and therefore are not particularly useful or unbiased (although maps and information about current museum exhibitions can be helpful).

If you don't have everything planned when you arrive, drop by one of several visitor information centers in Manhattan. They include:

- **Chinatown Visitor Information Center**—Walker, Canal, and Baxter streets (weekdays and Sunday from 10 to 6, Saturday from 10 to 7)
- **City Hall Visitor Information Center**—Broadway at Park Row (weekdays from 9 to 6, weekends from 10 to 6)
- **Embassy Theater Information Center**—Seventh Ave bet 46th and 47th St (daily 10 to 6)
- **Harlem Visitor Information Center**—163 W 125th St, at Seventh Ave (weekdays from 9 to 6, weekends from 10 to 5)
- **NYC & Company**—810 Seventh Ave, at 53rd St (weekdays from 8:30 to 6, weekends from 8:30 to 5)

The front section of the Manhattan Yellow Pages is a good place to look for information and ideas. In addition to useful telephone numbers, it includes diagrams of major concert halls and sports stadiums. It also includes a short calendar of major annual events and maps of the subway and bus systems.

Finally, the Internet has made accessing tourist information about New York as easy as clicking a mouse. Typing "New York City" into a search engine will generate several million hits. Here are several of the most useful sites:

- **www.ci.nyc.ny.us**: the official site of the city of New York, with great information for residents and visitors alike, including transportation resources, links to attractions and events, and even the New York Yellow Pages
- **www.centralparknyc.org**: the official site of the Central Park Conservancy, with a huge array of information about all that this remarkable park has to offer

- **www.cityguidemagazine.com**: restaurant reviews and numerous links to tours, museums, and other sites
- **www.GoCityKids.com**: helpful ideas for parents about parks, restaurants, play spaces, stores, and babysitting services
- **www.mta.nyc.ny.us**: the official site of the Metropolitan Transportation Authority, with helpful information about the bus and subway systems
- **www.newyork.citysearch.com**: current schedules for plays, concerts, and movies, good descriptions of clubs, and a weekly calendar
- **www.newyorkmetro.com**: information from *New York* magazine
- **www.nycgovparks.org**: extensive information about parks and recreation centers in all five boroughs
- **www.nycvisit.com**: the NYC & Company site, where you can request publications, maps, and event calendars
- **www.nytoday.com**: produced by the *New York Times,* with access to its reviews, calendars, and classified ads

If you're coming to New York in a wheelchair, you ought to know about a couple of resources. First, make sure to get a copy of "Access for All," an exceptional guide to the city's cultural institutions that describes in detail what sorts of facilities they have for people in wheelchairs (as well as the blind and deaf). This invaluable guide is available from **Hospital Audiences** (www.hospaud.org). This organization also runs a hotline (888/424-4685) on weekdays. Second, the **New York City Transit Authority** has a special phone number (718/596-8585) for information about routes accessible to people in wheelchairs and postage-paid fare envelopes for disabled riders. The **City of New York's Office for People with Disabilities** (212/788-2830, www.nyc. gov/html/mopd) is also a great resource. Finally, many Broadway theaters offer deeply discounted tickets for people in wheelchairs and their companions. Call individual theaters for more information.

The New York Philharmonic's marketing tag line sums it up perfectly: "Expect the Extraordinary. This Is New York."

Index

(Note: Bolded page numbers indicate major listings' main entries; index is in strict alphabetical order.)